ROOKWOOD VII & KERAMICS 1997

Featuring important ceramics from the Collection of Mr. and Mrs
Albert Jung, from the Collection of Mr. Edwin J. Kircher and from
other fine collections. Included will be over 500 lots of Rookwood
Pottery and over 400 lots of other American and European Art
Potteries. Examples from **Rookwood Pottery the Glorious Gamble**
and **From Our Native Clay** will be offered.

Auction
Keramics 1997 - Saturday, June 7th from 9:30 am until 5 pm
Rookwood VII - Sunday, June 8th from 9 am until 4 pm
Both Sales to be held at the Cincinnati Club Building
30 Garfield Place in Downtown Cincinnati

Preview
Friday, June 6th from 1 until 8 pm
Saturday, June 7th from 8 until 9:30 am
and from 5 until 7 pm
Sunday, June 8th from 8 until 9 am

Sale Coordinator
Riley Humler

Auctioneer
J. Louis Karp

Associate Auctioneer
Brad Karoleff

Sales Consultant
Louis Aronoff

Cincinnati Art Galleries

Michele and Randy Sandler
635 Main Street
Cincinnati, OH 45202

phone • (513) 381-2128   fax • (513) 381-7527   email • cincar19@mail.idt.net

ISBN: 0-943633-10-9

Terms of Sale

The buyer is the person making the final and highest bid. In the event of a disputed bid, the auctioneer shall determine who is the successful bidder, or the auctioneer may resell the lot in dispute, but in all instances the judgment of the auctioneer shall be final.

Sales Tax

A 6% Ohio Sales Tax applies to all retail purchases. Ohio Sales Tax exemption forms must be executed and filed with the auction clerk at the time of auction registration.

NOTE: Purchasers of items shipped out of state are subject (where applicable) to report and pay use tax to the state into which the items are being shipped.

Withdrawal

The auctioneer reserves the right to withdraw any lot before or at the time of the sale.

Credit, Methods of Payment

Cash, Visa, Mastercard, certified check and bank letters of credit are acceptable methods of payment. If you are known to us, your credit, and your credit only, can be established. Please check with the sale clerk. No company or personal references are accepted. We would appreciate credit arrangements being made in advance of the auction date. Persons not making prior credit arrangements can pay by personal check, but no merchandise can be removed until all checks have cleared. Any packing and shipping expenses will be borne by the purchaser. All items must be paid in full within 72 hours of the end of sale or the Auctioneer retains the right to resell the property, either at auction or by private sale. Purchaser will be liable for any deficiencies and all costs incurred, including collection and legal fees.

Bidding

Lots will be sold in the order in which they appear in the catalog. The normal bidding increments are as follows:

Up to $500	Bids will increase in $25 increments
$500-$1000	Bids will increase in $50 increments
$1000-$5000	Bids will increase in $100 increments
$5000-$10000	Bids will increase in $250 increments
$10000 up	Bids will increase in $500 increments

The Auctioneer reserves the right to vary the bidding increments.

The final bid is the price at which the lot is knocked down to the buyer.

This final bid, in all cases, is subject to a 10% buyer premium, the purchase price being the total of the two sums.

If the purchase price is not paid in full, the auctioneer may either cancel the sale, and any partial payment already made shall be there upon forfeited as liquidated damages or the auctioneer may resell the lot, without notice to the buyer.

Absentee, Written and Telephone bids

Absentee bids are welcomed. Absentee bids will be executed as if the bidder were present at the auction with the earliest bid received having preference in case of a tie between absentee bidders. Floor bids will be taken over absentee bids in case of a tie. Absentee, written or telephone bids are subject to the same 10% buyer's premium, and all credit requirements as listed above. The auctioneer, Cincinnati Art Galleries, and their employees are not responsible for absentee, written or telephone bids that are not properly executed. We have a limited number of telephone lines available during the auction. These will be reserved on a first come first served basis for telephone bidding. Due to the limited number of lines, we may not be able to accomodate telephone bidding on lots with low estimates of under $500. We will be happy to accept absentee bids on any lots not eligible for telephone bidding. All packing and shipping cost of items purchased by Absentee, Written or Telephone bids will be borne by the purchaser.

Buyer's Premium

The final bid ("hammer" price) is subject to a 10% premium. The purchase price is the total of these two sums.

Reserves and Estimates

The estimated value of each lot is printed in the catalog, and merely reflects the price range into which a lot might fall. All lots have a reserve price below which they will not be sold. The reserve price is not published in the catalog, but in no case is it higher than the lower amount of the estimated price.

Removal

All lots are to be removed by their buyers not later than 9:00 PM, Saturday, June 10th, 1995. Lots are released to buyers upon presentation of proof of payment.

Packing and Shipping

We have made arrangements to assist in packing and shipping your puchases should you desire. We will pack any item and arrange shipping through U.P.S., Federal Express or other shippers, as long as the items are insured. International shipping is likewise available. Packing and shipping will be done on a "time and material" basis and all cost will be billed directly to the purchaser. We fully expect excellent results and moderate prices from our new packing and shipping arrangement.

Guarantee

All lots in this catalogue are guaranteed as described and are guaranteed to be free of other problems or repairs. Crazing is only mentioned if objectionable. Sizes are approximate. (See Peck Book II for shape number references). We guarantee the authenticity of all lots in this auction.

Advice to Bidders

The Cincinnati Art Galleries staff is available to discuss all lots with potential buyers at all presale exhibitions, or by telephone (513-381-2128) Monday thru Friday 9AM-5PM, Saturday 9AM-4PM.

Prices Realized

The list of prices realized at the auction will be mailed shortly after the sale. Lots that have been withdrawn from the sale or that have failed to reach the reserve price will be excluded from the prices realized.

CONSIGNMENTS WANTED

For Rookwood VIII and Keramics 1998

Cincinnati Art Galleries is now accepting consignments for Rookwood VIII and Keramics 1998 which will take place in June of 1998. We have consistently set new levels of excellence in selling Art Pottery and would be pleased to assist you in making decisions about your single piece or collection.

Cincinnati Art Galleries is unique in the world of auctions. We have unmatched expertise in dealing with Rookwood and are quickly establishing our place as a trusted and appreciative seller of all Art Pottery. We operate our sales with the greatest attention to detail, honesty and scholarship and no one can offer consignors and sellers alike, a more friendly and efficient atmosphere in which to buy or sell.

We have established great credibility in dealing with fellow pottery lovers and we encourage anyone interested in learning about us to talk with others who have dealt with Cincinnati Art Galleries. Our reputation is important to us and we believe it should be of importance to you.

If you would like a professional and confidential opportunity to discuss the sale of a single piece or your entire collection, please call Riley Humler at 513-381-2128.

Cincinnati Art Galleries also offers extensive advertising for its sales. We target National and Regional magazines and newspapers, ensuring best possible exposure of your merchandise to potential buyers.

We purchase Rookwood and American and European Art Pottery.

Cincinnati Art Galleries is also interested in purchasing Rookwood and American and European Art Pottery. If you do not wish to pursue the auction method of selling your pottery, we would like to talk with you about outright purchase. Whether you have a $200 vase or a $2,000,000 collection, Cincinnati Art Galleries is ready and willing to review your needs. If you would like a Confidential, no obligation discussion with the experts at Cincinnati Art Galleries, please call Riley Humler or Randy Sandler at 513-381-2128.

Sell with the Record Setters

Below are listed some of the records we have set for selling American Art Pottery. We have listed only those over $20,000 to keep the list manageable. With very few exceptions, Cincinnati Art Galleries has achieved the highest prices for every type of Rookwood made. We also attempt to give our consignors the utmost in personal and professional service.

1. Glover Lot 724 Shirayamadani Sea Green Copper Overlay Vase.................$ 198,000.00*
2. Glover Lot 241 Shirayamadani Standard Copper Overlay Vase..........................88,000.00
3. Glover Lot 1087 A. R. Valentien Standardware Vase...66,000.00
4. Rookwood V Lot 429 Schmidt Black Iris Vase with Irises................................62,700.00
5. RW II Lot 223 H. E. Wilcox Dull Finish Carved Vase......................................56,000.00
6. RW IV Lot 187 Shirayamadani Black Iris Daisy Vase..51,700.00
7. RW II Lot 95 Shirayamadani Black Iris Scenic Vase..45,100.00
8. RW II Lot 600 Shirayamadani Black Iris Scenic Vase.......................................41,800.00
9. RW II Lot 132 Schmidt Black Iris Vase with Irises..40,700.00
10. RW IV Lot 443 W. P. McDonald Carved Black Iris Lotus Vase.......................39,600.00
11. RW VI Lot 1446 Schmidt Iris Glaze Vase with Thistles....................................38,500.00
12. RW III Lot 1667 Shirayamadani Black Iris Scenic Vase....................................37,400.00
13. Keramics 1995 Lot 250 Weller Aurelian vase by Haubrich...............................36,300.00
14. RW IV Lot 191 Schmidt Vellum Venetian Harbor Plaque.................................35,200.00
15. Glover Lot 328 Schmidt Vellum Venetian Harbor Plaque.................................35,200.00
16. RW III Lot 653 Grace Young Standardware Native American 34,100.00
17. Glover Lot 653 Grace Young Standardware Native American Plaque..................34,100.00
18. Glover Lot 118 Wareham-McDonald Advertising Plaque..................................34,100.00
19. RW VI Lot 1557 Grace Young Iris Glaze Plaque...33,000.00
20. RW VI 1568 Schmidt Iris Glaze Vase with Wisteria..33,000.00
21. RW IV Lot 592 Sara Sax French Red Vase...31,900.00
22. RW VI Lot 1545 Grace Young Standard GlazeNative American Portrait..............29,700.00
23. Rookwood V Lot 587 Iris Glaze Scenic Vase by Shirayamadani........................28,600.00
24. RW VI Lot 1770 Arthur Conant High Glaze Scenic Vase..................................28,600.00
25. RW VI Lot 1462 Arthur Conant High Glaze Peacock Vase...............................24,200.00

*Word Record for American Art Pottery at Auction

THE STAFF OF CINCINNATI ART GALLERIES

Ralph Allalouf	Jim Fleming	Michele Sandler
Richard Bitting	Riley Humler	Randy Sandler
Paul Findsen	Mark Lario	Rick Santa
Tom Deaton	Cal Long	Brian Sparks
	Pam Kirchner	

Selected Bibliography

Altman	Seymour and Violet	The Book of Buffalo Pottery	Bonanza Books	1969	New York
Atterbury	Paul	Moorcroft	Dennis & Edwards	1990	Somerset, England
Barr	Margaret Libby et.al.	University of North Dakota Pottery The Cable Years	Published by the Authors	1977	Grand Forks, ND
Bartlett	John	English Decorative Ceramics	Kevin Francis Publishing Ltd.	London 19898	
Blasberg	Robert W.	The Unknown Ohr	Peaceable Press	1986	Milford, PA
Borich	Ballard	Auspicious Circumstance	Ballard Borich	1988	Cincinnati
Burt	S.G.	2292 Pieces of Early Rookwood Pottery in the Cincinnati Art Museum in 1916 (Reprinted in 1978)	Herbert Peck	1978	Tucson
Buxton	Virginia Hillway	Roseville Pottery for Love or Money	Tymbre Hill Publishing Company	1977	Nashville
Clark	Garth & Margie Hughto	A Century of Ceramics in the United States 1878-1978	E.P. Dutton	1979	New York
Clark	Garth et.al.	The Mad Potter of Biloxi The Art and Life of George E. Ohr	Abbeville Press Inc.	1991	New York
Cox	Warren E.	The Book of Pottery and Porcelain Combined Edition	Crown Publishers	1944	New York
Cummins	Virginia Raymond	Rookwood Pottery Potpourri (Reprinted in 1991)	Cincinnati Art Galleries	1991	Cincinnati
Dale	Sharon	Frederick Hurten Rhead: An English Potter in America	Erie Art Museum	1986	Erie, PA
Darling	Sharon	Teco Art Pottery of the Prairie School	Erie Art Museum	1989	Erie, PA
Dietz	Ulysses G.	The Newark Museum Collection of American Art Pottery	Peregrine Smith Books	1984	Salt Lake City
Eidelberg	Martin, Editor	From Our Native Clay Art Pottery from the Collections of the American Ceramic Arts Society	Turn of the Century Editions	1987	New York
Ellis	Anita J.	Rookwood Pottery The Glorious Gamble	Rizzoli	1992	New York
Evans	Paul	Art Pottery of the United States Second Edition	Feingold & Lewis	1987	New York
Gifford	David Edwin	The Collector's Encyclopedia of Niloak	Collector Books	1993	Paducah, KY
Goodman	Marcia and William	American Art Pottery	Cooper-Hewitt Museum	1987	New York
Henzke	Lucile	Art Pottery of America	Schiffer Publishing Ltd.	1982	Exton, PA
Hibel	John et.al.	The Fulper Book	Published by the Authors	1994	New York
Humler	Riley, Editor	The Glover Collection: Rookwood Pottery	Cincinnati Art Galleries	1991	Cincinnati
Humler	Riley, Editor	Rookwood II	Cincinnati Art Galleries	1992	Cincinnati
Humler	Riley, Editor	Rookwood III	Cincinnati Art Galleries	1993	Cincinnati
Humler	Riley, Editor	Keramics 1993	Cincinnati Art Galleries	1993	Cincinnati
Humler	Riley, Editor	Rookwood IV & Keramics 1994	Cincinnati Art Galleries	1994	Cincinnati
Humler	Riley, Editor	Rookwood V & Keramics 1995	Cincinnati Art Galleries	1995	Cincinnati
Humler	Riley, Editor	Rookwood VI & Keramics 1996	Cincinnati Art Galleries	1996	Cincinnati
Huxford	Sharon and Bob	The Collectors Encyclopedia of Roseville Pottery First Series	Collector Books	1976	Paducah, KY
Huxford	Sharon and Bob	Early Roseville	Collector Books	1977	Paducah, KY
Huxford	Sharon and Bob	The Collectors Encyclopedia of Weller Pottery	Collector Books	1979	Paducah, KY
Huxford	Sharon and Bob	The Collectors Encyclopedia of McCoy Pottery	Collector Books	1980	Paducah, KY
Huxford	Sharon and Bob	The Collectors Encyclopedia of Roseville Pottery Second Series	Collector Books	1980	Paducah, KY
King	Lyndel	American Studio Ceramics 1920-1950	University of Minnesota	1988	Minneapolis
Kircher	Edwin J.	Rookwood Pottery, An Explanation of its Marks and Symbols	Published by the Author	1984	Cincinnati
Kircher	Edwin J. et.al.	Rookwood: Its Golden Era of Art Pottery 1880-1929	Published by the Authors	1969	Cincinnati
Kovel	Ralph and Terry	The Kovels' Collector's Guide to American Art Pottery	Crown Publishers, Inc.	1974	New York
Kovel	Ralph and Terry	Kovel's American Art Pottery	Crown	1993	New York
Lehner	Lois	Lehner's Encyclopedia of U.S. Marks on Porcelain & Clay Pottery	Collector Books	1988	Paducah, KY
McDonald	Ann Gilbert	All About Weller	Antique Publications	1989	Marietta, OH
Montgomery	Susan J.	The Ceramics of William H. Grueby	Arts & Crafts Quarterly Press	1993	Lambertville, NJ
Nelson	Scott, et al.	A Collector's Guide to Van Briggle Pottery	A.G. Halldin Publishing	1986	Indiana, PA
Pear	Lillian Myers	The Pewabic Pottery	Wallace-Homestead Book Co.	1976	Des Moines, IA
Peck	Herbert	The Book of Rookwood Pottery	Cincinnati Art Galleries	1968	Cincinnati
Peck	Herbert	The Second Book of Rookwood Pottery	Cincinnati Art Galleries	1985	Cincinnati
Perry	Barbara, Editor	American Ceramics, The Collection of Everson Museum of Art	Rizzoli	1989	New York
Poesch	Jessie	Newcomb Pottery	Schiffer Publishing Ltd.	1984	Exton, PA
Postle	Kathleen R.	The Chronicle of the Overbeck Pottery	Indiana Historical Society	1978	Indianapolis
Purviance	Louise et.al.	Zanesville Art Pottery in Color	Mid-America Book Company	1968	Leon, IA
Sanford	Martha and Steve	The Guide to Brush-McCoy Pottery	Published by the Authors	1992	Campbell, CA
Sasicki	Richard and Josie Fania	The Collector's Encyclopedia of Van Briggle Art Pottery	Collector Books	1993	Paducah, KY
Schneider	Norris F. Editor	Rozane Ware Catalog (Reprint)	The Roseville Pottery Company	1906	Zanesville, OH

ROOKWOOD POTTERY
An Explanation of Its Marks and Symbols
by Edwin J. Kircher

HISTORY

The Rookwood Pottery was founded in 1880 at Cincinnati, Ohio by Mrs. Maria Longworth Storer. The establishment was named for the Longworth Estate in the nearby countryside. The family home had large numbers of crows roosting in the trees on its grounds, and acquired its name from their presence.

The first plant was an abandoned schoolhouse at 207 Eastern Avenue. This address has been changed due to street renumbering, and the building has been razed, but the location was near the present intersection of Kemper Lane and Eastern Avenue. The factory remained in this location until construction of its Mount Adams site in 1893.

Mrs. Storer was the granddaughter of Nicholas Longworth, a wealthy pillar of the early Cincinnati community, and daughter of Joseph Longworth who endowed the Cincinnati Art School. Her husband, Bellamy Storer, was the son of a prominent judge, and himself a barrister. He served two terms as Congressional Representative before being appointed in 1887 by President McKinley to the post of Ambassador to Belgium. He later became Minister to Spain.

Mrs. Storer had been an active participant in the development of artistic interest in Cincinnati in the decade preceding the founding of Rookwood. She had worked at the Frederick Dallas Pottery as did members of the Cincinnati Women's "Pottery Club" of which Mrs. Storer was not a member, but from which she later drew heavily for artists with which to stock her company.

Admiration of the Japanese ceramics exhibit at the 1876 Centennial Exposition in Philadelphia crystallized Mrs. Storer's intention to manufacture "Art Pottery" in Cincinnati. Her experience made her realize that the existing local equipment and potteries were not adequately designed to fulfill this objective. She then set about assembling her plant and equipment, and Rookwood Pottery was born.

Mrs. Storer gathered around her the finest chemists, potters and decorators available in the local area. She also brought in the Japanese artist, Kataro Shirayamadani, to inject the influence of an advanced pottery technique which she had admired so much.

At the Paris Exposition of 1889 Rookwood Pottery received a gold medal and "the world awakened" to Rookwood. The Pottery began to pay its own way by 1890 and monetary support by the Longworth family was no longer necessary. In 1891 Mrs. Storer turned over management of the Pottery to the capable direction of W. W. Taylor. It was under the leadership of Mr. Taylor that the Pottery attained its greatest significance in pursuit of a unique American contribution to western culture.

During the years 1890-1925 Rookwood probably realized its greatest profit both in money and talent. At this time the Vellum finish was developed; the Iris glaze and Rookwood Porcelain came into being. It was also at this time that the Rookwood Faience architectural tiles and ornaments were fully developed. Such talents as Carl Schmidt, E. T. Hurley, Fred Rothenbusch, Ed. Diers, and Sturgis Lawrence were at their zenith. Kataro Shirayamadani, Matt Daly, and A. R. Valentien enjoyed international reputations. An extraordinary array of experience and talent underpinned by the many years of technical development had built the finest Art Pottery the world has ever known.

FACTORY MARKS

The factory mark identifies the manufacturer of the ware. Rookwood has used a number of factory marks. It has employed both its name, in various forms, as well as the picture-symbol type of representation associated with most European furnaces. The symbol that comes quickly to mind is the world famous monogram mark of the reversed R and P, with its wreath of flames.

This unique factory mark was used longer than any other, and was in use at the time the pottery enjoyed its greatest prestige. As a result it is this mark that is most often found on the finest of Rookwood productions. Prior to its institution the factory marks were widely varied in design and survived but a short time. They are herein explained and illustrated in the order of their occurrence, beginning with the earliest.

The most common marks prior to 1882 were the name of the pottery and the date of manufacture, either painted or incised on the base of the piece by perhaps the decorators or potters. A variation of this consisted of the initials of the Pottery, and of the founder: R.P.C.O.M.L.N. (Rookwood Pottery, Cincinnati, Ohio, Maria Longworth Nichols. Mrs. Nichols remarried in 1886 and became Mrs. Storer.) Illustrations of two of these marks are below:

From 1880 to 1882 another design used was that prepared by the famous Cincinnati artist, H. F. Farny. This factory mark was printed in black beneath the glaze, and represents a kiln with two Rooks.

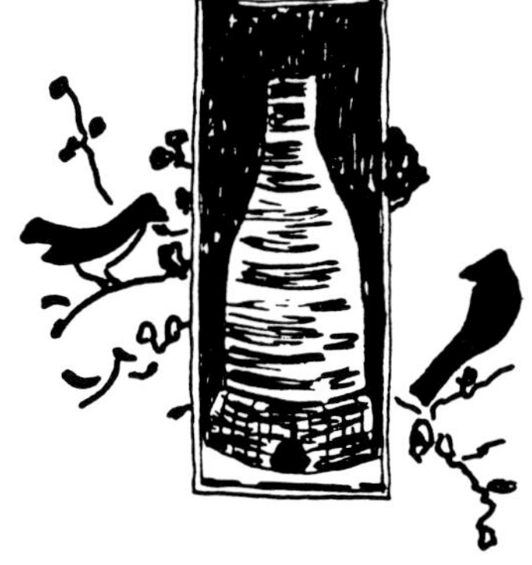

The following oval mark bearing the name and address of the factory was also used for a short time.

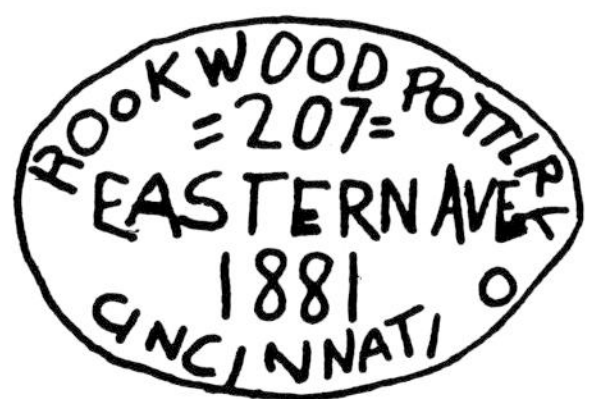

In 1882 the following two types of marks were used. Both were impressed in a raised ribbon, and the upper one appeared on a commercial project - a large beer tankard made for the Cincinnati Cooperage Company.

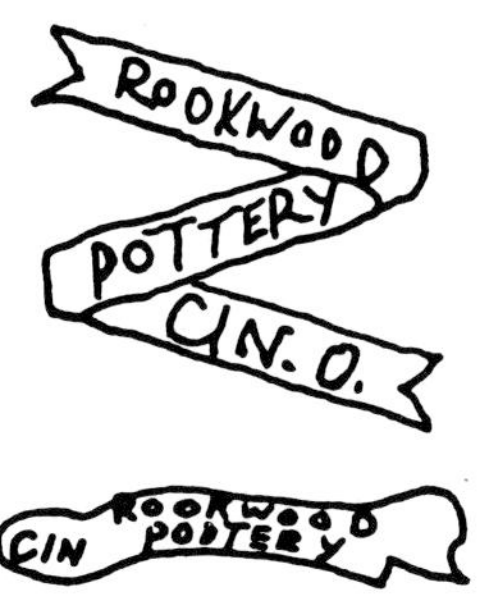

Prior to 1883 an anchor was sometimes impressed or placed in relief. It occasionally occurred in connection with an impressed date, and often in conjunction with a decorator's mark. (The illustration to the left is impressed; the one to the right appears in relief.)

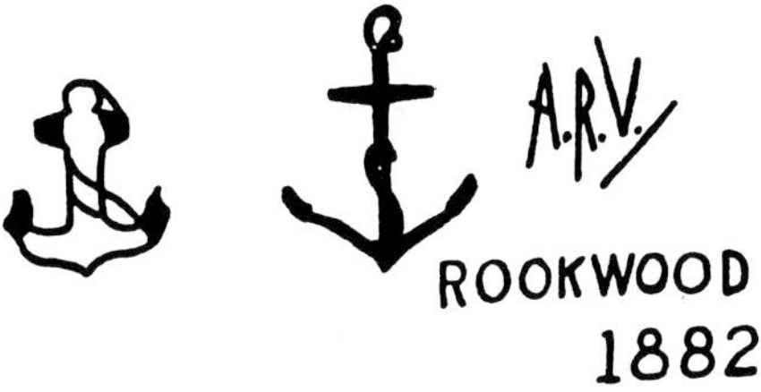

The regular mark adopted in 1882 was the word ROOKWOOD and the date in arabic numerals, impressed. This mark was in continuous use until 1886, the date being changed each year.

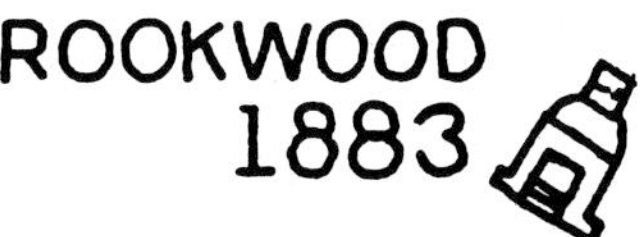

In the year 1883 a small kiln mark was impressed in the ware, and may or may not appear with the word ROOKWOOD and the date, also impressed.

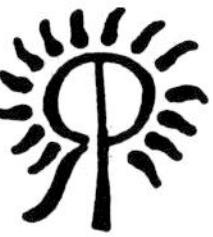

The monogram mark of the reversed R, and P was adopted in 1886, although it has been found upon ware dated as early as 1882. The monogram mark and the "ROOKWOOD 1886" both exist denoting the year 1886, the ROOKWOOD mark having been used in the earlier part of the year. In 1887 a flame point was placed above the RP monogram, and one point was added each year until 1900, at which time the monogram mark was encircled by 14 flame points.

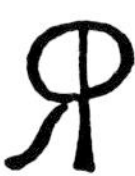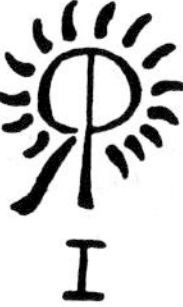

In 1901 the same mark used to indicate 1900 was continued, and the Roman numeral I was added below, to indicate the first year of the new century. The Roman numeral was subsequently changed to denote the correct year.

SHAPE NUMBERS AND SIZE SYMBOLS

Shape numbers are impressed in the clay just below the factory mark, and are usually followed by the size symbol if applicable. These numbers were assigned consecutively, and bear no direct relationship to year of manufacture or quantity produced. On early pieces the size symbol sometimes precedes the pattern number. It is also known to have appeared immediately below the pattern number, particularly on items upon which the area available for marking is limited. An example of each arrangement is shown on the following page:

568B   A7   9 0 1
              C

There are three categories of shapes. 1.) The regular series which comprise the majority of the pieces produced. 2.) The "Trial" series, in which the pattern number is preceded by a "T". ("E" for experimental could not be used — "E" is a size symbol.) 3.) Those items bearing no pattern numbers at all. (These were often the result of gifts for friends, etc., and in these cases were singular items.) Each of the categories excepting #3 were numbered consecutively.

2191   T1250

Clarence Cook, in "The Studio," said "Rookwood Pottery shows good taste in adhering to the principles which are the foundation of the system of forms called classical." In later years some patterns were duplicated, (same shape different pattern number) but despite exceptions, the patterns over the years have been generally quite artistic and tastefully executed.

Size symbols are impressed in the clay next to the pattern number and are represented by six letters. The sizes of the patterns were always lettered with A representing the largest, diminishing through F. If no size letter is shown, only the one size of the pattern exists. If an A exists, at least a B must have been constructed. However, there is no basis for assuming a C existed. Likewise, if an E is encountered, an A, B, C, and D were created, but not necessarily an F. Occasionally another was created at a later date, necessitating an insertion of a new size, such as "BB". An example of each single letter is shown:

A   B   C   D   E   F

Different pattern numbers having the same size letters bear no relation to each other. That is, a 907C and a 6308C have no relation in size, the former being a 14" high vase, and the latter a 7" high vase. Size ratio exists only within the category of a particular pattern or shape and is of no defined scale.

CLAY SYMBOLS

Rookwood Pottery employed a series of letter-symbols to indicate the clay used in the manufacture of the body. The clays were classified only in regard to color. The symbols were six in number and were impressed. The following letters were employed:

G   O   R   S   W   Y

These indicate Ginger, Olive, Red, Sage Green, White, and Yellow. The Ginger colored clay is one that would be termed a "Buff" clay. The letter "G" and the title Ginger" were employed to avoid confusion with the size symbol "B". The letter "S" is also used in another category, that of a special symbol.

The symbols refer only to the color of the various bodies, and as such do not take into consideration the possible chemical variations within a color. The White body was the most popular and undoubtedly the one most frequently used by the potters. This color was developed and compounded in at least seven chemically different varieties to fit glazes in use at the Pottery. Often no distinction was made in them when marking the ware. In later years the clay symbol "W" was sometimes omitted.

Rookwood experimented with artificially tinted bodies as have most of the world's leading potteries, but their existence in relation to the total production is quite small. Tinted grey, blue and black bodies were utilized for the most part after 1920.

Rookwood also experimented with foreign clays to some extent; but domestic clays, and particularly those from the Ohio Valley, were most popular. The Ohio region is rich in fine clays. These are naturally colored, having been stained by the mineral deposits of the area. The Red clay was from Buena Vista, Ohio and the Yellow from Hanging Rock, Ohio.

A Yellow clay was obtained from Georgia, and a Cream colored one from Chattanooga, Tennessee; still another clay came from Florida. The existence of a Cream colored clay, as well as examples of Cream colored ware, creates speculation that there may have been a symbol for "Cream" clay in use at one time, for relatively early pieces have been found marked with a double "C".

PROCESS MARKS

At Rookwood all experiments or changes in clay, decorative materials, and glaze were carefully recorded and studied. To do so, it was necessary to identify the items after their return from the fire. Therefore the chemists, and sometimes the potters, placed identifying symbols on the pieces. They did this by incising or impressing impromptu, but recognizable designs, much as Westerners brand cattle. The precise meaning of these symbols could only be known through access to the notebooks kept by these men. For the benefit of those who may come across such symbols a few are illustrated:

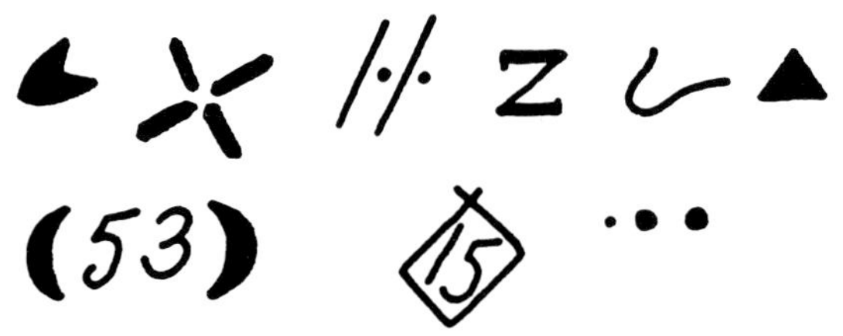

SPECIAL MARKS AND SYMBOLS

In the following paragraphs are collected and defined those marks and symbols which do not fit precisely into a prior category. These marks are not to be considered of any lesser importance than those comprising the other categories, because they also contribute invaluably to the understanding of the history and significance of the piece of Rookwood Pottery in question. Some are old. Others are of more recent composition. None are without precise meaning and purpose, though that be temporarily unknown.

The first mark to be considered, is the one that will be encountered most frequently. This is the "X" mark used to indicate a piece of secondary quality. Rookwood ware from its inception was graded into three classifications. These are: (1.) Those items of the best quality, that is, most nearly flawless. (No critisism of art work was involved, according to my friend Virginia Cummins, who was employed in the salesroom.) (2.) Those items displaying obvious technical faults, such as glaze bubbles, minor discolorations, kiln cracks, warp, and other manufacturing defects. It was this category of ware which was so designated by the "X" mark. (3.) Those items defective to the point of ruination of either their utility, decoration, or both. These were destroyed.

The "X" mark indicating secondary quality was usually cut into the underside of the piece, by means of a grinding wheel, much the same as that used to remove excess glaze from the resting surface of an item. The mark was also known to have been cut into the decorated surface of some pieces, and in these cases, undoubtedly contributes additionally to the undesirableness of the piece. The mark was not generally accurately cut, and as a result may appear as a "V" like score in the body, however, there is no reason to confuse this with the Vellum "V" mark, which is explained later in this same category. The "X" mark is generally large, and appears as a deeply ground score in the body, as follows:

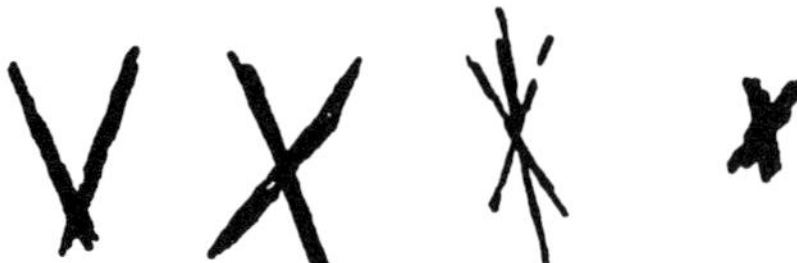

The category of second quality was usually determined in the showroom, by those in charge. The sales personnel had access to a grinding wheel, and cut the second mark themselves. It is presumed that the decorators could also request that an item of their work be adjudged as secondary quality. The extent to which this was done, if any, is not known. The third example from the left is a wheel ground "X" with an additional cut through the center which was used for items to be given away. "Give away" recipients ranged from visitors of note to unsold pieces "raffled" at company sponsored parties for employees. In later examples (circa 1940) a single wheel ground line has been found, which may have been the equivalent of an "X".

As any collector can attest, the judgment of secondary items over a period of years as represented by pieces of varying age, appears rather whimsical. Many items so marked contain only flaws of a very minor nature. In contrast, items are known with kiln cracks of several inches or more, and are not marked seconds. Regardless of the apparent overlapping of categories, and inconsistent application of standards, a second is less valuable. The second quality items were placed on a separate table at the Pottery, and marked down, in relation to items of first quality.

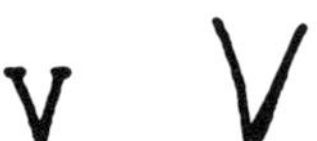

The examples above show the two varieties of the "V" mark which was used to designate the Vellum line. This particular glaze was first introduced in 1904 and is credited to the efforts of the plant chemist Stanley G. Burt.

The Vellum mark always appears on the bottom of the item, apart from the factory mark, so that it can never be confused with the date 1905 (V). It is either impressed, in which case it is in the form of a printed "V", or incised. It is believed the impressed "V" refers to a "vellum" body, and the hand incised "V" refers to the decorators desire to have the piece "vellum" glazed. This explanation is based upon empirical evidence, and the double "V" occurs mostly within the mid-range years of vellum production. The possibility of mismarked items is rather remote, and although this has undoubtedly occurred, the Pottery was rather well organized at the time Vellum was manufactured, and an error of this type would be unusual. After seeing several Vellum pieces and examining them closely, it becomes increasingly easier to identify, and reference to the "V" mark serves only as a verification of one's knowledge.

The Vellums are one of the most beautiful and unusual of all the Rookwood creations. To describe Vellum in its simplest terms Rookwood's master potter, Earl Menzel, said, "It is merely a transparent mat, developed in the fire." The implication of this, is that Rookwood was the first pottery to develop this glaze without the aid of chemical or mechanical means. The Vellum glaze won a Gold Medal at the St. Louis World's Fair in 1904.

S

The above letter "S" was impressed in the clay of Rookwood as an indication that the particular item had been created as a "special" shape (perhaps at the request of a decorator) and was not assigned a normal sequential shape number. However, one must be careful to distinguish between the "S" indicating the Sage Green clay (see: clay marks) and the "S" indicating the potter's handiwork. This is a relatively easy distinction to make, for the Sage Green clay is a pale olive color, and is easily recognized on the unglazed portions of the under surface. In addition, Sage Green bodies usually lent themselves to decoration in tones of green, brown, and yellow.

In the case of a Sage Green clay piece which was thrown by hand, the piece would bear two "S's". Examples of this nature do in fact exist, as do all the other combinations of clay marks and the potter's "S".

P

The above letter, impressed in the paste, represents the term, "Porcelain." It was introduced at Easter, 1915, after Rookwood had developed a "porcelainized" body, and accompanying high gloss glaze. The body is not a true porcelain, but should be more correctly termed a "soft-porcelain" or "semi-porcelain."

These pieces were generally decorated in light colors. This was probably due to the high glaze maturity and body vitrification temperatures, conditions which tend to "burn out" deeper colors. This body has a slightly irridescent appearance, and in the thinner pieces a translucence will be evident when exposed to a strong light. The colors and manner of decoration surpassed those of the Copenhagen furnaces, and magnificent blues had been developed. The ware was quite costly to produce, and was subsequently abandoned for a ware referred to as "Jewel Porcelain."

Jewel Porcelain was also a "porcelainized" or vitreous body, but employed a distinctively different glaze, which was characterized by a running of the colors. This ware was manufactured for quite some time. It bore no body or glaze mark of its own, nor did it bear the "P" mark.

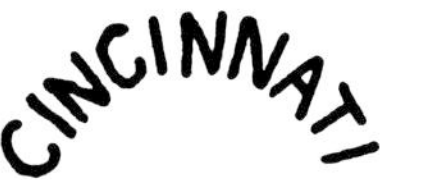 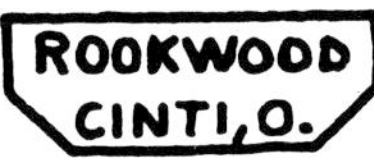

The "L" mark, as illustrated above, is found incised into older pieces of Rookwood in conjunction with the "Standard" glaze. The items are decorated, and the "L" is often under the decorator's mark, as shown in the second example, having been incised by the decorator himself. There is no apparent relationship between this mark and that of a specific decorator. It is found with the marks of all decorators of the period.

The letter refers to the decorator's choice of glaze to be employed. "L" refers to a lightly colored standard glaze and an M (not illustrated) refers to a Mahogany tinted standard glaze, The "D" for a dark standard glaze, was also used, and the script "G" (example 3) refers to the sea green glaze. The sea green glaze "G" is also found impressed as a capital G.

 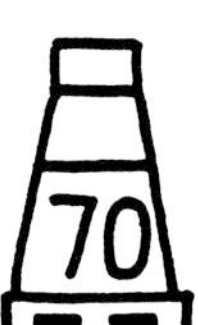 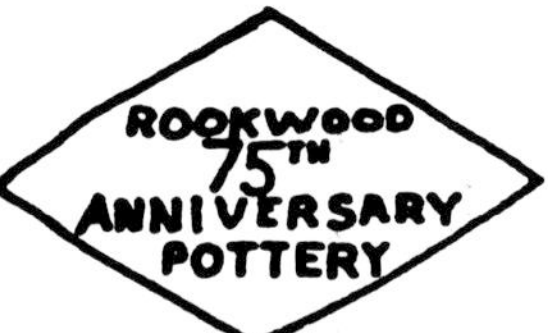

The above examples of the printed name "CINCINNATI" were used in an effort to identify the name of Rookwood with the city in which it was founded and had prospered. The impressions were always used in addition to the other standard symbols, factory marks, etc. This practice was originated circa 1920, and the symbol used from time to time on various productions. The mark on the extreme left appeared as a wreath over the factory symbol, RP with flames. The marks to the right appeared as later examples. The correlation between years and the use of these marks does not have any significance beyond the fact that the Pottery was attempting to hold its position of prestige in relation to its competitors; hence the inclusion of the name of the Pottery. Other varieties of the city name are known to exist.

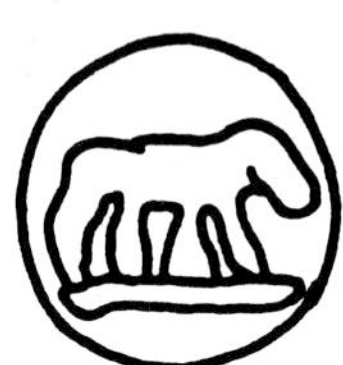

The above marks were created for the pieces of Rookwood ware produced during the year of an anniversary. The first such anniversary mark is the one signifying Rookwood's Fiftieth Year, 1930. This mark was usually applied in the form of an underglaze color, (blue or black) and represents a kiln with the number 50 within it. The mark used for the Seventieth Year is also a kiln with the number 70 contained in it, but differs in that it is also found impressed in the clay, and often accompanied by the name ROOKWOOD impressed alongside. The third anniversary mark at the right took the form of a diamond and signified Rookwood Pottery's 75th birthday.

This mark appears on the underside of a Rookwood ashtray depicting one of the masks of drama, but is not a Rookwood mark. The pattern is an exact reproduction of an item brought from Italy by Mr. J.D. Wareham, director of the Pottery. The original pattern bore the mark in question, and therefore, it was preserved in the reproduction. The relief form represents Romulus, Remus and their Wolf Mother of Roman Mythology.

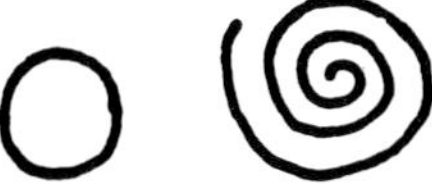

The above marks were instituted by Rookwood's master potter, Earl Menzel. The whorl was impressed on the underside of many thrown pieces and was merely an idiosyncrasy of the potter. The mark was made on the lathe, and is usually unaccompanied by Mr. Menzel's signature. It can be assumed to be a synonym for his mark, for these pieces were produced by his hand. The circle was applied, as an impression, to pieces whose shape might make them suitable for use as lamps, and was intended as a guide for drilling.

Initials, names, and inscriptions are also found incised into the decorative surface of some Rookwood. These are not marks, but the results of creation of pieces for friends, and commemoration of special events, and as such do not require further explanation.

ARTISTS' AND DECORATORS' MARKS

It became the custom at the Rookwood Pottery for the artists to incise or paint their initials or monograms on the pieces decorated or sculptured by them but this was not always so. In the fledgling days of the Pottery the signing of work was discouraged. Soon, however, a preference for the signed pieces made itself felt in the market, and the Pottery changes its policy. One must remember that these Artists' initials are presented here in their most ideal state — many hurriedly written examples exist, making the commonest of monograms sometimes impossible to decipher.

The artists not only cut their initials into the bottom of the ware, but painted them on, using some of the underglaze "paint" or engobe that was in use at the moment. This method was also employed when the artists signed pieces on the decorated surface. Many used their full names if their pieces were a special effort.

Marks were also impressed. This was done through the construction of a die, much the same as that employed to impress the factory mark. The decorators or potters formed these from clay, and once fired, they were permanent in nature and could be used repeatedly. It was necessary, of course, to construct them in reverse, the same as a rubber stamp. One artist intentionally failed to observe this rule, and as a result Carl Schmidt's mark is "mirrored," or reversed.

The use of dies was practiced primarily by the decorators of later years. Readily recognizable examples of these dies are the marks of Margaret Helen McDonald and Mary Graze Denzler.

There are decorators in the accompanying list. Some of these have as many as four different marks attributed to them. They are presented in the order of what is believed to be their earliest mark, first. An effort has been made to limit this presentation to only those marks and symbols which have been positively identified, and no full signatures have been included for these are self-explanatory.

Approximately one dozen other "decorators" marks will be found accompanying ware, circa 1946. These people are not identified in the following listing for they were designated as "junior artists" and did not participate in projects of original composition as did the staff artists. Their marks are found applied in underglaze color, and their duties consisted of applying specific colors to prepared designs.

Abel, Edward		Cranch, E. Bertha I.	
Abel, Louise		Cranch, Edward P.	
Altman, Howard		Crofton, Cora	
Asbury, Lenore		Daly, Matt A.	
Auckland, Fannie		Demarest, Virginia B.	
Auckland, William		Denzler, Mary Grace	
Baker, Constance A.		Dibowski, Charles John	
Barrett, Elizabeth		Diers, Edward	
Bishop, Irene		Duell, Cecil A.	
Bonsall, Caroline F.		Epply, Lorinda	
Bookprinter, Anna M.		Fechheimer, Rose	
Brain, Elizabeth W.		Felten, Edith R.	
Brennan, Alfred		Foertmeyer, Emma D.	
Breuer, W. H.		Foglesong, Mattie	
Caven, Alice		Fry, Laura A.	
Conant, Arthur P.		Furukawa, Lois	
Conant, Patti M.		Glass, William T.	
Cook, Daniel		Goetting, Arthur	
Covalenco, Catherine		Hall, Grace M.	
Coyne, Sallie E.		Hanscom, Lena E.	
Crabtree, Catherine		Harris, Janet	

Hentschel, W. E.

Hickman, Katharine

Hicks, Orville

Hirschfeld, N. J.

Holtkamp, Loretta

Horsfall, Bruce

Horton, Hattie

Humphreys, Albert

Hurley, Edward T.

Jensen, Jens

Jones, Katherine

King, Flora

King, Ora

Klemm, William

Klinger, Charles

Koehler, F. D.

Laurence, Sturgis

Lawrence, ELiza C.

Ley, Kay

Lincoln, Elizabeth N.

Lindeman, Clara C.

Lindeman, Laura E.

Lunt, Tom

Lyons, Helen M.

Markland, Sadie

Matchette, Kate C.

McDermott, Elizabeth F.

McDonald, Margaret Helen

McDonald, William P.

McLaughlin, Charles J.

Menzel, Reuben Earl

Mitchell, Marianne D.

Moos, Herman

Munson, Albert

Newton, Clara Chipman

Nichols, Maria Longworth

Noonan, Edith

Nourse, Mary

Perkins, Mary Luella

Peters-Baurer, Pauline

Pons, Albert

Pullman, J. Wesley

Rauchfuss, Marie

Reed, O. Geneva

Rehm, Wilhelmine

Rettig, Martin

Rothenbusch, Fred

Sacksteder, Jane

Sax, Sara

Scalf, Virginia

Schmidt, Carl

Sehon, Adeliza D.

Seyler, David W.

Shirayamadani, Kataro

Smalley, Marian H.

Sprague, Amelia B.

Stegner, Carolyn

Steinle, Carrie F.

Storer, Maria Longworth (Nichols)

Strafer, Harriette R.

Stuntz, H. Pabodie

Swing, Jeanette

Taylor, Mary A.

Tischler, Vera

Todd, Charles S.

Toohey, Sallie

Valentien, Albert R.

Valentien, Anna M.

Van Briggle, Artus

Van Briggle, Leona

Van Horne, Katherine

Vreeland, Francis W.

Wareham, John D.

Wenderoth, Harriet

Wilcox, Harriet E.

Wildman, Edith L.

Willitts, Alice

Workum, Delia

Young, Grace

Zanetta, Clotilda

Zettel, Josephine E.

ALPHABETICAL LIST OF ARTISTS AND THEIR WORKS BY CATALOG NUMBER

ROOKWOOD

Abel, Ed, 660, 905,963

Abel, Louise, 720, 772, 923, 968

Asbury, Lenore, 558, 573, 617, 689, 739, 750, 809, 854, 878, 883, 888, 950, 957, 977, 999, 1010

Auckland, Fannie, 904, 907

Baker, Constance, 504, 774, 900, 978, 1004

Barrett, Elizabeth, 553, 836, 982, 1009

Bishop, Irene, 505, 955, 983

Bookprinter, Anna, 729

Conant, Arthur, 502, 520, 732, 804, 841, 910, 917

Covalenco, Catherine, 741

Coyne, Sallie, 540, 563, 576, 605, 614, 623, 706, 768, 866, 962

Curry, Kate, 570

Daly, M.A., 603, 618, 703, 733, 747, 783, 789, 806, 884, 932, 935, 995

Denzler, Mary Grace, 616, 843

Diers, Ed, 562, 581, 582, 596, 680, 684, 713, 765, 770, 842, 845, 849, 864, 887, 893, 896, 903, 915, 934, 969, 974, 981

Duell, Cecil, 636, 723, 800

Epply, Lorinda, 511, 552, 589, 740, 852, 858

Fechheimer, Rose, 515, 881, 890, 914, 927

Felten, Edith, 538, 556

Foertmeyer, Emma, 507

Fry, Laura, 737, 766

Gest, Joseph Henry, 790

Harris, Janet, 663

Hentschel, William, 598, 727, 752, 794, 846

Hickman, Katherine, 980

Hirschfeld, N.J., 539

Horsfall, Bruce, 919

Horton, Hattie, 611

Humphreys, Albert, 716

Hurley, E.T., 509, 523, 527, 531, 572, 584, 608, 625, 649, 650, 651, 652, 653, 654, 707, 725, 792, 815, 885, 886, 920, 928, 958, 976, 1002, 1008

Jensen, Jens, 557, 560, 659, 677, 810, 856, 859, 916

Jensen, Jens attribution, 662

Jones, Katherine, 529, 575, 607, 831, 897, 953

Keenan, Mary Virginia, 788, 791

King, Flora, 637

Klinger, Charles, 964

Laurence, Sturgis, 628

Ley, Kay, 692, 913

Lincoln, Elizabeth, 541, 579, 624, 683, 839, 862, 926, 954, 997

Lindeman, Clara, 814, 912, 918

Lindeman, Laura, 638, 701

McDermott, Elizabeth, 921

McDonald, Margaret, 566, 613, 682, 702, 771, 838, 879, 902

McDonald, William, 593, 787, 793, 501

Menzel, Ruben Earl, 513, 734

Mitchell, Marianne, 555, 656

Noonan, Edith, 898

Nourse, Mary, 583, 634, 690, 717

Peck, Herbert, 781

Pons, Albert, 724

Reed, Olga Geneva, 536, 615, 709, 808

Rehm, Wilhelmine, 676

Rookwood Architectural Faience 580, 610, 693, 695, 696, 697, 698, 714, 851, 901

Rookwood Commercial, 510, 512, 524, 533, 542, 543, 544, 545, 546, 547, 548, 549, 550, 551, 554, 571, 585, 600, 635, 639, 640, 641, 642, 643, 644, 645, 646, 647, 648, 658, 665, 666, 667, 668, 669, 670, 671, 699, 704, 735, 753, 754, 755, 756, 757, 758, 759, 760, 761, 762, 763, 784, 817, 818, 819, 820, 821, 822, 823, 824, 825, 826, 835, 850, 867, 868, 869, 870, 871, 872, 873, 874, 875, 876, 877, 882, 891, 899, 936, 937, 938, 939, 940, 941, 942, 943, 944, 945, 946, 949, 956, 967, 985, 986, 987, 988, 989, 990, 991, 992, 993, 994, 998

Rothenbusch, Fred, 508, 559, 595, 612, 629, 630, 673, 674, 691, 718, 736, 742, 780, 782, 880, 892, 965, 975, 984

Sax, Sara, 500, 517, 569, 577, 588, 602, 661, 679, 711, 731, 743, 744, 764, 777, 802, 812, 827, 834, 848, 894, 906, 959, 996, 1007

Schmidt, Carl, 514, 587, 590, 597, 622, 626, 681, 687, 719, 722, 746, 776, 785, 807, 840, 847, 857, 908, 925, 948, 966, 1005

Sehon, Adeliza D., 592

Shirayamadani, Kataro, 518, 519, 526, 528, 532, 535, 565, 568, 578, 601, 606, 609, 632, 657, 675, 686, 688, 700, 708, 710, 728, 738, 769, 786, 813, 816, 837, 853, 930, 933, 951, 960, 970, 1001, 1003

Sprague, Amelia, 591, 721, 748

Steinle, Carrie, 574, 594, 620, 664, 833, 855

Strafer, Harriette, 895

Swing, Jeanette, 599, 685

Tischler, Vera, 534

Todd, C.S., 537, 621, 631, 801, 828

Toohey, Sallie, 564, 775, 860, 961, 972, 979

Unknown, 506, 522, 561, 749, 751, 795, 796, 861, 1000

Valentien, Albert R., 525, 604, 633, 655, 712, 715, 805, 863, 924, 947, 952

Valentien, Anna, 586, 678, 745, 773, 829, 911, 971, 973

Van Briggle, Artus, 844, 929

Wareham, John Dee, 521, 627, 672, 730, 734, 889, 909, 1009

Wenderoth, Harriet, 779, 922

Wilcox, Harriet, 530, 705, 726, 778, 811, 931, 1006

Willitts, Alice, 767

Young, Grace, 516, 619, 694, 803

ALPHABETICAL LIST OF ARTIST AND GLAZE LINES BY CATALOG NUMBER

KERAMICS

ALPHABETICAL LIST OF POTTERIES AND THEIR WORKS BY CATALOG NUMBER

KERAMICS

A.E.T.Co., 9

Amphora, 378, 380, 382, 383, 386, 387, 401

Ball and Bohrod, 404

Brush, 11

Buffalo, 265, 266, 267, 268, 269, 270, 271

Cabat, 251, 253, 254

California Faience, 199, 203

Charlotte Rhead, 340

Chicago Crucible, 305

Cincinnati Art Pottery, 798

Clarice Cliff, 338

Clement Massier, 390

Clewell, 260, 262, 263, 264

Clifton, 8

Cowan, 197, 198, 202, 252

Dalpayrat, 396

Deleherche, 393

Delphin Massier, 388, 391

Doulton Lambeth, 337

Forester & Son, 397

Fulper, 291, 292, 293, 294, 295, 296, 297, 298, 299, 300, 301, 302, 331, 332, 333, 334, 335, 336, 355, 356, 357, 358, 359, 360, 366, 367, 368, 369, 370, 371

Gladding McBean, 200

Gordy, 276

Grueby, 309, 311

Hamilton Tile Works Company, 312, 313, 315

Harris Strong, 325

Jervis, 206

Jugtown, 272

Julius Dressler, 394

Kenton Hills, 830, 832

Marblehead, 317, 322

Matt Morgan, 795

Merrimac, 310

Montigny sur Loing, 92

Moorcroft, 344, 345, 346, 347, 348, 349, 350, 351, 352, 353, 354, 361, 362, 363, 364, 365, 365, 372, 373, 374, 375, 376, 377

Moravian, 318

Mosaic Tile Company, 12

Muncie, 193, 196, 201

Natzler, 248, 249, 250

Newcomb, 185, 186, 187, 191, 192

Niloak, 273, 277

Northwestern Terra Cotta Company, 314

Overbeck, 13, 14, 15, 323, 324

Owens, 174, 175, 176, 177, 178, 179, 180, 195, 328

Pergamon, 385

Peters and Reed, 275

Pewabic, 330

Picasso, 406

Pillin, 244, 246

Pisgah Forest, 247, 274

Radford, 10

Rambervillers, 399

Red Wing, 212, 213

Rorstrand, 395

Roseville, 17, 20, 22, 23, 24, 25, 26, 27, 54, 55, 56, 57, 58, 59, 60, 78, 79, 80, 81, 82, 83, 84, 92, 93, 94, 95, 96, 108, 109, 110, 111, 112, 113, 114, 115, 116, 117, 118, 121, 122, 123, 135, 136, 137, 138, 139, 140, 153, 154, 181, 182, 183, 184, 204, 205, 208, 210, 236, 237, 238, 239, 240, 241, 242, 278, 279, 280, 281, 282, 283, 284, 285, 286, 287, 288, 289, 290

Royal Bonn, 381

Royal Copenhagen, 384

Royal Doulton, 337, 341, 342, 343

Royal Worcester, 400

Ruskin, 389

Scheier, 243, 245

Stellmacher, 379

Stonelain, 402, 403, 405, 407, 408

Teco, 303, 304, 306, 307

Trent Tile Company, 234

UND, 28, 29, 30, 31, 32, 33, 34

Unknown, 160

Van Briggle, 188, 189, 190

Vance-Avon, 207, 209

Vance-Avon and Clewell, 264

Walley, 261

Weller, 1, 2, 3, 4, 5, 6, 7, 16, 18, 19, 21, 35, 36, 37, 37, 38, 39, 40, 41, 42, 43, 44, 45, 46, 47, 48, 49, 50, 51, 52, 53, 61, 62, 63, 64, 65, 66, 67, 68, 69, 70, 71, 72, 73, 74, 76, 76, 77, 85, 86, 87, 88, 89, 90, 91, 97, 98, 99, 100, 101, 102, 103, 104, 105, 106, 107, 119, 120, 124, 125, 126, 127, 128, 129, 130, 131, 132, 133, 134, 141, 142, 143, 144, 145, 146, 147, 148, 149, 150, 151, 152, 155, 156, 157, 158, 159, 161, 162, 163, 164, 165, 166, 167, 168, 169, 170, 171, 172, 173, 194, 211, 214, 215, 216, 217, 218, 219, 220, 221, 222, 223, 224, 225, 226, 227, 228, 229, 230, 231, 232, 233, 235, 255, 256, 257, 258, 259, 316, 319, 321

Wheatley, 308, 320, 326, 327, 329, 797, 799

Wood & Sons, 339

KERAMICS 1997
SATURDAY
JUNE 7TH
1997
LOTS 1 - 408

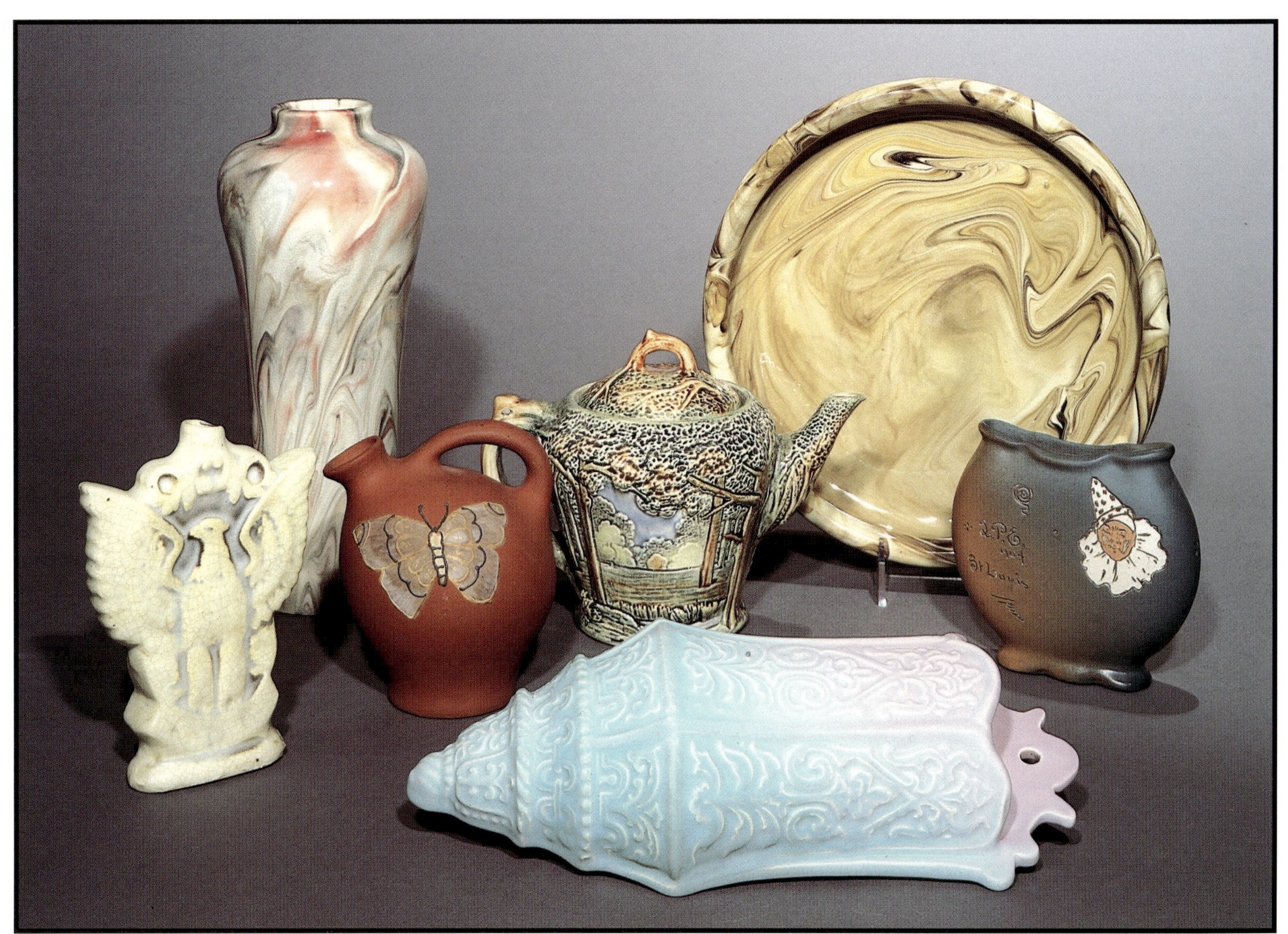

1   Weller creamware flask in the form of an eagle, made for the Fraternal Order of Elks. Marked F.O.E. on both sides. Otherwise unmarked. Height 5 3/4 inches. $100-150

2   Nice Weller Marbleized vase with interesting shape and colors of red, cream and brown. Incised "Weller" on the base. Height 10 1/8 inches. $200-300

3   Rare souvenir of the St. Louis World's Fair of 1904, a ewer of red clay decorated with a butterfly, outlined by slip trailing. Incised "Weller" in block letters on the bottom. $200-300

4   Weller Lavonia wall pocket with stylized Victorian designs embossed in the body and covered in mauve shading to aqua mat glaze. Unmarked. Height 10 3/4 inches. Uncommon. $200-300

5   Rare Weller Forest teapot in high glaze. Unmarked. Height 5 7/8 inches. There is a small chip on the end of the spout. $150-200

6   Weller Marbleized low bowl in shades of brown and cream. Marked "Weller" in large block letters. Diameter is 10 1/4 inches. $150-200

7   Rare St. Louis World's Fair (Louisiana Purchase Exposition) souvenir pillow vase made by Weller in 1904. The 2nd Line Dickensware piece is incised with the image of a clown and the notation "L.P.E. 1904 St Louis". The base is impressed "Dickensware Weller" and incised with the number "400". Height 4 1/2 inches. $200-300

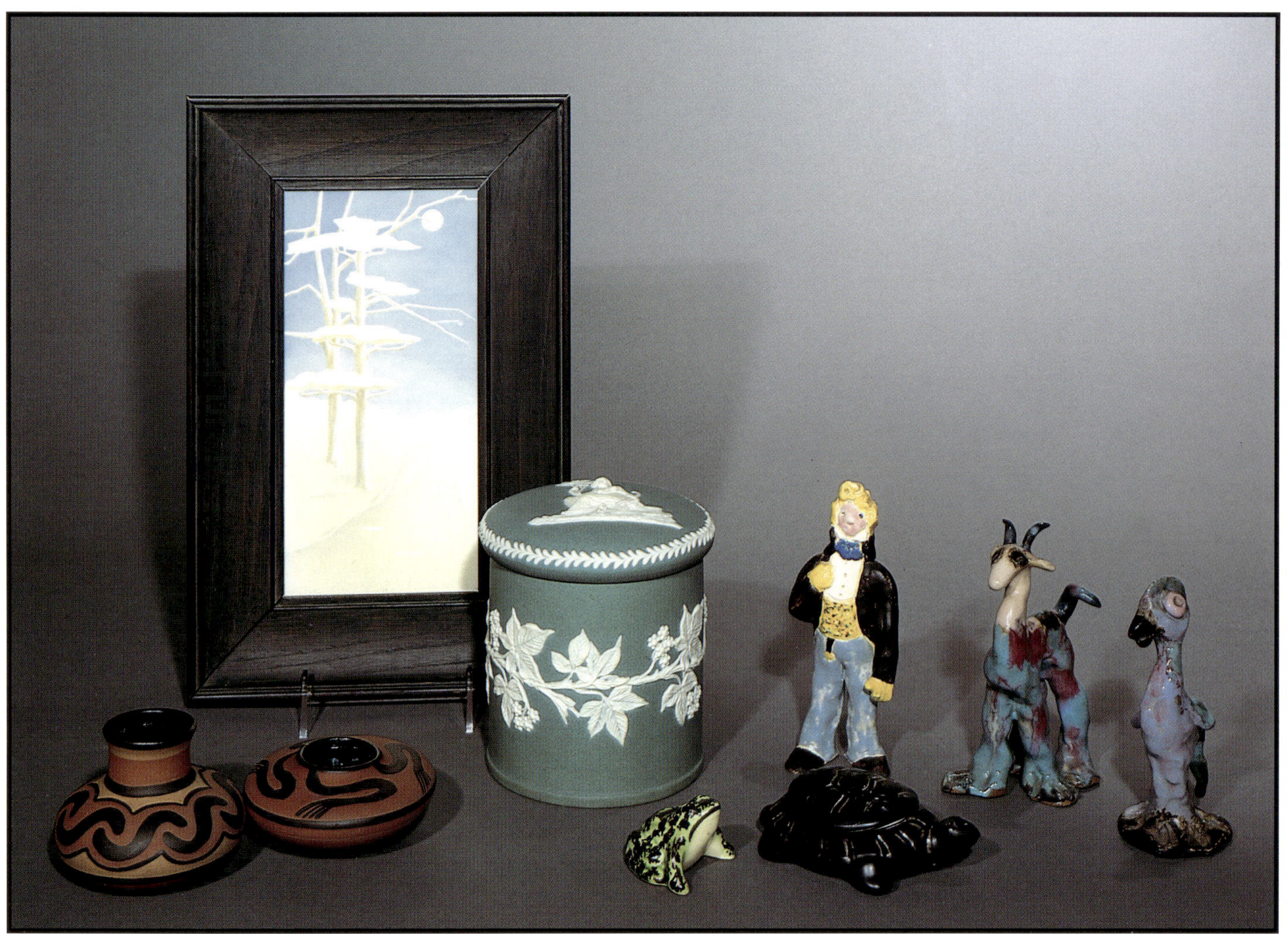

8	Nice pair of Clifton Indian Ware cabinet vases in bisque with Native American designs in black and tan slip. The taller vase carries the impressed "Clifton" name and the name "Mississippi" along with an incised Native American symbol and numbers "209" and "7". The smaller vase is impressed "Clifton" and is incised with the same symbol, the name "Florida" and the number "184". Height of the taller vase is 2 5/8 inches.	$300-400
9	Arts & Crafts style American Encaustic Tile Company tile, hand painted with a wintery snow scene by an unknown artist and covered with a vellum like glaze. Embossed on the back is "Patent Grip Back A.E.T. CO.". Size is 9 by 4 1/2 inches. Older ebonized oak frame.	$1000-1500
10	Radford Jasper covered box made by Albert Radford in Tiffin, Ohio circa 1896. Decoration consists of a classical seated figure holding a cornucopia and a branch applied to the lid and vine and berry decor encircling the body. The piece is stamped "Radford Jasper". Height 5 5/8 inches. A base chip has been professionally repaired.	$600-800
11	Brush figural frog in the smallest size. Unmarked. Height 1 1/2 inches. This size is rare and hard to find.	$100-200
12	Mosaic Tile Company ceramic box in the form of a turtle, covered in the company's blue mat glaze. The bottom of the turtle is incised "Mosaic Company Zanesville". Height is 1 3/8 inches while nose to tail length is 4 1/4 inches. We are still waiting for measurements with the head and tail retracted.	$150-200
13	Overbeck "Colonial Gentleman" figurine done in both gloss and matt glazes. Marked with the Overbeck monogram, the piece stands 5 3/4 inches high. Minor glaze nicks on both feet.	$175-225
14	Amusing Overbeck Grotesque goat done in maroon, teal and cream high glazes with accents in black matt glaze. Marked with the Overbeck logo on the bottom of one foot. Height 5 3/8 inches. Minor repairs to the tail and both horns.	$150-250
15	Overbeck Grotesque chicken figurine. Marked with the Overbeck monogram on the base. Height 5 inches. There is repair to base and a broken tail has been glued.	$100-150

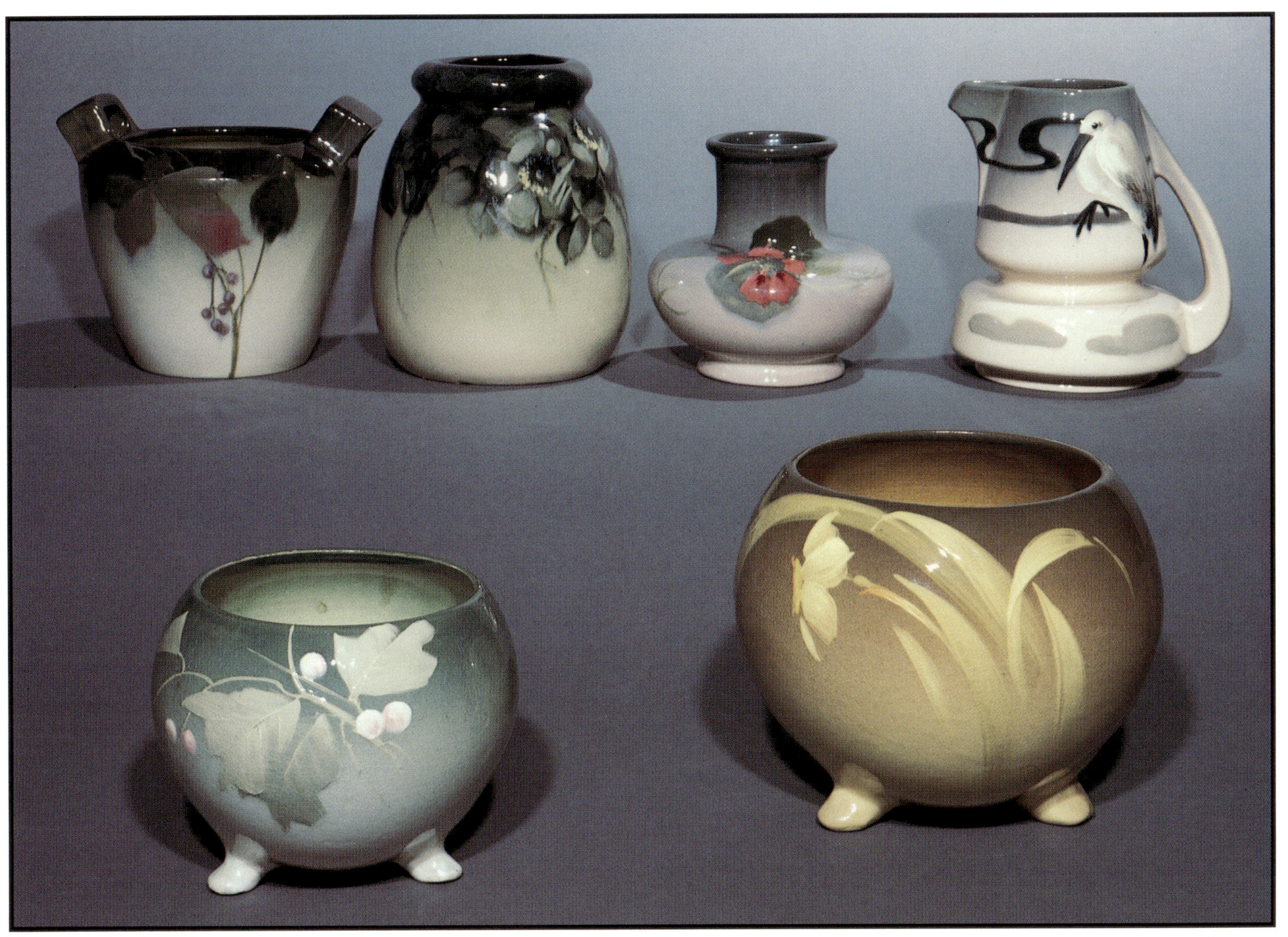

16   Weller Eocean vase with two square handles and Virginia creeper decoration, most likely the work of Levi J. Burgess. Incised "Eocean Weller" and "S" on the bottom. Initials which are somewhat blurred appear just below the left handle and seem to be those of Burgess. Height 5 3/4 inches. There is a tight line at the rim, just beside one of the handles. $300-400

17   Roseville Rozane Light three-footed vase with leaf and berry decoration done by an unknown artist. Unmarked. Height 3 7/8 inches. Minor roughness inside rim and small glaze nick on one of the feet. $150-200

18   Weller Eocean vase with wild rose decoration, done in shades of green and cream by an unknown artist. Marks on the base include "Weller" in small block letters, the name "Eocean" incised and the number "6906", also incised. Height 6 1/2 inches. $400-500

19   Weller Eocean vase with pink nasturtium decoration done by an unknown artist. Incised marks include "Eocean Weller" and an esoteric mark. Impressed on the base in the number "4". Height 4 7/8 inches. $300-400

20   Roseville Rozane Light vase with jonquil decoration and three stubby shoe feet, done by an unknown artist. Marked only with an impressed number "6" on the bottom. Height 5 inches. $200-300

21   Weller Eocean pitcher, an English Arts & Crafts form, showing a stork with ribbon-like clouds behind and lily pads below. Marked with two embossed rectangles; inside of one is the name "Weller" and inside the other the number "46". Incised inside the second rectangle is the number "90". Height 6 1/8 inches. A very similar piece signed by Frank Ferrell sold in last year's sale. $1750-2250

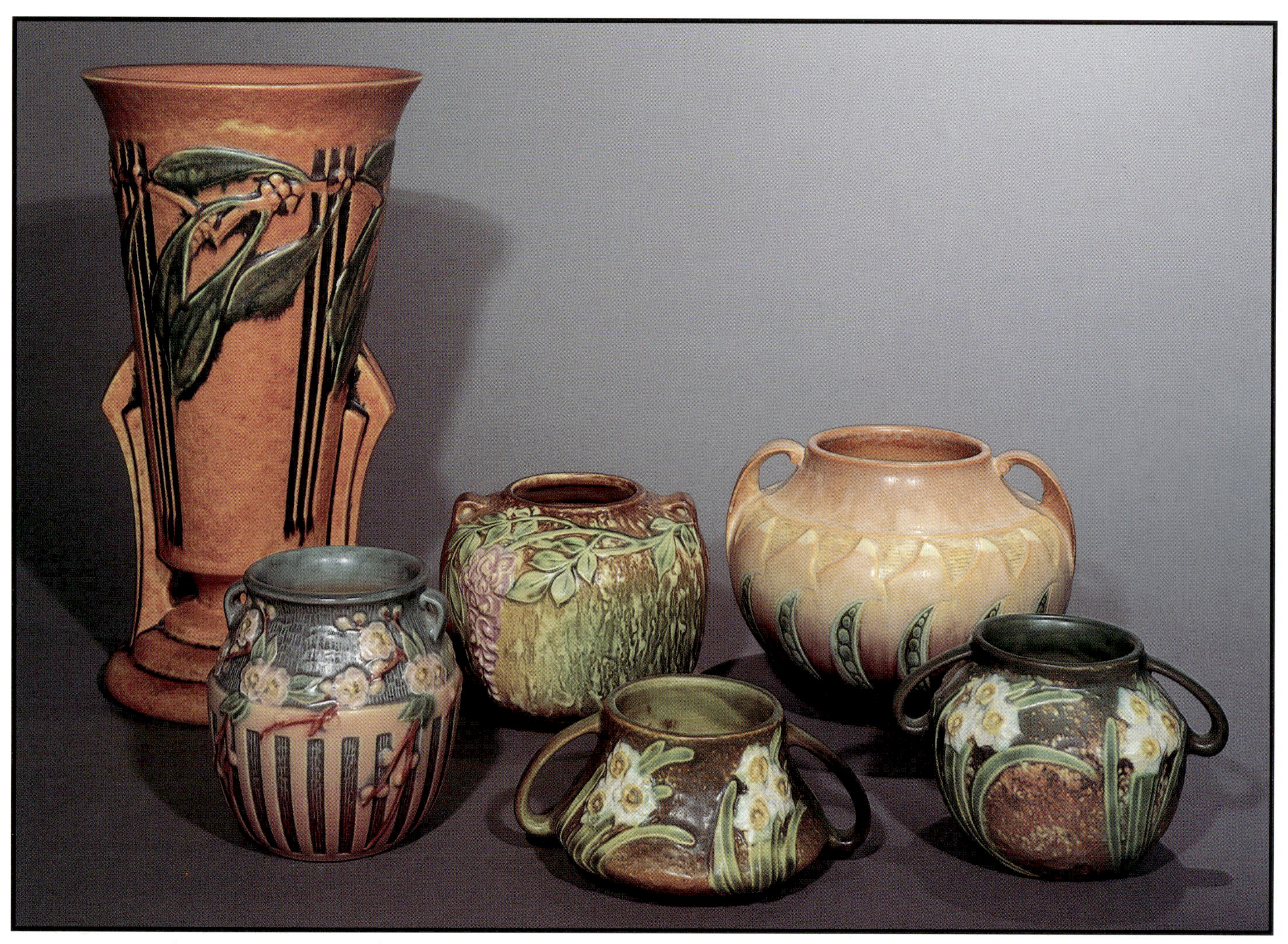

22 Tall Roseville Laurel vase in orange, green and black having two small handles. Marked only with an "X" and an "N" painted on the bottom in blue slip. Height 14 1/4 inches. Small rim chips have been professionally repaired. Great glaze and mold. $500-700

23 Roseville Cherry Blossom two-handled vase in pink and blue. Marked only with the number "9" painted on the bottom. Height 5 1/8 inches. Good mold and color. $250-350

24 Roseville Wisteria vase with two small loop handles. The only marking on the base is the number "6" painted on the bottom in blue slip. Height 6 inches. Excellent mold and color. $400-500

25 Roseville Jonquil vase with two wide loop handles. Unmarked. Height 3 inches. Good mold and color. $200-300

26 Roseville Falline two-handled vase in tan, brown and green. The only mark on the piece is an incised "9" on the bottom. Height 6 1/8 inches. There is a glaze nick on the inside of one of the handles and a flat chip off the base which is invisible from the side. Good color and mold. $400-600

27 Roseville Jonquil two-handled vase. Unmarked. Height 4 1/8 inches. Decent mold and color. $200-300

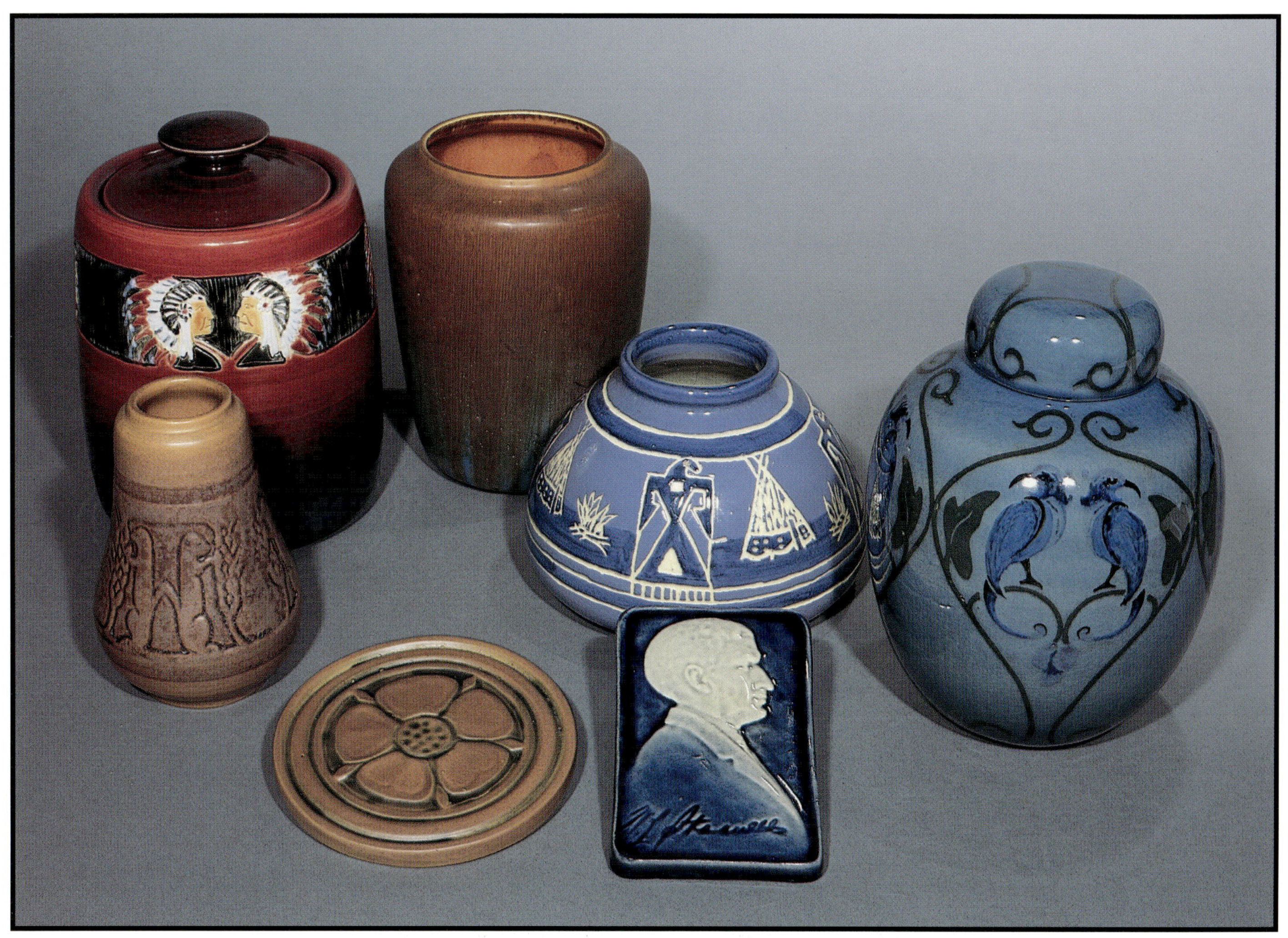

28   Unique carved and painted UND humidor with the profiles of six Native Americans in full headdress done by $2000-2500
      Margaret Cable. The hand-thrown body is lightly carved and the figures are painted in white, red, black and tan
      colors. Marked with the UND inkstamp logo. Painted in blue slip above and below the seal are respectively,
      Cable's name and the notation "Tob. 4". Height 7 3/4 inches. A chip in the lid has been professionally repaired.
      This is a fabulous example of Cable's work.

29   UND vase in shades of brown picturing what appear to be prairie dogs standing on their hind legs, braced $300-400
      against wheat stalks. The scene repeats several times in a band around the center of the vase. Marks include
      the UND inkstamp logo, incised initials which appear to be those of Julia Mattson and the number "43". Height
      5 1/4 inches. Clearly this is a cast piece but it does bear an artist's mark.

30   UND trivet with embossed prairie rose design. Marked on the back with the UND circular inkstamp logo and $100-150
      the incised number "85". Diameter is 4 7/8 inches.

31   Very rare and extremely early UND glaze effect vase done in 1913 by an unknown artist whose monogram $500-700
      appears to be L.B. Decoration consists of coffee brown mat glaze flowing over blue and green mat. Marks
      include the initials "U.N.D." and the date, painted on in dark blue slip. Incised marks include the artist's mono-
      gram and the number "912". Height 6 3/4 inches.

32   Rare and unusual high glaze UND vase with carved and painted Native American decoration done in 1934 by $2000-3000
      M. Helen Davies. Pictured are four teepees with fires and four eagle symbols, deeply carved into the body and
      colored in with dark and medium blues. Marks include the UND logo, the date and the full signature of the
      artist. Height 4 1/2 inches.

33   UND hanging commemorative "Stockwell" high glaze plaque done in 1933 for the North Dakota Grand Council $300-500
      of Royal and Select Masters and signed on the reverse by Julia Mattson. The embossed image on the front is a
      Mr. Stockwell, whose signature appears below his smiling visage. Marked with the circular UND inkstamp logo
      and the following inkstamp notation: "18th Triennial Assembly General Grand Council R. & S. M. Washington,
      D.C. October 9, 10, 1933 North Dakota Grand Council of Royal and Select Masters". Size is 5 by 3 1/4 inches.

34   Early and rare UND covered ginger jar painted by Freida L. Hammers in 1926. The high glaze jar is decorated $500-700
      with pairs of birds separated by elaborate scroll work. Marks include the rare circular UND inkstamp logo
      which includes the date and the name "M. Cable". Incised on the base are the artist's initials and the date
      "'25". Painted on the base in blue slip are the artist's initials and the date "'26". Height 7 7/8 inches. The lid has
      a one inch crack and there are two small glaze nicks on the inside rim.

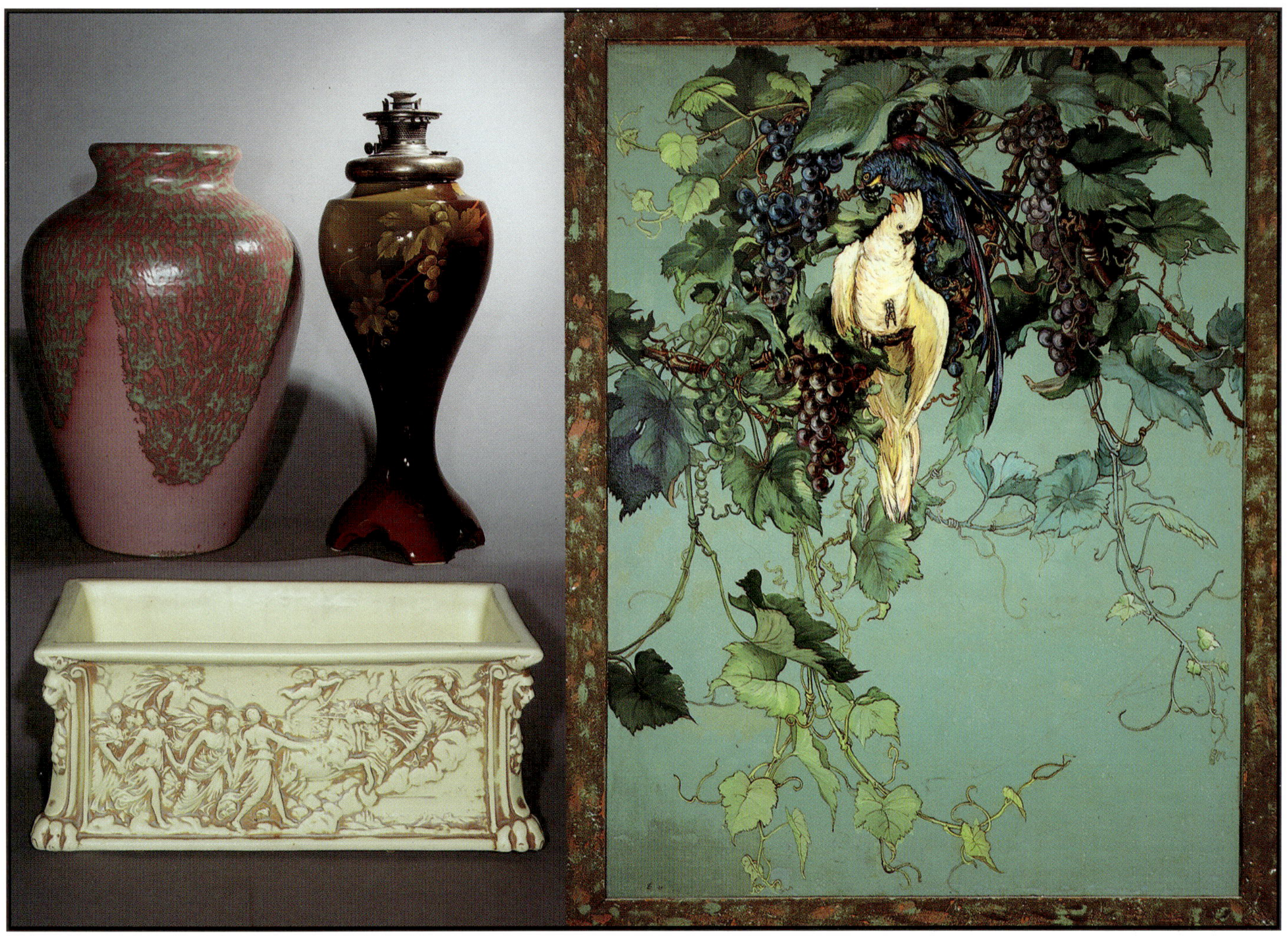

35   Large Weller floor vase in sponged-on green over pink. Unmarked. Height 22 1/4 inches. Minor roughness on the base. The consensus is that this is a Weller vase. The shape is decidedly Weller, the green looks very much like Coppertone green and the background color is Juneau pink. A very handsome piece in today's colors. $700-900

36   Rare Weller Ivory planter with molded classic scenes, cherubs, putti, griffins and horses. Impressed with "Weller" in large block letters. Height 8 inches and length 20 3/8 inches. Repairs to small chips at high points and to one handle but not broken or cracked. $500-700

37   Very tall Weller Louwelsa oil lamp decorated by Hester Pillsbury with grapes, leaves and vines. The original copper insert inside the rim accommodates a Bradley and Hubbard copper font and burner which appear to be in excellent condition. Marked inside the base with an impressed "Louwelsa Weller" logo and the numbers "617" and "0". Pillsbury's monogram is painted on the side of the vase in black slip. Excellent original condition. $1500-2000

37A   Large oil painting on board done in 1920 by Zanesville pottery artist, Claude Leffler. Shown are a cockatoo and a macaw perched in a grape arbor. The painting is signed with Leffler's monogram and the date in the lower left hand corner. Size is 46 by 36 inches. Another painting of a soaring eagle is on the back side of the work. Good original condition with a frame thought to be original. $800-1200

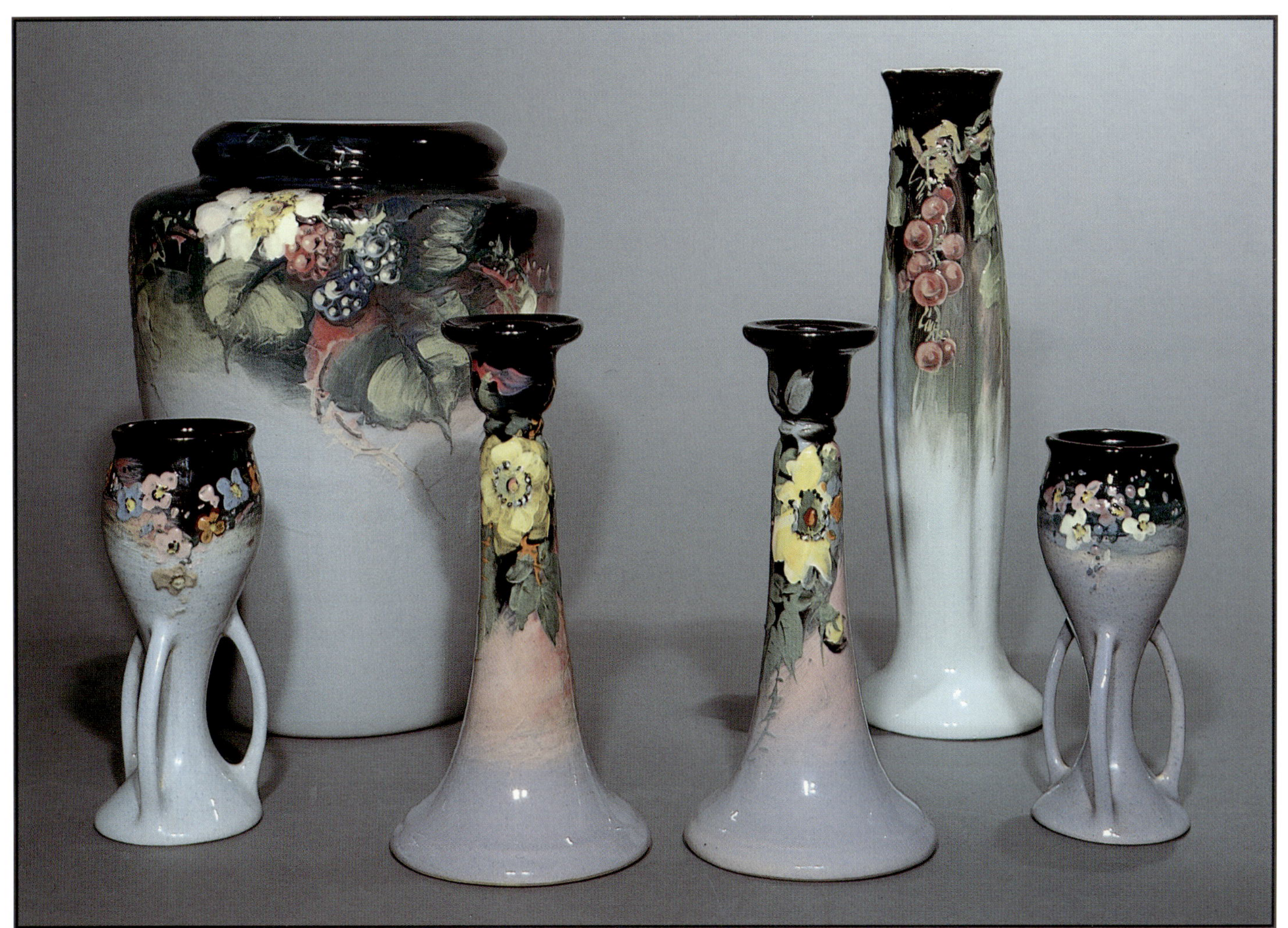

<table>
<tr><td>38</td><td>Weller Late Eocean three-handled urn shaped vase. Unmarked. Height 6 1/8 inches.</td><td>$150-250</td></tr>
<tr><td>39</td><td>Unusually large Weller Late Eocean vase with colorful blackberry decoration done by an unknown artist. Unmarked. Height 10 7/8 inches. A drill hole through the bottom has been professionally repaired.</td><td>$800-1000</td></tr>
<tr><td>40</td><td>Nice pair of Weller Late Eocean candlesticks with colorfully detailed yellow wild rose decoration done by an unknown artist. Stamped "Weller" in large block letters. Height of each is 7 7/8 inches.</td><td>$300-400</td></tr>
<tr><td>41</td><td>Tall Weller Late Eocean fluted vase with nicely detailed seedless grapes, grape leaves and vines, done in very heavy slip by an unknown artist. Unmarked. Height 12 1/8 inches.</td><td>$350-450</td></tr>
<tr><td>42</td><td>Weller Late Eocean three-handled urn-shaped vase. Unmarked. Height 6 inches.</td><td>$150-250</td></tr>
</table>

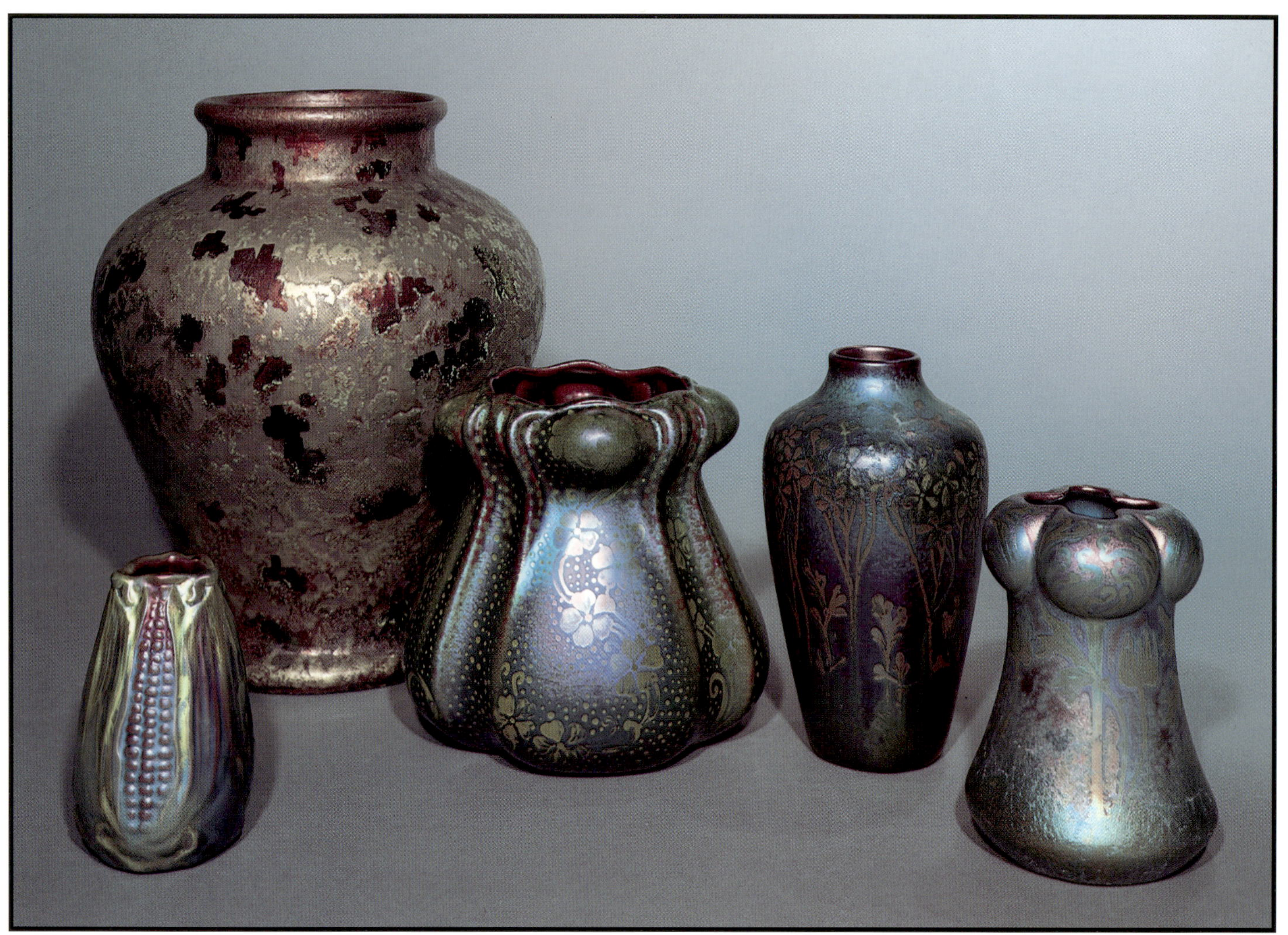

43   Weller Sicard vase on a blank with embossed ears of corn done by Jacques Sicard. Signed "Weller Sicard" $600-800
      on the side. Height 4 3/4 inches. Good color.

44   Large and important Weller Bronze Ware lamp vase, thought by some to be the finest example of Bronze $1000-1500
      Ware extant. Die stamped "Weller" in a long oval. Also marked with a paper label "From the White Pillars
      Museum". Height 12 inches. Accompanying the vase is a note of authentication from White Pillars dated
      1977 and signed by Louise Purviance and Harold Nichols. The surface texture and color of this vase need to
      be seen. It is a fabulous Arts & Crafts item.

45   Weller Sicard vase with swirling four leaf clover decoration. Marked "Sicard Weller" on the side and im- $1000-1250
      pressed "Weller" in small block letters on the bottom. Also incised on the bottom is the number
      "46". Height 6 7/8 inches. There is a small chip on the inside of the rim that has been professionally repaired.
      Good color and decoration.

46   Weller Sicard vase decorated with flowering trees and other vegetation. Marked "Sicard Weller" on the side $1500-2000
      and impressed with the number "6" on the bottom. Height 7 1/2 inches. Very good color and unusual
      decoration. Exhibited: Delaware Art Museum, Wilmington, Delaware, **American Art Pottery 1875-1930**,
      March 10th - April 23rd, 1978.

47   Good Weller Sicard vase with an unusual blown out four part top and stylish floral decoration. Marked $1000-1500
      "Weller Sicard" on the side of the vase and stamped with the number "11". Height 5 3/4 inches. Strong, rich
      coloring.

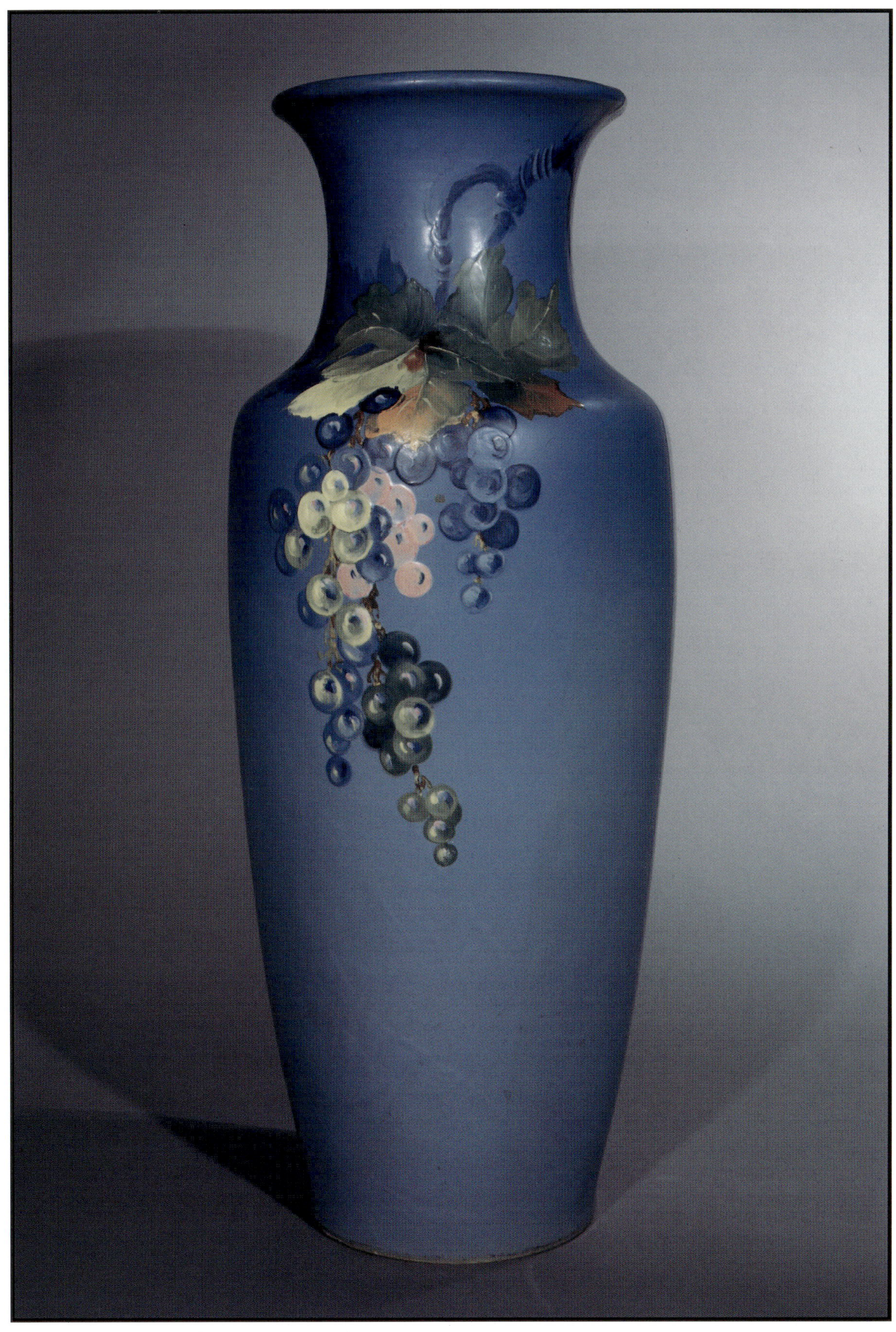

48 Monumental Weller Hudson vase with grape decoration painted by Sara Reid McLaughlin. The grapes on $2000-3000
the front side of the vase are done in shades of blue, green, pink and orange while those on the reverse
are painted tonalistically in shades of blue. Marks include a "Weller Ware" inkstamp logo on the base and
the artist's signature on the side of the vase, painted on in dark blue slip. Height 27 1/8 inches. Minor
grinding roughness on the base. Accompanying the vase is a custom-made wrought iron stand which
adds another four or five inches to the size of the piece.

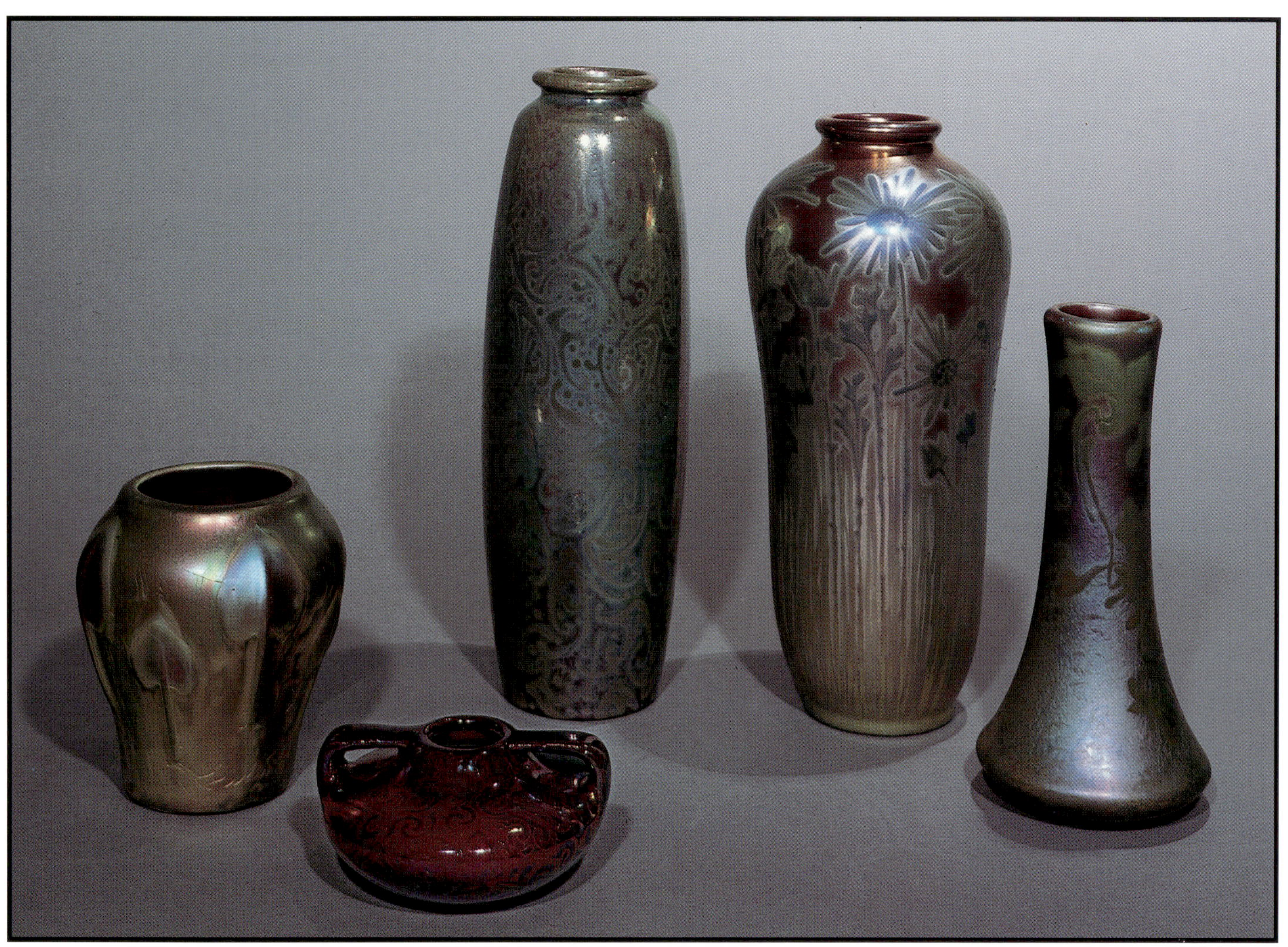

49   Weller Sicard vase with blown out arrowroot leaves. Marked "Weller Sicard" on the side. Height 4 3/8 inches. $600-800
Good color and an unusual shape.

50   Weller Sicard cabinet vase with two loop handles and stylized floral decoration. The only mark on the vase is $400-500
an impressed number "15". Height 1 7/8 inches. Strong, deep colors.

51   Tall Weller Sicard vase with stylized arrowroot decoration. The vase is signed "Weller Sicard" on the side and $800-1000
bears an older paper label which reads "Whitlow Collection". Stamped numbers on the base are difficult to
read. Height 10 1/8 inches. Good variety of color, although a bit shiny.

52   Weller Sicard vase with profusions of daisies encircling the body, the work of Jacques Sicard. Signed "Sicard $1750-2250
Weller" on the side of the vase. Height 9 1/2 inches. Decent color on an unusual Weller shape. There is a pin-
head size glaze flake off the rim.

53   Weller Sicard vase with flared bottom and tapering neck having cyclamen decoration. Unmarked but cer- $400-600
tainly a Weller form. Height 7 1/8 inches. Decent color. Minor abrasions to the rim.

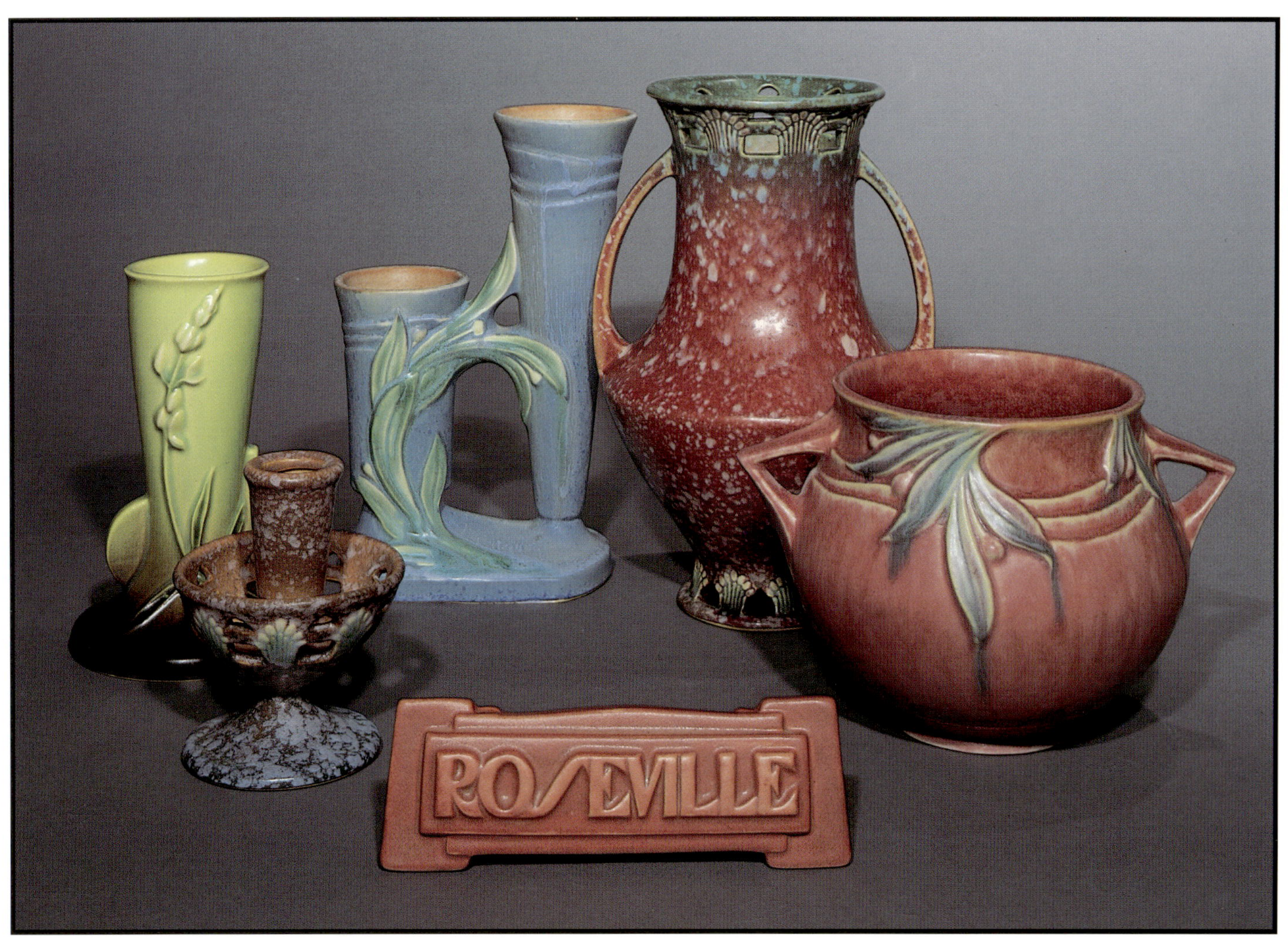#

54   Roseville Wincraft vase, possibly with experimental glaze. Embossed "Roseville U.S.A. 2V-6" on the bottom. Also on the bottom is the notation "Exp." painted on in blue slip. Height 6 1/4 inches. The glaze is more matt than gloss which may be the experiment. $200-400

55   Roseville Ferella candlestick done in rich, mottled gray and tan glazes. Unmarked. Height 4 1/8 inches. Good mold and interesting glaze. $150-200

56   Roseville Velmoss double bud vase in blue. Marked only with an"X" painted on the bottom in blue slip and an undecipherable, incised letter. Height 8 3/8 inches. There is a 1/4 by 1/4 inch flat chip off the bottom which does not show from the side. $250-350

57   Rare Roseville advertising sign in a soft dusty rose mat glaze. Embossed "Roseville" in Art Deco style lettering on the front. Height 1 7/8 inches and length 6 1/4 inches. This telescoping Art Deco form has not been seen by us before. $2000-2500

58   Rare Roseville Ferella two-handled vase in red and green. Marked with a black paper label. Height 9 1/8 inches. Excellent mold, glaze, color and condition. $1250-1750

59   Roseville Velmoss two-handled vase in red and green. Marks include a Roseville gold foil label and the letter "X" painted on in blue slip. Height 5 1/8 inches. $100-150

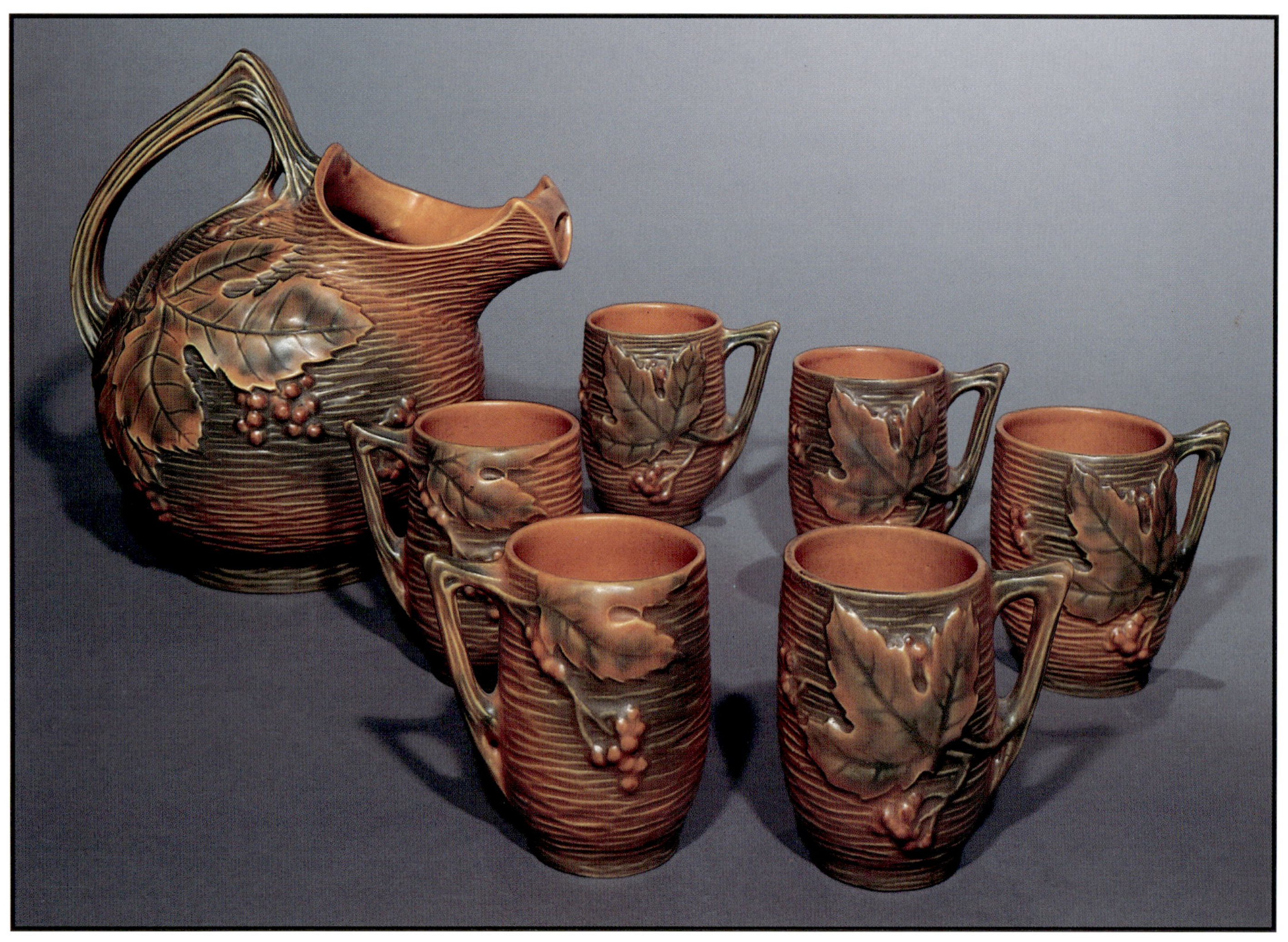

60 Hard to find Roseville Bushberry cider set in brown consisting of ice lip pitcher and 6 mugs, all in excellent $1000-1250
    original condition. The pitcher is embossed "Roseville U.S.A. 1325" and each mug is embossed "R U.S.A. 1-3
    1/2". The number 8 is painted on the bottom of the pitcher. Height of the pitcher is 8 3/4 inches. Height of
    each mug is 1 3/4 inches. Excellent mold and color.

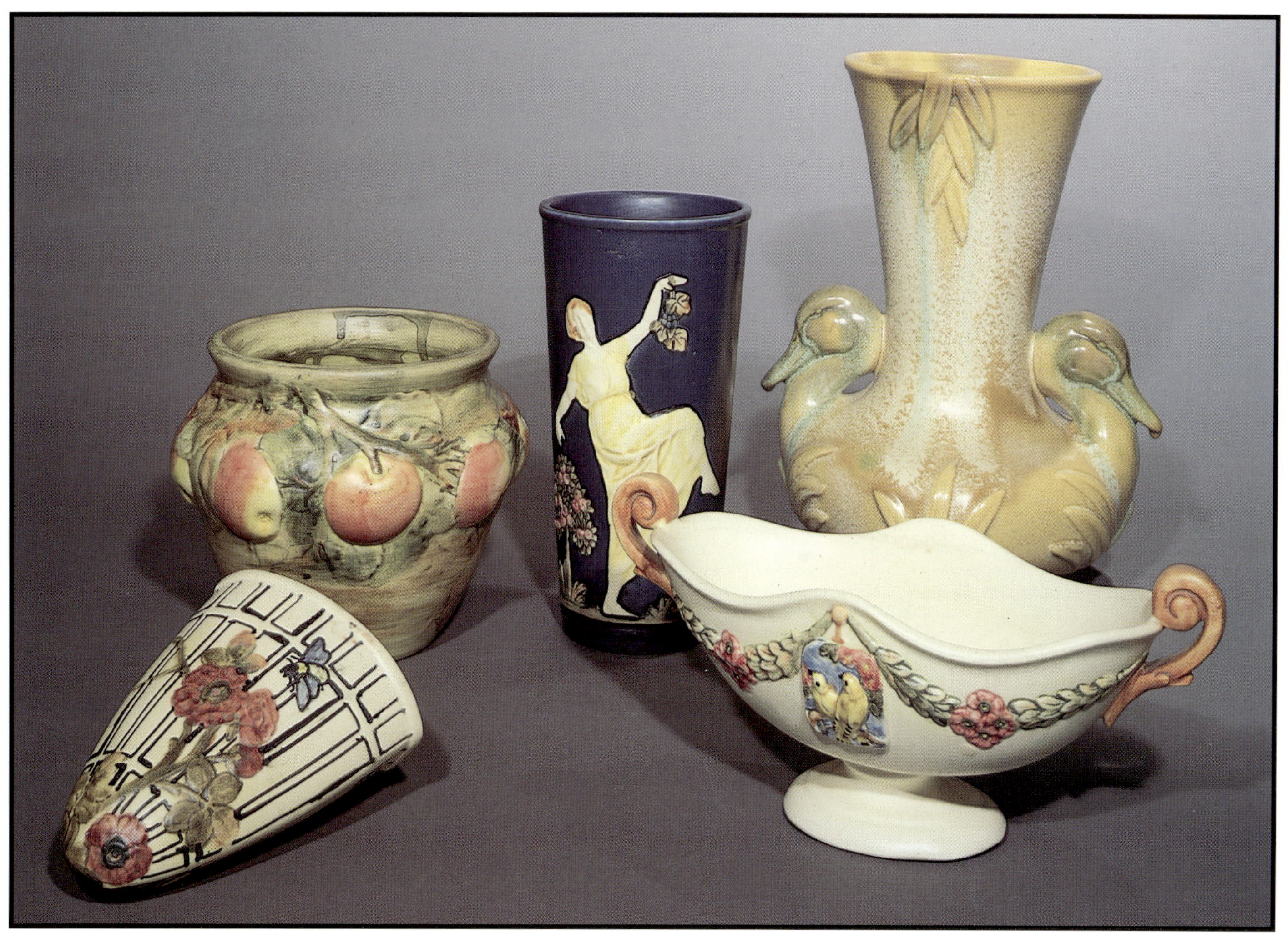

61 Weller Roma wall pocket with flowers on a trellis being checked out by a fat bumble bee. Stamped "Weller" in large block letters on the back. Height 5 5/8 inches. An unusual piece of Roma. $250-350

62 Weller Baldin vase with pink and yellow apples on a mottled green and brown ground. Impressed "Weller" in large block letters. Height 6 1/8 inches. $250-350

63 Weller Blue Ware vase showing a young woman in a toga balancing on one foot while holding a cluster of grapes and grape leaves. Looks like a fraternity party to me. Stamped "Weller" in large block letters. Height 8 3/4 inches. $200-250

64 Weller Roma compote in classical form having garlands of leaves and small plaques on each side with bright yellow birds and flowers. Unmarked. Height is 4 7/8 inches and length is 11 inches. $150-200

65 Tall Weller Patricia vase with two duck heads on the sides, covered with a fabulous gold, tan and green crystalline glaze. Marked "Weller Pottery" in script on the bottom. Height 11 5/8 inches. Good mold and great glaze. $300-400

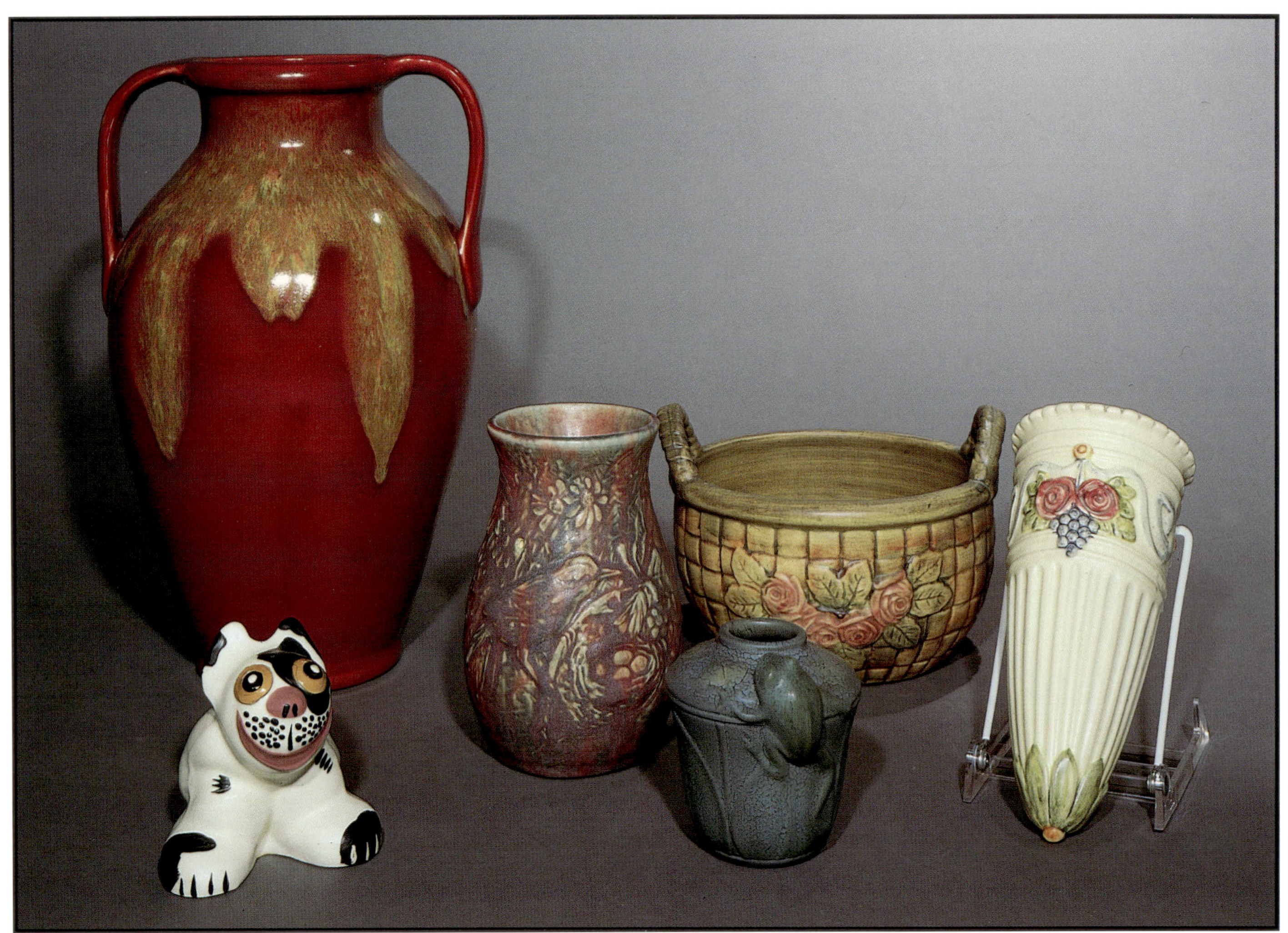

66   Weller "Pop Eye" dog in pink, black, brown and white. Marked "Weller Pottery" in script on the bottom. Height 4 1/2 inches. A cute little fellow. $400-600

67   Weller Turkish two-handled vase in rare large size. Unmarked. Height 14 inches. Good glaze and impressive size. Minor glaze scratches. $300-400

68   Experimental Weller Glendale vase with a typical bird beside her nest but done in a mottled pink mat glaze with green highlights. Unmarked. Height 6 3/4 inches. $300-400

69   Good Weller Fru Russet vase molded with a full sized, three dimensional frog climbing the side of the vase which itself is embossed with water lilies. There is a slight yellow cast to the leaves of the water lilies which contrasts nicely with the mottled blue glaze over the rest of the piece. Marked "Weller" in small block letters. Height 3 7/8 inches." $500-700

70   Weller Flemish two-handled basket. Marked "Weller" in large block letters. Height 5 1/2 inches. Diameter is 8 1/2 inches. $100-150

71   Weller Roma wallpocket. Unmarked. Height 8 3/8 inches. $200-250

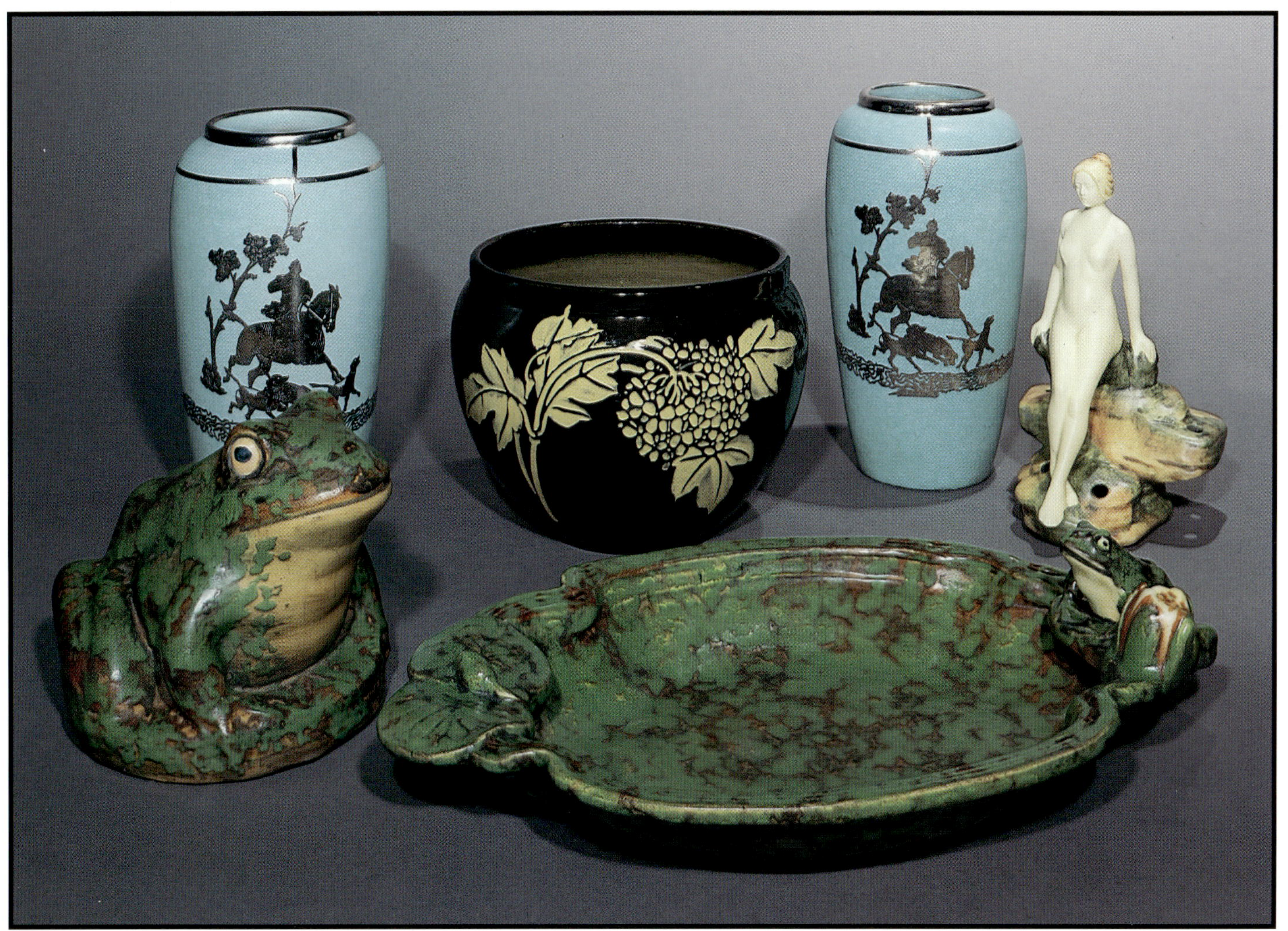

72   Weller Coppertone frog in unusual size. Marks include the inkstamp half kiln "Weller Pottery" logo and the number "12" painted on in black slip. Height 5 1/2 inches. Excellent glaze. $1000-1200

73   Weller Chase vase with a silver overlaid hunting scene on its mottled blue mat ground. The silver is marked "Sterling" and the bottom of the vase is impressed "Weller Pottery" in script. Height 8 7/8 inches. $600-800

74   Weller Coppertone centerpiece bowl with a frog and lotus blossom at one end and a lotus pad at the other. Marked with the "Weller Pottery" black inkstamp half kiln logo and the numbers "12" and "7" painted on in black slip. Height 3 1/2 inches and length 15 inches. Small firing separation at the rim. Excellent color and glaze. $600-800

75   Unusual Weller jardiniere, possibly early Dickensware, done with a black background color and cream slip decoration of flowers, signed on the side by Claude Leffler. The base is incised "Weller" in crude script. Height 5 7/8 inches. There is a tight spider crack in the bottom which extends up the sides about 1/4 inch in two spots. $250-350

76   Weller Chase vase with a silver overlaid hunting scene on its mottled blue mat ground. The silver is marked "Sterling" and the bottom of the vase is impressed "Weller Pottery" in script. Height 8 7/8 inches. $600-800

77   Rare Weller Muskota "Bathing Beauty" flower frog in excellent color and mold. Pictured in Huxford. Marked in black slip with what looks like the conjoined letters "NJ". Height 9 inches. $1000-1250

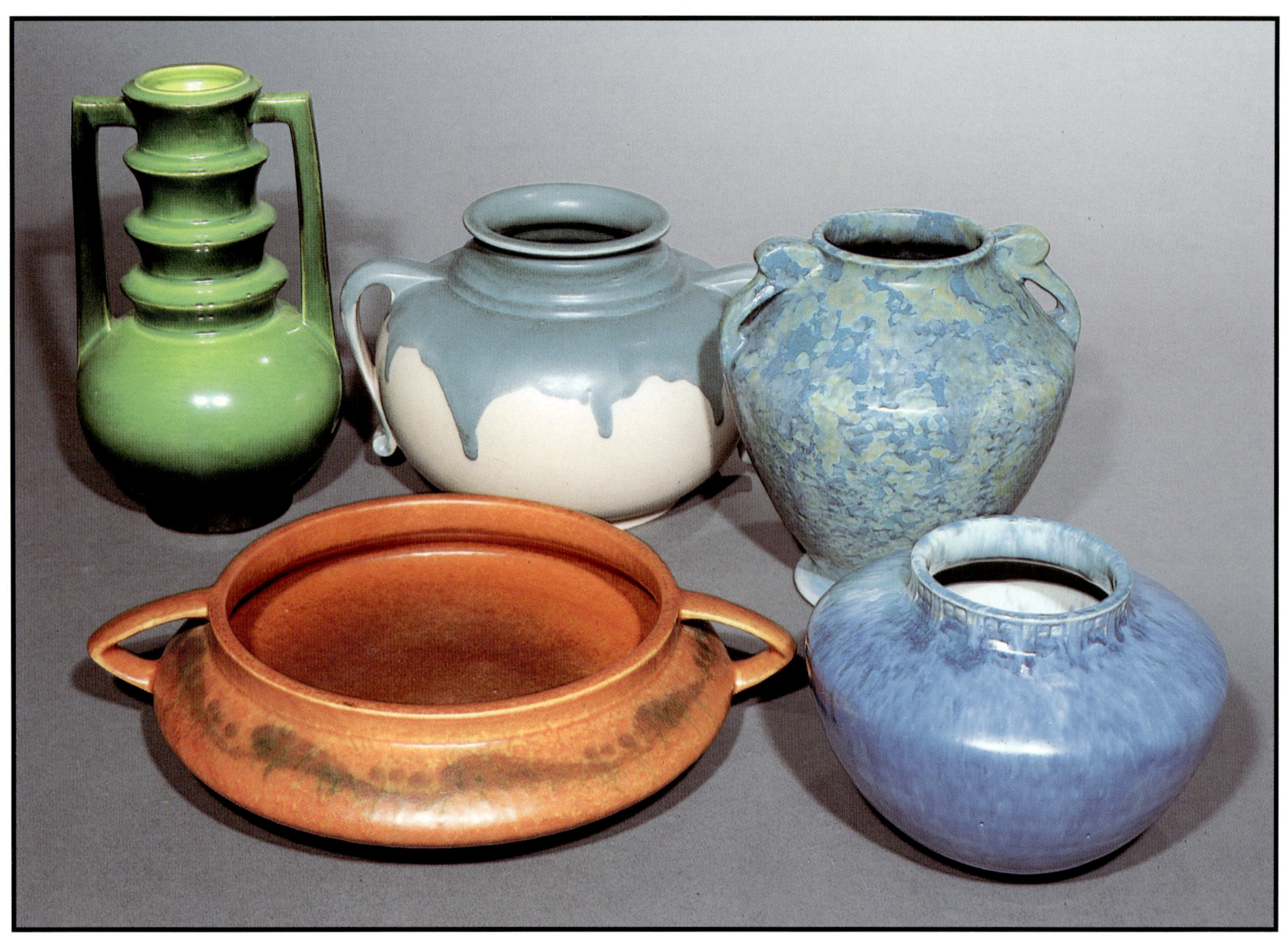

78	Roseville Futura "Emerald Urn" in green and black. Unmarked. Height 9 inches.	$400-600
79	Roseville Windsor low bowl with two strap handles done in a wonderful rust colored mat glaze with stylized leaf and berry decoration around the shoulder in green, brown and red. Unmarked. Height is 2 3/4 inches while the diameter of the bowl is 12 inches. A strong Deco form with excellent glaze.	$300-400
80	Roseville Carnelian I two-handled vase in blue and gray. Marked with the "RV" inkstamp logo. Height 6 inches.	$250-350
81	Roseville Carnelian II vase with what may be an experimental mottled blue and green glaze. Marked with the RV blue inkstamp logo and what appears to be a large "X" painted on the bottom in blue slip. Height 7 1/8 inches.	$200-250
82	Roseville Imperial II vase with embossed designs around the collar, done in a rich blue flambé type glaze. Marked with a gold foil label and incised with the number "9". Height 4 5/8 inches.	$150-200

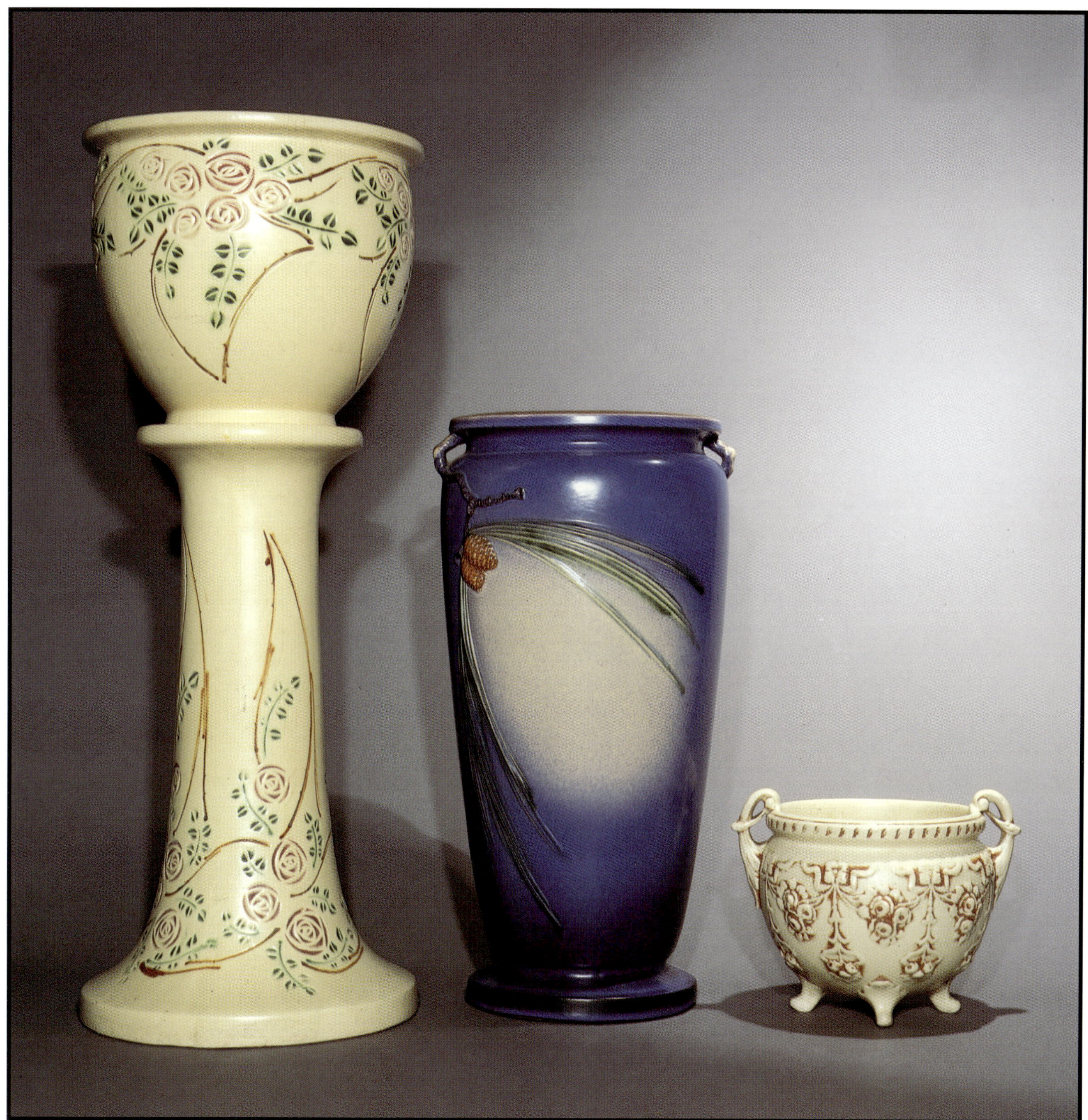

83   Roseville Velmoss Scroll jardiniere and pedestal. Unmarked. Height 29 1/2 inches. Slightly dirty crazing inside $900-1200
the jardiniere.

84   Fine Roseville Pinecone umbrella stand in blue. Marked "Roseville 777-20" on the bottom. Height 20 3/8 $1500-2000
inches. Excellent mold, color, glaze and condition. A marvelous, large example.

85   Weller Ivory jardiniere with two handles, three stubby shoe feet and embossed rose decoration. Marked $150-200
"Weller" in large block letters. Height 7 1/2 inches.

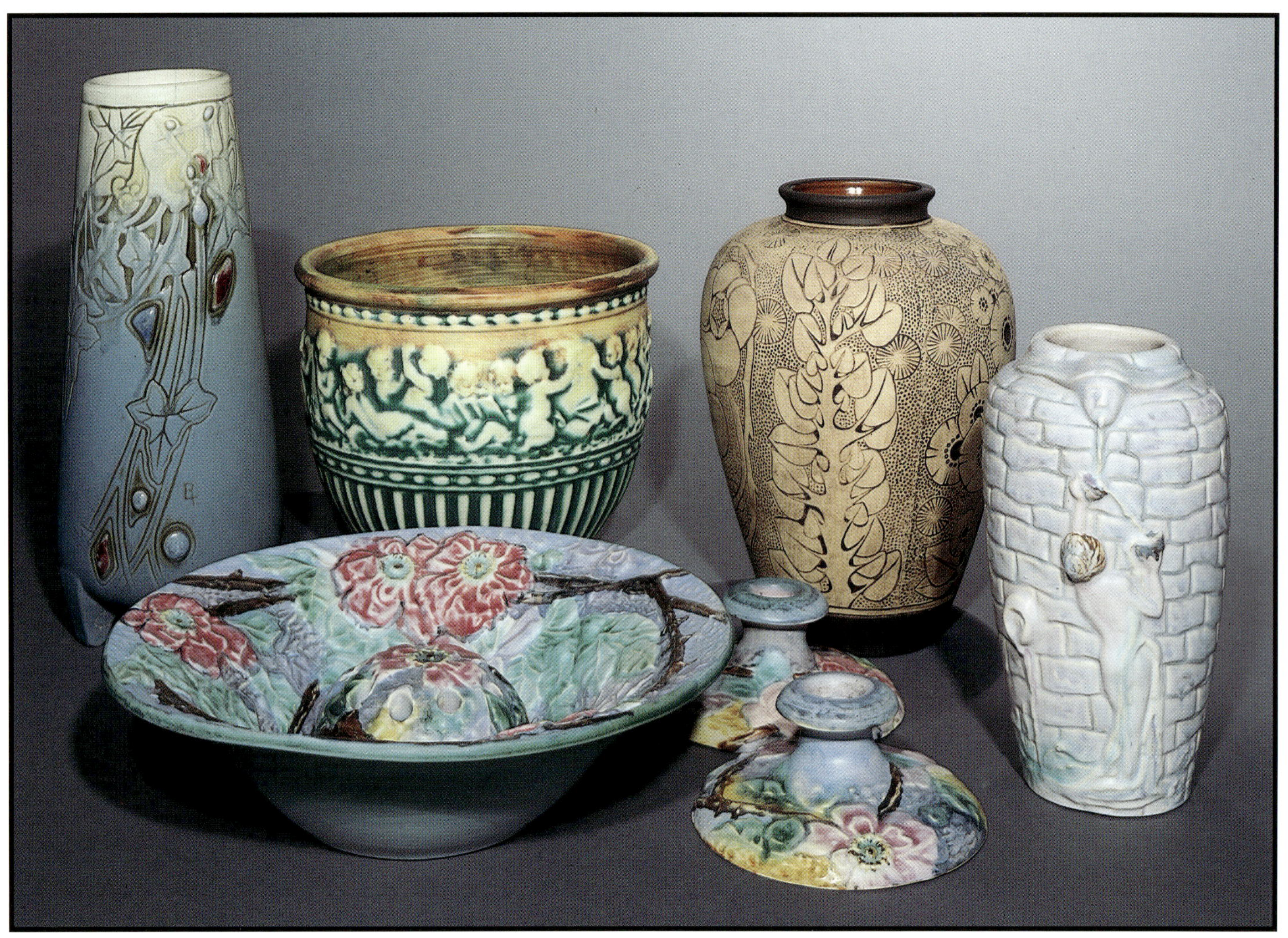

86	Rare Weller Cameo Jewel vase designed by Rudolph Lorber with both raised and relief decoration of English ivy encrusted with jewels in red and blue. The vase sits on four stubby feet. Marks include Lorber's monogram in the side of the vase and a slightly obscured Weller logo on the bottom. Height 13 inches. There are three lines descending from the rim and small nicks off three of the feet.	$400-600
87	Weller Silvertone bowl with matching flower frog done with wild rose decoration. The bowl is marked with the circular "Weller Ware" inkstamp and the number "12" is painted on in blue slip. The frog has the semi-circular "Weller Pottery" inkstamp and the letter "F" painted on. Height 3 1/2 inches and diameter is 12 1/4 inches.	$300-400
88	Weller Fairfield jardiniere in green, brown and cream. Unmarked. Height 7 7/8 inches.	$200-300
89	Pair of Weller Silvertone candlesticks in wild rose pattern. Both pieces are marked with the semi-circular "Weller Pottery" inkstamp. One piece is marked with a painted-on "F" while the other has a painted-on "3" and two interesting Weller labels. One label is a rectangular paper label which reads "Weller Silvertone Ware". The other is a silver foil label in the form of the semi-circular "Weller Pottery" inkstamp. Height of each is 2 1/2 inches. There is a small flat nick off one piece which is not visible from the side.	$125-175
90	Tall Weller Burntwood vase with several varieties of exotic vegetation. Marked "Weller" in block letters. Height 10 1/2 inches. Minor roughness off the base.	$150-250
91	Rare Weller figural vase showing what we believe to be "Rebecca at the Well", executed in Hudson Perfecto colors and signed by Edith Hood. Hood's last name appears on a stone in the wall at the base of the wall. Stamped "Weller" in large block letters on the bottom. Height 8 5/8 inches. This appears to be a cast piece but we haven't talked to anyone who has seen another.	$700-900

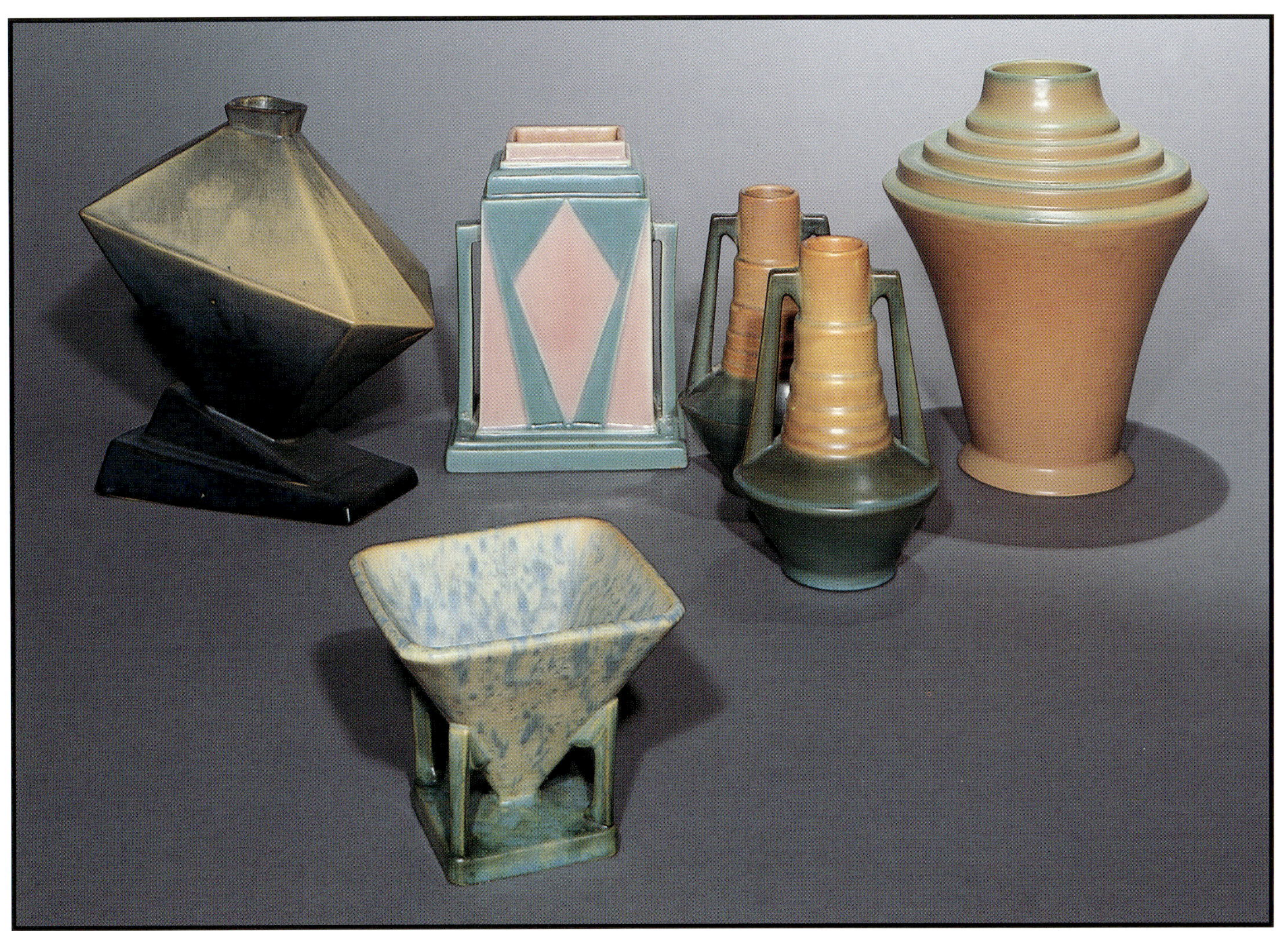

92	Rare Roseville Futura "Tank" vase. Marked with a small silver foil label. Height 9 3/8 inches. Small chips to the back side of the base. This is considered the ultimate in Futura, matched only in value by the elusive "Chinese Bronze" vase.	$6000-8000
93	Rare Roseville Futura "Sandtoy" form done in a mottled gray, blue and green glaze. Unmarked. Height 4 1/4 inches. Excellent original condition."	$700-900
94	Roseville Futura "Jukebox" vase in pink and green. Unmarked. Height 8 1/8 inches. Small glaze flakes off the base.	$400-500
95	Pair of Roseville Futura "Telescope Urns" in green and tan. Unmarked. Height of each is 7 1/8 inches. One of the urns has a small rim repair.	$500-700
96	Roseville Futura "Stepped Urn" in green and orange mat glaze. Unmarked. Height 10 inches. Rim repairs.	$200-300

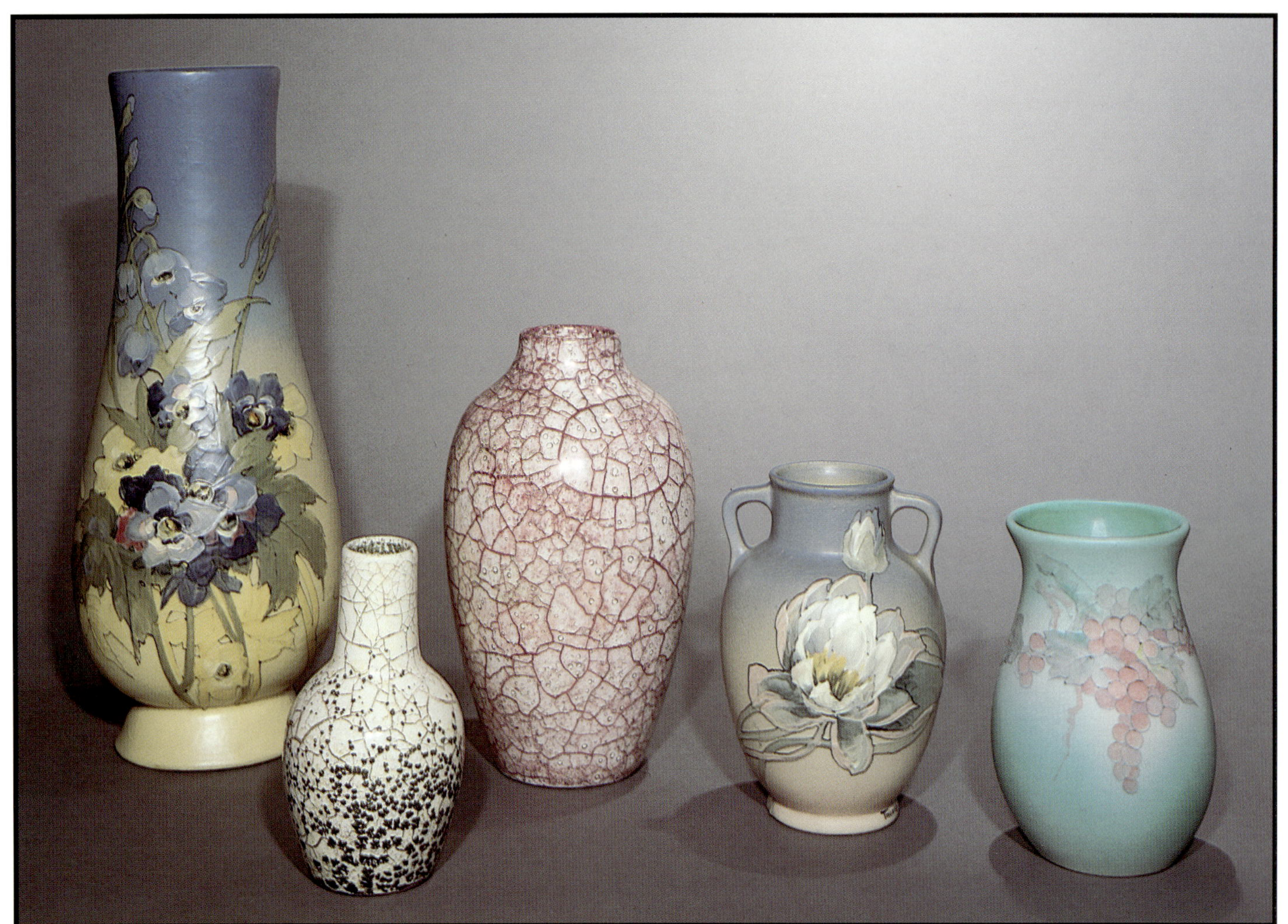

97   Tall and well painted Weller Hudson vase with multicolored floral decoration, done by Sarah Reid $1500-2000
      McLaughlin. Marks include the semi-circular "Weller Pottery" inkstamp logo and the artist's last name,
      painted on the surface of the vase in black slip. Height 17 1/4 inches. There are two small flat chips off the
      base which are barely visible from the side.

98   Nice Weller Cloudburst vase with green over white and crackle glaze. Marked with an unusual gold "Weller" $200-300
      oval transfer. Height 7 1/8 inches. There is a firing separation on one side of the rim and a tight line opposite.

99   Large Weller Cloudburst vase glazed in luster colors of purple, gray and white. Unmarked. Height $150-200
      10 3/4 inches. This is an extremely pleasant color combination in excellent shape.

100   Nice Weller Hudson two-handled vase with colorful water lily decoration in heavy slip, done by Mae $400-500
      Timberlake. Marked "Weller Pottery" in script on the bottom. Timberlake's last name is painted on the side
      of the vase near the bottom. Height 7 3/4 inches.

101   Weller Hudson Perfecto vase with grape decoration done by an unknown artist. Stamped "Weller" in large $200-300
      block letters. Height 7 1/4 inches.

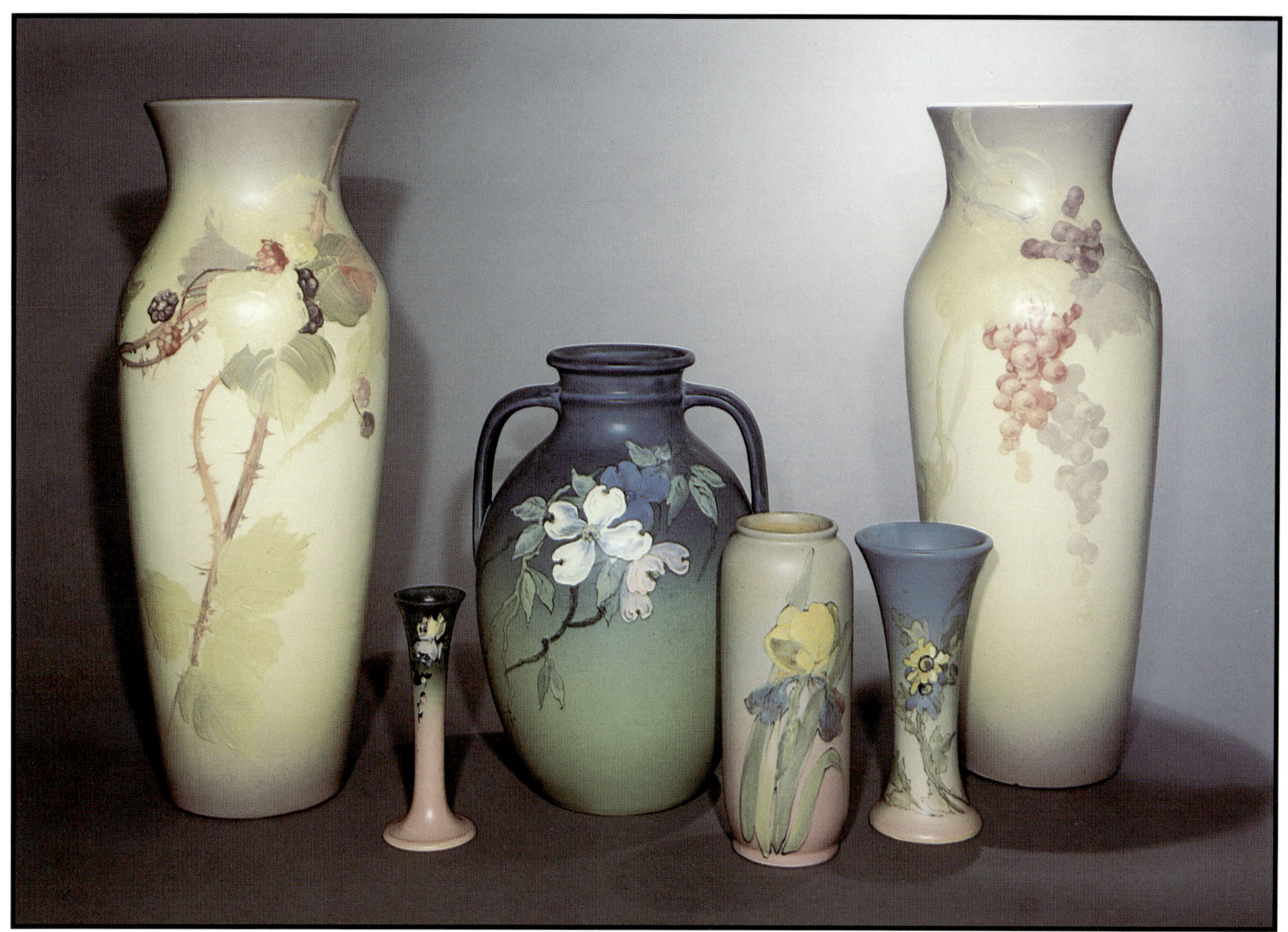

102   Monumental Weller Hudson Light floor vase decorated by an unknown artist with detailed blackberries, leaves and canes. Stamped "Weller" in large block letters. Height 22 inches. Strong artwork and delicate, subtle colors. The purchaser of this lot will be allowed to purchase lot 107 for the same price. $1750-2250

103   Weller Hudson bud vase with pink and yellow rose decoration by Hester Pillsbury, whose monogram appears just below the roses, painted on in black slip. The base is stamped "Weller" in large block letters. Height 7 1/8 inches. $150-200

104   Tall Weller Hudson two-handled vase with blue background and white, pink and blue dogwood flowers painted by Naomi Walch. Flowers on the back side of the vase are done in shades of blue. Marks on the base include the semi-circular "Weller Pottery" inkstamp and the letter "A" painted on in blue slip. The artist's last name is painted on the side of the vase in black slip. Height 13 3/4 inches. $1250-1500

105   Weller Hudson vase with a large yellow iris painted by Dorothy England. Unmarked. Height 9 1/2 inches. There are two tight lines at the rim and some glaze flakes off the base. $300-500

106   Weller Hudson vase with flaring rim painted by Sarah Timberlake. Decoration consists of multi-colored leaves and flowers. Marks include "Weller" stamped in large block letters, the artist's initials painted on the side of the vase and an original "Weller Hudson Ware" paper label. Height 8 3/4 inches. $250-350

107   Monumental Weller Hudson Light floor vase decorated by an unknown artist with detailed red and white grapes, leaves and vines. Stamped "Weller" in large block letters. Height 22 1/8 inches. There is a small chip off the base. The purchaser of lot 102 will be allowed to purchase this lot for the same price. $1750-2250

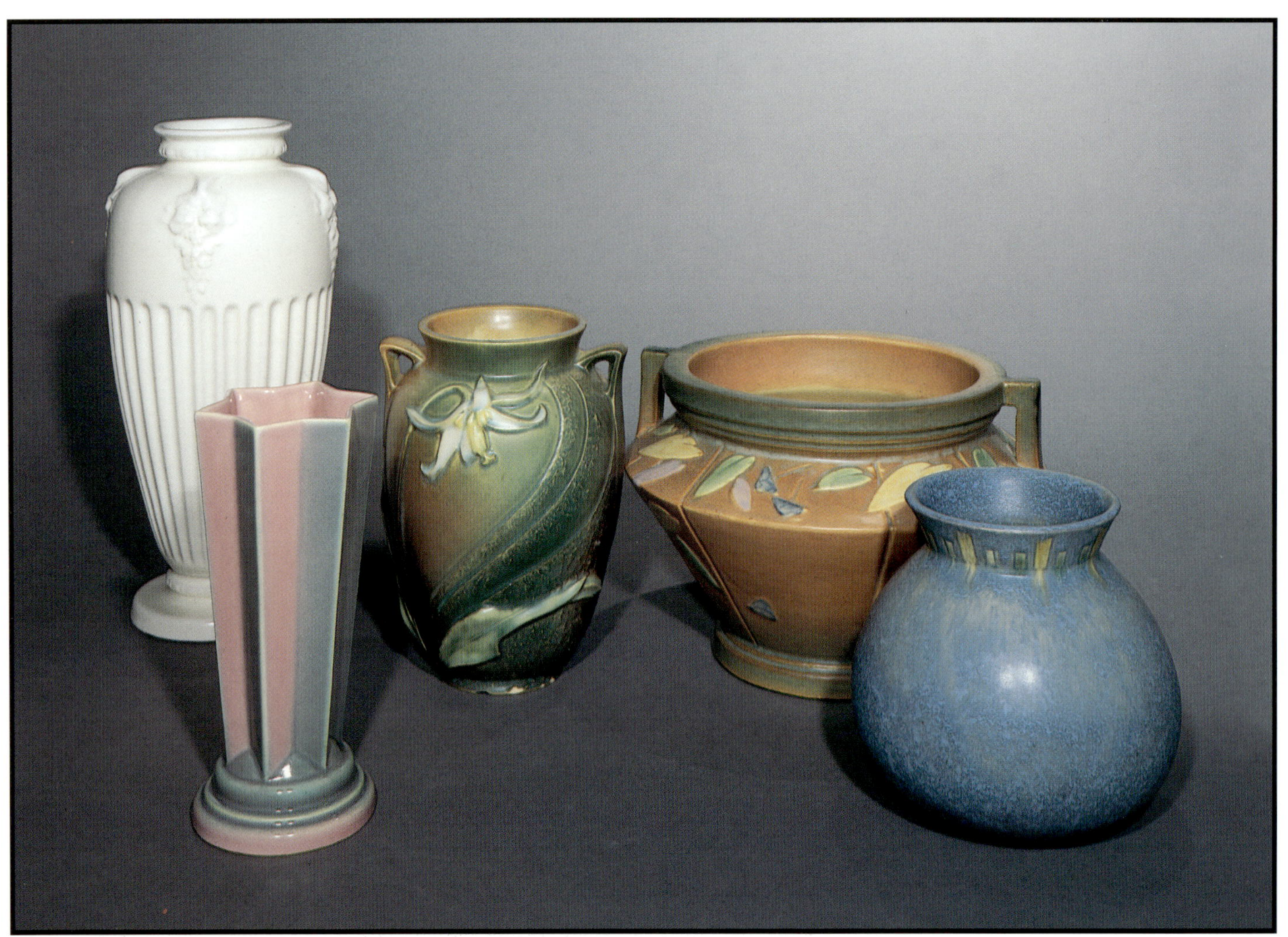

108   Tall Roseville Volpato vase in white semi-gloss glaze. Marked with a partial gold foil label. Height $200-300
       12 5/8 inches. There is a small glaze nick off the base.

109   Roseville Futura "Pleated Star" vase in pink and green gloss finish. Unmarked. Height 8 1/8 inches. $400-600

110   Rare Roseville experimental "Trout Lily" vase with two handles. Incised on the back side is the notation $500-700
       "Trout Lily White, Pink, Cream, Bright Yellow, Yellow or Orange Centre". Height 8 1/4 inches. There are
       several small base chips and a small rim chip.

111   Roseville Futura jardiniere in pink, green, yellow, blue, mauve and orange. Unmarked. Height 7 inches. Paul $300-400
       Findsen says this is a very irritating shape to photograph but he loves it anyway.

112   Roseville Windsor vase with embossed rectangles around the collar in alternating yellow and green. Overall, $200-300
       the vase is glazed in a mottled blue mat. Unmarked. Height 6 1/8 inches.

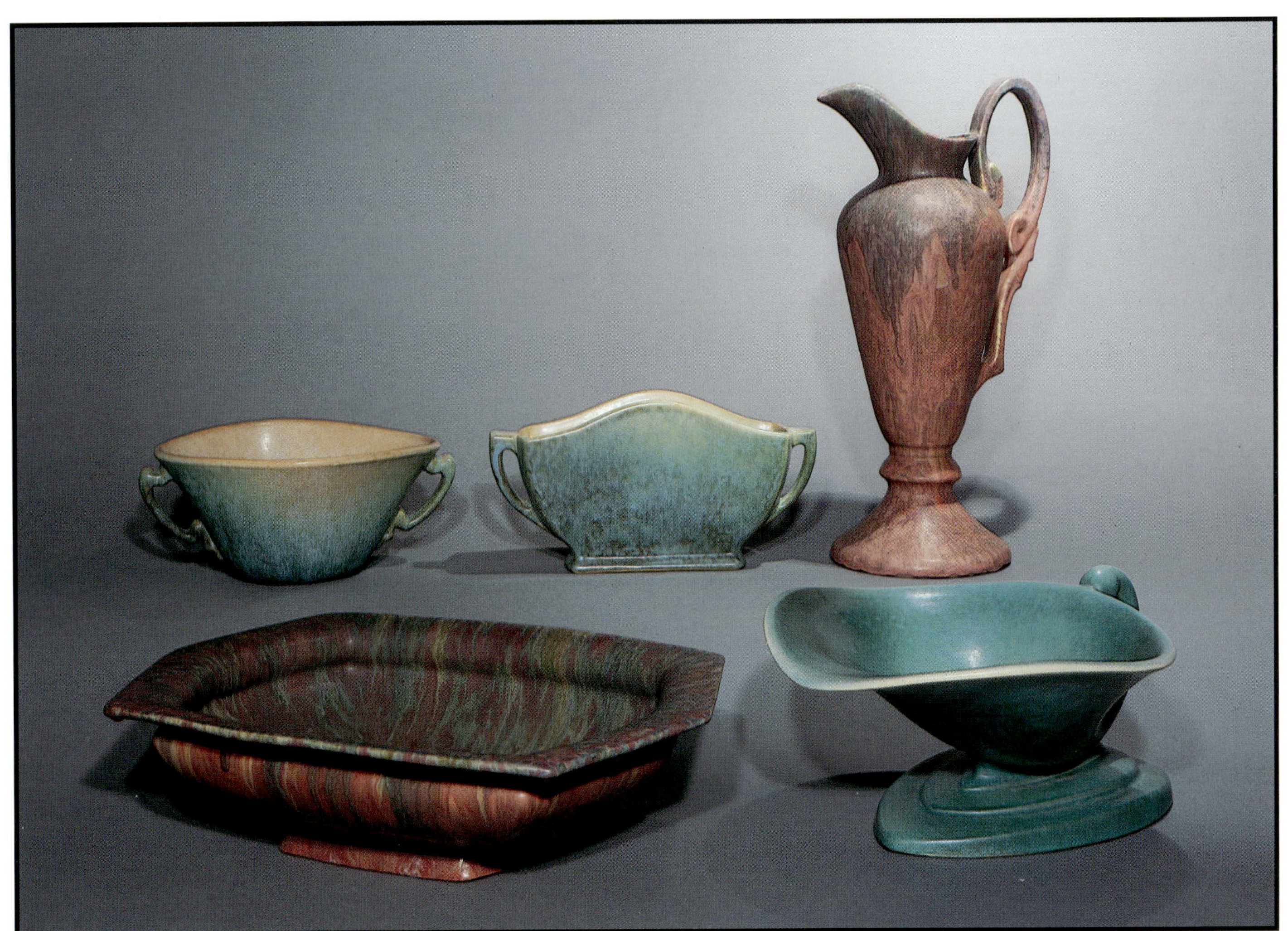

113	Roseville Earlam two-handled open bowl form with excellent blue- green glaze on the exterior and salmon color inside. Unmarked. Height 4 1/8 inches.	$200-300
114	Roseville Carnelian II rectangular bowl done in fabulous organic drip glaze in shades of rose, gray, green and tan. Unmarked. Height 3 5/8 inches and length 15 inches. Small firing separation at the rim.	$500-700
115	Roseville Earlam two-handled planter. Unmarked. Height 5 1/4 inches. Excellent glaze.	$200-300
116	Roseville Rozane Pattern cornucopia in green mat glaze. Marked "Roseville U.S.A. 2" on the bottom. Height is 5 1/8 inches while length is 11 3/4 inches. Rare form and size.	$200-300
117	Tall Roseville Carnelian II ewer with long swooping handle done in fabulous pink, mauve, green and black mottled gloopy mat glaze. Unmarked. Height 15 inches. Strong form and even stronger glaze.	$700-900

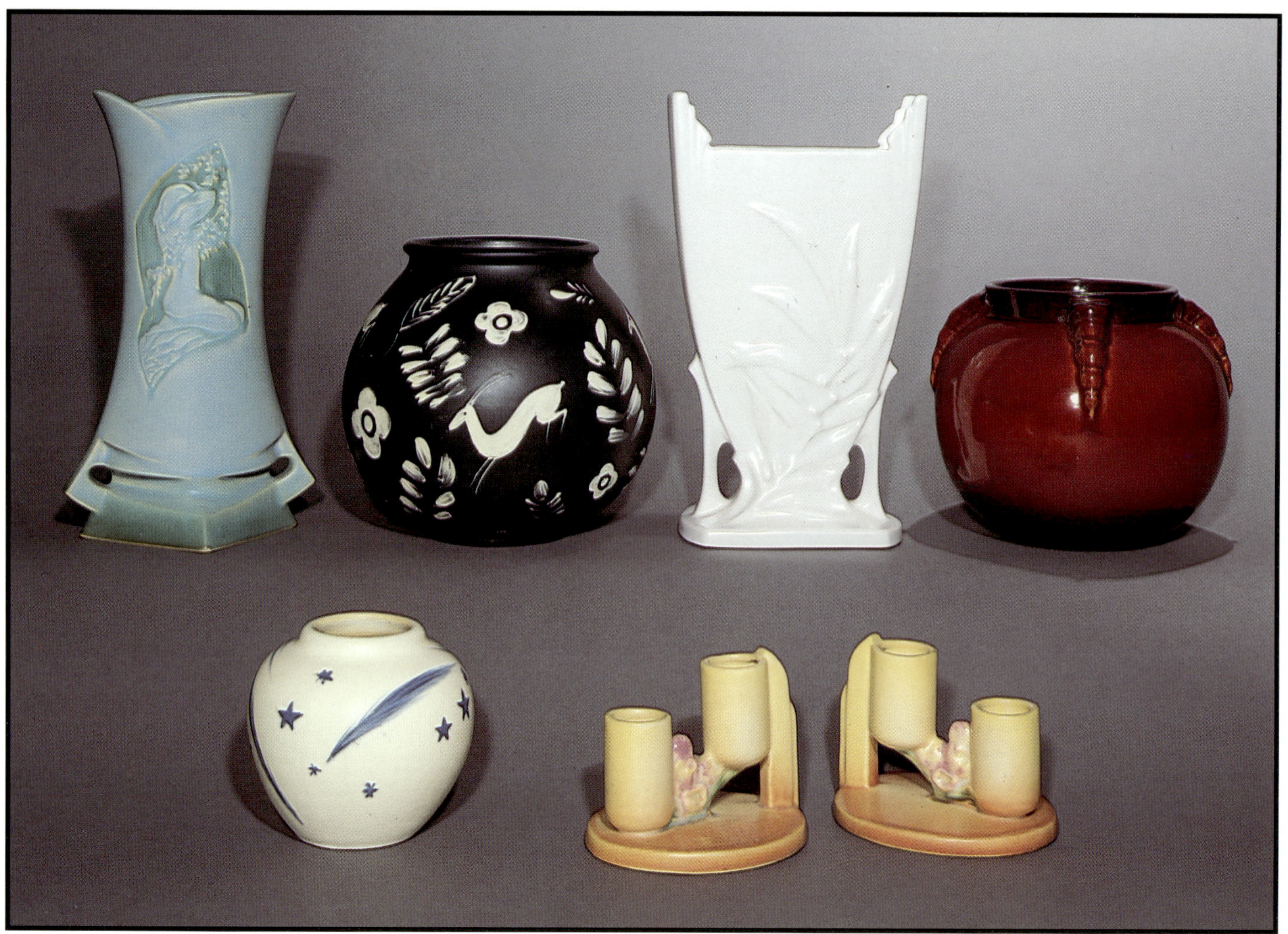

118   Roseville Silhouette vase in blue mat glaze with two small handles near its base. In each of the two panels, $500-700
front and back, is found a nude female modestly covered by a judiciously placed bough. The base is embossed "Roseville U.S.A. 787-10" and painted with a letter "g". Height 10 3/8 inches. Minor flake off one
corner of the base. Rare shape. Excellent color and mold.

119   Weller Geode vase with blue stars and comets. "Weller" in script and the initials "TM" are incised on the $200-300
bottom. Height 3 3/4 inches.

120   Weller Cretone vase signed by Hester Pillsbury with Art Deco deer and flower designs in cream colored slip $300-400
painted over a mat black background. Marked "Weller Pottery" in script. Pillsbury's monogram is painted on
the side of the vase. Height 6 7/8 inches.

121   Pair of Roseville Ixia candlesticks in yellow and pink. Impressed "Roseville 1127" faintly on the bottom of $125-175
each. Height 3 inches.

122   Roseville Ivory II vase done in an almost opalescent white mat glaze. Impressed "Roseville 943-10". Height $150-250
10 1/2 inches. Rare form.

123   Roseville Topeo vase done in a rich red glaze. Marked with a gold foil label. Height 6 inches. $150-200

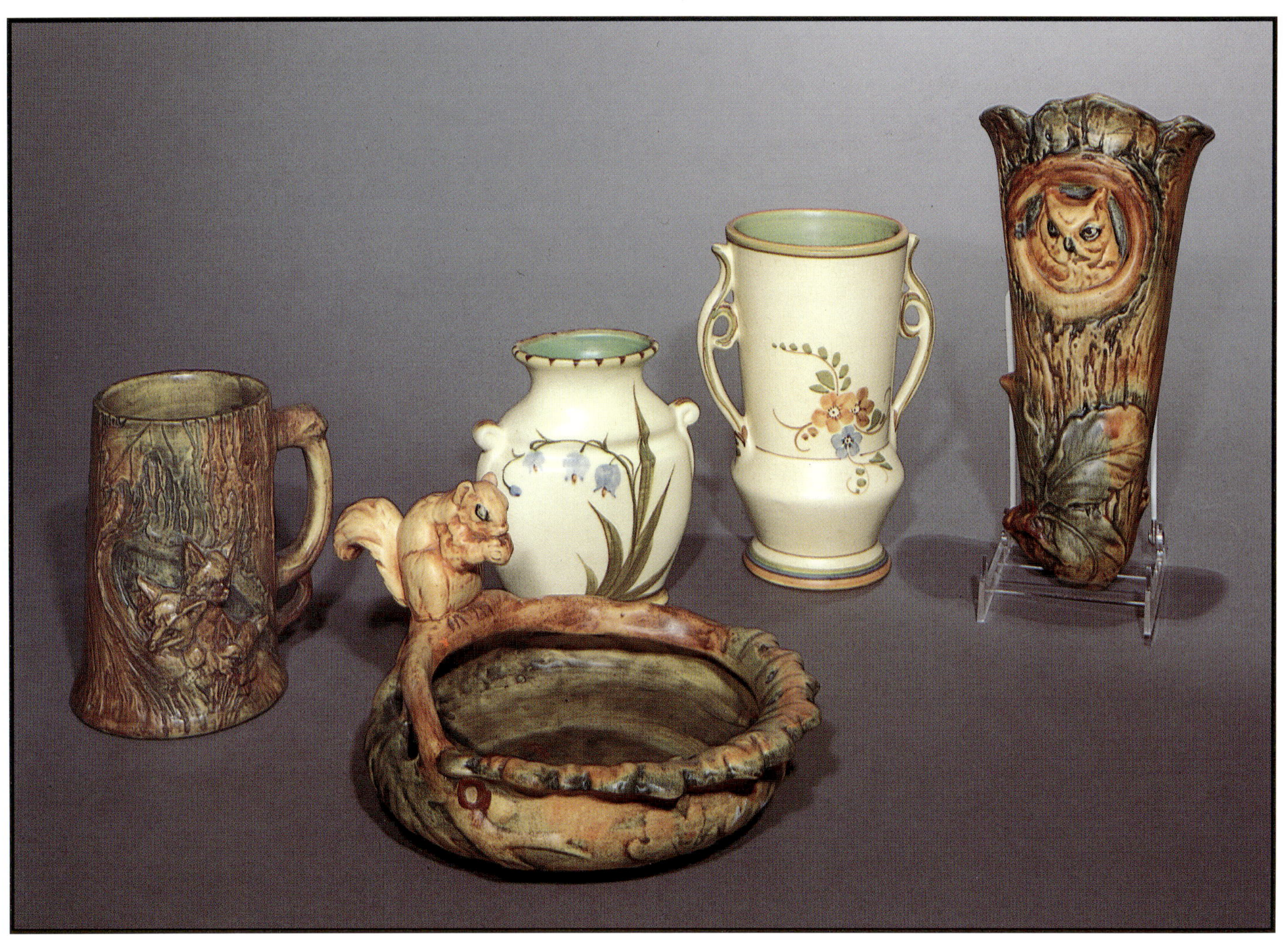

124   Weller Woodcraft mug with baby foxes inside a log. Marked "Weller" in large block letters. Height 6 inches. $150-200
Small flake off the nose of one fox.

125   Weller Woodcraft nut dish with a squirrel sitting on the rim. Impressed "Weller" in large block letters. Height 5 $200-300
1/4 inches. There is a small nick on the squirrel's left ear which has been professionally repaired.

126   Weller Bonita vase with bluebell decoration. Marked "Weller" in script on the bottom. Also painted on the $75-100
bottom are an "X" and an "O". Height 5 7/8 inches.

127   Weller Bonita two-handled vase with floral decoration done by an unknown artist. Incised "Weller Pottery" in $200-300
script on the bottom. Also marked with a letter "O" painted on the bottom in brown slip. Height 7 7/8 inches.

128   Weller Woodcraft owl wall pocket. Marked with the semi-circular "Weller Pottery" inkstamp logo. Height 10 3/4 $250-350
inches. Good mold, color and condition.

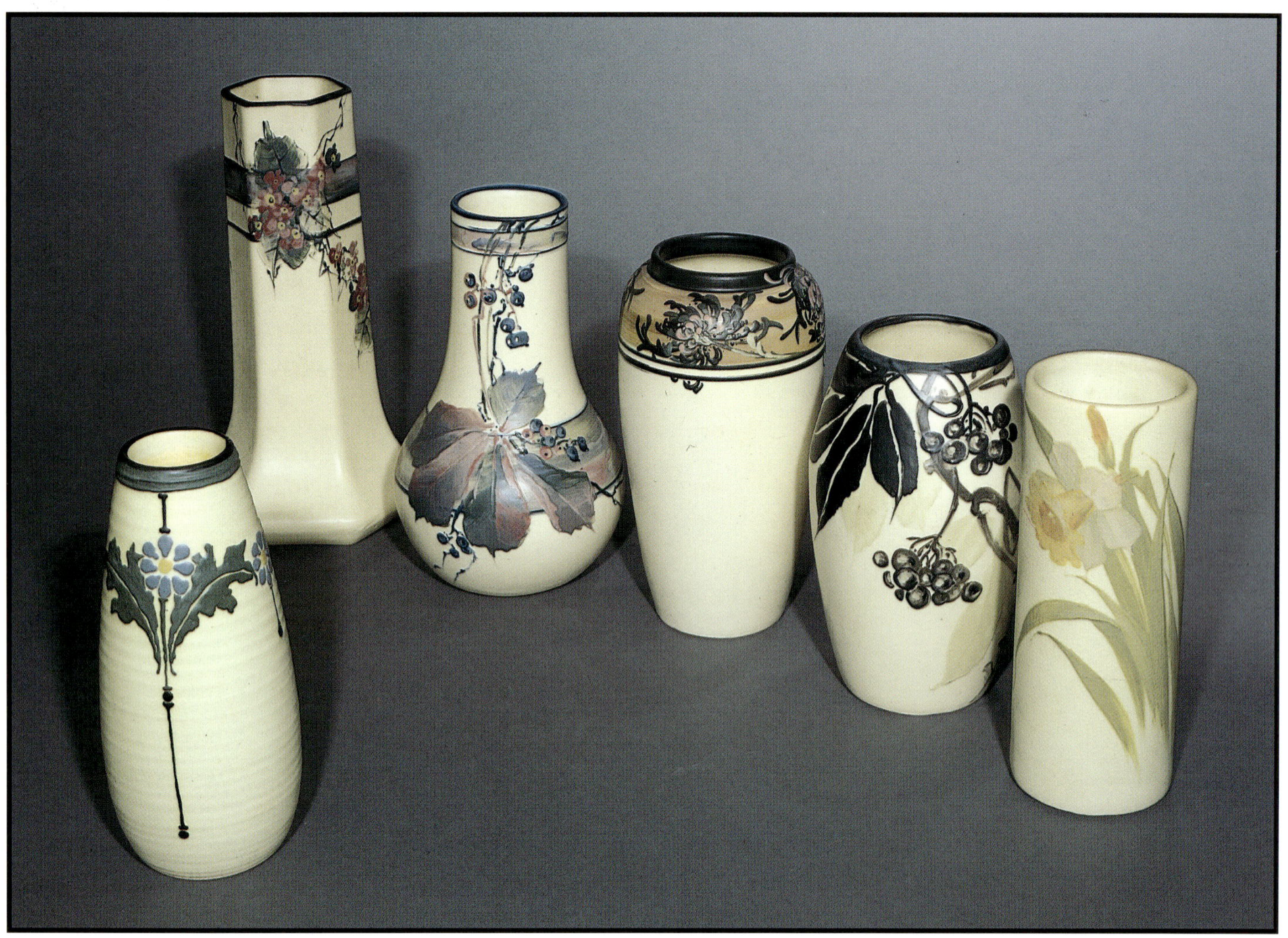

129	Rare and unusual hand thrown Weller White and Decorated vase with stylized floral decoration done by an unknown artist. Unmarked. Height 8 1/4 inches. This is a very heavy piece with repeating floral sprays and flowers, done in heavy slip.	$500-700
130	Weller hexagonal White and Decorated vase done by an unknown artist with Oriental prunus blossoms in red, yellow, green and black. Impressed "Weller" in large block letters. Height 11 1/8 inches.	$400-500
131	Weller White and Decorated vase decorated by an unknown artist with colorful Virginia creeper leaves, vines and berries. Bands outlined in dark blue encircle the rim and the fat portion of the vase. Unmarked. Height 9 3/8 inches.	$500-700
132	Pretty Weller White and Decorated vase done by an unknown artist with very stylish chrysanthemum decoration in pink, green, cream and black. Stamped "Weller" in large block letters. Height 8 7/8 inches.	$300-500
133	Weller White and Decorated vase with grapes, grape leaves and vines which are painted in black and pale green slip. Stamped "Weller" in large block letters. Height 8 inches. An unusual use of color with a very pleasant effect.	$200-300
134	Weller White and Decorated cylindrical vase with yellow jonquils with green stems done by an unknown artist. Stamped "Weller" in small block letters. Height 8 5/8 inches.	$400-600

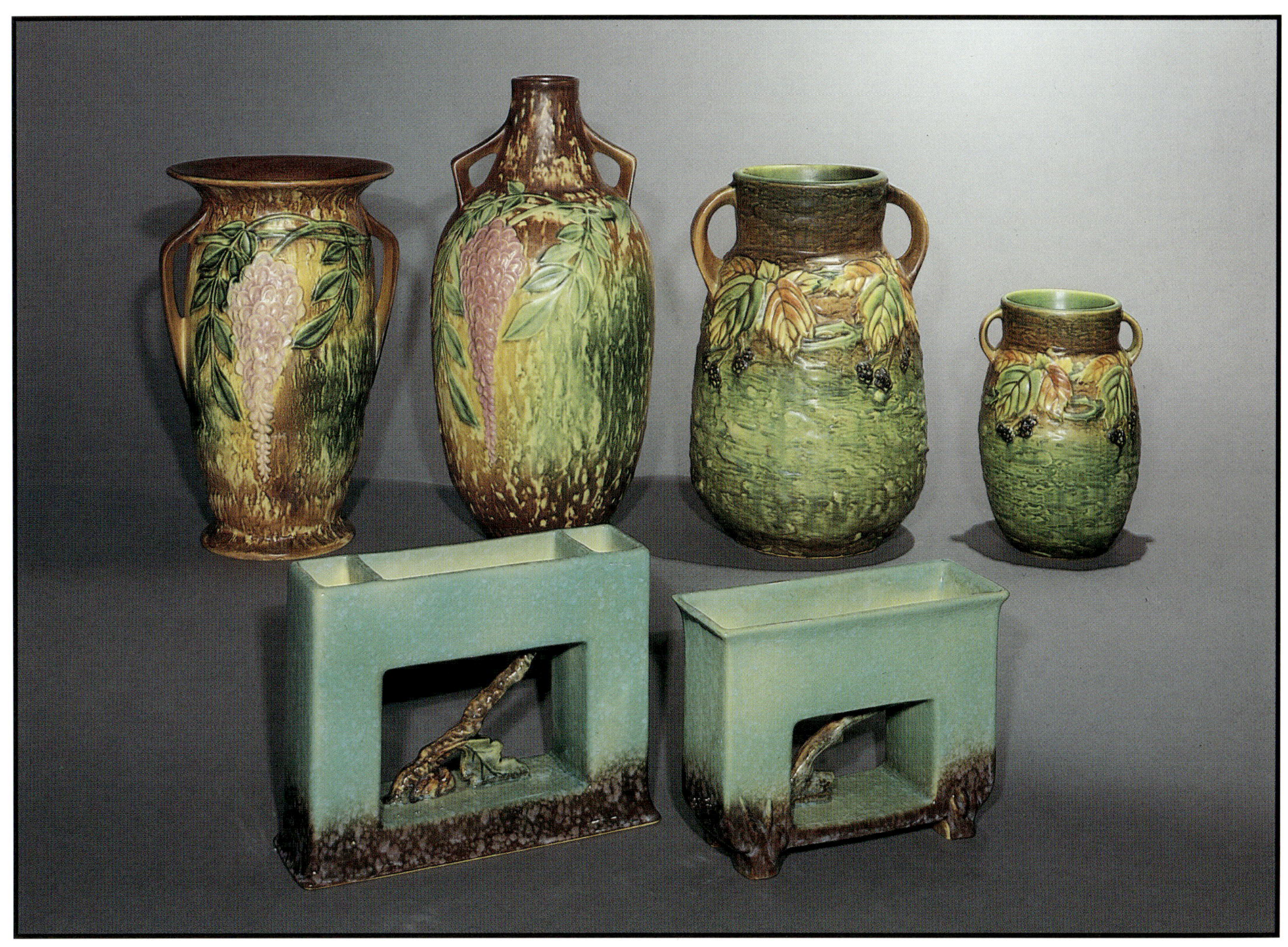

135   Tall Roseville Wisteria vase in brown, a hard to find shape and size. Marked only with the number "5" painted on the bottom in blue slip. Height 12 1/4 inches. Excellent mold and color. $1750-2250

136   Roseville Artcraft planter in green, brown and gray with the planter area divided into three sections. The oak limb in the recessed part of the piece has leaves and acorns. Marked with the embossed "Roseville USA" logo and shape number 1055-9. A small blue "X' is painted on the bottom, under the glaze. A number "3" or the letter "W" is incised in the bottom. Height is 7 1/8 inches and width is 9 1/2 inches. $150-200

137   Tall Roseville Wisteria two-handled vase with brown background. Marked only with the number "2" painted on the bottom in blue slip. Height 15 1/4 inches. A line at the rim has been professionally repaired. Excellent mold and color and a very hard to find size. $1500-2000

138   Roseville Artcraft planter in green, brown and gray. Marked with the embossed "Roseville USA" logo and shape number 1054-8 1/2. A small blue "X" is painted on the bottom, under the glaze. Height is 6 1/4 inches and width is 8 3/4 inches. $150-200

139   Tall Roseville two-handled Blackberry vase. Marked only with a number "5" painted on the bottom in blue slip. Height 12 1/4 inches. Decent mold and color with a small kiln kiss on one of the handles. $1500-2000

140   Roseville Blackberry two-handled vase. Marked with a gold foil logo and the letter "p" painted on in blue slip. Height 8 1/4 inches. Good mold and color. $600-800

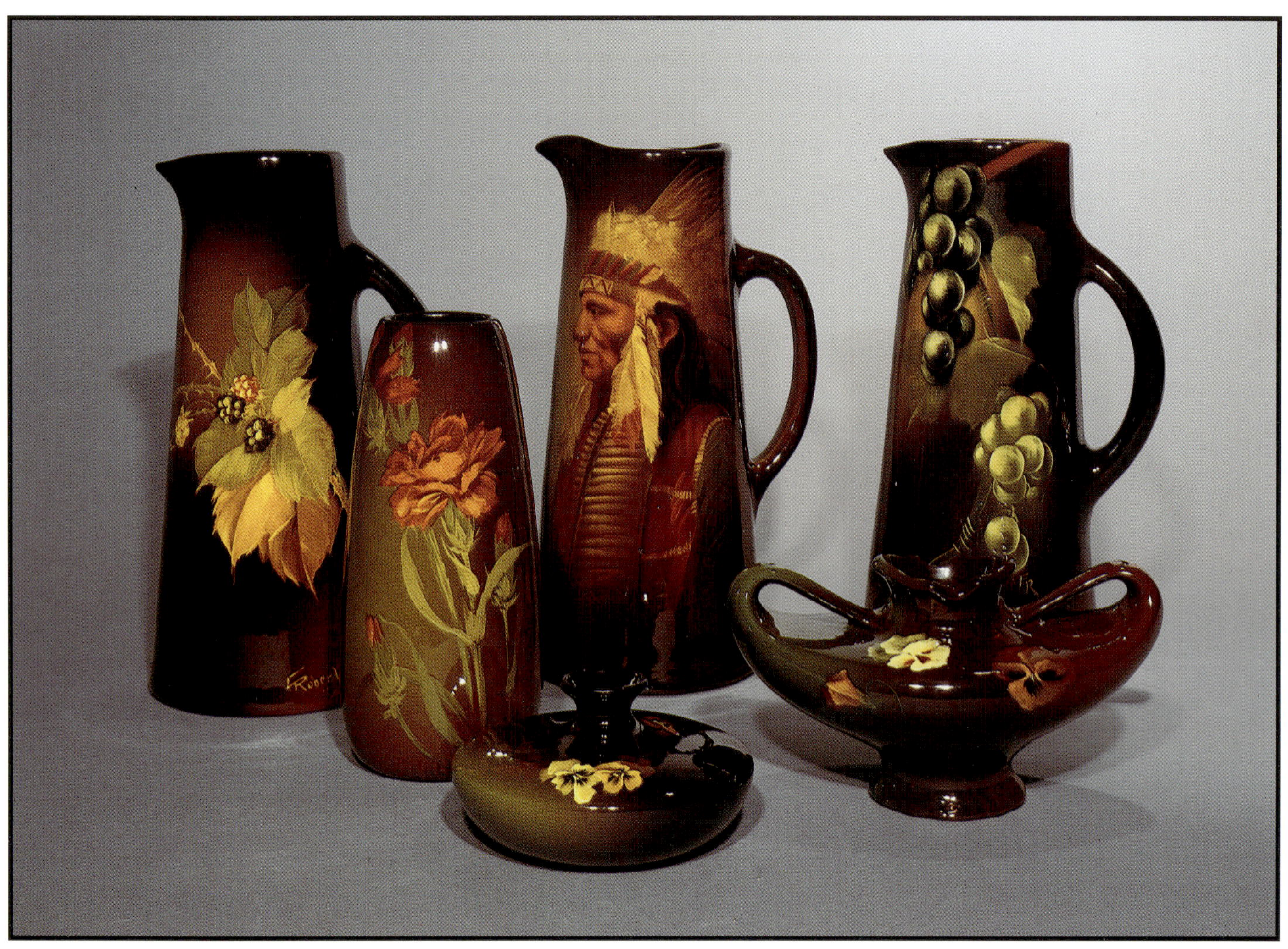

141   Nice Weller Louwelsa tankard with strong blackberry decoration by Eugene Roberts, whose name appears on the side of the piece. Impressed marked include the Louwelsa Weller semi-circular logo and numbers "580" and "7". Height 12 1/4 inches. Minor glaze scratches. $300-400

142   Weller Louwelsa vase with bright red rose decoration done by an unknown artist. Stamped "Weller" in small block letters. Height 8 7/8 inches. $100-150

143   Weller Louwelsa squat vase with pansy decoration in yellow, orange and black, done by Minnie Mitchell. Impressed marks include the "Louwelsa Weller" logo and numbers "481" and "9". The artist's initials are painted on the side of the vase in red slip. Height 2 3/4 inches. $125-175

144   Handsome Weller Louwelsa tankard with the portrait of a Native American chief in full headdress, painted by Levi J. Burgess. Marks include the circular "Louwelsa Weller" stamped logo and the impressed numbers "580" and "5". Height 12 1/2 inches. Small flake off base. A wonderfully detailed portrait with great color by one of Weller's best. $1000-1500

145   Weller Louwelsa two-handled vase with pansy decoration done by Mary Gillie on a brown and dark green ground. The artist's initials are painted on the side of the vase below the flowers. Impressed "Louwelsa Weller", "X 332" and "8". Height 4 5/8 inches. Glaze scratches on the back side. $150-200

146   Weller Louwelsa tankard with grape decoration boldly painted by Eugene Roberts, whose initials appear on the side of the piece. Impressed marks on the base include the "Louwelsa Weller" logo, notations "S" and "2" and shape number 580. Height 12 3/8 inches. Seepage throughout the crazing. $200-300

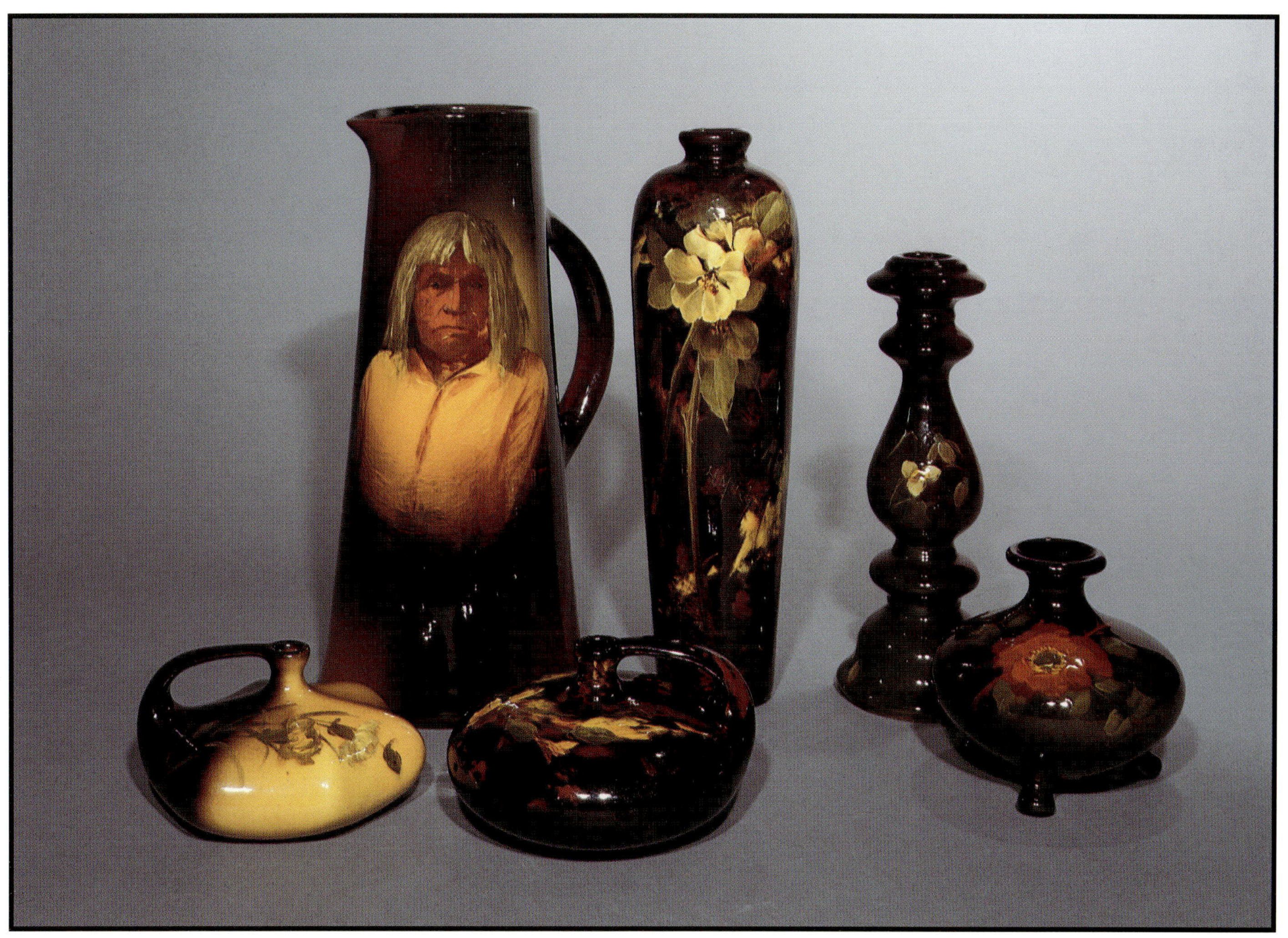

147 Cute Weller Louwelsa ewer with yellow carnation decoration done by an unknown artist, whose initials appear on the back side of the handle. Unfortunately, they are difficult to read. Other marks include the impressed semi-circular "Louwelsa Weller" logo and the impressed numbers "5", "521" and "2". Height 2 7/8 inches. $100-150

148 Colorful Weller Louwelsa tankard painted by Anthony Dunlavy with what is thought to be a portrait of Geronimo. The artist's monogram is painted on the side of the piece near the sitter's left arm. Impressed marks include the semi-circular "Louwelsa Weller" die-stamp and the numbers "580" and "12". Height 12 5/8 inches. A copy of a photograph of Geronimo comes with the tankard along with some biographical data. $1200-1500

149 Weller Aurelian squat ewer with carnations painted on by William Hall. Hall's initials are also painted on the side of the vase, just below the handle. Incised "Aurelian Weller K" and impressed with the numbers "519" and "8". Height 3 1/4 inches. Minor discoloration to the glaze. $300-400

150 Elegant Weller Aurelian vase with wild rose decoration, the work of Hattie Mitchell, whose full name appears on the side of the vase. Incised on the base is the notation, "Aurelian Weller". Stamped on the base are the numbers "9" and "409". Height 12 1/4 inches. Minor glaze scratches. $300-400

151 Weller Louwelsa candlestick with floral decoration done by an unknown artist whose initials appear on the side of the piece. Impressed marks on the base include the semicircular "Louwelsa Weller" logo and the numbers "4", "X 260" and "8". Height 9 1/2 inches. $150-200

152 Weller Louwelsa vase with three bun feet and wild rose decoration done by an unknown artist. Impressed marks include the semi-circular "Louwelsa Weller" logo and the notation "X 409 8". Height 4 1/4 inches. $100-150

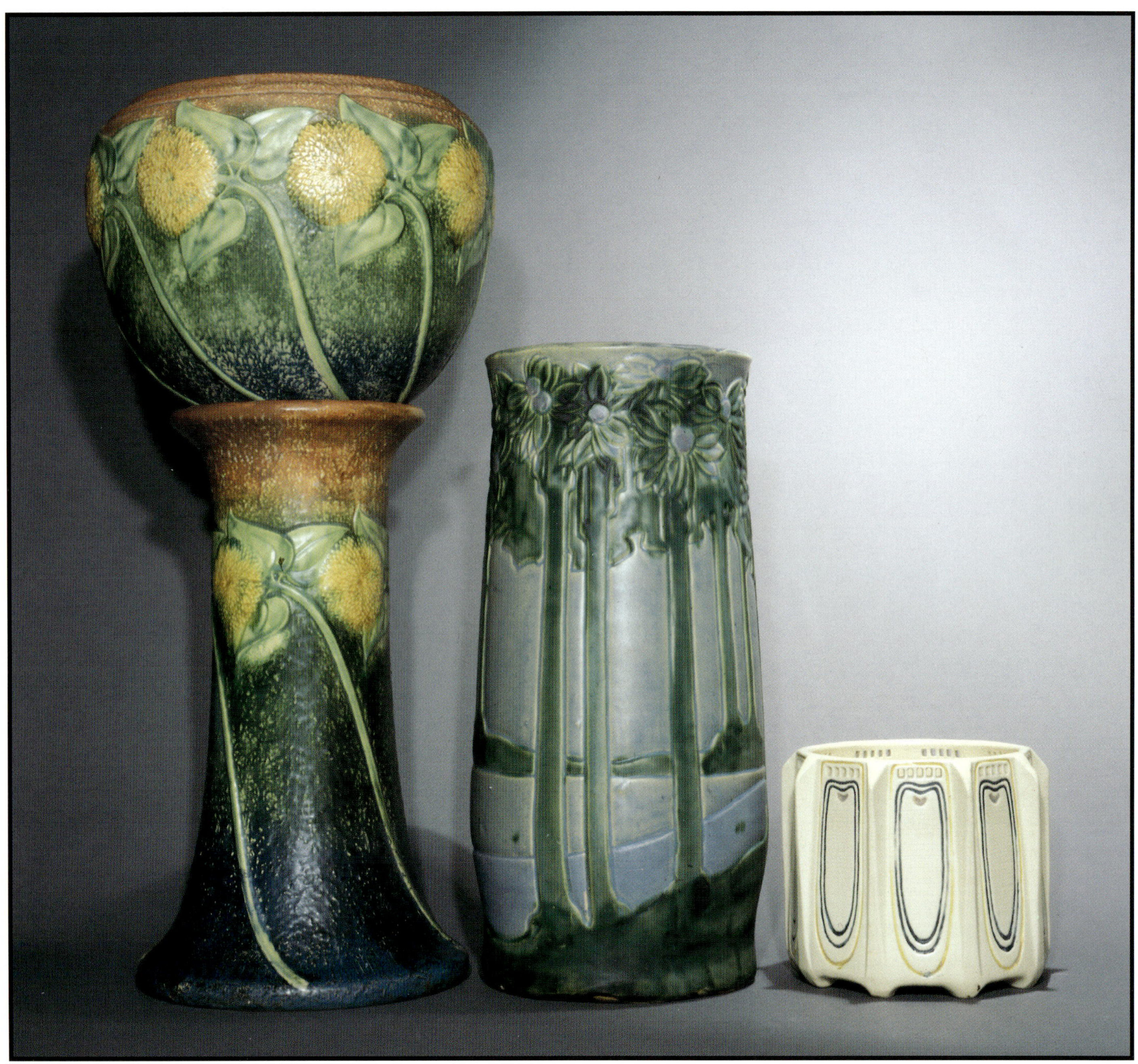

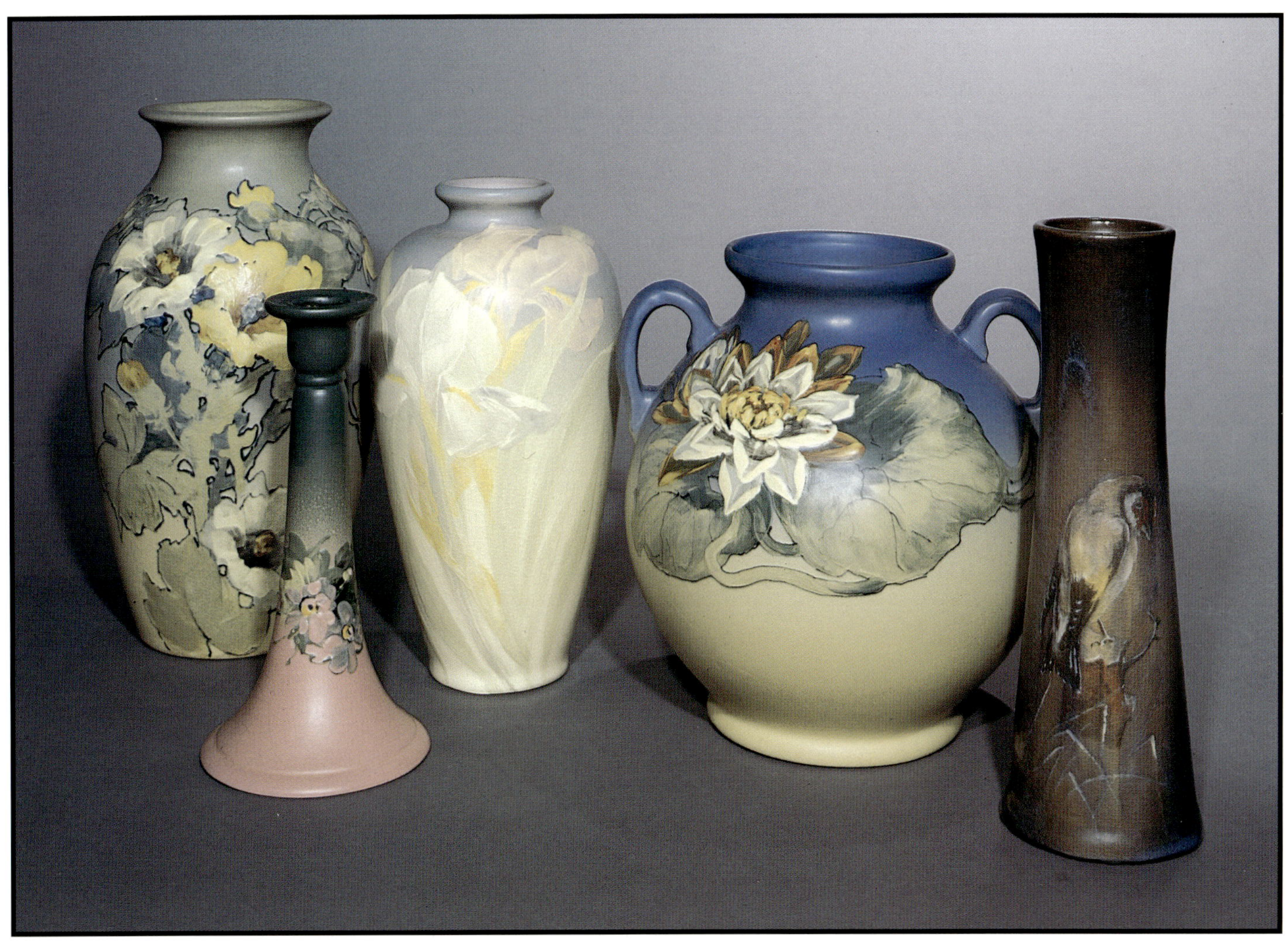

| 156 | Tall and colorful Weller Hudson vase, most likely the work of Hester Pillsbury, with showy hibiscus flowers and leaves, all outlined in black. Marked with "Weller Hudson Ware" paper label, impressed "Weller" in large block letters and inkstamped with a full kiln "Weller Ware" logo. Height 11 7/8 inches. Lot 1056 in Keramics 1996 was done by Pillsbury and is the mate to this piece. | $2000-2500 |

| 157 | Weller Hudson candlestick with flower decoration done by Mae Timberlake. The artist's initials are painted on among the flowers in black slip. Height 8 5/8 inches. | $200-300 |

| 158 | Weller Hudson Light vase decorated with two large irises, one white and the other mauve, done by an unknown artist. Impressed "Weller" in small block letters. Height 10 3/8 inches. A very strong example. | $800-1000 |

| 159 | Good Weller Hudson two-handled vase with showy lotus blossoms on front and back, painted by Hester Pillsbury. Lotus pads and vines encircle the vase, running through the handles. Pillsbury's signature appears on the back of the vase, painted on with black slip. The bottom of the piece is marked with the half kiln inkstamp "Weller Pottery" logo. Height 9 3/8 inches. | $1500-2000 |

| 160 | Interesting vase painted by Ed Abel in 1906. Abel worked at Rookwood in the early 1890's and later at Weller. A good artist, Abel consistently used difficult motifs in his work, with birds and fish a frequent topic at both potteries. In the past 10 years, we have seen about a dozen pieces signed by Abel and dated 1906 and 1907. These bear the logo of an unknown pottery, most likely one that Abel operated himself. Most of these pieces resemble Rookwood's Standard or Weller's Louwelsa glazes. This piece seems more like Rookwood's Vellum or Weller's Hudson, though it predates Hudson by several years. The artwork is typically good, being a small bird perched on a stump. Abel's initials are incised in the base along with the date and company logo which a large letter "T" over a large letter "O" with smaller letters "c" and "o" on either side of the "T" but inside the "O". We assume the pottery was located near Cincinnati since most of these vases have come from the area. Height is 10 5/8 inches. | $600-800 |

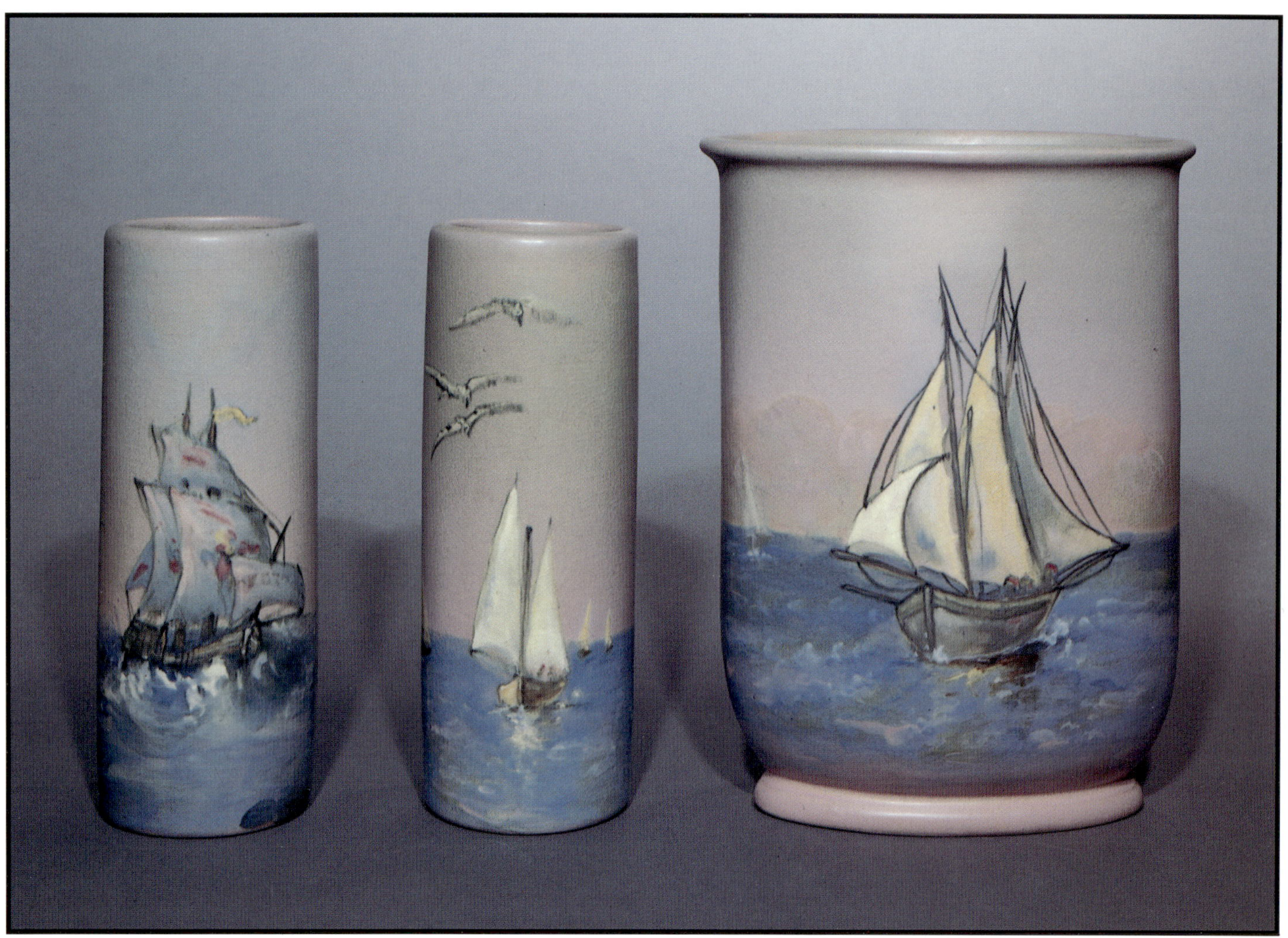

161   Good Weller Hudson scenic vase painted by Hester Pillsbury. A Spanish caravel under full sail moves over $5000-7000
       moderate seas with two other craft behind. Sea gulls accompany the boats which may represent the three
       ships of Christopher Columbus, the famous boat builder from central Ohio. Signed in black slip on the side
       of the vase and marked "A", also in black slip on the bottom. Height 8 5/8 inches. Great color and a very
       pleasant scene. The purchaser of this lot will be allowed to buy lot 162 for the same price.

162   Good Weller Hudson scenic vase painted by Sarah Reid McLauglin showing several sail boats plying quiet $5000-7000
       seas while sea gulls fly overhead. Signed by the artist in black slip on the side of the vase. The letter "A" is
       painted on the bottom in black slip. Height 8 1/2 inches. The purchaser of lot 161 will be allowed to buy this
       lot for the same price.

163   Weller Hudson scenic vase painted by Sarah Reid McLaughlin. The flat side vase has a large sailing vessel on $2000-3000
       the front side and several smaller craft on the back side. Clouds swirl around in the background from horizon
       to about half way up the vase. Signed by the artist in black slip on the back side. The base carries a letter "A"
       in black slip and the half kiln "Weller Pottery" inkstamp. Height 9 7/8 inches. Four hairlines descending from
       the rim have been professionally repaired.

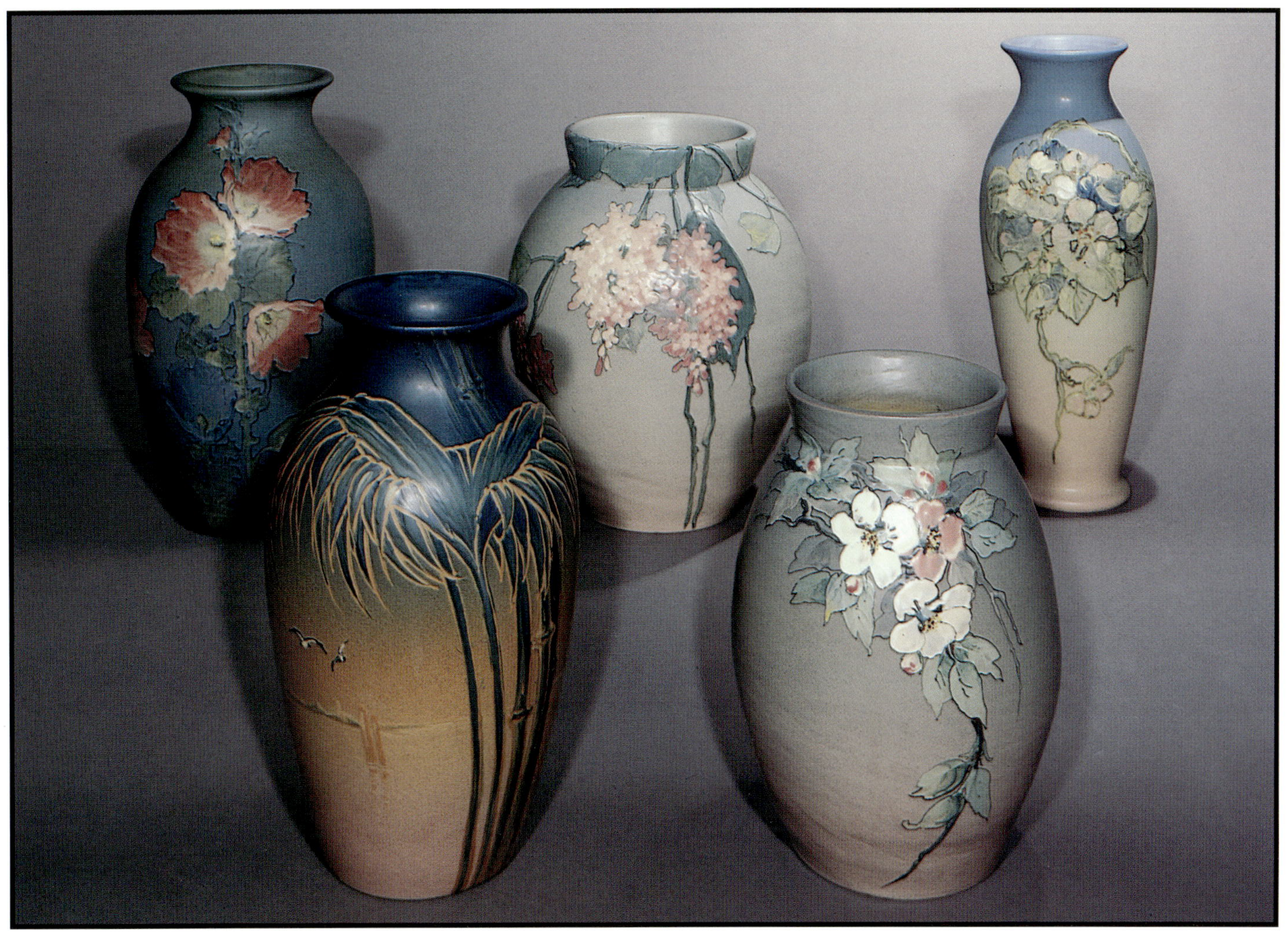

164	Pretty Weller Hudson vase with red and blue hollyhocks on a medium blue ground painted by Mae Timberlake. Impressed "Weller" in large block letters. Timberlake's signature is painted on the side of the vase in the same dark blue slip used to outline the flowers. Height 12 1/8 inches. A rim chip has been professionally repaired.	$400-600
165	Rare Weller Hudson scenic vase showing a distant city across a bay. Tall bamboo shoots and leaves tower over sea gulls flying toward wood pilings in the bay. Marked only with the impressed "Weller" logo in large block letters. Height 12 1/4 inches. A 1/2 inch drill hole in the bottom has been professionally repaired. A very nicely conceived scene, well executed by an unknown artist.	$2000-3000
166	Showy Weller Hudson vase with lush pink lilac decoration, done in very heavy slip by Sarah Timberlake, whose initials are painted on the side of the vase in black slip. An unusual and pleasant touch is the hollowing out of each small flower center with a stylus which gives the thick decoration even more dimension. Incised "Weller Pottery" in script on the bottom. Height 10 5/8 inches. Minor glaze flakes off the base. There is wonderful shading and detail in the work of Ms. Timberlake.	$1500-2000
167	Pretty Weller Hudson vase with red and white fruit blossoms painted by Naomi Walch, whose last name appears on the side of the vase in black slip. The base is incised "Weller Pottery" in bold script. Height 10 1/8 inches. Flowers on the back side of the vase are done in tonalistic shades of gray and white. There are two small burst glaze bubbles on the back.	$700-900
168	Tall hand thrown Weller Hudson vase with multicolored vining flowers painted by Edith Hood, whose last name is painted on the side of the vase in black slip. Otherwise the vase is unmarked. Height 12 7/8 inches.	$1000-1250

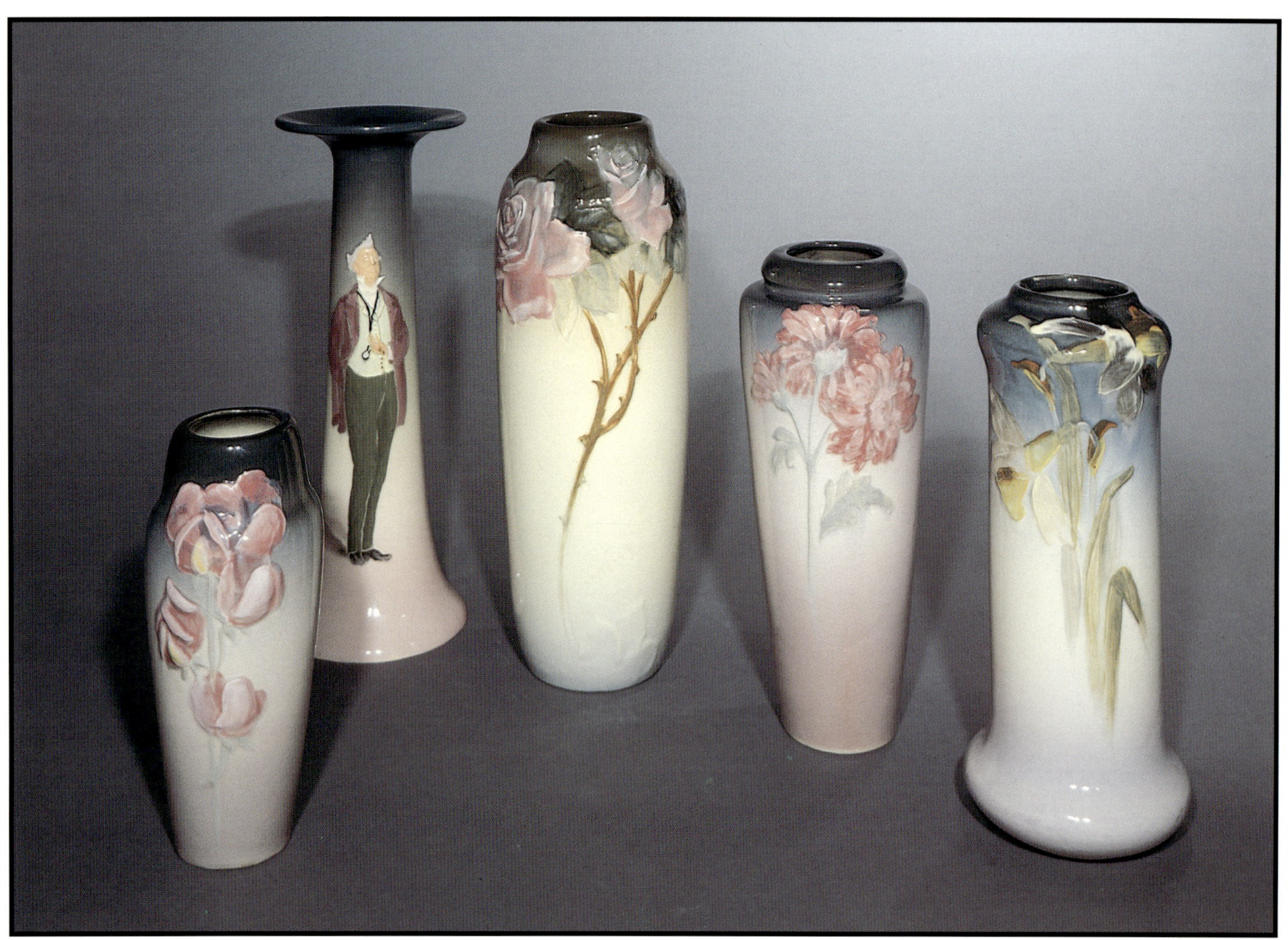

169   Weller Etna vase with embossed flowers in pink and yellow. Stamped "Etna Weller" in large block letters. Height 8 3/8 inches. $200-300

170   Tall Weller 3rd Line Dickensware vase with the colorful image of Mr. Pecksniff. A wafer seal on the back side of the vase carries Mr. Pecksniff's name. Embossed on the bottom are two rectangles, one of which contains the name "Weller" and the other, the number "12". Incised on the bottom is the notation "Dickens" and the letter "S". Height 12 7/8 inches. Damage to the rim has been professionally repaired. $300-500

171   Large and well defined Weller Etna vase with embossed pink roses. Impressed "Weller" on the side of the vase. Height 13 3/8 inches. $600-800

172   Weller Etna vase with embossed carnation decoration. Stamped "Etna Weller" on the bottom. Height 10 7/8 inches. Minor glaze scratches. $200-300

173   Weller Etna vase with embossed and colored jonquils. Impressed marks include "Weller" on the side of the vase and "Etna Weller" in large block letters on the bottom. Height 11 inches. $200-300

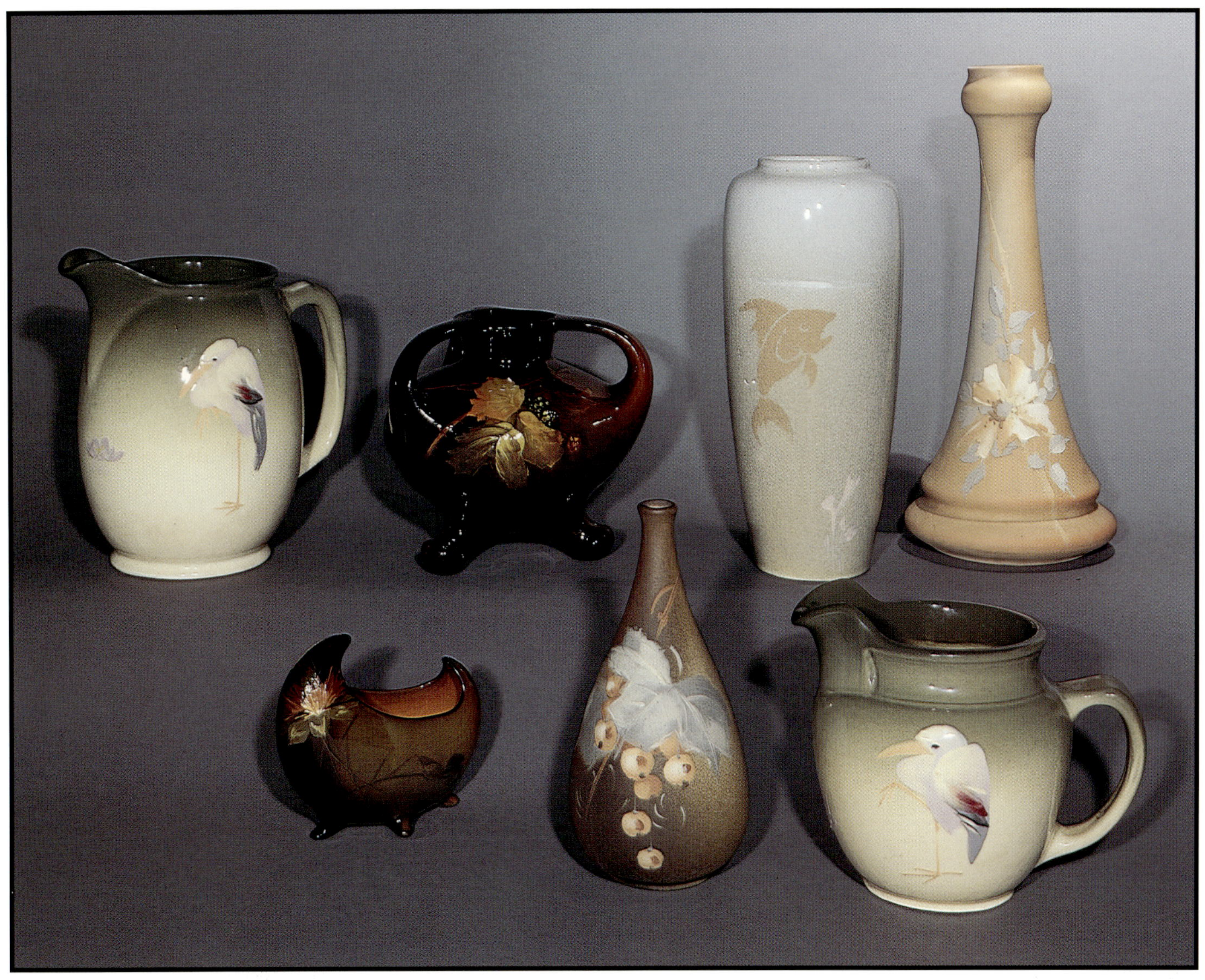

174   Owens Lotus pitcher with a wading bird and lotus blossom. Unmarked. Height 8 5/8 inches. Some staining $400-600
       from use.

175   Owens Utopian crescent shaped flower boat with four bun feet. Decoration consists of red clover, done by an $200-300
       unknown artist whose monogram appears on the back side of the vase. Impressed on the base is the notation
       "Utopian J.B. Owens" and shape number 872. Height 4 1/4 inches.

176   Owens Utopian three-handled and three-footed vase with excellent blackberry decoration done by an unknown $250-350
       artist. The base is stamped "Utopian Owens" and has several other numbers which are glaze obscured. Height
       6 3/4 inches. Small glaze nick on the back side of the piece.

177   Owens Matt Utopian vase with red cherry decoration done by Hattie Eberlein. The artist's monogram appears $300-500
       on the side of the vase. Impressed marks include "Owens Utopian" and shape number 817. Height 7 7/8
       inches.

178   Owens Lotus high glaze vase with stylized fish and seaweed, done in the manner of Frank Ferrell. The $1000-1500
       vase is unmarked but the style is identical to Ferrell pieces in the new Owens books. Height 11 1/8 inches.
       Fairly heavy crazing and a scuff mark on the back side of the vase.

179   Owens Lotus pitcher showing a single lotus blossom and a tall wading bird. Marked only with an incised "4" on $400-500
       the bottom. Height 6 inches. Minor staining from use.

180   Tall Owens Matt Utopian vase with wild rose decoration painted by Tot Steele. The base is impressed "Owens" $400-500
       in tiny script and bears shape number 123. The artist's monogram is painted on the side of the vase in slip.
       Height 13 5/8 inches.

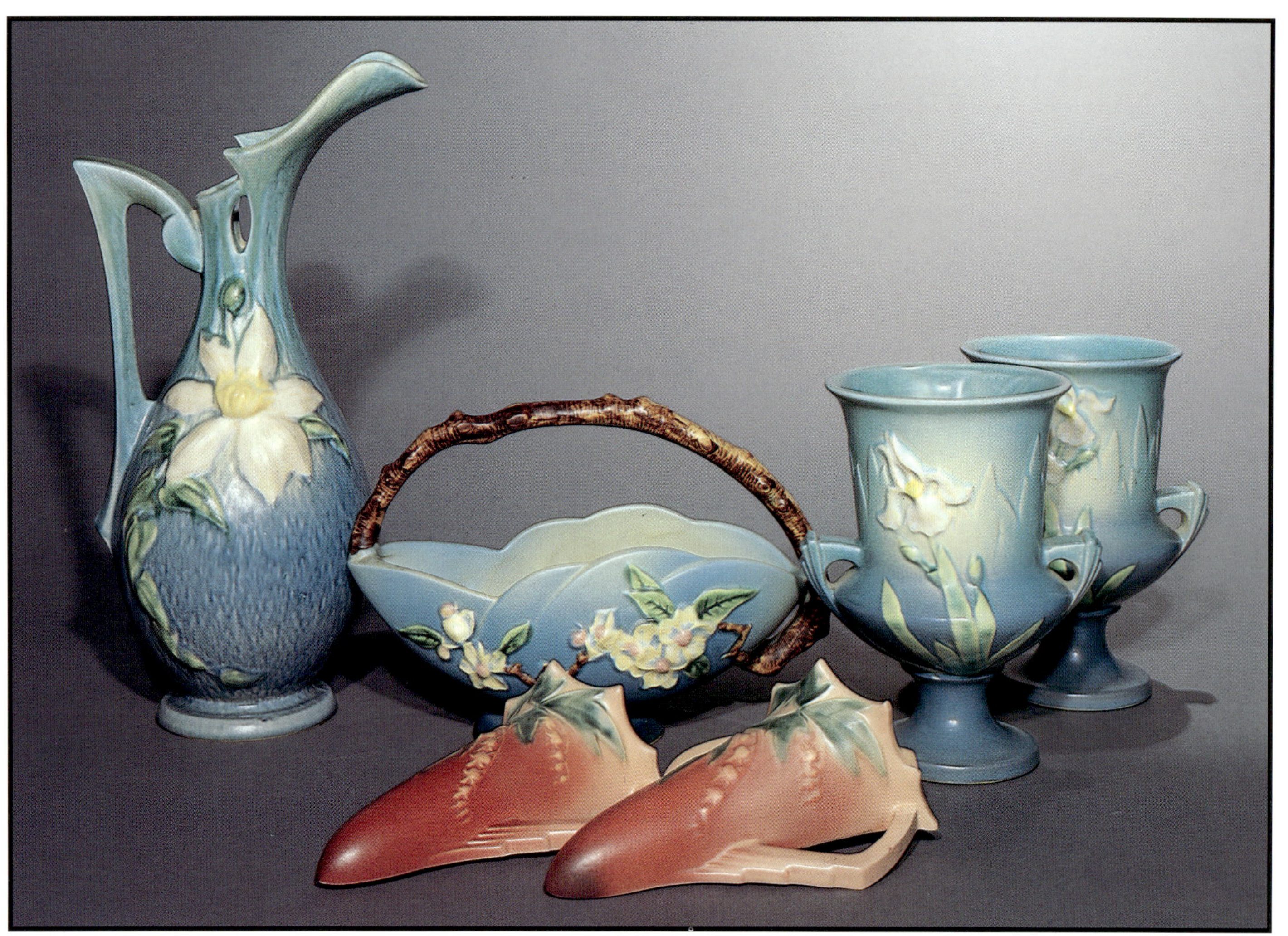

181   Roseville Clematis ewer in blue. Marked with the embossed "Roseville USA" logo and shape number "18-15". Painted on the bottom in blue slip are the letter "r" and the number "10". Height 15 1/4 inches. $200-300

182   Pair of Roseville Bleeding Heart wall pockets in pink. Marked with the embossed "Roseville U.S.A." logo and shape number "1287-8". Painted on the back of each piece is an "X" in blue slip. Height of each is 8 5/8 inches. $400-500

183   Roseville Apple Blossom basket with long handle. Embossed "Roseville USA 310-10" on the bottom. Height is 5 3/4 inches and length is 11 5/8 inches. Good mold and color. $150-200

184   Pair of Roseville Iris two-handled pedestal vases. Stamped "Roseville 923-8" on each. Height 8 1/4 inches. $150-200

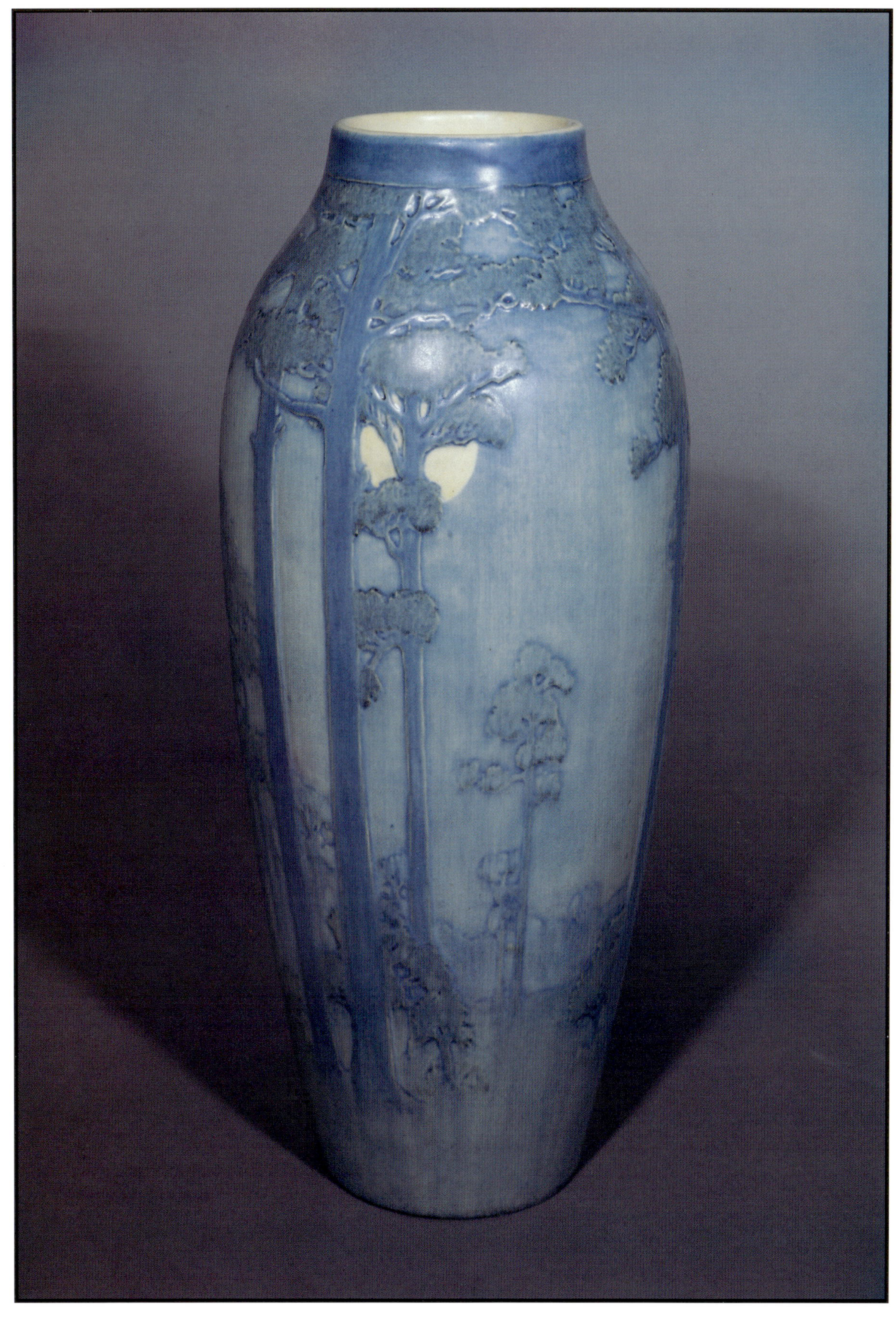

185   Tall and beautiful Newcomb scenic vase done in mat glaze, carved and painted in 1918 by Sadie Irvine. $10000-12500
Pictured are tall Southern pines in green and dark blue outlined against a pale blue ground. A large full
moon peeks through the dense pine boughs which are finely detailed and carved. Impressed marks
include the Newcomb logo, the date (JH 20), shape number 232 and the initials of potter Joseph Meyer.
Incised is the monogram of the artist. Height 13 1/2 inches. There are two pin-head size grinding flakes
off the base.

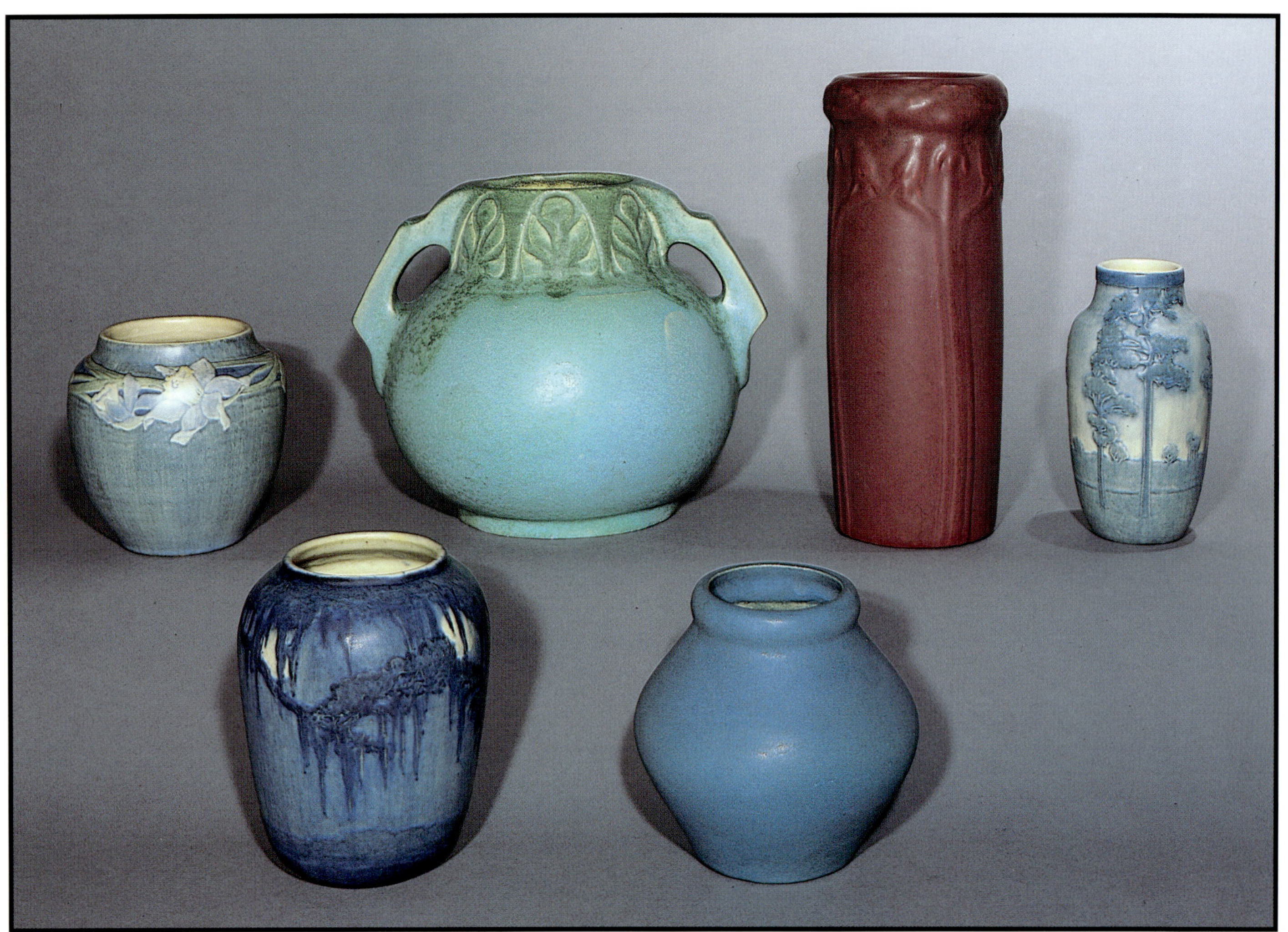

186	Newcomb vase with a band of carved and painted jonquils surrounding the shoulder, the work of Cynthia Pugh Littlejohn in 1913. Impressed marks include the Newcomb logo, shape number 49, the initials of potter Joseph Meyer and the letter B in a circle for buff clay. Incised and painted on the base is the monogram of the artist. Incised next to the monogram is the number "51". Painted on the bottom is the date code, "GF 18". Height 4 5/8 inches. Nice detailing and color.	$1500-2000
187	Rare and unusual Newcomb scenic mat glaze vase carved and painted in 1933 by Henrietta Bailey. Basically, a typical Newcomb scenic with Spanish moss hanging from gnarled live oak trees but just when you feel like everything is all right and it's safe to come out you see (gasp!) two full moons lurking through the moss. This might be a case for Fox Mulder and the X-Files since we don't usually see such phenomena in real life (or on a Newcomb vase.) Despite what Mulder says, you can trust us on this one. It is a true oddity and still a very pretty vase. Marks include the Newcomb logo and date (UL 32) along with the incised initials of potter Kenneth Smith and decorator Henrietta Bailey. Height 5 1/2 inches	$1750-2250
188	Van Briggle two-handled vase with embossed, stylized dandelion decoration around the collar, done in the 1907-1912 period with a curdled green mat glaze over a slightly lighter green. Incised marks include the AA logo, "Van Briggle Colo. Spgs.", shape number 756 and finisher numbers "6" and "17". Height 7 5/8 inches.	$500-700
189	Van Briggle blue mat glaze vase from the 1907 to 1912 period. Incised marks include the conjoined AA logo, "Van Briggle Colo Sprgs", shape number "119" and finisher numbers "18" and "14". Height 4 7/8 inches.	$300-400
190	1903 Van Briggle vase done in a rich maroon mat glaze over embossed, stylized dandelion decoration. Incised marks on the base include the "AA" logo, "Van Briggle" and the date signified by Roman numeral III. Stamped in the base is shape number 135. Height 10 inches.	$700-900
191	Well defined Newcomb mat glaze "Southern Pine" scenic vase done by Sadie Irvine in 1916. Impressed marks include the Newcomb logo, the date (IG 3), shape number 237 and the initials of potter Joseph Meyer. Incised in the base are the monogram of the artist and the number "233". Height 5 7/8 inches. This vase has no moon!	$2000-2500

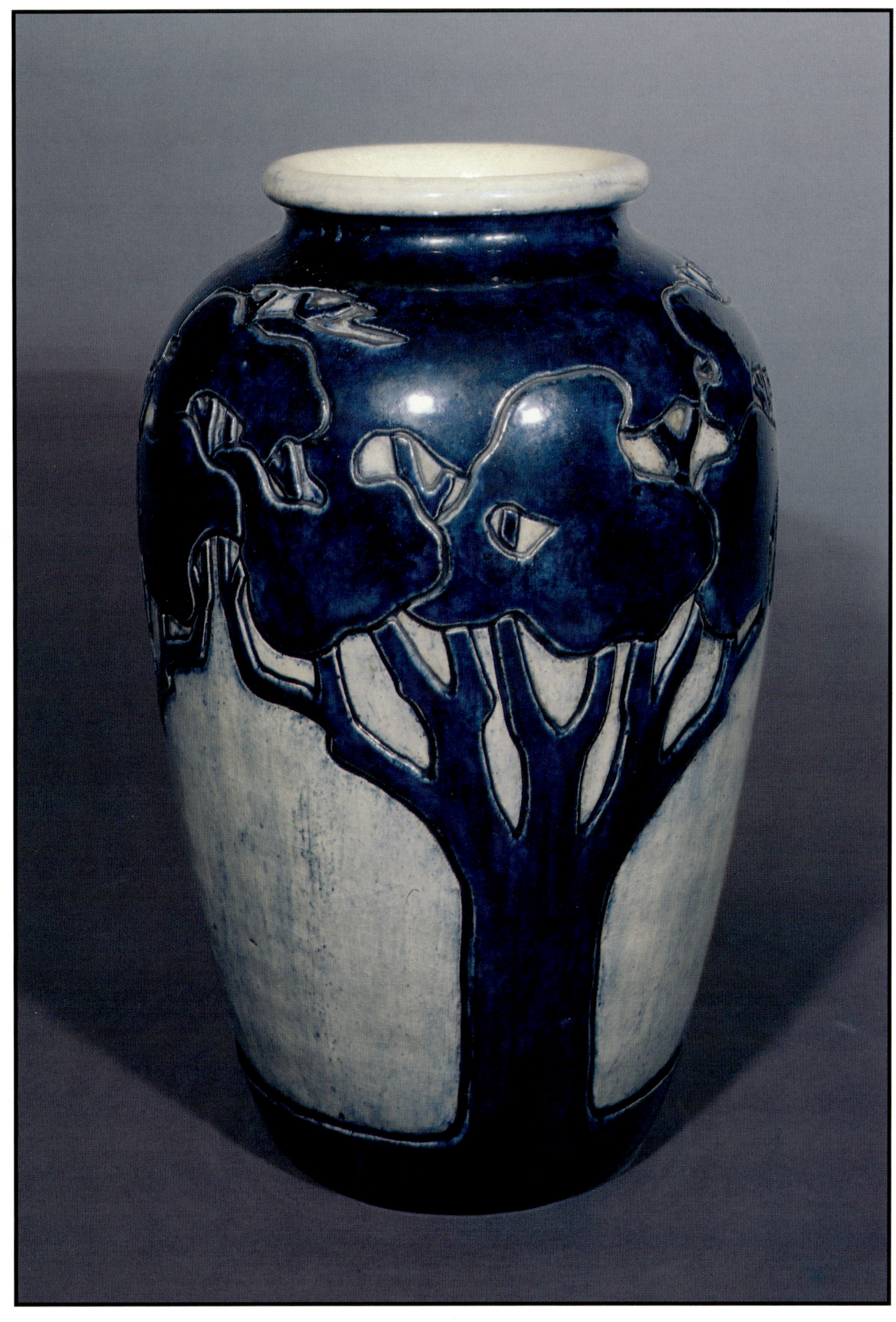

192   Rare and important high glaze Newcomb Pottery scenic vase, deeply carved and painted by Leona Nicholson in 1902. The conventionalized treatment of trees utilizes large, flat areas of cobalt blue against a gray ground. The ground color is deeply cut back into the body of the vase and is more reminiscent of Frederick Hurten Rhead's Della Robbia for Roseville than later Newcomb. Though flatly painted, the trees have much dimension, due to the deep, sharp edged carving. Marks include the impressed Newcomb logo, the impressed initials of potter, Joseph Meyer, an impressed "Q" for buff clay, the incised monogram of the artist and the painted-on date (R 25). Height 12 7/8 inches. There are two small, flat, base chips which are not visible from the side. Exhibited: From Our Native Clay Art Pottery From the Collections of the American Ceramic Arts Society, Martin Eidelberg, Editor, New York, 1987. Pictured on page 74 as item number 126. $50000-60000

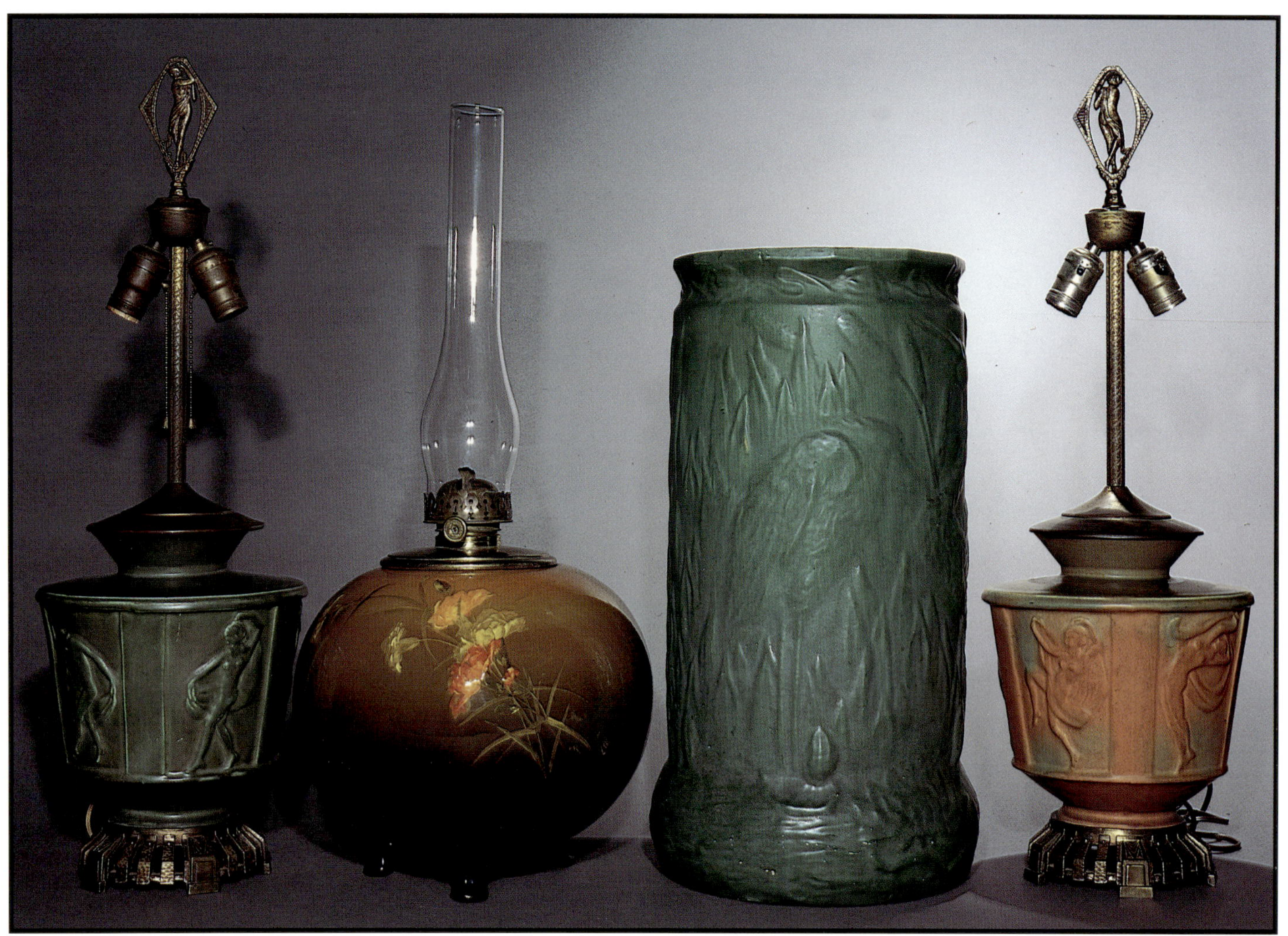

193   Rare Muncie Pottery lamp in green mat glaze with six panels, each having a different view of an Art Deco nude. The lamp has original Deco fittings, including the finial, which is in the form of a nude. The ceramic base is incised "IS". Height of the ceramic portion is 9 3/4 inches. $800-1000

194   Weller Louwelsa oil lamp base with carnation decoration done by Eugene Roberts, whose initials appear on the side of the vessel. The lamp sits on three stubby shoe feet and is impressed "Louwelsa Weller" and "K". The base is also incised with the number "367". Height 10 1/8 inches. There is a tight line at the rim and minor glaze scratches. An older font, burner and chimney accompany the lot. $300-400

195   Arts & Crafts style umbrella stand in green mat glaze with embossed scene of cranes and water plants, possibly the work of Owens Pottery. Unmarked. Height 20 5/8 inches. There is a tight line at the rim. $500-700

196   Rare Muncie Pottery lamp in orange and green mat glaze with six panels each having a different view of an Art Deco nude. The lamp has original Deco fittings, including the finial, which is in the form of a nude. The ceramic base is incised "IA". Height of the ceramic portion is 9 3/4 inches. $800-1000

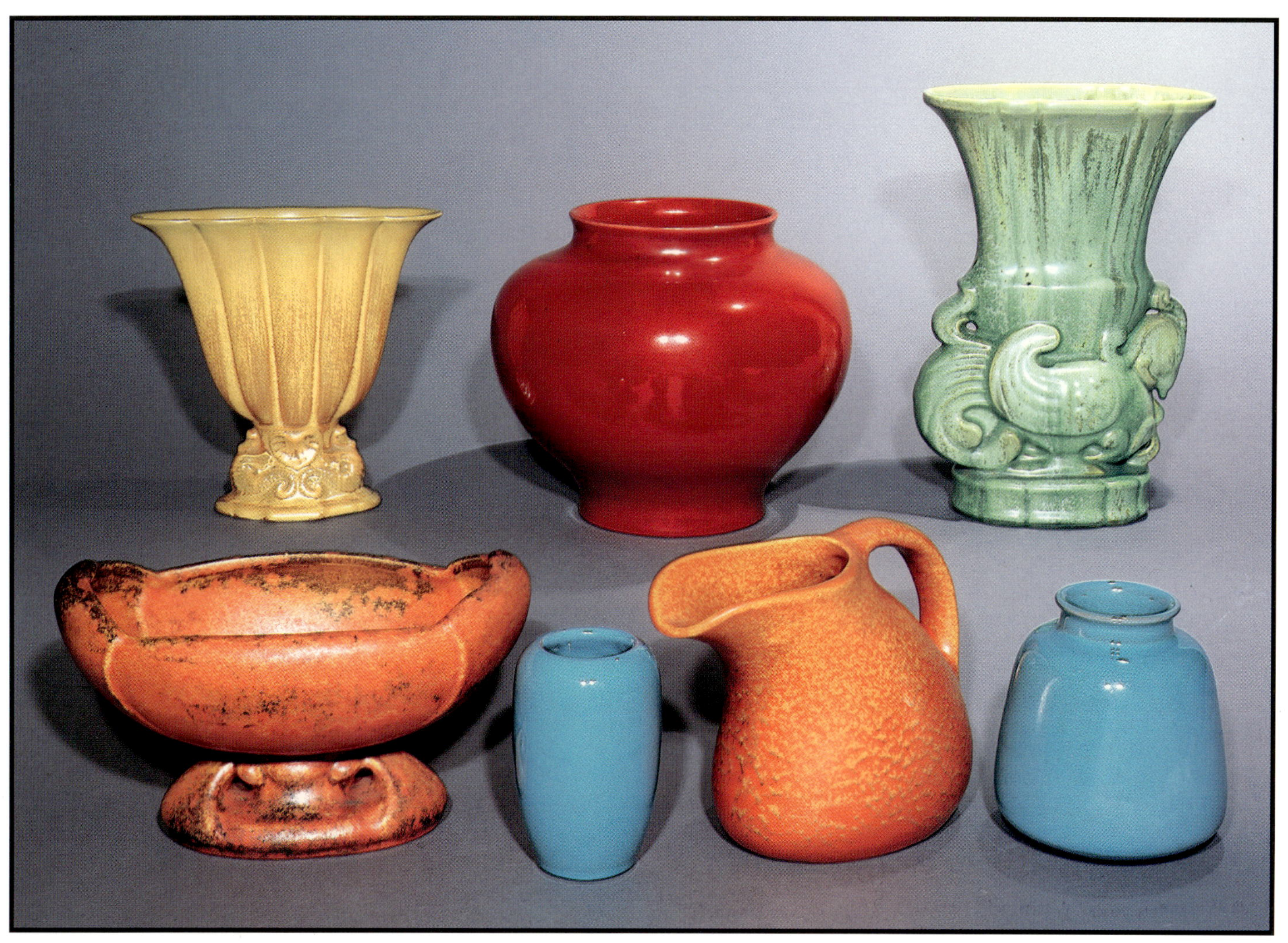

197   Cowan console bowl done in their wonderful Oriental Red glaze. Impressed with the Cowan logo and the name "Cowan". Height 5 7/8 inches. $400-500

198   Cowan Seahorse fan vase covered with a lush gold and tan crystalline glaze. Impressed Cowan logo. Height 7 7/8 inches. $200-300

199   California Faience vase made of red clay and covered with a rich, blue high glaze. The base is incised "California Faience". Height 4 5/8 inches. Very minor glaze scratches. $200-300

200   Handsome Gladding McBean vase covered with a brilliant red glaze with tiny gray crystals. Marked with the inkstamp GMcB in an oval logo. Height 8 inches. $500-700

201   Muncie pitcher covered with a striking Uranium orange glaze. Stamped "Muncie" in block letters on the bottom. Height 6 1/8 inches. A very strong glaze. $150-200

202   Cowan "Chinese Bird" vase done in a wonderful green and brown crystalline mat glaze. Impressed with the Cowan logo. Height 11 1/8 inches. $600-800

203   California Faience vase of red clay covered with a mottled blue high glaze. Incised "California Faience" on the bottom. Height 5 1/8 inches. Uncrazed. $150-200

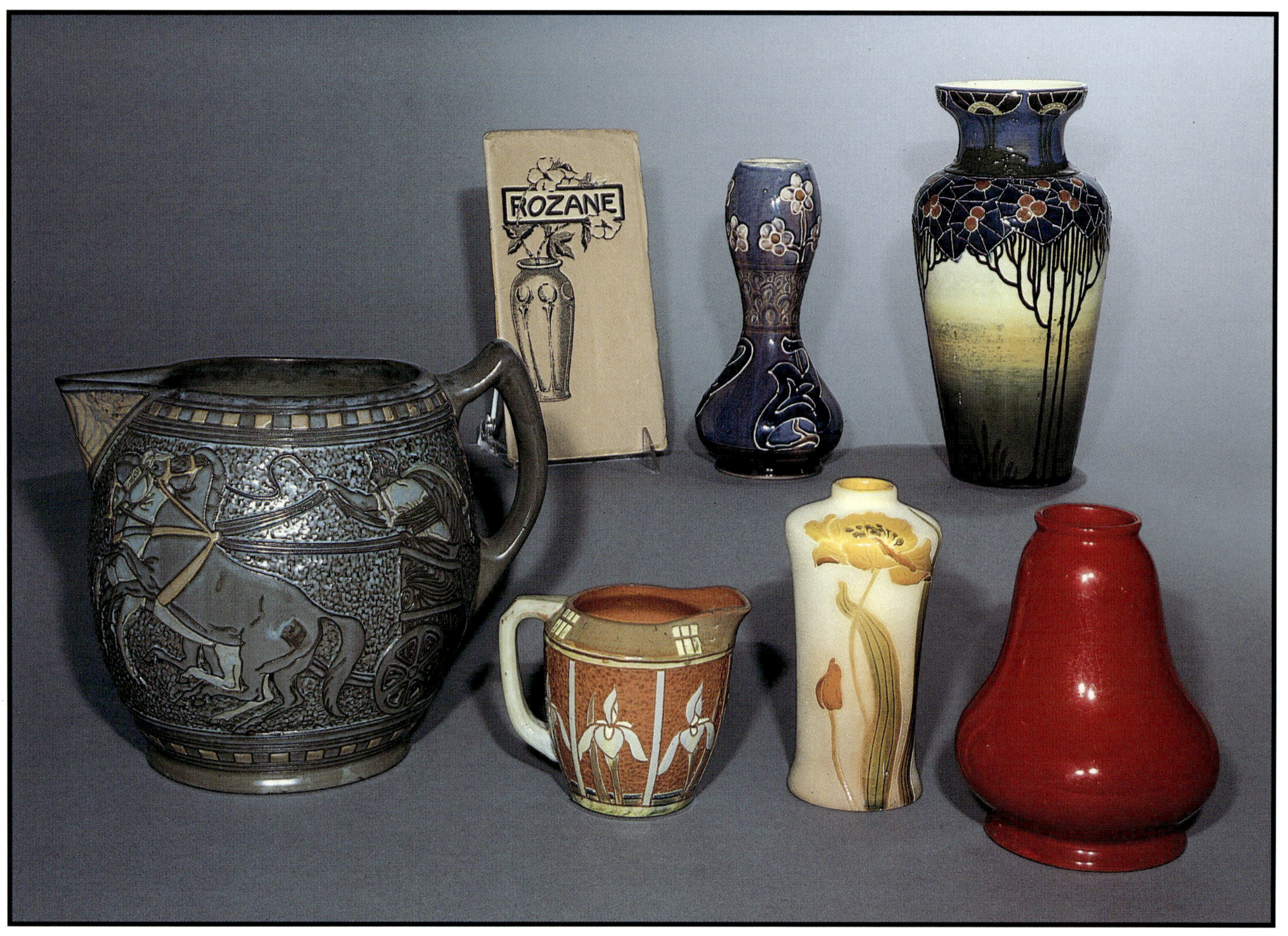

<table>
<tr><td>204</td><td>Fine Roseville Della Robbia "Roman Charioteer" pitcher deeply carved and painted in an exceptional glaze by an unknown artist early in this century. Marked with a Rozane Ware wafer seal and an old toothed circular paper label. Well detailed and finely carved with a chariot, driver and team of three horses, this piece is blessed with wonderful glazes which we have not seen. There are light blue and tan colors for accent but the primary glaze is a gun metal blue which Roseville should have used more often. The color and texture are impressive. Height is 8 3/4 inches. Very minor nicks to a few high points.</td><td>$3000-4000</td></tr>
<tr><td>205</td><td>Rare Roseville catalog from 1905 showing several important Rozane glaze lines in color. Included are Rozane Royal, Mongol, Egypto, Mara and Woodland. The catalog is 40 pages long and includes 20 color plates. The front and back cover are blindstamped with the name "Rozane". Size is 9 1/2 by 5 inches. Good condition with a minimum of wear. Rookwood published a similar catalog in 1904 and this would seem to be Roseville's attempt to "test the waters" with a showy advertising piece.</td><td>$300-400</td></tr>
<tr><td>206</td><td>Rare Jervis high glaze pitcher with cut-back panels each framing a stylized iris. Influenced by Frederick Hurten Rhead, production at Jervis was fairly limited and often exciting. This pitcher, a derivative of Rhead's Della Robbia for Roseville, is done in several colors with the red clay showing through behind the flowers. Marked with the incised vertical Jervis mark and an obscured shape number. Height 4 1/8 inches. There are two small chips on the spout.</td><td>$600-800</td></tr>
<tr><td>207</td><td>Good Vance-Avon corset shaped vase done in the manner of Frederick Hurten Rhead and William P. Jervis, circa 1903. Under a clear high glaze are found two distinctive styles of decoration for the stylized flowers. At top and bottom the leaves, stems and flowers are outlined by slip trailing which serves to keep the colors in place. A band at the waist is lightly carved in repeating floral patterns. Both techniques would continue to be Rhead's stock in trade as he moved to other potteries, particularly Weller and Roseville. The piece is marked with the cast "Avon Wheeling Potteries" logo and there is also an incised mark, partially obscured by glaze. Height 8 3/4 inches. There is a very tight 1/2 inch line at the rim which is difficult to find.</td><td>$1000-1500</td></tr>
<tr><td>208</td><td>Roseville Woodland vase with poppy decoration in green, tan and brown. Marked with the Rozane Ware wafer seal. Height 6 3/8 inches. Typical tiny glaze flakes off the base.</td><td>$1000-1250</td></tr>
<tr><td>209</td><td>Rare vase decorated by Albert Cusick, most likely during his tenure at Vance-Avon. Cusick has used slip trailing to outline and define the stylized trees which are loaded with blossoms at the shoulder. Around the collar of the vase is found another band of stylized vegetation, possibly lotus blossoms and pads, also outlined by slip trailing and then colored. The name "Cusick" is incised in the side of the vase, near the bottom. Height 11 1/8 inches. There are two chips inside the rim and half of one red flower is also chipped off.</td><td>$2000-4000</td></tr>
<tr><td>210</td><td>Roseville Rozane red glaze vase marked with a Mara wafer seal. This looks more like Mongol than Mara but in either case it is an impressive color. Marked also with the impressed number "16". Height 6 3/8 inches. Very minor glaze scratches.</td><td>$1000-1500</td></tr>
</table>

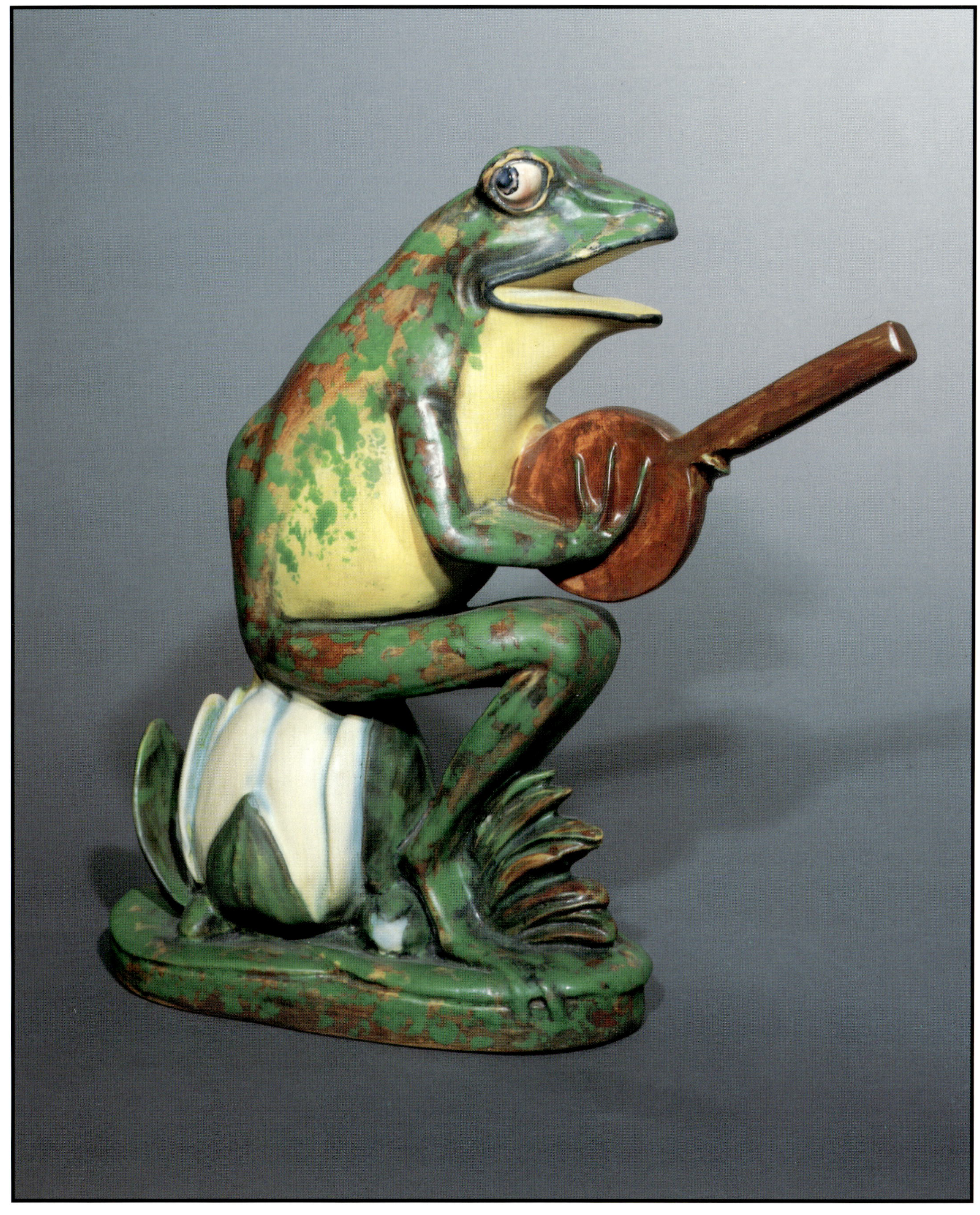

211 Rare Weller Coppertone "Banjo Frog" garden ornament. Marked "Weller Pottery" in script on the base. $7000-9000
Height 12 1/4 inches. We sold this fellow's cousin last year and made the mistake of claiming him to be
the largest of four "Banjo Frogs" made by Weller. We were informed that a larger version does exist, so
our current frog is also the second largest in the series. Like his cousin, our frog has broken his banjo but
we have managed to get it fixed and tuned in time for the auction. There is also a small glaze flake off a
leaf in front of the frog's feet and a small nick off the his left eyebrow. For more information please see
Huxford, The Collectors Encyclopedia of Weller Pottery, page 291.

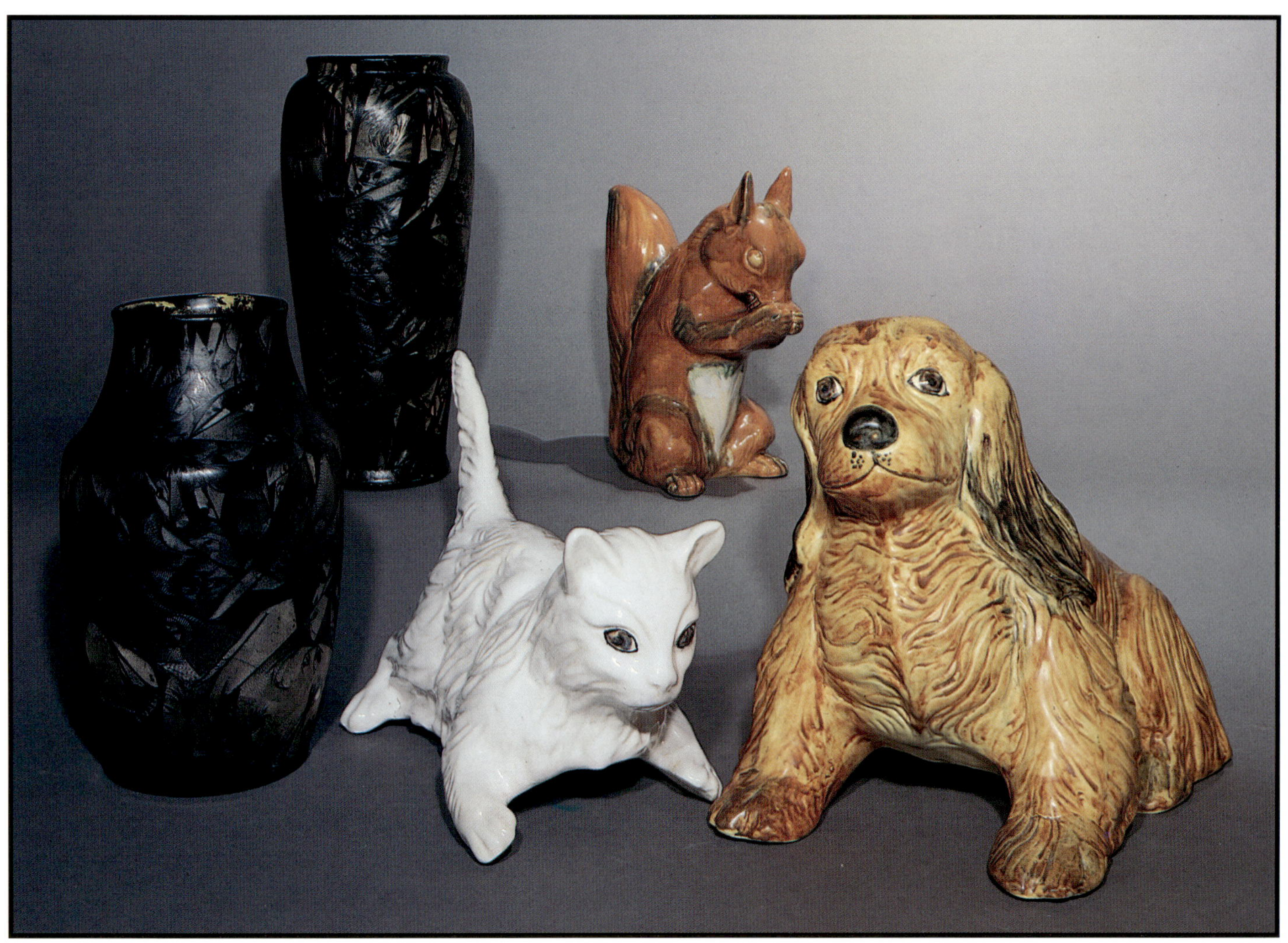

212   Rare Red Wing vase with a most unusual surface decoration. Done on a Nicomas blank, we see what looks $800-1200
like a fabulous crystalline glaze in black and silver in random patterns. Closer examination shows the black
and gray work to be hand done in a cold painting process. In the last 20 years or so, a half dozen or fewer of
these vases have appeared, all done on Red Wing Nicomas blanks. We have two examples in this sale. We
can only assume the work to be either something special done at Red Wing or something special done by
someone with access to Red Wing Nicomas blanks. Marked with the "Red Wing Art Pottery" circular
inkstamp. Height 10 3/8 inches. Minor loss of surface paint. The work on this vase and its cousin is remarkable regardless of artist.

213   Another rare Red Wing vase done on a Nicomas blank with cold painted crystalline-like decoration in gray $1000-1500
and black. Marked with the "Red Wing Art Pottery" inkstamp and impressed with shape number 197. Height
12 7/8 inches. Minor loss of surface paint.

214   Weller cat in white high glaze with multicolored eyes. Marked with the semi-circular "Weller Pottery" $1000-1250
inkstamp logo. Height to the tip of the cat's tail is 8 1/4 inches. About an inch of Tabby's tail was broken off
but it has been re-attached and professionally repaired. The cat's right front paw also had a large chip off its
bottom which has been reconstructed by noted paw expert, Billy Wiebold. Bill said he had to start from
scratch on the job but he was able to keep his fee in line. Fortunately the cat had been de-clawed by its
previous owner.

215   Rare Weller garden squirrel in high glaze. Unmarked. Height 9 1/4 inches. Huxford shows the squirrel in mat $2000-3000
glaze on page 289. At this time, no other high glaze version is known to us.

216   Rare Weller Terrier dog in mat glaze. Marked with the semi- circular "Weller Pottery" inkstamp. Height 10 3/4 $2500-3500
inches. Minor chips on the dogs feet have been professionally groomed.

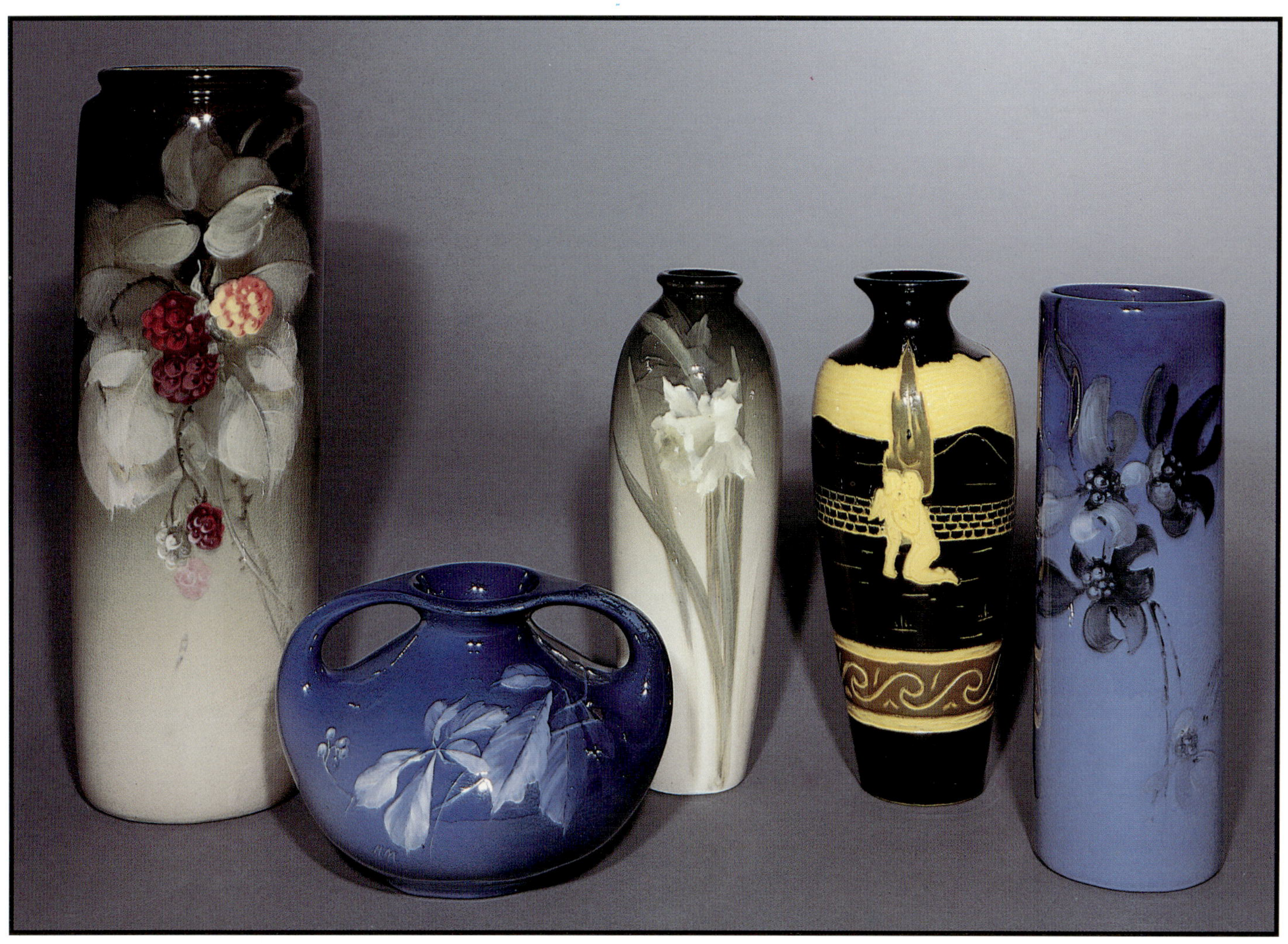

217   Tall Weller Eocean vase with colorful raspberry decoration. Incised "Weller" on the base. What might be an $2500-3500
       artist's monogram appears just below the raspberries in the form of a letter "A". Height 14 1/8 inches. Minor
       glaze scratches.

218   Rare Weller Blue Louwelsa two-handled vase with Virginia creeper decoration done by Hattie Mitchell. Im- $800-1200
       pressed "Louwelsa Weller" on the base. The artist's initials appear just under the flowers on the surface of the
       vase. Height 5 inches. Blue Louwelsa is rare and artist signed examples are very difficult to find.

219   Weller Eocean vase with nice jonquil decoration done by an unknown artist. Incised "Eocean Weller" and "F". $700-900
       Impressed "X 461". Height 10 inches.

220   Unusual Weller Dickensware vase with deeply incised and carved scene of a garden in which a mother and $400-500
       winged child embrace. The base is stamped "Dickensware Weller" and contains other obscured numbers. A
       small "X" is incised into the base. Height 10 1/8 inches. Minor damage to the rim has been repaired. A very
       similar example appears in Huxford on page 69, row 2. It is nearly the identical scene on a slightly different
       blank and it, too, bears no artist mark.

221   Weller Blue Louwelsa vase with white and blue dogwood decoration done by an unknown artist. The sides of $400-600
       the vase near the rim are dimpled. Marked with the impressed circular "Louwelsa Weller" logo and the number
       "9072". Height 10 1/8 inches. A crack at the rim has been professionally repaired.

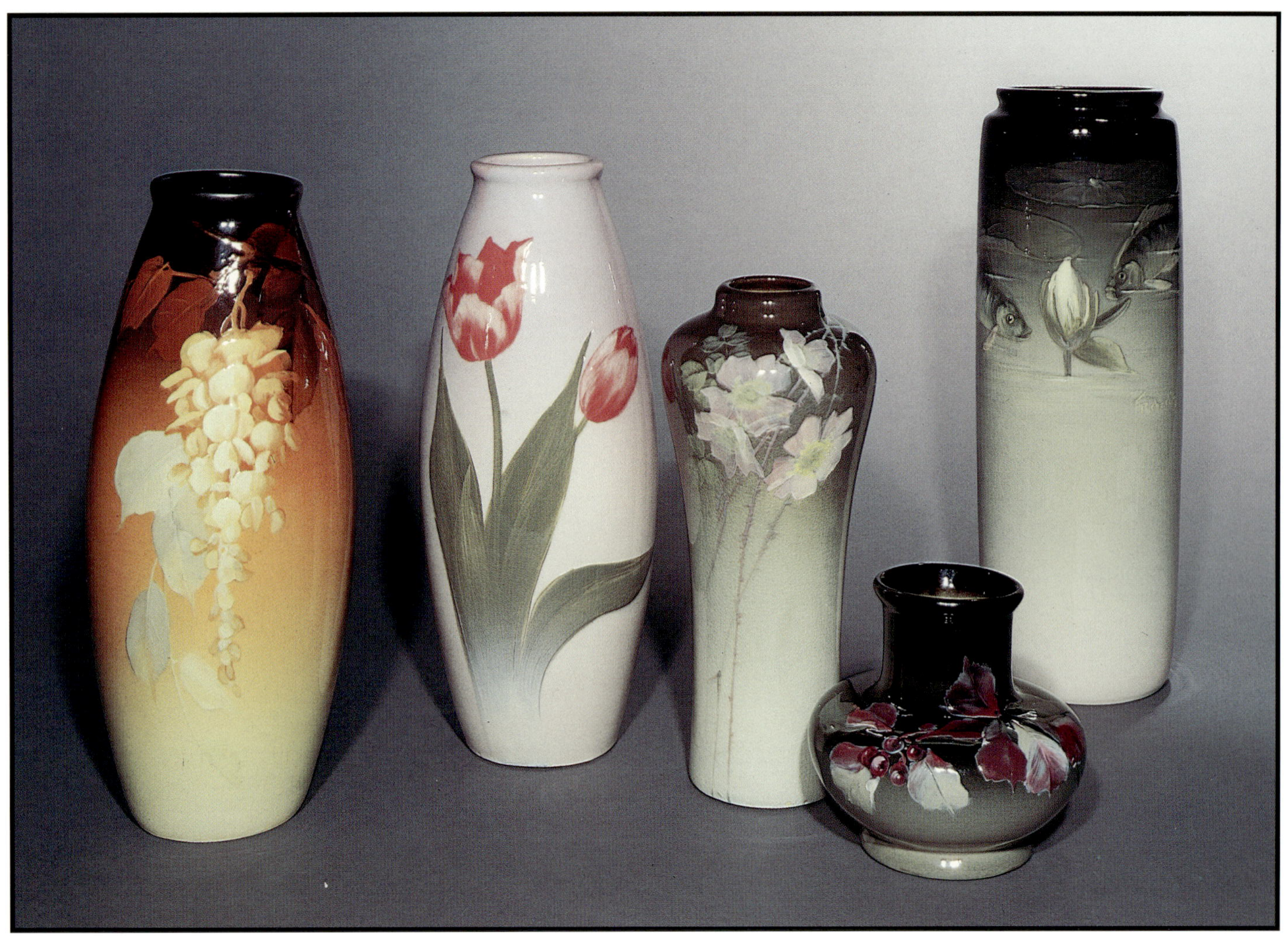

222   Weller Eocean vase with wisteria decoration, possibly done by Mae Timberlake. Marks include an incised "X" on the bottom and the artist's initials painted on the side in white slip. Height 12 7/8 inches. There is a tight, two inch line descending from the rim. Unusual colors. $400-600

223   Tall Weller Eocean vase with bright red tulip decoration most likely painted by Albert Haubrich. Marks on the base include "Eocean Weller" incised, a large incised letter "F" and the impressed notation "X 467". The artist's full name is painted on the side of the vase in white slip but it is difficult to see. Height 12 3/4 inches. $2000-2500

224   Good Weller Eocean vase with pink wild rose decoration painted by Levi J. Burgess. The artist's initials are painted on the surface of the vase, near the base, in white slip. Stamped "Weller" in small block letters. Incised "Eocean", "X" and "501" on the base. Height 10 3/8 inches. $800-1200

225   Weller Eocean Rose vase with maroon and gray Virginia creeper leaves and berries painted by Claude Leffler. Incised "Eocean Rose Weller" on the bottom and stamped with the number "9056". Leffler's initials, C.L.L., are painted on the side of the vase on the foot. Height 5 1/8 inches. Small glaze nicks on the rim and foot have been professionally repaired. $250-350

226   Exceptional Weller Eocean Rose vase decorated by Eugene Roberts with two finely detailed fish swimming among lily pads and flowers. Signed "E. Roberts" on the side in white slip. Incised on the bottom is "Eocean Rose Weller" and impressed with shape number 579. Height 14 1/8 inches. A strong piece by one of Weller's most consistent artists. $3000-4000

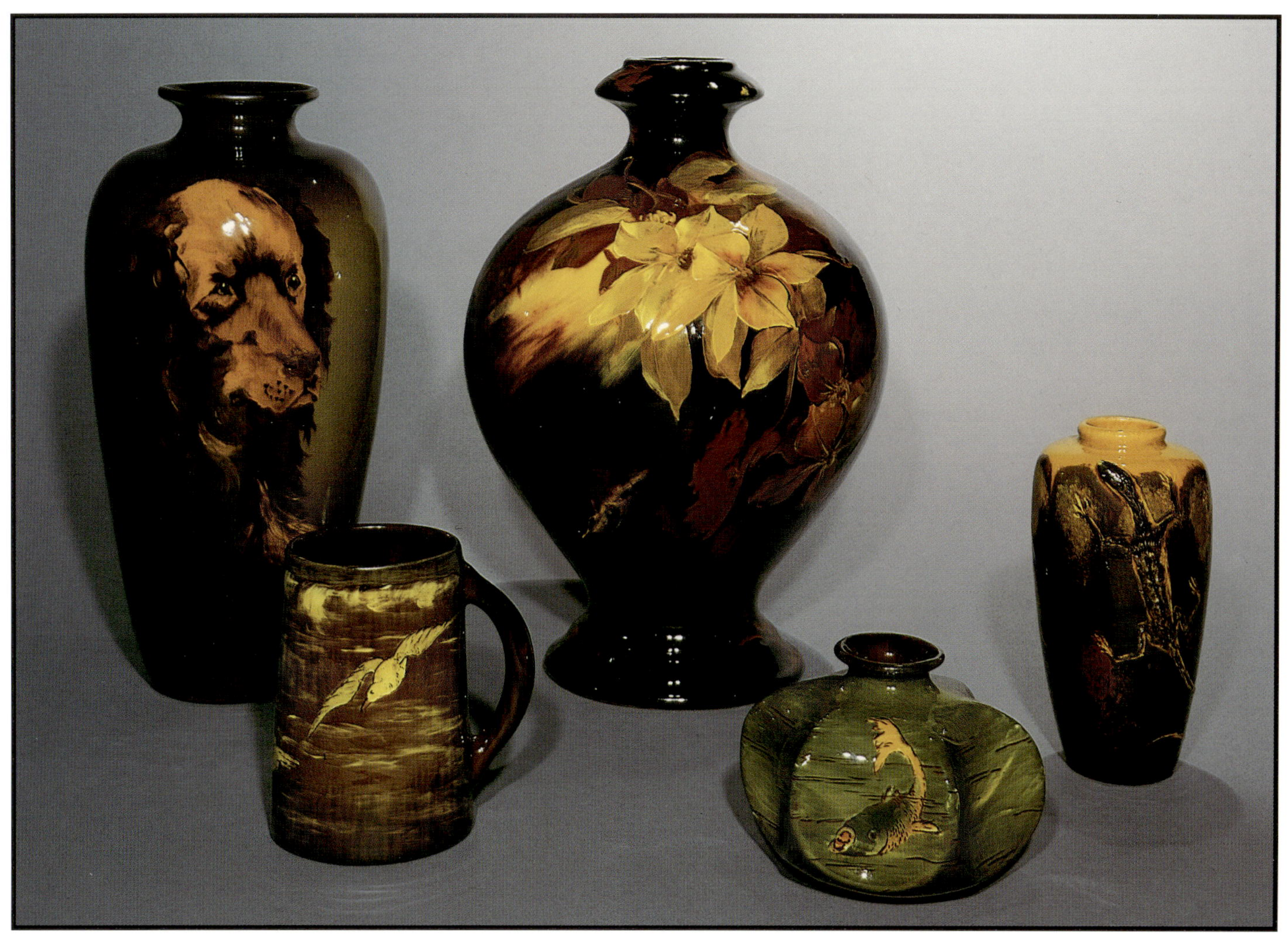

227 Tall Weller Louwelsa vase with a sensitive portrait of a Golden Retriever dog, done by Albert Wilson, whose last name is painted on the side of the vase in white slip. Marks on the base include the circular "Louwelsa Weller" stamp and shape number "X 635". Height 14 1/4 inches. Damage to the rim has been professionally repaired. $600-800

228 Weller Hunter mug with several sea birds and crashing waves, incised and painted by Charles B. Upjohn. The base is impressed with the numbers "562" and "7". Upjohn's distinctive monogram is incised on the mug, just below the handle. Height 5 5/8 inches. An above average example of Hunter. $400-600

229 Fabulous Weller Aurelian vase with brilliant floral decoration done around the turn of the century by former Rookwood artist Charles Dibowski. Dibowski's name is painted on the side of the vase in white slip. Incised marks include the name "Aurelian", an "X" and the letter "K". Impressed marks include "Weller" in small block letters and the numbers "56" and "2". Height 14 3/4 inches. Unimportant firing separation on the rim. Superior artwork and glaze. $2000-2500

230 Weller Hunter vase painted by an unknown artist whose initials appear on the side of the vase. The star shaped, six-sided vase has three fish in various poses on three of its panels. All the artwork is incised and then painted. There are several impressed marks on the bottom which are obscured by glaze. Height 4 1/8 inches. $600-800

231 Rare carved and painted Weller Louwelsa style vase done by an unknown artist at the turn of the century. A nicely detailed lizard in life-like three dimensions clings to the side of the vase, watching intently as a small beetle walks across the shoulder. Impressed marks include the numbers "99" and "5". Height 7 3/8 inches. What might be initials in red slip appear just below the lizard's right hind leg. $1500-2000

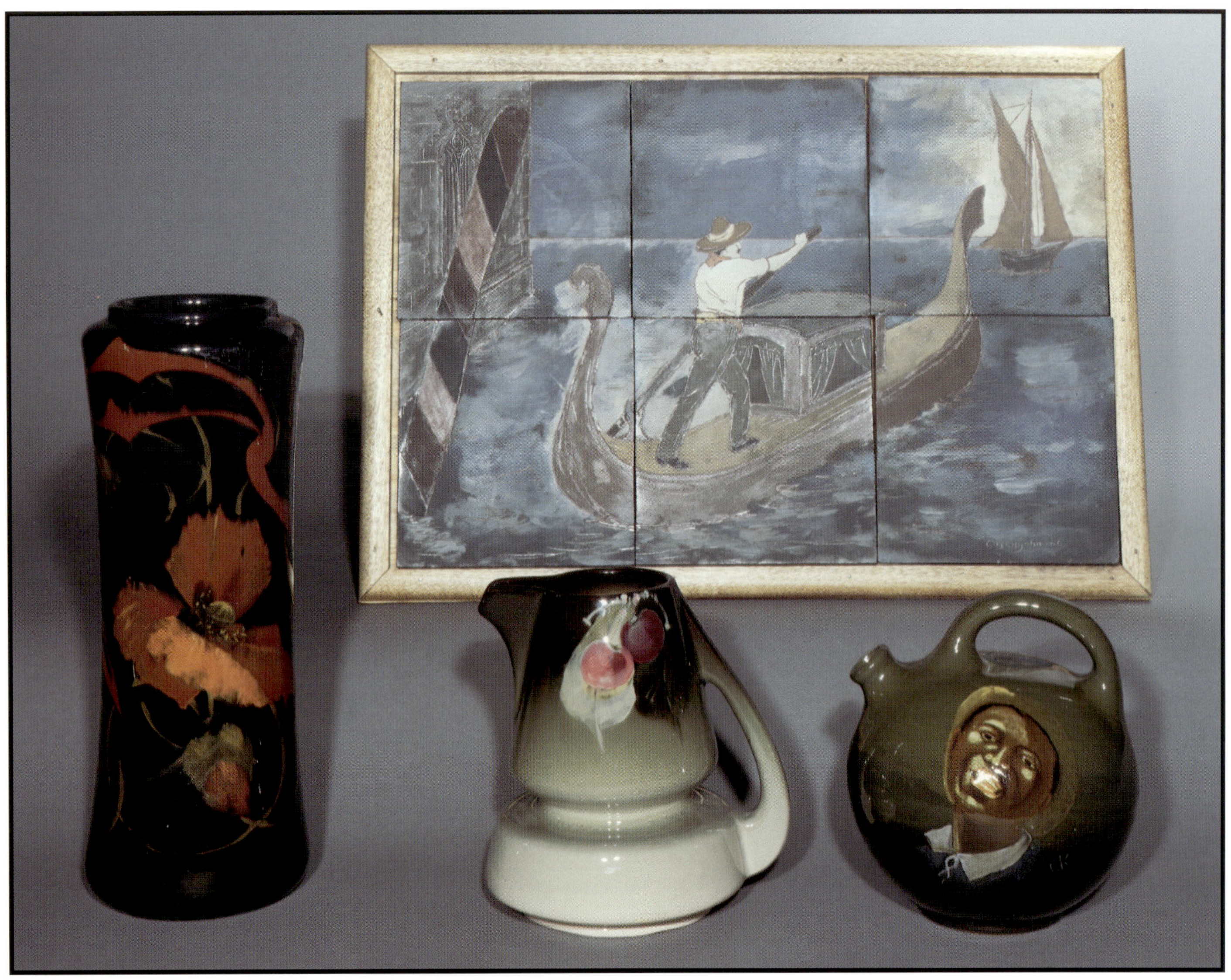

232   Striking Weller Dickensware vase with bright orange poppies and orange stylized leaves, all on a deep blue ground, thought to be the work of Charles Fouts. Impressed marks on the bottom include a partially obscured "Dickensware Weller" semi-circular logo and the number "581". Painted on the side of the vase is the artist's name, which is difficult to read. Height 11 1/2 inches. Crudely drilled through the bottom and slightly scuffed. Overall a very stylish example of Art Nouveau decoration at Weller. $500-700

233   Weller Eocean Arts & Crafts style pitcher decorated by an unknown artist with cherries. The base is marked with the double rectangles, one containing the Weller name. Height 6 1/8 inches. $300-400

234   Rare Trent Tile Company six tile tableau incised and painted by Charles B. Upjohn in 1906. The scene is of a Venetian gondolier rowing his craft through the city's waterways. Like 2nd Line Dickensware, which Upjohn introduced at Weller, the tiles are first incised with the outline of the scene and subsequently painted by the artist. Upjohn joined Trent Tile around this time, after the failure of his own pottery in Zanesville. Each red clay tile carries the Trent name and the letters "CH". The lower right hand tile is incised on the front "C.B. Upjohn '06" and is incised on the reverse "Aug 11, 1906". There are very minor firing separations in the tiles but the overall condition is original and excellent. $3000-4000

235   Rare Weller Dickensware whiskey jug decorated by an artist with the initials "CK", which appear on the side of the vase in blue slip. The artist has given us a portrait of an African-American man wearing a straw hat and a navy blue shirt with light blue collar. Stamped "Dickensware Weller" and "330" on the bottom. Height 6 inches. Very minor glaze scratches. $800-1000

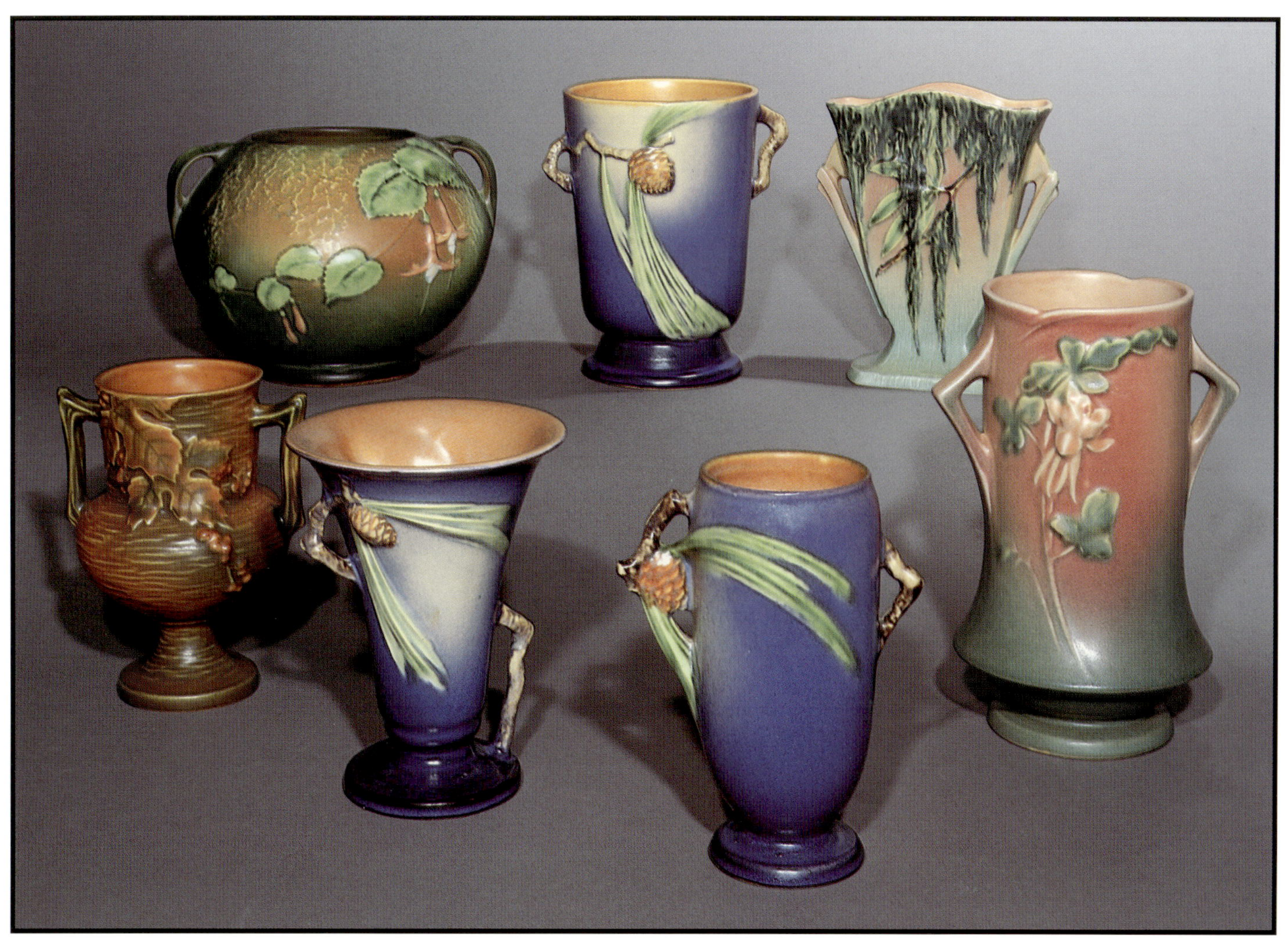

236	Roseville Bushberry two-handled vase in brown. The base bears the embossed "Roseville USA" logo and shape number 156-6. A small blue "x" is painted on the base. Height 6 1/4 inches.	$125-175
237	Roseville Fuschia two-handled vase in green. The only mark is an "X" painted on the bottom in blue slip. Height 6 inches. Good mold and color.	$250-350
238	Roseville blue Pinecone two-handled vase. Marked "Roseville 906- 6" and with a painted letter "C". Height 6 3/8 inches. Excellent color and mold.	$300-400
239	Roseville blue Pinecone two-handled vase. Marked "Roseville 704- 7". Height 7 1/8 inches. There is a small glaze flake of the top of the foot. Good color mold and glaze.	$300-400
240	Roseville blue Pinecone vase. Marked "Roseville 748-6". Height 6 3/8 inches. Good mold, color and glaze.	$200-300
241	Roseville Moss two-handled vase. The bottom of the vase is marked "Roseville" and the rest of the characters present are difficult to read. Height 7 3/8 inches.	$150-200
242	Roseville Columbine vase with two angular handles. The vase carries the embossed "Roseville USA" logo and the shape number "20-8". Height 8 1/4 inches. Good mold and color.	$125-175

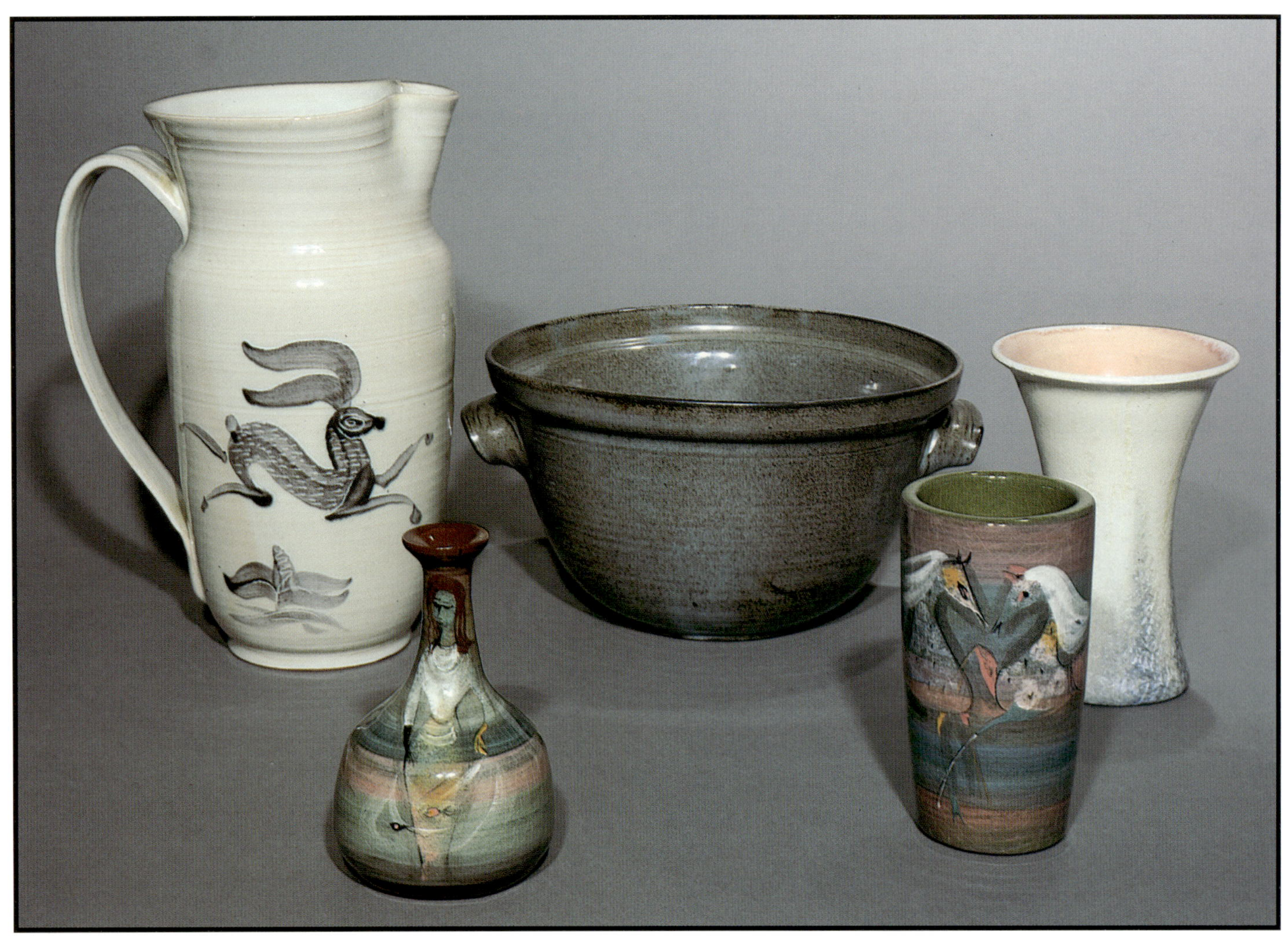

243	Red clay pitcher with gloss finish made by Edwin and Mary Scheier, circa 1949. Shown are leaping deer on both sides done in a light gray background color with the deer and plants in dark gray. Incised "Scheier" on the bottom. Height 9 1/2 inches.	$300-400
244	Polia Pillin vase in high glaze showing two female figures seining for fish. The vase is marked "Pillin" in black slip on the base. Height is 4 1/2 inches.	$200-250
245	Bowl with two attached handles done in a mottled blue to gray glaze by Edwin and Mary Scheier, circa 1949. Incised "Scheier" on the base. Height 4 3/4 inches.	$200-300
246	Polia Pillin vase in high glaze with two frolicking horses. Marked "Pillin" in black slip on the base. Height is 4 3/4 inches.	$200-250
247	Handsome Pisgah Forest flared vase with snowflake blue and white crystals, done by Walter Stephen in 1949. Raised marks include the Pisgah Forest logo and the date. Height 5 1/2 inches.	$200-300

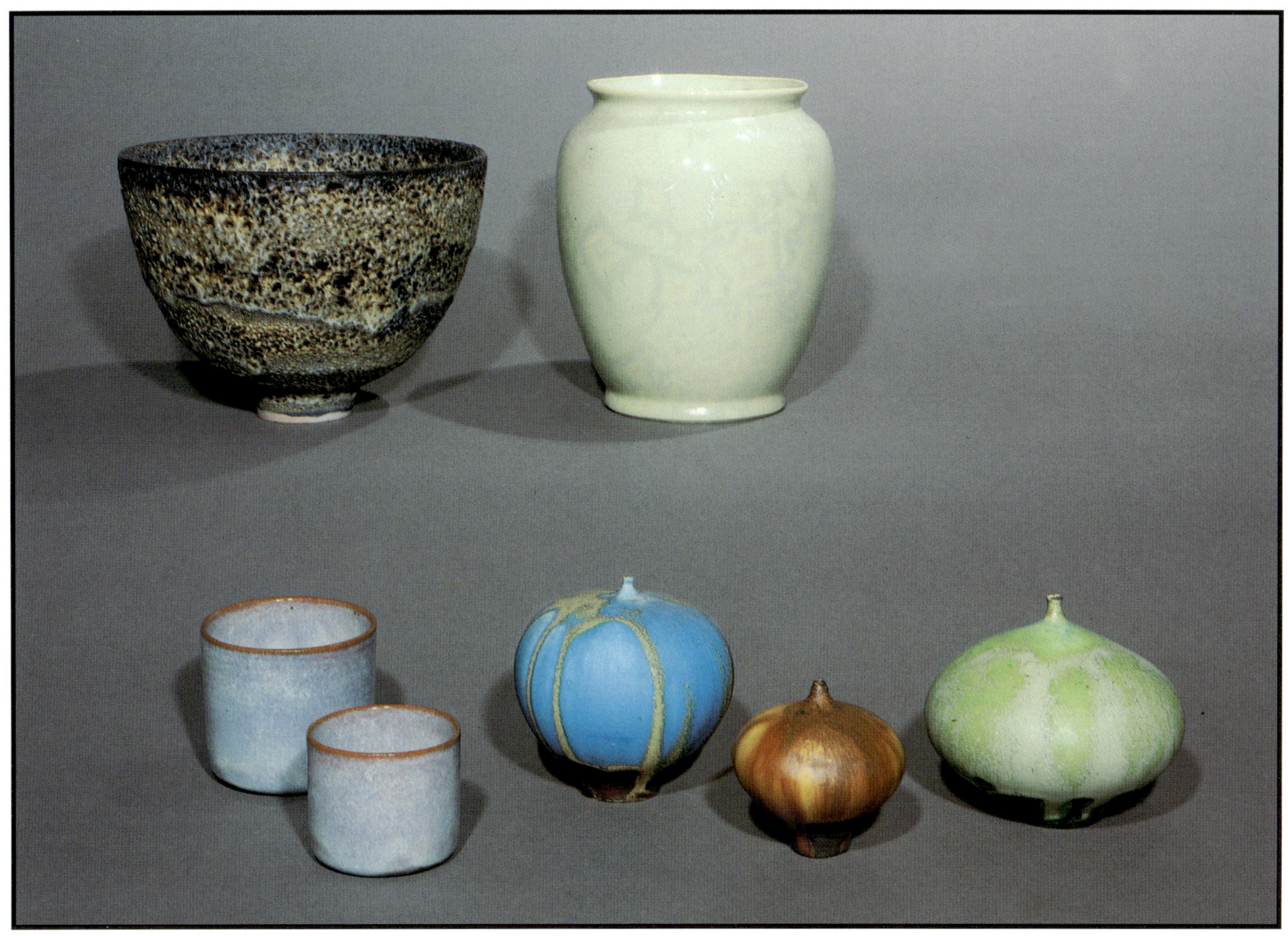

248   Fine Otto and Gertrud Natzler open vase form covered in a wonderful volcanic glaze in shades of gray, brown and black over the red clay body. Signed "Natzler" in black slip on the bottom. Height 5 inches, diameter 6 7/8 inches. Fabulous glaze and pristine original condition. $3000-4000

249   Natzler cup done in the same "grey opal" glaze as lot 253. Marked also with a small letter "n" painted on in black slip. Height 2 1/4 inches. $300-400

250   Small Natzler cup covered in a mottled gray glaze over the thin red clay body. The bottom of the piece is marked with a letter "n" painted on in black slip. On the side of the cup is an old label which reads "C 458 3.00 grey opal". We assume the glaze is grey opal and the original price to be $3.00. Height 1 3/4 inches. $200-300

251   Cabat "Feelie" vase in blue mat glaze with gold crystals. Incised "Cabat" on the base. Height 3 1/4 inches. $250-350

252   Rare experimental crystalline glaze vase made at Cowan in 1925 by Arthur Baggs and Richard Hummel. A letter written and signed by Hummel in 1969 accompanies the vase. Hummel goes into great technical detail about the chemistry and firing conditions used by Baggs and himself to make the piece. Hummel, who owned the vase in 1969, says of the crystals, "As far as we can determine, they are still growing at a very slow rate. In 40 years they have probably grown 1/16th inch." Hummel also notes, "The Cowan Pottery Studio made many outstanding masterpieces in their day but pieces such as this are among the finest, as well as most scarce." Marked with the impressed "Cowan" logo and number "39" in an oval, painted on in slip. Height 6 1/8 inches. Uncrazed and loaded with large, fern-like crystals having slight iridescence. $1000-1500

253   Cabat "Feelie" vase done in a striated brown to tan mat glaze interspersed with copperdust crystals. Incised "Cabat" on the bottom. Height 2 1/4 inches. $250-350

254   Cabat "Feelie" vase covered with lime to medium green mat glazes and lots of gray crystals. Incised "Cabat" on the bottom. Height 3 inches. $350-450

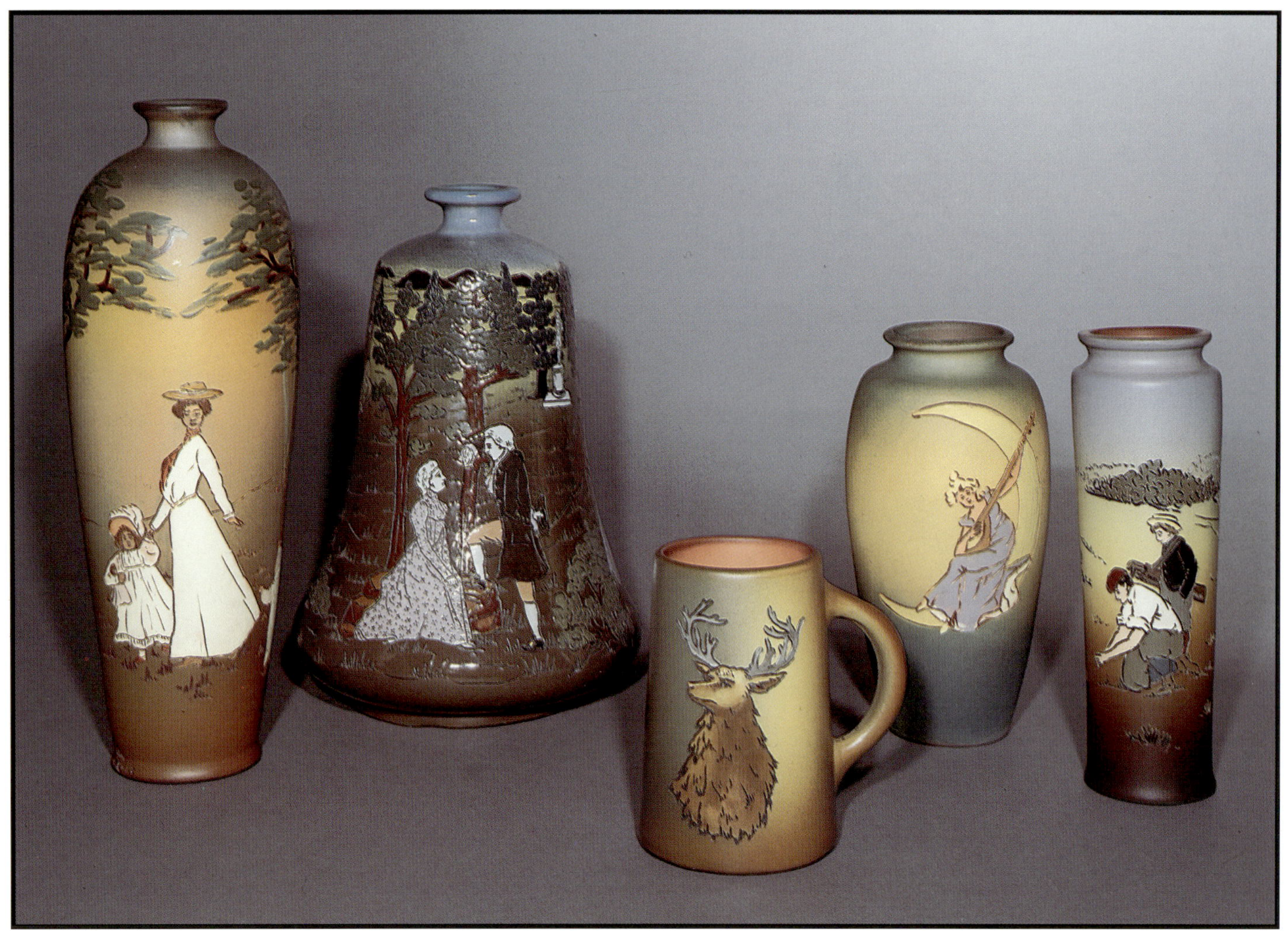

255   Tall and unusual Weller 2nd Line Dickensware vase done by both Anthony Dunlavy and Helen Smith showing a young mother walking through a wooded area with her two daughters. The older daughter carries a small doll and the younger one seems to be just barely able to carry herself. The base is stamped three times with semi-circular "Dickensware Weller" die and once with the notation "X 290 0". The initials of Smith and Dunlavy are painted on the side of the vase at the bottom. Height 14 inches. There is a small chip on the rim. $600-800

256   Rare high glaze Weller 2nd Line Dickensware vase with an intricately carved and colorfully painted scene of Colonial life. Pictured are seven people, three horses and two statues in a densely wooded area, all in costumes from the late 18th century. Impressed marks include the semi- circular Dickensware Weller logo and numbers "X 48" and "8". Incised is a large letter "W". Height 11 7/8 inches. A rim chip has been professionally repaired. There is an amazing amount of work in the vase. It is a shame we cannot identify the artist. $1500-2000

257   Weller 2nd Line Dickensware mug with the nicely detailed image of a deer. Impressed marked include "Dickensware Weller", shape number 562 and the number "12". The initials "K B" are incised on the base. Height 5 1/2 inches. Very crisp and clean. $250-350

258   Weller 2nd Line Dickensware vase with a young woman sitting in a crescent moon playing a long-necked mandolin, done by Anthony Dunlavy. Marks include the impressed "Dickensware Weller" logo and the notation "X 31". Incised on the base is the letter "M". Painted on the side of the vase in white slip is the monogram of the artist. Height 8 7/8 inches. Glaze nicks on the rim. $200-300

259   Rare and well-executed Weller 2nd Line Dickensware vase with a highly detailed golfing scene featuring a golfer and caddy, trees and a fence. Marks include the Dickensware Weller logo, impressed "X 169" and "12" and the incised initials, "KVV". Height 9 1/4 inches. Excellent color and crisp incising. $2500-3000

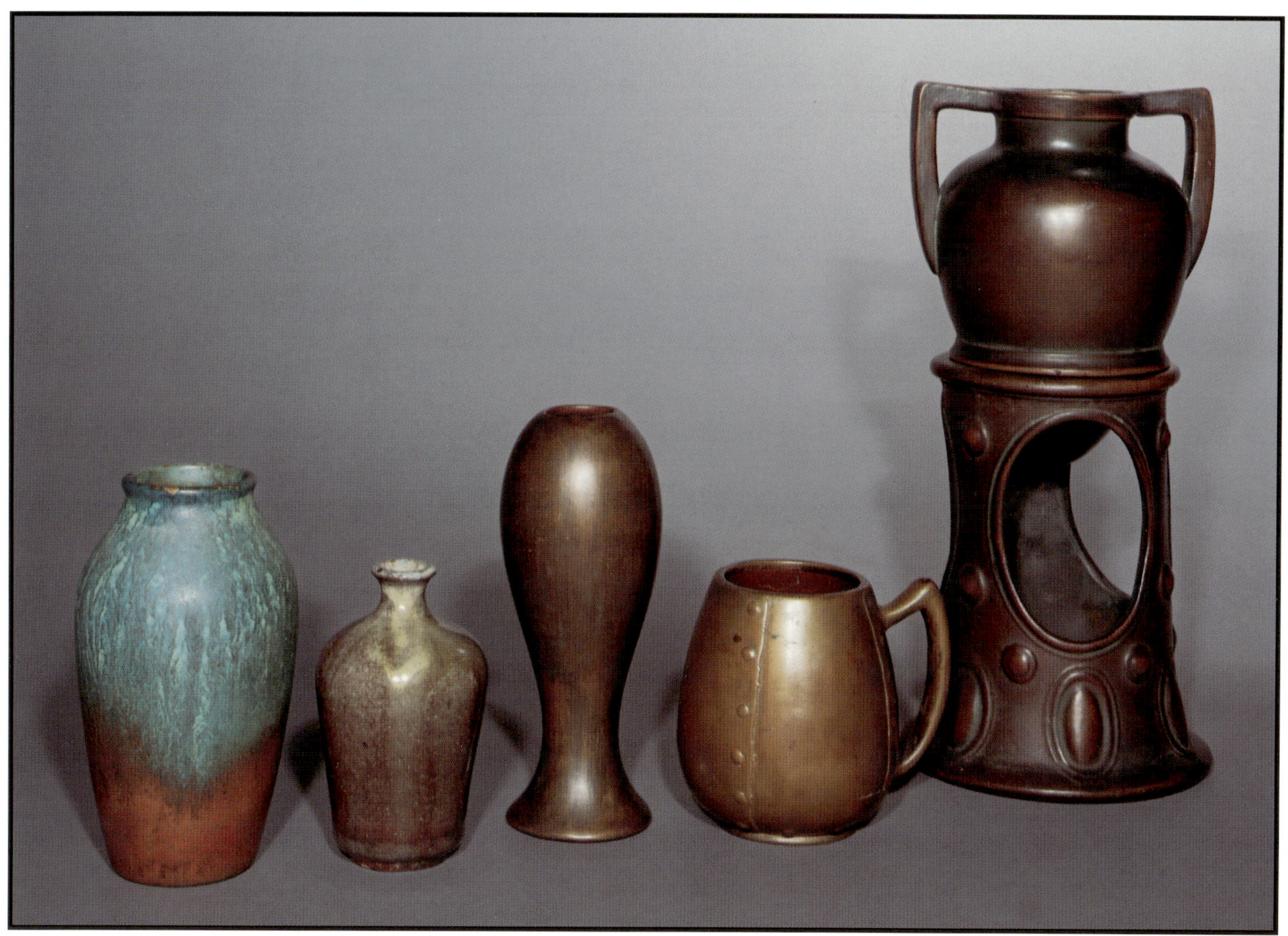

260   Clewell copper-clad vase with a strong crusty green patina over the orange copper body. Marked "Clewell 321-24" on the bottom with a stylus. Height 6 1/4 inches. Very minor loss of patina. $700-900

261   W.J. Walley vase done in red clay with a mottled gray and brown high glaze. Stamped W.J.W. on the bottom. Height 4 3/4 inches. Minor glaze losses on the underside of the foot. $300-400

262   Unusual Clewell vase with typical copper cladding. Worked into the copper surface is slightly raised decoration of a dragonfly above a daisy. How the scene is applied is a mystery. There are Owens pieces with underglaze slip decoration which have been electroplated by Clewell so that the decoration shows through in the copper. This work may have been done with a reverse electroplating process where metal is removed from the surface leaving the flower and dragonfly. The vase is marked with a remnant of a rare Clewell paper label which seems to read "Clewell Canton, Ohio". Height 7 inches. $500-700

263   Clewell copper clad mug with external rivets. Marked "Clewell Coppers" in an embossed circle on the base. Height 4 1/8 inches. A small bruise in the pottery under the copper can be seen at the rim. $100-150

264   Most unusual pottery vase and stand with copper cladding. The clay bodies are the product of Vance-Avon as the base is clearly marked "Vance F.CO. No. 122." which shows through the copper. As to the origin of the copper, we can only speculate. The most obvious answer would be Clewell. Since Vance-Avon was out of business before Clewell began production, we must assume that Clewell bought some old stock on which to work, including this piece. We know that Clewell used a wide variety of Ohio pottery blanks in his work so this is not an unreasonable scenario. Our interesting combination stands 12 3/8 inches tall and has excellent original brown patina. $1000-1500

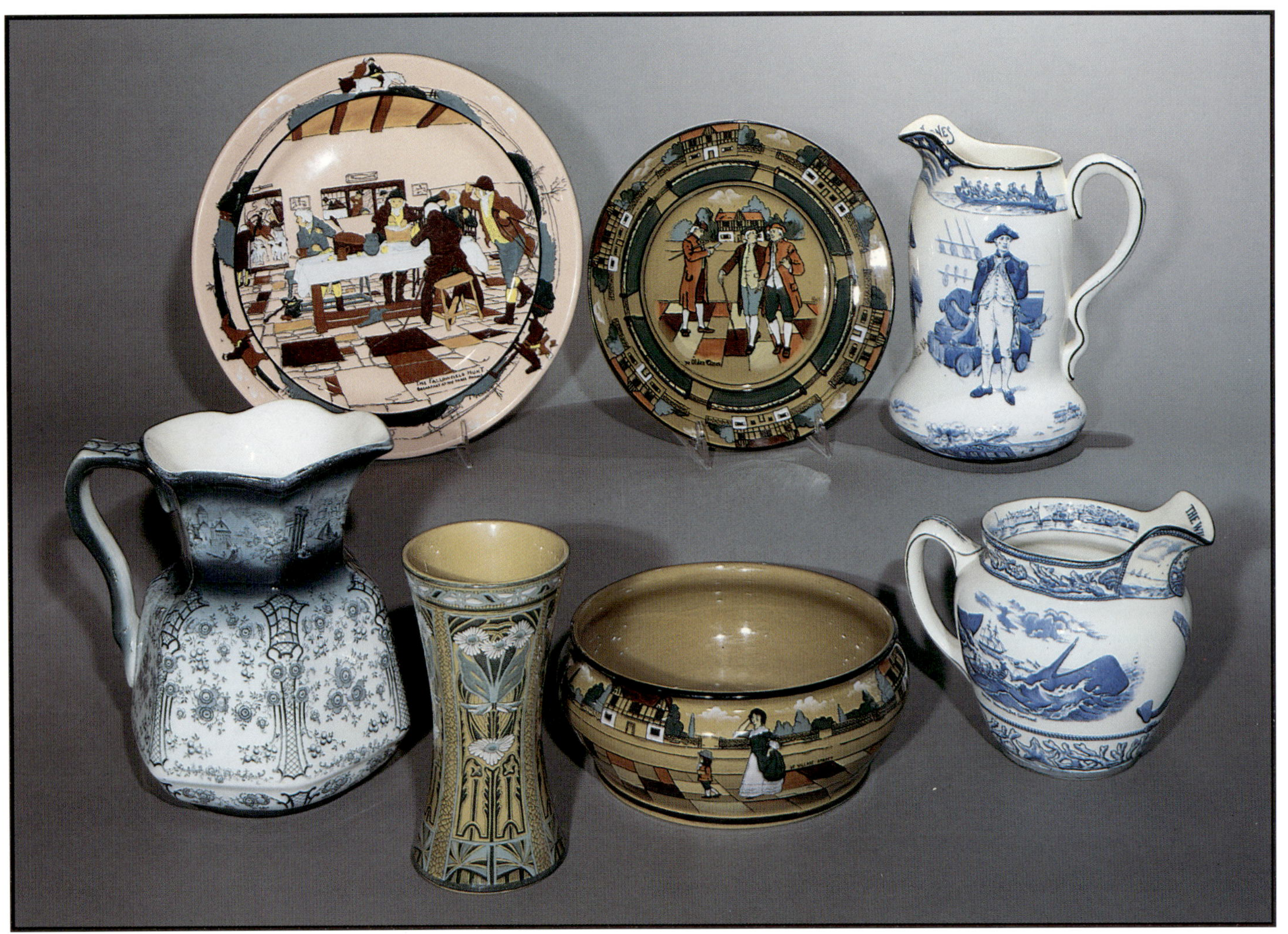

265 Rare Buffalo Pottery "Mason Jug" dated 1907. Marked with the Buffalo logo and date inkstamp, the name $1200-1500
"Mason Jug" and the numbers "3" and "1420" painted on in blue slip. Height 8 1/4 inches. Very few Mason
Jugs are known to exist and this one is in excellent condition.

266 Unusual Buffalo China Rouge Ware chop plate with a scene from "The Fallowfield Hunt" entitled "Breakfast $500-700
at the Three Pigeons", done sometime in the early 1920's. The pink ground color is actually the clay itself.
Marked with the "Buffalo China Rouge Ware" inkstamp logo. Diameter is 11 3/8 inches. Minor glaze
scratches on the front.

267 Rare Buffalo Emerald Deldare corset shaped vase with beautifully stylized designs of daisies and butterflies $600-800
decorated in 1911 by an unknown artist. Marks include the Emerald Deldare inkstamp logo and date and the
number "7". Height 6 3/4 inches. A horizontal crack near the base has been professionally repaired.

268 Buffalo Deldare bowl decorated by W. Foster with scenes from "Ye Village Street" in 1909. Marks include the $300-400
Buffalo inkstamp logo and date and the number "1". The artist's name and the title appear on the surface of
the bowl. Height 3 1/4 inches and diameter is 6 1/4 inches.

269 Buffalo Deldare plate in the "Ye Olden Times" pattern painted in 1908 by H. Ball. Inkstamp marks include the $200-300
Buffalo logo, the date and the number "1". The artist's name and title of the piece appear of the surface of
the plate. Diameter is 9 1/2 inches. Minor surface scratches.

270 Buffalo Pottery "John Paul Jones" pitcher done in 1907. Marked with the Buffalo blue inkstamp logo and date $600-800
and the numbers "1433" and "1". Inside the lip is the notation "John Paul Jones". On the front of the pitcher
one finds the notation "Fredericksburg, VA. 1773" done in fired-on gold. Height 9 3/8 inches. Good original
condition although somewhat stained from use.

271 Rare Buffalo Pottery "Whaling" pitcher made in 1908. The piece is marked with the blue inkstamp Buffalo $600-800
logo and date, the notation "Made Expressly for Bliss & Nye, New Bedford, Mass." and the numbers "1329"
and "3" painted on in blue slip. On the inside of the lip is the notation "The Whaling City Souvenir of new
Bedford, Mass". Height 6 1/8 inches.

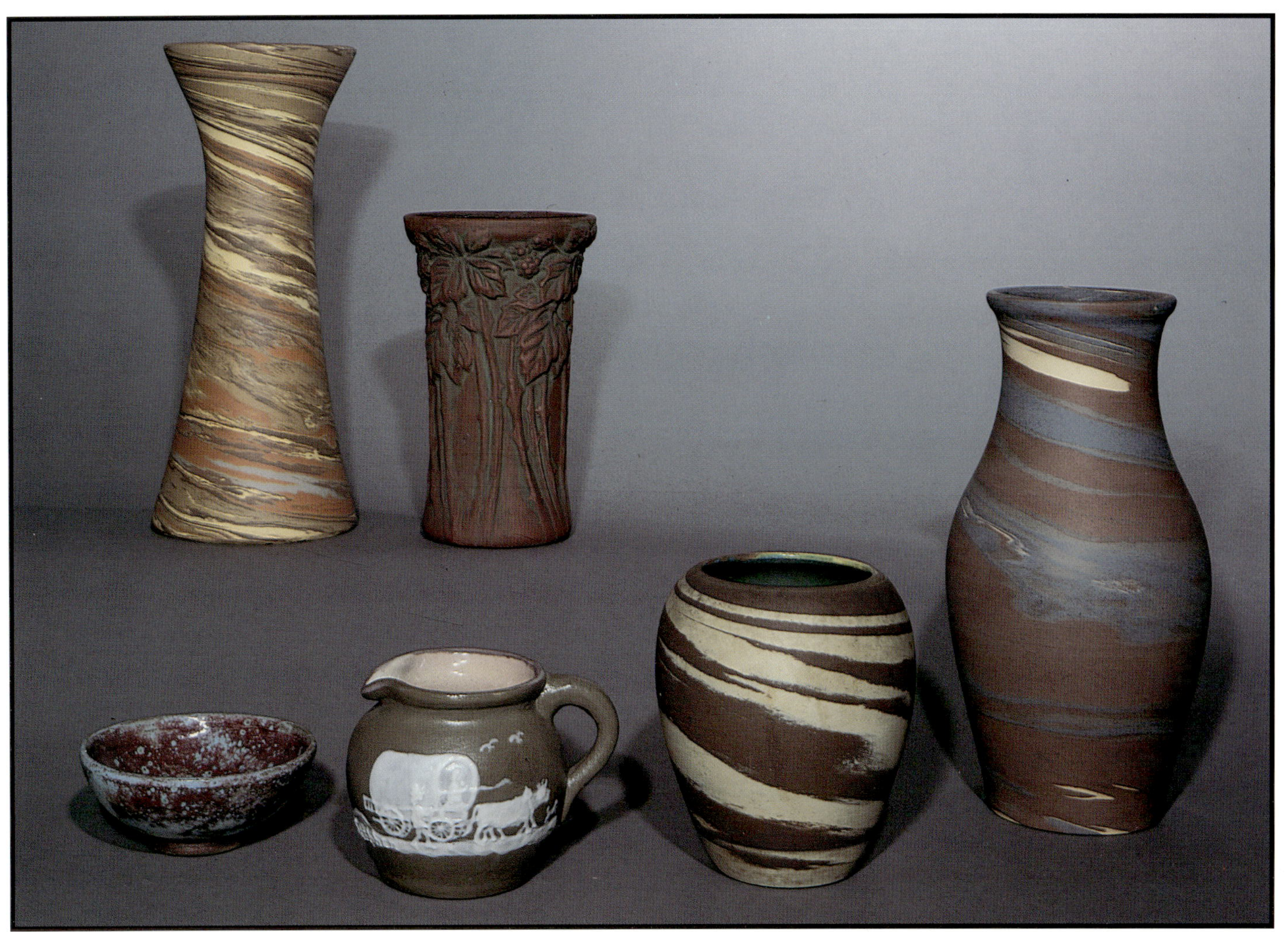

272   Jugtown bowl in Chinese Blue glaze on a graceful Oriental shape. Marked with the die-stamped "Jugtown" $200-300
       logo. Height is 1 7/8 inches and diameter is 4 3/8 inches.

273   Tall Niloak mission swirl vase using cream, brown, blue and red clays. Unmarked. Height 11 7/8 inches. Some $400-600
       roughness around the base but a great Arts & Crafts shape and style.

274   Pisgah Forest creamer with cameo scene of settlers with a Conestoga wagon painted by Walter Stephen. $400-500
       Stephen's name is worked into the design, just behind the wagon. The base carries the embossed Pisgah
       Forest logo and the date, which is hard to decipher. Height 3 5/8 inches.

275   Peters and Reed Moss Aztec vase with crisp blackberry designs. Unmarked. Height of the vase is 7 3/4 inches. $150-200

276   Mission Swirl vase in brown and cream clays made by W.J. Gordy of Georgia, sometime after 1935. Impressed $150-250
       "Hand Made by W.J. Gordy" on the base. Height 5 1/4 inches.

277   Tall Niloak vase with red, blue and cream colored clays swirled together. Faintly stamped "Niloak". Height 10 $200-250
       inches.

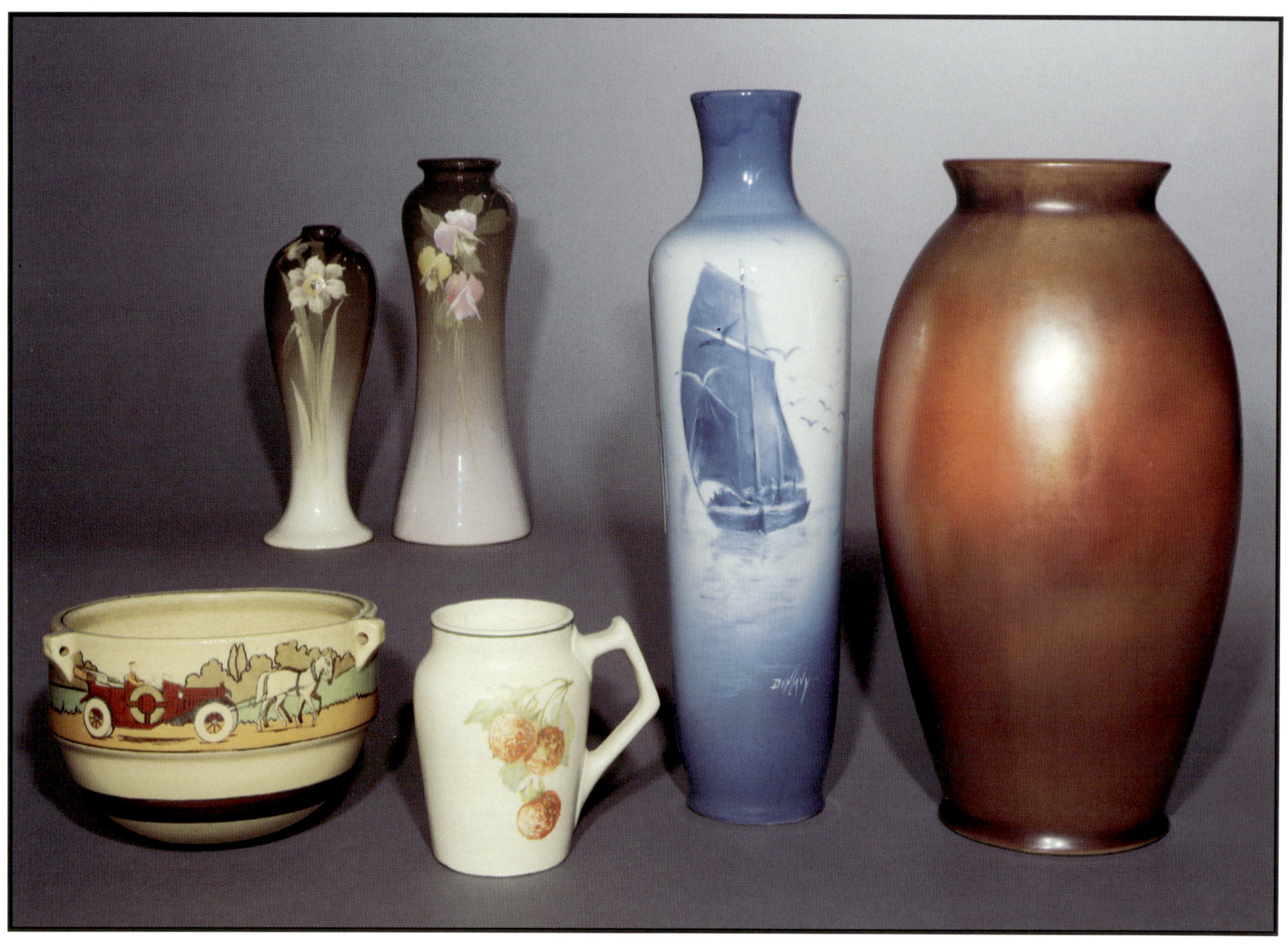

278   Rare Roseville Tourist hanging basket showing a red touring car being towed by a team of horses. A sign $2250-2750
       beside the road reads "Garage 10 Miles". Unmarked. Height 4 1/2 inches. There is a a dark craze line at the
       rim which does not extend to the outer surface of the piece and two small burst glaze bubbles on the rim.

279   Roseville Rozane Royal Light vase with jonquil decoration done by Josephine Imlay, whose name is painted $400-600
       on the side of the vase in white slip. The base carries the Rozane Royal wafer seal. Height
       8 1/2 inches.

280   Good Roseville Rozane Royal Light vase decorated by Josephine Imlay with delicate sweet pea blossoms in $1000-1250
       mauve and yellow. Marks include the Rozane Royal wafer seal, the impressed number "1" and the artist's
       name, painted on the side of the vase in white slip. Height 10 3/8 inches. Truly a wonderful example.

281   Roseville creamware mug with transfer strawberry decoration. Marked only with the number "2" painted on $100-125
       the bottom in black slip. Height 4 3/4 inches.

282   Rare Roseville Azurean vase painted by Anthony Dunlavy. Pictured is a heavily laden sailing vessel and many $1500-2500
       sea gulls moving near a buoy. Signed "Dunlavy" on the side of the vase in white slip. Impressed "Azurean
       Rozane A 322 R.P.Co. 7". Height 15 1/8 inches. There is a 1 inch by 1/2 inch kiln kiss on the back side of the
       piece and prominent craze line just to the right of the kiss. This is a rarely seen form and a strong scene.

283   Tall Roseville Pauleo vase with luster glaze in reds and golds. Unmarked. Height 14 inches. Very minor glaze $400-500
       scratches. A neat drill hole in the base has been professionally repaired.

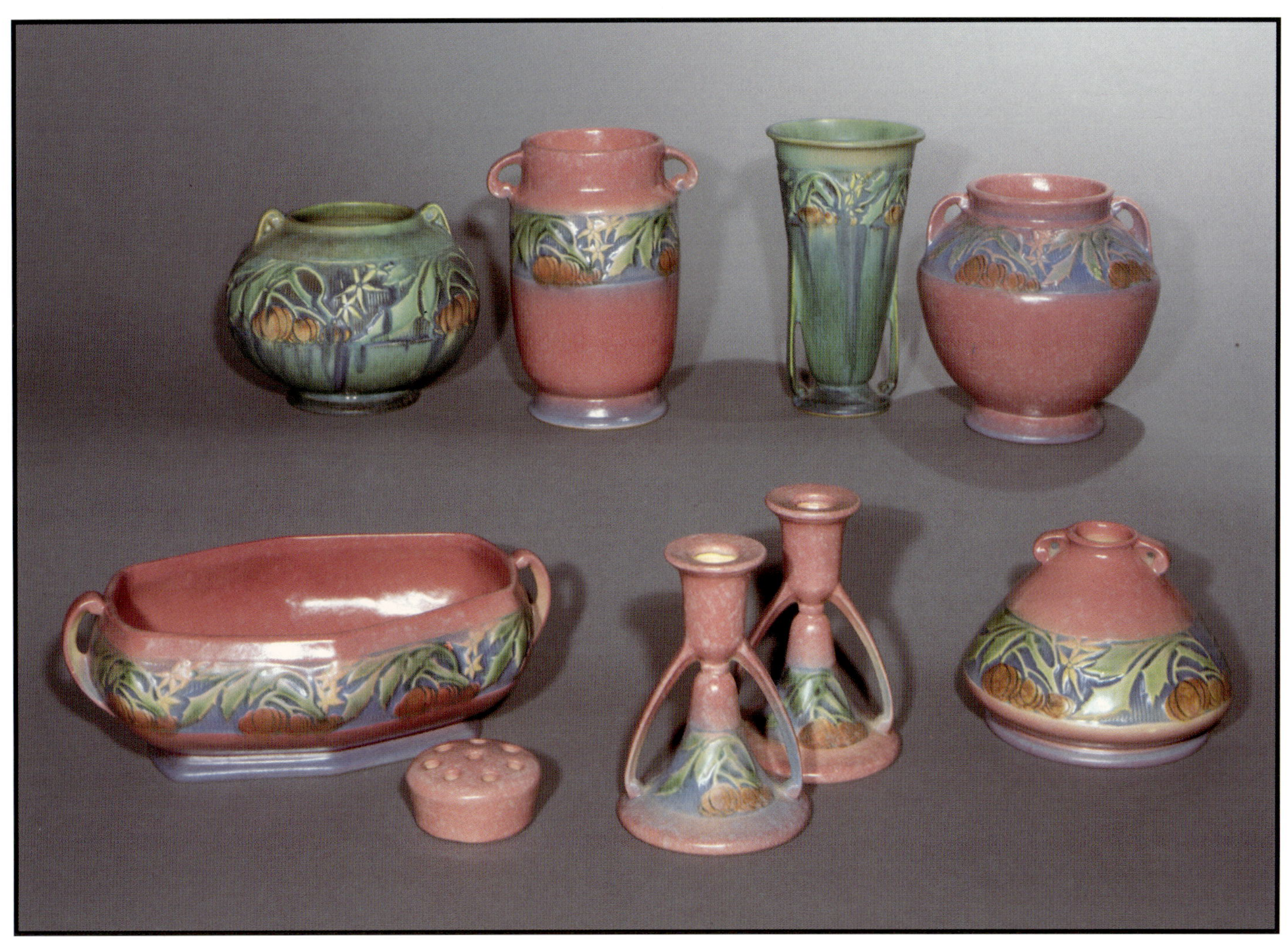

284	Roseville pink Baneda console bowl with matching flower frog. Marked with a gold foil label. Height 3 1/2 inches and length 10 1/4 inches. Excellent mold and color.	$400-600
285	Roseville Baneda two-handled vase in green crystalline mat glaze. Marked with a black paper label and the number "3" painted on in blue slip. Height 5 inches. Good mold and color.	$300-500
286	Roseville Pink Baneda vase with two small loop handles. The only mark is the number "3" painted on the bottom in blue slip. Height 7 1/8 inches. Good color and mold.	$400-600
287	Pair of Roseville Baneda candlesticks in pink. One stick is unmarked while the other bears an incised number "4" and a painted-on number "2". Height of each is 5 1/4 inches. Unusual shape with good color and mold.	$400-600
288	Roseville Baneda vase in rare trumpet shape with two long handles done in a variegated green mat glaze. Marked with an incised "4" and the imprint of a foil label. Height 7 3/8 inches. A small chip on the interior of one handle has been professionally repaired.	$300-400
289	Roseville Baneda two-handled vase in pink. The only mark on the bottom is the number "2" painted on in blue slip. Height 6 1/4 inches. A small chip on one handle has been professionally repaired.	$300-400
290	Roseville Baneda two-handled vase in pink. Marks include a large Roseville gold foil label and the number "4" incised in the bottom. Height 4 1/8 inches. Excellent mold and color.	$300-400

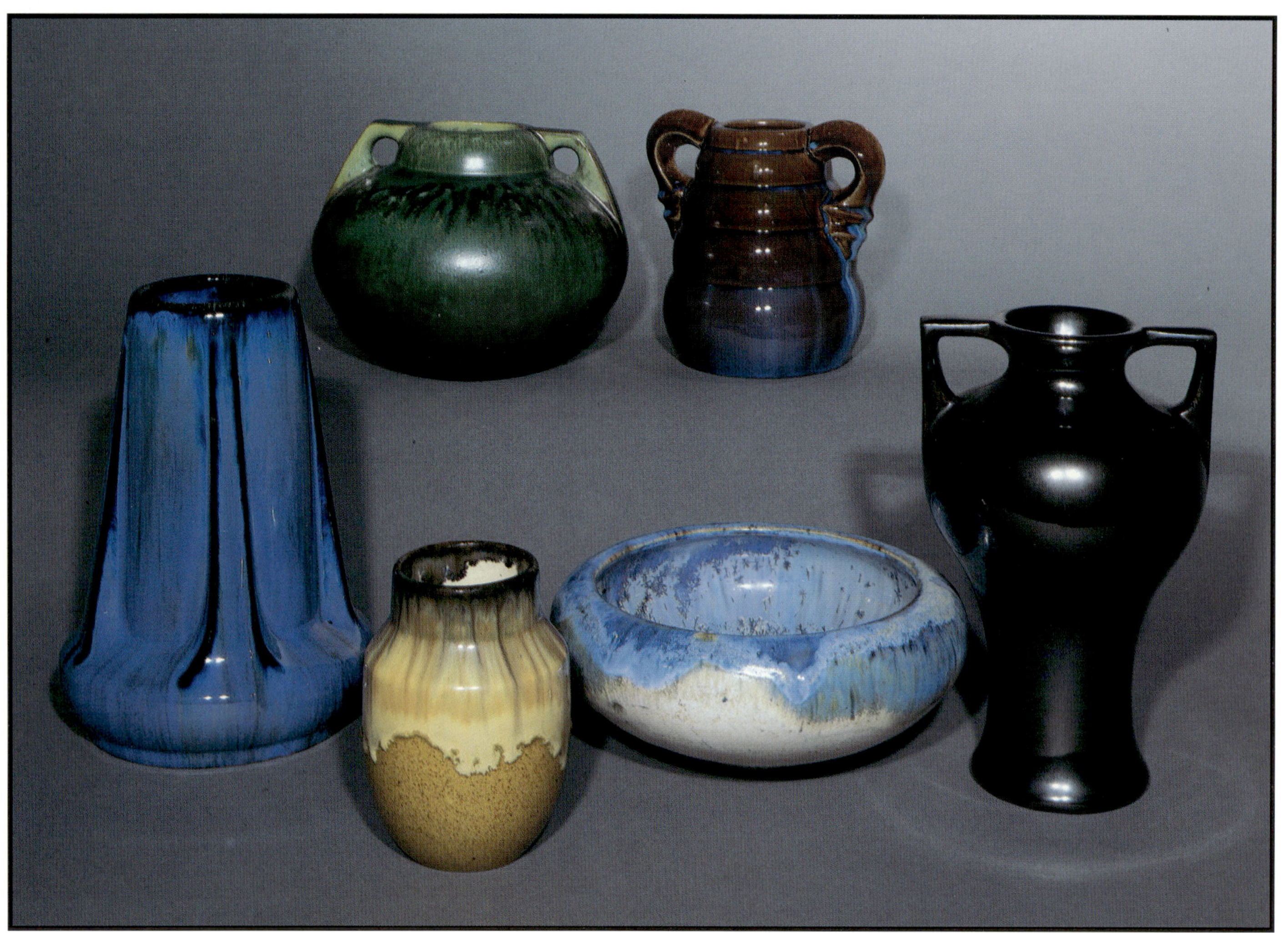

291   Fulper buttressed vase done in Chinese Blue Flambé with cobalt blue highlights. Marked with the vertical incised logo. Height 8 inches. A very striking piece. $600-800

292   Fulper two-handled vase with a green matt glaze having some Cucumber Crystalline effect. Marked with the vertical inkstamp logo with Oriental lettering. Height 6 1/8 inches. $500-700

293   Early Fulper vase having a thick Cat's Eye Flambé over Mustard Matt glazes. Marked with the squat vertical inkstamp logo. Height 4 5/8 inches. $200-300

294   Fulper bowl with blue snowflake crystalline over cream mat glazes. Marked with the early "squat" vertical inkstamp logo. Height is 3 1/8 inches and diameter is 7 5/8 inches. $200-300

295   Fulper two-handled Art Deco vase form done in a brown high glaze with blue highlights. Marked with the vertical racetrack inkstamp logo. Height 6 1/8 inches. $300-400

296   Fulper two-handled vase with bulbous top, done in a crisp, even Mirrored Black glaze. Marked with the vertical "incised" logo. Height 8 inches. $400-600

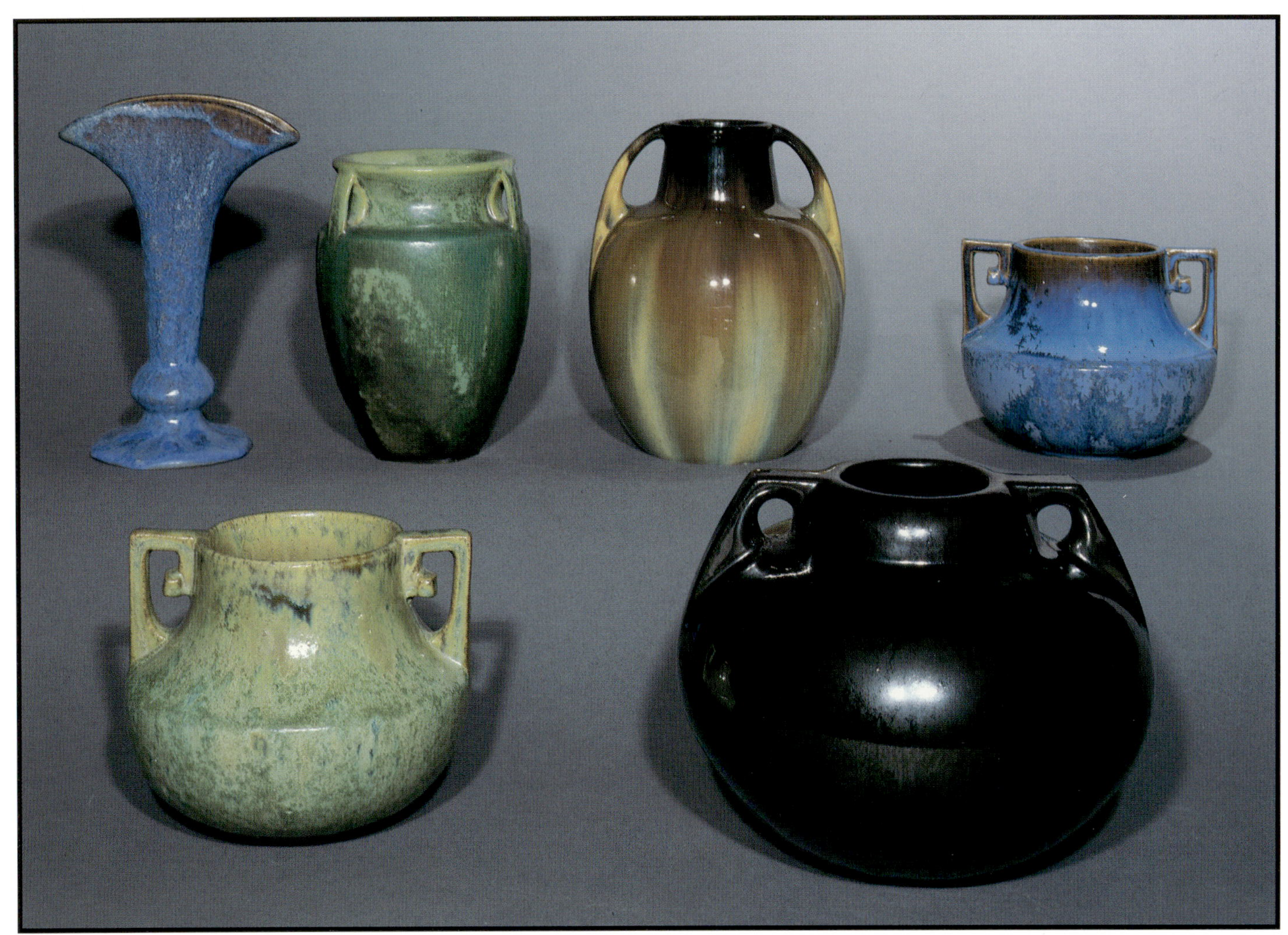

| 297 | Fulper vase form with flattened and flared rim covered with a dense Blue Snowflake Crystalline glaze. Marked with the vertical racetrack inkstamp Fulper logo. Height 8 inches. Typical grinding chips on the base. | $200-300 |

| 298 | Fulper two-handled vase with a thick, gloopy green high glaze over green mat. Marked with the vertical inkstamp logo with Oriental lettering. Height 4 5/8 inches. | $300-400 |

| 299 | Fulper "Bullet" vase done in a thick glossy green over mat green glaze. Marked with the vertical inkstamp logo with Oriental letters. height 6 3/4 inches. | $400-500 |

| 300 | Fulper two-handled vase done in a good Cat's Eye Flambé glaze. Marked with the incised vertical logo and a tiny part of a Vasecraft label. Height 7 1/2 inches. | $400-500 |

| 301 | Fulper two-handled vase in Mirrored Black. The glaze is fairly thick and gloopy with swirls of gray giving it dimension. Marked with the vertical incised logo. Height 6 inches. There is a 1/8 inch glaze flake off one of the handles. | $400-500 |

| 302 | Fulper two-handled vase covered with a lush Blue Snowflake crystalline glaze. Marked with the impressed vertical racetrack logo. Height 4 3/4 inches. | $400-500 |

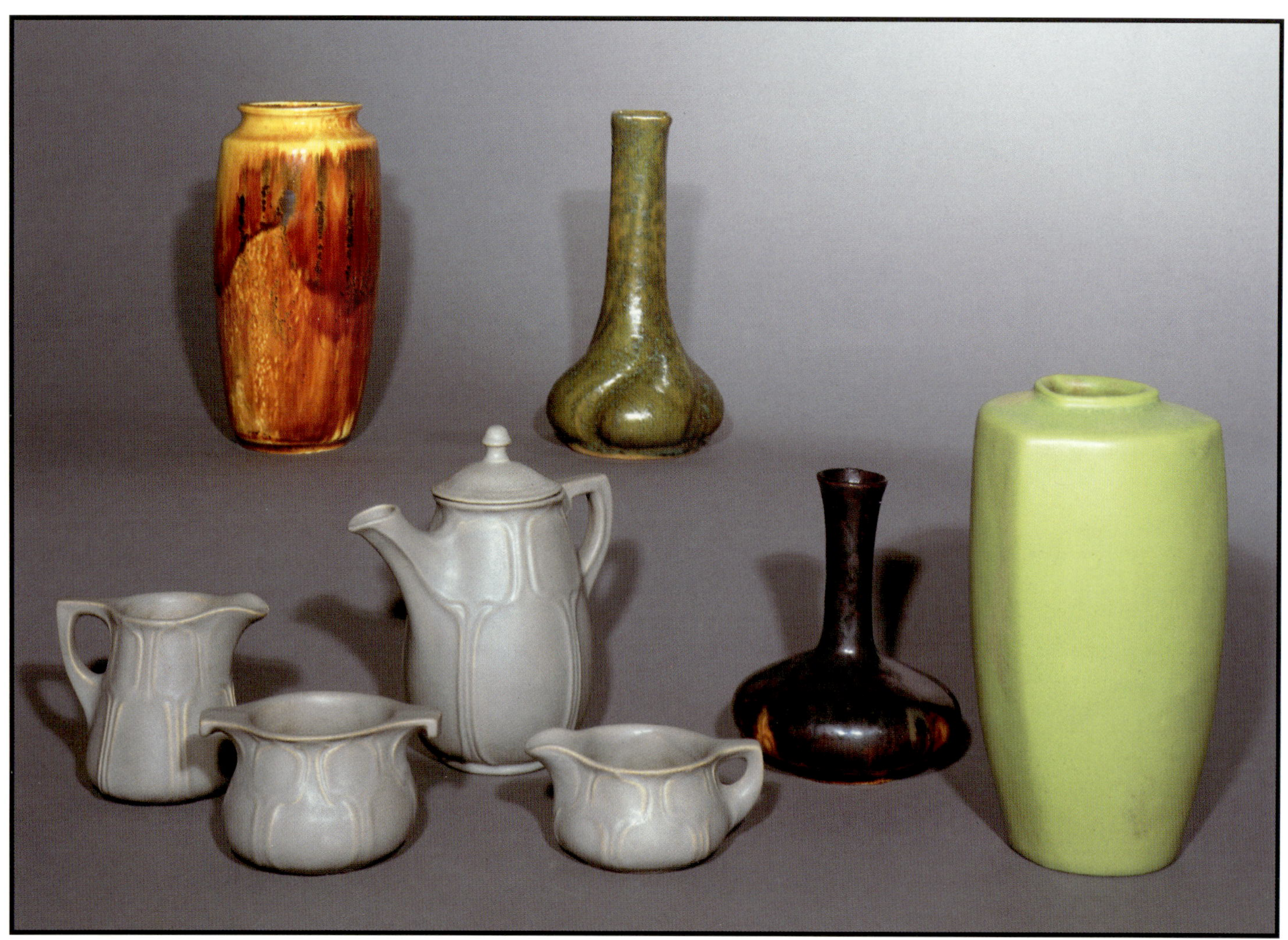

303   Teco five piece tea set consisting of lidded tea pot, creamer, sugar bowl and lemon pot, all nicely designed $600-800
      with the same embossed Art Nouveau design and covered with a pleasant gray-beige mat glaze. All bodies
      are stamped with the vertical Teco logo. Height of the tea pot is 6 inches. There is a small flake off the spout
      of the lemon pot. Excellent design and glaze.

304   Teco crystalline glaze vase in shades of orange, yellow, red and black. The base is stamped "Teco". Height $1000-1500
      8 1/8 inches.

305   Chicago Crucible vase with twisted body, done in mottled green and brown glazes. Unmarked but a classic $300-400
      shape for Chicago Crucible. Height 8 inches.

306   Teco crystalline glaze vase with round bottom and long flaring neck. Die-stamped "Teco" on the base. Height $300-400
      5 3/8 inches. Minor roughness on the rim. A rare Teco glaze line but fairly skimpy on crystals.

307   Teco three sided vase (shape 336) designed by Fritz Albert and covered in a yellow-green mat glaze. Im- $500-700
      pressed "Teco" twice on the bottom. Height 7 5/8 inches.

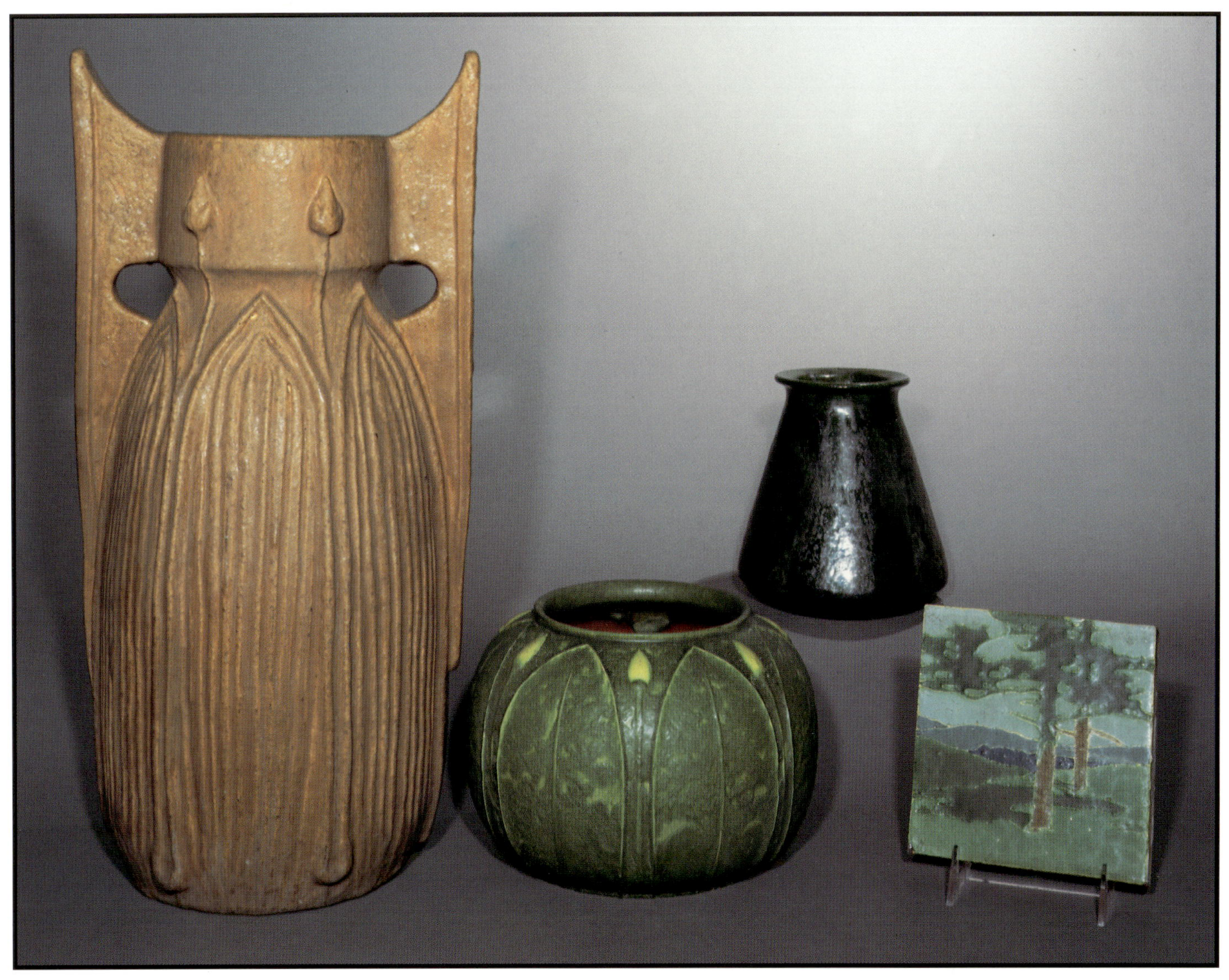

308   Monumental Wheatley Arts & Crafts style vase with buttressed bat wing handles and overlapping leaves with $4000-6000
       buds, done in a wonderful cafe'-au- lait glaze. Unmarked. Height 20 5/8 inches. Two 1/2 inch chips, one off a
       handle and the other off the side of the vase, have been professionally repaired. The form has shown up a
       time or two but to our knowledge, never in this color. Besides being a very pleasant shade of brown, the
       glaze is knobby and warty and full of character. A superb addition to most Arts & Crafts settings.

309   Good Grueby vase with seven yellow flower buds spaced between seven flat leaves, done by an artist with $4000-5000
       the initials "E.R." Marks include the die-stamped Grueby logo, the incised initials of the artist and the notation
       "3/6". Height 6 3/8 inches and diameter 9 1/4 inches. Two 1/2 by 1/4 inch chips on the rim have been profes-
       sionally repaired. Minor glaze nicks to the high points of some leaves. The glaze is particularly consistent and
       gloopy and the colors are strong and precise.

310   Good Arts & Crafts vase with fabulous green mat glaze having black crystalline-like striations, thought to be $700-900
       Merrimac Pottery. Unmarked. Height 7 1/2 inches. There is a small burst bubble on the rim. The glaze on this
       vase is worth noting.

311   Grueby scenic mat glaze tile showing pine trees with hills in the background. Marked "MD" in green slip on $800-1000
       the back. Size is 6 by 6 inches. Edge chips and a few surface nicks.

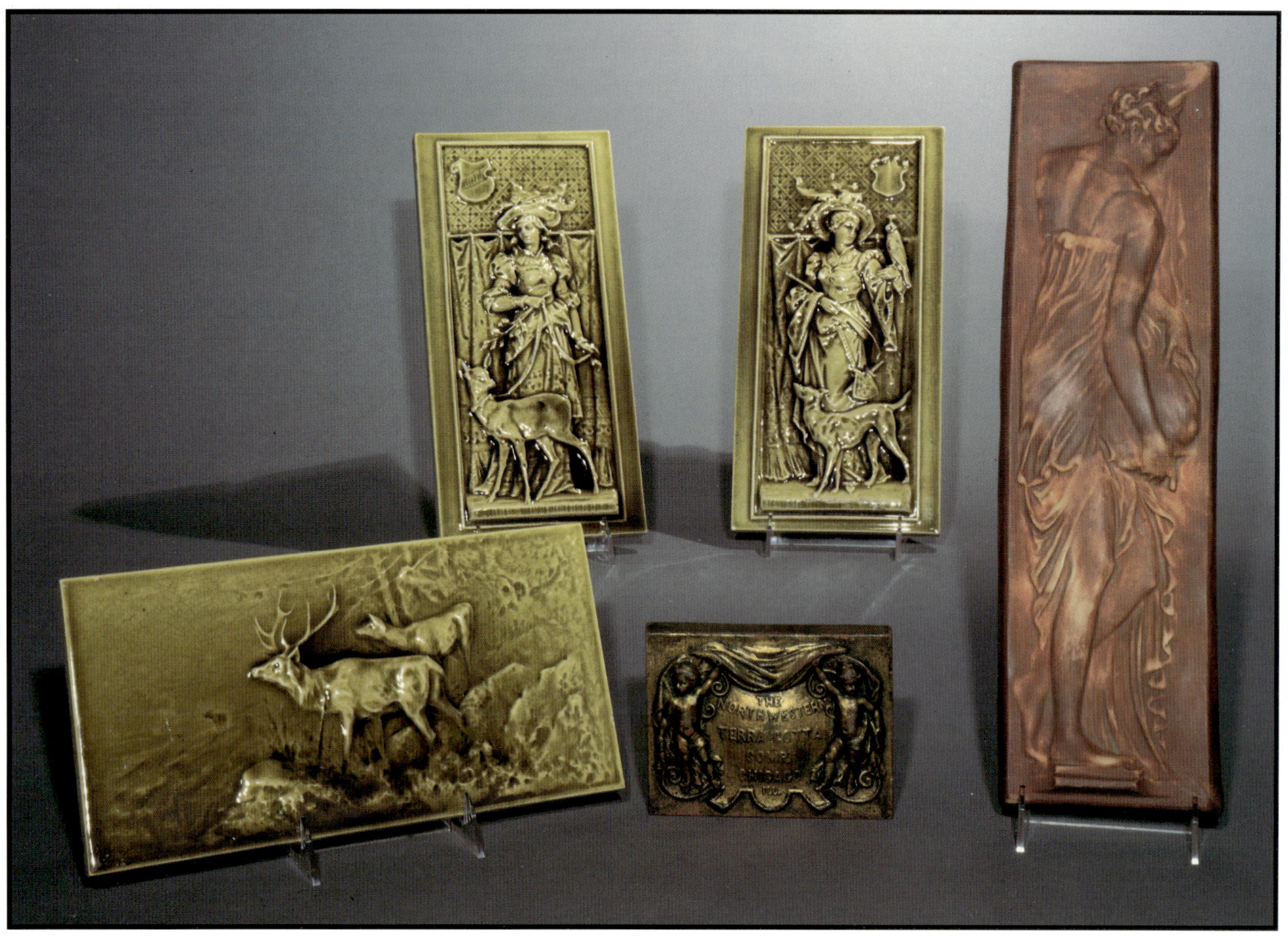

312   Hamilton Tile Works Company tile showing two deer in a woodland setting. The tile is covered with a green high glaze and is marked on the reverse "The Hamilton Tile Works Co. Hamilton Ohio". Size is 6 by 12 inches. Minor roughness on the edges. The purchaser of this lot will be allowed to buy lot 315 at the same price. $200-300

313   Hamilton Tile Works Company tile in green high glaze showing a Victorian woman in an interior with a fawn on a leash. The back is embossed "The Hamilton Tile Works Co. Hamilton Ohio". Size is 12 by 6 inches. Minor abrasions to high points on the tile. $200-300

314   Northwestern Terra Cotta Company advertising tile showing two putti holding up a heavy cloth border. Embossed on the front is the message "Northwestern Terra Cotta Comp. Chicago Ill." Size is 4 1/8 by 5 1/2 inches. The terra cotta tile is cold painted in gold which appears to be quite old. Minor wear to the gilt paint and a small edge chip. $300-400

315   Hamilton Tile Works Company tile in green high glaze showing a Victorian woman in an interior. A dog waits at her feet while she holds a falcon in her left hand . The back is embossed "The Hamilton Tile Works Co. Hamilton Ohio". Size is 12 by 6 inches. There are several abrasions to high points on the tile. The purchaser of lot 312 will be allowed to purchase this lot at the same price. $200-300

316   Unusual Weller bisque tile with the embossed image of a classical female figure. Stamped "Weller" in small block letters on the reverse. Height is 16 7/8 inches. A small chip on the lower left hand corner has been repaired. $300-500

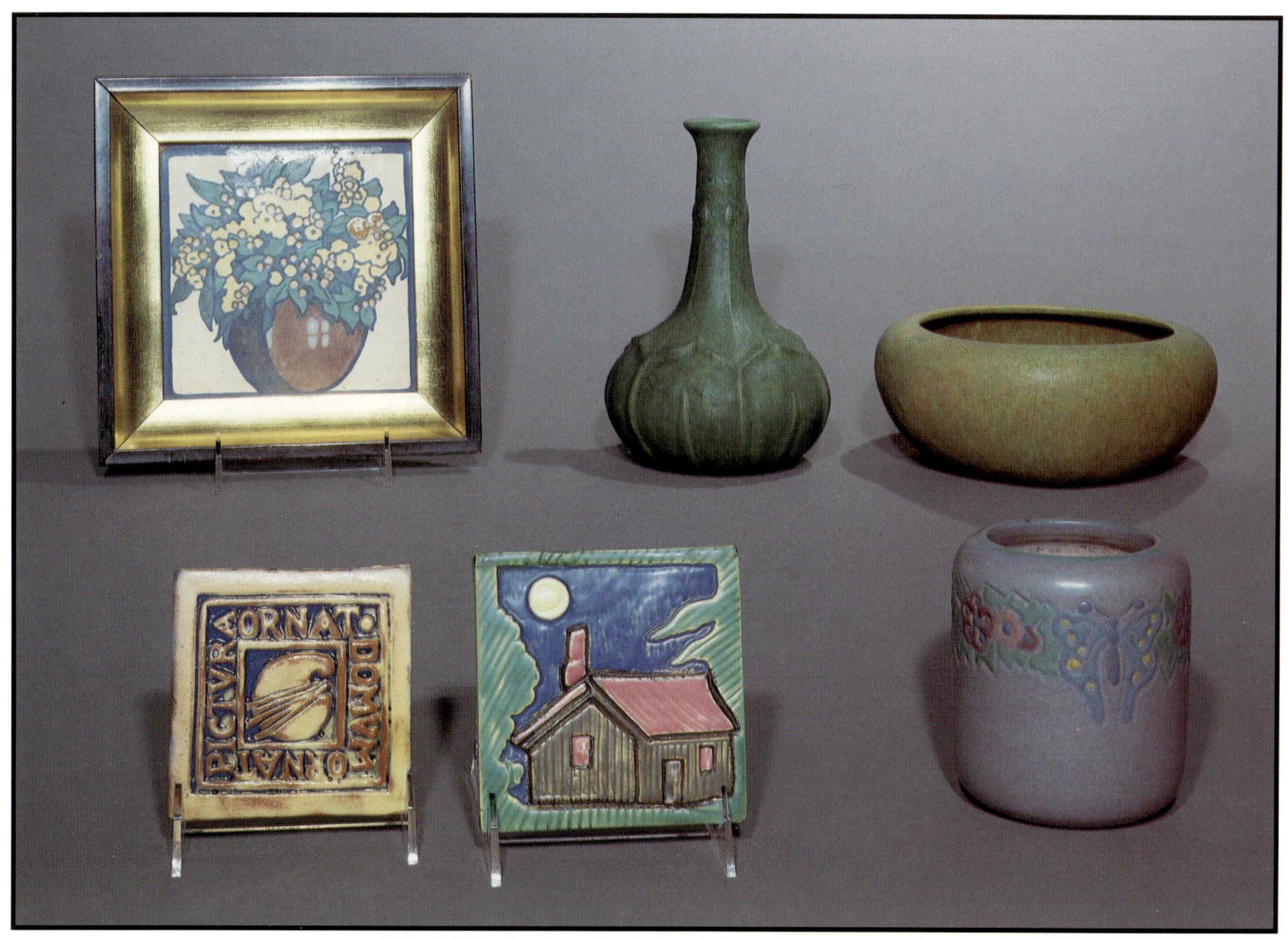

317 Good Marblehead mat glaze tile in seven colors signed by both Arthur Baggs and Hannah Tutt. Pictured is a colorful still life with stylized flowers in a large vase. The back is impressed with the Marblehead logo and bears the monograms of Baggs and Tutt, painted on in black slip. Size is 5 7/8 by 5 7/8 inches. Uncrazed and very pretty. Minor edge chips covered by a very new frame. $800-1000

318 Moravian tile showing an artist's palette with a Latin inscription around the border which reads "Pictura Ornat-Domum Ornat". Otherwise unmarked. Size is 3 3/4 square. Minor edge flakes. $125-175

319 Rare Weller hand carved tile in green, blue, yellow, brown and pink mat glazes showing what is probably the original Weller Pottery building under a full moon. Incised "Weller Art Tiles" enclosed in a square. Painted on the back in black slip is the number "2026-79". This tile appears to have never been installed and is most likely a salesman's sample or a display tile. Size is 4 1/4 by 4 1/4 inches. Strong color, deep carving, wonderful subject and great condition. $700-900

320 Wheatley Arts & Crafts style vase with bulbous bottom and long flaring neck having overlapping leaves on the bottom and thin flower buds going half way up the neck. Some of the Wheatley logo is obscured by glaze. Height 7 3/4 inches. Excellent form and very rich, organic glaze. $1000-1250

321 Weller Frosted Matt bowl done in green and pink. Unmarked. Height is 3 1/4 inches and diameter is 7 3/4 inches. $150-200

322 Extremely colorful hand thrown Marblehead vase with carved and painted butterfly and flower decoration done by an unknown artist. On a mauve ground, the artist has used blue, gray, green, maroon, yellow and pink slip on the flowers and butterflies. Marked with the impressed Marblehead logo. Two tight lines, one opposite the other, descend from the rim. $2000-2500

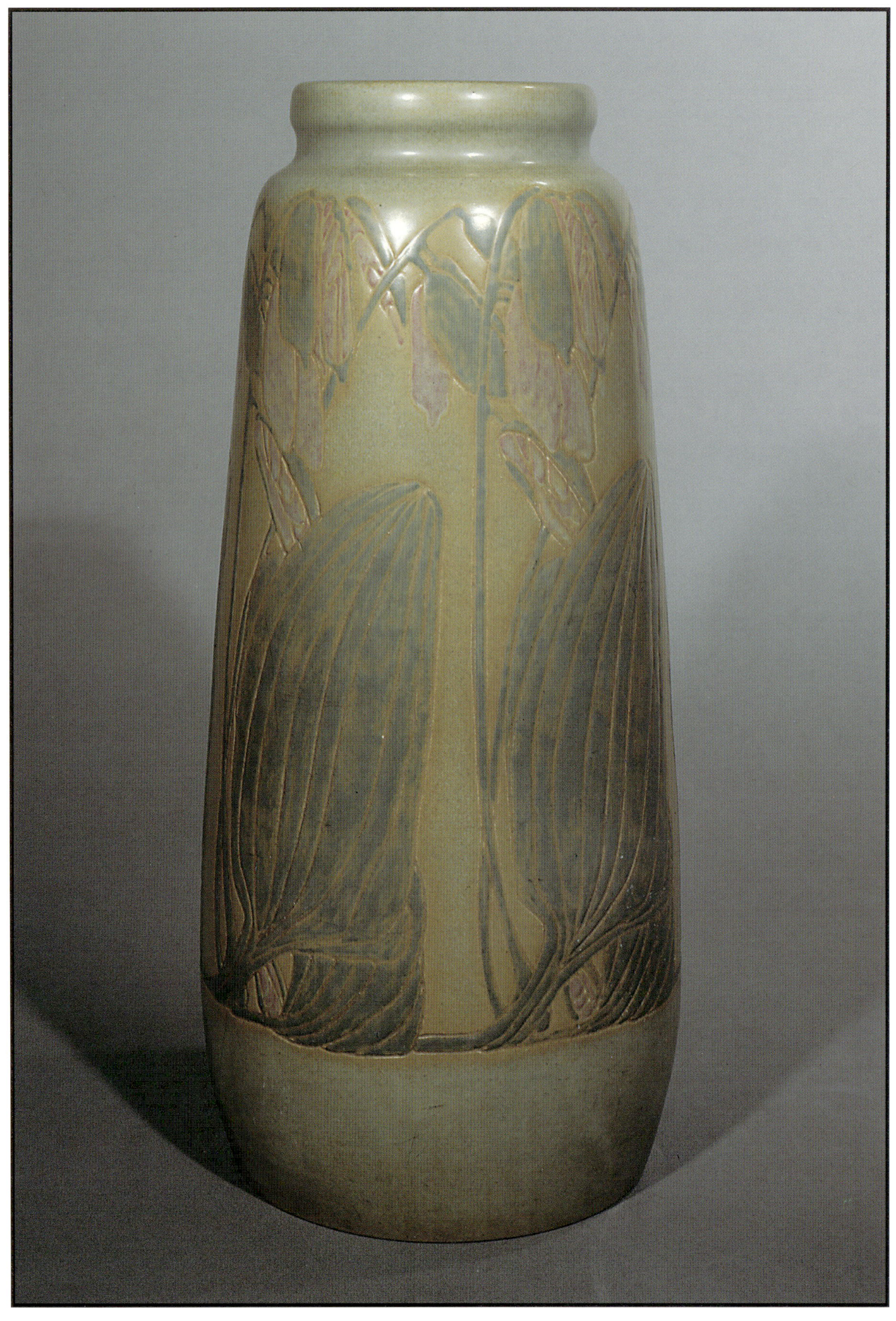

323   Rare and important Overbeck vase made by potter Elizabeth Overbeck and decorated by her sister, Mary Frances. Decoration consists of hosta flowers, leaves and stems, lightly carved and painted in shades of green, mauve, gray and tan on the gray clay body. The base is incised with the Overbeck logo and the initials of the two sisters. Height 14 1/4 inches. $12500-17500

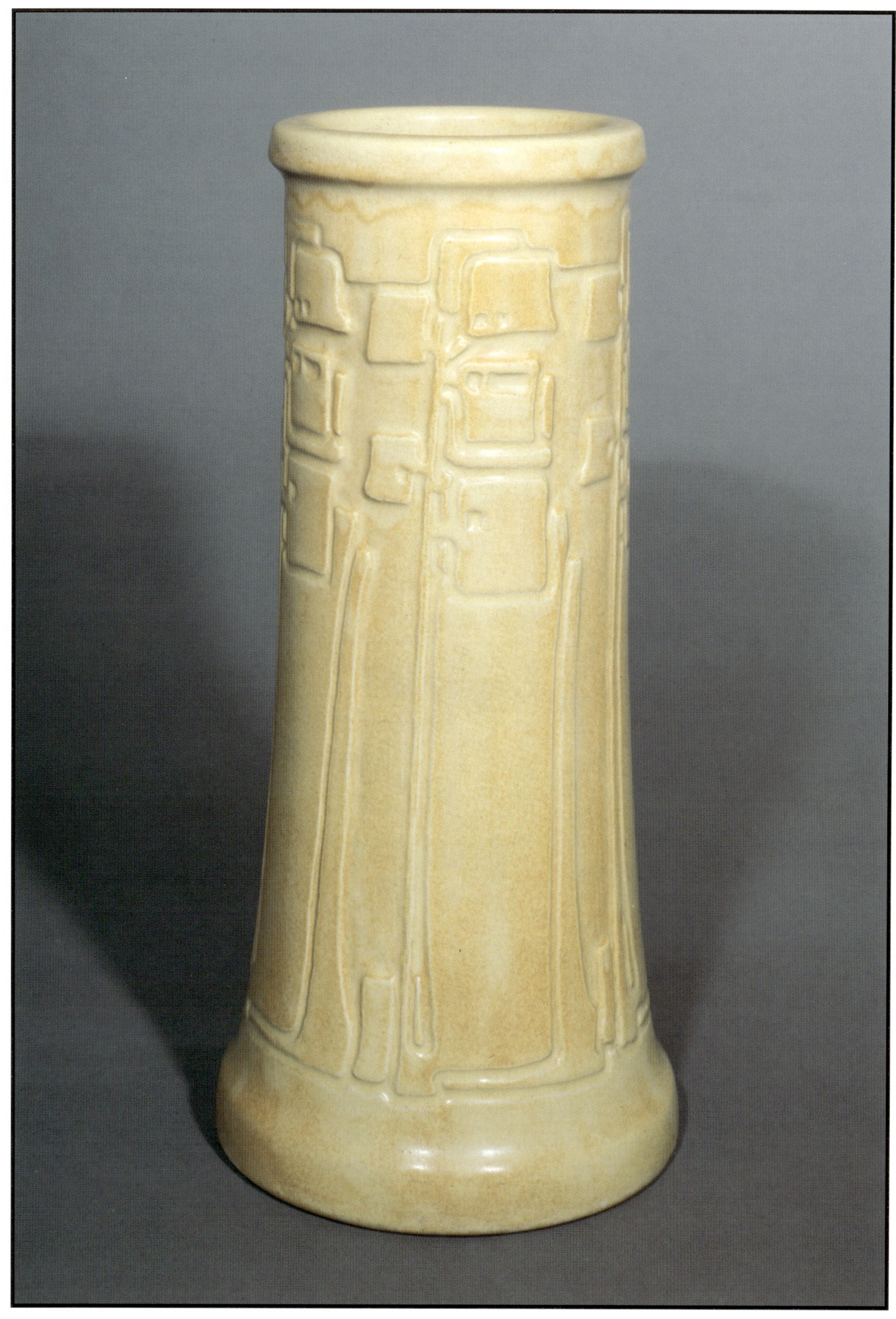

324   Rare, large and important Overbeck vase, deeply carved with stylized floral decoration done by Elizabeth and Mary Frances Overbeck. The floral motif is one that seems to have been an Overbeck favorite, appearing in drawings by the sisters and in smaller examples of their pottery. Deeply carved and glazed in subtle shades of tan and pale orange, the long stems and leaves reflect the Overbecks' interest in and knowledge of European design. Incised marks include the Overbeck logo and the initials of Elizabeth and Mary Frances. Height 11 3/8 inches. $8000-10000

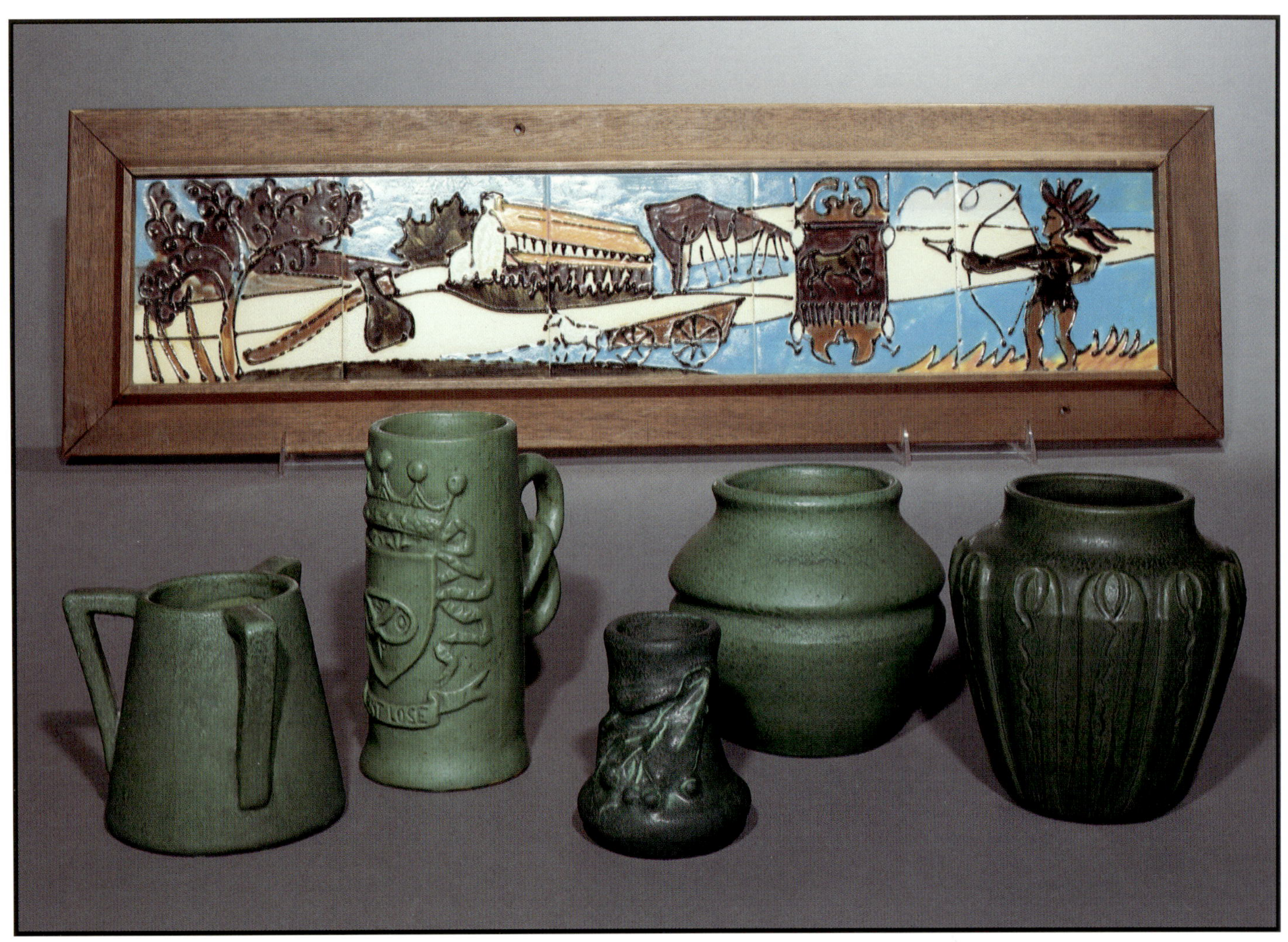

325   Harris Strong frieze consisting of five high glaze tiles which make up a stylized Western tableau depicting a barn and wagon and a Native American with bow, arrow and axe. Unmarked. Size is approximately 6 by 30 inches. Original frame. $200-300

326   Interesting Wheatley green vase with three angular handles or buttresses covered in a nice, gloopy glaze. Unmarked. Height 4 1/2 inches. $350-450

327   Amusing Wheatley mug with a fancy shield on the front and a pretzel handle. Incised on the bottom of the mug is the Wheatley logo and the notation "Compliments of the Fleischman Co". The shield bears the letters "OSOP" and the motto "Can't Lose". Possibly made for Cincinnati's Fleischmanns, makers of yeast for brewing and baking. Height 7 1/4 inches. Small glaze nicks off the rim and foot. $200-300

328   Arts & Crafts green mat glaze vase with deeply embossed leaves and berries, thought to be Owens. Unmarked. There are several small burst bubbles in the glaze. Height 4 inches. $200-300

329   Wheatley Arts & Crafts style vase done in a thick, organic green mat glaze. A nice architectural touch is the indentation around the belt line of this piece. Unmarked. Height 5 5/8 inches. $300-400

330   Green mat glaze Arts & Crafts style vase with hand incised squiggles on the raised panels, possibly early Pewabic pottery. Height 6 1/4 inches. Unmarked. Flat grinding chips on the base and a pin-head sized glaze nick on the rim. $400-600

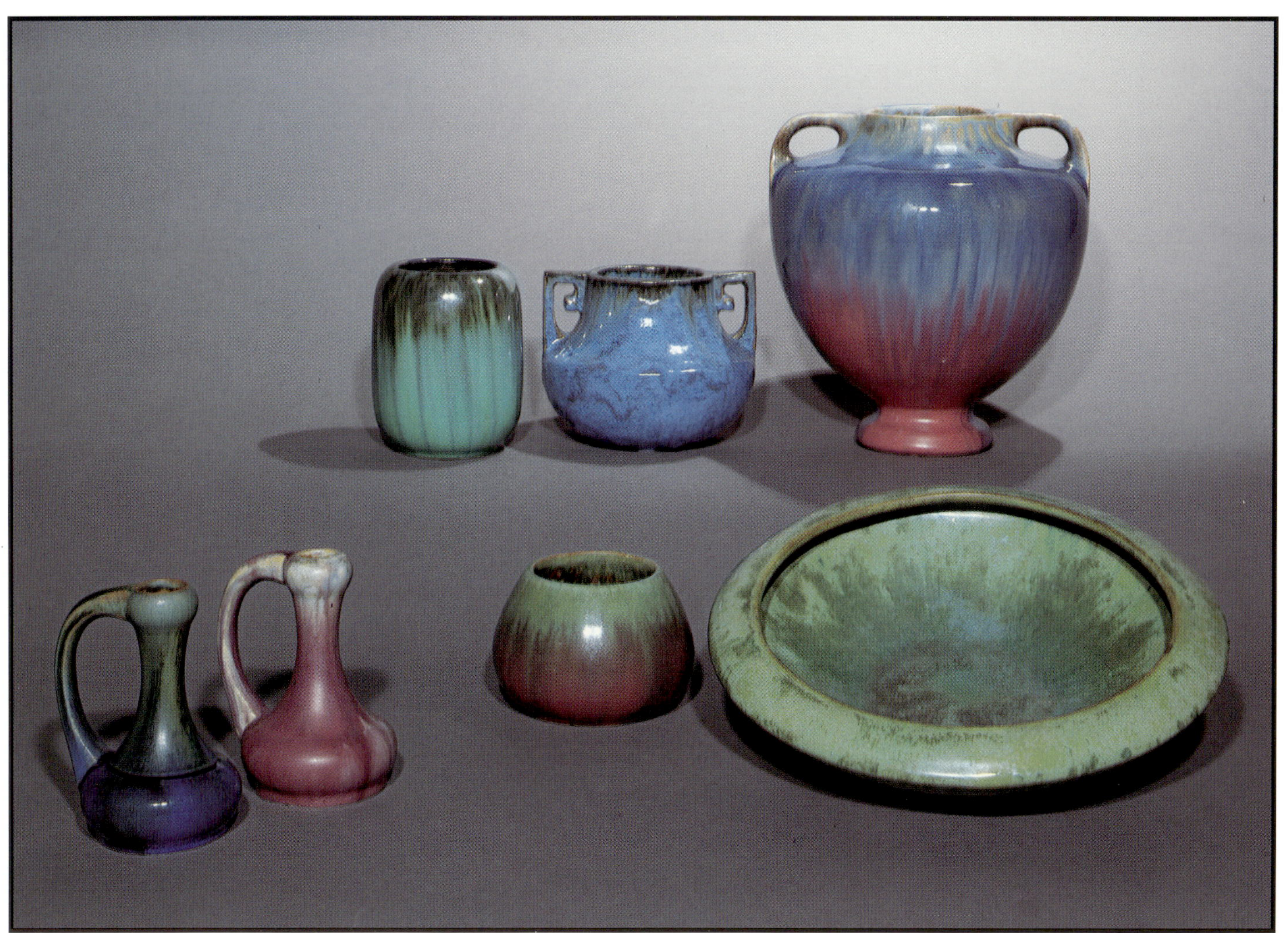

331   Pair of Fulper bud vases with handles, one done in Wisteria glaze, the other in a green over blue flambé. Both are marked with the vertical racetrack inkstamp. Height of each is 4 1/2 inches. $200-300

332   Fulper vase in Flemington Green glaze. Marked with the vertical racetrack inkstamp logo. Height 4 7/8 inches. $150-200

333   Fulper vase done in Flemington Green over Famille Rose glazes. Marked with the vertical racetrack inkstamp. Height 3 inches. Minor grinding chip off the base. $100-150

334   Fulper two-handled vase done in a rich, thick Chinese Blue Flambé which has pooled and clumped in interestingly irregular patterns. Marked with the vertical racetrack inkstamp. Height 4 5/8 inches. $200-300

335   Fulper low bowl done in green mat over green gloss glazes. Marked with the vertical inkstamp logo with Oriental letters. Height 2 5/8 inches and diameter is 10 5/8 inches. Unusual form. $300-400

336   Good Fulper two-handled vase with Chinese Blue Flambé over Famille Rose glazes. Marked with the raised vertical racetrack Fulper logo. Height 9 inches. $600-800

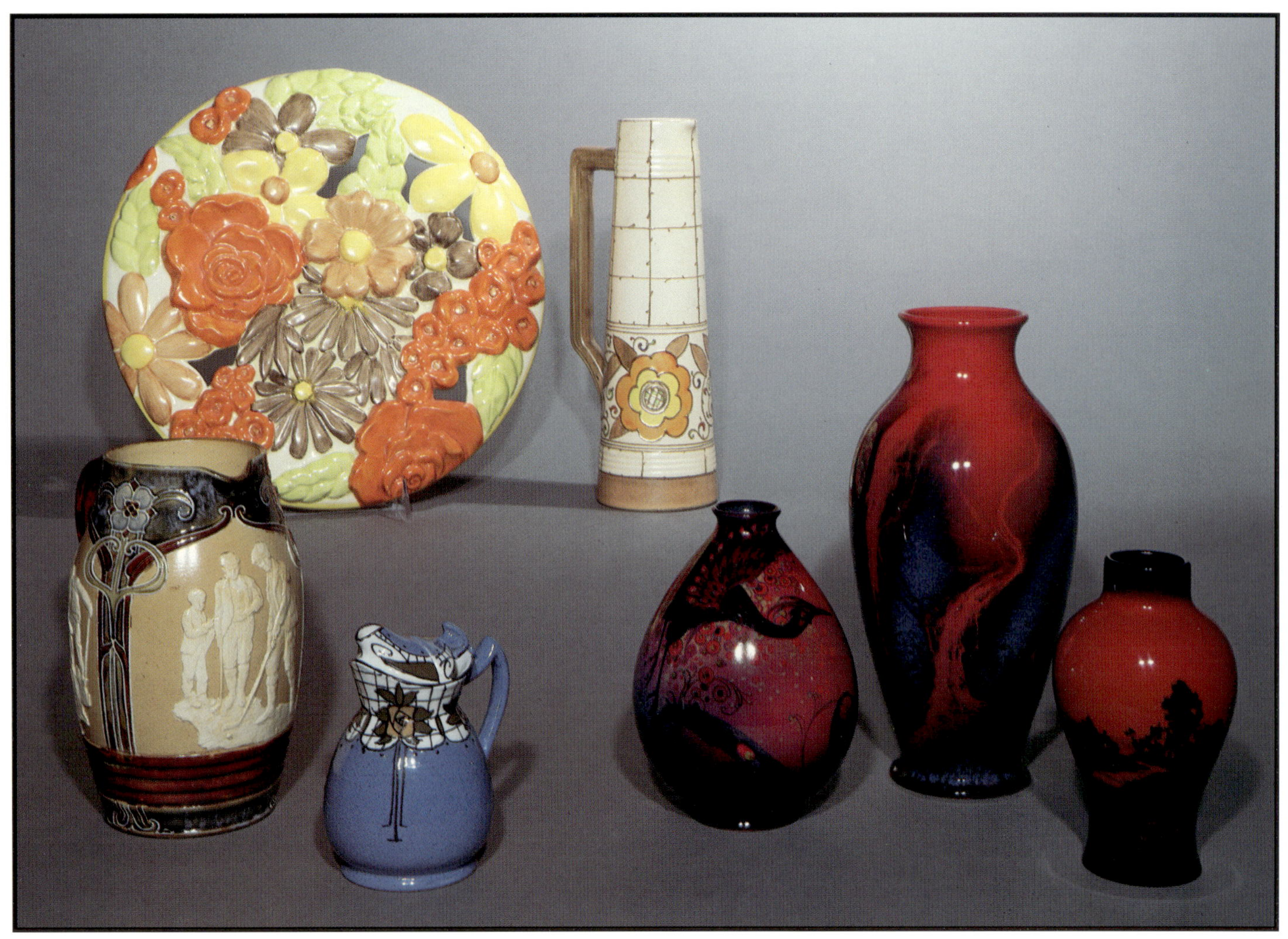

337	Rare Doulton Lambeth pitcher with three different golfing scenes done just before the turn of the century by an unknown artist. Impressed with the "Doulton Lambeth England" logo, the letter "M", the number "165" and other, arcane marks. Incised initials of the artist are also on the bottom of the pitcher. There are a few minor spots of discoloration in the applied clay of the golfers themselves. Height 7 3/4 inches.	$1000-1500
338	Clarice Cliff hanging charger with embossed multi-colored floral design and some articulation. Marked on the reverse with a Clarice Cliff ink stamp logo and the ink stamp notation "Made in England". Diameter is 13 inches. There is a tight 1/2 inch internal line which is only visible from the reverse.	$600-800
339	Wood & Sons Bursley Ware "Cosy" teapot with lid done in the Trellis pattern, a design by Frederick Alfred Rhead. Marks include the Wood & Sons inkstamp logo and the painted on number "9". Height 5 inches. The stylized Art Nouveau design is outlined by tube lining.	$200-300
340	Colorful Charlotte Rhead tankard in the Trellis pattern done in semi-gloss and luster glazes, all outlined by slip trailing. Marked with the "Burley Ware Charlotte Rhead England" inkstamp logo and impressed with the numbers "258" and "788313". Painted on the base in brown slip is the number "723" and the number "1". Also painted on in blue slip is the letter "H". Height 11 1/8 inches. Good color and glaze.	$400-500
341	Rare decorated Royal Doulton Sung vase painted by Charles Noke in the 1920's. An Art Deco peacock with outstretched tail struts among dozens of bubbles on the colorful Flambe' ground. Marks include the Royal Doulton Flambé logo and, in black slip, the names "Noke" and "Sung" and the reference "No. 3124 E". Height 6 1/2 inches. There are a few tiny glaze bubbles on the lip of the rim.	$1750-2250
342	Rare Royal Doulton Sung Ware vase decorated by Charles Noke and possibly by Fred Moore, most likely during the 1920's. The vase bears the Royal Doulton Flambe' transfer logo, Noke's last name, the name Sung and Moore's monogram, painted on in black slip and the incised numbers 7798 and 1471. Height 10 1/2 inches.	$1000-1500
343	Royal Doulton Flambé vase with village scene possible painted by an artist with the initials "HE". Marks include a transfer Royal Doulton logo, an incised number "7681" and the painted-on initials of the artist. Height 6 1/8 inches. Very clean.	$200-300

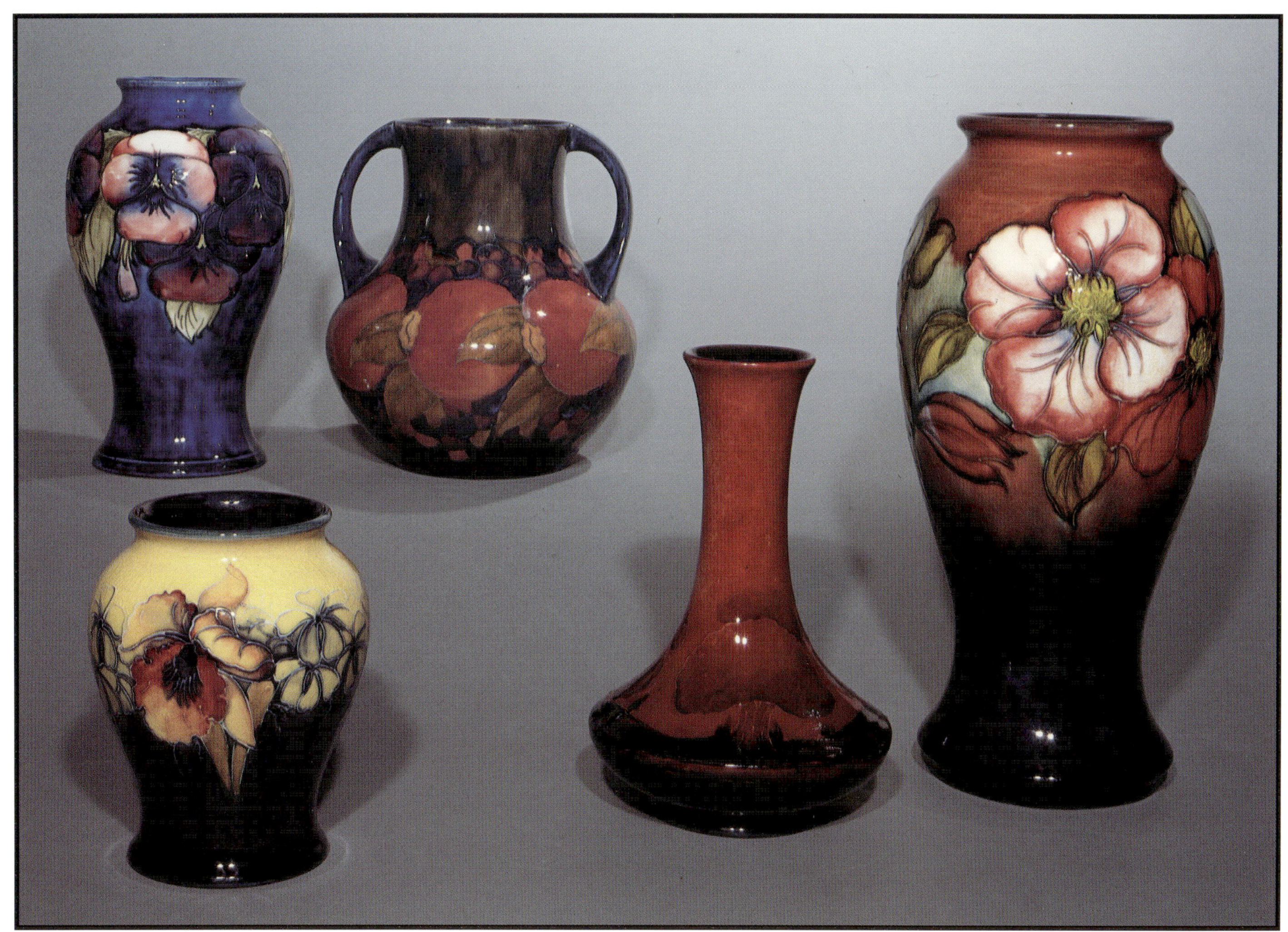

344   Moorcroft Pansy vase with slightly bulbous upper portion. Marks include impressed "Moorcroft Made in England", a small incised circle and the painted signature of William Moorcroft. Height 9 1/8 inches. $400-500

345   Moorcroft Orchid vase with cobalt and orange ground. Marks include the impressed factory logo with facsimile signature, impressed "Made in England" and the painted initials of Walter Moorcroft. Height 5 5/8 inches. $300-400

346   Early Moorcroft two-handled Pomegranate vase. Marks include impressed "Moorcroft Burslem England", an impressed number "5" and the painted signature of William Moorcroft. Height 8 1/4 inches. Unusual form from a good period. $500-700

347   Striking Moorcroft landscape vase done in a rich Flambé glaze. Impressed marks include "Moorcroft Made in England" and what appears to be the number "88". Painted on the base is the signature of William Moorcroft and a small circle. Height 8 inches. A rare combination of subject and glaze. $2000-2500

348   Tall Moorcroft Clematis vase done in a strong Flambé glaze. Marks include the impressed factory mark with facsimile signature, the painted signature of William Moorcroft, impressed "Made in England" and an impressed cross in a circle. Height 12 1/8 inches. $600-800

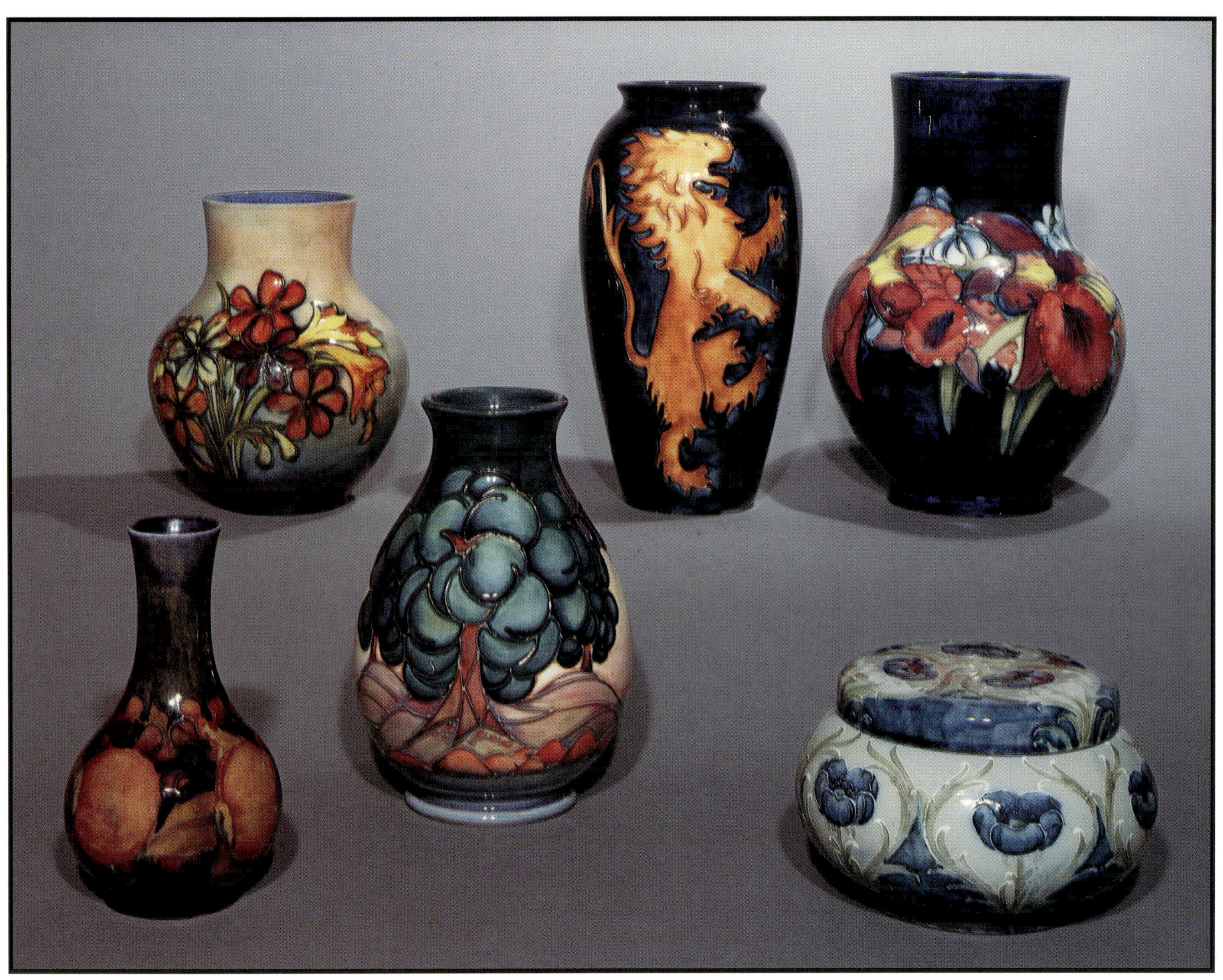

349   Moorcroft Pomegranate vase with bulbous bottom and tall flaring neck. Marks include the painted initials of William Moorcroft in green slip, impressed "Moorcroft Made in England" and also an obscured shape number. Height 6 1/8 inches. $250-350

350   Moorcroft Spring Flowers vase finished in a pale Flambé glaze. Marks include impressed "Moorcroft Made in England" and the painted-on initials of Walter Moorcroft. Height 7 inches. $300-400

351   Unusual Moorcroft landscape vase done in bright colors in the 1980's. Marks include impressed "Moorcroft Made in England", the painted initials of Walter Moorcroft, tube liner Alison Neale and paintress Jennifer James. Height 7 1/2 inches. $400-500

352   Limited edition Moorcroft "Lions Den" vase showing a rampant lion on a cobalt ground, this being number 13 of 50 pieces done in 1988. Impressed marks include "Moorcroft" and "Made in England". Painted on the base are the initials of Walter Moorcroft, the designation "13/50" and the monogram of paintress Julie Dolan. Height 9 3/4 inches. $300-400

353   Rare Moorcroft Florian tobacco jar with a screw-on lid, decorated with blue poppies on a green and blue ground. The only mark is the painted signature of William Moorcroft on the bottom. Height 3 3/4 inches. This is an early piece in an extremely unusual form. $2000-3000

354   Tall Moorcroft Orchid vase featuring many multicolored flowers on a cobalt ground. Marks include impressed "Moorcroft Made in England", incised number "8" and the painted Walter Moorcroft initials. Height 10 inches. $400-500

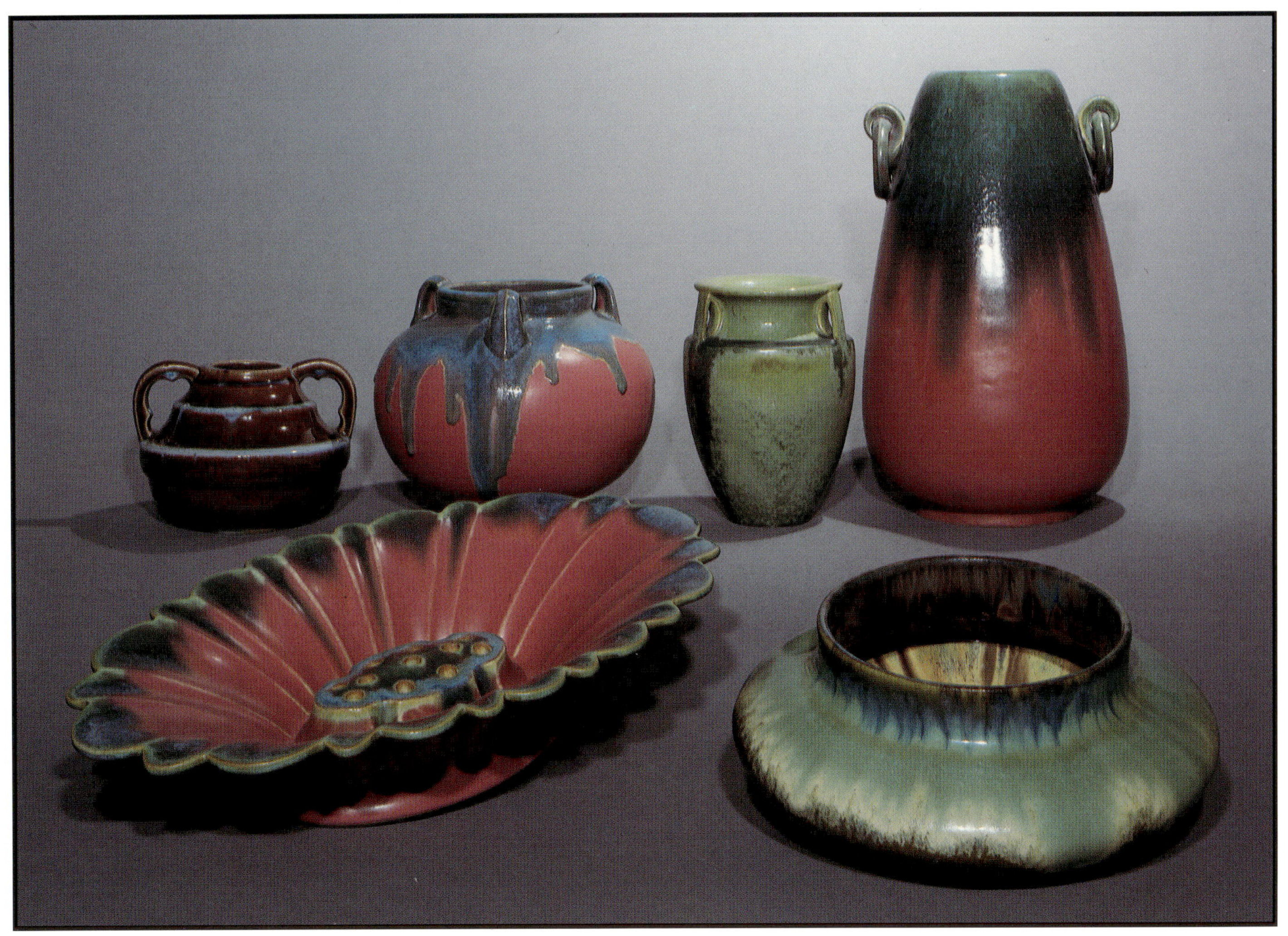

355   Fulper Art Deco centerpiece with separate flower frog done in Famille Rose glaze with touches of green and blue at the edges. The centerpiece is marked with the vertical racetrack inkstamp. The flower frog is unmarked. Height is 3 1/2 inches and longest distance across is 12 inches. $300-400

356   Fulper two-handled Art Deco vase form done in a brown to tan high glaze with blue highlights. Marked with the vertical racetrack inkstamp with Oriental lettering. Height 4 1/2 inches. $200-300

357   Late Fulper three-handled vase form with strong glaze and color. The vase was first coated with a thick Famille Rose glaze over which an even thicker mat blue-gray flambe' glaze with slight iridescence has been applied. Marked with the die-stamped Fulper logo and shape number 564. Height 6 3/4 inches. $400-600

358   Fulper "Bullet" vase done in a Cucumber Crystalline glaze. Marked with the vertical racetrack inkstamp Fulper logo. Height 6 3/4 inches. $200-300

359   Fulper low vase form done in blue to green to cream Flambé over dark Mustard Matte glazes. Marked with a large vertical rectangular ink stamp logo. Height is 4 inches while diameter is 10 1/2 inches. $400-600

360   Tall Fulper vase with loop handles and rings done in a mottled green flambé over Famille Rose glaze. Marked with the vertical racetrack inkstamp Fulper logo. Height 11 3/4 inches. A handsome and clean example. $700-900

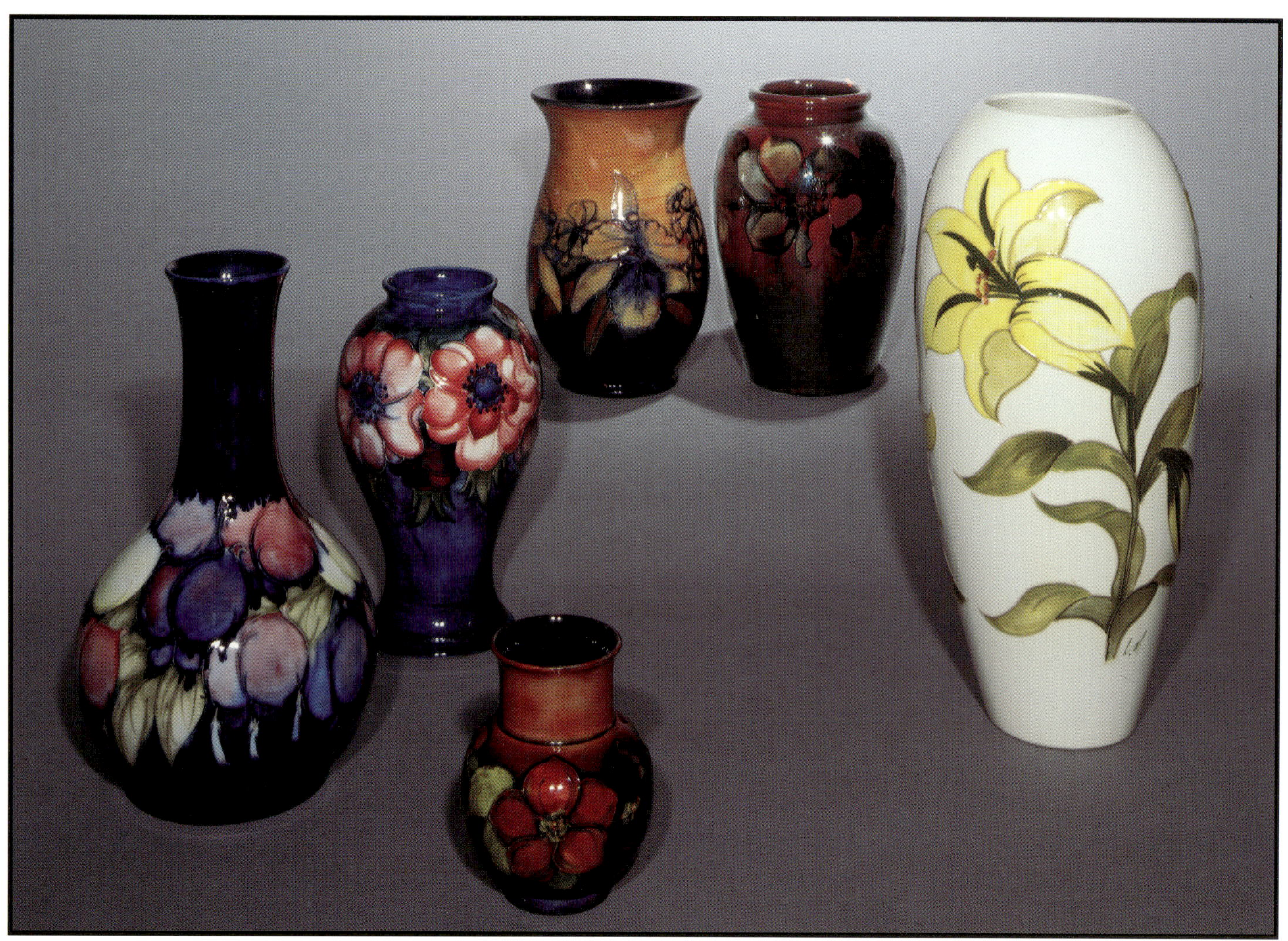

361   Tall Moorcroft Wisteria vase with bulbous bottom done on a cobalt ground. Marks include impressed "Moorcroft" and "Made in England", the painted signature of William Moorcroft, an impressed "B" and an impressed "O". Height 11 1/2 inches. $500-700

362   Moorcroft Anemone vase with bulbous top half of the body. Marks include the impressed factory mark with facsimile signature, an incised number "3" and painted Walter Moorcroft signature. Height 9 1/8 inches. Slight unevenness to the base. $400-500

363   Moorcroft Clematis vase done in a bright Flambé glaze. Marks include "Moorcroft" and "Made in England" impressed and the letter "B" painted on. Height 5 inches. $200-300

364   Handsome Moorcroft Orchid vase with unusual orange background color, possibly Flambé glaze. Marks include the impressed factory mark with facsimile signature, painted signature and the impressed notation "Made in England". Height 9 1/8 inches. $600-800

365   Striking Moorcroft Clematis vase done in a deep maroon Flambé glaze which is subtly infused with hundred of snowflake crystals. Marks include the impressed factory mark with facsimile signature, the painted signature of Walter Moorcroft and impressed "Made in England". Height 9 1/2 inches. Crystalline glaze examples of Moorcroft are quite unusual. $500-700

365A   A tall, possibly unique, Moorcroft Bermuda lily vase made sometime in the 1970's. Marked on the base only with the Royal Warrant paper label. On the side of the vase is the monogram of Walter Moorcroft, painted on in green slip. We assume the vase to have been painted by Moorcroft himself. Height 14 5/8 inches. $1000-1500

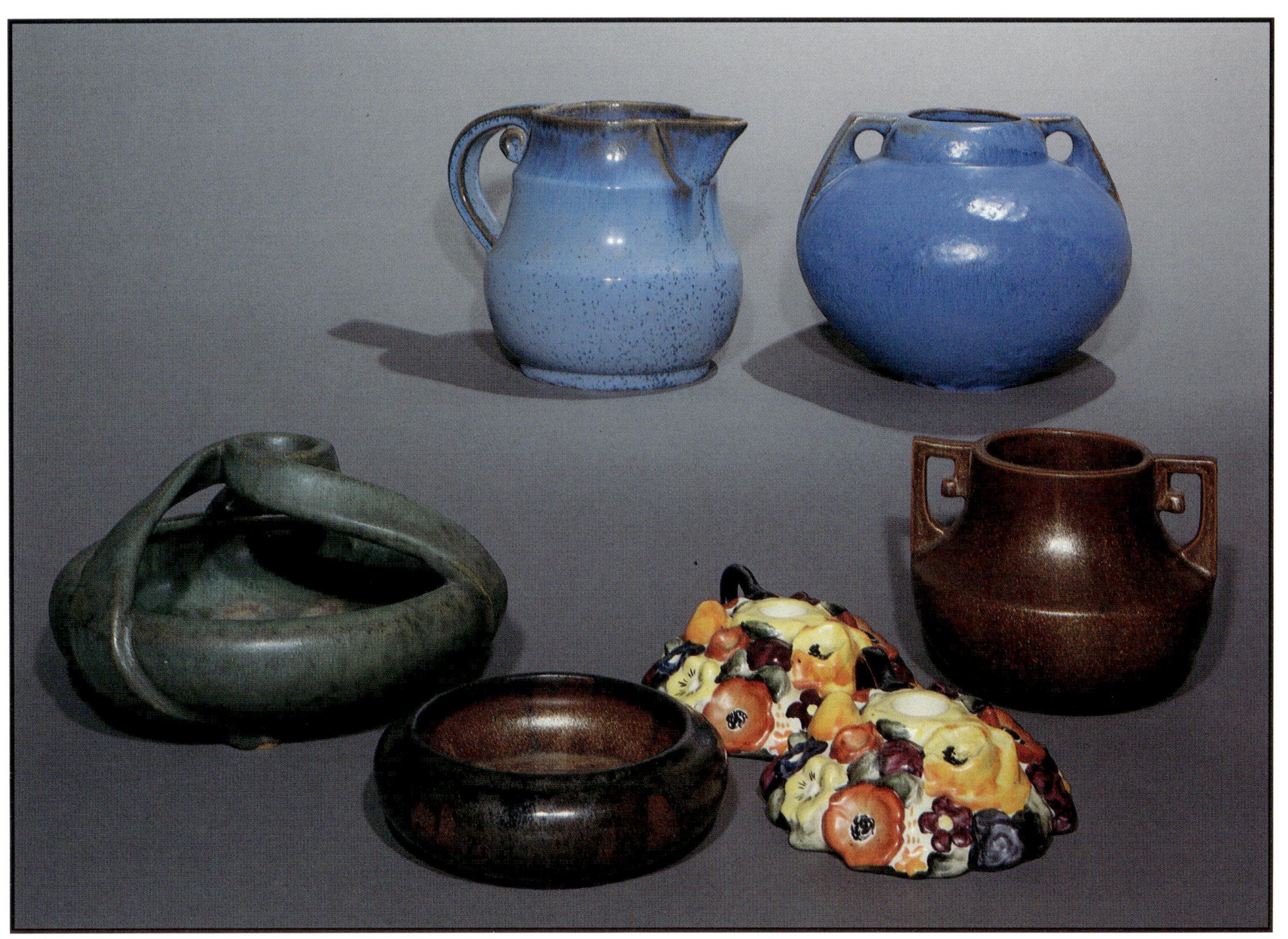

366   Fulper "Vaz" bowl in green mat glaze complete with three swirl handles which meet in the middle to hold flowers or perhaps even a candle. The interior of the bowl is covered with a gray to green high glaze. Marked with the large rectangular inkstamp. Height 4 7/8 inches. An unusual form in excellent original condition. $500-700

367   Beautifully glazed Fulper bowl done in Mirrored Black over Copperdust Crystalline. Marked with the vertical racetrack inkstamp. Height is 1 7/8 inches and diameter is 6 inches. $250-350

368   Late Fulper pitcher covered with Blue Snowflake crystalline glaze. Marked with impressed horizontal Fulper name, the notation "EL" and shape number 830. Height 6 3/8 inches. $250-350

369   Pair of multicolored Fulper candlesticks in the form of floral bouquets. Each is marked with the vertical race track inkstamp with Oriental letters and each bears an original paper showroom label which lists the price at $6.00 for the pair. One stick has the number "75" painted on in black slip. Height is 2 inches. $200-300

370   Fulper two-handled vase done in a gloopy mottled blue mat glaze with touches of green. The glaze is very organic, pooling and curdling in irregular patterns. Marked with the vertical racetrack inkstamp with Oriental letters. Height 6 1/4 inches. $400-600

371   Sharp looking Fulper two-handled vase with great over-all Copperdust Crystalline glaze. Marked with the vertical inkstamp logo with Oriental letters. Height 4 5/8 inches. $800-1000

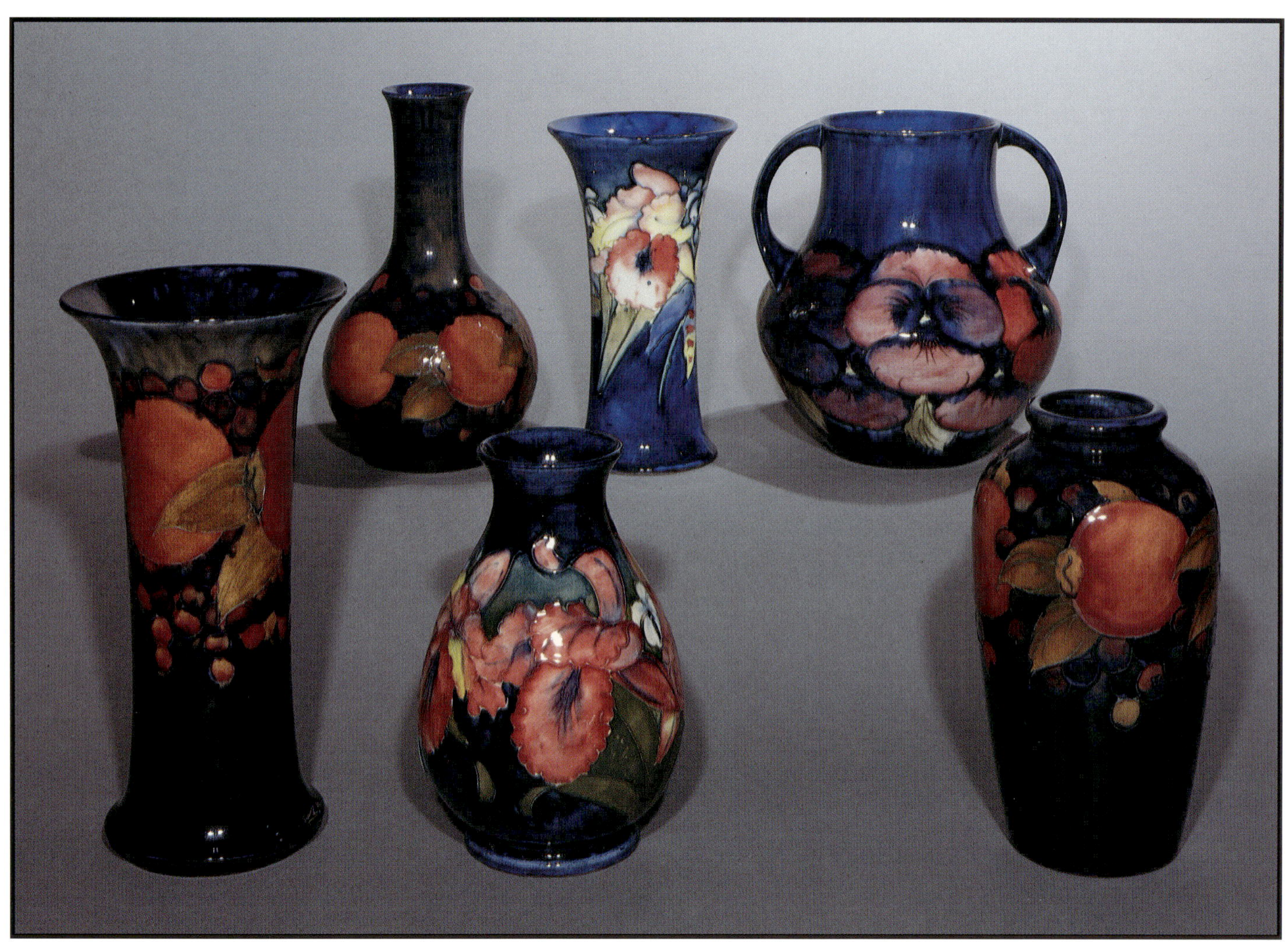

372	Early Moorcroft Pomegranate vase with flared rim, made around the time of World War I. Marks include the impressed "Moorcroft Burslem England" mark, an impressed number obscured by glaze and the painted-on signature of William Moorcroft. Height 10 1/4 inches.	$500-700
373	Moorcroft Pomegranate vase with bulbous bottom and tall neck. Marks include the impressed "Moorcroft Made in England" logo, a number obscured by glaze, a printed paper Royal Warrant label and the painted-on signature of William Moorcroft. Height 9 inches.	$400-600
374	Moorcroft Orchid vase done in crisp colors on a cobalt ground. Marks include the impressed factory mark with facsimile signature, the painted initials of Walter Moorcroft, impressed "Made in England" and impressed number "5". Height 7 3/8 inches.	$300-400
375	Moorcroft corset shaped Orchid vase done in slightly pastel colors. Marks include the impressed factory mark with facsimile signature and impressed "Made in England". Height 8 1/8 inches.	$300-400
376	Two-handled Moorcroft Pansy vase done on a deep cobalt ground. Marks include "Moorcroft" and "Made in England" impressed, the painted signature of William Moorcroft and the impressed number "5". Height 8 1/8 inches.	$400-500
377	Moorcroft Pomegranate vase done with a deep cobalt ground. Marks include the impressed factory mark with facsimile signature, impressed "Made in England", a small incised circle and the painted initials of Walter Moorcroft. Height 8 1/8 inches. Minor glaze scratches.	$300-400

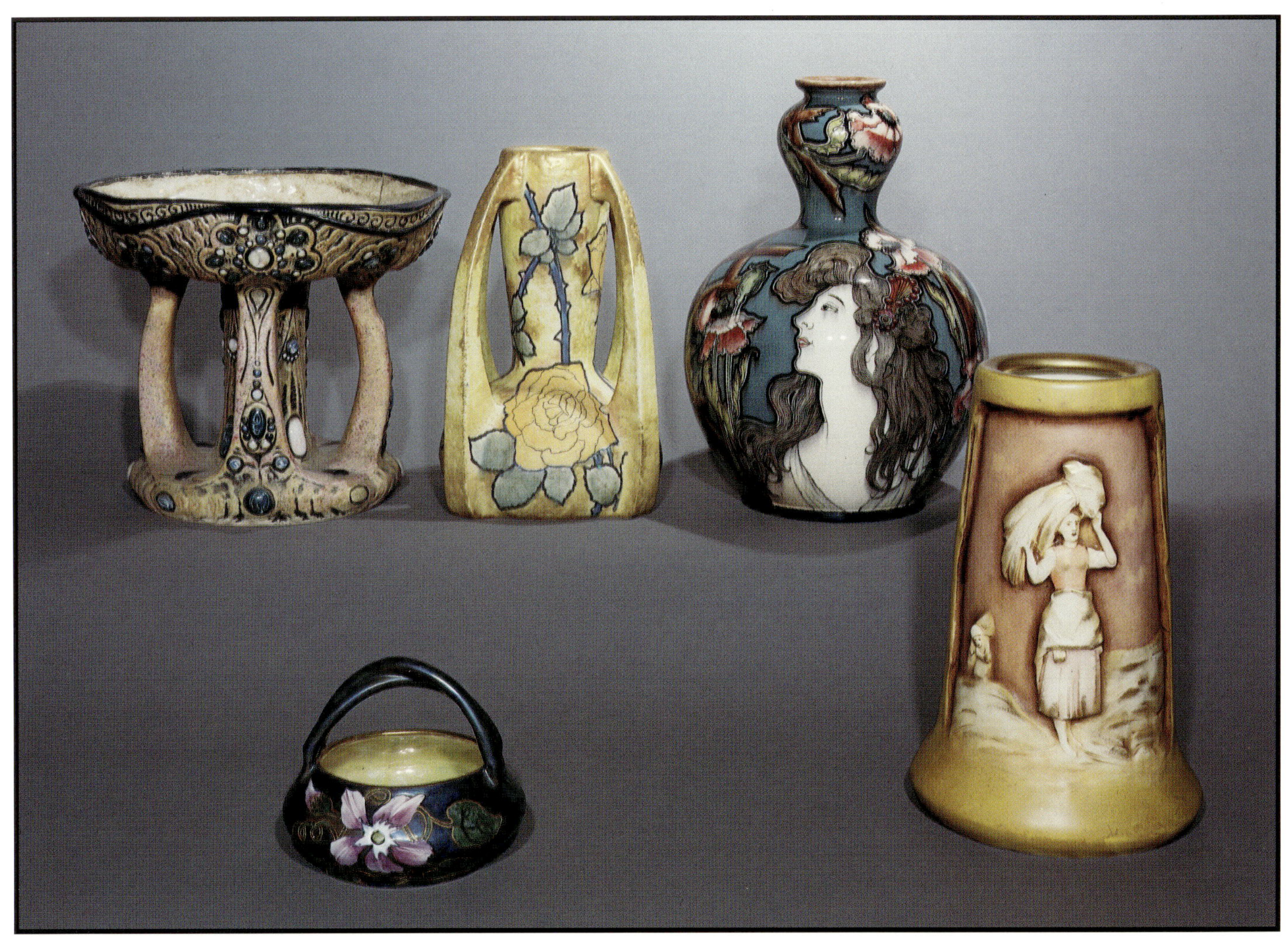

378   Curious Amphora compote vase with four buttress handles and many simulated jewels in a variety of colors. Marked with a transfer "Amphora Made in Czecho-Slovakia" oval logo. Height 9 1/4 inches. There is a firing separation in the bowl. $300-400

379   Stellmacher two-handled basket with enameled floral decoration on an iridescent blue ground. Marks include an embossed "Stellmacher Potterie Teplitz" logo, a "Stellmacher Teplitz" transfer logo, the number "510" painted on in blue slip and the impressed numbers "21", "11" and "14". Height 4 1/4 inches. $200-300

380   Amphora vase with four buttress handles and rose decoration outlined in black. The top of the vase is enhanced with fired-on gold. Impressed marks include a crown, the notation "Austria Amphora" and the numbers "3883" and "42". Painted on is the letter "B". Height 10 3/8 inches. $300-400

381   Stylish Royal Bonn high glaze vase decorated with Art Nouveau women and stylized poppies on trellises. Marked "Royal Bonn Art Nova 221 Germany 3838/5 22" in black slip. Impressed marks include a Royal Bonn logo and the numbers "8" and "2562". Height 12 5/8 inches. $1000-1500

382   Amphora vase with embossed decoration of women harvesting wheat, done in various mat glazes with gold highlights. Impressed with a crown and two ovals which contain the words "Amphora" and "Austria". Also impressed are the numbers "44" and "11563". Height 10 1/8 inches. $400-500

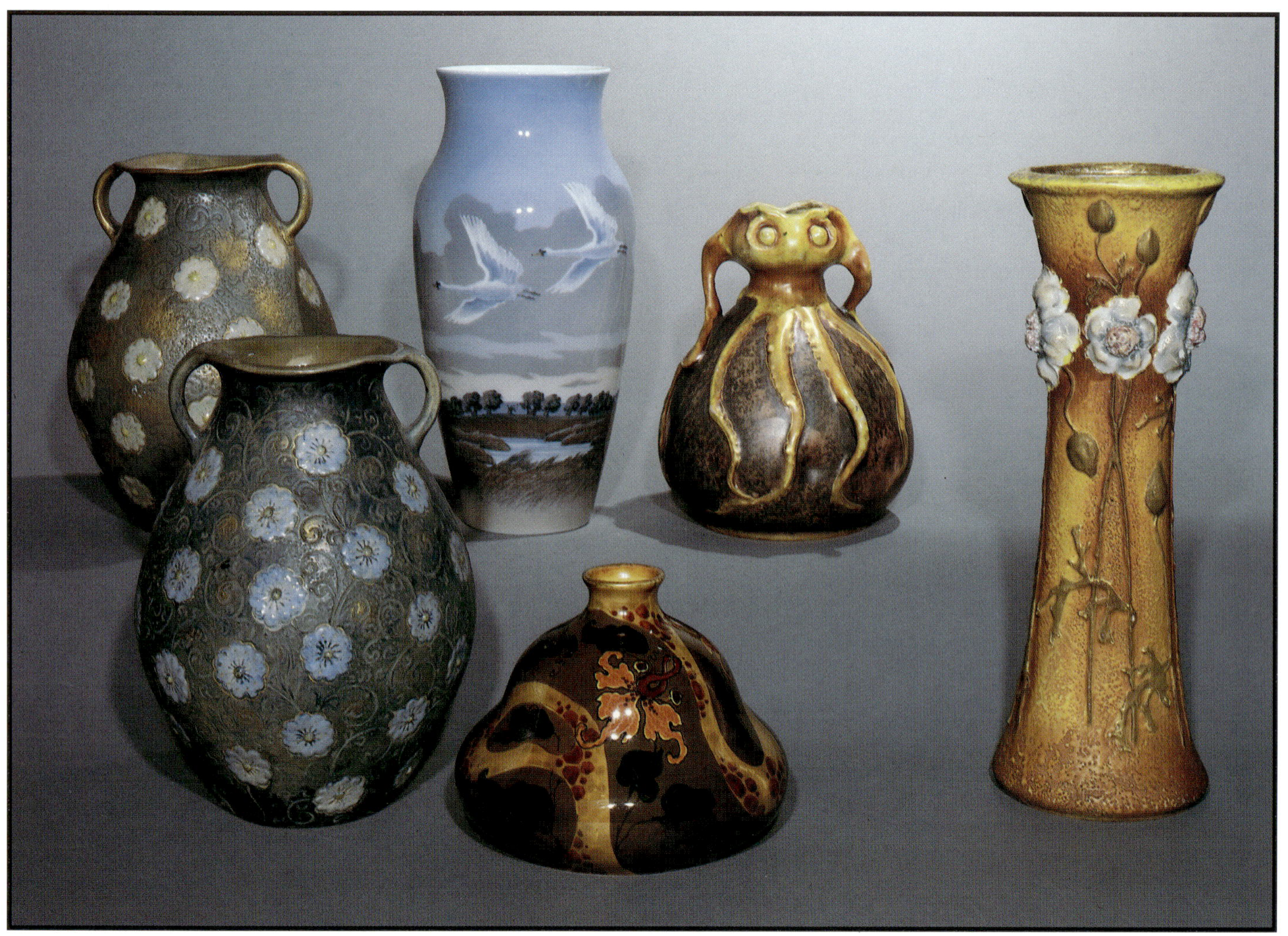

383 Pair of Amphora two-handled vases done in mat and gloss glazes. The two differ slightly in color but the form $300-400
and concept are the same. Impressed marks include a crown, the names "Amphora" and "Austria" in ovals
and the numbers "11663" and "46". One of the vases is impressed with a circular "Imperial Amphora" logo.
Height of each is 10 inches. One of the vases has a 1/4 by 1/2 inch chip off the underside of the rim.

384 Tall Royal Copenhagen landscape vase showing two flying white swans. Marks include the Royal $400-500
Copenhagen logo, the initials of the artist, the number 1955 (possibly the date) and the number 137. Height
12 1/2 inches. Uncrazed and very clean.

385 Pergamon vase done in beautiful luster colors of purple, gold, green, orange and maroon. Marks in black slip $200-300
include the name "Pergamon" and the notations "5665/2418" and "x". Incised in the base is the number
"5665". Height 5 5/8 inches. Pergamon is thought to have been associated with Ernst Wahliss in Austria.

386 Interesting Amphora vase in the form of a two-sided octopus with the head forming the neck and rim and $400-500
free standing tentacles giving the impression of handles. The background glaze is a mottled gray with red
touches while the octopus is done in fired-on gold. Marks include the impressed crown and ovals reading
"Austria" and "Amphora". Impressed numbers "4547" and "50" are also present on the bottom. Height 8 3/4
inches. A small chip on the inside of the rim has been professionally repaired.

387 Tall Amphora vase with embossed floral decoration, mostly covered with gold mat glaze while the three $500-700
dimensional flowers themselves are coated with a glossy, opalescent glaze. Impressed with a crown mark
and two ovals in which appear the words "Amphora" and "Austria". Other impressed marks include the letter
"G" and numbers "2138" and "46". Height 14 1/8 inches.

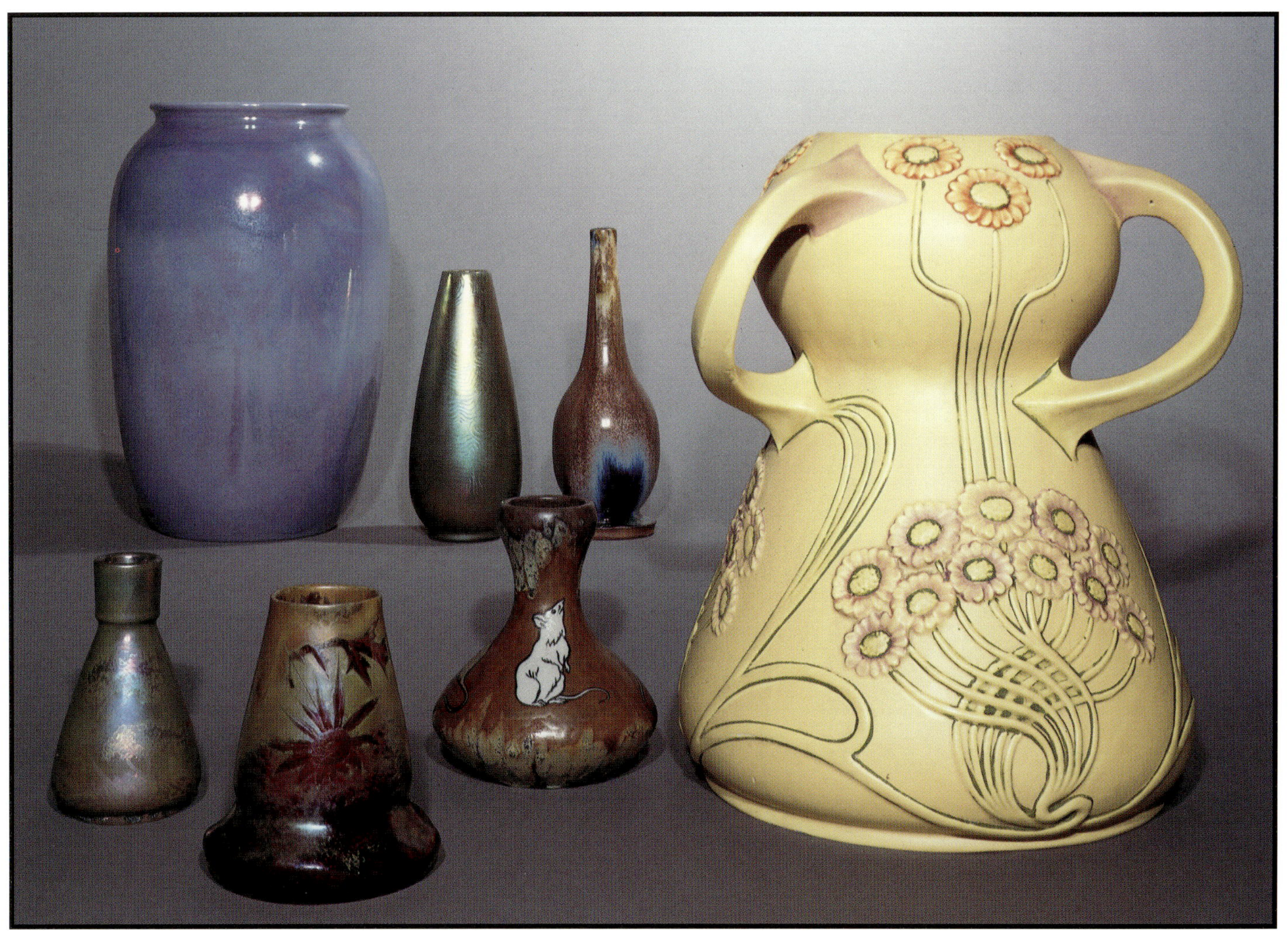

388	Delphin Massier vase done in metallic glazes and made in France at the turn of the century. This vase shows a woodland scene. Painted marks on the base read, "Delphin Massier Vallauris AM". Height 5 3/8 inches. Several burst bubbles around the foot.	$200-300
389	Large Ruskin vase done in purple luster glaze in 1920. Impressed "Ruskin England 1920". Height 12 7/8 inches. Very minor glaze scratches.	$300-400
390	Clement Massier vase with leaf and flower decoration, possibly painted by L. Levy. Marks include the painted notation, "Clement Massier Golfe Juan AM" and the name "L.Levy". Impressed marks are obscured by glaze. Height 5 3/8 inches. Minor glaze nicks at the rim.	$300-400
391	Delphin Massier metallic glaze vase with painted swirls on the colorful surface. The base is marked "DM Vallauris". Height 7 3/4 inches. Good color and condition.	$200-300
392	Fine Art Nouveau faience piece decorated by sculptor Charles Virion, for Montigny sur Loing. Along with a fabulous multicolored glaze, Virion has painted three mice in enamels, each in different color and pose. Impressed marks include the name "Montigny s/Loing," the profile of a rooster, the letters "B.P." and shape number 287. Painted on the side of the vase is the artist's name. Height 6 1/4 inches. There is a 1/4 by 1 inch chip off the base.	$500-700
393	Fabulous footed vase in mottled, multicolored glaze made by August Delaherche. The brown mat glaze over most of the body is interrupted by shades of cobalt, pink, green and gray in gloss finishes. Incised "A Delaherche" on the bottom. Height 8 7/8 inches.	$800-1200
394	Huge Amphora style vase made by Julius Dressler in Austria at the turn of the century. The vase has three long sweeping handles which begin at the rim and connect at the waist. Embossed Art Nouveau flowers in red, green and purple swirl around the entirety of the vase. Marked with the Dressler raised kiln mark and impressed "Austria" and "714". Height 14 7/8 inches. Excellent color, mold and condition.	$1000-1500

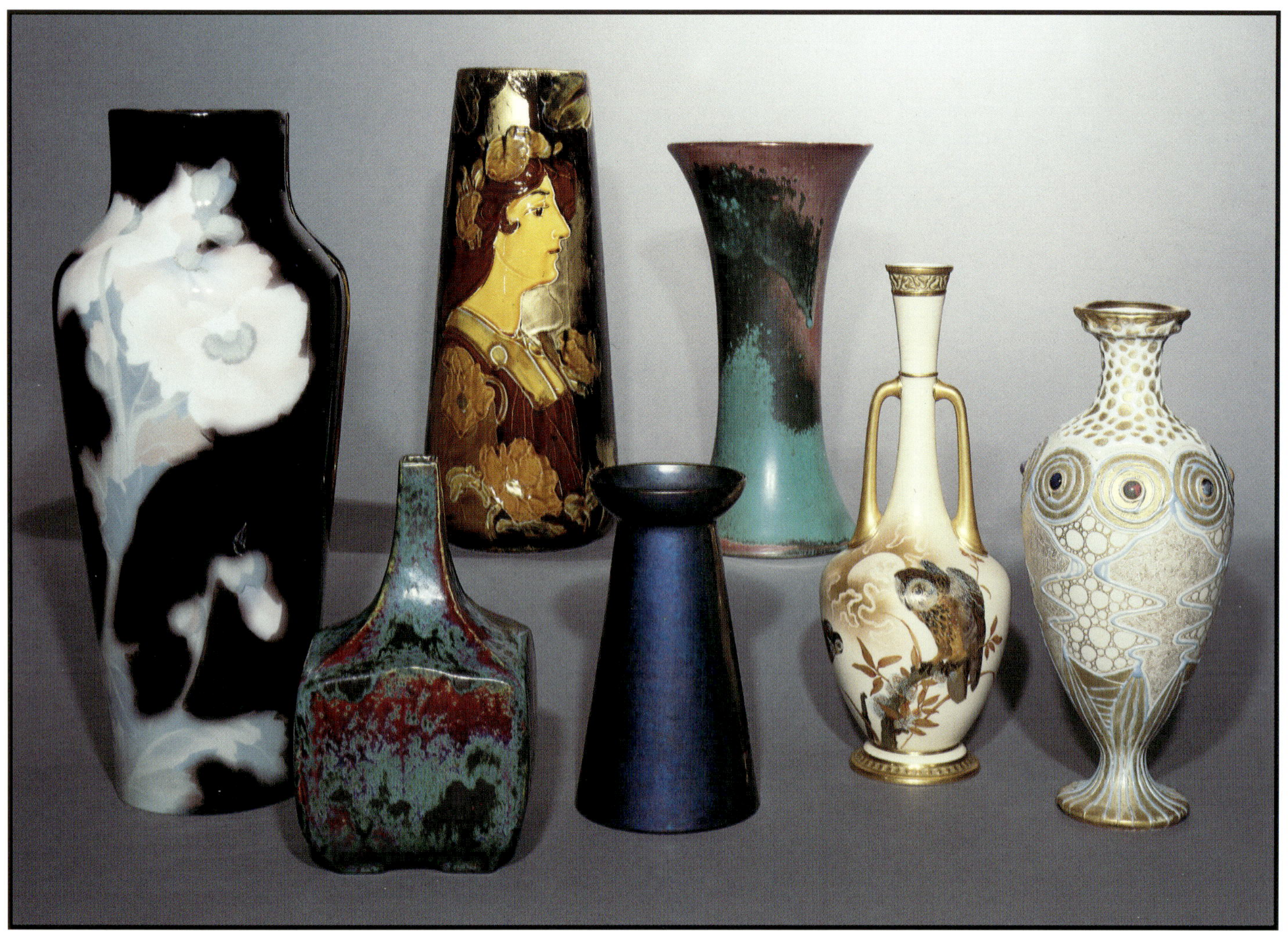

395	Tall and showy high glaze Rorstrand vase with pink and green poppies on a black ground, painted in 1904 by Algot Erikson. Marked with the inkstamp "Rorstrand" logo and the artist's initials, painted on in green slip. Also marked on the base is the notation "Algot Erikson Rorstrand 1904" painted on in gold. Height 16 1/2 inches. A 1/2 by 3/4 inch base chip has been professionally repaired.	$1000-1500
396	Good Dalpayrat four-sided lamp vase done in a rich mat red, purple, black and teal Chinese-style glaze. Impressed "Dalpayrat Made in France" and "310". Height 8 5/8 inches. There is a cast hole in the base.	$500-700
397	Forrester's & Son Phoenixware vase with embossed decoration of an Art Nouveau woman in multiple colors under a clear high glaze with fired-on gold highlights. Unmarked. Height 14 1/8 inches. Made in England circa 1910.	$400-600
398	Zsolnay vase done in metallic glaze in shades of blue, red and purple. The base is marked with Zsolnay Pecs transfer logo and the notation "Made in Hungary". Height 7 3/4 inches.	$200-300
399	Handsome Rambervillers corset-shaped vase done in wonderful luster mauve glaze over dark green gloss and medium green mat glazes, all of which flow and mingle and do strange and wonderful things. Impressed "Gres de a Cetere Rambervillers". Height 12 1/8 inches.	$400-600
400	Tall Royal Worchester two-handled vase, circa 1883, with exacting decoration of owls, one perched and the other flying under a cloudy, moonlit sky. Swallows cavort on the back side of the vase. Slip trailing in a greenish-white slip is used to highlight the owls. Fired-on gold is used on the handles, collar and foot. Marks include the impressed and inkstamped Royal Worcester logos, the numbers "850" and "U7" and the initials "C.F.", most likely those of the artist. Height 12 1/2 inches.	$700-900
401	Unusual Amphora vase decorated with much fired-on gold in geometric patterns and lots of outlining done with slip trailed white glaze. Around the shoulder of the vase are eight ceramic cabochons in different colors, which mimic semi-precious stones. Marks include the name "Amphora" and impressed crown and impressed numbers "2023" and "41". Height 11 3/4 inches. Very modern and very clean.	$400-600

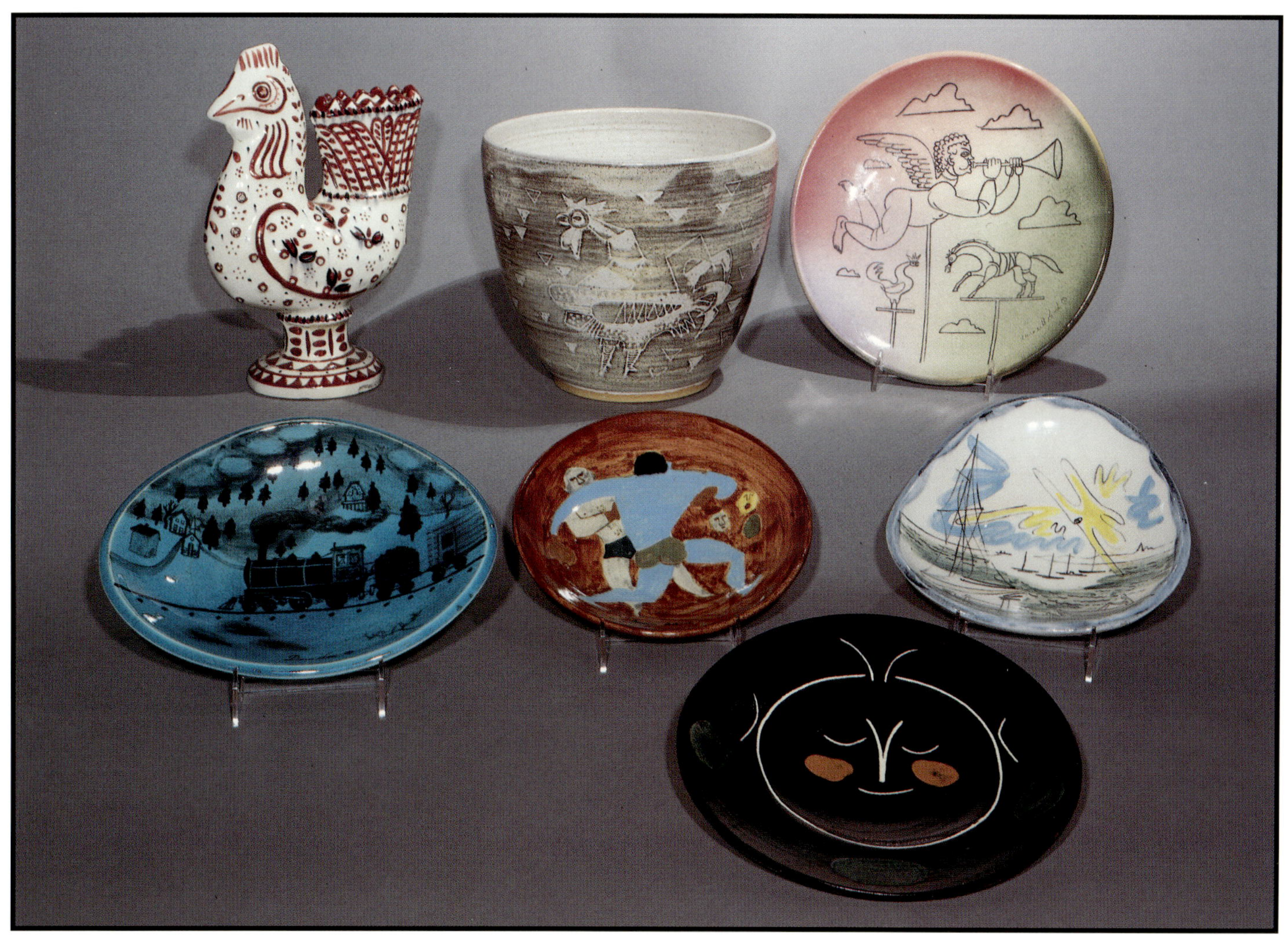

402   Stonelain irregularly shaped bowl with a scene designed by Doris Lee, noted Woodstock, New York artist. In $700-900
        typical Doris Lee fashion, a steam train passes through a small village while birds roost on a bare tree. Lee's
        work has a deceptive simplicity which belies her wonderful ability as a story teller. Her paintings are in great
        demand. The artist's name appears on the front of the bowl and the impressed Stonelain logo appears on the
        reverse.

403   Stonelain chicken designed by Carl Walters. Done in a gloss finish, the white porcelain body, is outlined and $800-1200
        enhanced with maroon. Marked on the base with the impressed Stonelain logo and Walters' signature. Walters
        is well known for his whimsical three dimensional animal sculpture. That he did a piece for Stonelain only
        makes sense. Height 10 7/8 inches. There is a minor glaze flake off the chicken's tail.

404   Large high glaze ceramic vessel with incised and painted roosters and triangles designed by Aaron Bohrod and $300-400
        executed by noted potter F. Carlton Ball. Hand signed by both Ball and Bohrod on the base. Height 8 inches
        and diameter at the rim is 9 1/2 inches. Ball and Bohrod collaborated on a wide range of pots in the early
        1950's. Most of the works were based on sketches made by Bohrod and several dozens of vessels were
        produced. Both Ball and Bohrod were instructors at Southern Illinois University at Carbondale during the period
        when the school employed Buckminster Fuller.

405   Early Stonelain plate decorated by noted artist Aaron Bohrod in the early 1940's. Bohrod has given us a $1250-1500
        wonderful period image of two beefy prize fighters sizing each other up while people at ringside look on with
        apparent boredom. The plate is done in high glaze with Bohrod's full name painted on the front in black slip.
        The reverse offers an unusual set of markings. A crudely incised palette contains the letters "AAA" and "SS".
        The AAA of course stands for Stonelain's parent company, Associated American Artists, which produced prints
        by famous American painters from the early 30's to the present. The SS most likely refers to Master Potters
        William Soini and Frances Server who were in charge of production and technical aspects at Stonelain.
        Diameter is 8 3/8 inches.

406   Picasso "Face" plate in orange, green and white slip on a semi- gloss black ground. Impressed "Madoura Plein $600-800
        Feu" and "D'Apres Picasso" on the reverse. Also painted on the reverse in black slip is the notation "Edition
        Picasso A". Diameter 9 1/2 inches.

407   Colorful Stonelain charger designed by Aaron Bohrod in the 1940's. Shown are three weathervanes and a few $600-800
        puffy clouds. The central weathervane figure is most likely Saint Gabriel blowing his horn. Bracketing Gabe is
        one of Bohrod's patented roosters and a race horse. Marked with the impressed Stonelain logo on the reverse
        and Bohrod's signature in the lower right hand corner of the charger. Diameter is 10 5/8 inches.

408   Stonelain porcelain bowl in high glaze decorated with a scene of sailboats at dockside under a blazing sun, the $400-500
        work of noted American artist Joe Jones. Originally from St. Louis, Jones is best known for his regionalist
        works. This piece for Stonelain is very modern in concept, reminiscent of John Marin. Marked with the Stone-
        lain logo on the reverse and Jones' signature in the lower center of the front. Greatest distance across is 8 1/4
        inches.

ROOKWOOD VII
SUNDAY
JUNE 8TH
1997
LOTS 500-1010

10% Buyers Premium
will be added to all lots purchased

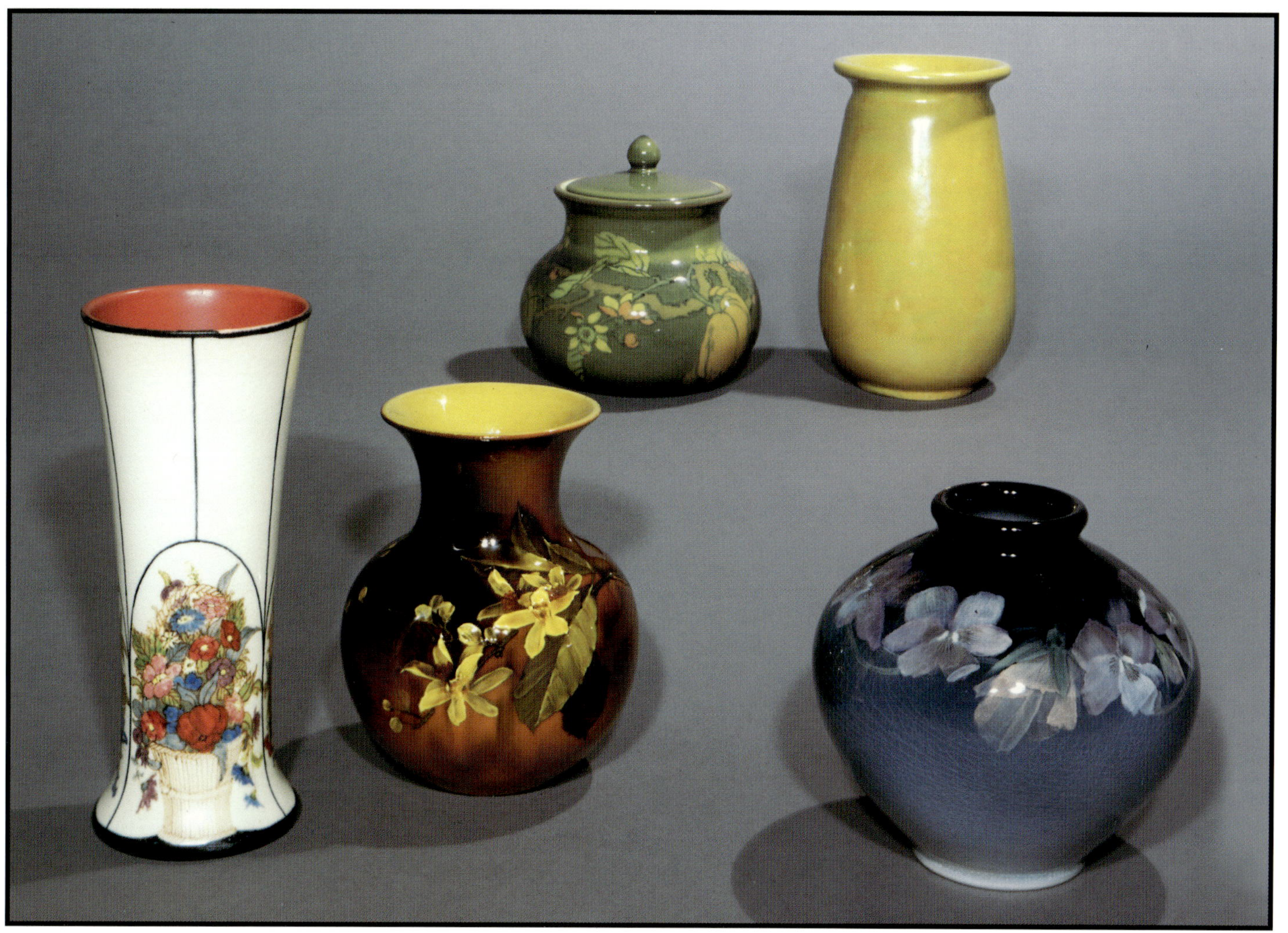

| 500 | Very unusual Vellum glaze vase done in 1922 by Sara Sax. The vase is divided by black lines into three panels. Within each panel is found a basket loaded with a variety of flowers. While the baskets are basically alike, each grouping of flowers is completely different. Marks include the Rookwood logo, the date, shape number 1357 E, an incised V for Vellum glaze and the incised monogram of the artist. Height 7 5/8 inches. Strong color and very fine detail. | $800-1000 |

501 — Nicely painted Standard glaze vase with floral decoration, done by William McDonald in 1891. Marks include the Rookwood logo, the date, shape number 402, an impressed W for white clay, an incised L for light Standard glaze and the incised initials of the artist. Height 5 5/8 inches. — $400-500

502 — High glaze lidded scent jar decorated by Arthur Conant in 1921. Pictured are vines, leaves, flowers and some unusual orange colored fruit. Marks include the Rookwood logo, the date, shape number 478 and the incised monogram of the artist. Height 5 inches. Uncrazed and very crisp. — $2000-2500

503 — Nacreous glaze vase in mustard with luster highlights made at Rookwood in 1915. Impressed marks include the Rookwood logo, the date, shape number 1910 and a Y. Height 6 5/8 inches. — $400-500

504 — Iris glaze vase with purple and gold pansies against a cobalt blue ground painted in 1902 by Constance Baker. Marks include the Rookwood logo, the date, shape number 964 C and the incised initials of the artist. Height 5 1/8 inches. — $1250-1750

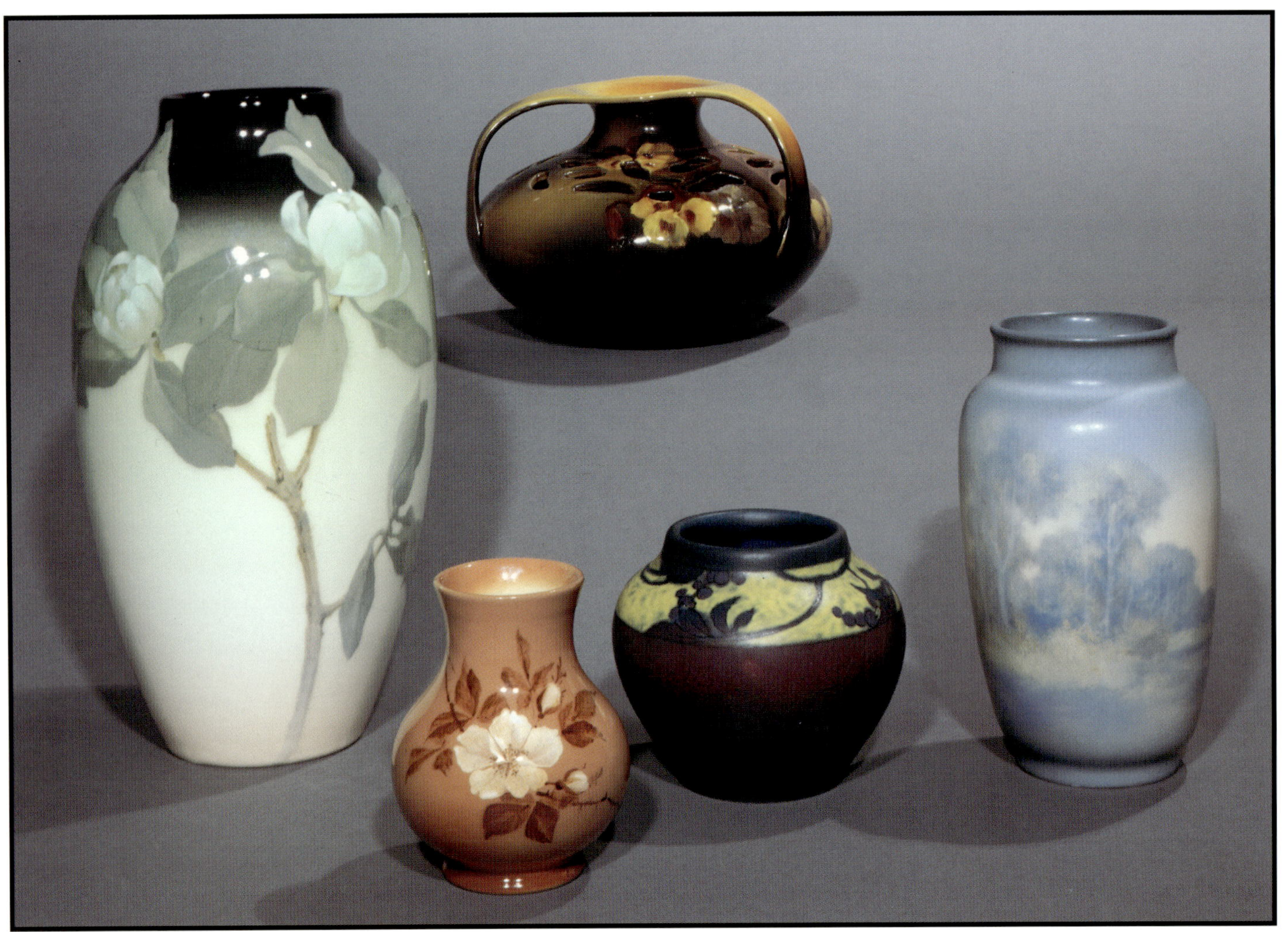

505   Tasteful Iris glaze vase with nicely applied magnolia decoration, done in 1908 by Irene Bishop. Impressed marks $2500-3500
include the Rookwood logo, the date, shape number 900 C, an incised W for white (Iris) glaze and the incised
monogram of the artist. Height 8 1/8 inches. Very slight amount of crazing restricted to some of the slip
decorated areas.

506   Cameo glaze vase with wild rose decoration done by an unknown artist in 1887. Marks include the incised date $150-200
and the painted-on letter "W" for white (Cameo) glaze. Also incised in the base is what appears to be the name
"Mazy Barnum". Size is 3 1/8 inches. This piece may have been made as a gift for Ms. Barnum, hence her
incised name and the absence of other Rookwood marks. Uncrazed.

507   Standard glaze vase with three handles and reticulation under the handles, decorated with yellow and blue $500-700
pansies by Emma Foertmeyer in 1892. Marks include the Rookwood logo, the date, shape number 503 B, W for
white clay and the incised initials of the artist. Height 4 3/8 inches. Pictured: Rookwood Its Golden Era of Art
Pottery 1880-1929 by Kircher and Agranoff, color plate 6, row two, number three. Good work and an unusual
shape.

508   Snappy Painted Mat vase done in 1910 by Fred Rothenbusch. The rim and lower portion of the vase are painted $1000-1250
colors reminiscent of Van Briggle's Persian Rose. Around the shoulder is a yellow band on which are painted
purple and maroon Virginia creeper flowers, vines and berries. Marks include the Rookwood logo, the date,
shape number 890 F, an impressed V for Vellum glaze body and the artist's monogram, painted on in dark slip.
Height 2 7/8 inches.

509   Small but extraordinary Vellum glaze scenic vase painted by E.T. Hurley in 1938. Pictured is a finely detailed $1000-1500
woodland scene with tall Summer trees reflecting in a lake in the foreground. Marks include the Rookwood
logo, the date, shape 6730 and the incised initials of the artist. Height 5 1/4 inches. Uncrazed and extremely
crisp and clean.

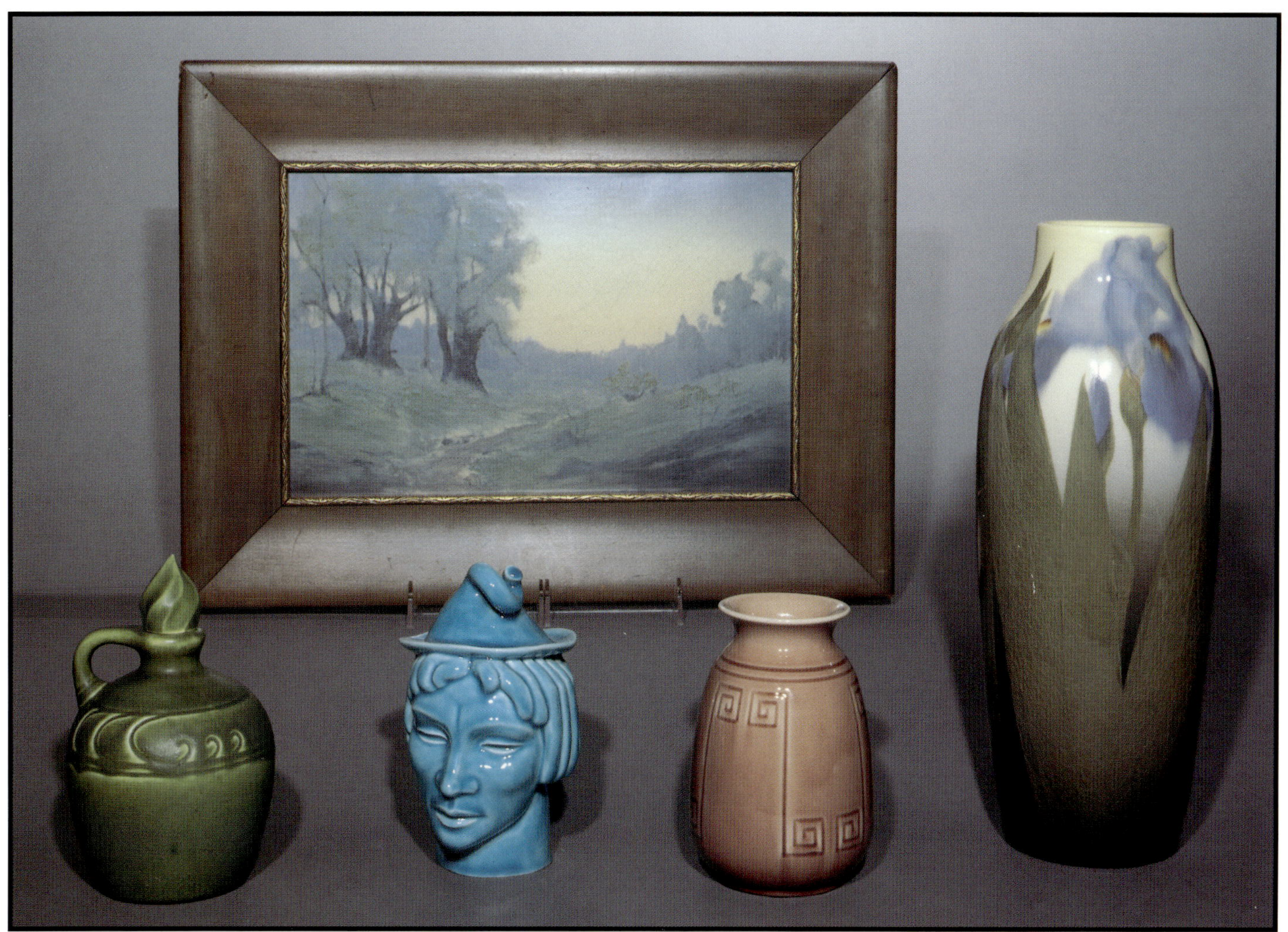

510   Arts & Crafts style mat glaze stoppered whiskey jug with incised patterns around the shoulder, made at Rookwood in 1904. Impressed marks include the Rookwood logo, the date and shape number 512 C. Height 7 3/8 inches. $400-500

511   Large Vellum glaze scenic plaque painted in 1919 by Lorinda Epply. Epply's monogram appears in the lower right hand corner. Marks on the back include the Rookwood logo and the date. An original Rookwood typewritten label on the frame carries the title, "Dawn L. Eppley (sic)". Size is approximately 9 1/4 by 14 1/2 inches. Original frame. $4000-5000

512   Rare Art Deco figural piece designed by David Seyler and made at Rookwood in 1938. The head of a young person with a hat is covered in a blue high glaze. Marks include the Rookwood logo, the date and shape number 2724 which should actually be 6724. Height 7 inches. Seyler worked at Rookwood as a student before joining Harold Bopp at Kenton Hills Porcelains in Erlanger, Kentucky. His sculptural pieces from the late 30's are very fresh and this one is seldom seen. $400-600

513   High glaze vase with incised geometric decoration done by Earl Menzel in 1951. Marks include the Rookwood logo, the date, S for Special shape and the incised monogram of the artist. Height 6 inches. Uncrazed. $300-500

514   Tall Iris glaze vase with large blue iris flowers and buds painted in 1903 by Carl Schmidt. Marks include the Rookwood logo, the date, shape number 932 B, an incised W for white (Iris) glaze and the impressed monogram of the artist. Height 14 3/8 inches. A two inch long crack descending from the rim and a small flake off the base have been professionally repaired. $2500-3000

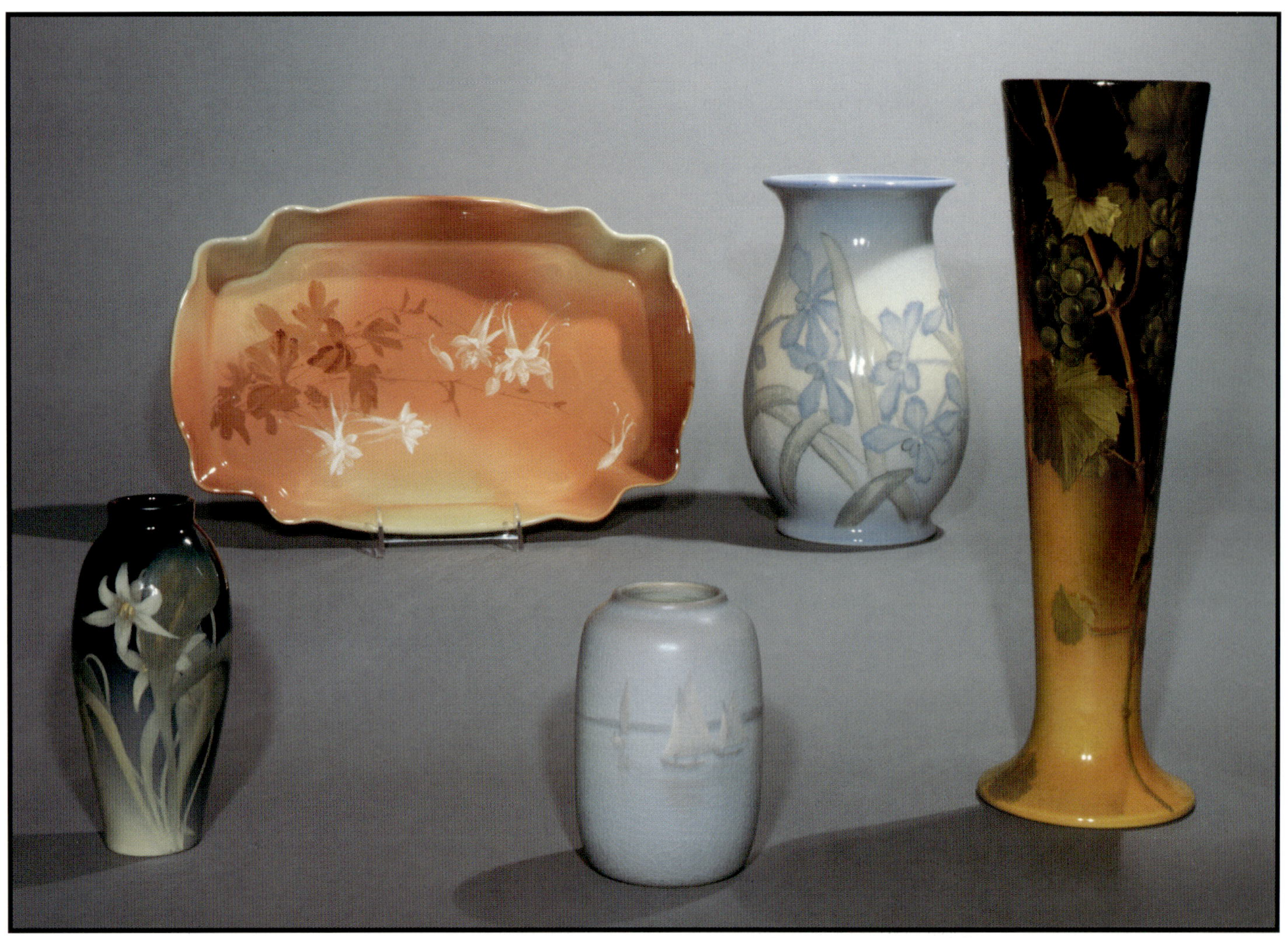

515   Pretty high glaze vase with star flower decoration done in 1900 by Rose Fechheimer. Marks include the Rookwood logo, the date, shape number 901 D, an incised W for white (Iris) glaze and the incised monogram of the artist. Height 6 3/4 inches. Although clearly marked by the artist to be coated with Iris glaze, the vase has the look of Sea Green from its blue-green top to its pale green lower regions. The bottom of the piece looks fairly clear although it might have a very pale greenish cast. In any event, it's an attractive example of Fechheimer's work. $2000-2500

516   Cameo glaze tray with floral decoration on a coral ground painted in 1890 by Grace Young. Impressed marks include the Rookwood logo, the date, shape number 289 and W for white clay. Incised marks include the artist's monogram and W for white (Cameo) glaze. Greatest distance across is 14 1/4 inches. $400-600

517   Charming Vellum glaze scenic vase with four pink sailboats on the water, done in 1912 by Sara Sax. Marks include the Rookwood logo, the date, shape number 1373, an impressed V for Vellum glaze body, an incised V for Vellum glaze and the impressed monogram of the artist. Height 5 3/8 inches. $800-1000

518   High glaze vase with blue floral decoration by Kataro Shirayamadani, done in 1946. Impressed marks include the Rookwood logo, the date and shape number 2782. Incised are the artist's initials and the number 6323. Height 9 1/2 inches. $1000-1250

519   Tall Standard glaze vase of special form with rich and colorful grape decoration done in 1895 by Kataro Shirayamadani. Marks include the Rookwood logo, the date, Special shape number S 1172 and the incised cypher of the artist. Height 15 1/4 inches. A good large form with exacting art work. $3000-4000

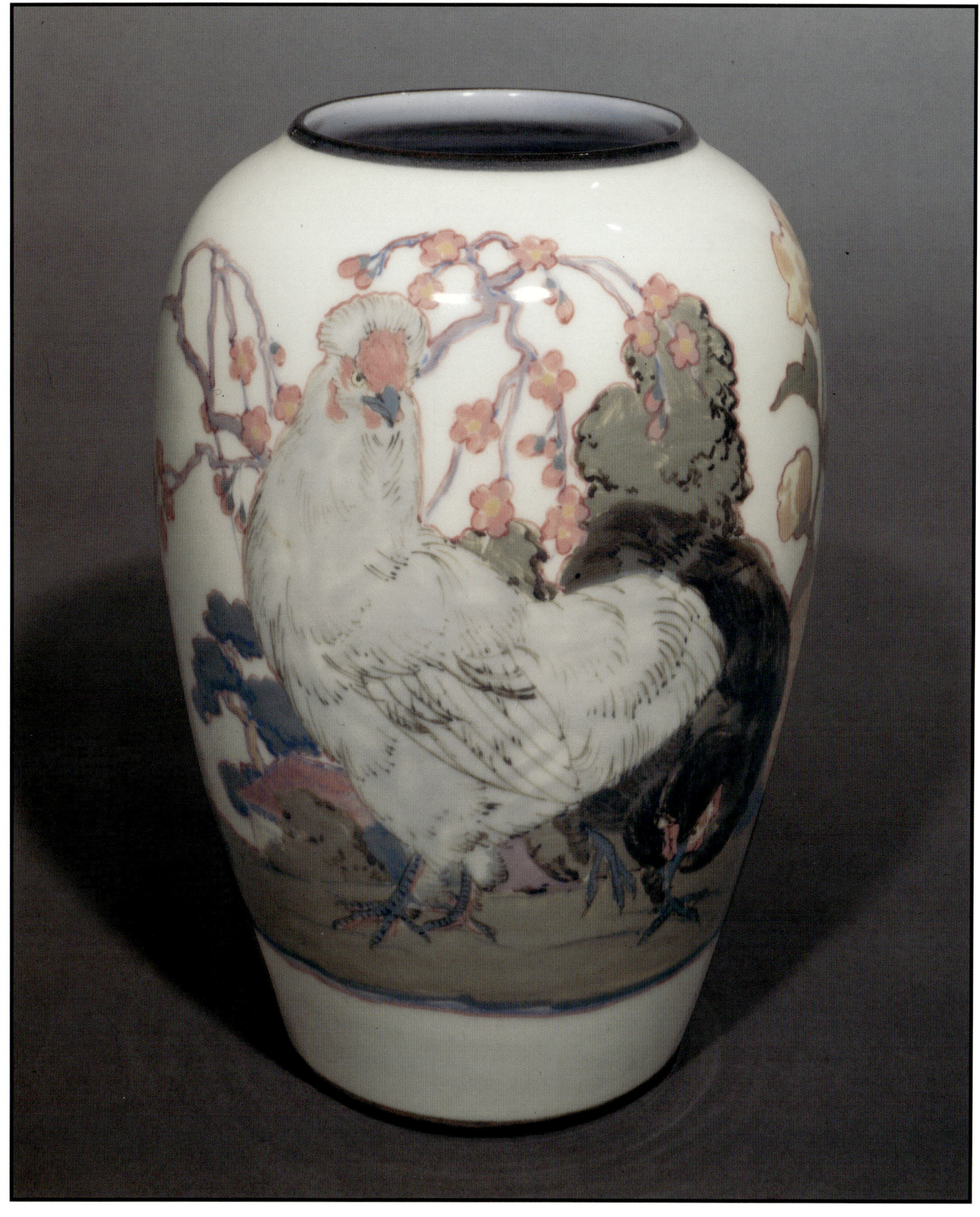

520   Exceptional scenic vase done in high glaze by Arthur Conant in 1919. Always unpredictable, Conant has $7000-9000
created a very Japanesque scene consisting of two chickens, one white one black, in a setting comprised of
blossoming cherry trees, blooming exotic flowers, a bridge and two large buildings among tall trees. As usual,
Conant's palette is bold and quite varied. Marks include the Rookwood logo, the date, shape number 999 C
and the incised monogram of the artist. Height 9 inches. Uncrazed and very clean.

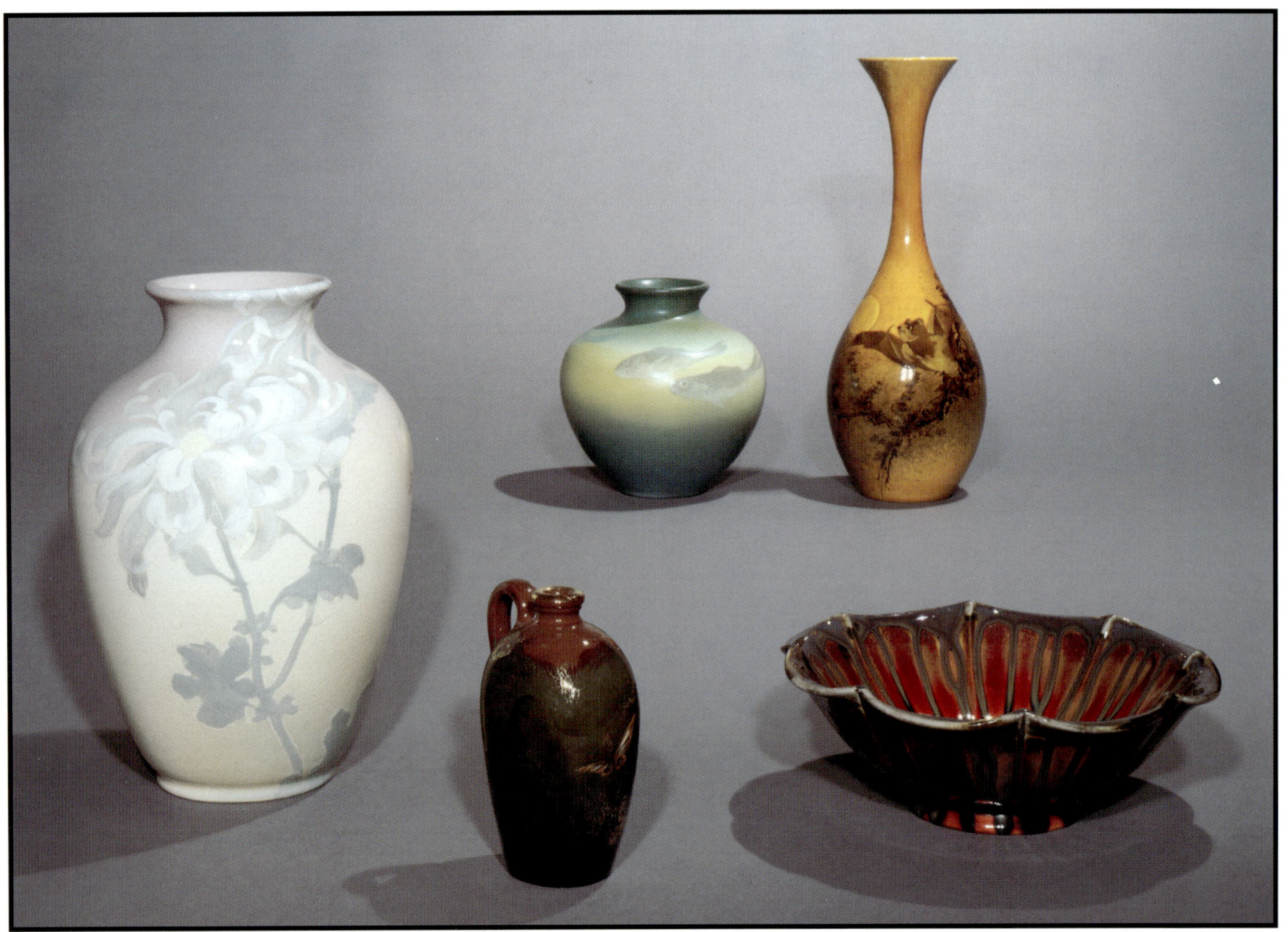

| 521 | Incised and painted Iris glaze vase with bold chrysanthemum decoration done in 1898 by John Dee Wareham. Close examination reveals incised lines at the edges of the flowers and leaves which may have been done to keep colors in place or to give dimension to the slip decoration. The pale green leaves and stems are outlined in white slip to make them stand out even more. Marks include the Rookwood logo, the date, shape number 814 A, an arrow shaped esoteric mark and the incised initials of the artist. Done in typical pastel shades used by Wareham after his return from studies in Europe " | $2000-2500 |

| 522 | Flat side perfume jug in Limoges-style glaze, painted by an unknown artist in 1882. Decoration consists of a single butterfly and Oriental grasses highlighted with fired-on gold. Impressed marks include Rookwood in block letters, the date, shape number 60, R for red clay and a small kiln mark. Height 4 3/4 inches. | $200-250 |

| 523 | Good Vellum glaze vase with three finely detailed fish, done in 1906 by E.T. Hurley. Marks include the Rookwood logo, the date, shape number 1127, an impressed V for Vellum glaze body, an incised V for Vellum glaze and the incised initials of the artist. Height 5 1/4 inches. Besides being a nice example of Hurley's undersea art, this vase is a true prize winner. Inside the vase were found a paper tag and a paper scorecard from the Minnesota State Fair (year unknown). The scorecard gives the vase a 95 out of a possible 100 points. We concur. | $2000-2500 |

| 524 | Fluted bowl covered with rich Coromandel glaze made at Rookwood in 1932. Marks include the Rookwood logo, the date and shape number 6313. Height is 3 inches and diameter is 8 1/4 inches. | $300-400 |

| 525 | Standard glaze vase with speckled background painted in 1885 by Albert Valentien. Pictured is a toothy bat soaring over a pine bough while the full moon shines above. Impressed marks include Rookwood in block letters, the date, shape number 141, Y for yellow clay and the incised initials of the artist. Height 10 7/8 inches. A thumbnail size chip out of the rim has been glued in place. | $300-500 |

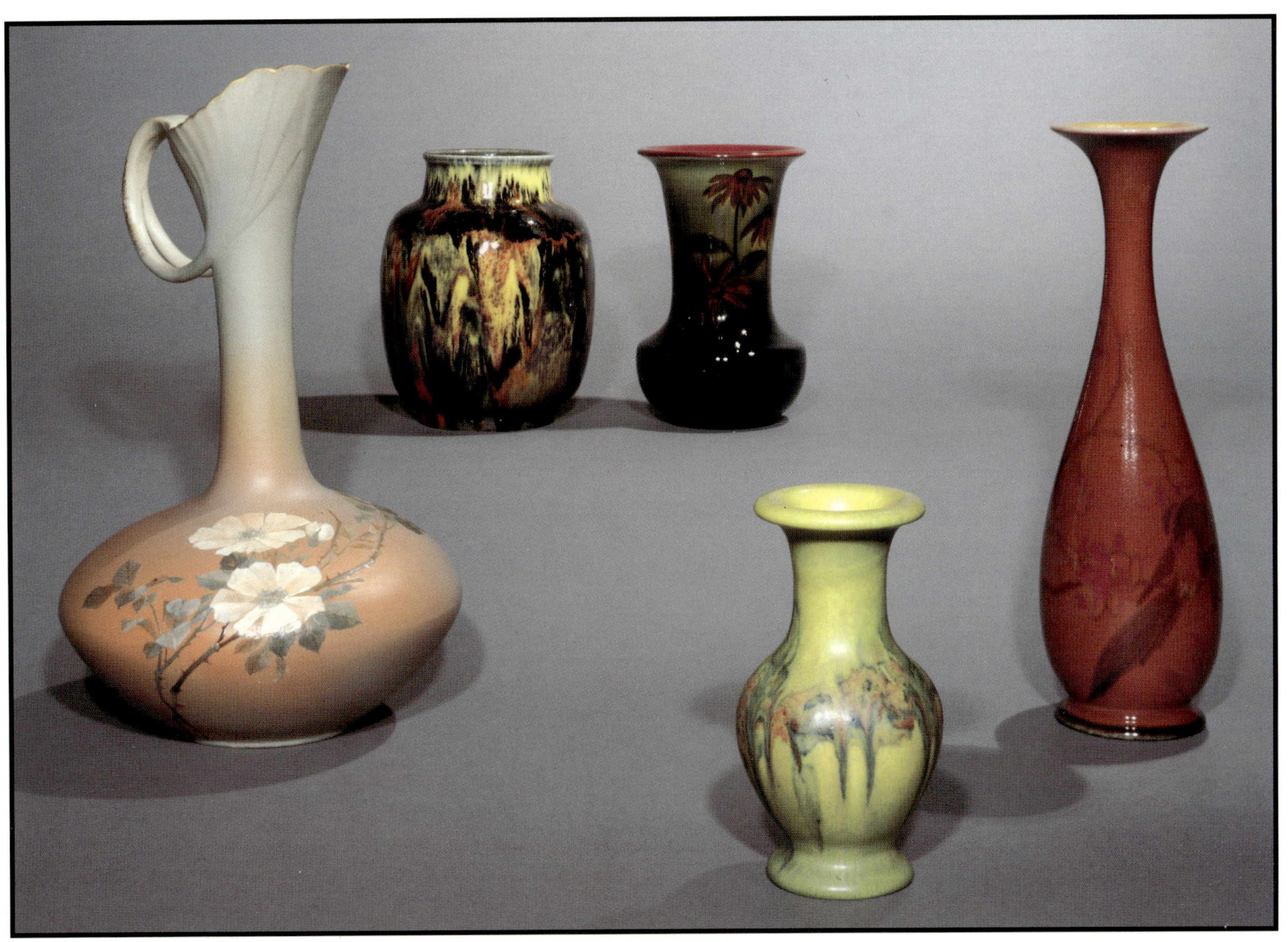

526 Beautiful dull finish ewer with elegant neck and spout, painted by Kataro Shirayamadani in 1889. Decoration is $1500-2000
     of precisely detailed wild roses on a soft salmon colored ground. The spout and handle are enhanced with
     fired-on gold. Marks include the Rookwood logo, the date, shape number 471 B, W for white clay, an incised S
     for smear (dull finish) glaze and the incised cypher of the artist. Height 11 5/8 inches. Very clean and crisp.

527 High glaze vase with abstract drip decoration done in 1930 by E.T. Hurley. Marks include the Rookwood logo, $400-600
     the date, shape number 2917 E, a fan shaped esoteric mark and the artist's initials, painted on in black slip.
     Height 6 1/4 inches. Uncrazed.

528 Yellow tinted high glaze vase with orange daisies on a ground shading from pale green to cobalt blue at the $1500-2000
     bottom, the work of Kataro Shirayamadani in 1925. The interior of the vase is lined in Shirayamadani's maroon
     glaze. Marks include the Rookwood logo, the date, shape number 2719, a wheel ground x and the incised
     cypher of the artist. Height 6 3/8 inches. A small spot of lost glaze on the rim has been professionally restored.

529 Mat glaze ribbed vase with floral decoration painted by Katherine Jones in 1927. Marks include the Rookwood $300-400
     logo, the date, shape number 2972 and the artist's initials painted on in blue slip. Height 5 1/2 inches.

530 High glaze vase painted in 1922 by Harriet Wilcox. Decoration consists of red flowers and black stems on a $800-1000
     reddish-brown background while an exotic bird perches in the flowers. The interior of the vase is done in a
     slightly lustrous glaze that resembles peachblow glass. Marks include the Rookwood logo, the date, shape
     number 2545 C and the incised initials of the artist. Height 10 1/2 inches. Uncrazed.

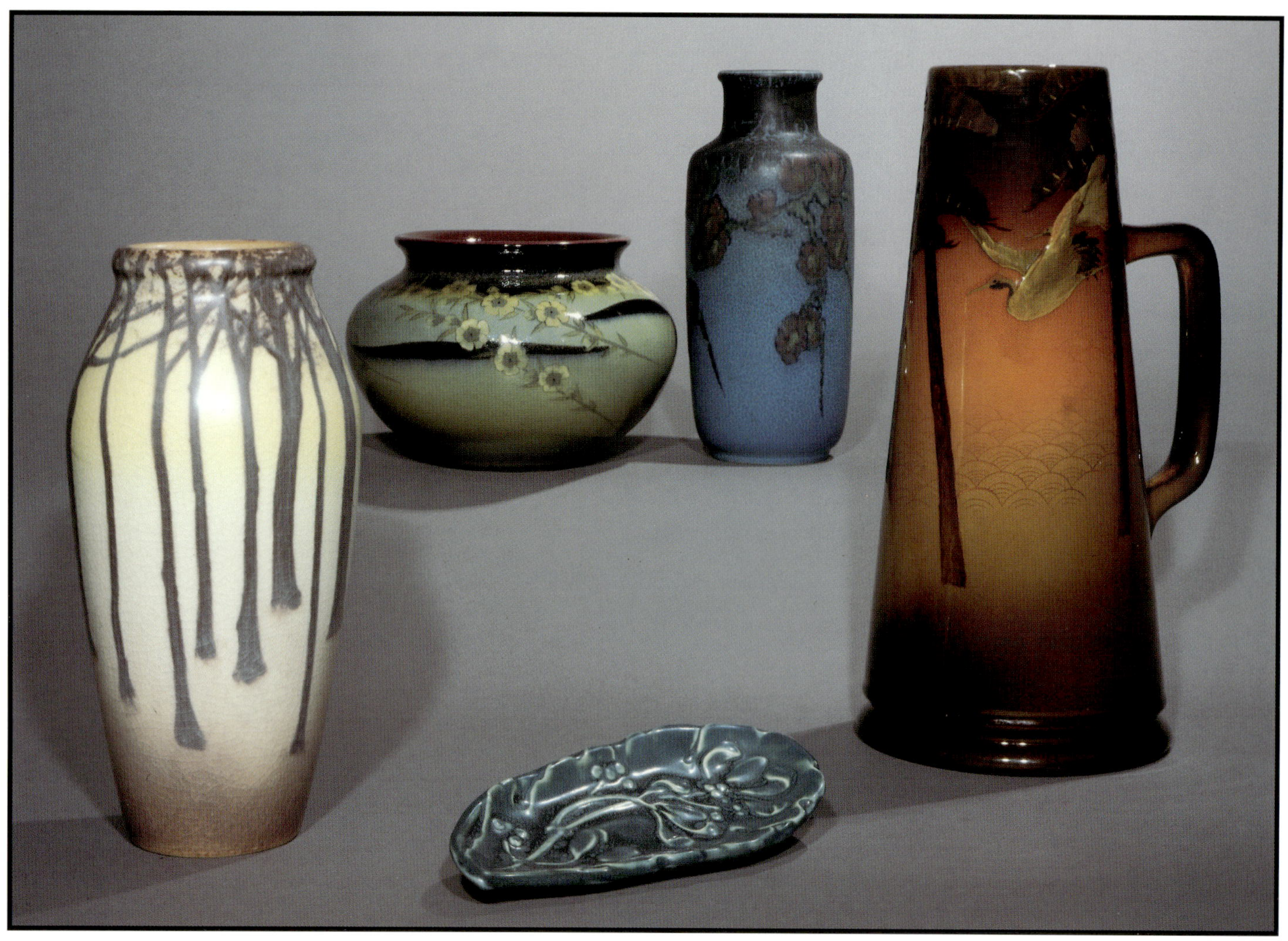

531   Unusual Vellum glaze landscape vase painted in 1908 by E.T. Hurley. The tall trunks of the trees are silhou- $1500-2000
etted against a lemon yellow sky and almost reach the rim before leaves appear. The perspective and
treatment are different and fun. Marks include the Rookwood logo, the date, shape number 925 D, an
impressed V for Vellum glaze body, an incised V for Vellum glaze and the incised initials of the artist. Height
8 1/2 inches.

532   High glaze vase with stylized yellow flowers around the shoulder, accented with long, thin black leaves. $1500-2000
Painted by Kataro Shirayamadani in 1925 the vase is lined with Sherry's Maroon. Marks include the Rookwood logo, the date, shape number 494 B and the incised cypher of the artist. Height is 4 3/4 inches and
diameter is 7 1/8 inches.

533   Interesting mat glaze card tray with embossed floral decoration made at Rookwood in 1920 for use as a $200-300
party invitation. Besides the usual Rookwood logo and date we find the incised notation "Mr. & Mrs. Harold
Willis Nichols At Home New Years Day Nineteen Hundred and Twenty One Four Until Seven". Length is 6 5/8
inches.

534   Bottle shaped mat glaze vase with stylized cherry blossoms painted in 1923 by Vera Tischler. $400-600
Marks include the Rookwood logo, the date, shape number 2528 and the artist's initials, painted on in dark
blue slip. Height 8 1/4 inches.

535   Handsome Standard glaze tankard done in an Arts & Crafts manner by Kataro Shirayamadani in 1897. Tall $2500-3500
pine trees seem to rise from stylized clouds while three cranes fly through the tops of the trees. Marks
include the Rookwood logo, the date, shape number 564 B, a diamond shaped esoteric mark and the incised
cypher of the artist. Height 11 1/4 inches. There is a tiny glaze nick off the rim and an unobtrusive line at mid
body on the back of the piece which does not appear on the inside.

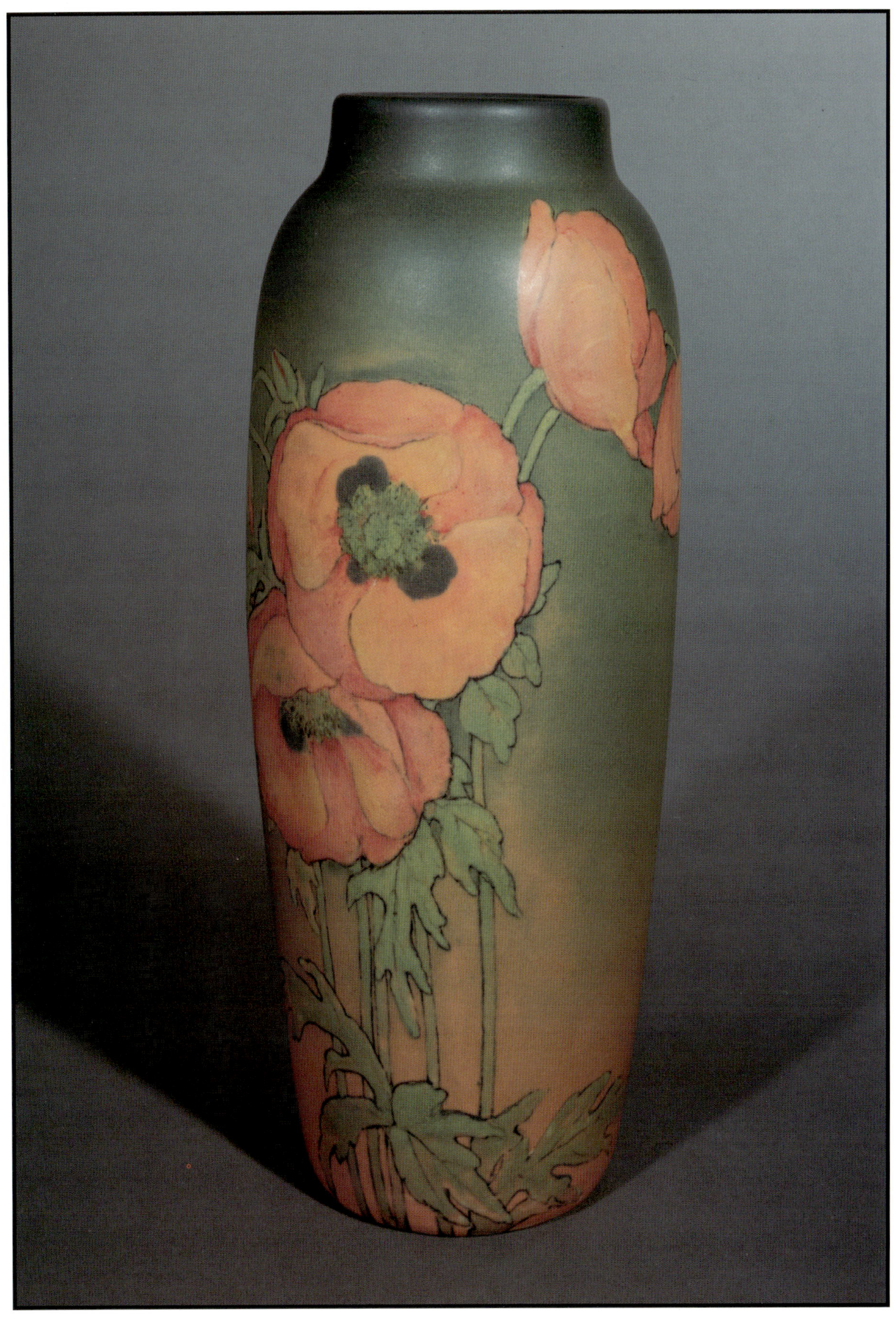

536   Exceptional Painted Mat vase done by Olga Geneva Reed in 1906. Pictured are bright red and orange $17500-22500
poppies on a dark green to salmon colored ground. All flowers, buds and leaves are cleanly outlined in black.
Marks include the Rookwood logo, the date, shape number 907 D and the artist's initials, painted on in black
slip. Height 10 5/8 inches. Crisp and clean with exceptional detail. Uncrazed. This is one of the finest Painted
Mat examples known to exist.

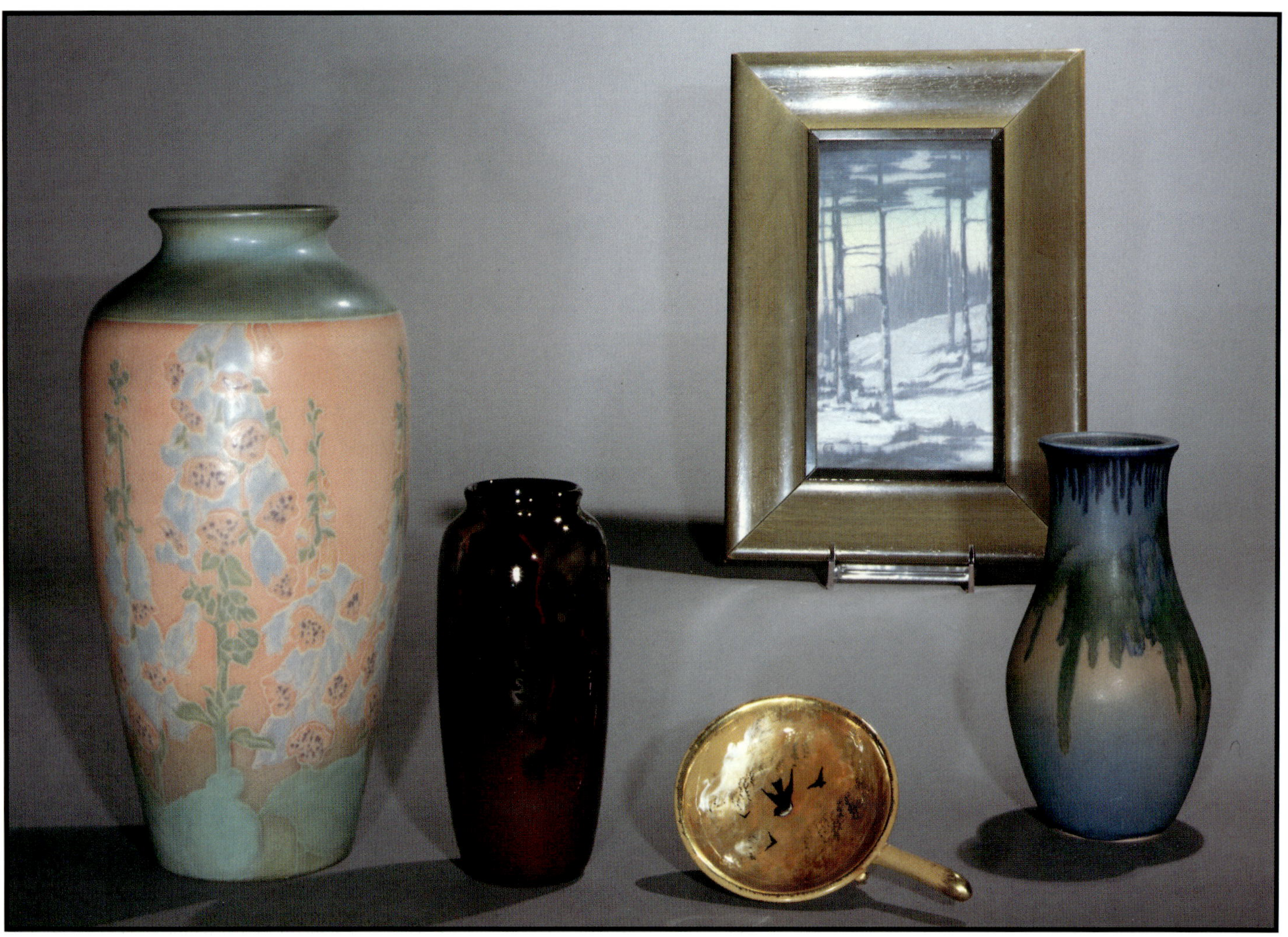

537   Vellum glaze vase with incised and painted flowers in pink, blue and green, done by C.S. Todd in 1916. The $1500-2000
        bluebell-like flowers are first outlined by incising, perhaps to keep the colors in place and then the colors are
        applied. Marks include the Rookwood logo, the date, shape number 614 C, V for Vellum glaze body, an
        incised V for Vellum glaze, a wheel ground x and the incised initials of the artist. A neat piece with flowers all
        the way around the body. Height 13 3/8 inches. There is a small spider crack confined only to the bottom of
        the vase and a pin-head size nick off the base. Neither of these are visible from the side.

538   Standard glaze vase with grape decoration by Edith Felten in 1903. Marks include the Rookwood logo, the $300-400
        date, shape number 904 D and the incised initials of the artist. Height 7 3/4 inches. A bit on the dark side and
        with minor glaze scratches.

539   Limoges style ramekin with flying birds and clouds done in 1882 by N.J. Hirschfeld. Marks include Rook- $200-300
        wood in block letters, the date, G for ginger clay, an impressed kiln mark and the incised initials of the artist.
        Length is 6 5/8 inches.

540   Good Arts & Crafts style Vellum glaze plaque painted in 1914 by Sallie Coyne. Shown is a snowy landscape $4500-5500
        with tall pine trees, Coyne's monogram is painted on the front of the plaque in the lower left hand corner.
        Impressed marks on the back include the Rookwood logo and the date. Affixed to the original frame is a
        typewritten title "A Cold Day S.E. Coyne". Size is approximately 9 by 5 inches.

541   Bottle shaped mat glaze vase with abstract floral decoration and drip glaze at the rim, done in 1926 by $300-400
        Elizabeth Lincoln. Marks include the Rookwood logo, the date, shape number 2885 and the initials of the
        artist painted on in blue slip. Height 8 3/8 inches.

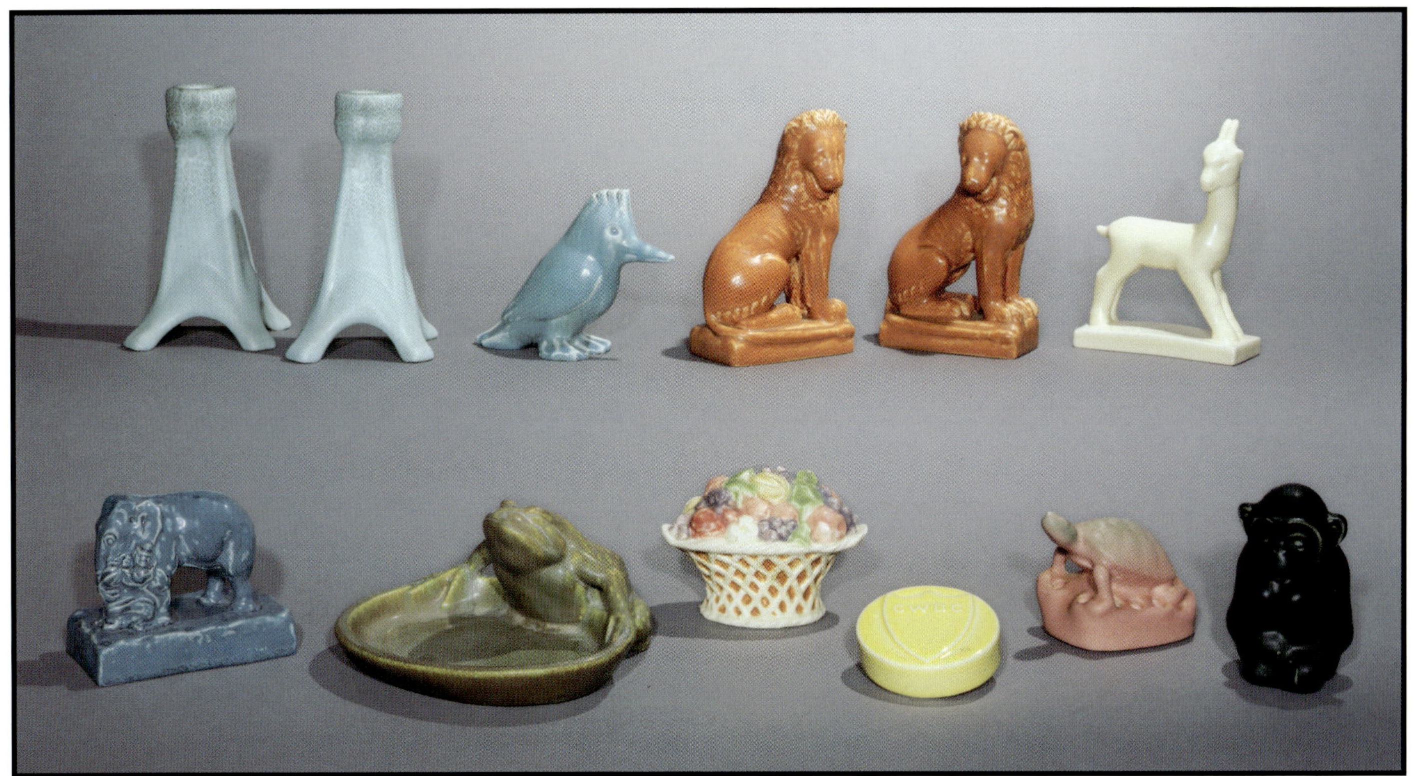

542   Rare blue mat glaze elephant and clown paperweight made at Rookwood in 1922. There are two clowns, one on either side of the elephant's head. Marks include the Rookwood logo, the date and shape number 2628. Height 3 1/2 inches. $300-400

543   Pair of Arts & Crafts style candlesticks in mottled blue mat glaze made at Rookwood in 1921. Marks include the Rookwood logo, the date, shape number 1194 and a wheel ground x. Height 6 7/8 inches. $200-300

544   Mat glaze frog pintray made at Rookwood in 1935. The glaze should be called Frogskin 'cause that's what it looks like. Impressed marks include the Rookwood logo, the date and shape number 2602. Height is 3 1/4 inches. $400-500

545   Art Deco kingfisher paperweight in blue mat glaze made at Rookwood in 1931. Marks include the Rookwood logo, the date, shape number 6277 and the cast-in monogram of designer, Louise Abel. Height 4 3/8 inches. $350-450

546   Polychromed fruit basket paperweight made at Rookwood in 1927. Impressed marks include the Rookwood logo, the date, shape number 6020 and the monogram of designer, Sallie Toohey. Height 3 1/8 inches. Two small glaze nicks on high points. $300-400

547   Pair of mat glaze Art Deco lions designed by Louise Abel and made at Rookwood in 1929. Marks include the Rookwood logo, the date, shape number 6019 and Abel's cast-in monogram. Height of each is 6 1/2 inches. Nice reddish-tan glaze and an uncommon form. $400-600

548   Yellow high glaze paperweight made at Rookwood in 1949. Embossed on the front is a shield with the letters "CWBC". Marks on the back include the Rookwood logo and the date. Diameter is 2 7/8 inches. Uncrazed. $150-200

549   Rare Rookwood turtle flower frog made in 1930 and done in green over pink mat glazes. Marks include the Rookwood logo, the date and shape number 2994. Height 2 7/8 inches. $400-500

550   White semi-gloss glaze goat paperweight made at Rookwood in 1930. Marks include the Rookwood logo, the date, shape number 6170, a fan shaped esoteric mark and the cast-in monogram of designer, Louise Abel. Height 6 1/4 inches. $200-300

551   Dark green mat glaze monkey paperweight made at Rookwood in 1929. Marks include the Rookwood logo, the date and shape number 6084. Height 4 3/8 inches. $400-500

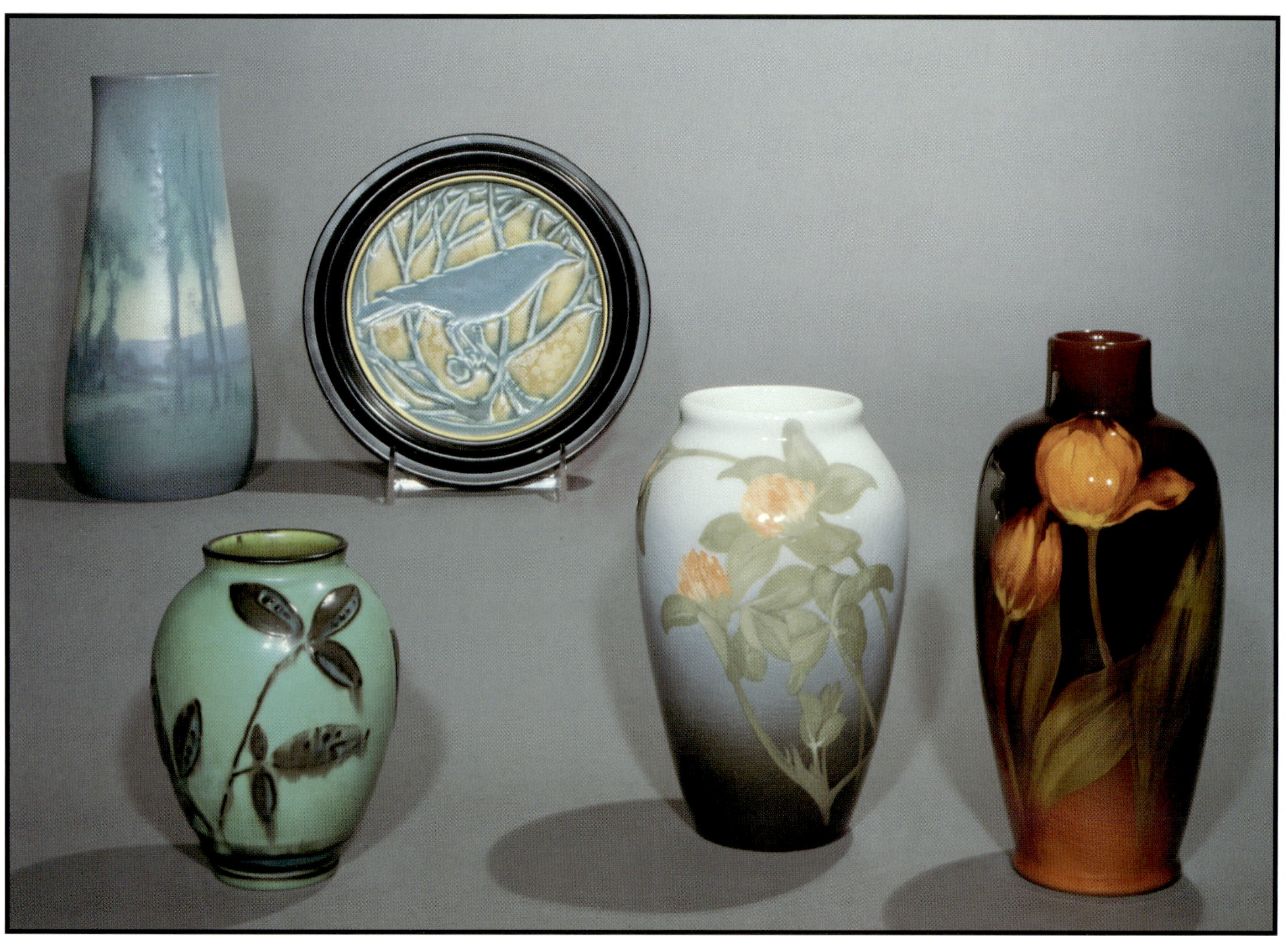

552   Vellum glaze landscape painted in 1915 by Lorinda Epply. Marks include the Rookwood logo, the date, shape $1000-1500
number 950 D, an impressed V for Vellum glaze body, an incised V for Vellum glaze and the incised monogram of the artist. Height 9 inches. There is a fair amount of peppering in the glaze.

553   Mat glaze vase with Art Deco leaves, painted and outlined by slip trailing in 1930 by Elizabeth Barrett. Marks $400-500
include the Rookwood logo, the date, shape number 2191, a fan shaped esoteric mark and the incised
monogram of the artist. height 5 1/8 inches.

554   Circular mat glaze trivet showing a blue bird in a tree, made at Rookwood in 1919. Marks include the $400-500
Rookwood logo, the date and shape number 2349. Diameter is 6 inches. Good color and nice, slightly
crystalline glaze.

555   Pretty Iris glaze vase with bright red clover decoration done in 1903 by Marianne Mitchell. Impressed marks $2500-3000
include the Rookwood logo, the date and shape number 913 D. Incised marks include the artist's monogram
and W for white (Iris) glaze. Height 7 1/8 inches. There is a faint spider line on the inside of the vase which is
not visible on the front. Nice color and contrast.

556   Standard glaze vase with bright red tulips painted in 1899 by Edith Felten. Marks include the Rookwood logo, $400-600
the date, shape number 786 D and the incised initials of the artist. Height 8 3/8 inches. Some glaze scratches
and burst glaze bubbles.

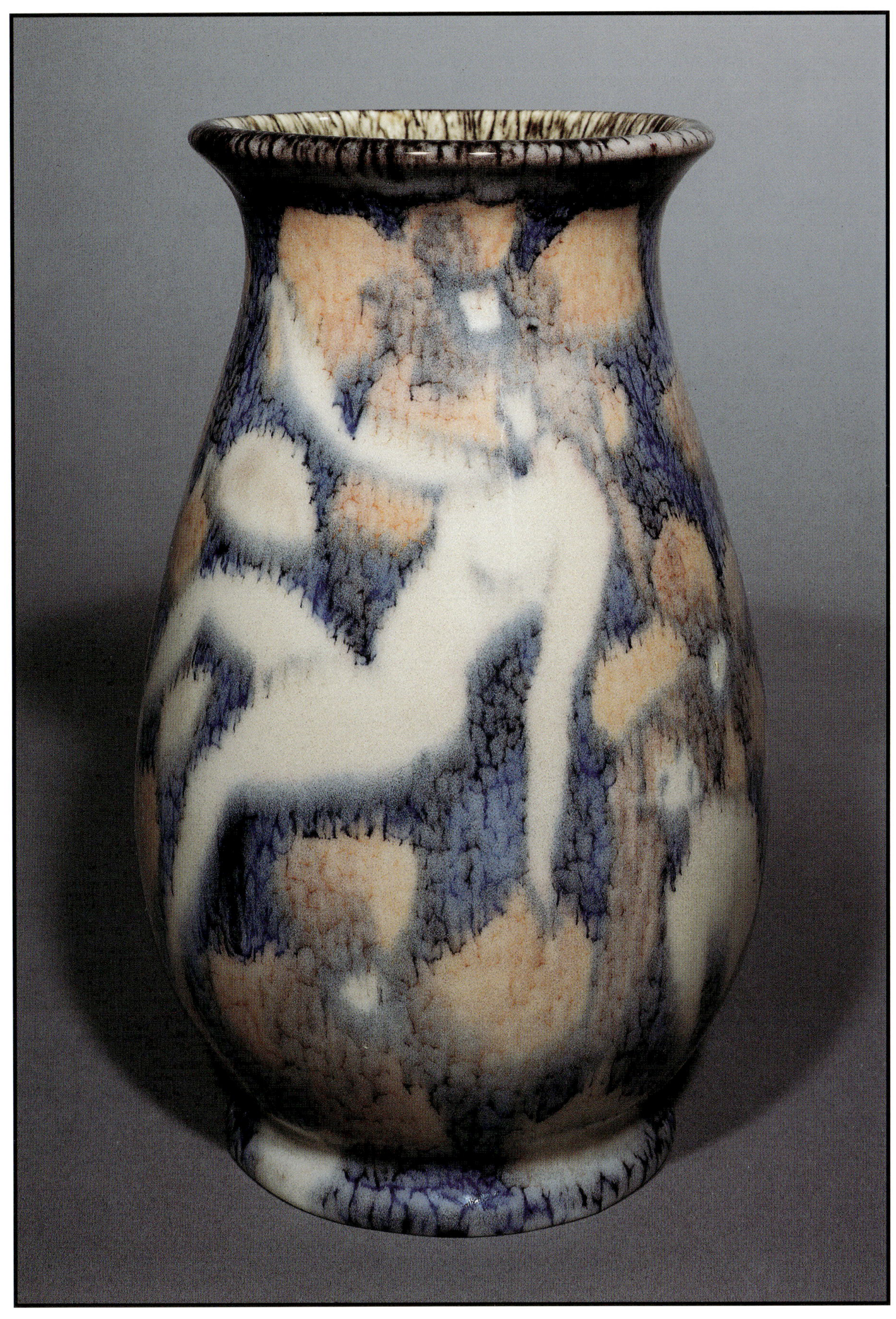

557   Rare and important high glaze vase with overall decoration of four female nudes and large blossoms done by $10000-12500
Jens Jensen in 1927. Jensen officially began his tenure at Rookwood in 1928, so this is one of his first efforts.
Flowers and nudes cover most of the surface in a complex yet subtle relationship. The interior of the vase is
covered with a mottled gray glaze which extends down the rim about 1/2 inch. Jensen, fresh from Europe, is
also influenced by the Art Deco ceramics of French arts, Rene' Buthaud, Jean Mayodon and Edouard Cazaux.
Marks include the Rookwood logo, the date, shape number 2782 and the painted-on monogram of the artist.
Height 9 5/8 inches. Uncrazed and extremely clean. Exhibited: Rookwood Pottery The Glorious Gamble,
Cincinnati Art Museum, 1992. Color plate 91 on page 156.

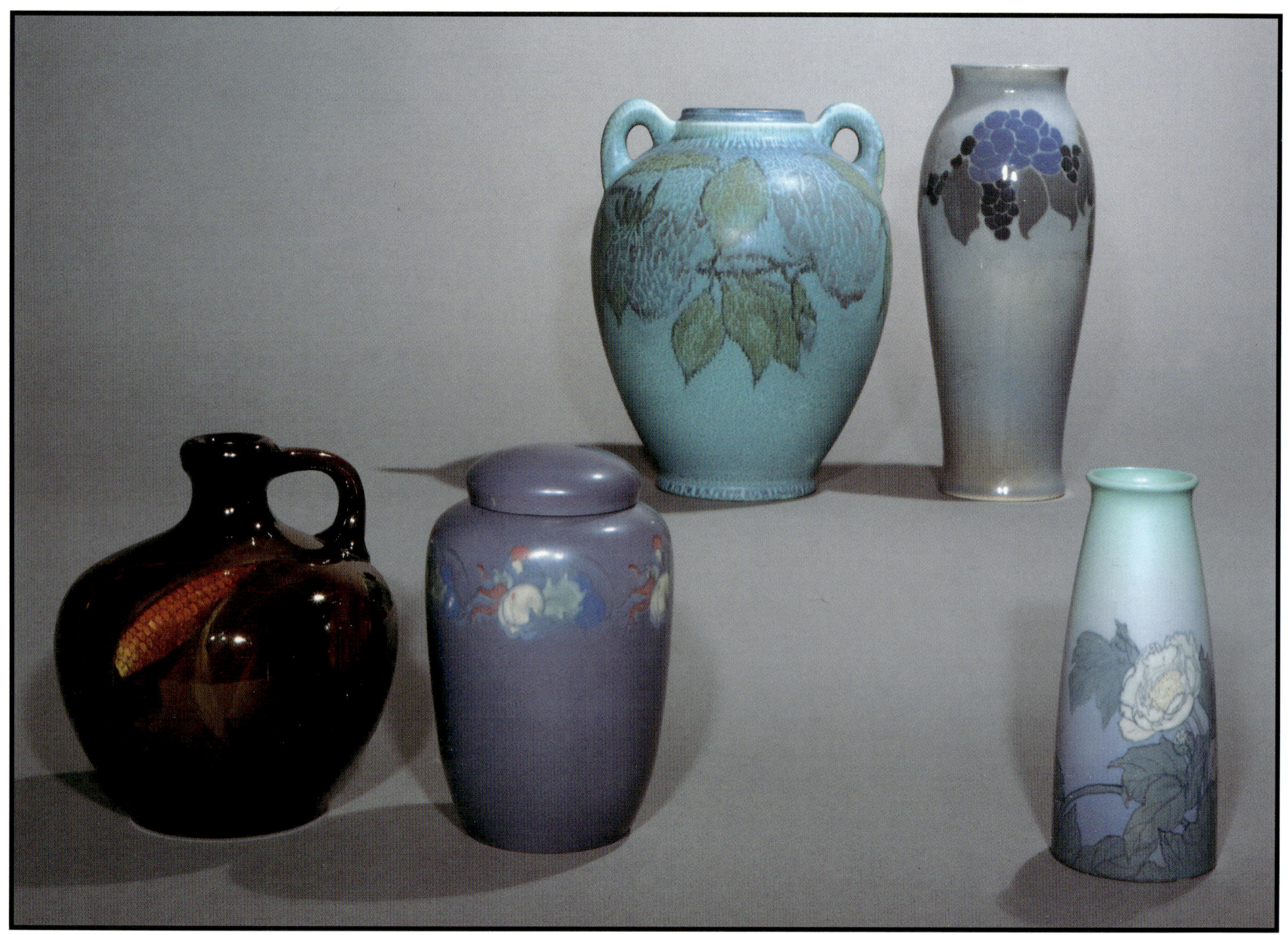

558 Standard glaze whiskey jug with corn and wheat decoration done by Lenore Asbury in 1899. Marks include the Rookwood logo, the date, shape number 675 and the incised initials of the artist. Height 6 3/8 inches. Minor glaze scratches and one or two tiny glaze bubbles. $500-800

559 Vellum glaze lidded vase with stylized fruit and flower decoration painted by Fred Rothenbusch in 1922. Marks include the Rookwood logo, the date, shape number 47 C, a sideways P for porcelain body, impressed V for Vellum glaze and incised monogram of the artist. Height 6 1/2 inches. Uncrazed with lots of color. $800-1000

560 Mat glaze two-handled vase with blue hydrangea and green leaves, painted in 1930 by Jens Jensen. Marks include the Rookwood logo, the date, shape number 2640 E, a fan shaped esoteric mark and the artist's monogram, painted on in black slip. Height 9 inches. $1250-1500

561 High glaze vase from 1919 decorated with flatly painted outlines of fruit and flowers in many colors, decorated by an unknown artist. Marks include the Rookwood logo, the date, shape number 937 and the incised monogram of the artist, which looks like an E inside a C. Height 9 7/8 inches. Interesting design and uncrazed. We have seen two examples of work signed by the same hand in 1919. $1000-1500

562 Pretty Vellum glaze vase with snappy floral decoration by Ed Diers, done in 1924. The flowers and leaves are outlined in black. Marks include the Rookwood logo, the date, shape number 1660 F, an incised V for Vellum glaze and the incised monogram of the artist. Height 6 1/4 inches. Uncrazed and very crisp. A small base chip has been professionally repaired. $600-800

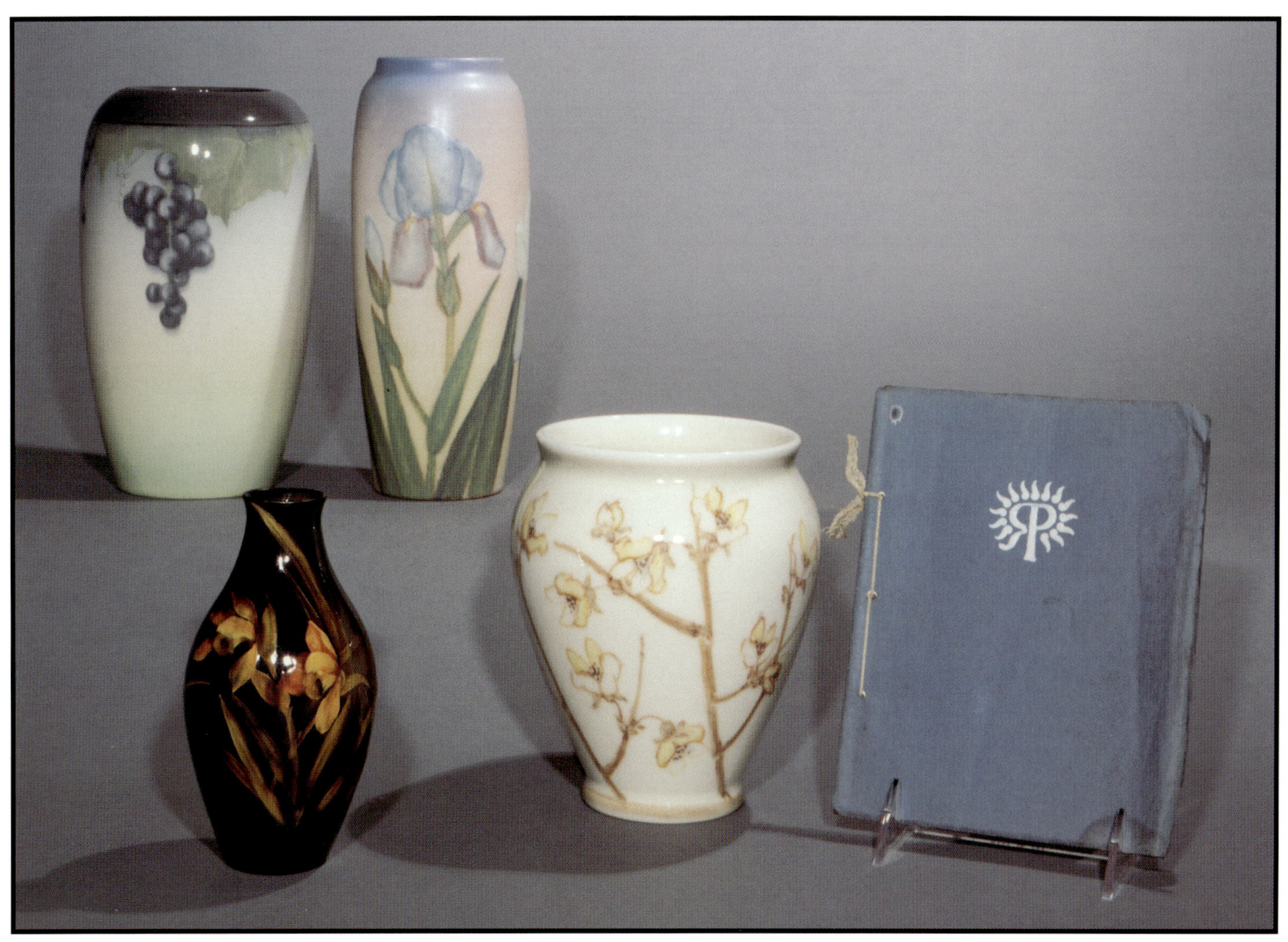

563	Interesting Iris glaze vase painted in 1910 by Sallie Coyne. From a gray band at the shoulder descend several lifelike bunches of grapes and grape leaves. Marks include the Rookwood logo, the date, shape number 1126 C, an incised W for white (Iris) glaze and the incised monogram of the artist. Height 8 1/2 inches.	$1250-1750

564	Standard glaze vase with orange and yellow jonquils nicely contrasted against a deep brown ground, painted in 1894 by Sallie Toohey. Marks include the Rookwood logo, the date, shape number 41 C, an impressed W for white clay and the incised monogram of the artist. Height 5 5/8 inches.	$250-350

565	Unusually crisp and colorful Vellum glaze floral vase painted by Kataro Shirayamadani in 1942. Pictured are several blue and white irises with yellow centers and bright green stems. Marks include the Rookwood logo, the date, shape number 951 D and the incised initials of the artist. Height 9 1/4 inches. Uncrazed. This is certainly one of the nicest late Vellums by Shirayamadani.	$2500-3500

566	High glaze vase decorated by Margaret McDonald in 1944 with white and yellow flowers and brown stems. Marks include the Rookwood logo, the date, shape number 2190 and the artist's monogram, painted on in brown slip. Height 6 1/4 inches. Uncrazed.	$400-500

567	Rare Rookwood 1904 "Bluebook" mail order catalog consisting of 36 pages with many black and white reproductions of pottery and 8 color plates. This is one of only two Rookwood publications to be dated. Size is 7 by 5 1/2 inches. Good original condition with some staining and wear on the cover.	$300-400

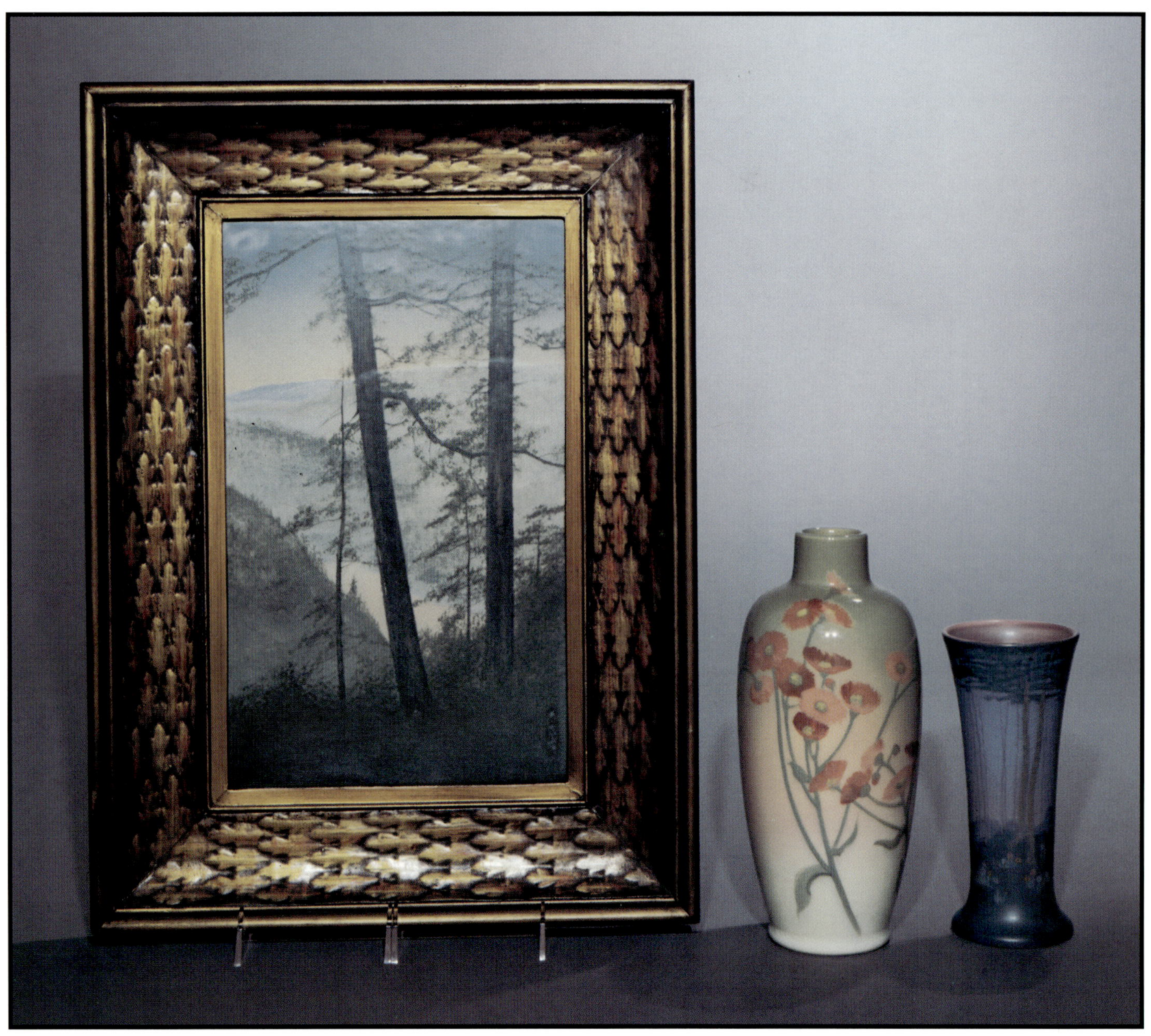

568   Large and handsome Arts & Crafts style Vellum glaze scenic plaque painted in 1912 by Kataro Shirayamadani. $12500-15000
The artist's cypher is incised on the lower right hand corner of the plaque. Marks on the back include the
Rookwood logo, the date and V for Vellum glaze body. Size is 14 1/4 by 9 inches. Pictured is a view of a river
valley seen from high atop a pine covered ridge.

569   Stylish and showy Iris glaze vase painted in 1901 by Sara Sax. Sax has laid a profusion of coral colored $5000-7000
bachelor's buttons on a green to salmon to cream ground with nice contrast leading to a wonderful effect.
Impressed marks include the Rookwood logo, the date, shape number 786 C and the artist's monogram.
Incised on the base is a W for white (Iris) glaze. Height 10 inches. Minimal crazing.

570   Remarkable Vellum glaze scenic vase painted by Kate Curry in 1917. Curry, whose work is seldom seen, has $3000-3500
given us a wonderful, almost dream-like, nocturnal landscape with tall stylized trees which leaf out near the
top of the vase and through which can be seen a yellow, full moon. Growing among the trees are flowers in
blue, orange, pink and green. Small white birds can be seen in the sky. The ground color is a pale mauve
with purple trees growing in the background. Marks include the Rookwood logo, the date, shape number
1357 E, an impressed V for Vellum glaze body and the incised monogram of the artist. Height 7 3/8 inches.
All in all, a rather unique piece.

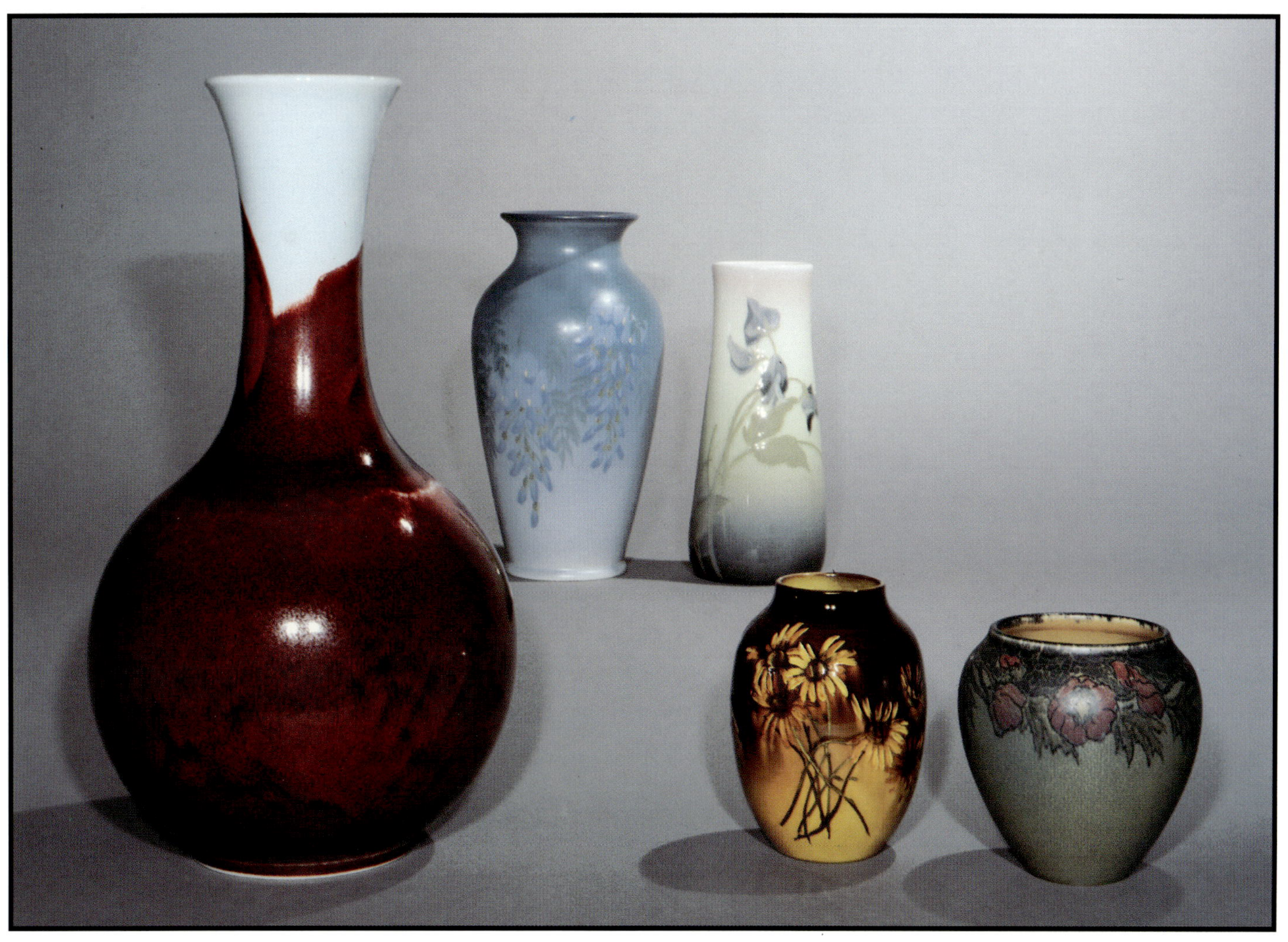

571   Large and impressive Oxblood vase made at Rookwood in 1926. Marks include the Rookwood logo, the date $800-1000
       and shape number 2983. Height 15 5/8 inches. A very large example of Oxblood with a wonderful variegated
       glaze.

572   Good Vellum glaze vase with crisp wisteria decoration by E.T. Hurley in 1927. The blue flowers have yellow $1500-2000
       centers and dark blue buds. Marks include the Rookwood logo, the date, shape number 546 C, an incised V for
       Vellum glaze and the incised initials of the artist. Height 9 1/2 inches. Uncrazed and very clean.

573   Pretty Iris glaze vase with sweet pea decoration done in 1906 by Lenore Asbury. Marks include the Rookwood $3000-4000
       logo, the date, shape number 950 D, an incised W for white (Iris) glaze and the incised initials of the artist.
       Height 8 1/4 inches. Uncrazed and nicely done.

574   Standard glaze vase with daisy decoration done in 1893 by Carrie Steinle. Marks include the Rookwood logo, $300-400
       the date, shape number 654 C, an impressed W for white clay and the incised initials of the artist. Height 5 1/2
       inches. Small glaze chip off the base.

575   Mat glaze vase with pretty red wild roses encircling the shoulder, done in 1924 by Katherine Jones. Marks $400-600
       include the Rookwood logo, the date, shape number 1343 and the initials of the artist, painted on in black slip.
       Height 4 3/4 inches.

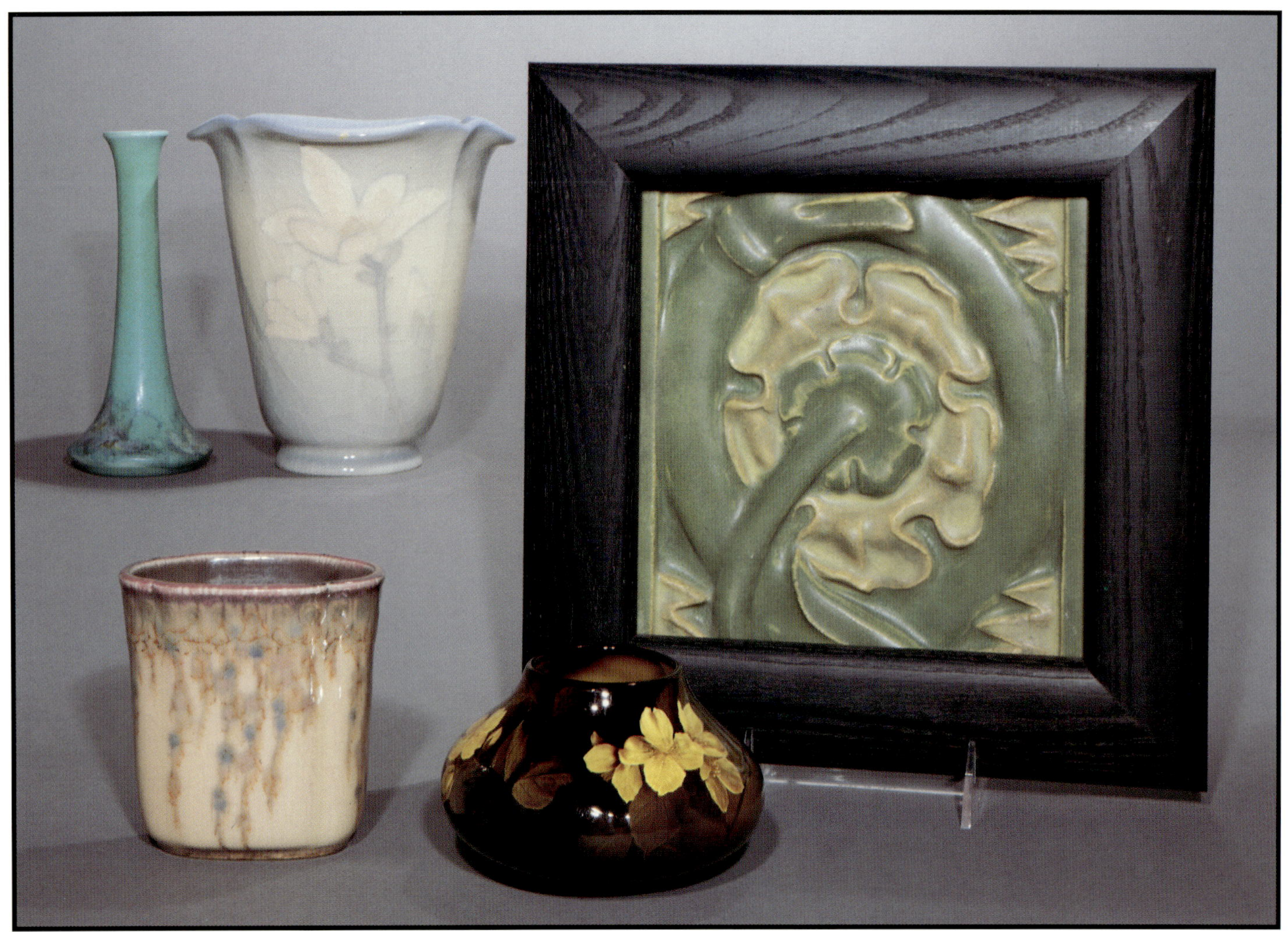

576   Mat glaze bud vase by Sallie Coyne with floral decoration Painted in. Marks include the Rookwood logo, the date 1929, shape number 2307 and the artist's monogram, painted on in blue slip. Height 7 inches. Glaze peppering. $200-300

577   High glaze, flat sided vase painted with trailing flowers by Sara Sax in 1929. The interior of the vase is nicely glazed in a mottled purple. Marks include the Rookwood logo, the date, shape number 6093 and the monogram of the artist, painted on in black slip. Height 4 1/4 inches. Uncrazed. $400-500

578   High glaze vase with fluted top decorated in 1946 by Kataro Shirayamadani. Decoration consists of white magnolia flowers. Marks include the Rookwood logo, the date, shape number 6314, the incised number 6554 and the incised initials of the artist. Height 7 1/2 inches. $1000-1500

579   Standard glaze vase with pretty, yellow wild rose decoration painted in 1897 by Elizabeth Lincoln. Marks include the Rookwood logo, the date, shape number 536 E, an impressed star shaped esoteric mark, a wheel ground X and the incised initials of the artist. Height 3 inches. Innocuous glaze pooling on the back side accounts for the X. $250-350

580   Rookwood Architectural Faience tile in green mat glaze with the deeply embossed floral pattern. What we see is the back of a flower head where the stem joins the bud, an unusual but interesting perspective. Impressed on the back "Rookwood Faience", "6" in a circle and shape number 1170 Y-2. Size is 7 7/8 by 7 3/4 inches. New ebonized oak frame. $500-600

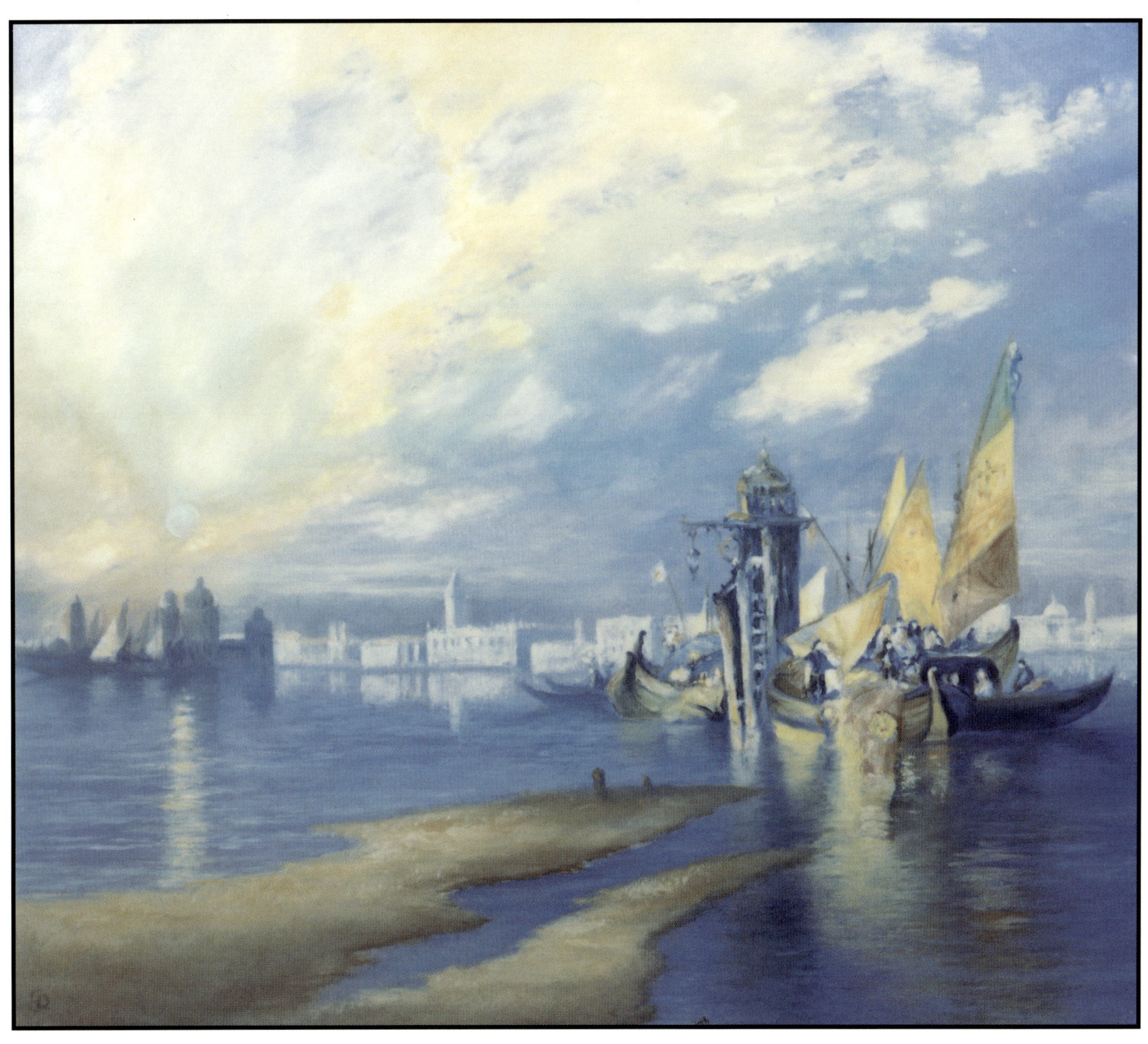

581   Large and important Vellum glaze scenic plaque painted by Ed Diers in 1929, showing an early morning view $25000-35000
of Venice with buildings, boats and people under a Turneresque sky. The large structure beyond the sand
bar, surrounded by boats, is a religious shrine maintained and frequented by those who make their living at
sea. Diers has signed the piece with his monogram in the lower left hand corner. Impressed marks on the
back include the Rookwood logo and the date. Size is 14 1/4 by 16 1/8 inches. Affixed to the original frame is
an original paper label with the typewritten notation "Venetian Shrine E. Diers". The plaque is uncrazed and
very colorful. This is one of Diers' finest efforts.

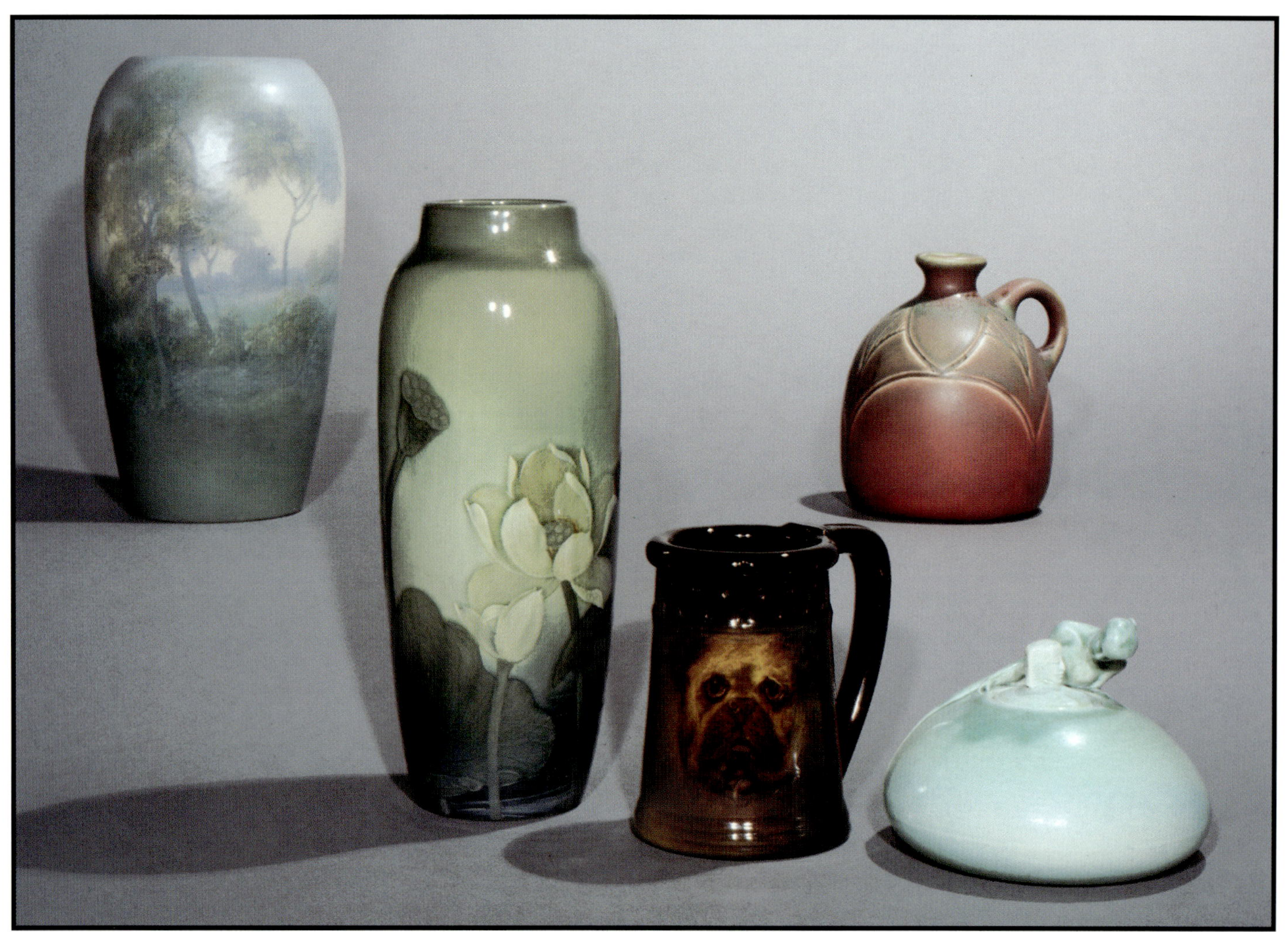

582 Nicely detailed Vellum glaze scenic vase done in 1920 by Ed Diers. Diers has made an extra effort on this $2000-2500
vase, for every leaf seems visible on the trees. Marks include the Rookwood logo, the date, shape number
1126 C, an incised V for Vellum glaze and the incised monogram of the artist. Height 9 5/8 inches.

583 Sea Green glaze vase painted in 1901 by Mary Nourse with lotus blossoms, pads, stems and seed pods. $1000-1500
Marks include the Rookwood logo, the date, shape number 907 D, an incised G for Sea Green glaze, the
incised initials of the artist and a wheel ground x. A firing crack and small area of glaze loss at the rim
account for the x and have been professionally repaired. Good detail and wonderful color.

584 Standard glaze puzzle mug with the face of a bulldog with collar, painted by E.T. Hurley in 1898. Marks $500-700
include the Rookwood logo, the date, shape number 711, a wheel ground x and the incised initials of the
artist. Height 4 7/8 inches.

585 Arts & Crafts style whiskey jug with incised geometric designs covered with a red mat glaze with green $400-500
highlights at Rookwood in 1906. Marks include the Rookwood logo, the date and shape number 747 C.
Height 5 3/8 inches.

586 Early modeled mat glaze inkwell with lid and inner cup made by Anna Valentien in 1901. A lithe female $1250-1750
nude clings to the top of the well and peers intently at the Sphinx-like finial on the lid, making for a mysteri-
ous allegory. Marks include the Rookwood logo and date, shape number 305 Z, a wheel ground x and the
incised initials of the artist. Height 3 1/2 inches. The glaze is a bit thin and uneven, most likely the reason
for the x but the thinness of the glaze allows the sharp detailing of Valentien's modeling to show through.

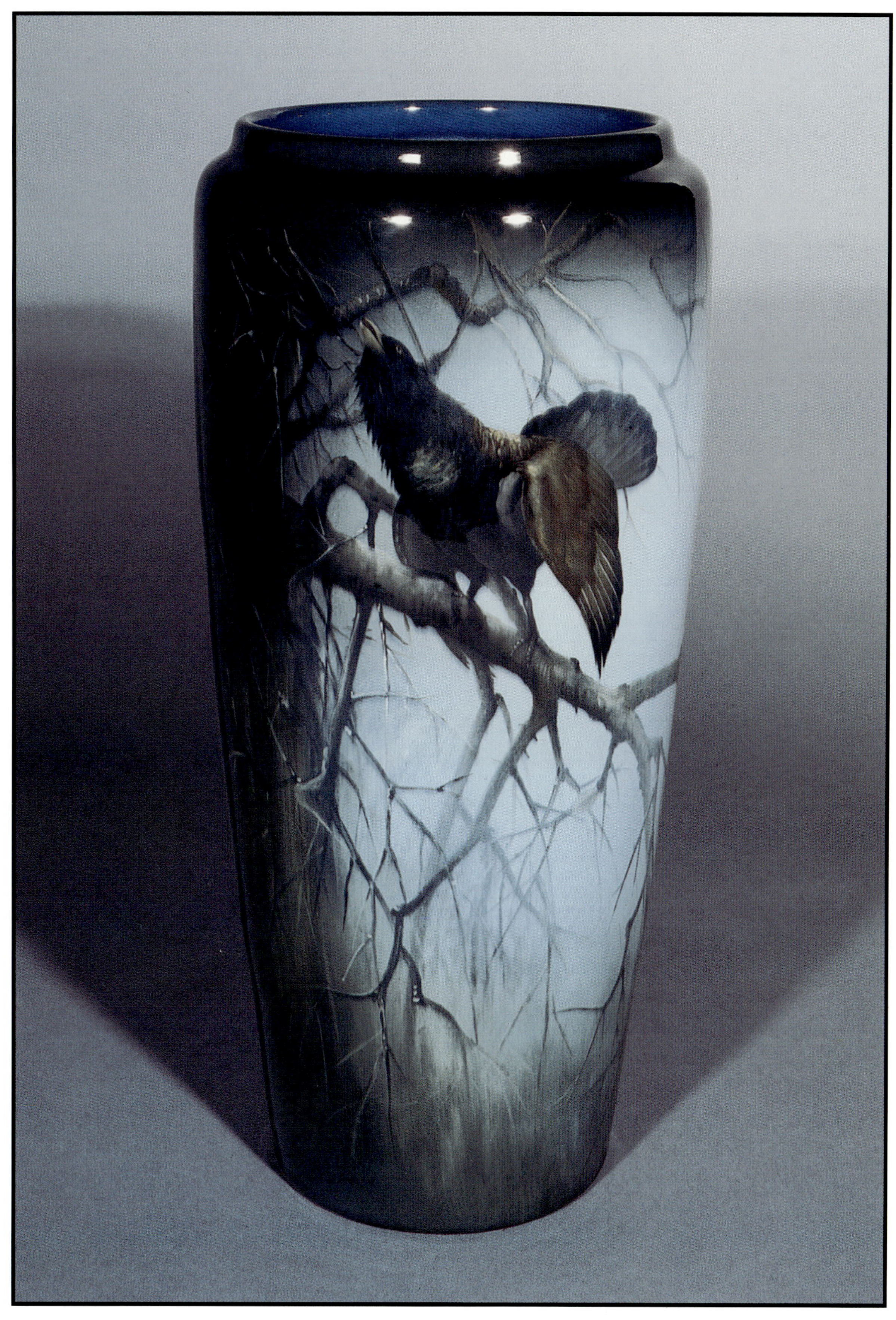

587   Large, rare and important Black Iris glaze vase painted by Carl Schmidt in 1909. Schmidt has crafted a $30000-40000
wonderful, moody scene with a beautifully detailed grouse perched in a tall tree having many branches.
The time period would seem to be winter, perhaps hunting season and the bird may be calling out an alert.
Typical of Schmidt's work, every branch and every feather is in place. Marks include the Rookwood logo,
the date, shape number 1369 B, an incised W for white (Iris) glaze and the impressed monogram of the
artist. Height 14 1/8 inches. Uncrazed and extremely clean. This incredible vase was purchased from
Rookwood's Cincinnati showroom in the 50's, shortly before the company moved to Starkville. The young
couple who bought the vase and lot 769 were told at that time that both pieces were "collector's items"
and extremely rare. We know that Rookwood maintained a small but powerful collection of pieces made
throughout its history that represented the best of every era. Many of these pieces were donated to the
Cincinnati Art Museum by the Schott group which bought Rookwood in 1940. Many others continued on
display in Cincinnati until the move to Mississippi. The purchaser of this lot will be its second caretaker in
over 40 years and can feel pride in knowing that Rookwood considered it a premier example.

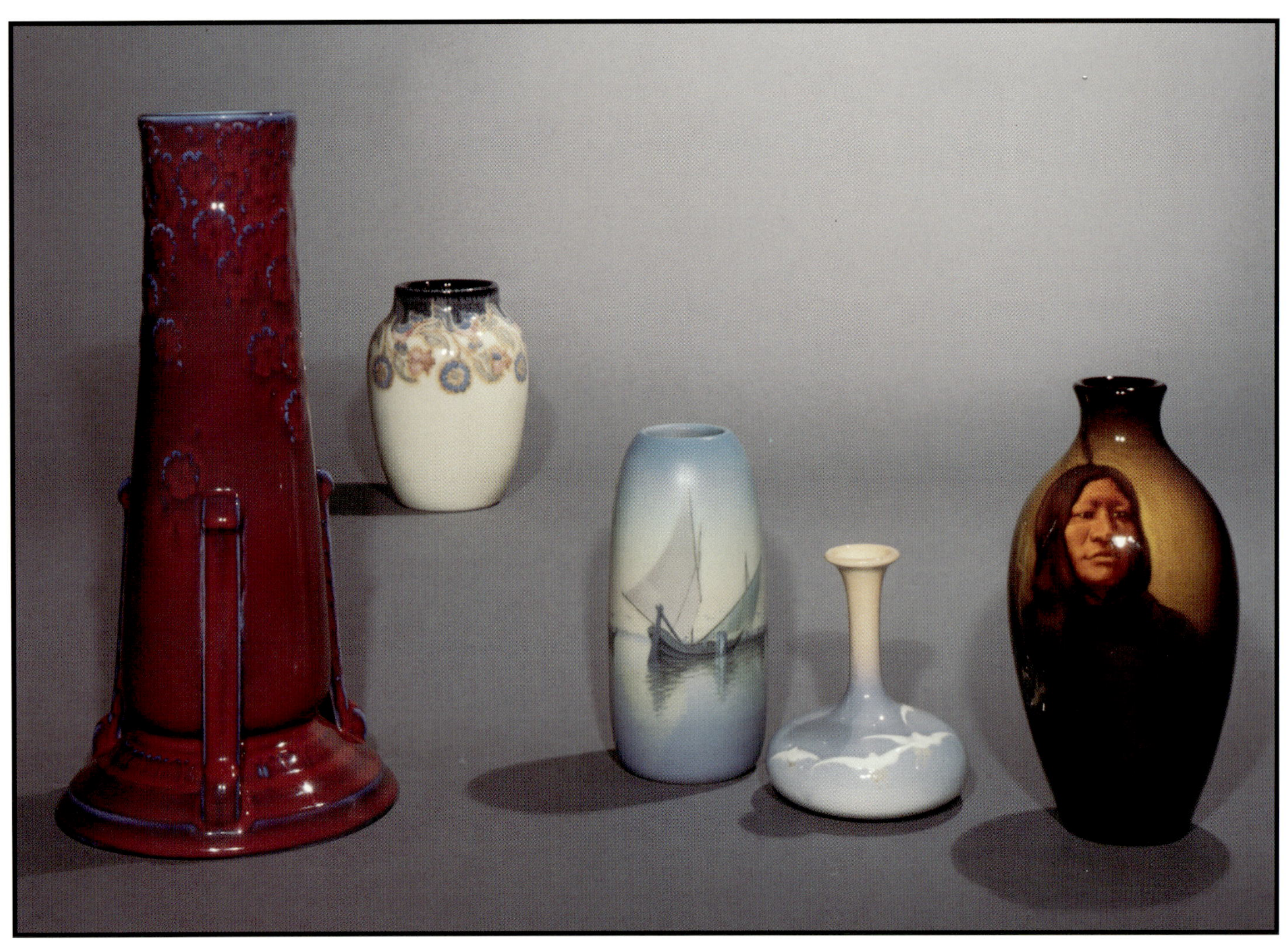

588	Handsome Black Opal-type glaze lamp base decorated by Sara Sax in 1922. The basic form is a cast piece with embossed flowers and three buttressed handles. Sax has added some decoration and most effectively has hand applied the strong colors common to the glaze. Although the overglaze here is clear, not the black tinted glaze commonly associated with Black Opal, the overall effect is very similar. Marks include the Rookwood logo, the date, shape number 2610 and the artist's monogram, painted on in black slip. Height 13 3/8 inches. Uncrazed and very snappy.	$1000-1500
589	Nice high glaze floral vase painted in 1926 by Lorinda Epply. A black mottled glaze lines the interior of the vase and drips down from the rim. Marks include the Rookwood logo, the date, shape number 654 C and the artist's monogram, painted on in black slip. Height 5 1/2 inches.	$800-1000
590	Vellum glaze Venetian harbor scenic vase decorated by Carl Schmidt in 1926. Impressed marks include the Rookwood logo, the date, shape number 2102 and the artist's monogram. Incised in the base is a V for Vellum glaze. Height 6 3/4 inches. A small rim chip has been professionally repaired.	$1500-2000
591	Pretty Iris glaze vase with four seagulls flying away from the viewer, painted in 1898 by Amelia Sprague. Marks include the Rookwood logo, the date, shape number 852 E, an incised W for white (Iris) glaze and the incised monogram of the artist. Height 4 7/8 inches. This is one of only a few Iris glaze pieces we have seen by Sprague.	$1500-2000
592	Sensitive Standard glaze portrait of a Native American done in 1900 by Adeliza D. Sehon. Marks include the Rookwood logo, the date, shape number 732 BB, a wheel ground x and the notation "Brule T-e-san-yan White Wash His Face". Height 8 1/4 inches. Minor glaze exudation.	$3000-4000

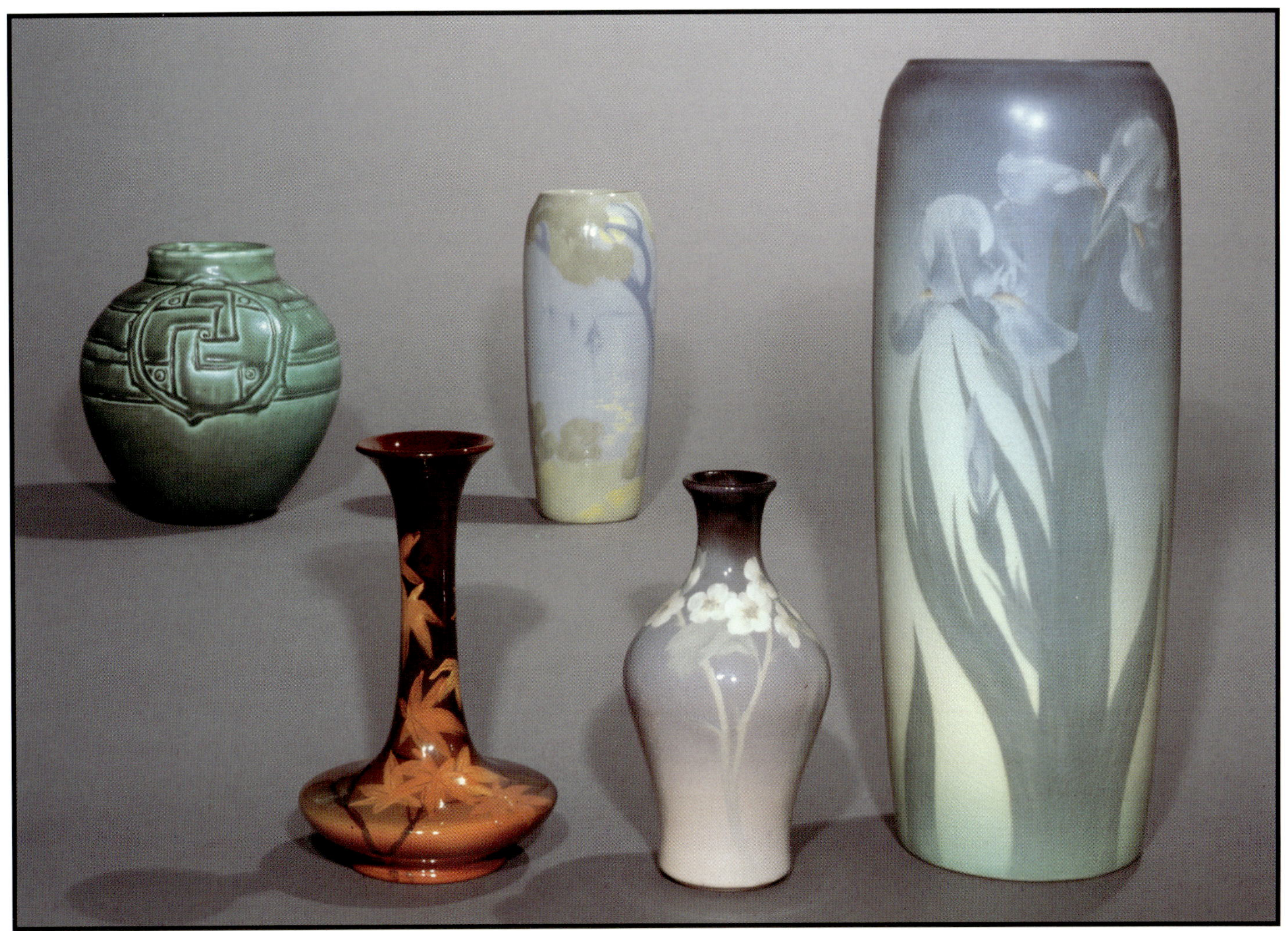

593   Mat glaze vase with incised Native American designs done in 1901 by William McDonald. Marks include the Rookwood logo, the date, shape number 1 Z, a wheel ground X and the incised monogram of the artist. Height 5 1/2 inches. Small glaze skips account for the X. $400-500

594   Standard glaze vase with Japanese maple leaves and stems painted by Carrie Steinle in 1900. Marks include the Rookwood logo, the date, shape number 566 D and the incised monogram of the artist. Height 6 1/2 inches. $300-400

595   Rare Iris glaze scenic vase with sailboats and stylized trees under a full moon, done in 1905 by Fred Rothenbusch. The scene is done in an Arts & Crafts style rather than the typical, naturalistic composition of the period. Marks include the Rookwood logo, the date, shape number 951 E, an incised W for white (Iris) glaze and the incised monogram of the artist. Height 6 5/8 inches. $3000-4000

596   Iris glaze vase with white wild rose decoration done by Ed Diers in 1901. The background shades from gray to mauve to peach. Marks include the Rookwood logo, the date, shape number 748 D, an incised W for white (Iris) glaze and the incised monogram of the artist. Height 6 1/8 inches. $1250-1500

597   Tall and handsome Vellum glaze vase with iris decoration by Carl Schmidt, painted in 1915. There are two life-like irises on the front of the vase and another on the back. Marks include the Rookwood logo, the date, shape number 951 B, V for Vellum glaze body, an incised V for Vellum glaze and the impressed monogram of the artist. Height 12 5/8 inches. $3500-4500

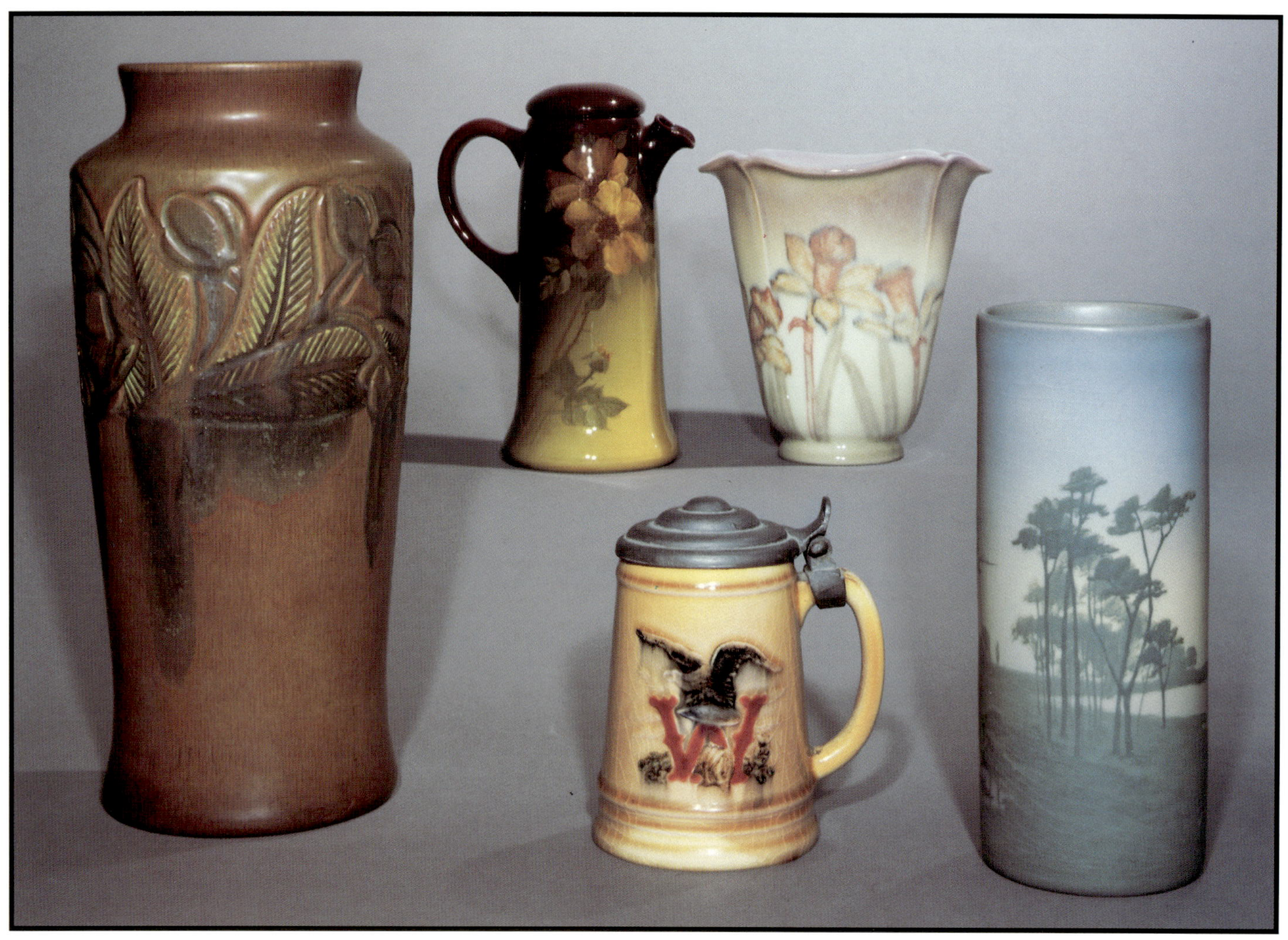

598	Tall Ombroso glaze vase with deeply carved floral decoration done by William Hentschel in 1915. Marks include the Rookwood logo, the date, shape number 1664 C and the incised monogram of the artist. Height 12 3/4 inches. Ombroso was introduced by Rookwood in 1910 and used with some frequency by Hentschel thereafter. The variegated glaze and deep incising lend themselves well to the Arts & Crafts style.	$1500-2000
599	Standard glaze chocolate pot with domed lid, decorated in 1901 by Jeanette Swing with pretty wild roses. Marks include the Rookwood logo, the date, shape number 772 and the incised monogram of the artist on both the base and lid. Height 9 inches. Excellent original condition.	$400-600
600	Wiedemann Brewing Company mug with pewter lid made at Rookwood in 1948. Marks include the Rookwood logo, the date and the notation "The Geo. Wiedemann Brewing Co. Inc.". Height 5 3/8 inches.	$400-500
601	High glaze vase with red and yellow daffodils painted by Kataro Shirayamadani in 1946. Impressed marks include the Rookwood logo, the date and shape number 6314. Painted on the base in black slip are the artist's initials and the number "6649". Height 7 3/8 inches. Uncrazed and rather colorful.	$1000-1250
602	Cylindrical Vellum glaze scenic vase painted by Sara Sax in 1911. The Arts & Crafts scenic features silhouetted trees around a body of water. Marks include the Rookwood logo, the date, shape number 1124 D, an incised V for Vellum glaze, an impressed V for Vellum glaze body and the impressed monogram of the artist. Height 8 3/4 inches. There is a minor 1/8 by 1/4 inch glaze skip at the base.	$1500-2000

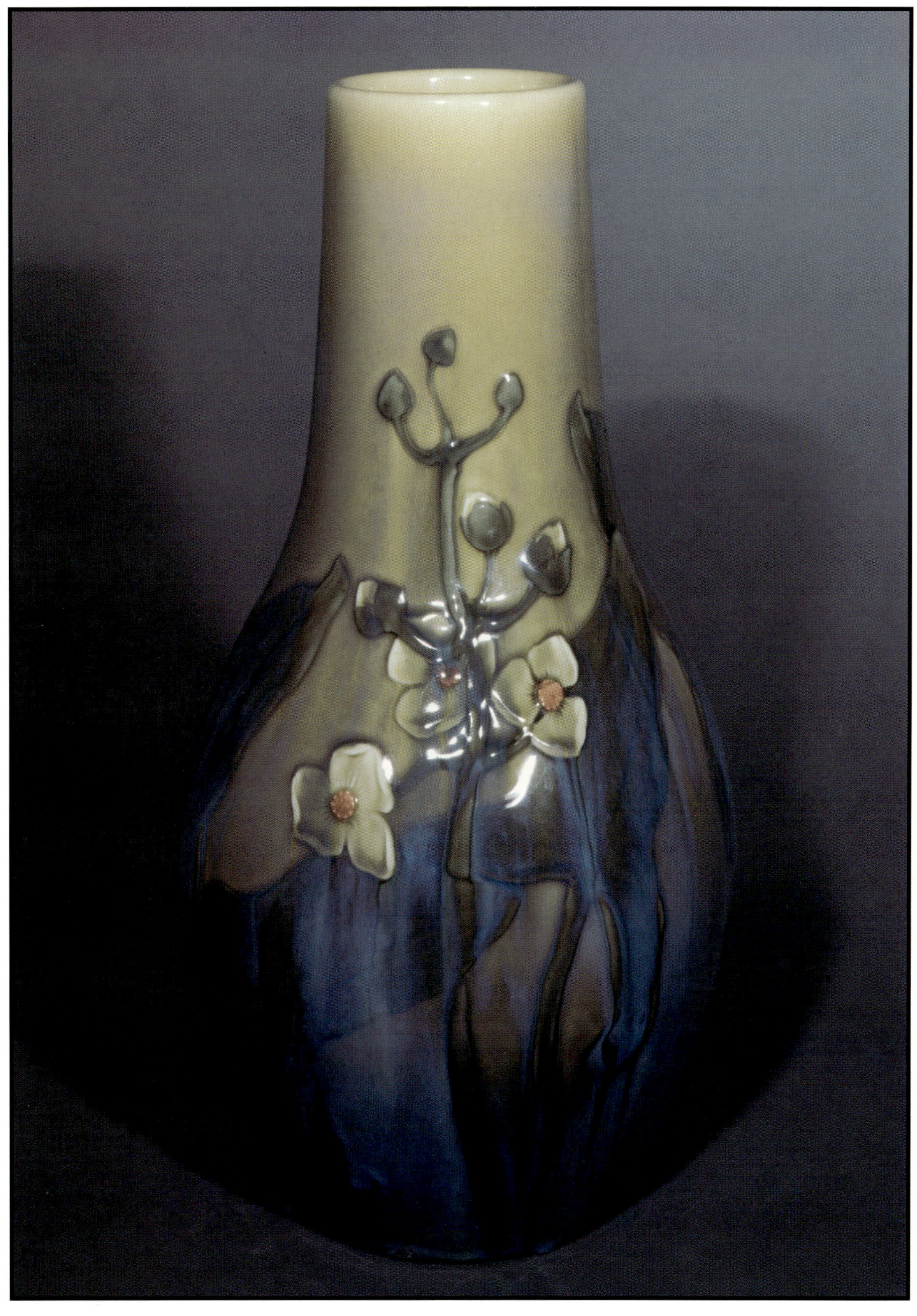

603   Rare and important Flowing glaze vase carved and painted by Matt Daly in 1901. Decoration consists of $25000-30000
white flowers with salmon colored centers and large green leaves, all of which are deeply and intricately
carved. The vase is then coated with a clear glaze blessed with sheets of hazy blue which are most prominent in its lower third. Impressed marks include the Rookwood logo, the date and shape number S 1702 A.
Incised are Daly's full name and the letter "F", which we feel is the artist's request of the glaze department
for Flowing Glaze. We know Rookwood experimented with Flowing Glaze at the turn of the century, going so
far as to name the glaze and even design a logo for it along with its more well known glaze lines. Apparently
the glaze was not easy to control because until now, no marked example has come to light. Lot 619 in this
year's sale (lot 706 in Rookwood II) is another 1902 piece by Daly which descended in the family of Rookwood artist Carl Schmidt. Schmidt always referred to this piece as "Flowing Glaze" and it is the same artist
and same year. Other pieces with similar effect have been noted over the years but this exceptional vase,
wonderful in any case, may be the first known marked example of an elusive glaze line. Flowing glaze would
seem a close relative of Iris glaze since it appears clear for the most part and since the blue sheeting occurs
in other examples of Rookwood usually designated as Iris.

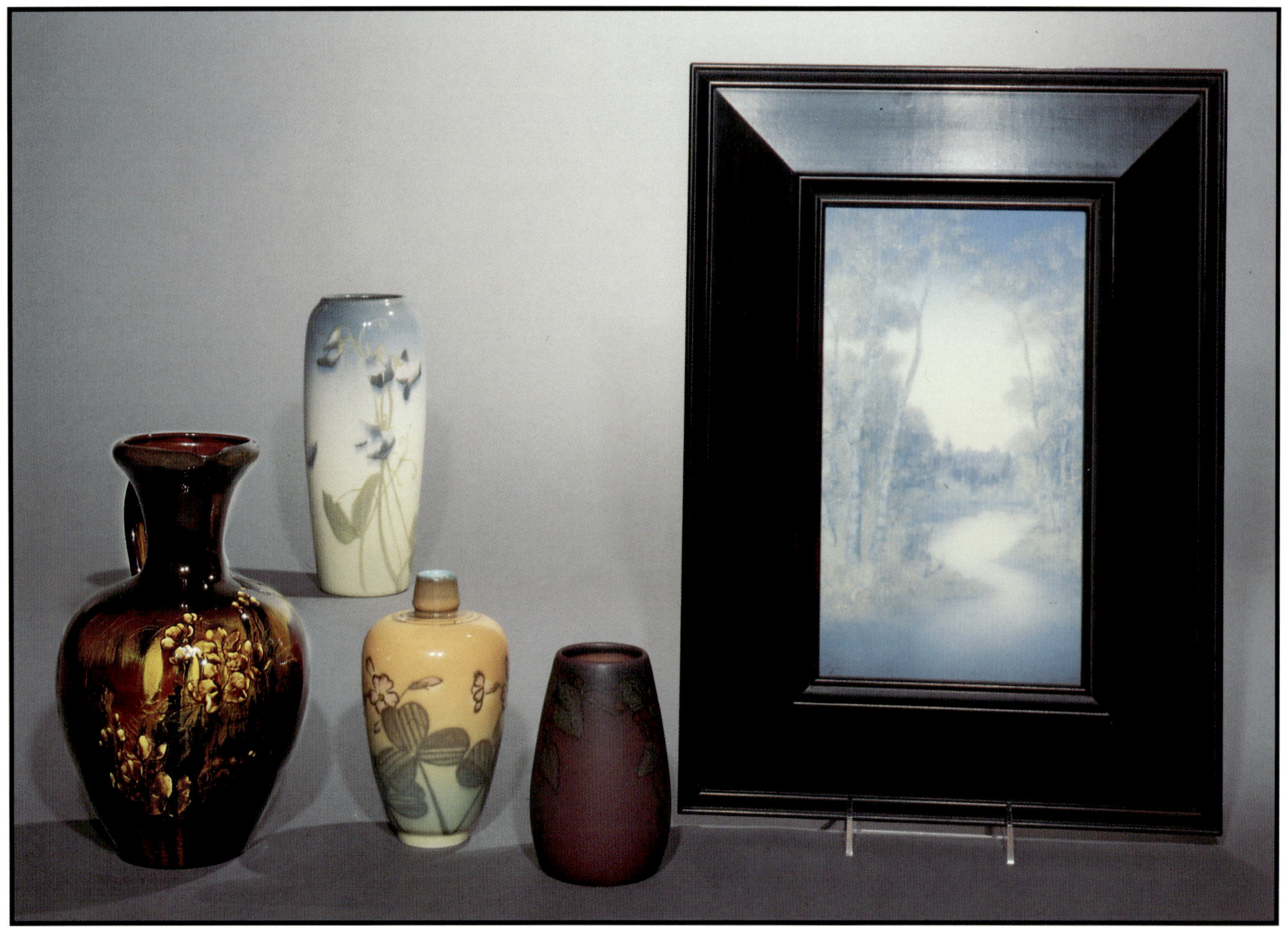

604	Standard glaze ewer with fabulous Tiger Eye effect decorated with simple flowers by Albert Valentien in 1886. Marks include Rookwood in block letters, the date, shape number 267, the incised initials of the artist and accession numbers from the Cincinnati Art Museum in red paint. Height 9 1/4 inches. A chip to the spout has been professionally repaired. The Tiger Eye here looks like liquid gold and is some of the finest we have ever seen.	$1000-1500
605	Iris glaze vase with blue and white sweet pea decoration painted in 1907 by Sallie Coyne. Marks include the Rookwood logo, the date, shape number 951 D, an incised W for white (Iris) glaze and the incised monogram of the artist. Height 8 3/8 inches.	$2000-2500
606	High glaze vase with very stylized, very modern, floral decoration done in 1934 by Kataro Shirayamadani. The vase form, a special shape, is itself quite modern for Rookwood. Concentric circles below the collar are also a nice touch. Marks include the Rookwood logo, the date, S for Special shape and the incised cypher of the artist. Height 6 inches. There is a thin glaze flake off the rim. Uncrazed.	$1000-1500
607	Mat glaze vase with leaf and berry decoration on a dark maroon ground, the work of Katherine Jones in 1923. Impressed marks include the Rookwood logo, the date and shape numbers 2105. Painted on the bottom in black slip are the initials of the artist. Height 4 3/4 inches.	$300-400
608	Vellum glaze plaque with dreamy woodland scene decorated by E.T. Hurley in 1939. Hurley's initials are incised in the lower left hand corner of the plaque. Marks on the back include the Rookwood logo and the date. Size is 11 1/2 by 6 3/4 inches. New frame. Uncrazed and very clean. Any decorated Rookwood done in the late 1930's is rare.	$4000-5000

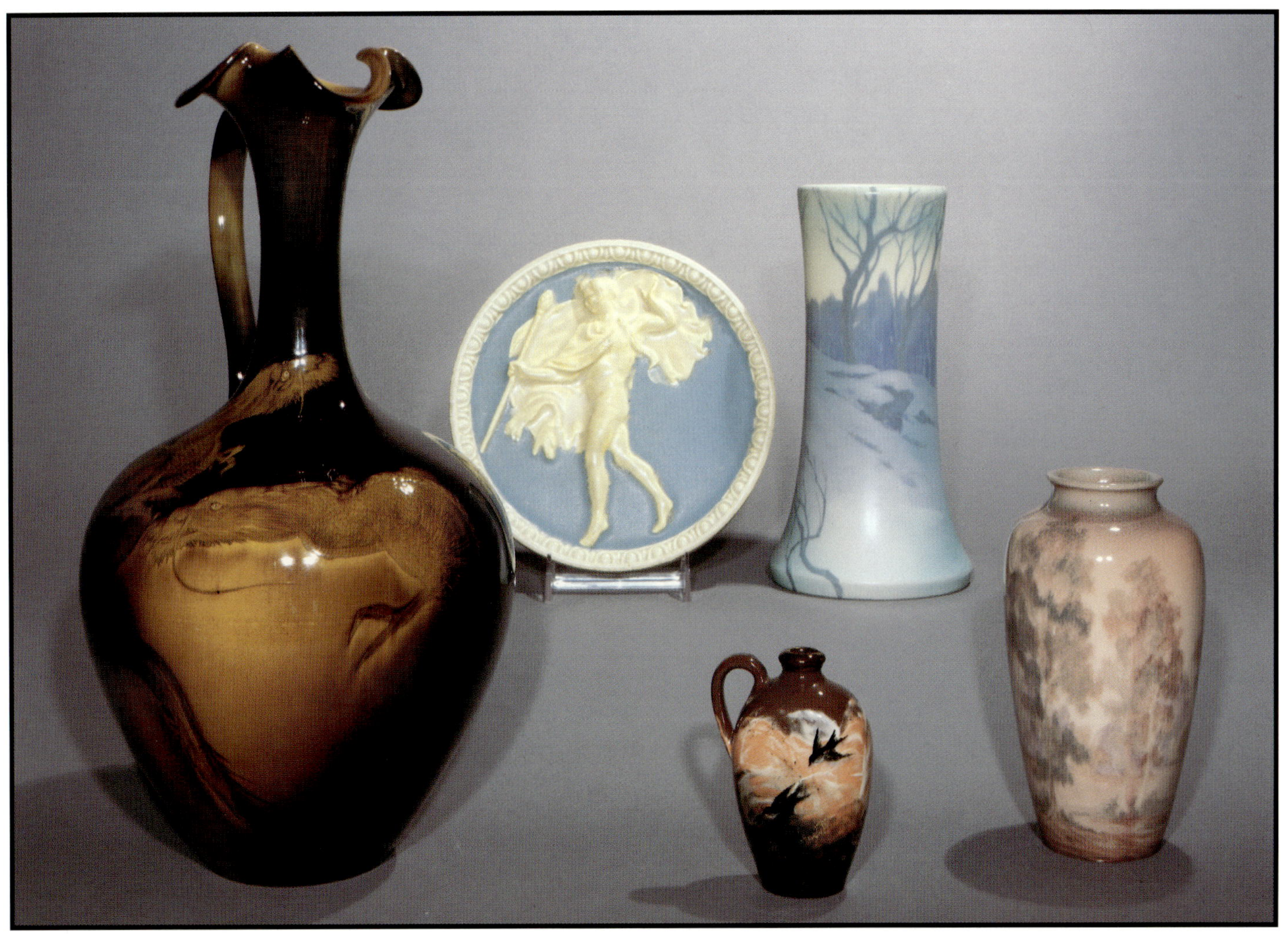

609   Large and impressive Standard glaze ewer gracefully decorated in 1894 by Kataro Shirayamadani. Pictured are four fierce-looking dragons arrayed around the body of the piece. These are three toed dragons with lots of scales and spines but no wings. Marks include the Rookwood logo, the date, shape number 578 A, W for white clay and remnants of a Rookwood showroom label. The artist's cypher is incised about four inches below the handle. Height 17 1/8 inches. Chips to the spout and breaks in the handle have been professionally repaired. $3000-4000

610   Round Rookwood Architectural Faience tile with a classical nude in white mat glaze on a blue ground. Marks include the Rookwood logo and the numbers "442", "J 50" and "3255 Y 2". Diameter is 8 7/8 inches. Minor edge chips. $300-400

611   Limoges style perfume jug painted by Hattie Horton, circa 1883. Decorative theme includes two small birds and Oriental grasses. Marks include R for red clay, shape number 60, an impressed kiln mark and the incised initials of the artist. Height 4 3/4 inches. $300-400

612   Very stylish Arts & Crafts Vellum glaze vase painted by Fred Rothenbusch in 1908. Rothenbusch has crafted a winter landscape of stark trees and snow which places the viewer in the middle of the scene, a very different treatment of a recurring Rookwood theme. Marks include the Rookwood logo, the date, shape number 1358 C, an impressed V for Vellum glaze body, an incised V for Vellum glaze and the impressed monogram of the artist. Height 10 5/8 inches. There is a bit of glaze peppering in the sky. $2500-3500

613   Rare high glaze scenic vase nicely rendered in a variety of pastel colors in 1939 by Margaret McDonald. Marks include the Rookwood logo, the date, shape number 614 E and the artist's monogram painted on in rose colored slip. Height 7 7/8 inches. Uncrazed and very clean. $1500-2000

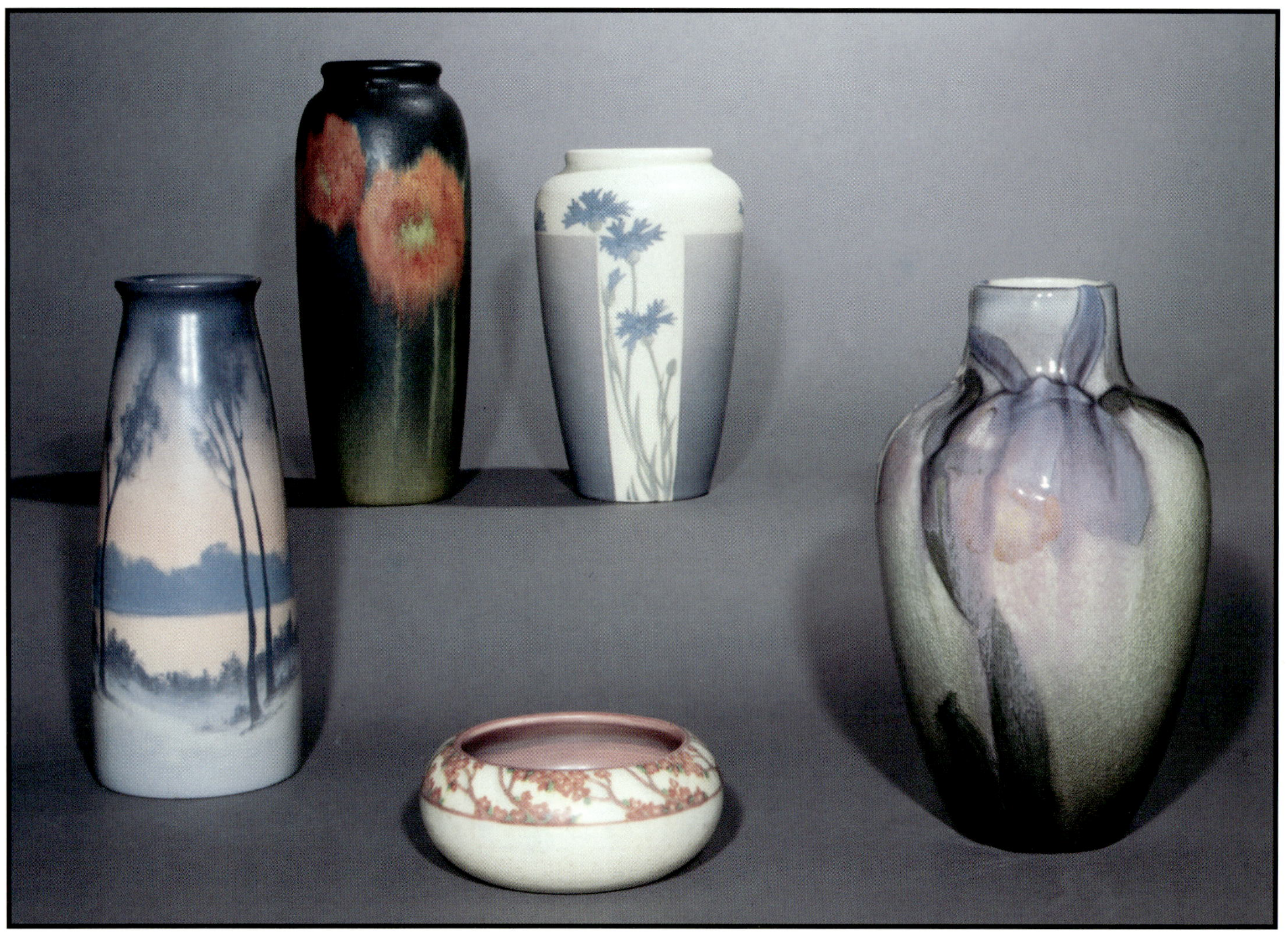

614   Vellum glaze snow scene with wonderful peach sky, painted in 1919 by Sallie Coyne. Marks include the Rookwood logo, the date, shape number 1660 D, a V for Vellum glaze and the incised monogram of the artist. Height 9 3/8 inches. There is a nearly undetectable line at the rim. $1000-1500

615   Rare Painted Mat vase with bright red poppies on a black to dark green ground painted by Olga Geneva Reed in 1904. Marks include the Rookwood logo, the date, shape number 188 CZ and the initials of the artist, painted on in black slip. Height 10 1/2 inches. Minor grinding chips. $3000-4000

616   Vellum glaze low bowl with a band of red, green and brown flowers on the shoulder, painted in 1917 by Mary Grace Denzler. Marks include the Rookwood logo, the date, shape number 2119, V for Vellum glaze body and the impressed monogram of the artist. Height is 2 inches and diameter is 6 inches. Glaze peppering $300-400

617   Interesting Vellum glaze vase with blue chicory flowers painted between gray panels by Lenore Asbury in 1908. The panels are outlined by incising and the flowers are very nicely detailed. Marks include the Rookwood logo, the date, shape number 938 C, an impressed V for Vellum glaze body, an incised V for Vellum glaze and the incised initials of the artist. Height 8 3/8 inches. $800-1000

618   Rare Flowing Glaze vase carved and painted by Matt Daly in 1901. Two orchids in shades of mauve, yellow and orange with green leaves adorn the vase with the leaves folding over the rim. Marks include the Rookwood logo, the date, shape number 905 C and Daly's incised name. Height 9 1/2". The exact nature of Flowing Glaze has been hinted at for a number of years but never proven. This vase descended in the family of Rookwood artist Carl Schmidt and was always referred to by Schmidt as Flowing Glaze. With the addition of lot 603 in this year's sale, clearly marked with an "F", the confusion seems resolved. Pictured: Rookwood Pottery The Glaze Lines by Ellis on page 52. $3000-4000

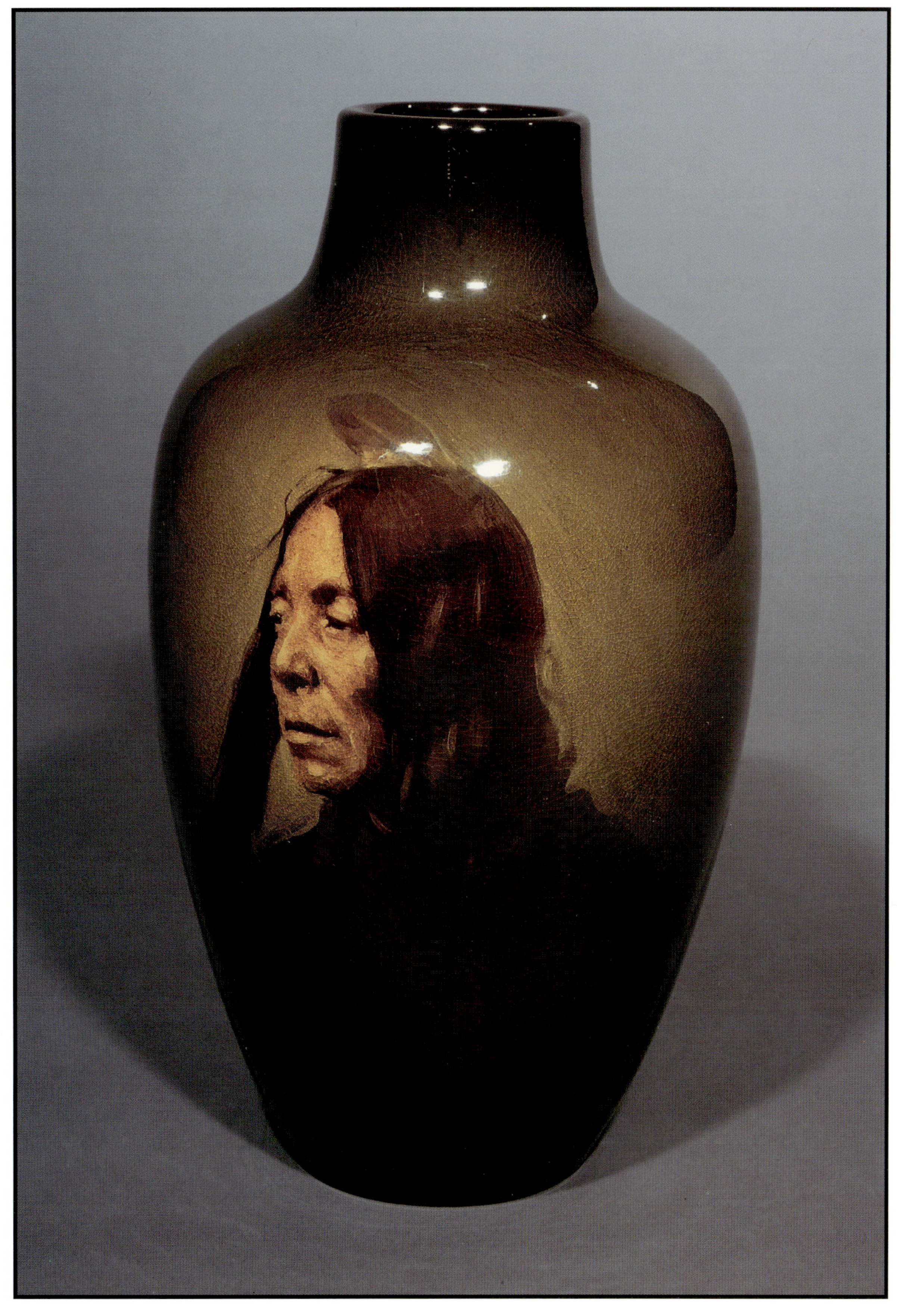

619   Lifelike portrait of a Native American male done in 1901 by Grace Young. Incised on the base is the name $5000-7000
      "- Akahedik -" which most likely is the name of the sitter. Other marks include the Rookwood logo, the date,
      shape number 905 C and the impressed monogram of the artist. Height 9 1/2 inches. Minor glaze scratches
      and a pin-head size glaze nick on the top of the rim. A good example of work by Rookwood's best portrait
      artist.

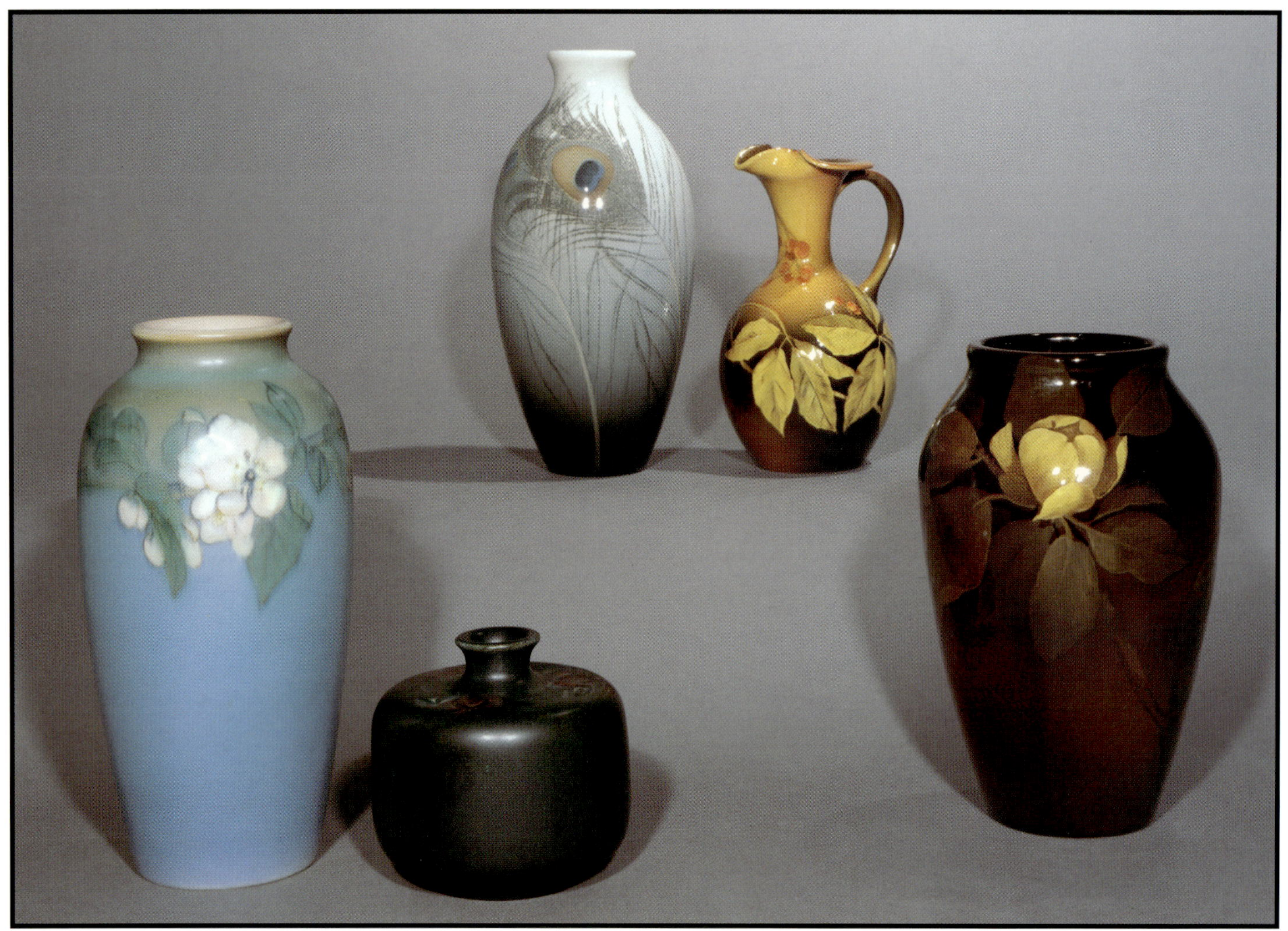

620   Vellum glaze vase with flowers encircling the shoulder, done in 1917 by Carrie Steinle. Marks include the Rookwood logo, the date, shape number 922 D, V for Vellum glaze body and the incised monogram of the artist. Height 7 7/8 inches. Uncrazed. Uncrazed Vellums from this period are rare. $600-800

621   Blue mat glaze vase with incised and painted lotus blossoms on the shoulder, done in 1914 by C.S. Todd. Marks include the Rookwood logo, the date, shape number 2116 and the incised initials of the artist. Height 3 3/8 inches. A small nick on the rim has been professionally repaired. $300-400

622   Iris glaze vase with delicate Peacock feather decoration, done in 1911 by Carl Schmidt. The shading and exacting artwork make this a very handsome example of Schmidt's work. Marks include the Rookwood logo, the date, shape number 732 BB, an incised W for white (Iris) glaze, a faint wheel ground X and the impressed monogram of the artist. Height 8 1/2 inches. Uncrazed. There is some sort of restoration at the rim, possibly covering a bit of missing glaze which necessitated the X. $3000-4000

623,   Standard glaze ewer with finely detailed Virginia creeper leaves, vines and berries, painted in 1893 by Sallie Coyne. Marks include the Rookwood logo, the date, shape number 685, W for white clay and the incised initials of the artist. Height 6 1/2 inches. $400-600

624   Standard glaze vase decorated by Elizabeth Lincoln in 1902. There is a single blooming flower with green leaves on the front of the vase and a full bud just to the side. Marks include the Rookwood logo, the date, shape number 913 D and the incised initials of the artist. Height 7 1/8 inches. $400-500

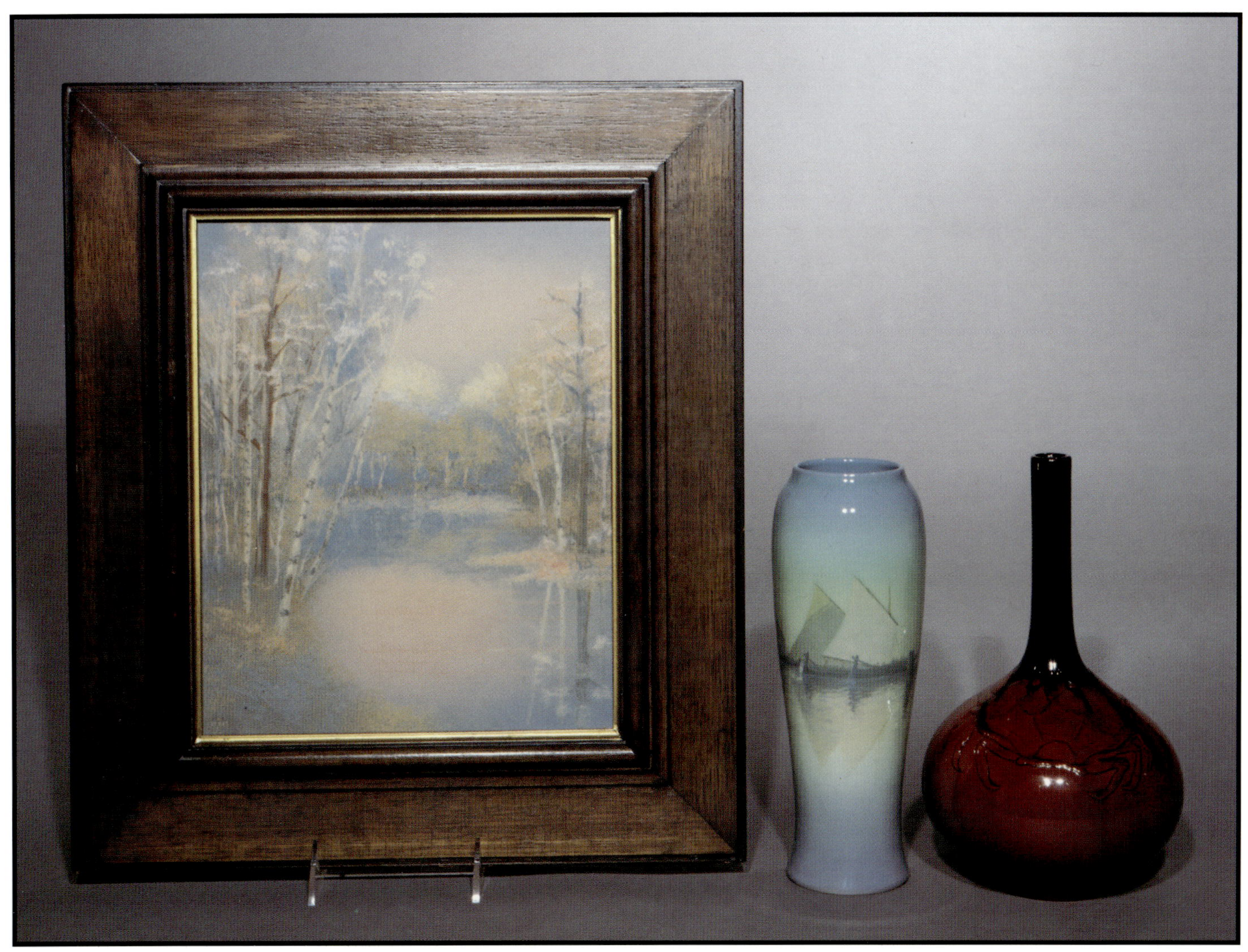

<table>
<tr><td>625</td><td>Good Vellum glaze plaque painted in 1948 by E.T. Hurley. This is a Hurley trademark plaque with a fall view of birch trees, mountains and a reflecting lake with a pinkish sky and water. Hurley's initials are incised in the lower left hand corner. Marks on the back include the Rookwood logo, the date and the size notation "10 x 12". Size is actually 11 7/8 by 9 7/8 inches. The frame is new and the plaque is uncrazed and very clean.</td><td>$4000-6000</td></tr>
<tr><td>626</td><td>Rare and impressive high glaze Venetian harbor scene vase painted by Carl Schmidt in 1922. Pictured are several boats with multicolored sails and the city of Venice in the background. The detail is such that many small figures can be seen working on the boats. Marks include the Rookwood logo, the date, shape number 2040 D, a P, obviously incised by Schmidt, which may be a call for the clear high (porcelain?) glaze and the impressed monogram of the artist. Height 9 1/4 inches. Uncrazed and extremely crisp and clean.</td><td>$4000-6000</td></tr>
<tr><td>627</td><td>Rare carved and painted Standard glaze vase with a long slender neck, done in 1899 by John Dee Wareham. Clutching and encircling the neck of the vase is a nicely detailed crab in relief. The neck is painted black, the only color other than the yellow glaze over the red clay body. Marks include the Rookwood logo, the date, shape number 743 A and the incised initials of the artist. Affixed to the base is an original Rookwood Show-room paper label listing the price at $35, a princely sum in 1899. Height 9 1/2 inches. Minor glaze blisters on the back side.</td><td>$4000-5000</td></tr>
</table>

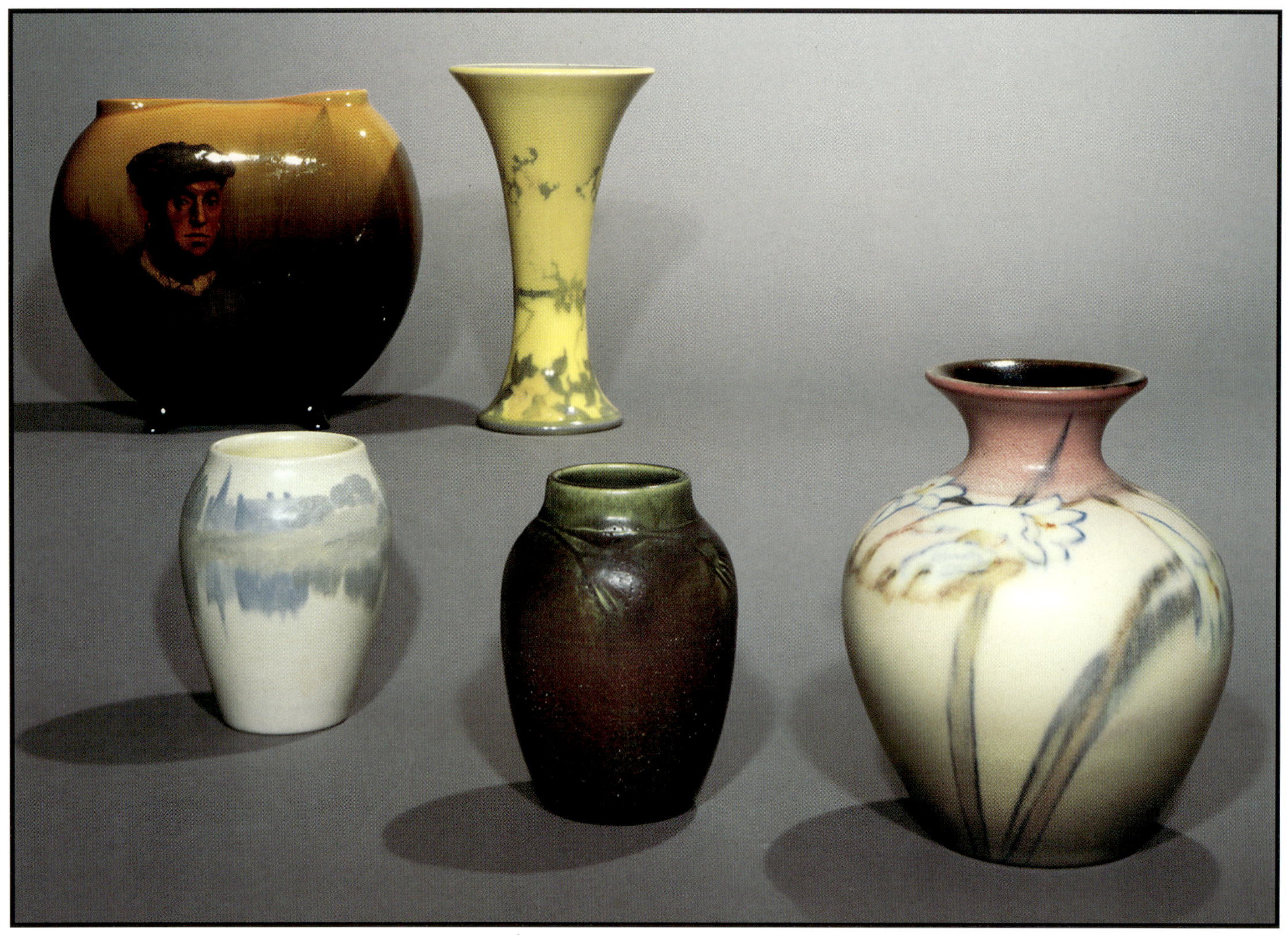

628   Standard glaze pillow vase picturing a sailor in front of a row of docked sailboats, painted in 1898 by Sturgis Laurence. Marks include the Rookwood logo, the date, shape number 90 A, a wheel ground x, part of an old paper label and the artist's last name, incised in the clay. Height 7 1/8 inches. There is a small glaze nick off the rim. $600-800

629   Early and unusual Vellum glaze vase painted by Fred Rothenbusch in 1905. Pictured is a small village with houses, trees and a church all reflecting in a body of water. Marks include the Rookwood logo, the date, shape number 942 E, an impressed V for Vellum glaze body, an incised V for Vellum glaze, a wheel ground X and the impressed monogram of the artist. Height 4 1/2 inches. Slight runs in the underglaze color probably account for the X. $700-900

630   Pretty yellow tinted high glaze flared vase with precise floral decoration done in 1923 by Fred Rothenbusch. Marks include the Rookwood logo, the date, shape number 2619 E, an incised P for porcelain body, an incised Y for yellow tinted high glaze and the incised monogram of the artist. Height 7 5/8 inches. Uncrazed and very crisp and clean. $1250-1750

631   Mat glaze vase with simple incising around the rim in the form of pine boughs, done in 1913 by C.S. Todd. Marks include the Rookwood logo, the date, shape number 654 D and the incised initials of the artist. Height 4 7/8 inches. A tight line at the rim is more visible from inside the vase than out. $300-400

632   Mat glaze vase with trumpet creeper decoration done by Kataro Shirayamadani in 1932. The interior of the vase is lined with metallic glaze which has the same visual effect as oil on water. Marks include the Rookwood logo, the date, S for special shape number, an original Rookwood showroom paper label which lists the glaze line as Decorated Mat and the artist's cypher, painted on in black slip. Height 6 5/8 inches. $800-1000

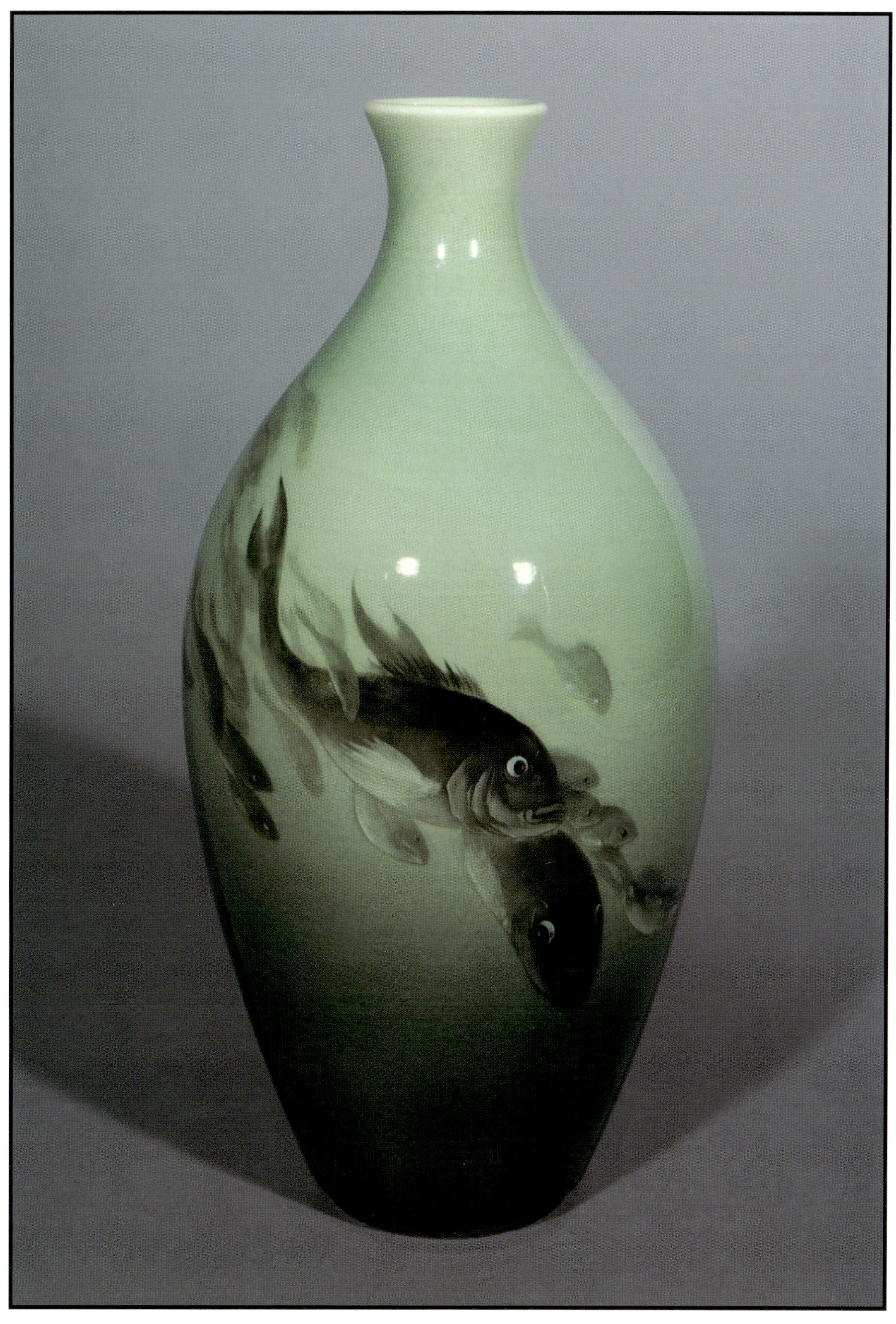

633   Good Sea Green glaze vase done by Albert Valentien in 1896 showing a large school of nearly thirty fish of $6000-8000
       various sizes swimming past. One of the larger fish stares directly at the viewer. This is an early example of Sea
       Green, done with great style by one of Rookwood's most talented decorators. Marks include the Rookwood
       logo, the date and shape number 745 A. The artist's full name is incised on the side of the vase, below and just
       to the right of the leading fish. Height 10 7/8 inches. There are a few small, unobtrusive glaze bubbles on the
       back side of the vase.

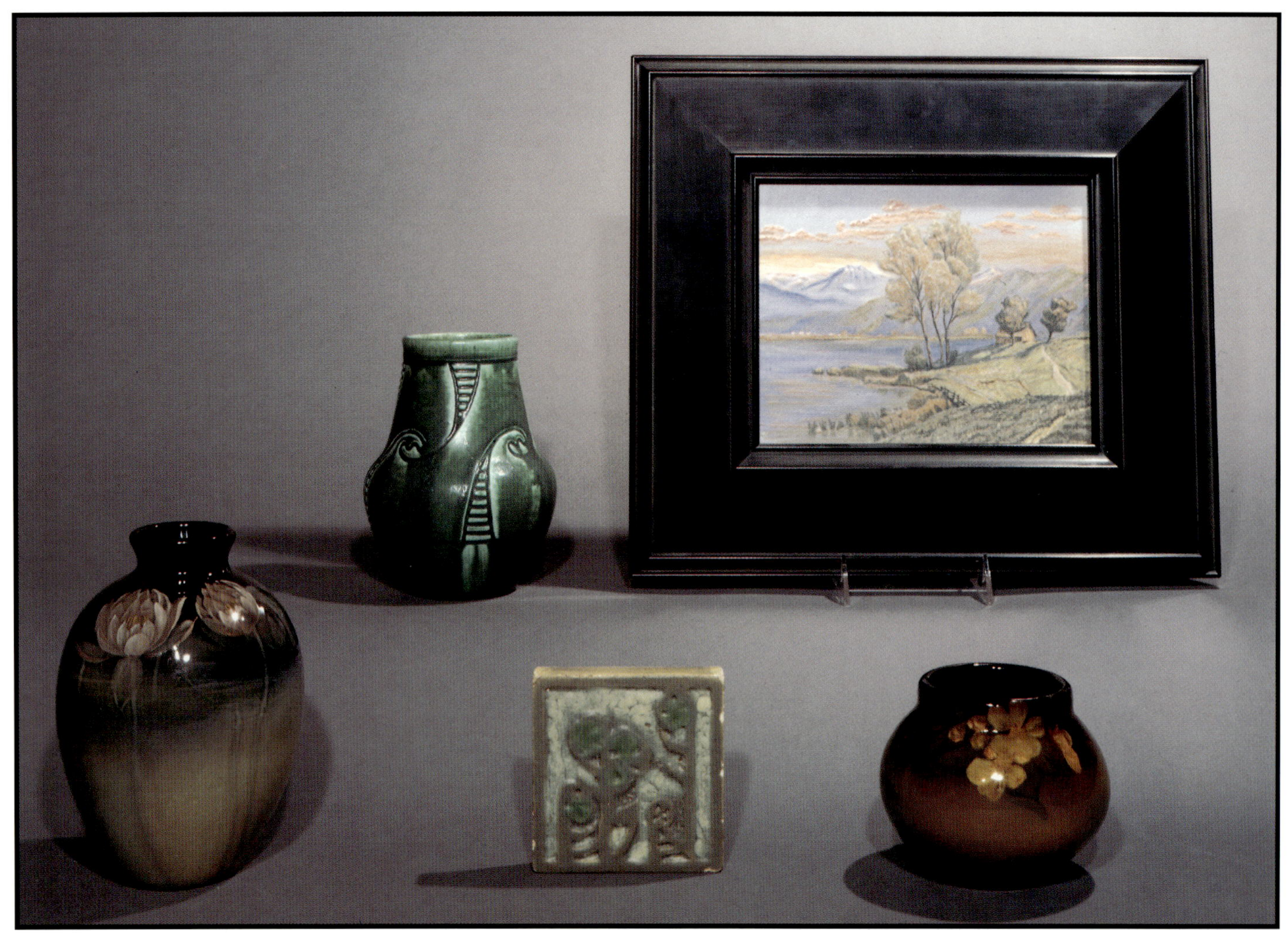

634   Pretty Sea Green vase with purple lotus blossoms floating in limpid waters, painted in 1901 by Mary Nourse. Marks include the Rookwood logo, the date, shape number 902 D, an incised L for light Standard glaze and the incised initials of the artist. Height 6 7/8 inches. Nourse obviously wanted Standard glaze on this vase and, fortunately for us, the glaze department had Sea Green on its' mind. Some sort of damage to mid-body has been professionally repaired. $2000-2500

635   Early mat glaze Arts & Crafts style vase with repeating geometric patterns made at Rookwood in 1901. Marks include the Rookwood logo, the date and shape number 191 DZ. Height 6 1/2 inches. Minor grinding chips on the base. $300-400

636   Rookwood Architectural Faience tile with fiddlehead fern decoration, hand carved by Cecil Duell, circa 1910. The back is impressed "Rookwood Faience 1157" and also bears the incised initials of the artist. Size is 4 inches square. Minor edge chips. $200-300

637   Rare Vellum glaze scenic tile painted in 1946 by Flora King. Shown is a hilly region with a barn and other small buildings sitting around the edge of a large lake. King's initials appear in the lower left hand corner. The back is marked with an unusual inkstamp Rookwood logo and date. Size is approximately 8 x 10 inches. There is some crazing, which is almost impossible to see. The King sisters were excellent at portraying animals. This is the only known landscape plaque done by either. New frame. $6000-6500

638   Standard glaze vase with wild rose decoration by Laura Lindeman, done in 1904. Marks include the Rookwood logo, the date, shape number 911 E and the incised initials of the artist. Height 3 7/8 inches. There are minor glaze flaws at the rim. $200-300

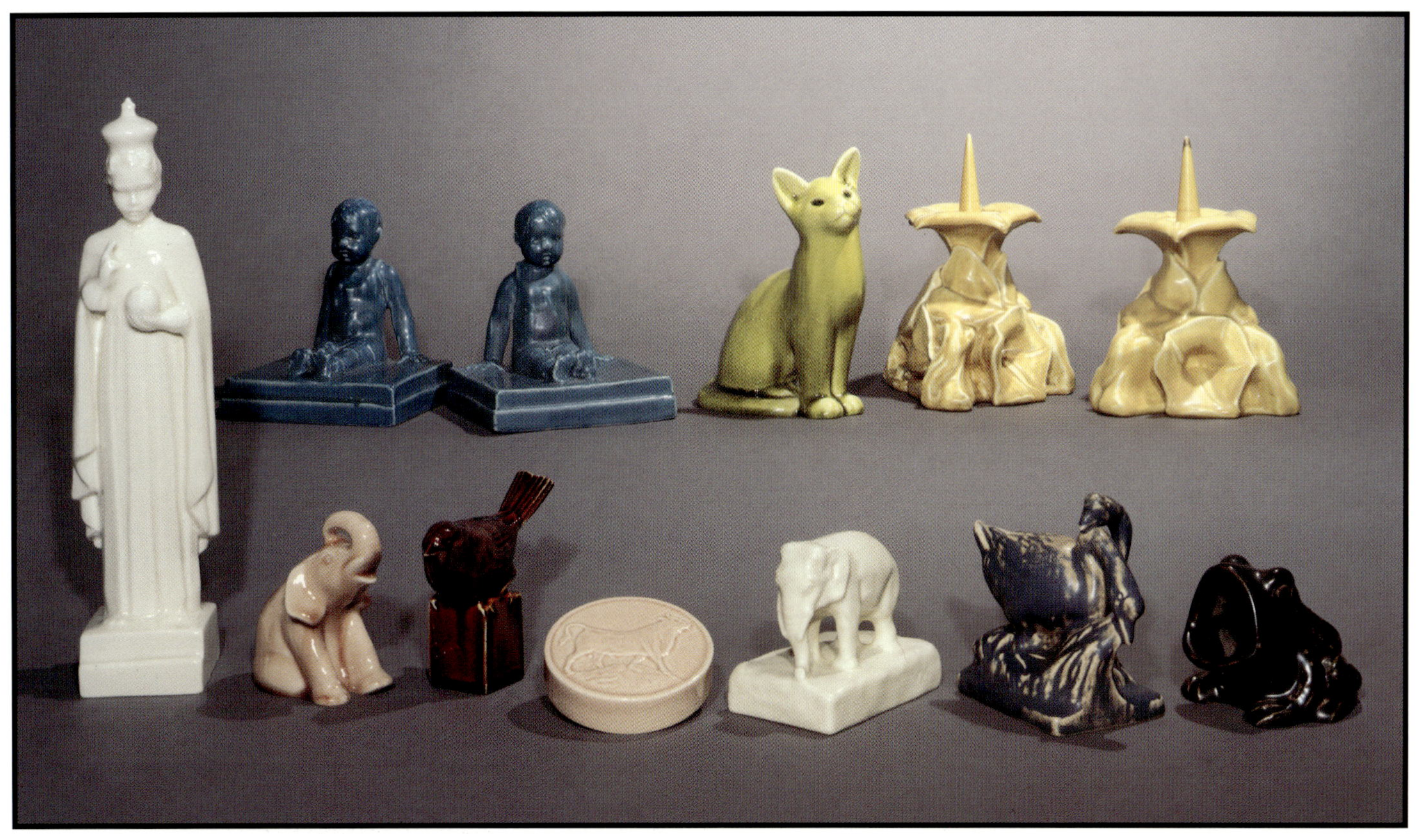

639	Tall Rookwood figural "Infant Jesus of Prague" statue in white high glaze, made in 1959. Marks include the Rookwood logo, the date, shape number 6950 and the notation "Rookwood Cinti, O." Height 11 7/8 inches.	$200-300
640	Pair of mat glaze "Little Boy" bookends in dark blue made at Rookwood in 1920. Marks include the Rookwood logo, the date, shape number 2447 and a wheel ground x. Height 5 3/8 inches. A small glaze skip on one of the bookends has been professionally repaired.	$400-500
641	Cute high glaze seated elephant paperweight designed by Kataro Shirayamadani and made at Rookwood in 1947. Marks include the Rookwood logo, the date and shape number 6409. Height 3 3/4 inches.	$300-400
642	Sparrow paperweight done in a glittery Coromandel glaze at Rookwood circa 1932. Marks are obscured with the exception of part of the Rookwood logo. Height 3 7/8 inches.	$300-400
643	High glaze paperweight made by Rookwood in 1948. On the front is the embossed image of a large bull. Marks on the back include the Rookwood logo, the date and the notation "Boss Chas. G. Schmidt The Cincinnati Butchers' Supply Company Cin. O." Diameter is 3 3/8 inches.	$200-250
644	Cat paperweight in chartreuse high glaze made at Rookwood in 1946. Marks include the Rookwood logo, the date, shape number 6182 and the cast-in monogram of designer, Louise Abel. Height 6 7/8 inches.	$300-400
645	White mat glaze elephant paperweight made at Rookwood in 1932. Marks include the Rookwood logo, the date and shape number 2797. Height 3 1/8 inches.	$300-400
646	Pair of Rookwood bagel holders in the form of morning glory flowers ad vines, done in 1923 with a variegated yellow mat glaze. Impressed with the Rookwood logo, the date and shape number 2513. Height of each is 6 7/8 inches. We were kidding, they're really candlesticks.	$500-700
647	Good Double Goose paperweight done in a rich blue over brown mat glaze at Rookwood in 1927. Marks include the Rookwood logo, the date and shape number 1855. Height 4 1/8 inches.	$400-600
648	Frog ashtray with a strong resemblance to our Auctioneer, done in a gunmetal brown glaze at Rookwood in 1932. Marks include the Rookwood logo, the date and shape number 6097. Height 2 3/4 inches.	$250-350

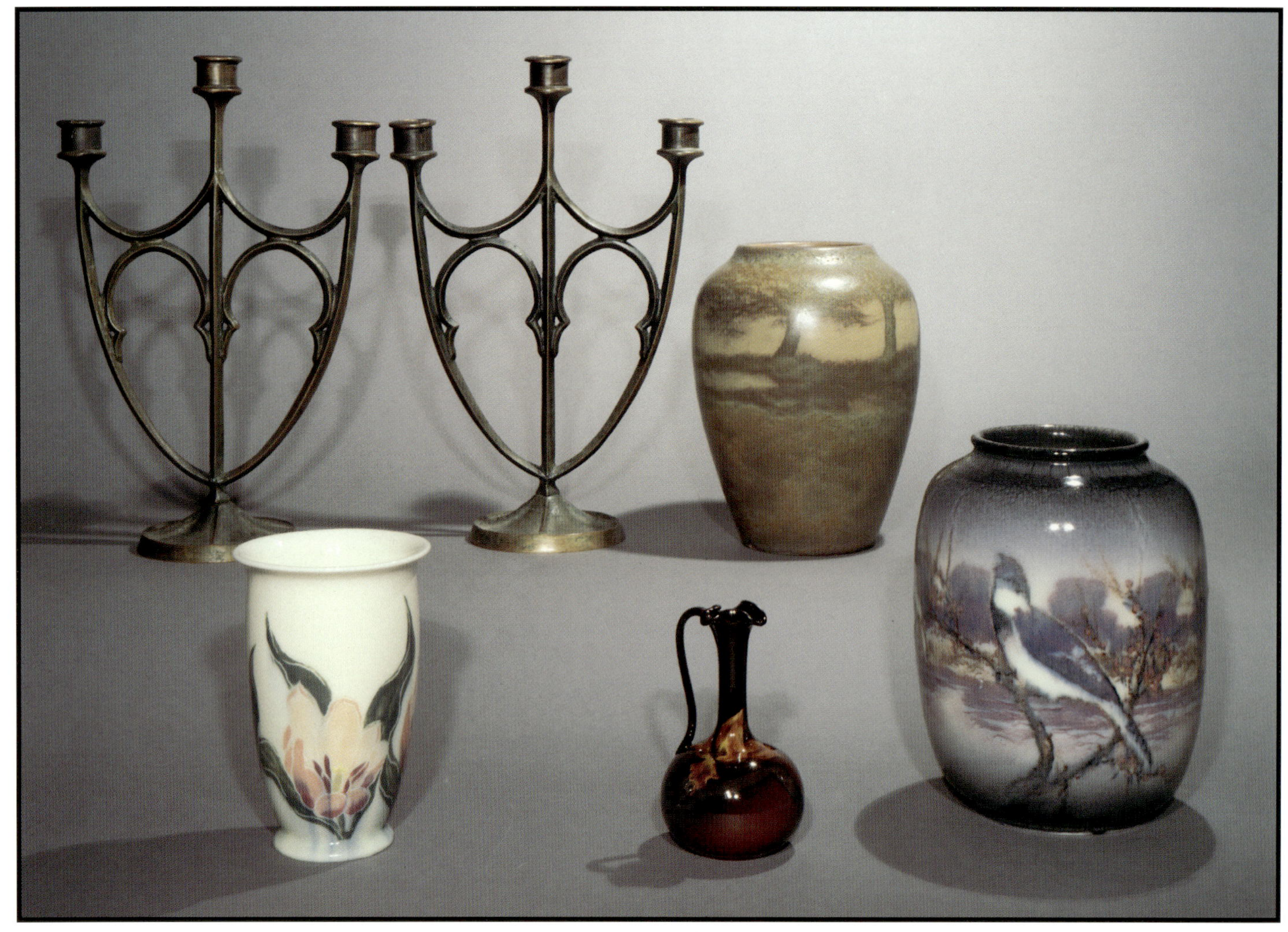

649   Pair of three-pronged bronze candelabra made by Rookwood artist E.T. Hurley, circa 1918. Each bears the cast-in notation "E.T. Hurley 1918". Height 14 3/4 inches. Good original medium brown patina. $1000-1500

650   High glaze vase with stylized lotus blossom decoration, painted and incised by E.T. Hurley in 1944. Marks include the Rookwood logo, the date, shape number 6357 and the incised initials of the artist. Height 6 1/2 inches. Uncrazed with good color and design. $1000-1500

651   Delicate Standard glaze ewer painted in 1898 by E.T. Hurley. Decoration consists of red and yellow parrot tulips with green leaves. Marks include the Rookwood logo, the date, shape number 844, a star shaped esoteric mark and the incised initials of the artist. Height 5 1/4 inches. $300-500

652   Good Arts & Crafts style Vellum glaze landscape vase painted by E.T. Hurley in 1908. Done in tonalistic shades of brown and green and using dusky winter images, flatly painted, the vase represents one of Hurley's strongest periods. Hurley painted a nearly identical frieze for the foyer of Rookwood Photographer Fritz Raymond's house in Cincinnati around this same time. Marks include the Rookwood logo, the date, shape number 999 C, an impressed V for Vellum glaze body, an incised V for Vellum glaze, a wheel ground x and the incised initials of the artist. A small burst bubble and small glaze miss near the base account for the x. There are a fair amount of glaze pits but these seem to fit in nicely with the overall organic nature of the vase. $1250-1750

653   Colorful high glaze scenic vase with four birds in the foreground in various poses around the vase, painted in 1945 by E.T. Hurley. Marks include the Rookwood logo, the date, shape number 6197 C, the number 5054 painted on in black slip and the initials of the artist, also painted on in black slip. Height 8 5/8 inches. A neat drill hole in the bottom has been plugged. Uncrazed. $1750-2250

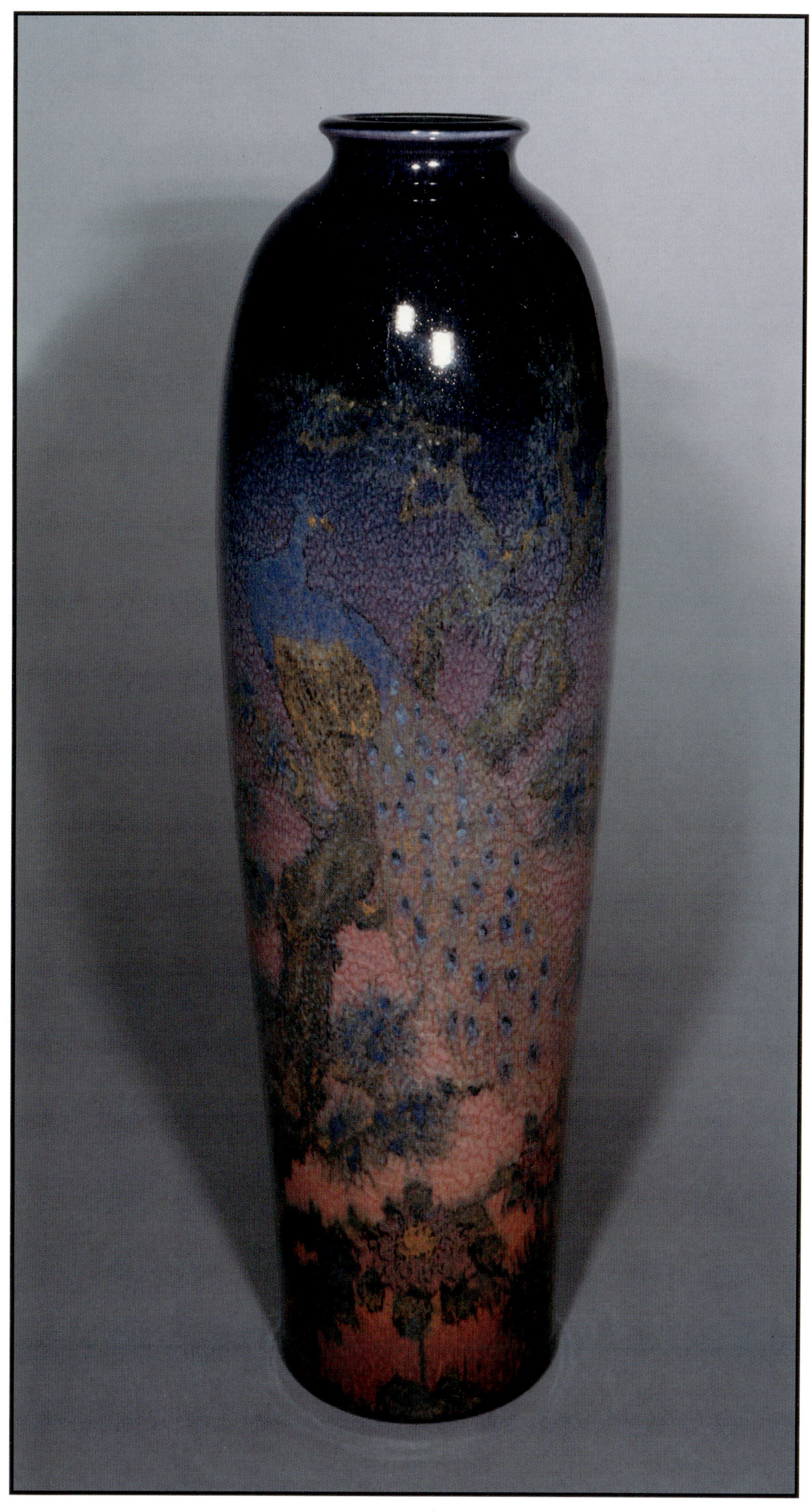

654   Tall hand thrown vase done by E.T. Hurley in 1925 which shows three peacocks perched among exotic flower- $6000-8000
ing plants. Marks include the Rookwood logo, the date, shape number 2499 A and the artist's monogram
painted on in black slip. Height 18 3/4 inches. Minor crazing. Hurley created a number of large pieces using
what has been described as a "watercolor" decorating style which utilizes lush colors that tend to intermingle
somewhat when applied. On occasion, layers of color can be seen, indicating multiple firings and glazes which
are finally finished with a clear high glaze. Typically, Hurley will incorporate exotic birds and foliage in his
scenes reminiscent of Japanese woodblock prints popular at the turn of the century.

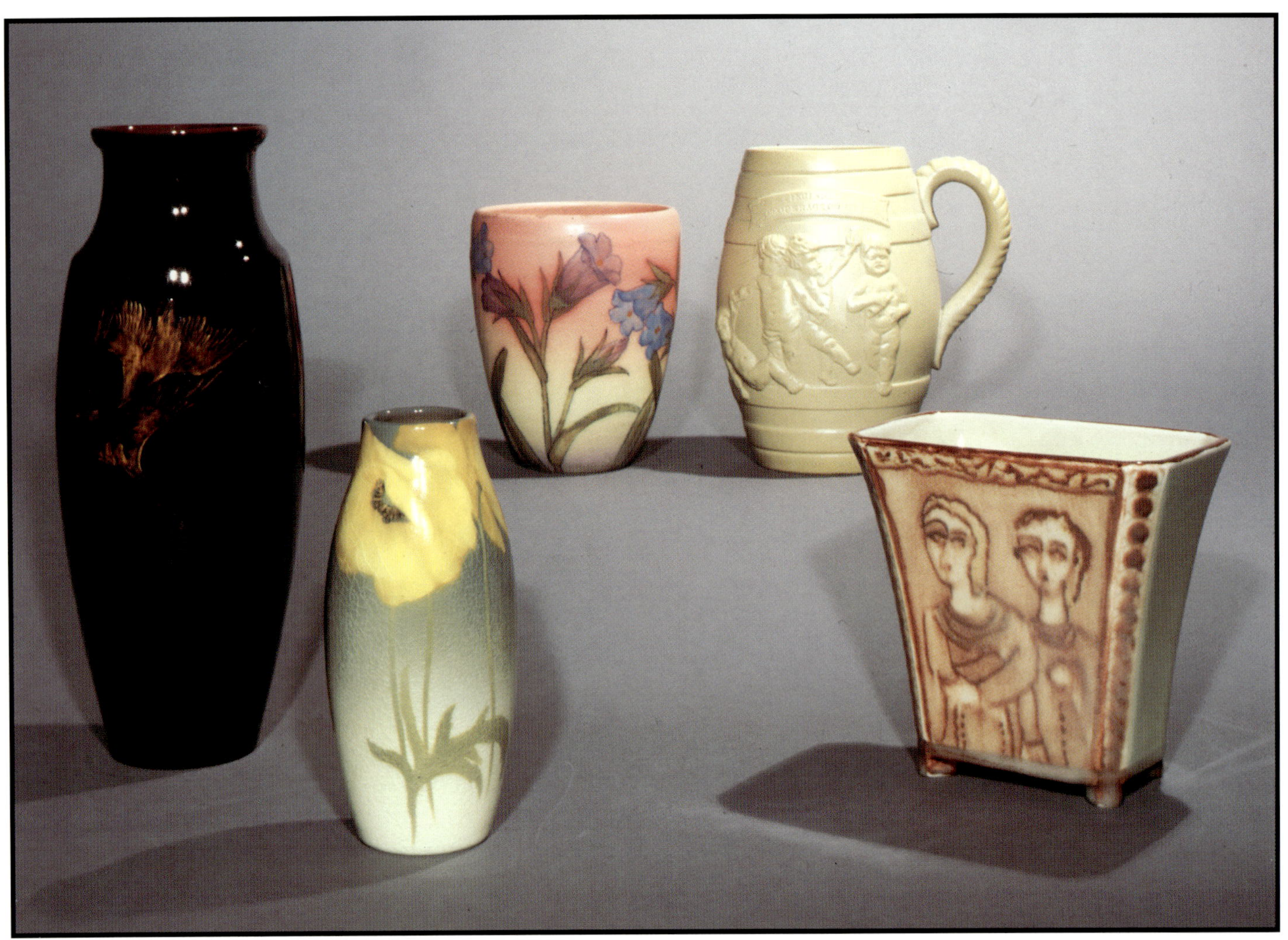

655	Fine Standard glaze vase showing two geese flying over a reeded marsh, decorated in 1893 by Albert Valentien. The vase is nearly covered with Tiger Eye and Goldstone effect. Marks include the Rookwood logo, the date, shape number 538 C, R for red clay, an incised L for light Standard glaze and the incised initials of the artist. Height 11 3/4 inches. Pictured: Rookwood Its Golden Era of Art Pottery 1880-1929 by Kircher and Agranoff, color plate 4, middle row, number two.	$1000-1500
656	Iris glaze vase with bright yellow poppies on a pale gray to cream ground, done in 1903 by Marianne Mitchell. Marks include the Rookwood logo, the date, shape number 939 D, an incised W for white (Iris) glaze and the incised monogram of the artist. Height 7 inches.	$1250-1500
657	Brightly painted Vellum floral vase done in 1930 by Kataro Shirayamadani. The flowers are outlined in black. Marks include the Rookwood logo, the date, shape number 6181 E, a fan shaped esoteric mark and the incised cypher of the artist. Height 6 inches. There is a crack and glaze peppering at the rim.	$500-700
658	Early Rookwood production mug made for Cincinnati Cooperage Company in the early 1880's. The only mark on the bottom of this piece is an S for sage green clay. The Cooperage name appears on the front of the mug. Height 7 1/2 inches. There is a small chip off the base.	$200-300
659	High glaze planter vase with four small feet decorated by Jens Jensen in 1946 with two human figures. Marks include the Rookwood logo, the date, shape number 6036, a wheel ground line, the number 8978 painted on in brown slip and the artist's monogram, also painted on in brown slip. Height 6 1/8 inches. The wheel ground line is most likely the 1940's equivalent of a wheel ground x. It serves the same purpose without dramatically marring the product.	$600-800

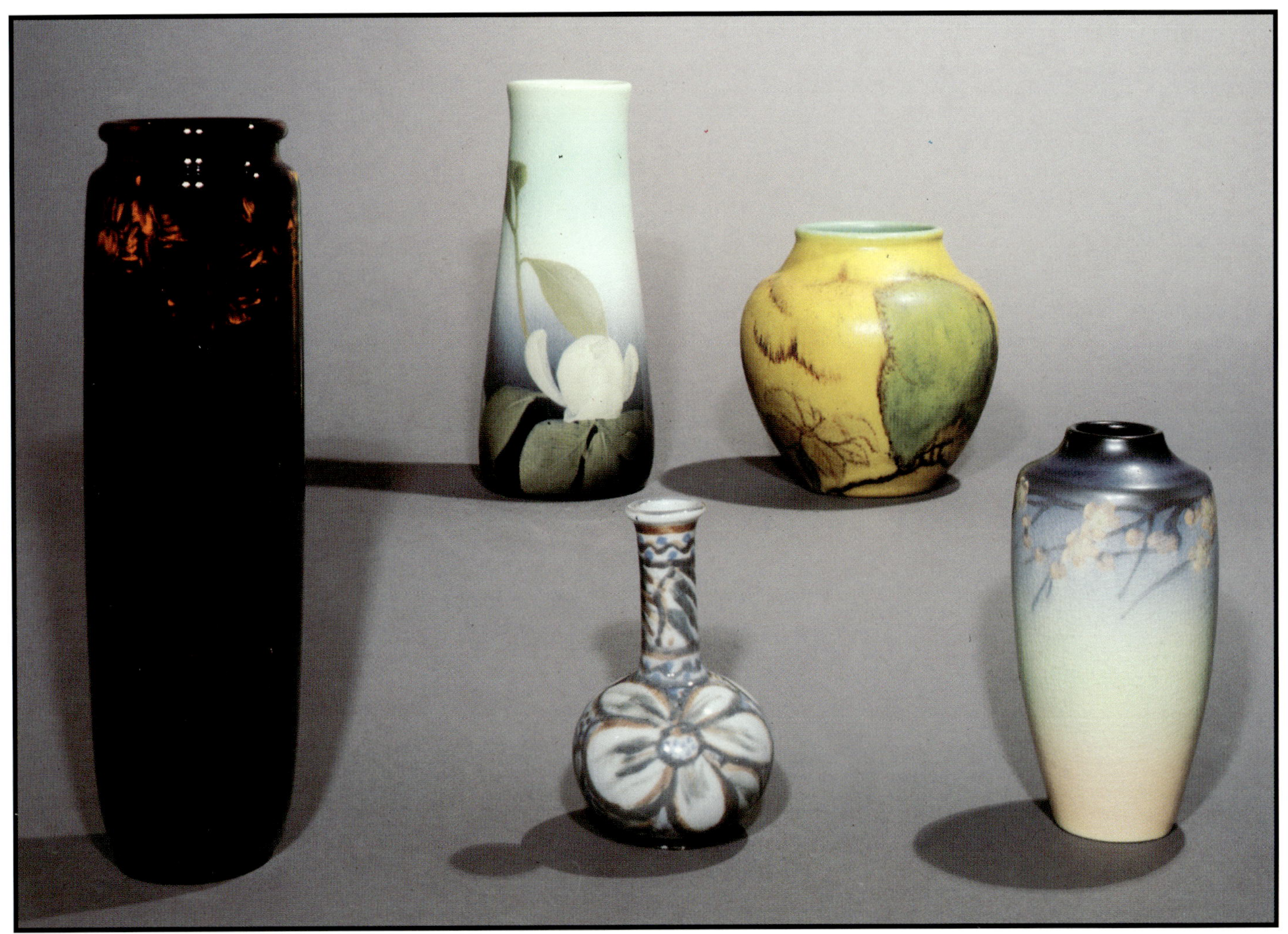

660   Standard glaze vase with daisy decoration done in 1892 by Ed Abel. This is a good example of Rookwood's "Mahogany", a Dark Standard glaze done over red clay and as often happened with this combination, large areas of Goldstone and Tiger Eye are present in this example. Marks include the Rookwood logo, the date, shape number 589 D, an impressed R for red clay, an incised D for Dark Standard glaze and the incised initials of the artist. Height 11 1/4 inches. A tight 1 1/2 inch line descends from the rim. $400-600

661   Iris glaze vase with nicely composed magnolia decoration painted in 1906 by Sara Sax. Marks include the Rookwood logo, the date, shape number 950 D, an incised W for white (Iris) glaze and the impressed monogram of the artist. Height 8 3/8 inches. $2000-2500

662   1945 High glaze vase with all over floral decoration, most likely the work of Jens Jensen. Marks include the Rookwood logo, the date and shape number 6910. Height 5 1/8 inches. Although unsigned, the style is certainly consistent with Jensen's. $300-400

663   Mat glaze vase with green and brown floral decoration on a bright yellow ground done in 1930 by Janet Harris. Marks include the Rookwood logo, the date, shape number 919 D and the monogram of the artist, painted on in black slip. Height 5 1/4 inches. Some peppering in the glaze. $300-400

664   Vellum glaze vase from 1914 with cherry blossoms painted by Carrie Steinle. Marks include the Rookwood logo, the date, shape number 1926, an impressed V for Vellum glaze body, an incised V for Vellum glaze and the incised monogram of the artist. Height 6 1/4 inches. Some peppering in the glaze. $400-500

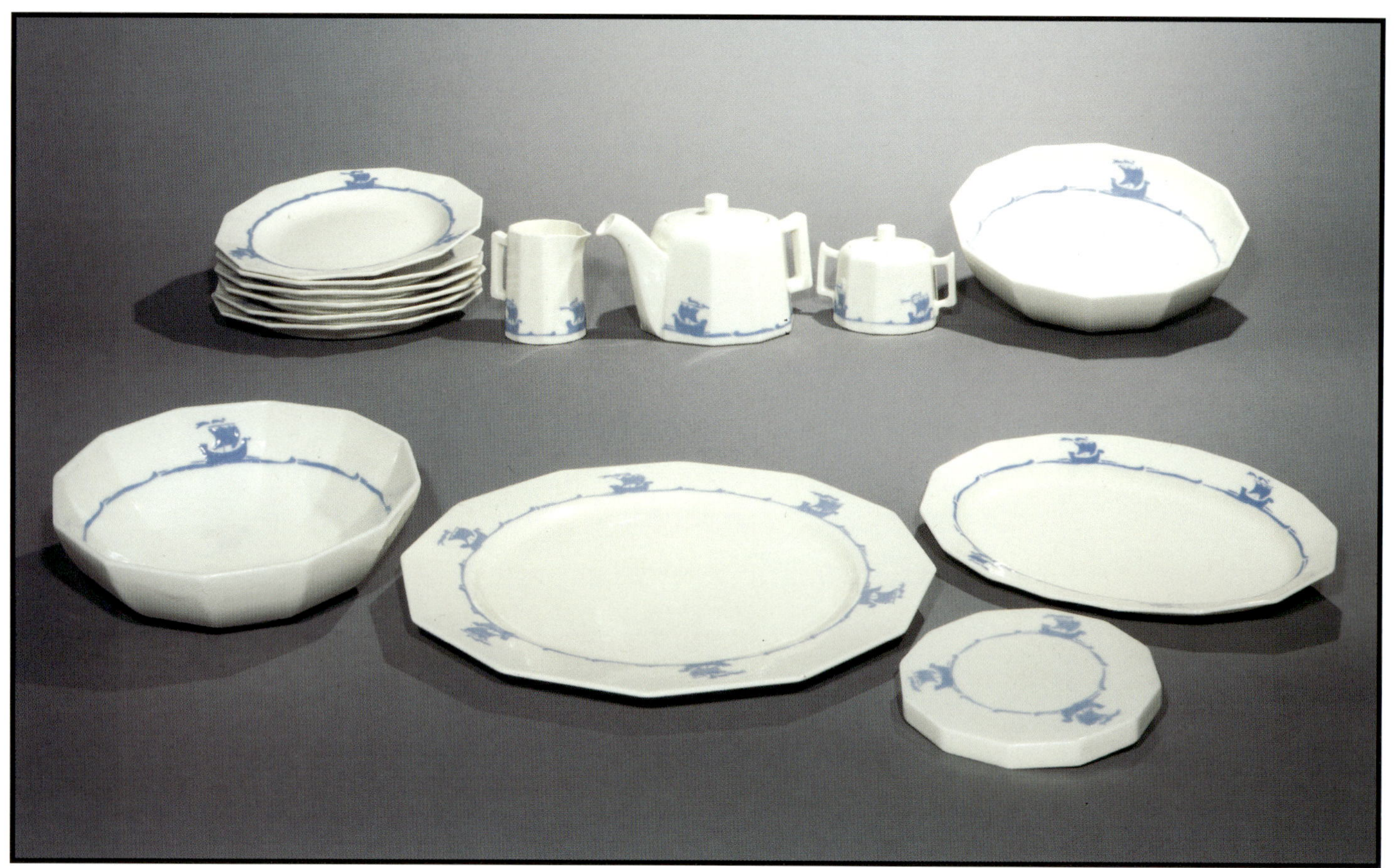

665	Rookwood Blue Ship Dinnerware vegetable bowl made circa 1930. Marks include the Rookwood logo and shape number M-29. Height is 2 7/8 inches and diameter is 9 3/4 inches.	$300-400
666	Set of six Rookwood Blue Ship Dinnerware luncheon plates made circa 1930. Marks include the Rookwood logo and shape number M-33. Diameter is 9 1/8 inches.	$300-400
667	Rookwood Blue Ship Dinnerware cake plate made in 1925. Marks include the Rookwood logo, the date and shape number 2701 L. Diameter is 14 inches. Although Rookwood designated its Blue Ship pieces with shape number 2701 and a different letter for each different piece, this is the first dated piece we have seen and the first to use the shape number.	$400-600
668	Rookwood Blue Ship Dinnerware three piece tea set consisting of covered teapot, covered sugar bowl and creamer. All pieces are marked with the Rookwood logo and a shape number. The teapot is M-15, the sugar bowl is M-19 and the creamer is M-20. Height of the teapot is 4 3/8 inches. Excellent condition except for a small nick on the bottom of the teapot's spout.	$400-600
669	Blue Ship dinnerware tea tile made at Rookwood circa 1925. Marks include the flameless Rookwood logo and shape number M 28. Diameter is 6 inches across. Blue Ship pieces are generally never dated but were produced from about 1920 until perhaps the 1940's.	$300-400
670	Rookwood Blue Ship Dinnerware oval platter made circa 1930. Marks include the Rookwood logo and shape number M-32. Greatest distance across is 12 inches.	$250-350
671	Rookwood Blue Ship Dinnerware vegetable bowl. Impressed with the Rookwood logo and shape number M-29. Height 2 3/4 inches and diameter 9 7/8 inches.	$300-400

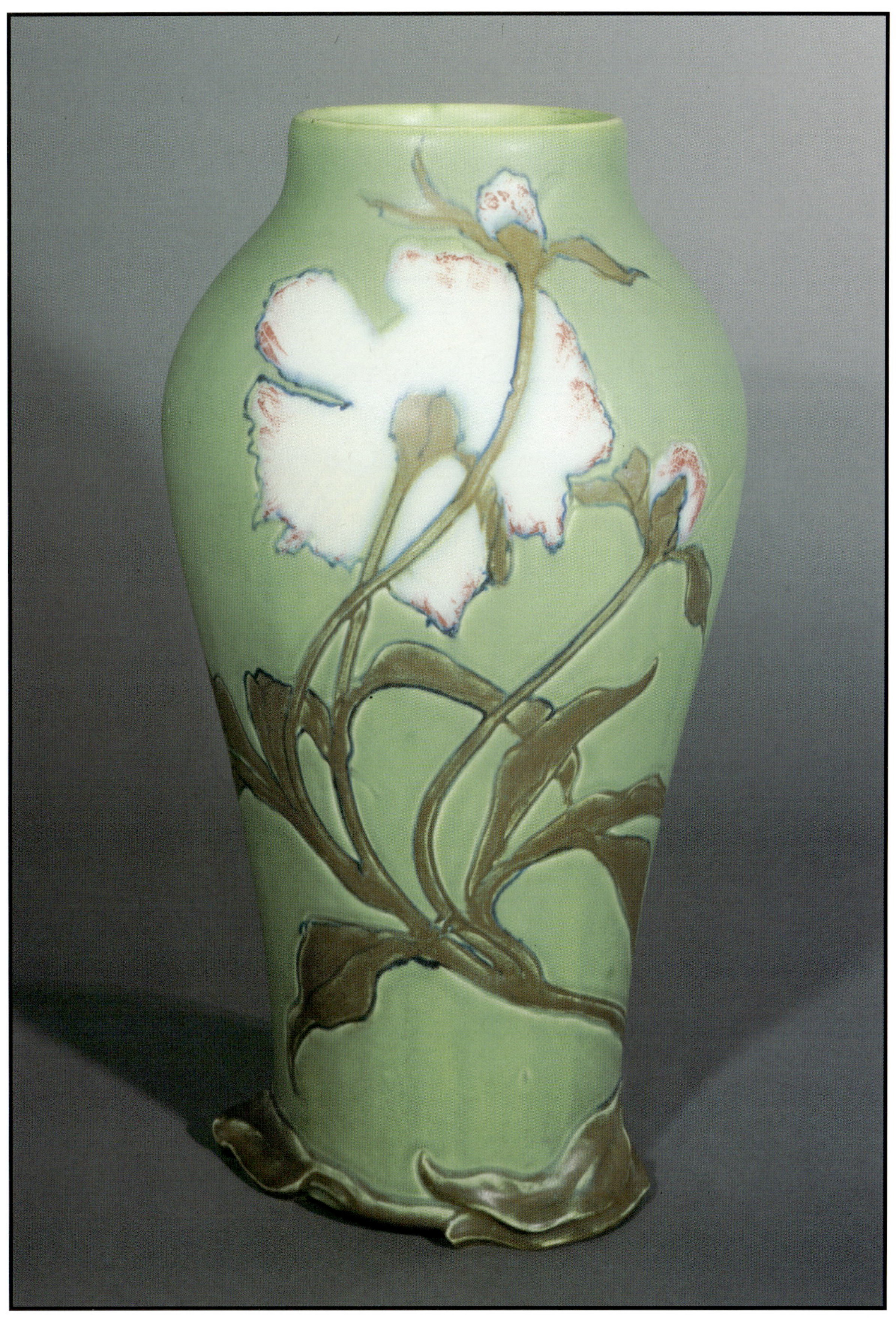

672   Tall and impressive mat glaze lamp base with conventional floral decoration and modeling at the base, done   7000-9000
in 1902 by John Dee Wareham. Decoration consists of white peonies with red highlights which are first
outlined by incising and edging in cobalt blue. The base of the piece is stabilized and elevated slightly by
three feet carved in the form of low growing leaves. A cast hole in the bottom allows for the exit of wiring
although this piece most likely had an oil font and burner given the size of the opening at the top. Marks
include the Rookwood logo, the date and shape number 429 Z. Wareham's initials are painted in blue slip on
one of the feet. Height 16 inches. A small chip to one of the feet has been professionally repaired. Two
prominent decorators at Rookwood created most of the carved lamp bases from this period, these being
Wareham and Shirayamadani. Both tended to use extensive modeling or carving in preparation of the pieces
which are usually done in mat or Iris glaze and which are, by their nature, large by usual Rookwood
standards. Wareham again shows a wonderful flair for decoration, creating stylish designs without
overdecoration. His works are almost always understated, graceful and dramatic at the same time.

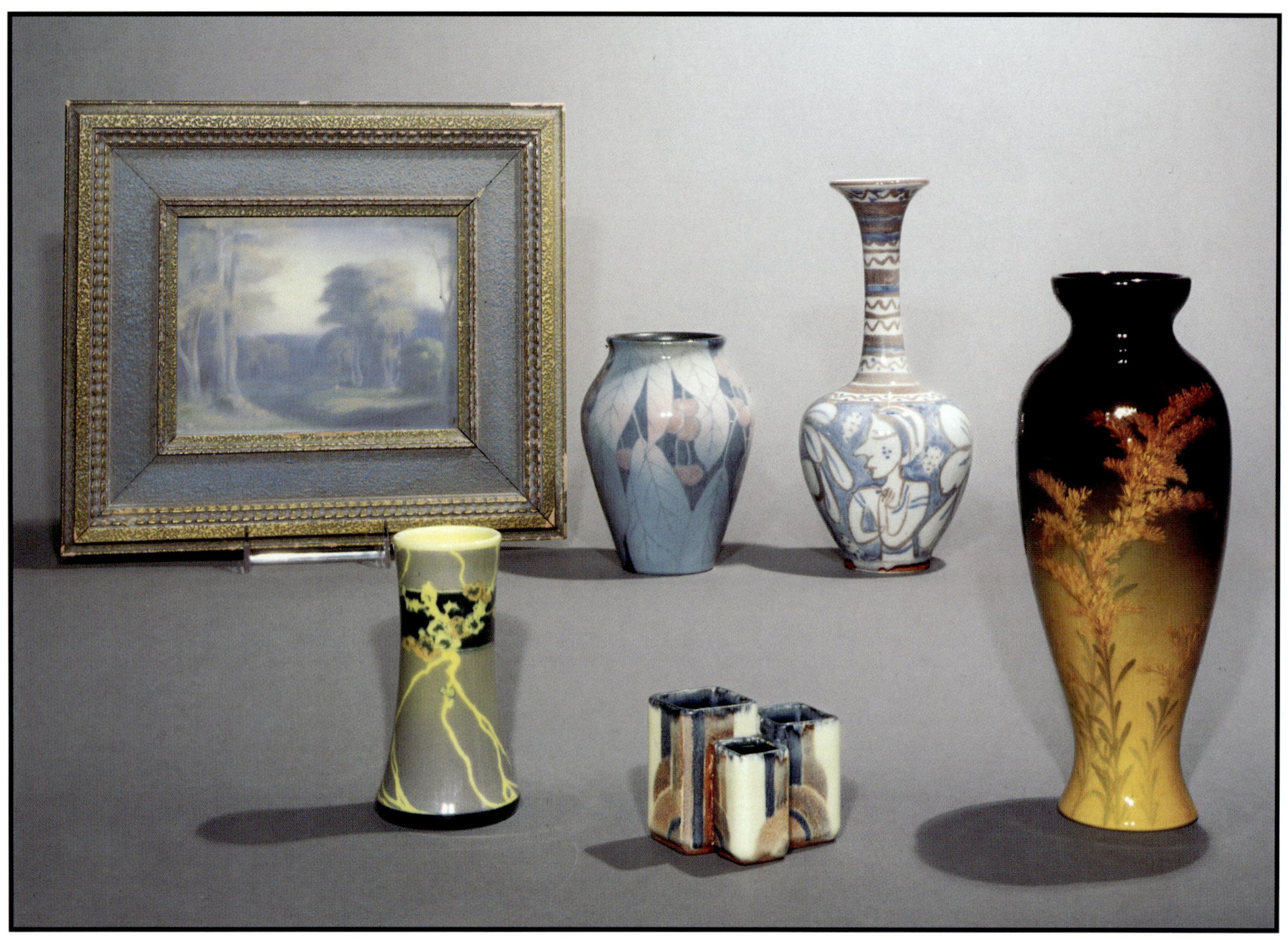

673 Vellum glaze woodland scenic plaque painted by Fred Rothenbusch, circa 1925. The artist's monogram is painted on the lower left hand corner in white slip. Marks on the back have not been examined because the plaque is in its "as made" condition. We assume it to be marked with the Rookwood logo and a date. Affixed to the back is an original Rookwood typewritten label with the title "Morning Fred Rothenbusch". Size is approximately 6 by 8 inches. Uncrazed and very crisp and clean. $3000-4000

674 Unusual yellow tinted high glaze vase with very stylish fruit blossoms and vines painted by Fred Rothenbusch in 1922. Marks include the Rookwood logo, the date, shape number 1358 F, an incised Y for yellow glaze and the incised monogram of the artist. Height 5 3/4 inches. Uncrazed and pleasantly different. $1250-1500

675 Crisp and colorful high glaze vase painted by Kataro Shirayamadani in 1927. Shown are overlapping leaves and bright red cherries, all on a black ground. The interior of the vase is covered in a black mat glaze. Marks include the Rookwood logo, the date, shape number 915 E and the incised cypher of the artist. Height 5 7/8 inches. Uncrazed. $2500-3500

676 Art Deco three compartmented vase with Deco designs in mat glaze, painted by Wilhelmine Rehm in 1930. Marks include the Rookwood logo, the date, shape number 6127, a fan shaped esoteric mark and the artist's monogram, painted on in black slip. Height 2 7/8 inches. Very clean. $400-600

677 Fanciful high glaze vase with long neck and flared rim painted in 1946 by Jens Jensen. Pictured are a young woman, a long-necked bird and several of Jensen's oversized flower blossoms. Marks include the Rookwood logo, the date, shape number 776, the painted on number "911" and the painted-on monogram of the artist. Height 9 7/8 inches. $2500-3500

678 Good Standard glaze vase with several sprays of goldenrod, painted by Anna Valentien in 1899. Marks include the Rookwood logo, the date, shape number 792 C and the incised initials of the artist. Height 11 1/4 inches. Very crisp and clean. $1000-1250

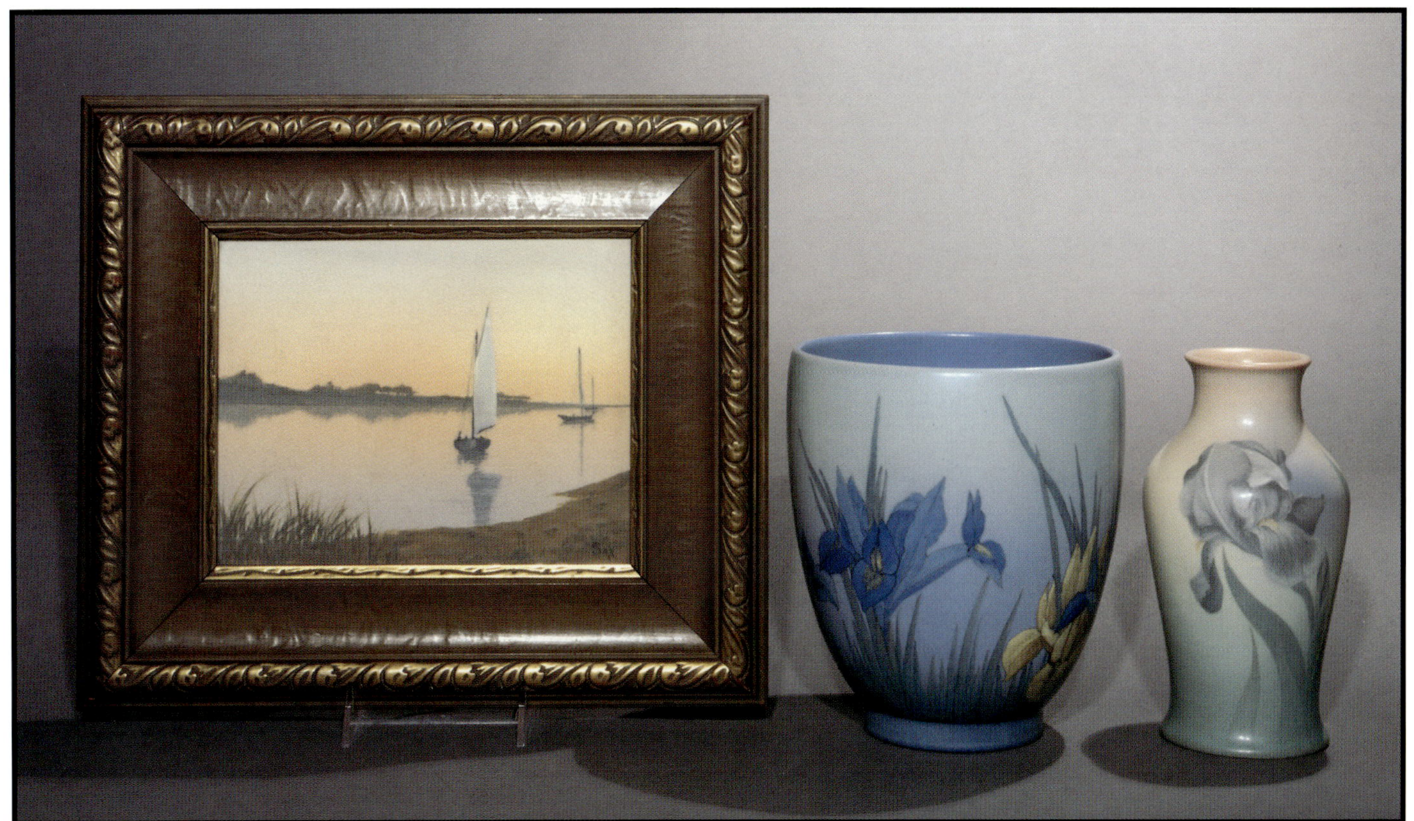

679   Pleasant Arts & Crafts style Vellum glaze plaque in unusual, warm colors showing two sailboats on calm waters $6000-8000
near the end of the day. Painted in 1916 by Sara Sax, whose last name appears in the lower right hand corner.
Marks on the back include the Rookwood logo, the date and V for Vellum glaze body. Size is 7 1/4 by 9 3/8
inches. Affixed to the original frame is a typewritten label with the notation "Yachting S. Sax". A Rookwood
circular paper logo is also affixed to the backing.

680   Finely crafted Vellum glaze vase with tan and blue Japanese irises, painted in 1931 by Ed Diers. The flowers $5000-7000
and green stems are all outlined in black, giving extra contrast to the pale blue ground. Marks include the
Rookwood logo, the date, shape number 6112, an impressed fan shaped esoteric mark, an incised V for Vellum
glaze and the incised monogram of the artist. Height 8 inches. Uncrazed and extremely clean.

681   Fine Vellum glaze vase by Carl Schmidt with a large blue iris on the front and iris buds on the back, painted in $2500-3500
1925. Marks include the Rookwood logo, the date, shape number 2301 E, an incised V for Vellum glaze and the
impressed monogram of the artist. Height 8 inches. Uncrazed. Floral Vellums of this quality are rare indeed.

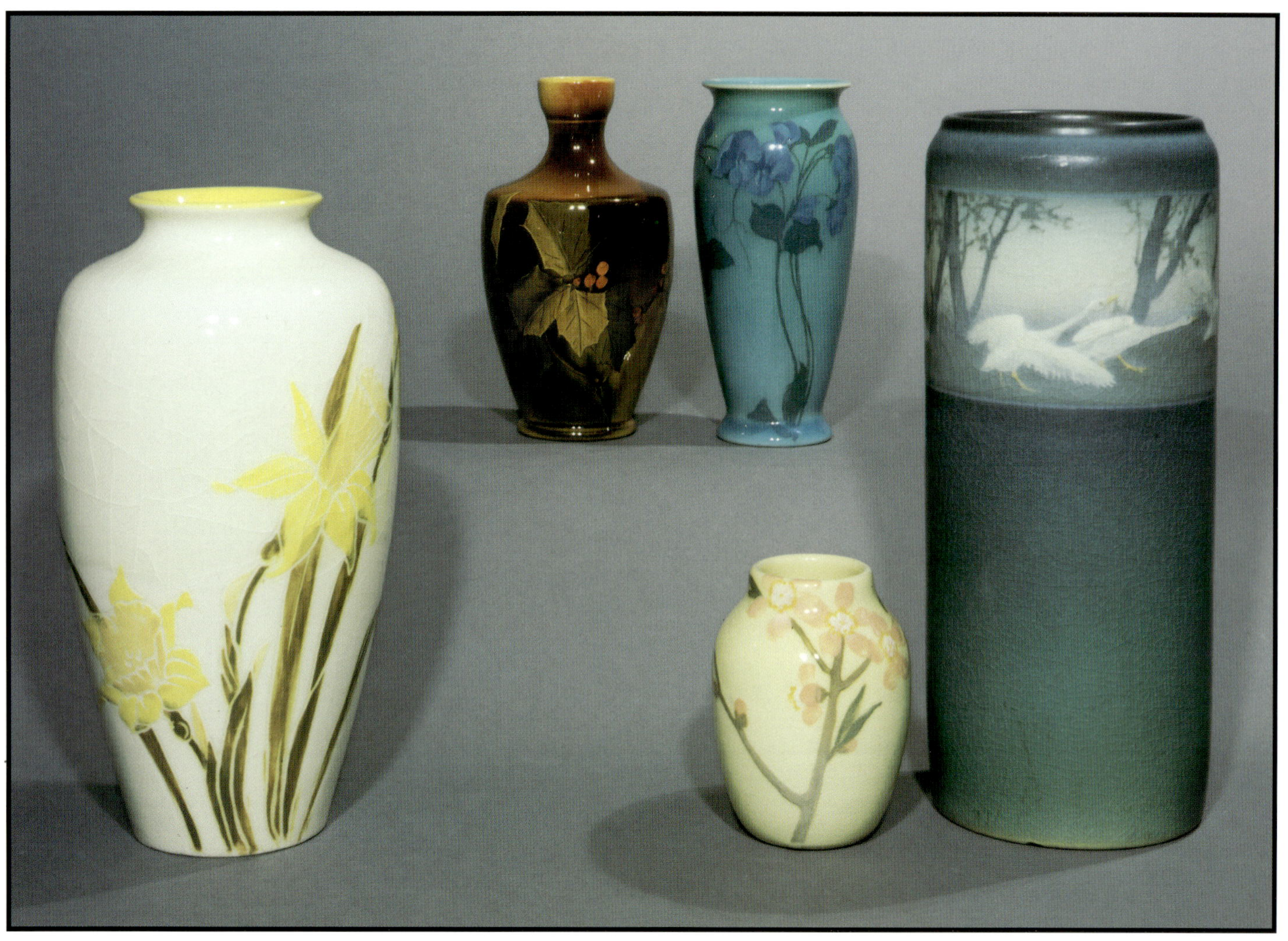

682 High glaze vase with incised and painted jonquils done in 1943 by Margaret McDonald. Marks include the Rookwood logo, the date, shape number 614 E and the incised monogram of the artist. Height 8 1/4 inches. Some glaze pooling on the top half of the vase. $300-400

683 Standard glaze vase decorated with holly by Elizabeth Lincoln in 1893. Marks include the Rookwood logo, the date, shape number 667, W for white clay and the incised initials of the artist. height 6 1/8 inches. $250-350

684 Good blue tinted high glaze vase with exacting decoration of sweet peas, done in 1924 by Ed Diers. Marks include the Rookwood logo, the date, shape number 2721 and the incised monogram of the artist. Height 6 1/8 inches. Uncrazed and very nice. Pictured: Rookwood Its Golden Era of Art Pottery 1880-1929 by Kircher and Agranoff, color plate 14, top row, number three. $1000-1500

685 Iris glaze cabinet vase with red cherry blossoms painted by Jeanette Swing in 1904. Marks include the Rookwood logo, the date, shape number 654 E, an incised W for white (Iris) glaze and the incised monogram of the artist. Height 3 3/8 inches. Some discoloration under the glaze. $400-500

686 Banded Vellum glaze scenic vase showing five white geese running through a wooded area, the work of Kataro Shirayamadani in 1909. Marks include the Rookwood logo, the date, shape number 952 D, an impressed V for Vellum glaze body and the incised cypher of the artist. Height 9 1/4 inches. There is a small chip on the base, obviously in the making and clearly glazed over. $2000-2500

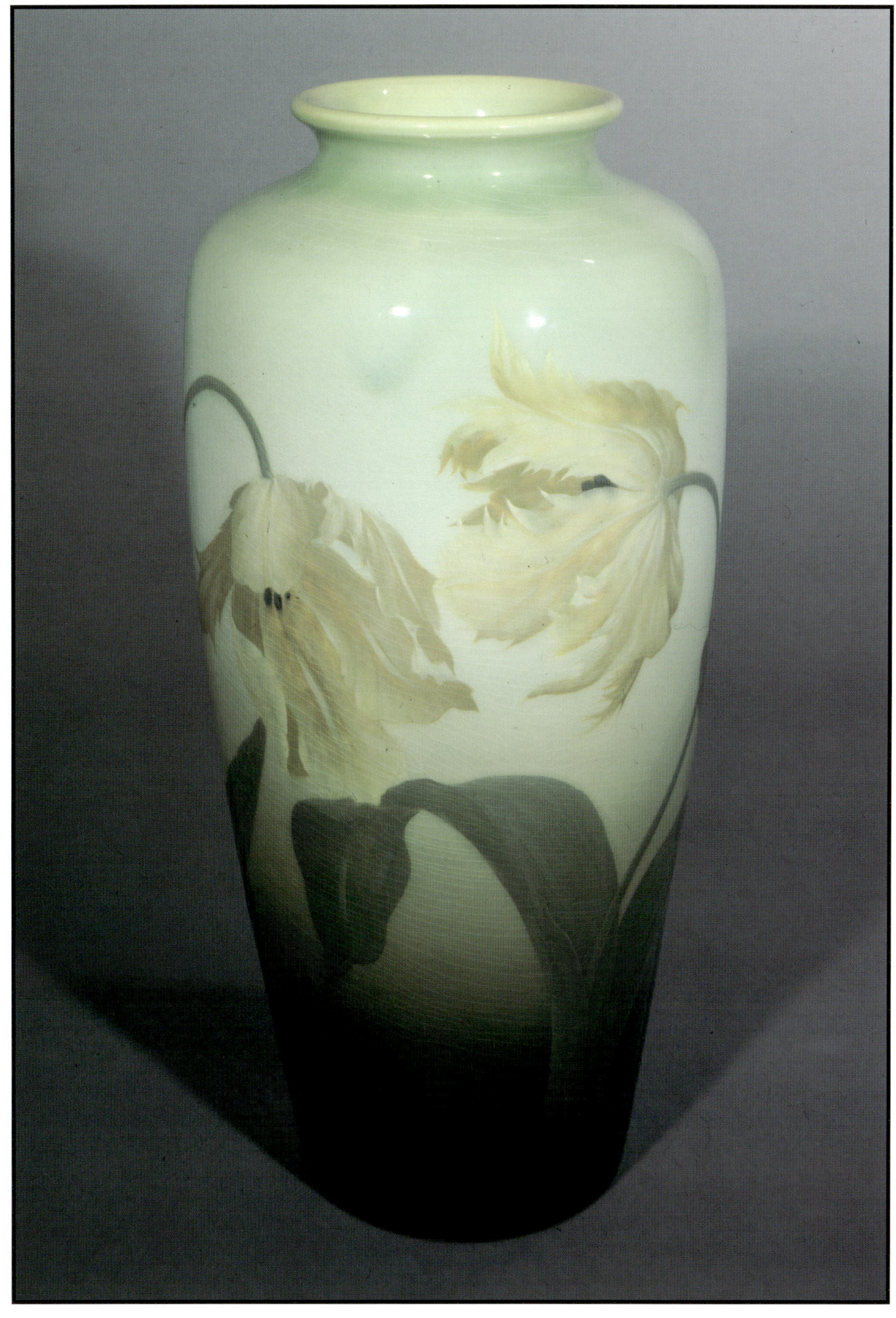

687   Tall and impressive Iris glaze vase with parrot tulip decoration by Carl Schmidt, done in 1910. Parrot tulips $15000-18000
were a favorite at Rookwood, lending themselves naturally to an Art Nouveau aesthetic because of their
languid, undulating appearance which Schmidt has captured in his exacting style. Marks include the
Rookwood logo, the date, shape number 614 B, an incised W for white (Iris) glaze and the impressed
monogram of the artist. Height 14 inches. Minor crazing and minor glaze scratches.

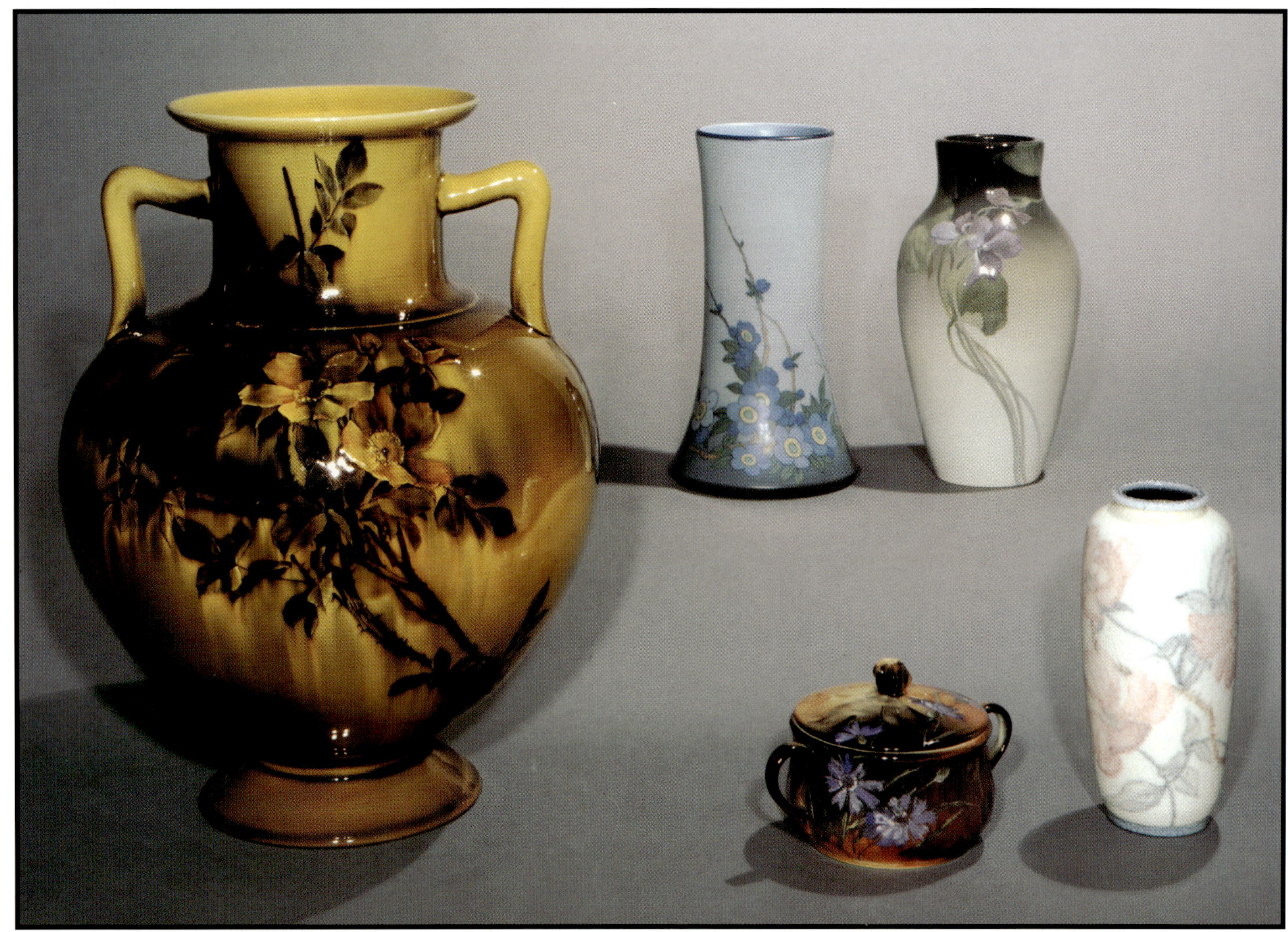

688	Handsome two-handled urn with lifelike wild rose decoration done in 1890 by Kataro Shirayamadani and covered with Standard glaze. Marks include the Rookwood logo, the date, shape number 425, an impressed W for white clay, an incised L for light Standard glaze and the incised cypher of the artist. Height 13 3/4 inches. A triangular 1 inch piece broken out of the foot has been re-glued and professionally repaired. This is a magnificent piece with exceptional artwork and wonderful glaze.	$2000-2500
689	Good Vellum glaze floral vase with Art Deco flowers painted in 1923 by Lenore Asbury. The flowers, leaves and stems are outlined in black. Marks include the Rookwood logo, the date, shape number 1358 D, an incised V for Vellum glaze and the incised initials of the artist. Height 8 3/4 inches. Uncrazed with great color and design.	$2500-3500
690	Good Cameo glaze sugar bowl with blue cornflower decoration on a tan to rust to brown background, painted in 1892 by Mary Nourse. Marks include the Rookwood logo, the date, shape number 473, W for white clay, an incised L for light Standard glaze and the incised initials of the artist. Painted on both the bottom of the bowl and inside the lid are the numbers "67:00" which are acquisition numbers from the Cincinnati Art Museum indicating the piece was on loan from Rookwood. Listed: 2,292 Pieces of Early Rookwood Pottery in the Cincinnati Art Museum in 1916 by Stanley Burt, page 100, item 35. Nourse has clearly marked the piece to receive Standard glaze but somehow it ended up with Cameo. The shading is consistent with Standard glaze and the overall effect gives us a clue as to why and how Iris glaze came into being.	$500-700
691	Iris glaze vase with stylish Art Nouveau treatment of wild violets, painted in 1903 by Fred Rothenbusch. Marks include the Rookwood logo, the date, shape number 928 C, an incised W for white (Iris) glaze and the incised monogram of the artist. Height 8 3/8 inches.	$2500-3000
692	Butterfat glaze vase with bright floral decoration done in 1945 by Kay Ley. Marks include the Rookwood logo, the date, shape number 6644 E, the number 4237 and the artist's monogram, painted on in black slip. Height 6 3/8 inches. A nice example of an uncommon glaze line.	$600-800

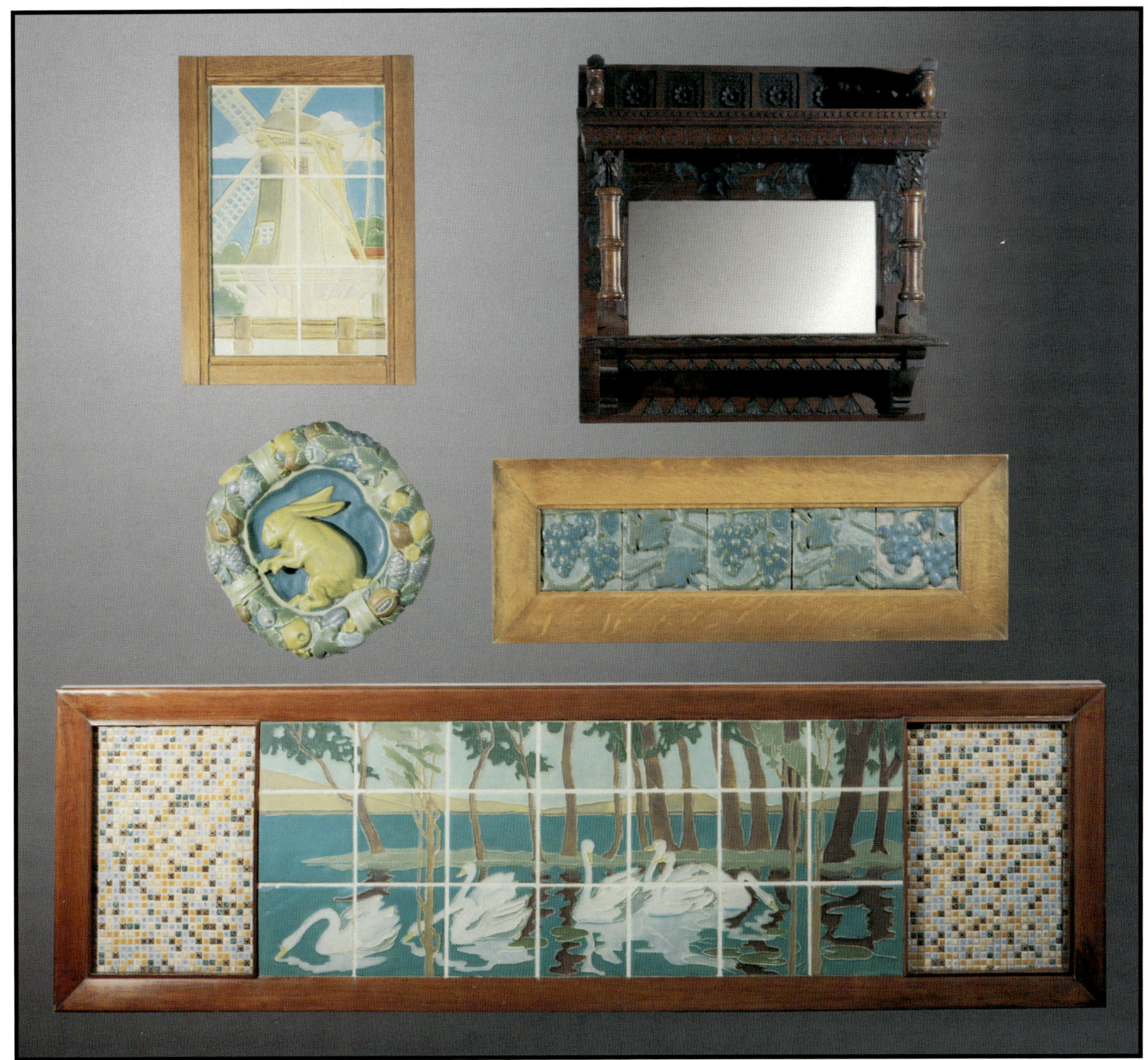

693   Set of six Rookwood Architectural Faience tiles from Mills Restaurant in Cincinnati. Mills featured lots of Rookwood Faience on the walls, all showing scenes of Holland. Windmills were a recurrent theme tieing in with the name of the eatery which was razed a number of years ago. Size is approximately 18 by 12 inches. Not examined out of the frame. $800-1200

694   Good example of Cincinnati art carved furniture in the form of a walnut etagere, done before the turn of the century by Rookwood decorator Grace Young. The design is the common trumpet creeper which grows in abundance in the area. Wood carving was quite the rage in Cincinnati in the 1880's and later. A style of carving on native woods, especially Walnut developed through the influence of the Fry and Pittman families. Young, like most of her craftsman contemporaries, worked in wood in addition to her pottery decoration and painting. Descended in the family of the artist until sold to the consignor in the 1980's. Unsigned. Height is 25 inches, length is 25 inches and depth is a maximum of 9 inches. $1000-1500

695   Rare Rookwood Architectural Faience plaque in colorful mat glaze showing a three dimensional rabbit surrounded by a wreath made up of fruit and leaves. The back is impressed "Rookwood Faience", "062 B" and "4 B". Diameter is 16 1/4 inches. Very minor chips to high points. $1000-1500

696   Framed set of five Rookwood Architectural Faience tiles with grape decor done in blue and green mat glaze. We have exposed the back of one tile and it is stamped "Rookwood Faience 1147". Size is 6 inches by 30 inches. Minor glaze chips. These would appear to be fairly early Rookwood Faience. $1000-1500

697   Handsome Rookwood Architectural Faience grouping showing swans swimming in a placid woodland setting. Made at Rookwood but never installed, the 21 tiles were given to a Rookwood employee by Dr. George Sperti after the Pottery closed. Not examined out of the frame. Size is approximately 17 by 42 inches. One tile is cracked and there are the usual minor chips. The mosaic pieces on either end are not Rookwood. $2500-3500

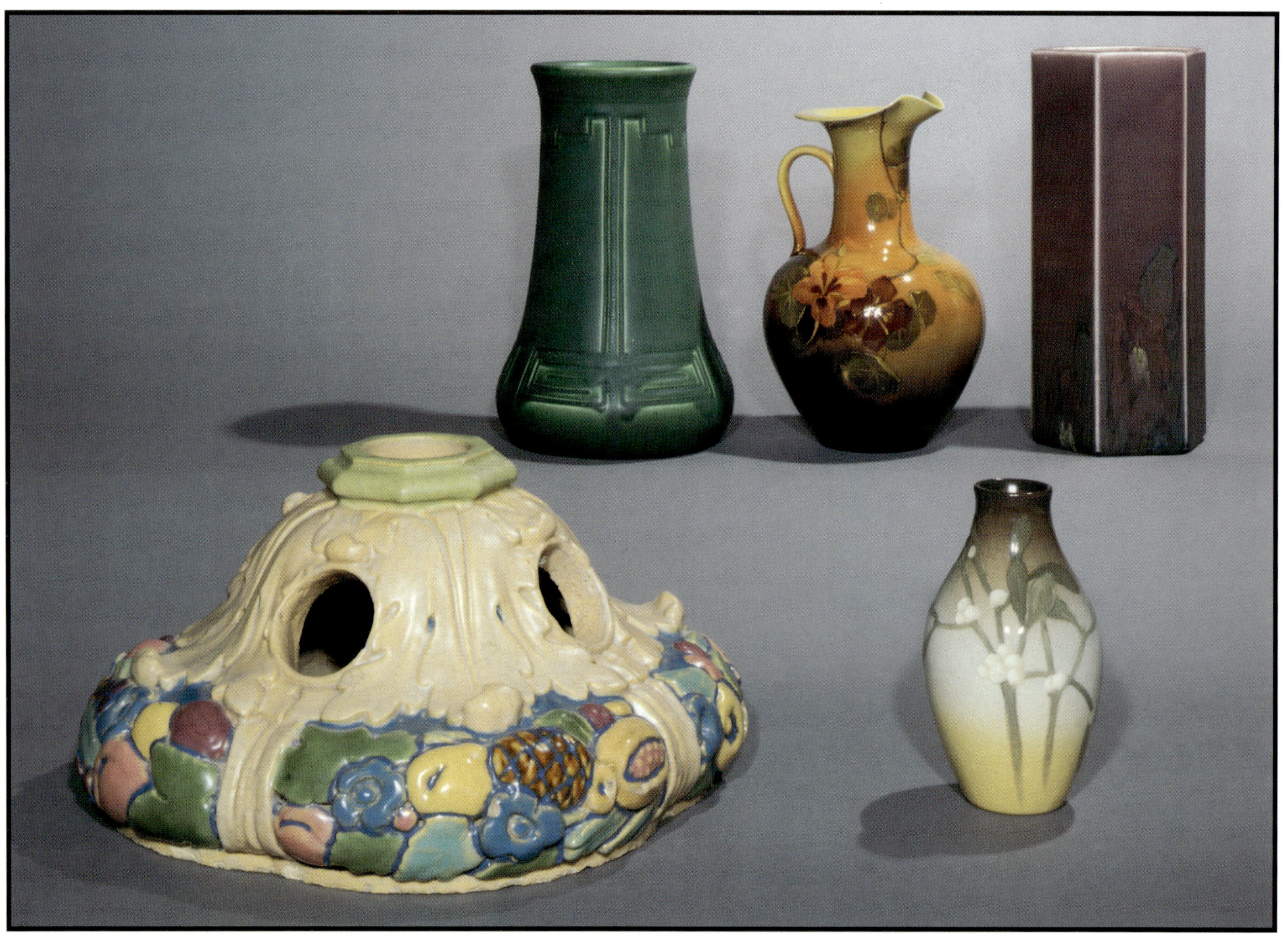

698   Rookwood Architectural Faience ceiling light fixture with embossed fruit in a variety of semi-gloss colors. $700-900
Impressed marks include "Rookwood Faience", the number 5 in a circle and shape numbers 8596 D and
38. Height 6 1/8 inches and diameter is 12 1/2 inches. Minor glaze nicks. Photographed upside-down for
convenience. Actually, it might make a neat centerpiece.

699   1905 Rookwood Arts & Crafts style production vase in green mat glaze having embossed Greek key $500-700
designs worked into the body. Marks include the Rookwood logo, the date, shape number 1097 C and an
impressed V for Vellum glaze body. Height 9 1/4 inches.

700   Good Standard glaze ewer with realistic nasturtium decoration done by Kataro Shirayamadani in 1890. $800-1200
Marks include the Rookwood logo, the date, shape number 62 B, S for sage green clay, an incised L for
light Standard glaze and the incised cypher of the artist. Height 8 1/2 inches. Very crisp and clean.

701   Iris glaze vase with mistletoe decoration done in 1903 by Laura Lindeman. Marks include the Rookwood $300-400
logo, the date, shape number 741 C, an incised W for white (Iris) glaze and the incised initials of the artist.
Height 5 5/8 inches. Rim repair of very average quality.

702   Six-sided mat glaze vase with rather abstracted floral decoration done in 1924 by Margaret McDonald. $300-500
Marks include the Rookwood logo, the date, shape number 2794 and the artist's monogram, painted on in
black slip. Also on the bottom is a ground off spot about 1/2 inch in diameter where some enterprising
person tried to obliterate a wheel ground x. Height 9 1/2 inches.

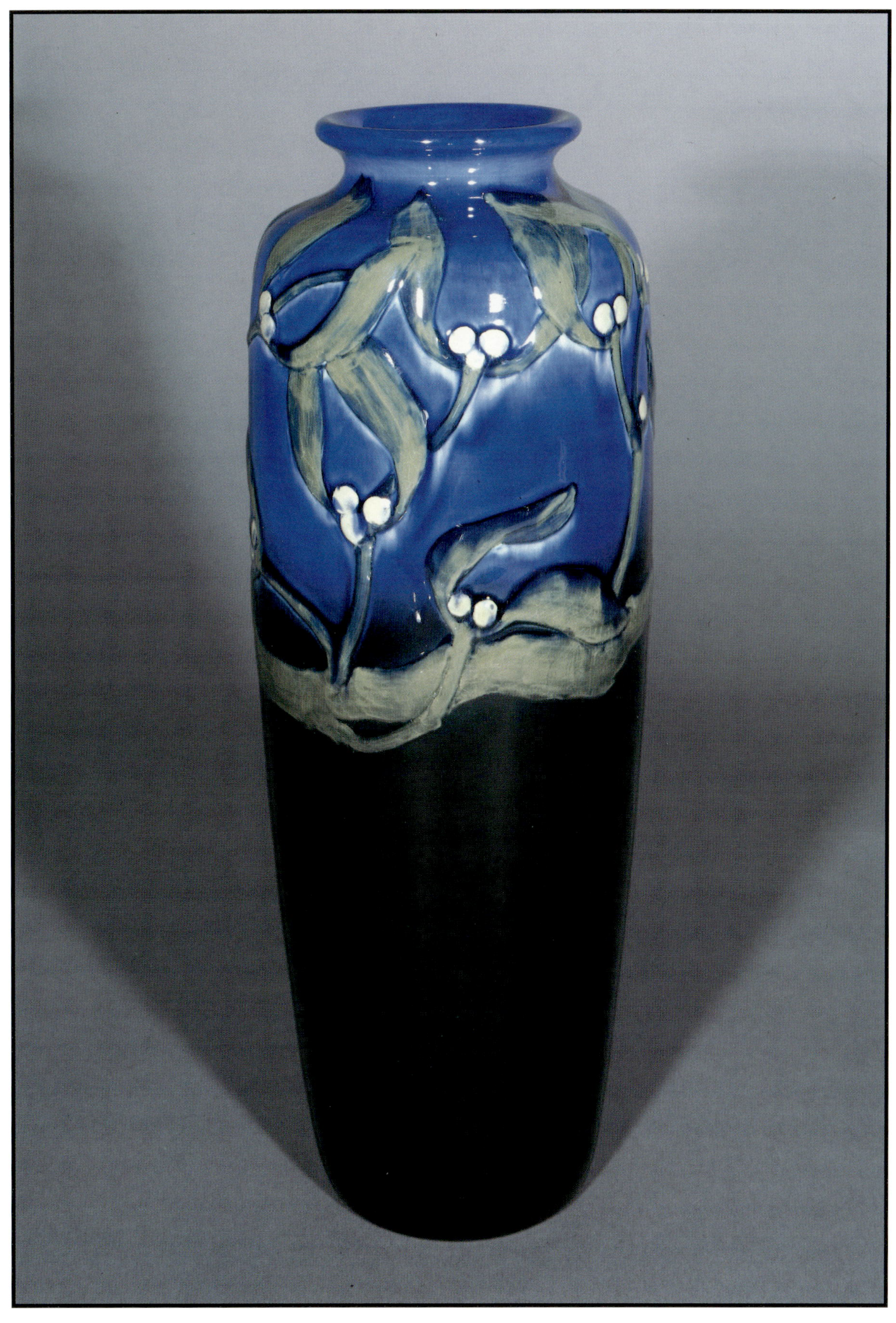

703   Rare, large and important carved Black Iris glaze vase with mistletoe decoration done by Matt Daly in 1900. $15000-20000
The leaves, berries and stems of the mistletoe are in relief indicating a fair amount of carving or modeling
for which Daly is well noted. Another interesting sidelight is the use of both black and cobalt in the background color. While many Black or Dark Iris pieces rely on deep cobalt or even deep green as a background,
this vase has cobalt shading at its top and the rarer, true black on the lower half. Impressed marks include
the Rookwood logo and date and shape number 904 B. Incised on the bottom is Daly's full signature and a
W for white (Iris) glaze. Height 13 inches. Minimal crazing.

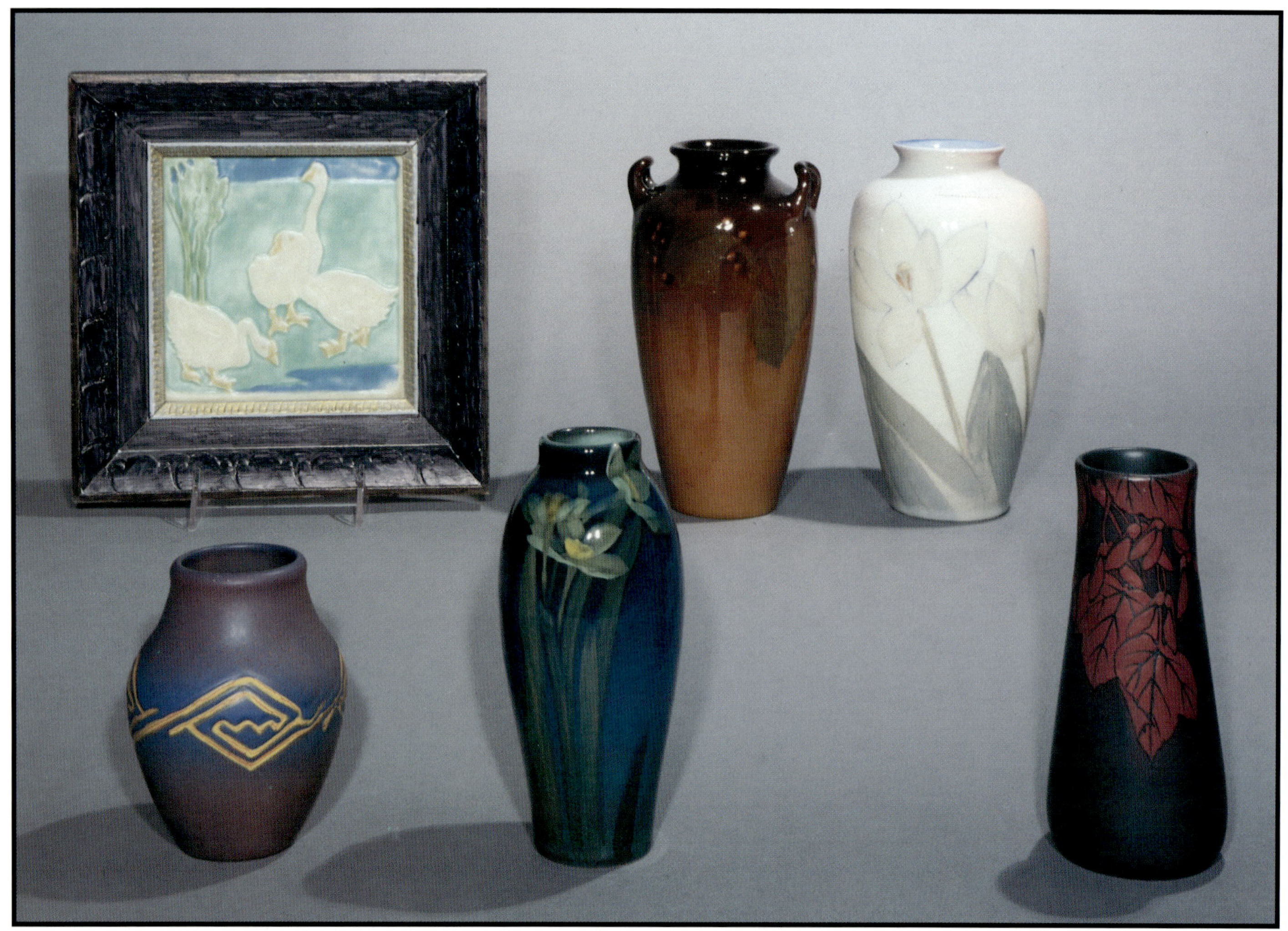

704	Multicolored mat glaze trivet from 1924 showing three white geese in an outdoor setting. Marks include the Rookwood logo, the date and shape number 3207. Size is 5 3/4 by 5 3/4 inches. Uncrazed and very nice. Recent frame.	$400-500
705	Painted Mat glaze vase with incised Native American geometric patterns inlaid with red and orange on a purple ground by Harriet Wilcox in 1905. Marks include the Rookwood logo, the date, shape number 914 F and the artist's initials, painted on in black slip. Height 5 inches.	$600-800
706	Sea Green vase with rich blue-green background on which are painted tall jonquils with yellow and white flowers and green leaves. The artist is Sallie Coyne and the work was done in 1902. Marks include the Rookwood logo, the date, shape number 901 D, an incised G for Sea Green glaze and the incised monogram of the artist. Height is 7 1/2 inches.	$1750-2250
707	Two-handled Standard glaze vase with holly decoration done in 1900 by E.T. Hurley. Marks include the Rookwood logo, the date, shape number 614 E and the incised initials of the artist. Height 8 1/8 inches.	$400-600
708	1943 High glaze vase with white tulips painted by Kataro Shirayamadani. Marks include the Rookwood logo, the date, shape number 614 E and the incised initials of the artist. Height 8 1/8 inches. Uncrazed with some minor glaze imperfections.	$1250-1750
709	Good Painted Mat vase with maple leaves, stems and seeds incised and painted by Olga Geneva Reed in 1909. In this example, the incised outline of the decoration is clearly visible. All outlining and the veins of the leaves are lined with black slip to enhance contrast. Marks include the Rookwood logo, the date, shape number 950 E and the artist's initials, painted on in black slip. Height 6 7/8 inches.	$2000-2500

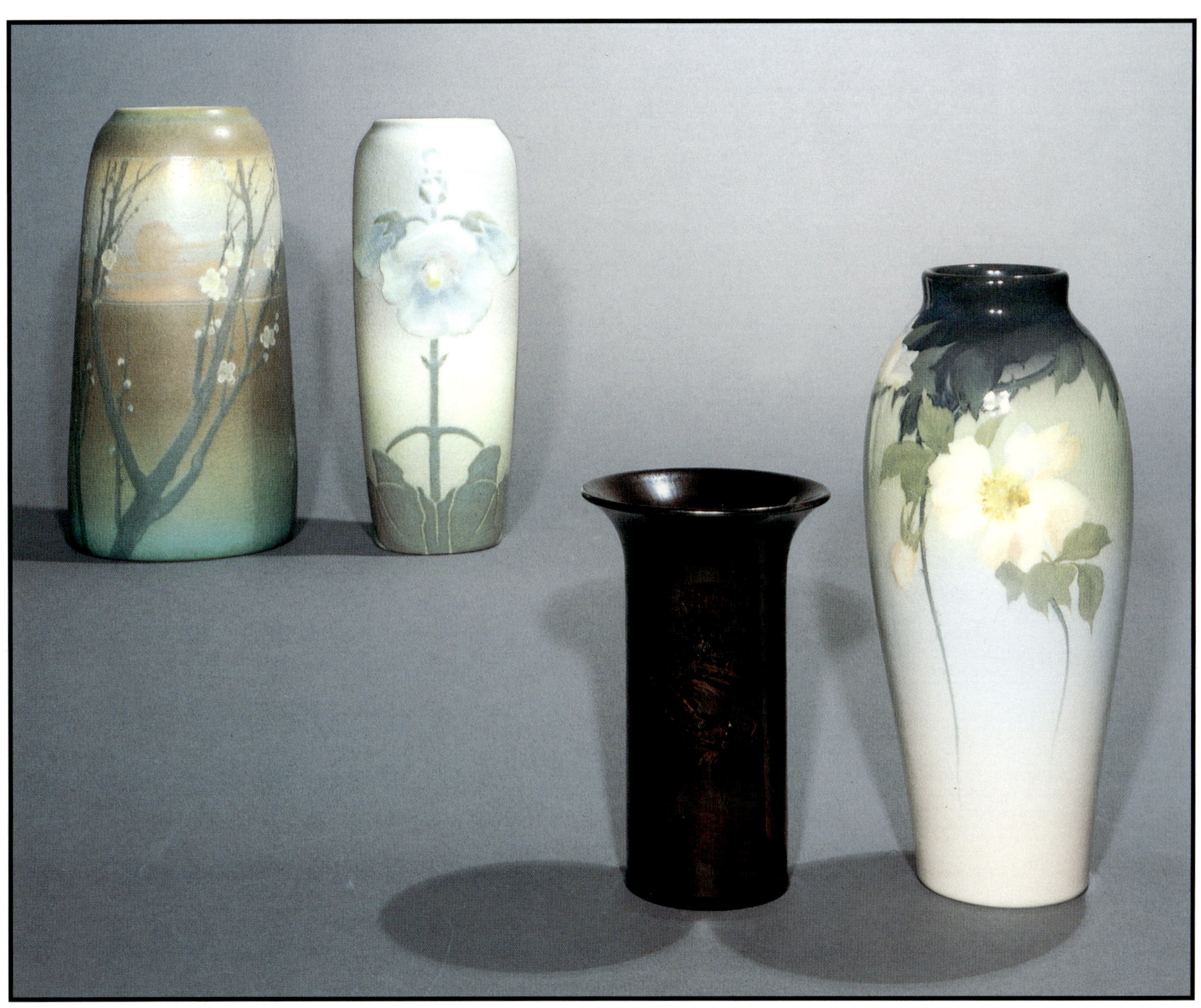

710   Unusual Vellum glaze scenic vase painted by Kataro Shirayamadani in 1909. In the foreground are blooming $2500-3500
       apple trees with black limbs and white blossoms. In the distance, an incised line represents the horizon
       above which is a pink setting sun. Clouds in the otherwise blue sky are turned pink by the sun. The treatment
       and perspective are very Oriental and a bit different for Rookwood. Marks include the Rookwood logo, the
       date, shape number 1654 D, an impressed V for Vellum glaze body and the incised cypher of the artist.
       Height 9 1/4 inches.

711   Rare carved Vellum vase with two stunning hollyhocks, done in 1908 by Sara Sax. On opposite sides of the $2000-2500
       vase, Sax has carved and outlined a symmetrically arranged hollyhock stalk with one flower and two buds.
       The leaves are also symmetrically arranged. Delicate shades of pink, yellow and green are used for the center
       of the flowers. Marks include the Rookwood logo, the date, shape number 951 D, V for Vellum glaze body, an
       incised V for Vellum glaze and the impressed monogram of the artist. Height 8 7/8 inches. There is a tight
       spider crack at the rim. Exhibited: Rookwood Pottery The Glorious Gamble as item 60 on page 125.

712   Good Standard glaze vase decorated by Albert Valentien in the late 1880's with a fierce looking dragon. The $1500-2000
       glaze is loaded with Tiger Eye effect both inside and out. Marks include "Rookwood" in block letters, the
       obscured date and shape number (which ends in the letter C) and the incised initials of the artist. Height 6 3/8
       inches. Strong decoration and fluid glaze.

713   Pretty Iris glaze vase painted in 1911 by Ed Diers. Diers began the decoration around the collar of the vase $3500-4500
       then allowed the vines and flowers to trail down the sides. Marks include the Rookwood logo, the date,
       shape number 901 C and the number 1 just above the logo. Incised are the artist's monogram and a W for
       white (Iris) glaze. Height 9 7/8 inches.

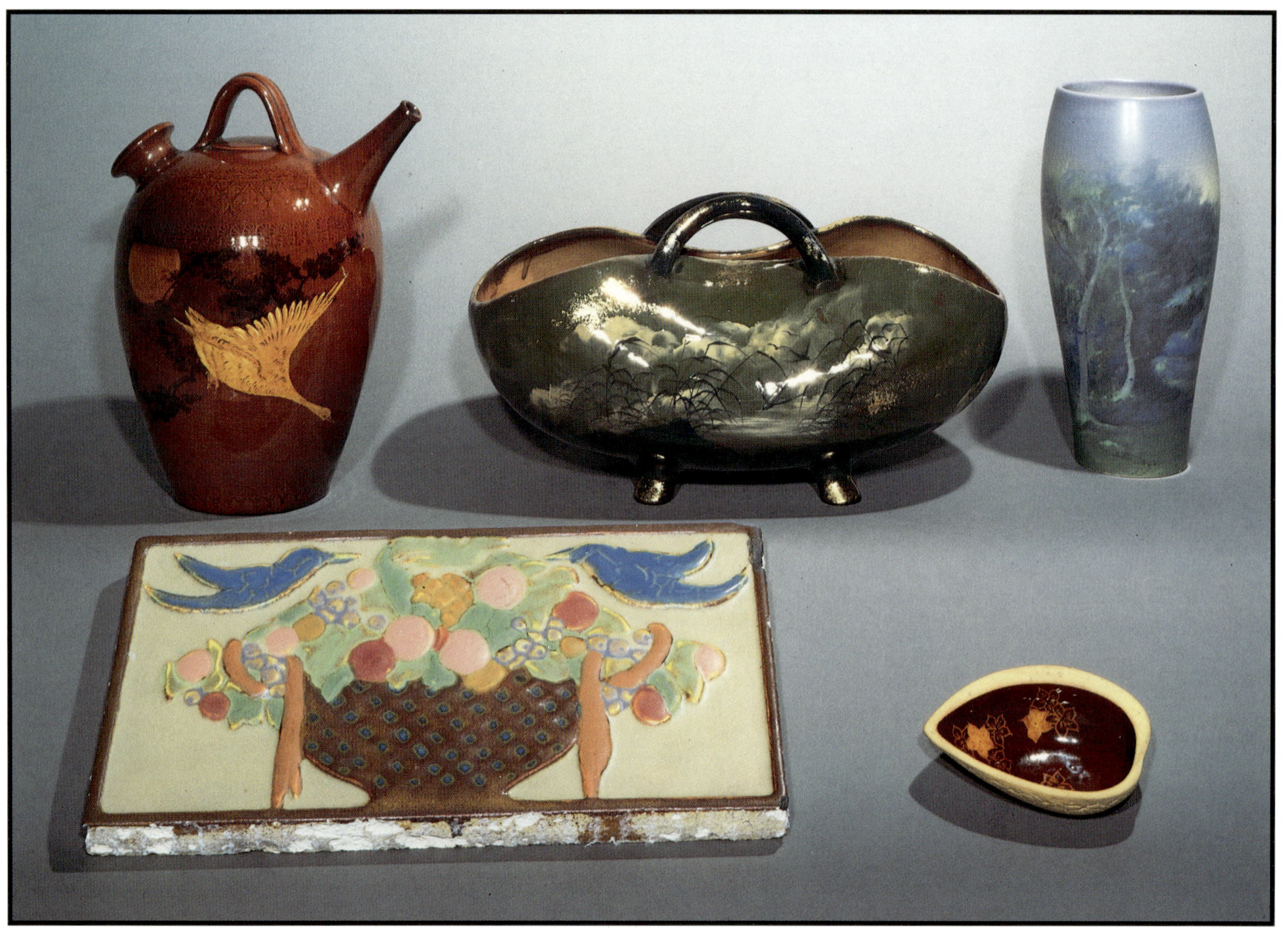

714   Rookwood Architectural Faience tile in multicolored mat glaze showing a basket of fruit with two blue humming birds. Impressed marks on the back include the Rookwood logo and the numbers "G 527", "3084 Y" and "416". Size is 6 by 12 inches. Uncrazed and very clean with the exception of some edge chips which would be hidden by a frame. $700-900

715   Early Standard glaze Spanish Water Jug decorated in 1885 by Albert Valentien. Shown is a large white goose flying through very Japanesque pine boughs while the full moon shines. Marks include "Rookwood" in block letters, the date, shape number 41, R for red clay and the incised initials of the artist. Height 8 inches. Very delicate decoration. $2000-2500

716   Early Limoges style flower basket with, birds, grasses, clouds and fired-on gold done in 1882 by Albert Humphreys. Incised marks include the name "Rookwood", the date and the artist's initials. Impressed is an anchor mark. Height 5 3/4 inches. There is a three inch crack descending from the rim. $300-500

717   Standard glaze almond dish with incised floral decoration inside the bowl, done in 1900 by Mary Nourse. Marks include the Rookwood logo, the date, shape number 279 C and the incised initials of the artist. Height is one inch and length is four inches. $100-150

718   Vellum glaze landscape vase painted by Fred Rothenbusch in 1922. Marks include the Rookwood logo, the date, shape number 2032 E, an impressed V for Vellum glaze and the impressed monogram of the artist. Height 7 3/4 inches. There is a pin-head sized nick off the base and a two inch line descending from the rim. $600-800

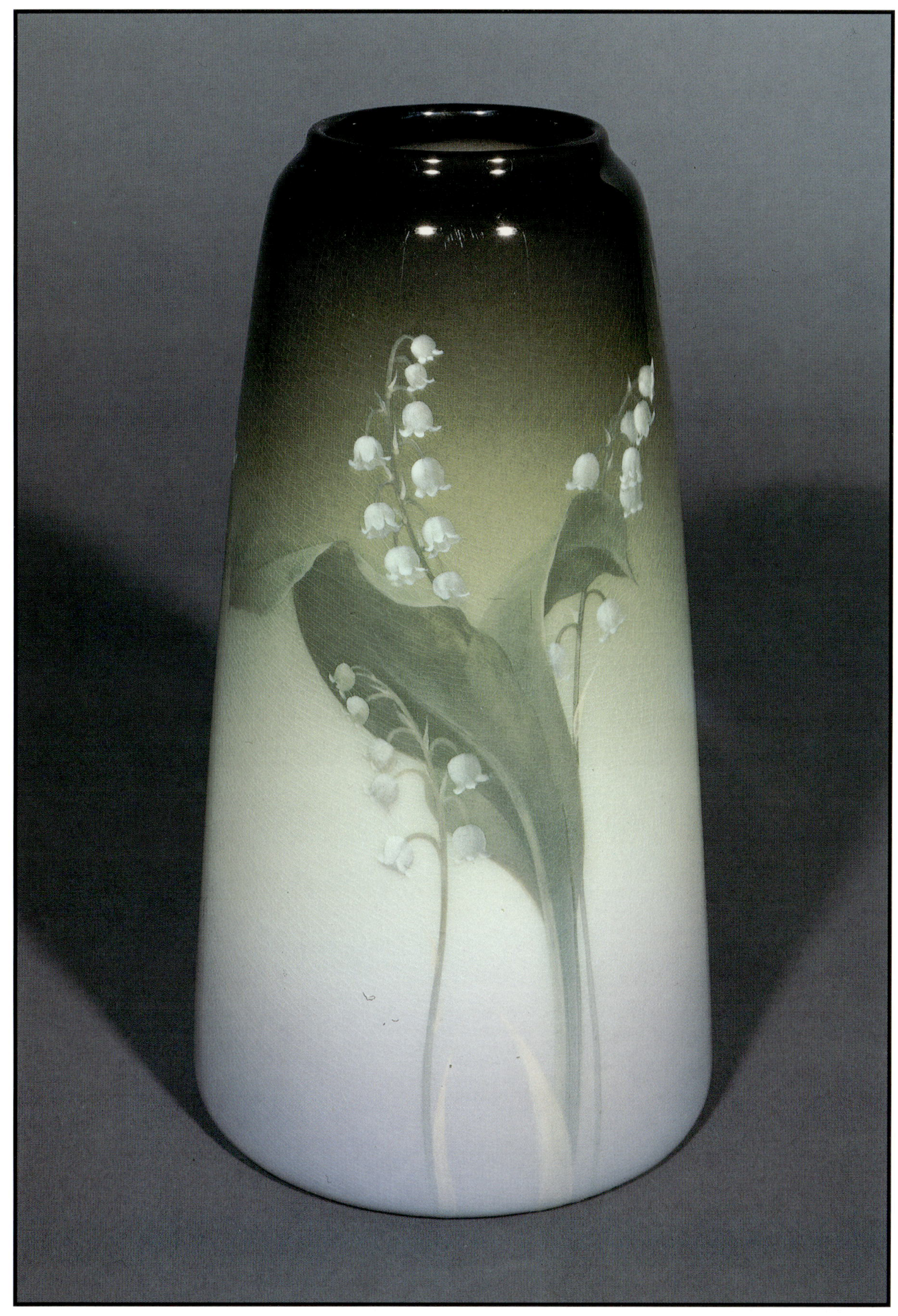

719   Beautiful Iris glaze vase with exacting lily-of-the-valley decoration, the work of Carl Schmidt in 1909. Marks $7000-9000
include the Rookwood logo, the date, shape number 1654 D, an incised W for white (Iris) glaze and the
impressed monogram of the artist. Height 9 1/8 inches. Fine overall crazing which is nearly invisible. Schmidt
frequently used lily-of-the-valley flowers in his work. This vase has a profusion of blossoms, all crisply applied
and also has a delicate pale blue aura at its base from which the plants seem to spring.

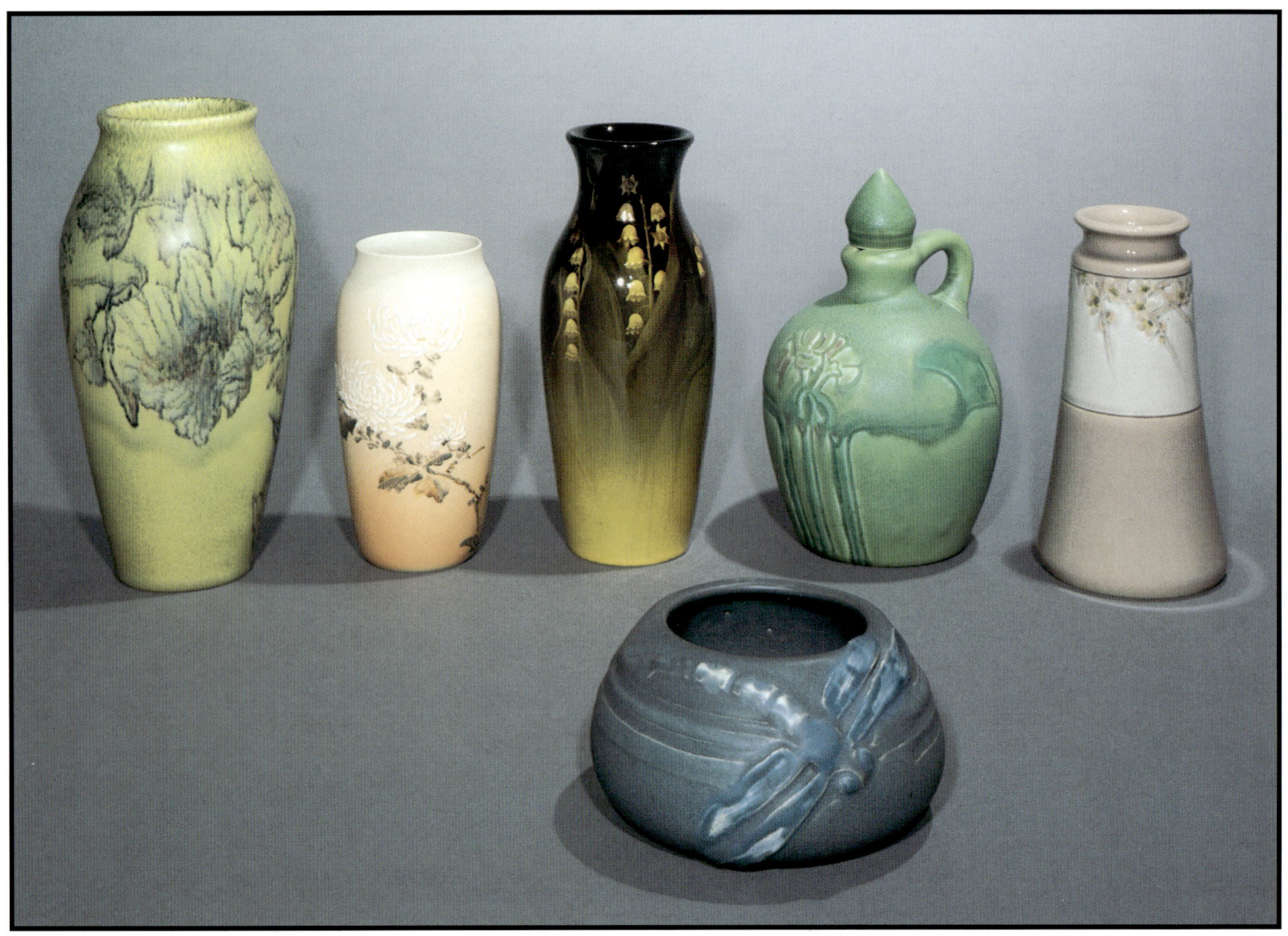

720   Mat glaze floral vase painted in 1924 by Louise Abel. Marks include the Rookwood logo, the date, shape number 939 D and the artist's monogram, painted on in black slip. Height 8 5/8 inches. $500-700

721   Crisp and clean dull finish vase with white spider mums done in heavy slip by Amelia Sprague in 1888. Marks include the Rookwood logo, the date, shape number 80 B, W for white clay, an incised S for smear (dull finish) glaze and the incised initials of the artist. Height 5 7/8 inches. Uncrazed. $500-700

722   Finely painted Standard glaze vase with lifelike lily-of-the- valley flowers done by Carl Schmidt in 1898. Marks include the Rookwood logo, the date, shape number 117 C and the incised monogram of the artist. height 7 7/8 inches. Minor glaze discoloration on the back side. $700-900

723   Good Arts & Crafts carved mat glaze vase done by Cecil Duell in 1908. Duell has carved a lifesize dragonfly in blue on the side of the gray body. Marks include the Rookwood logo, the date, shape number 1069 and the incised initials of the artist. Height 2 5/8 inches. There is a tight line at the rim. $800-1000

724   Arts & Crafts Mat glaze stoppered whiskey jug with incised decoration of stylized flowers, done by Albert Pons in 1906. Marks include the Rookwood logo, the date, shape number 512 C, a wheel ground x and the incised monogram of the artist. Height 7 1/8 inches. $400-600

725   Banded Iris glaze vase done in 1911 by E.T. Hurley. On a taupe ground are painted trailing apple blossoms, a recurrent theme for Hurley. Marks include the Rookwood logo, the date, shape number 1655 F, V for Vellum glaze body, a wheel ground x, the incised initials of the artist and the number 1 just above the logo. Height 6 1/2 inches. There is no obvious reason for the x. $600-800

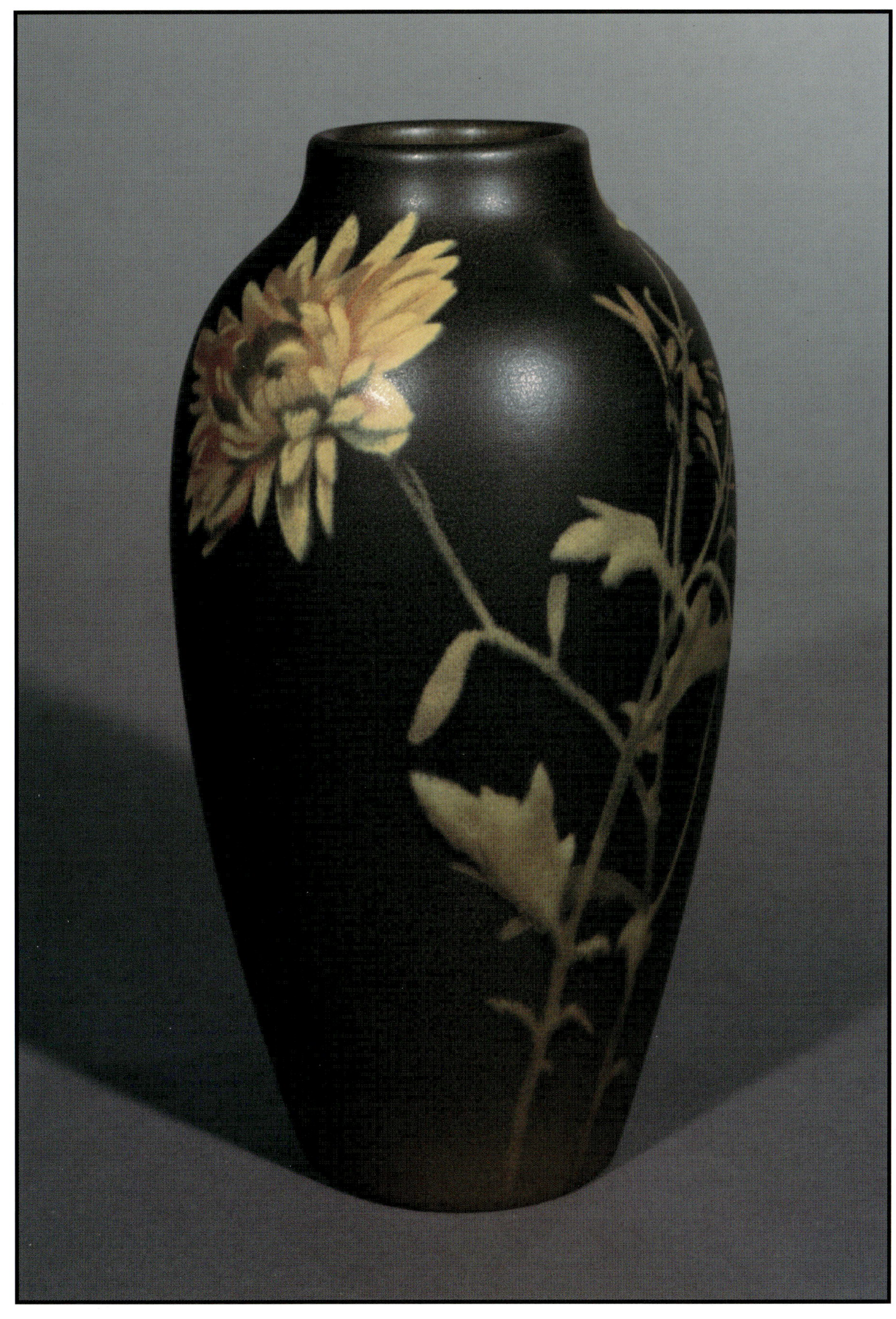

726   Beautiful and rare Painted Mat vase with stylish chrysanthemum decoration, done in 1902 by Harriet Wilcox. $8000-10000
Shown are three mature flowers and several buds in shades of orange, yellow and black, all nicely contrasted
on a greenish-black background. Marks include the Rookwood logo, the date, shape number 175 CZ and the
artist's initials, painted on in black slip. Height 8 3/8 inches. Wilcox has used delicate shading of color to
define the individual petals of each flower rather than the black outlining seen in other more well defined
Painted Mats. The overall effect is striking and condition is first rate.

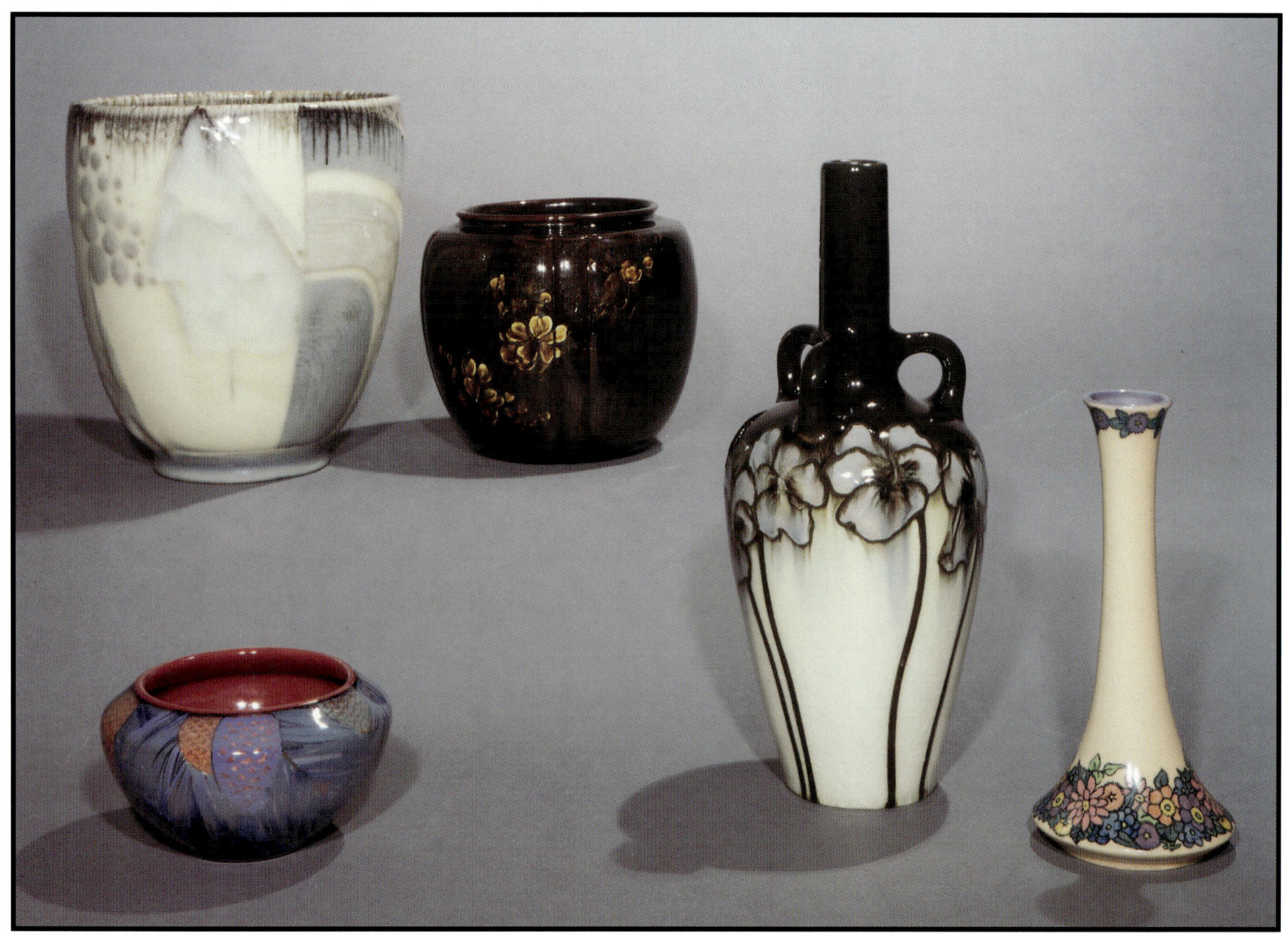

727   Strong Art Deco design which incorporates geometric forms and possibly bizarre human faces done in 1930 by William Hentschel. Although a glossy finish, the glaze is most likely Wax Mat. The interior of the vase is lined in Rookwood's Anniversary Glaze. Marks include the Rookwood logo, the date, shape number 6112, a fan shaped esoteric mark and the incised monogram of the artist. Height 8 inches. We're not sure about the faces but there are two profile-like images on the sides in which we see eyes, noses and chins. The Deco design is absolutely for real though. Uncrazed and very stylish. $2000-2500

728   Crisp and very colorful high glaze vase decorated by Kataro Shirayamadani in 1924 with pine boughs and cones. The interior is lined with Sherry's maroon. Marks include the Rookwood logo, the date, shape number 955 and the incised cypher of the artist. Height 2 1/2 inches. Uncrazed. $1000-1250

729   Rookwood Standard glaze ribbed vase with floral decoration by Anna Bookprinter, having large passages of Tiger Eye effect. Marks include the Rookwood logo, the date, shape number 244, R for red clay and the incised initials of the artist. Height 5 3/8 inches. $400-600

730   Good Iris glaze vase with Art Nouveau treatment of pansies and a modified form, done in 1898 by John Dee Wareham. Wareham spent several months in Europe in 1898 at Rookwood's expense and seems to have returned, charged with new ideas and techniques. The use of slip trailing to outline the flowers and the whip lash composition of the flower stems are ideas which Wareham would have seen and perhaps embraced. The three loop handles are not shown in the shape record book and add a nice architectural touch. Marks include the Rookwood logo, the date, shape number 765 C, a wheel ground x and the incised initials of the artist. Height 10 3/8 inches. The neck of the vase was broken off at some point and has been professionally repaired. $2000-3000

731   Neat high glaze bud vase decorated by Sara Sax in 1922 with bands of flowers just under the rim and at the base. Sax has used eight different colors in the flowers and outlined all of them in black. Marks include the Rookwood logo, the date, shape number 2307 and the incised monogram of the artist. Uncrazed and extremely crisp and clean. $1000-1500

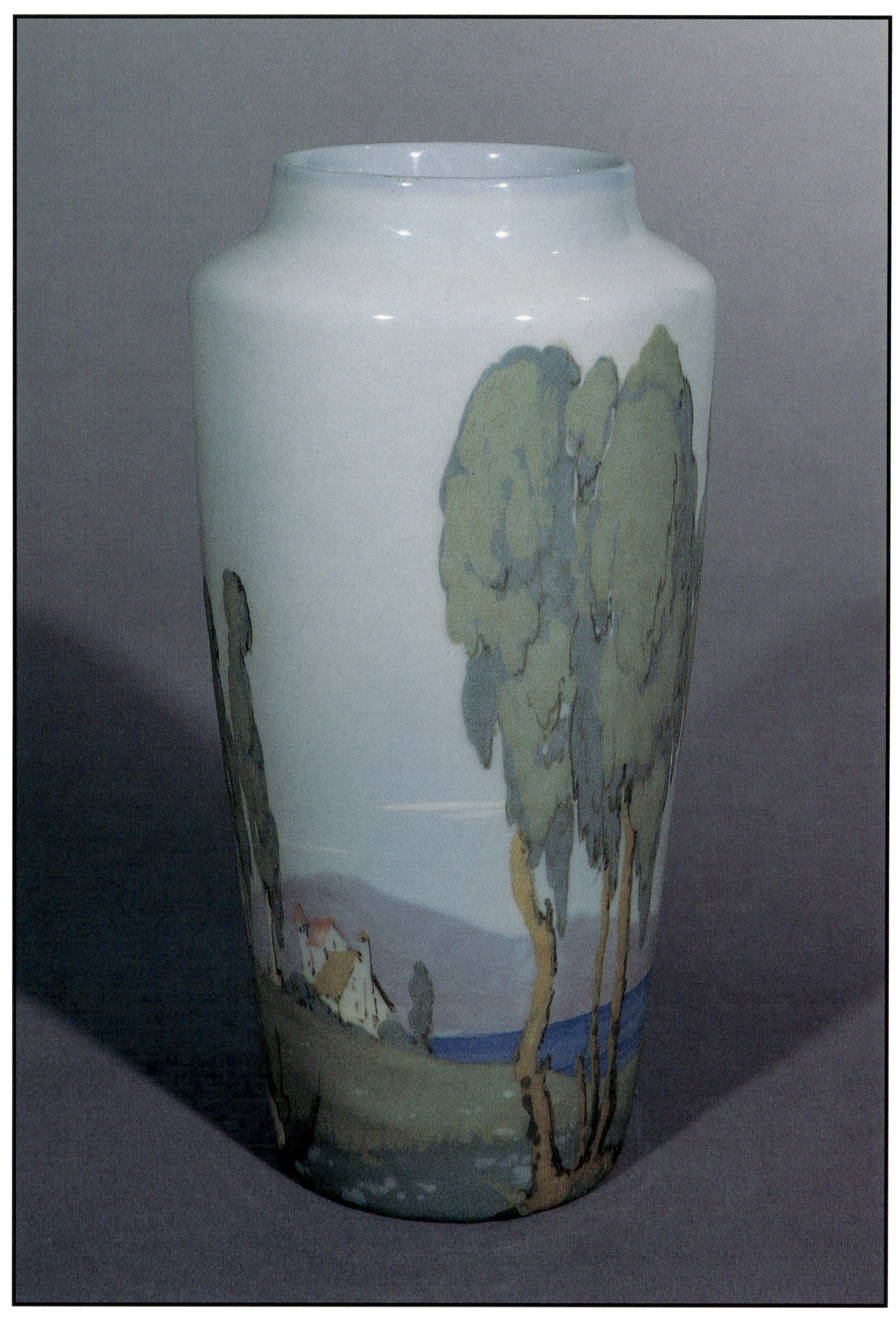

732   Rare and colorful high glaze scenic painted by Arthur Conant in 1921. Pictured is a fanciful castle on a $8000-10000
backdrop of purple hills with tall trees and exotic flowers growing near a lake of deepest blue water. Marks
include the Rookwood logo, the date, shape number 1918 and the incised monogram of the artist. Height
8 5/8 inches. Uncrazed. Conant's landscapes are some of the most unusual pieces ever produced at
Rookwood. Not only is the subject matter unique, done in Conant's signature style but the range of colors
is amazing by anybody's standards. We often wonder why the colors that frequent Conant's work are
foreign to most of his colleagues.

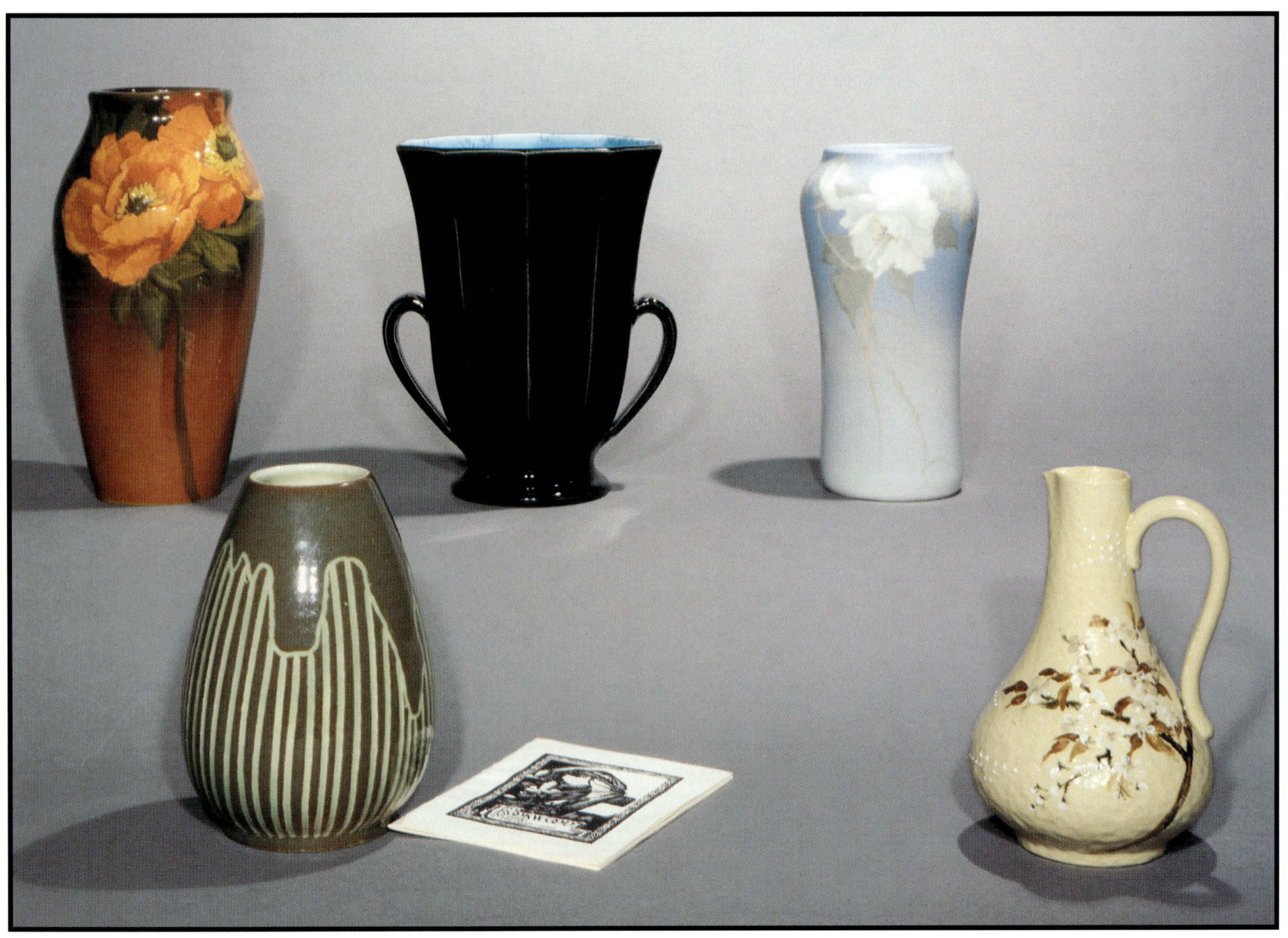

733 Matt Daly Standard glaze vase with bright orange flowers painted in 1901. Marks include the Rookwood logo, the date, shape number 925 C and the incised initials of the artist. Height 9 3/8 inches. $600-800

734 Late high glaze vase with deeply incised irregular lines, done by John Dee Wareham and Reuben Earl Menzel in 1952. Marks include the Rookwood logo, the date, S for Special shape, Menzel's swirl mark and the incised initials of Wareham. Height 6 1/8 inches. Included with the vase is a Rookwood booklet and an original Rookwood sales receipt for the vase which lists the price in 1960 as $12.50 plus tax. Artist decorated pieces from this period are some of the last ever produced at Rookwood. $400-500

735 Interesting two-handled trophy made especially for the Garden Club of Cincinnati by Rookwood in 1924. The exterior of the vase is done in a glossy, jet black glaze and the interior is done in medium blue. Marks include the Rookwood logo, the date, special shape number S 2041 and the notation "Garden Club of Cincinnati Trophy". Height 8 1/8 inches. $300-400

736 Vellum glaze vase by Fred Rothenbusch with pretty white rose decoration, done in 1906. Marks include the Rookwood logo, the date, shape number 935 D, an impressed V for Vellum glaze body, an incised V for Vellum glaze and the incised monogram of the artist. Height 8 inches. $500-700

737 Neat Limoges style ewer decorated by Laura Fry in 1883. In addition to the heavy slip decoration, Fry has hammered the surface giving it the look of beaten copper and then applied small dots of white slip in irregularly spaced lines. Impressed marks include Rookwood in block letters, the date, shape number 65, S for sage green clay and the number "1". Painted on the base in black slip is the monogram of the artist. Height 6 1/4 inches. $350-450

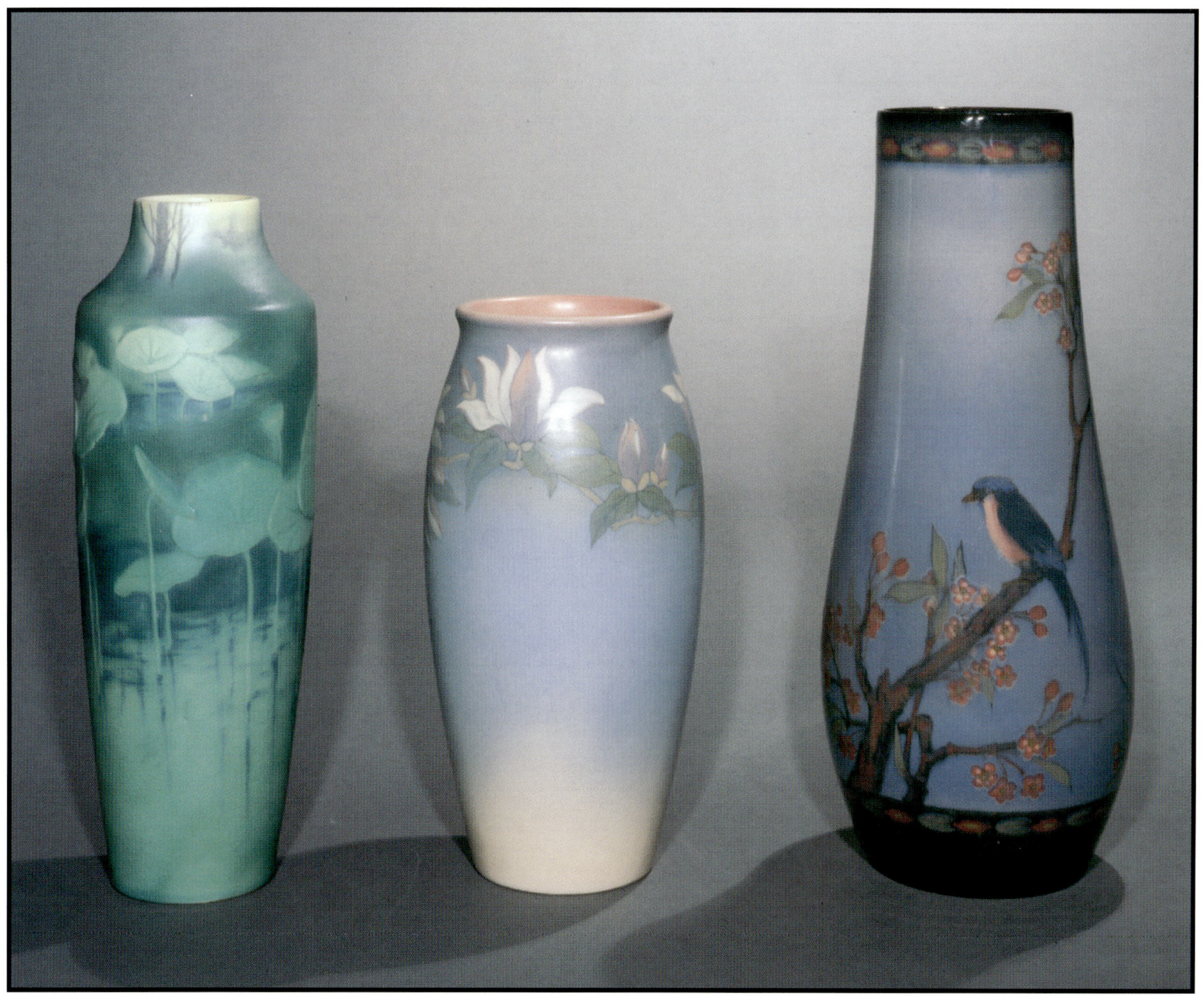

738   Early and rare carved and painted Vellum glaze scenic vase decorated in 1905 by Kataro Shirayamadani. $6000-8000
Below a small area painted on the collar and shoulder of the vase are profusions of lightly carved lotus blossoms, stems and pads in shades of green, purple and yellow which seem to be standing well above the water line, as they are casting shadows. Marks include the Rookwood logo, the date, shape number 946, V for Vellum glaze body and the incised cypher of the artist. Height 12 1/4 inches. Two lines descend from the rim and nearly meet on the shoulder. These have been professionally repaired. Carved Vellum pieces are rare and scenic ones are especially hard to find.

739   Very clean and crisp Vellum glaze vase with exotic floral decoration painted in 1928 by Lenore Asbury. $2000-2500
Marks include the Rookwood logo, the date, shape number 917 B, an incised V for Vellum glaze and the incised initials of the artist. Height 10 1/8 inches. Uncrazed and in superb original condition.

740   Tall, crisp and clean high glaze vase decorated in 1919 by Lorinda Epply. Epply has painted a scene of $4000-6000
exotic flowers in green, red, pink and brown along with three birds in the picture, one perched prominently on the tallest branch. Marks include the Rookwood logo, the date, shape number 2441 and the incised monogram of the artist. Height 13 3/4 inches. There is a small underglaze skip on the backside of the vase. Uncrazed.

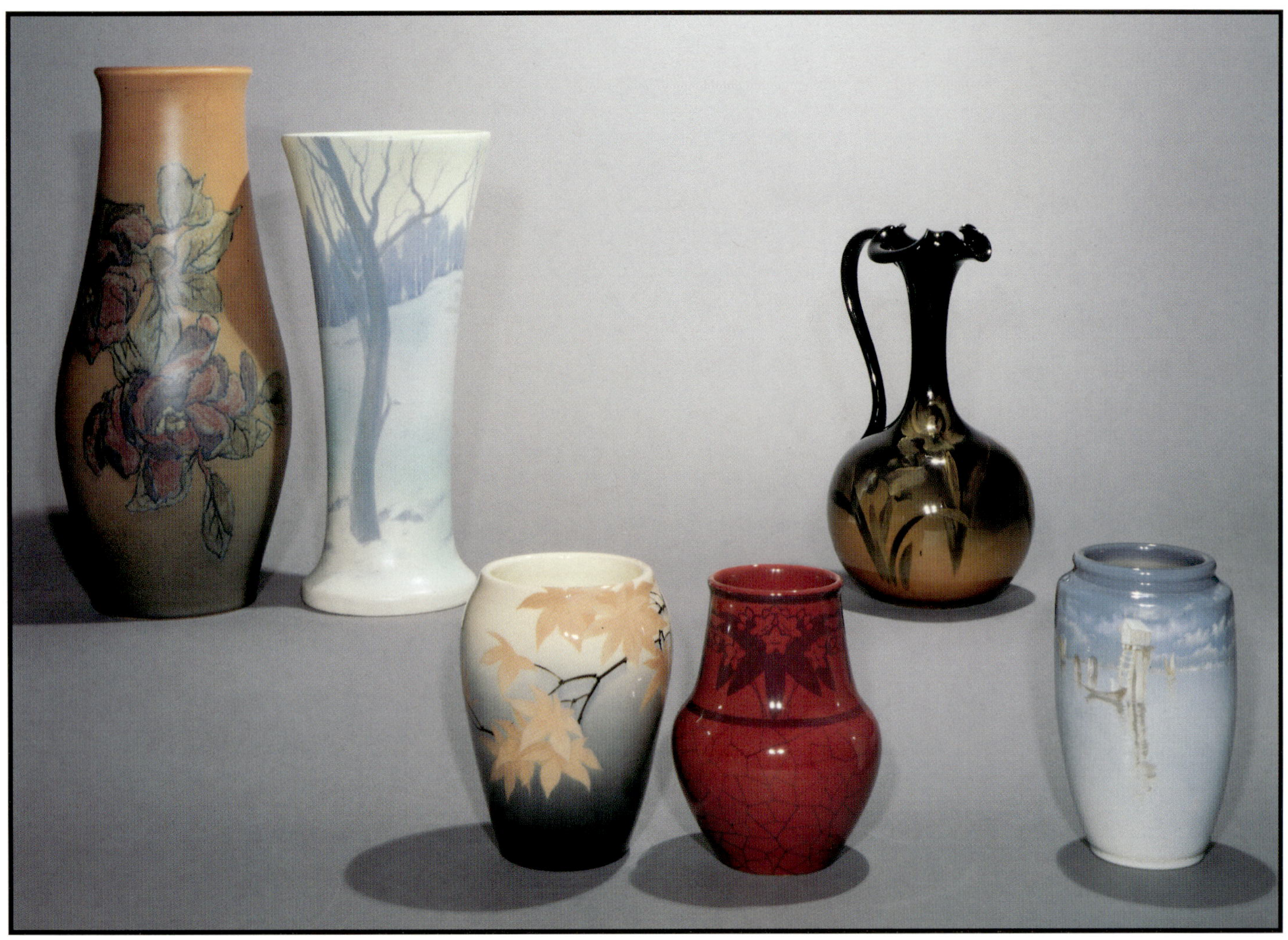

741   Tall mat glaze vase with colorful and well defined red rose decoration done in 1925 by Catherine Covalenco. Marks include the Rookwood logo, the date, shape number 838 A and the artist's monogram, painted on in black slip. Height 15 inches. There are lots of leaves and full blown roses arrayed around the body of the vase. $1750-2250

742   Tall and unusual Vellum glaze snow scene painted in an Arts & Crafts manner by Fred Rothenbusch in 1908. The artist places the viewer very close to the scene by having the leafless trees in the foreground. Marks included the Rookwood logo, the date, shape number 1357 B, an impressed V for Vellum glaze body, an incised V for Vellum glaze and the incised monogram of the artist. Height 13 inches. A tight line descends from the rim. $2000-2500

743   Subtle and stylish Iris glaze vase decorated with salmon colored Japanese maple leaves and black limbs on a cream to gray ground by Sara Sax in 1906. Marks include the Rookwood logo, the date, shape number 942 C, an incised W for white (Iris) glaze and the incised monogram of the artist. Height 6 3/8 inches. Uncrazed and very crisp. $4000-5000

744   Early French Red vase with stylized floral decoration around the collar, done in 1918 by Sara Sax. Marks include the Rookwood logo, the date, shape number 975 D, a sideways P for porcelain body and the impressed monogram of the artist. Height 6 3/8 inches. Most French Red pieces occur in the early 1920's. We have seen a few others from 1918 by Sax which must have been experiments with the new glaze. $1000-1500

745   Standard glaze ewer with blue iris decoration painted in 1895 by Anna Valentien. The artist has used deep blues and greens in the flowers and in the background color near the spout. Marks include the Rookwood logo, the date, shape number 387 C and the incised initials of the artist. Height 10 3/8 inches. $600-800

746   Rare Iris glaze Venetian harbor scenic vase painted by Carl Schmidt in 1900. Shown is a shrine on wooden pilings with other pilings, sailing ships and the city under cloudy skies in the background. Marks include the Rookwood logo, the date, shape number 734 D, an incised W for white (Iris) glaze and the incised monogram of the artist. Height 6 3/4 inches. There are a few dots of underglaze color in the image. $3500-4500

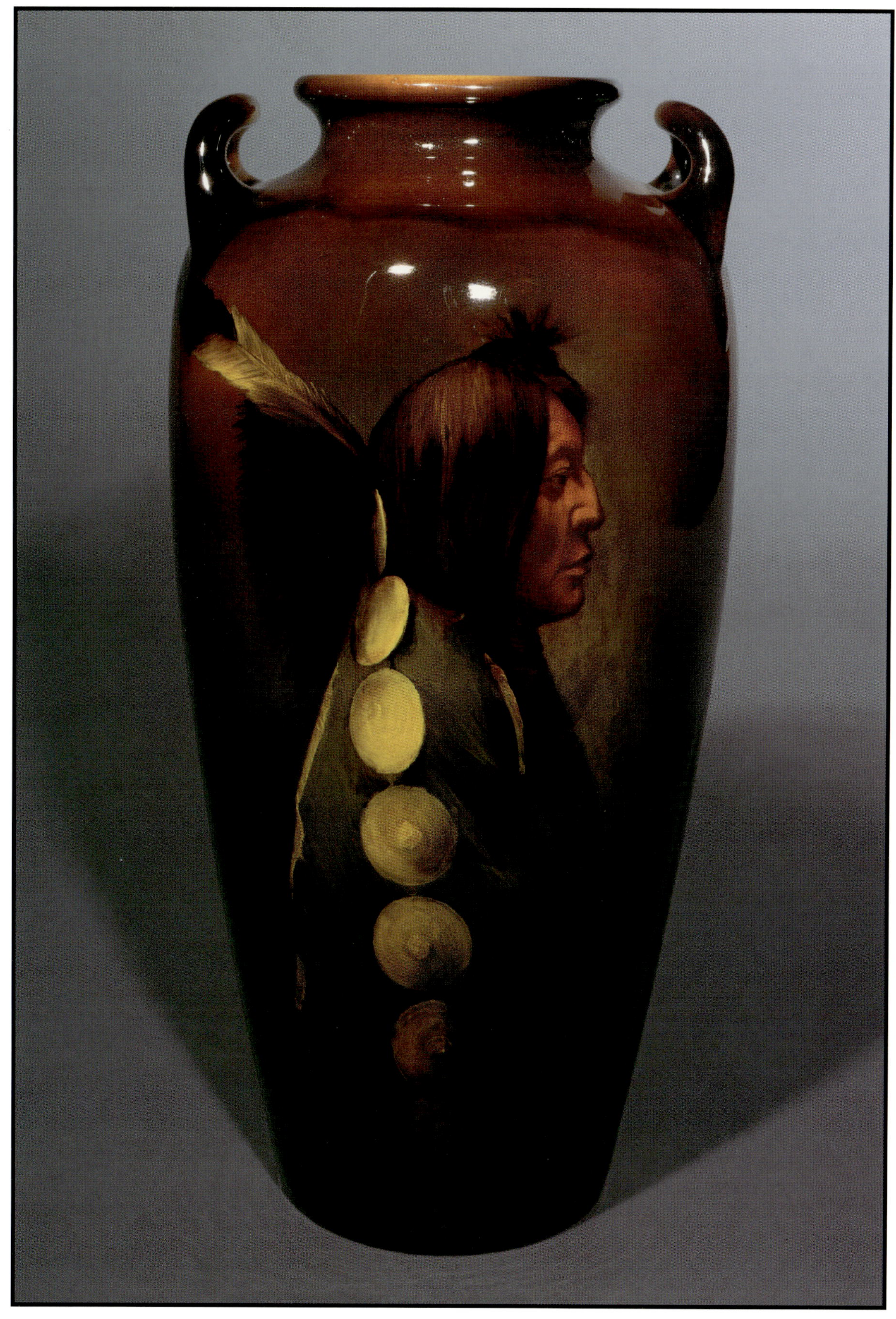

747   Tall and impressive Standard glaze vase with two loop handles which bears the portrait of a Native American, done in 1899 by M.A. Daly. For his subject, Daly has used an Arapaho named Binanset, who is profiled in three quarter length, and who is dressed in a fine headdress and blue robe with yellow piping and shell decoration down the side. Impressed marks include the Rookwood logo, the date and shape number 614 B. Painted on the base in black slip is the notation "M.A. Daly Binanset Arapaho". Incised on the base are three vertical lines whose meaning is unknown. The use of black slip to sign the piece indicates Daly did so after the a first firing but before the glaze was applied and fired. Height 13 7/8 inches. Minor glaze scratches. $12500-17500

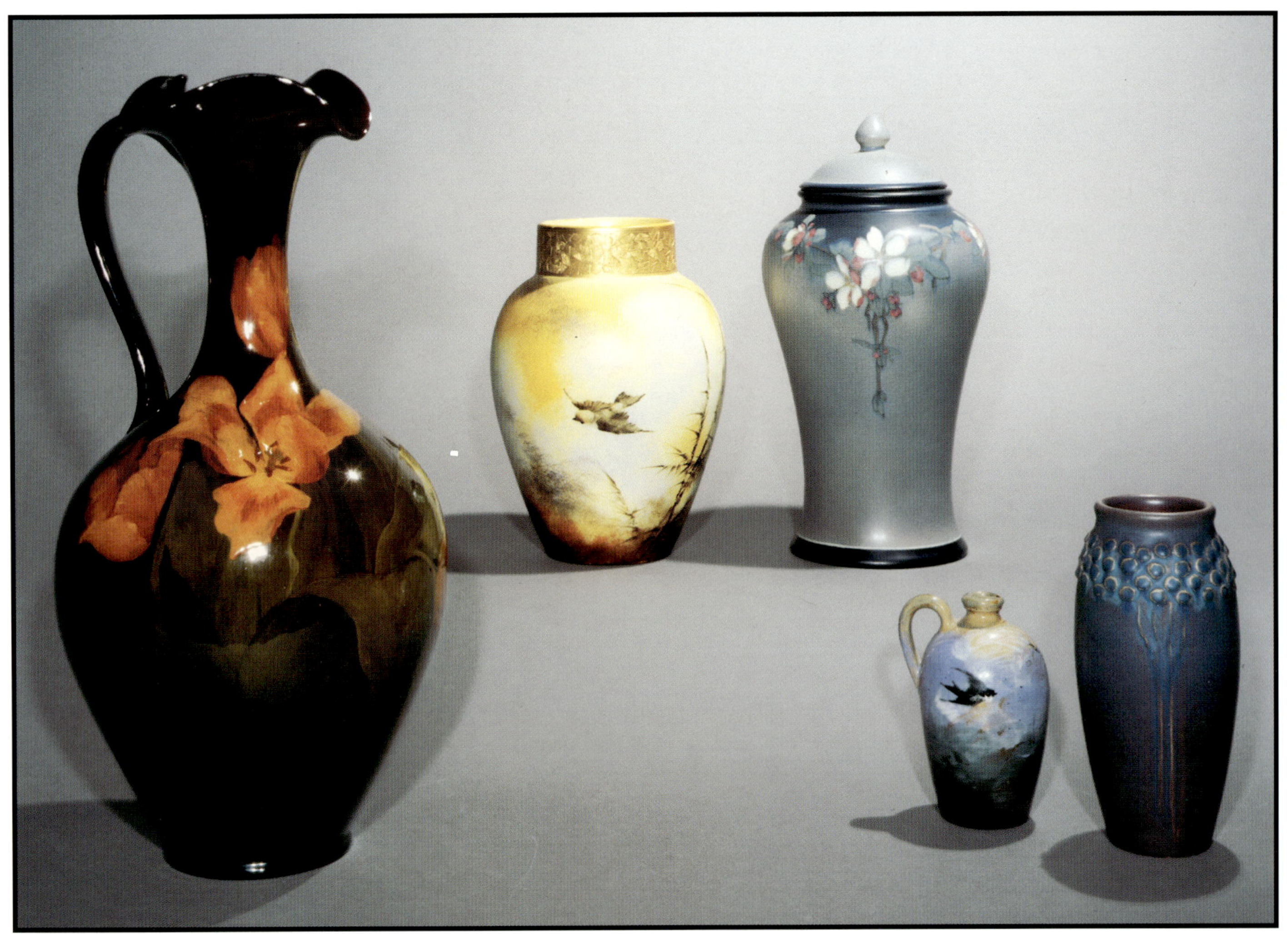

748   Large Standard glaze ewer with showy, bright orange tulips painted by Amelia Sprague in 1898. Impressed marks include the Rookwood logo, the date and shape number 578 B. Incised on the base is the monogram of the artist. Height 16 3/8 inches. Good decoration and very nice original condition. $1500-2000

749   Handsome dull finish vase decorated by an unknown artist in 1885 with a small sparrow flying over Oriental grasses. The collar of the vase is die-stamped with nail heads and chased with fired-on gold. Marks include the Rookwood in block letters, the date, shape number 162 C and Y for yellow clay. Height 9 inches. Although not artist signed, the quality of work suggests the hand of Matt Daly. Uncrazed and very clean. Pictured: Rookwood Its Golden Era of Art Pottery 1880-1929 by Kircher and Agranoff, color plate 2, middle row, number 3. $500-700

750   Vellum glaze lidded urn with floral decoration painted by Lenore Asbury in 1918. Marks include the Rookwood logo, the date, shape number 2303, a wheel ground x and the incised initials of the artist. Height 11 3/4 inches. There is a small chip off the foot and another on the edge of the rim. $1000-1250

751   Limoges style perfume jug with the usual sparrow and Oriental grass motif painted by an unknown artist in 1883. Marks include Rookwood in block letters, the date, shape number 61, G for ginger clay and an impressed kiln mark. Height 4 3/4 inches. Pictured: Rookwood Its Golden Era of Art Pottery 1880-1929 by Kircher and Agranoff, color plate 1, top row, number 2. $250-350

752   Unusual mat glaze scenic vase with applied decoration done by William Hentschel in 1910. Around the top of the vase, Hentschel has added small circles of clay which give the effect of leaves in the top of a tree. Trunks of three trees are incised in the side of the vase. Marks include the Rookwood logo, the date, shape number 917 C and the incised monogram of the artist. Height 7 inches. $800-1200

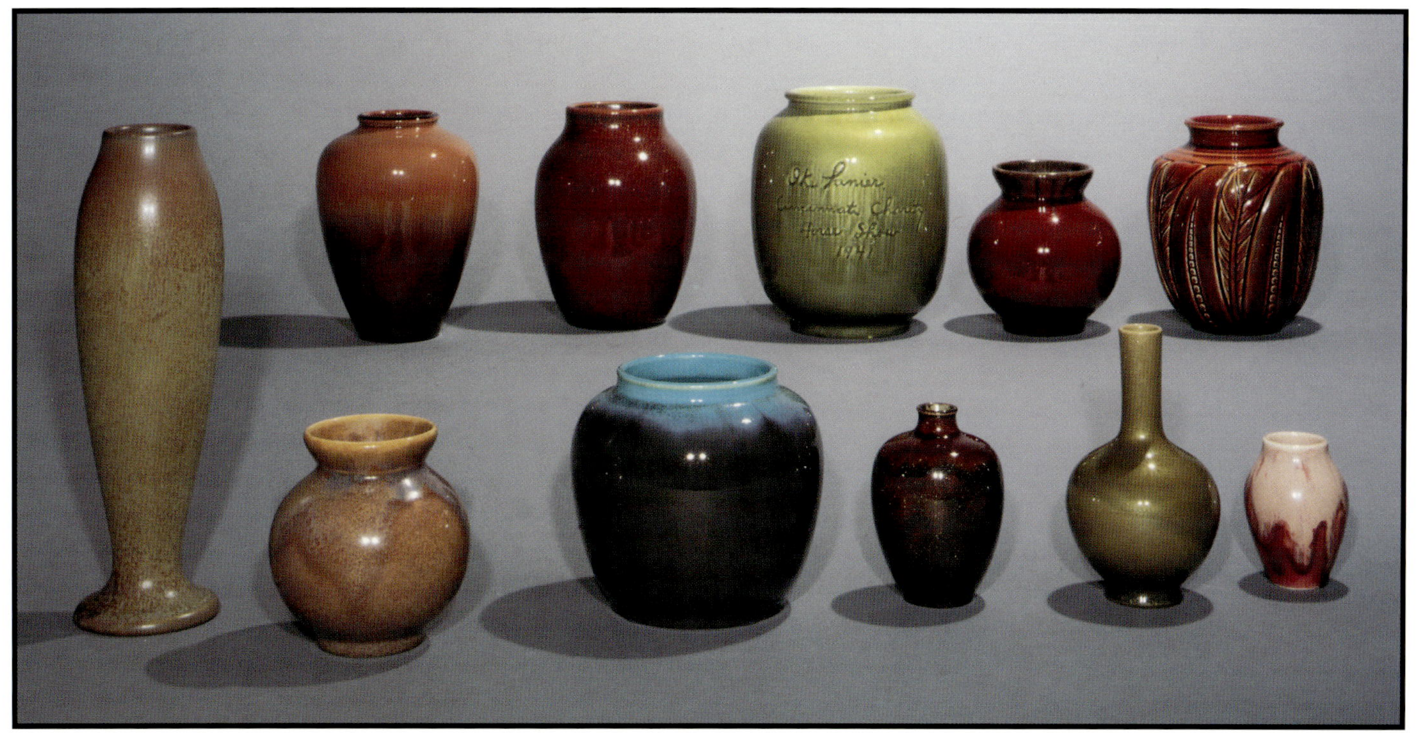

753	Good Arts & Crafts Rookwood production vase covered with a rust over mustard Ombroso glaze. Marks include the Rookwood logo, the date and shape number 949 D. Height 9 1/2 inches. Ombroso was introduced in 1910. This vase, from 1911, is loaded with micro-crystals which sparkle in strong light.	$400-500
754	Glaze effect vase done in Michele Purple over a rich, mottled Ralphie Tan at Rookwood in 1932. Marks include the Rookwood logo, the date and shape number 6303. Height 4 inches.	$200-300
755	Coromandel glaze vase with subtle shadings of color and fine crystals made at Rookwood, circa 1932. Marks include the Rookwood logo and a date and shape number which are obscured by glaze. Height 5 3/8 inches.	$300-400
756	Coromandel glaze vase with good crystals made at Rookwood in 1936. Marks include the Rookwood logo, the date and shape number 654 C. Height 5 3/8 inches.	$200-300
757	Rookwood glaze effect vase from 1933 done in Riley Blue over Randy Gray. Marks include the Rookwood logo, the date and shape number 6319 D. Height 4 5/8 inches. Minor grinding chips on the base.	$200-250
758	Rookwood Aventurine glaze vase made as a presentation piece in 1941. Incised on the front surface is the notation, "Ike Lanier Cincinnati Charity Horse Show 1941". Marks include the Rookwood logo, the date and S for special shape. Height 5 7/8 inches.	$200-300
759	Handsome Coromandel glaze vase made at Rookwood in 1932. Marks include the Rookwood logo, the date and shape number 6317 F. Height 3 3/4 inches. A small but spectacular example of Coromandel with sheets of small crystals throughout.	$400-500
760	Coromandel vase with some crystals done at Rookwood circa 1932. Marks include the Rookwood logo and the mostly obscured date and shape number. Height 4 inches. Good colors and shape.	$200-300
761	Superb example of Aventurine glaze on a Special shape made at Rookwood in 1937. Marks include the Rookwood logo, the date, S for Special shape and possible experimental number H 2052. Height 5 1/4 inches. Great glaze on an elegant form.	$400-500
762	Coromandel glaze on a body embossed with Art Deco flowers and leaves and made at Rookwood in 1935. Marks include the Rookwood logo, the date and shape number 6462. Height 5 inches. Good color on a stylish design.	$300-400
763	Rookwood glaze effect vase from 1930 done in a taupe over maroon high glaze. Impressed marks include the Rookwood logo, the date and shape number 604 H. Height 2 7/8 inches.	$200-300

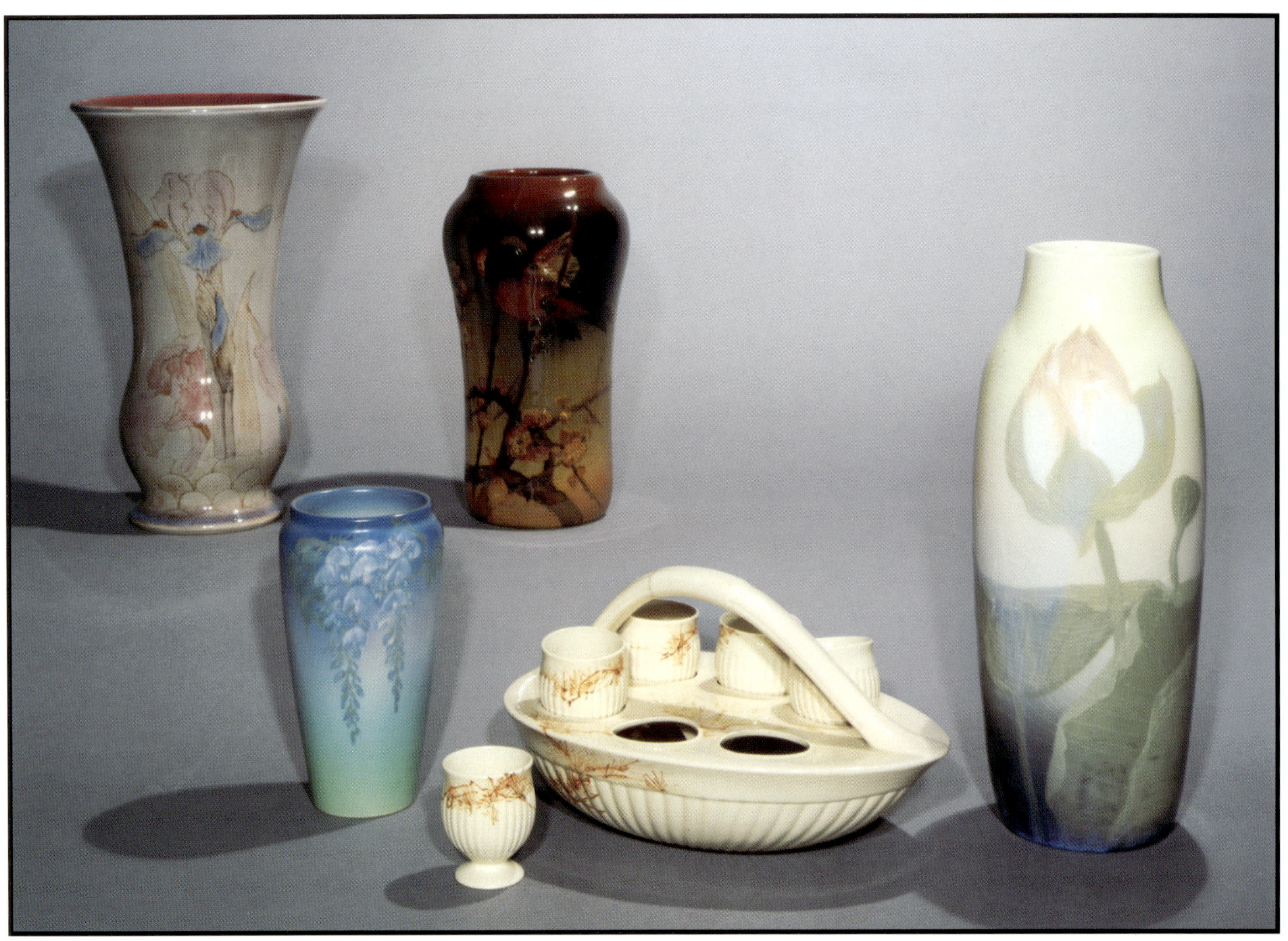

764   Black Opal glaze vase with red and blue irises painted by Sara Sax in 1924. Two interesting observations $3000-4000
about this vase. First of all, the Black Opal glaze, which is often somewhat obscuring, is quite clear with
only a bit of the blue hazing. Secondly, the decoration is done with stains rather than slip decoration giving
the flowers a slightly translucent quality. Overall the vase is quite extraordinary by any standard. Marks
include the Rookwood logo, the date, shape number 2733 and the artist's monogram, painted on in black
slip. Height 10 3/4 inches. Uncrazed.

765   Pretty Vellum glaze vase with wisteria decoration done in 1924 by Ed Diers. Marks include the Rookwood $1000-1250
logo, the date, shape number 1369 F, an incised V for Vellum glaze and the incised monogram of the artist.
height 6 1/8 inches. Uncrazed and very nice.

766   Rare Cameo glaze egg server with five egg cups painted in 1887 by Laura Fry. The basket and each of the $800-1200
egg cups have simple pine boughs painted on them in a rust color. Marks on the basket include the
Rookwood logo, the date, shape number 337, W 7 for a type of white clay, an incised W for white (Cameo)
glaze and the incised monogram of the artist. The five cups have the Rookwood logo and shape number
337. Four of the cups also have an impressed 7. Height of the basket is 5 inches. The basket is made to
hold six cups. One cup is missing. Pictured: Rookwood Its Golden Era of Art Pottery 1880-1929 by Kircher
and Agranoff, color plate 2, middle row, number 2. This set may be unique.

767   Good Standard glaze vase painted in 1906 by Alice Willitts. Willitts, whose work is seldom seen, has $1250-1750
presented us with a very Oriental theme, a bough of cherry limbs loaded with red blossoms and near the
top of those limbs is perched a small bird with red chest and blue head. Impressed marks include the
Rookwood logo, the date and shape number 935 C. Incised on the base is the monogram of the artist. Also
affixed to the base is an original Rookwood showroom label which lists the 1906 price as a princely $12.00.
Height 8 3/4 inches.

768   Colorful Flowing glaze vase with pink and white lotus blossoms painted in 1904 by Sallie Coyne. Is this Iris $1500-2000
or Flowing glaze? Good question. Since we now feel certain about the composition of Flowing glaze, i.e.
the blue striations seen on the two Matt Daly vases in this sale, it seems reasonable to think this might be
Flowing glaze or at least be said to have "Flowing Glaze Effect". Obviously, Flowing glaze is a very close
relative of Iris. Marks include the Rookwood logo, the date, shape number 932 C, an incised W for white
(Iris) glaze and the incised monogram of the artist. Height 11 5/8 inches. A neat drill hole in the bottom has
been professionally repaired.

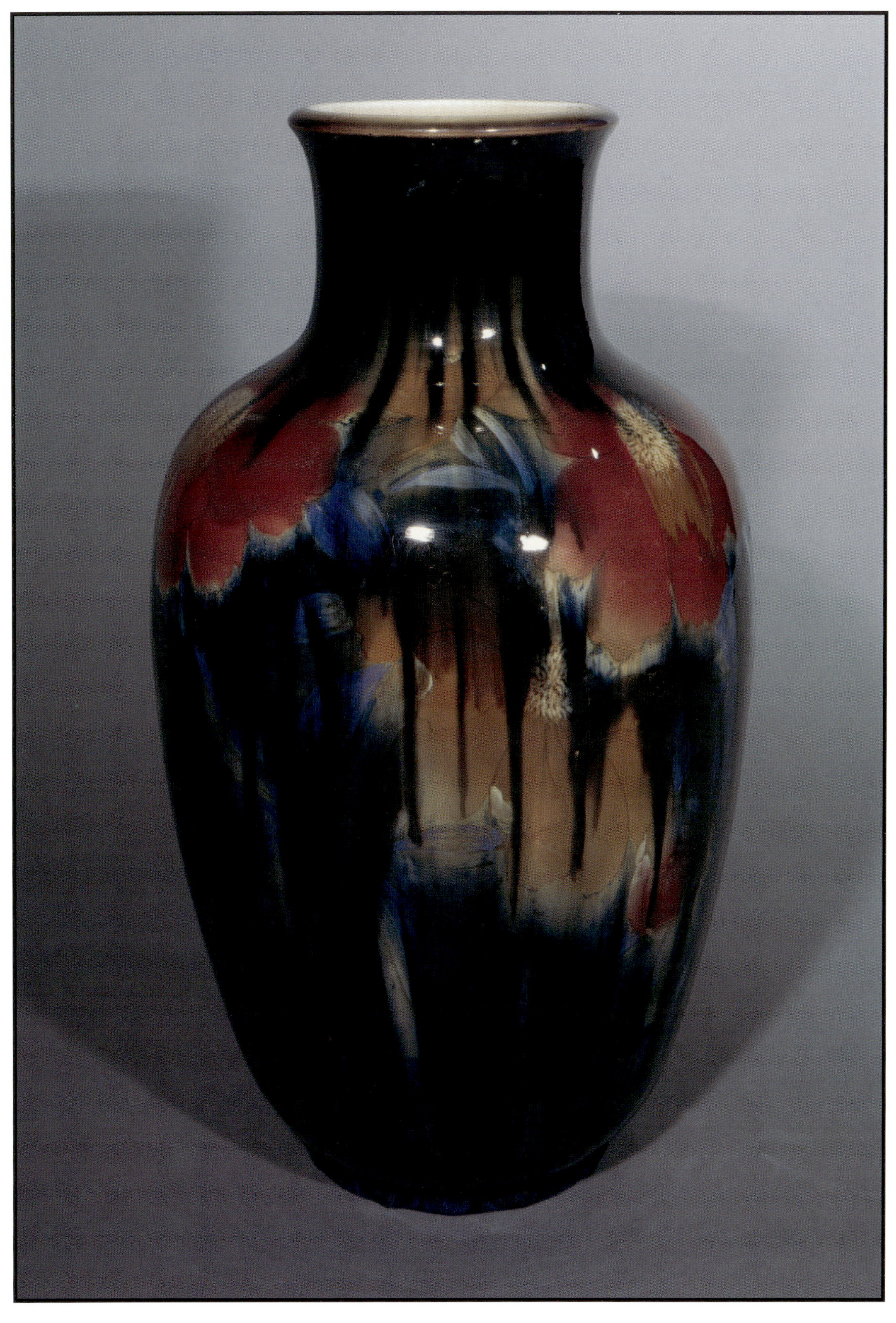

769   Tall and impressive high glaze vase with red and orange poppy decoration, most likely painted by Kataro $7000-10000
Shirayamadani in 1926. Along with the cover lot, this fabulous vase was purchased at Rookwood in the late
1950's by the consignor. A part of Rookwood's permanent museum collection for over 30 years, the two
vases were sold when Rookwood was about to move from Cincinnati to Starkville. The consignor and her
husband were told that both vases were collector's items (we agree) and well worth the discounted price.
(I wish I could have been there). This lot was sold as a Shirayamadani and in looking at the decoration, it
seems a certainty. Marks include the Rookwood logo, the date and shape number 2819. The vase appears
to be unsigned. There is a neat drill hole in the base (done by the consignor) which would not obscure the
artist's long, elegant cypher. We have not found a mark on the side but the black and cobalt blue drips may
be hiding the signature. Perhaps it was never signed but the overall effect is clearly that of Shirayamadani.
Height 17 1/2 inches. Minor grinding chips and a few burst bubbles.

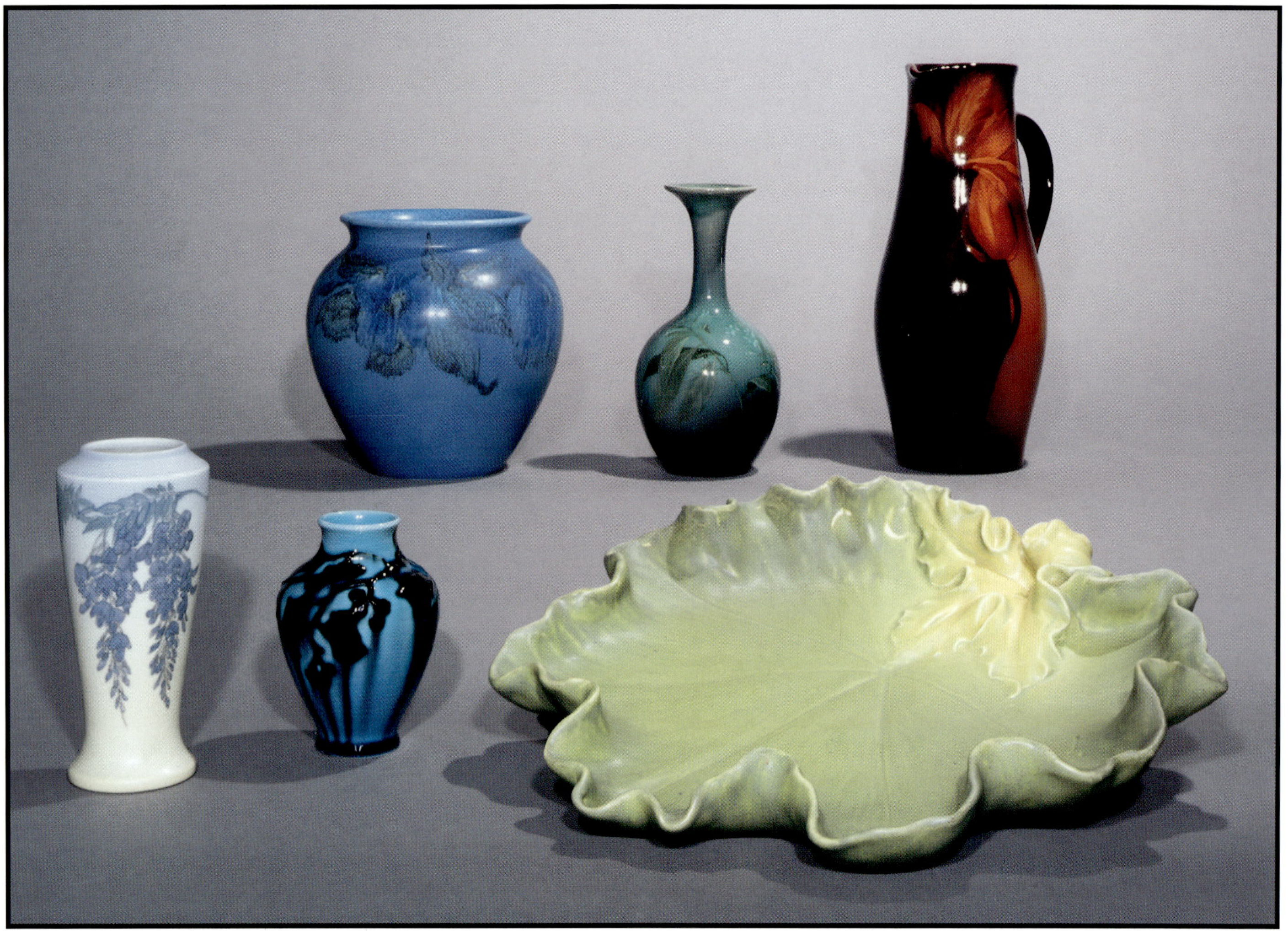

770   Vellum glaze vase with several naturalistic sprays of wisteria blossoms, painted in 1922 by Ed Diers. Marks include the Rookwood logo, the date, shape number 1356 F, an impressed V for Vellum glaze and the incised monogram of the artist. Height 6 1/8 inches. $700-900

771   Unusual high glaze vase with black leaf decoration in very heavy slip on a blue ground, done by Margaret McDonald in 1933. Marks include the Rookwood logo, the date, S for Special shape and the incised monogram of the artist. height 4 3/8 inches. There are two tiny grinding nicks on the base. $300-500

772   Mat glaze vase with floral decoration done by Louise Abel in 1924. Marks include the Rookwood logo, the date, shape number 130 and the artist's monogram, painted on in black slip. Height 6 1/2 inches. $400-500

773   Large mat glaze tray in the form of a water lily and pad, done in 1903 by Anna Valentien. Marks include the Rookwood logo, the date, shape number 372 AZ, the notation X 1023 X, a wheel ground x and the incised initials of the artist. Most likely cast in small quantity, the piece is hand colored in green and bright yellow and signed by Valentien. Distance across is 13 1/2 inches. There are firing separations in the clay on the back of the piece which account for the x. These are due to the thickness of clay used in creating the flower. $700-900

774   Sea Green glaze vase with tiny white flowers and green leaves painted in 1896 by Constance Baker. Marks include the Rookwood logo, the date, shape number 738 C, an incised G for Sea Green glaze, the incised initials of the artist and an incised X which, in this case, is an experimental mark for the artist. Height 7 1/8 inches. There is a tight line descending about one inch from the rim. $1500-2000

775   Standard glaze tankard with bold tulip decoration done in 1900 by Sallie Toohey. Impressed marks include the Rookwood logo, the date, shape number 838 C and the monogram of the artist. Height 10 1/4 inches. Minor glaze scratch. $400-600

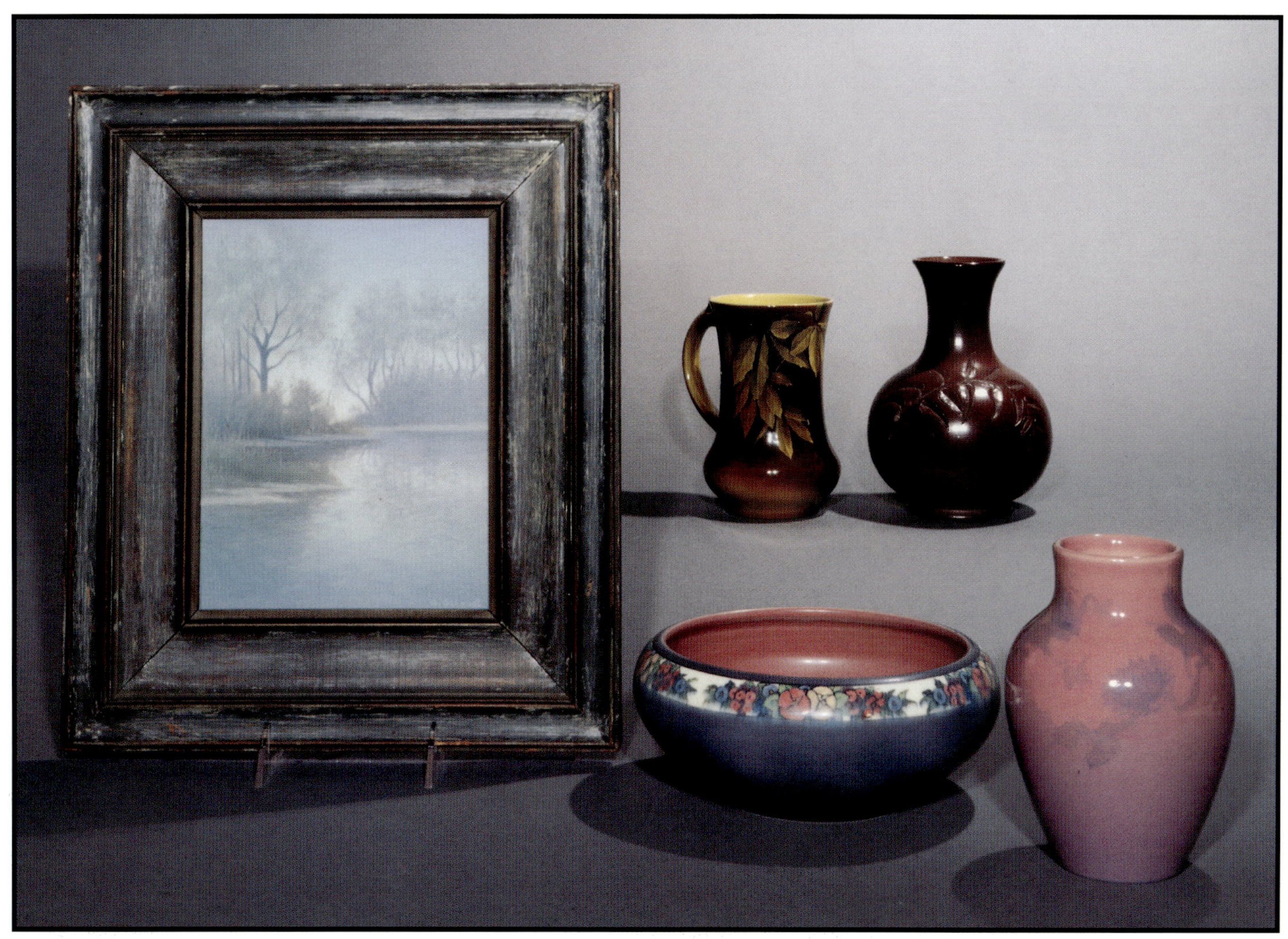

776   Vellum glaze woodland scenic plaque painted by Carl Schmidt in 1926. This a typical restful Schmidt with trees reflecting in a marshy pool. The artist's name appears in the lower right hand corner. Marks on the back include the Rookwood logo and the date. A partial paper label on the original frame carries the notation "Reflection C. Schmidt". Size is 9 by 7 inches. Uncrazed. There is pitting in the central region of the plaque and, in the same area, the glaze is noticeably thinner in certain light. $2000-2500

777   Vellum glaze bowl with pink interior and a band of multicolored flowers around the shoulder painted by Sara Sax in 1919. Marks include the Rookwood logo, the date, shape number 957 C, an impressed V for Vellum glaze body and the impressed monogram of the artist. Diameter is 7 7/8 inches and the height is 3 1/8 inches. Uncrazed. $400-600

778   Standard glaze mug with leaf and berry decoration done in 1889 by Harriet Wilcox. The work is very lifelike. Marks include the Rookwood logo, the date, shape number 461, S for sage green clay, incised LY for light yellow or Standard glaze and the incised initials of the artist. Height 5 3/4 inches. $350-450

779   1881 Rookwood dull finish vase with deeply carved leaves, done by Nettie Wenderoth. Incised marks read "Rookwood Pottery Cin O 1881 N.W.". Height 6 3/4 inches. Pieces with the incised marks from 1881 are uncommon. $300-500

780   Pink tinted high glaze vase with exotic floral decoration painted by Fred Rothenbusch in 1924. Marks include the Rookwood logo, the date, shape number 927 F, an incised P for porcelain body, another incised P for pink glaze and the incised monogram of the artist. Height 6 inches. Uncrazed. $800-1000

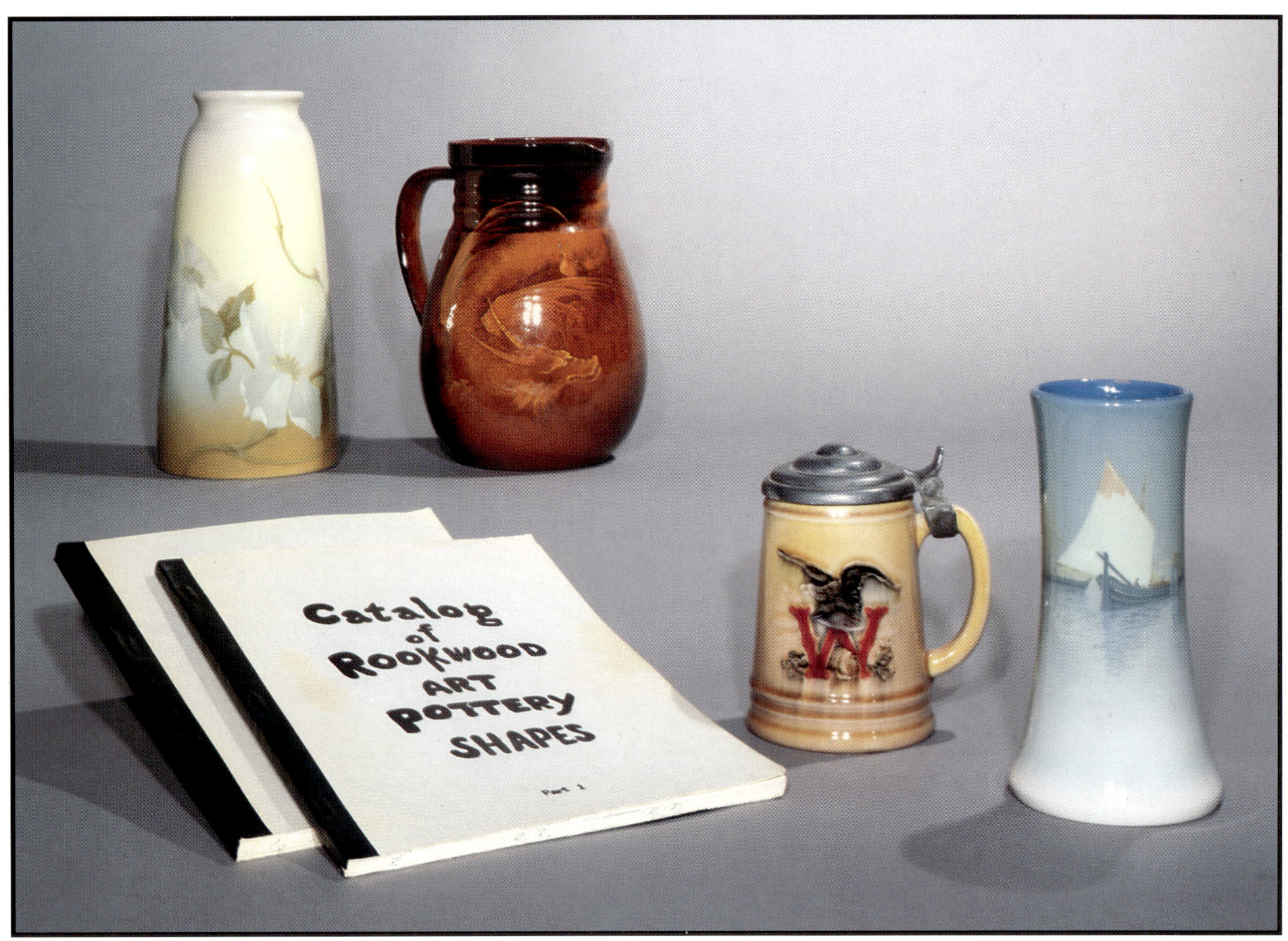

781   Set of Rookwood shape record books published from the originals in 1971 by Herbert Peck. These are $100-150
        numbered 127 out of 300 and are signed by Margaret Peck. Out of print for many years and still a valuable
        resource for Rookwood collectors. Good shape with evidence of usage.

782   Delicate Iris glaze vase with crisp wild rose decoration painted in 1909 by Fred Rothenbusch. The white $3000-4000
        flowers contrast nicely with the apricot ground. Marks include the Rookwood logo, the date, shape
        number 1658 D, an incised W for white (Iris) glaze and the incised monogram of the artist. Height 9 1/4
        inches.

783   Early Standard glaze pitcher painted in 1885 by Matt Daly. Glaring at us from the side of the pitcher is a $2500-3000
        fierce horned dragon with three toes and leathery wings who appears to emerge from the cloudy back-
        ground. Impressed marks include the date, shape number 54 A and R for red clay. Incised on the bottom
        are the artist's full name and the date 6/11/85. Height 8 inches. A small rim chip has been professionally
        repaired."

784   Wiedemann Brewing Company mug with pewter lid made at Rookwood in 1948. Marks include the $400-500
        Rookwood logo, the date and the notation "The Geo. Wiedemann Brewing Co. Inc.". Height 5 3/8 inches.

785   Snappy high glaze Venetian harbor scenic vase with wonderful depth and color, painted by Carl Schmidt in $3500-4500
        1923. Marks include the Rookwood logo, the date, shape number 1358 E and the impressed monogram of
        the artist. Height 7 1/8 inches. Uncrazed and very crisp. There are several small glaze bubbles just inside
        the rim which have caused a 1/8 by 1/2 inch section of glaze to come off. This would be a simple and
        invisible repair or simply a thing to be ignored.

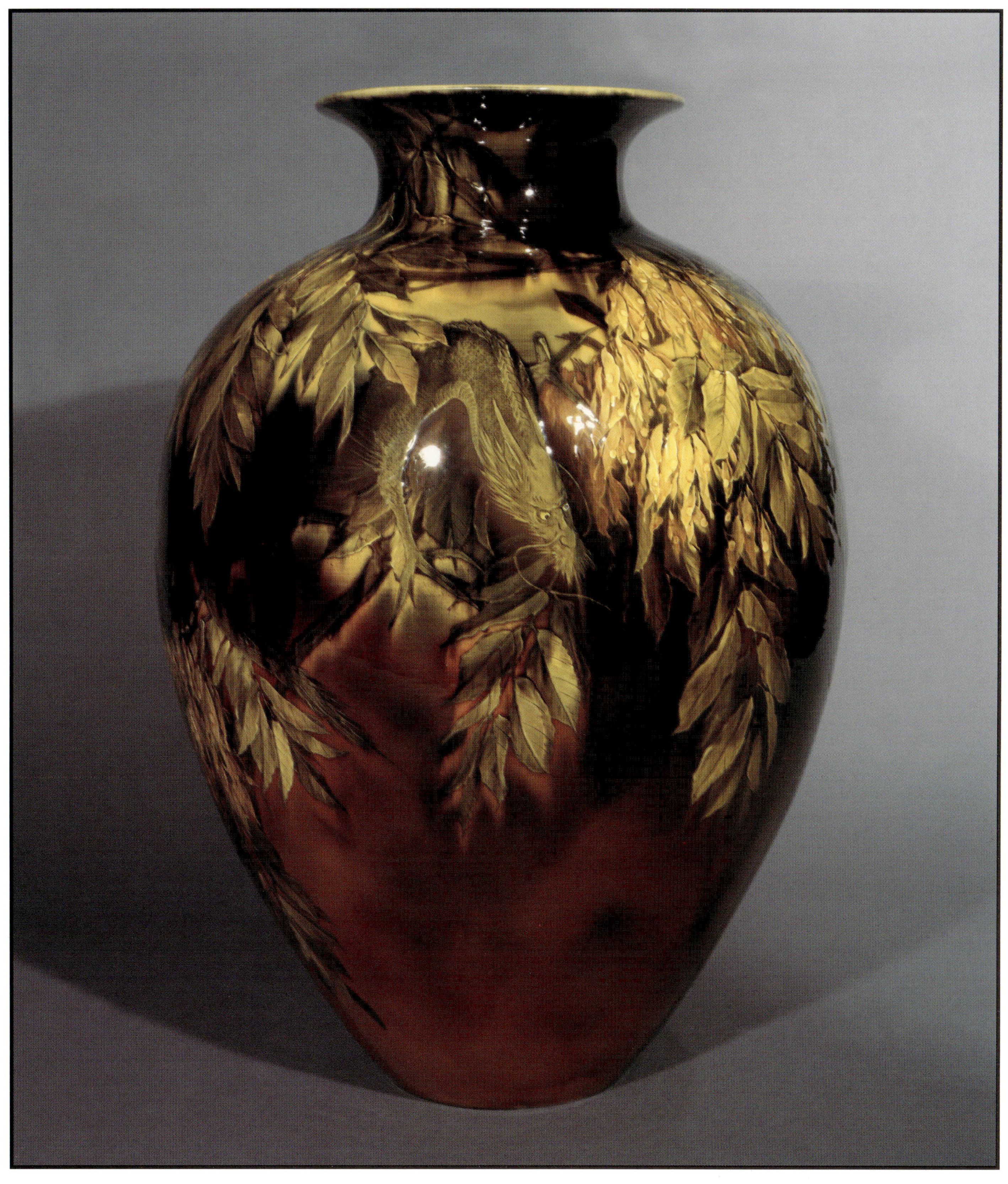

786   Monumental Standard glaze vase painted in 1891 by Kataro Shirayamadani showing five magnificently $15000-20000
        detailed three toed dragons climbing in and peeking out from ailanthus foliage. The ailanthus is a tree
        introduced from the orient which, in mythology, was a common resting place for dragons. Marks include
        the Rookwood logo, the date, shape number 488 X, an impressed W for white clay, an incised L for light
        Standard glaze and the incised cypher of the artist. Height 22 1/2 inches. This is a most impressive and
        large example of Rookwood's Standard glaze and certainly, of superior quality and condition.

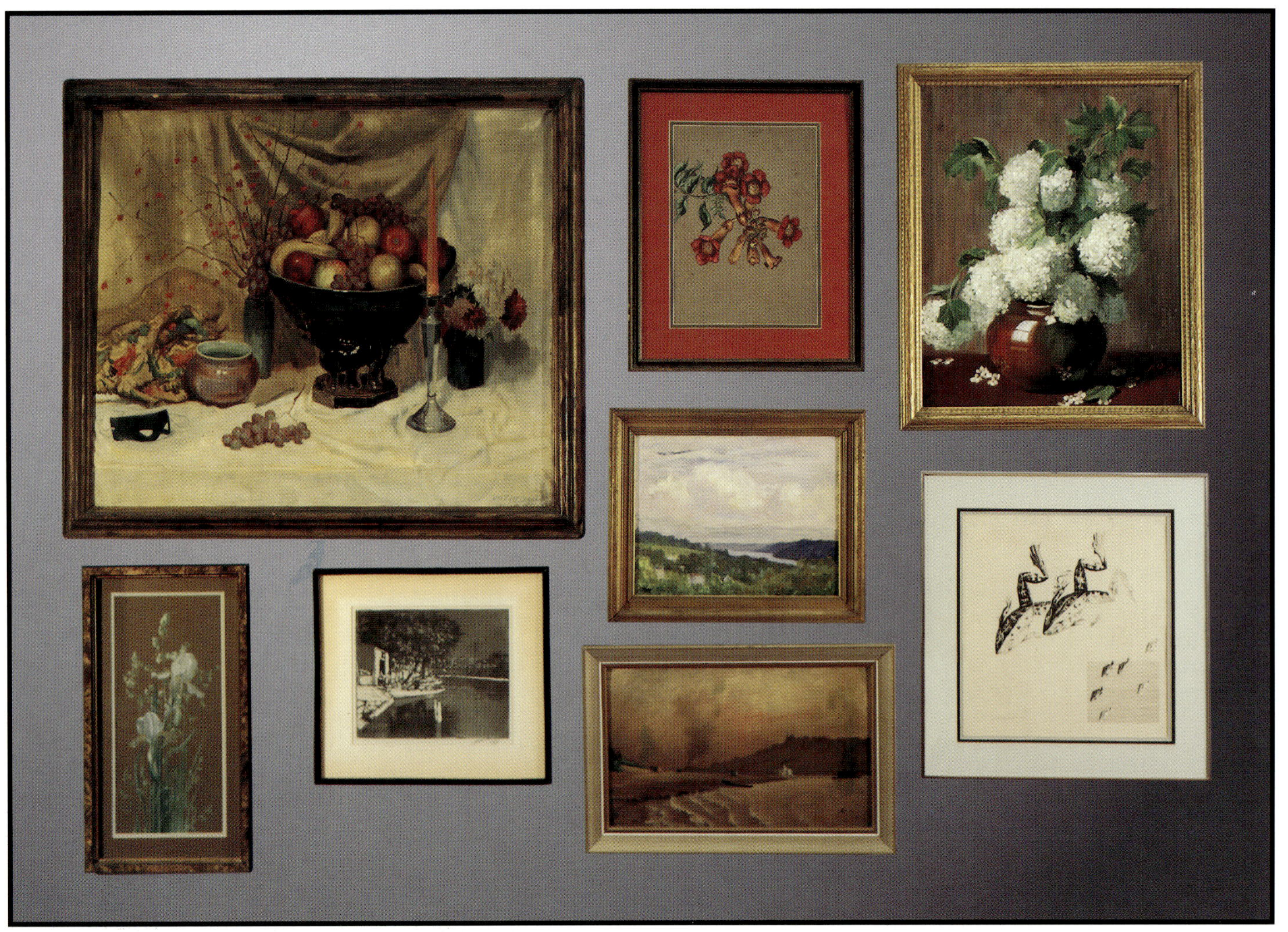

| 787 | Large oil painting on canvas, a still life with flowers, fruit and several Rookwood pieces, done by Rookwood artist William McDonald. The large black compote with elephants supporting the bowl is Rookwood's shape number 2512, a design created by Mr. McDonald. The painting is signed in the lower right hand corner. Size is 30 by 36 inches. Original, unrestored condition | $1250-1750 |

| 788 | Early watercolor of trumpet creepers painted by Cincinnati artist and potter, Mary Virginia Keenan, probably in the 1880's. Unsigned but with good oral provenance. Descended in the family of Virginia Cummins, Grace Young's step-daughter. Size is 15 x 11 1/2 inches. | $300-500 |

| 789 | Nice still life oil painting on canvas showing white hydrangea in a brown vase, painted in 1897 by Rookwood artist Matt Daly. Signed and dated in the lower right hand corner. Size is 24 by 20 inches. The painting appears to have been recently cleaned. Good overall condition with older frame showing some minor wear. | $700-900 |

| 790 | Oil painting on academy board done in 1930 by Joseph Henry Gest, Director of Rookwood Pottery. The view seems to be the Ohio River from Eden Park in Cincinnati. The painting is signed and dated in the lower left hand corner. Size is 12 by 16 inches. Recently cleaned and in an older frame. Accompanying the painting is a small, privately published book on the life of Joseph Henry Gest, done in 1937. The painting and the book have been together for many years. | $600-800 |

| 791 | Watercolor of blue irises painted by Cincinnati artist and potter, Mary Virginia Keenan, probably in the 1880's. Unsigned. This lot comes with a notarized letter from Edwin J. Kircher III detailing the provenance and family history. Size is 18 by 9 inches. | $300-500 |

| 792 | Original Etching done by Rookwood artist E.T. Hurley, circa 1920. Signed in the plate and in pencil by the artist in the lower right hand corner. Affixed to the back is an old label from the Closson Galleries in Cincinnati which lists the title as: "Hempelmans Boathouse Brighton", which is a Cincinnati suburb. Size is 9 1/4 by 11 3/4 inches. Original frame and mat, both of which are showing their age. | $200-300 |

| 793 | Oil painting on canvas mounted on board done by Rookwood artist William McDonald. Shown is a view of downtown Cincinnati and Mt. Adams from across the Ohio River in Northern Kentucky. A packet boat steams downriver and a small houseboat is tied up to a low pier. Size is 12 by 20 inches. The painting is unsigned but has descended in McDonald's family until consigned to this sale along with the McDonald still life. Generally in good condition with evidence of repair to a small tear. The frame is older but not contemporary with the painting. | $700-900 |

| 794 | Original pen and ink on paper drawing of frogs and fish, done in an Art Deco style by William Hentschel. Signed in the lower left hand corner. Size is 16 by 15 inches. Recent frame. | $300-500 |

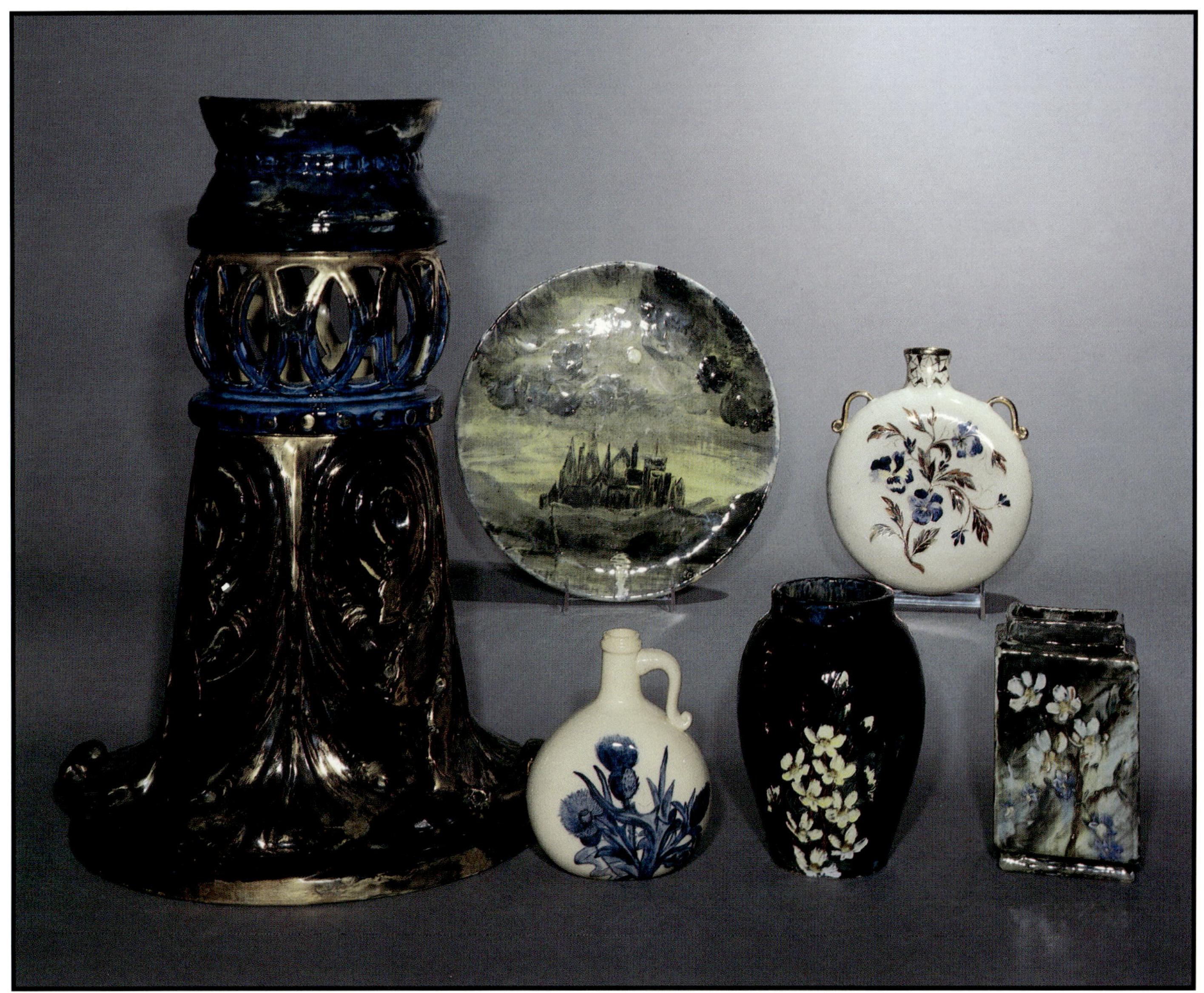

795A   Matt Morgan umbrella stand in blue gloss glaze with fired-on gold highlights. Stamped with the "Matt Morgan - Cin'ti O-Art Pottery Co" logo. Height 20 3/8 inches. A large piece of the base has been broken off and glued back in place. $300-400

795   Limoges style charger, possibly of Ohio origin, decorated by an unknown artist with a moonlit scene of a castle and lake. The artist's incised initials appear in the lower right hand edge of the charger. Diameter is 11 5/8 inches. $200-300

796   Rookwood Pilgrim flask with underglaze decoration of thistles and grasses painted by an unknown artist in 1885. Impressed marks include Rookwood in block letters, the date, shape number 85 and W for white clay. Height 6 1/8 inches. $400-500

797   Early Cincinnati Limoges style glaze vase with floral decoration made at the T.J. Wheatley Company, circa 1880. The base is incised "T.J.W. & Co. Pat. Sep 28 - 1880". Height 7 1/4 inches. $150-250

798   Cincinnati Art Pottery canteen vase with floral decor, done by an unknown artist. One side of the vase is decorated with Virginia creepers while the other has blue and yellow pansies. The handles, collar and sides are enhanced with fired-on gold. Unmarked. Height 8 1/8 inches. $200-300

799   Early Cincinnati Limoges style vase with simple floral decoration done by an unknown artist at the T.J. Wheatley Pottery, circa 1880. Incised on the bottom "T.J.W. Co. Pat Sep 28 1880". Height 6 5/8 inches. Wheatley's famous patent is in itself an interesting story. See Herbert Peck's **The Book of Rookwood Pottery** for details. $150-200

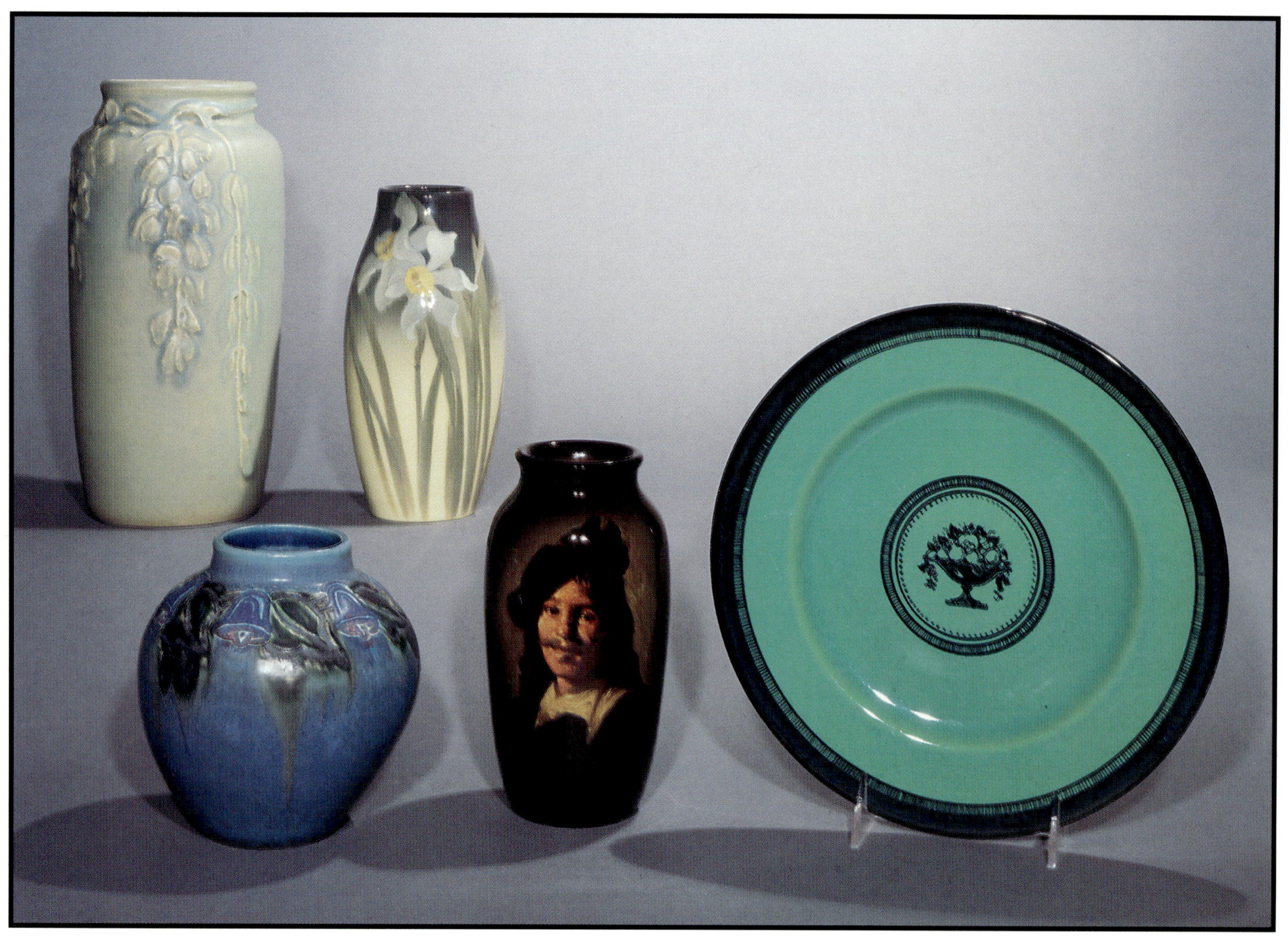

<table>
<tr><td>800</td><td>Deeply carved mat glaze Arts & Crafts style vase with wisteria flowers, leaves and thick vines, done in 1908 by Cecil Duell. Marks include the Rookwood logo, the date, shape number 1065 B, a fan shaped esoteric mark and the incised initials of the artist. Height 10 7/8 inches. There is a tight line in mid-body of the vase</td><td>$600-800</td></tr>
<tr><td>801</td><td>Neat Arts & Crafts style mat glaze vase with carved and painted bluebells, done in 1916 by C.S. Todd. Marks include the Rookwood logo, the date, shape number 912 and the incised initials of the artist. Height 5 3/8 inches. There is a pin-head sized nick off the inside of the rim.</td><td>$600-800</td></tr>
<tr><td>802</td><td>Iris glaze vase with yellow and white jonquils painted in 1904 by Sara Sax. Marks include the Rookwood logo, the date, shape number 939 C, an incised W for white (Iris) glaze and the impressed monogram of the artist. Height 8 1/8 inches. A two inch line descending from the rim has been professionally repaired.</td><td>$800-1200</td></tr>
<tr><td>803</td><td>Good Standard glaze Old Master-style portrait of a gentleman after Gerard Don, painted in 1901 by Grace Young. Marks include the Rookwood logo, the date, shape number 80 B, the impressed monogram of the artist and the incised notation "After Gerard Don". Height 7 inches.</td><td>$1000-1500</td></tr>
<tr><td>804</td><td>High glaze plate decorated by Arthur Conant around 1920. The plate is edged in cobalt blue with fine hatching as the center which contains the image of a fruit laden compote. Marks on the back include the flameless Rookwood logo and the incised monogram of the artist. The blank for the plate is most likely from the early 20's when Rookwood made its Blue Ship Dinnerware. Like the Blue Ship Dinnerware, it carries neither date nor shape number. Diameter is 9 7/8 inches. Uncrazed but showing minor scratches from use.</td><td>$600-800</td></tr>
</table>

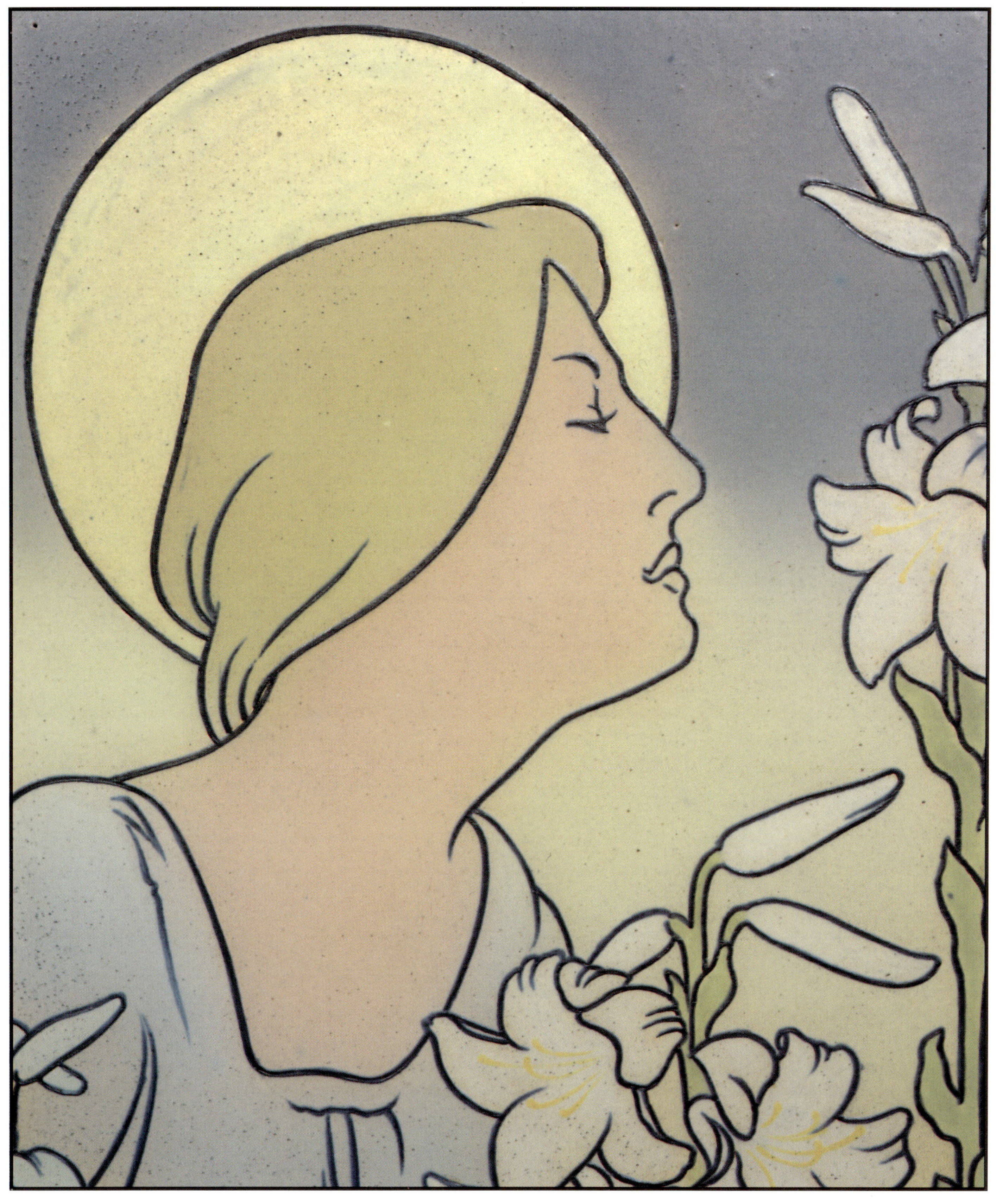

805   Large, rare and important Art Nouveau style mat glaze plaque painted by Albert Valentien in 1902. $25000-30000
Pictured is a young woman in a field of white lilies with the sun behind her head. She appears to be taking in the fragrance of the lilies. Valentien has drawn inspiration from Pre- Raphaelite paintings of similar subject matter. Close examination reveals the design to have been first incised in the damp clay and then the incised lines were filled with black slip by slip trailing. Several places in the flowers show incised lines that were not filled in favor of another. The slip trailing serves to isolate colors much like cloisonne' enamel. The only true painting on the plaque occurs in the yellow centers of the white lilies. Otherwise each color is broadly painted between the lines to give a two dimensional effect not unlike Japanese woodblock printing. The artist's initials are found in the lower left hand corner of the plaque, painted on in reddish-brown slip. Impressed on the back is a very large Rookwood logo and the date. Size is 21 by 15 inches. There is a fair amount of peppering in the glaze but no crazing. Certainly, this is one of the most unusual of all Rookwood plaques. Exhibited: **Rookwood Pottery The Glorious Gamble**, color plate 48 on page 113.

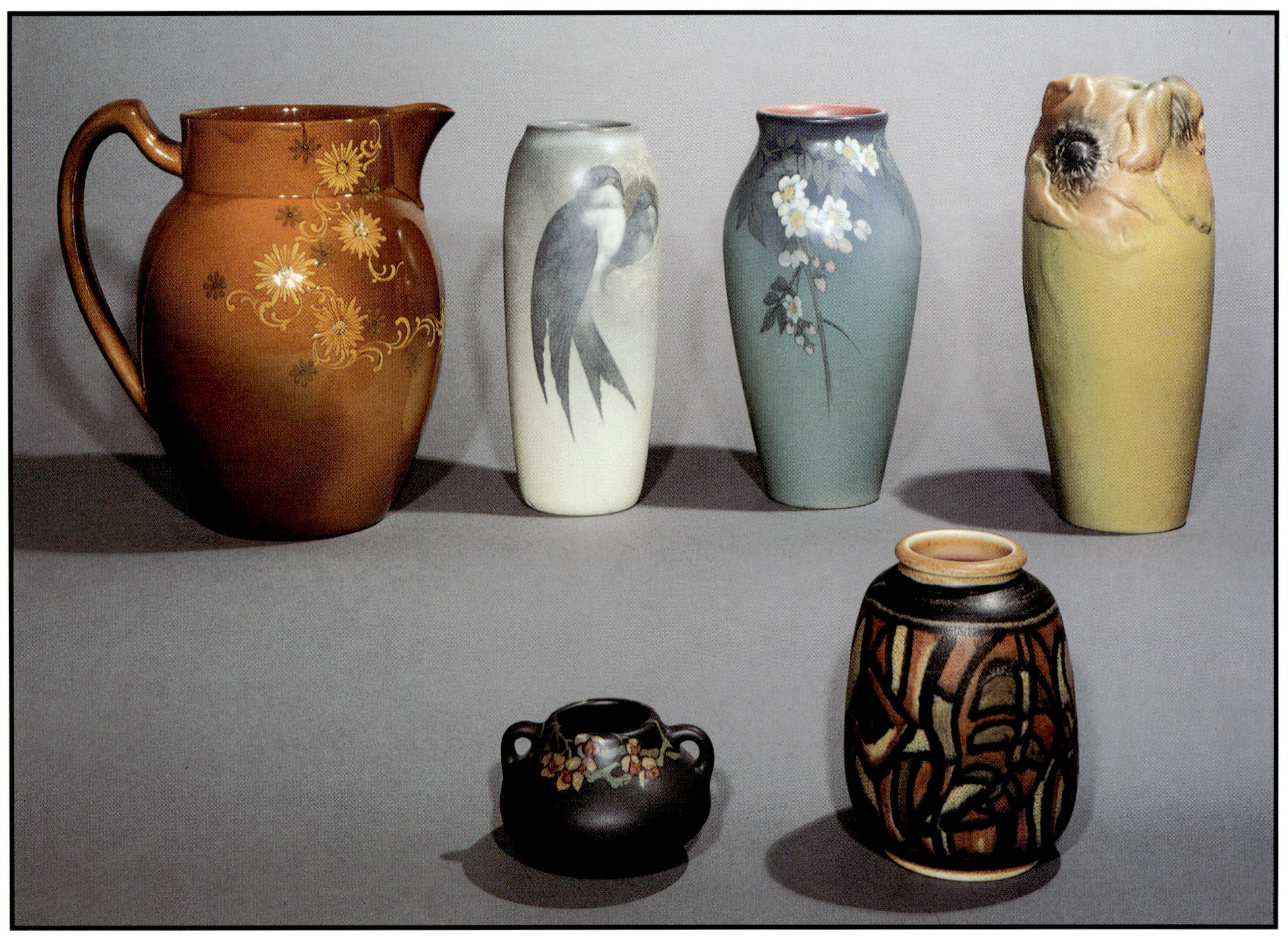

806   Standard glaze pitcher with highly stylized flowers in green and gold painted in 1886 by Matt Daly. Marks include the Rookwood logo, the date, shape number 293, R for red clay, an incised D for Dark Standard glaze and the incised initials of the artist. Height 8 7/8 inches. $600-800

807   Early Carl Schmidt Vellum glaze vase from 1905 showing an adult barn swallow perched outside its mud nest while another bird peers out from inside. Marks include the Rookwood logo, the date, shape number 951 D, V for Vellum glaze body, an incised V for Vellum glaze and the impressed monogram of the artist. Height 8 1/4 inches. There is a tight, three inch crack descending from the rim on the back side of the vase. $1500-2000

808   Sharp Painted Mat two-handled vase with colorful leaves, flowers and vines encircling the shoulder, painted in 1906 by Olga Geneva Reed. All decoration is outlined on black to add contrast with the purple body. Marks include the Rookwood logo, the date, shape number 536 F and the initials of the artist, painted on in black slip. Height 2 3/8 inches. $1250-1500

809   Sharp and flawless Vellum glaze vase with cherry blossoms painted in 1925 by Lenore Asbury. The life-like flowers and leaves are all outlined in black. Marks include the Rookwood logo, the date, shape number 925 D, an incised V for Vellum glaze and the incised initials of the artist. Height 8 5/8 inches. Uncrazed and extremely nice. $2000-2500

810   Mat glaze vase with very stylized floral designs in orange, gray and yellow, all outlined in black, decorated by Jens Jensen in 1930. Marks include the Rookwood logo, the date, shape number 6196 F, a fan shaped esoteric mark and the artist's monogram, painted on in black slip. Height 5 1/4 inches. A small but dramatic example of Jensen's floral work. $1000-1250

811   Rare mat glaze vase with molded poppies, hand colored by Harriet Wilcox in 1902. Clearly a cast form, much like the nude pieces done by Anna Valentien and Artus Van Briggle in Colorado, this vase carries an artist's initials because Wilcox has applied the glaze colors. Until about 1905, Rookwood advertised that no artist signed pieces were ever duplicated. Obviously this vase, which is still quite rare, and many of Valentien's nudes, are cast pieces which later became regular production pieces (this vase became shape number 1005). To make sure the claim of originality was not violated, the artist who signed the piece was obliged to do some hand work or glazing as in this case. Marks include the Rookwood logo, the date, shape number 391 Z and the artist's initials, painted on in black slip. Height 9 1/2 inches. Very crisp and clean. $1500-2000

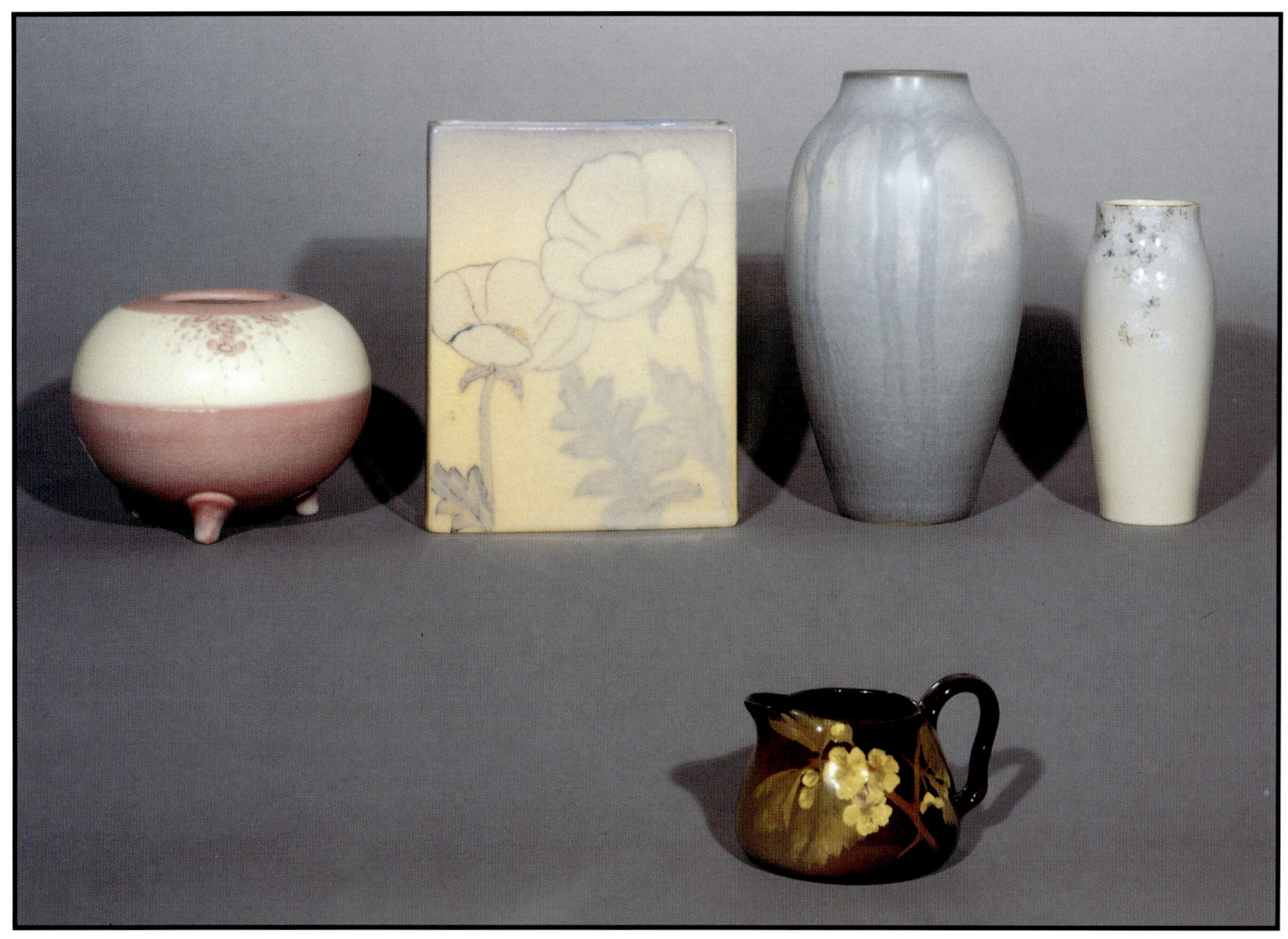

812   Round Vellum glaze vase with three small feet. Decorated by Sara Sax with small sprays of pink flowers. $300-400
       Marks include the Rookwood logo, the date, shape number 2038, an impressed V for Vellum glaze body, an
       incised V for Vellum glaze, a wheel ground x and the incised monogram of the artist. Height 4 1/4 inches.
       Minor glaze anomalies.

813   High glaze planter vase with white poppy decoration done in 1946 by Kataro Shirayamadani. Marks include $1000-1500
       the Rookwood logo, the date, shape number 6292 C, the incised number 6386 and the incised initials of the
       artist. Height 7 5/8 inches.

814   Standard glaze creamer with yellow wild rose decoration done in 1900 by Clara Lindeman. Marks include the $200-300
       Rookwood logo, the date, shape number 770 and the incised initials of the artist. Height 2 1/2 inches.

815   Misty Vellum glaze winter landscape vase painted by E.T. Hurley in 1912. Marks include the Rookwood logo, $600-800
       the date, shape number 900 C, an impressed V for Vellum glaze body and the incised initials of the artist.
       Height 8 5/8 inches. Moderate crazing.

816   Cameo glaze vase with pretty white flowers on a pale gray to cream ground, painted by Kataro Shiraya- $1000-1250
       madani in 1887 and signed with his earliest mark, a Japanese chop. Marks include the Rookwood logo, the
       date, shape number 30 C, W for white clay, an incised W for white (Cameo) glaze and the impressed chop
       mark of the artist. Height 6 inches. There is a tight line at the rim.

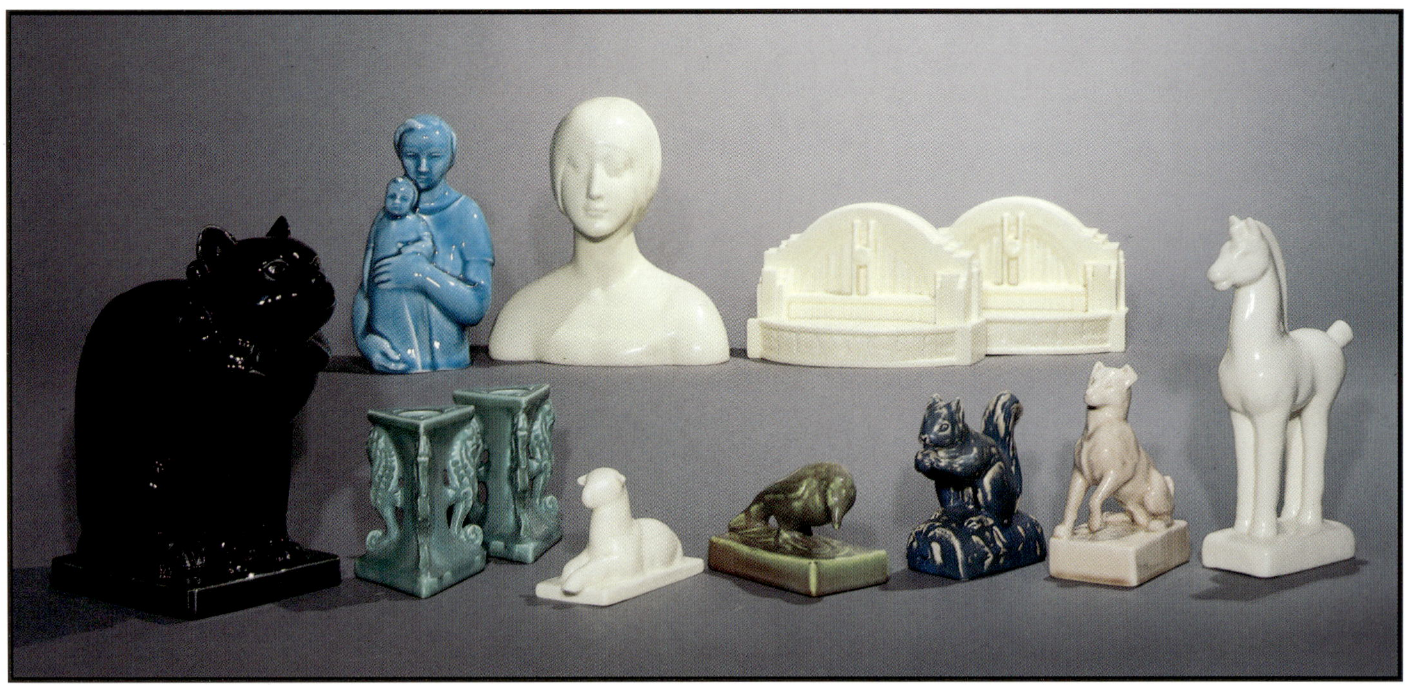

817   Rare Cat doorstop in cobalt high glaze made at Rookwood in 1924. Marks include the Rookwood logo, the date and shape number 2637. Height 8 1/2 inches. We know of three of these doorstops and this is the only one without damage. $1500-2000

818   Pair of triangular seahorse candlesticks done in a variegated green mat glaze at Rookwood in 1927. Marks include the Rookwood logo, the date and shape number 1773. Height of each is 4 inches. $200-250

819   Art Deco mother and child designed by David Seyler and made at Rookwood in 1939. Marks include the Rookwood logo, the date and shape number 6736. Seyler worked at Rookwood as a student before his involvement at Kenton Hills Porcelains. His figural pieces are generally very Deco in style. This piece is seldom seen. Height 7 1/2 inches. The blue high glaze is uncrazed. $500-700

820   Rookwood production bust of a young woman done in white mat glaze in 1924. Marks include the Rookwood logo, the date, shape number 2026 and an original Marshall Field, Inc. showroom label dated December, 1924. Height 7 7/8 inches. $300-400

821   Rare lamb paperweight in white mat glaze made at Rookwood in 1938. Marks include the Rookwood logo, the date and shape number 6663. Height 2 3/4 inches. $400-600

822   Green mat glaze Rook paperweight made in 1932. Marks include the Rookwood logo, the date and shape number 1623. Height 2 3/4 inches. $300-400

823   Rare Rookwood Union Terminal bookends in white mat glaze made in 1933 as presentation pieces. Marks include the Rookwood logo, the date, shape number 6378 and the notation on the back side of each "Presented to Col. H.M. Waite 1933 by Kiwanis Club of Cincinnati". Height of each is 4 5/8 inches. Very minor glaze chips. We know of only four sets of Union Terminal bookends. $2000-3000

824   Rare Rookwood squirrel paperweight done in 1928 in a neat blue and tan mat glaze. Marks include the Rookwood logo, the date, shape number 6025 and the cast-in monogram of designer Sallie Toohey. Height 4 1/8 inches. There is a small glaze skip on the front of the plinth. $300-400

825   High glaze, rose colored, dog paperweight made at Rookwood in 1948. Marks include the Rookwood logo, the date and shape number 2777. Height 4 7/8 inches. Uncrazed and sharp. $250-350

826   Rare white semi-gloss carousel horse made at Rookwood in 1946. Marks include the Rookwood logo, the date and shape number 6929. Height 8 1/4 inches. $400-600

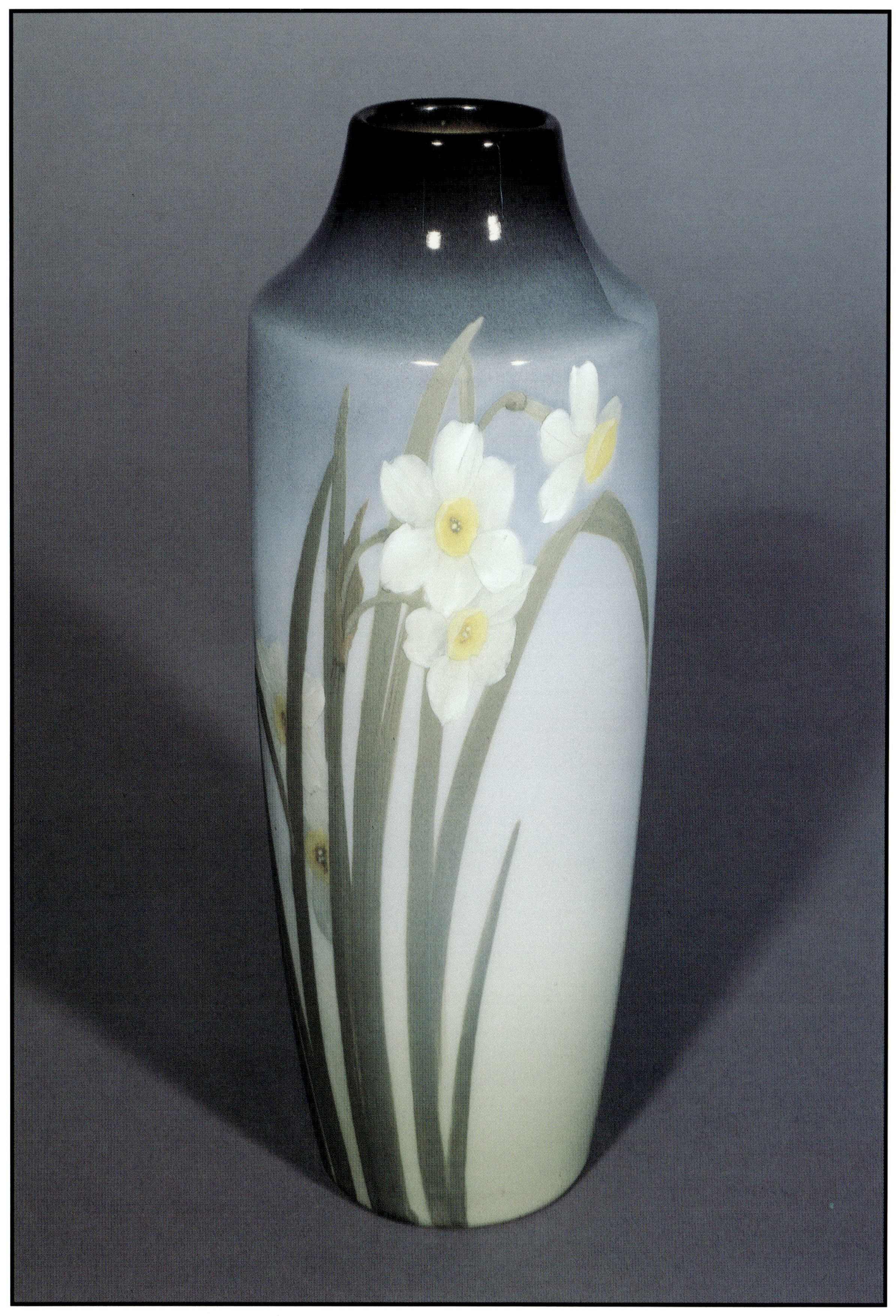

827   Beautifully detailed Iris glaze vase painted in 1908 by Sara Sax. Pictured are several sprays of white $8000-10000
jonquils with yellow centers which contrast nicely along with green stems on a pale gray to cream
ground. Marks include the Rookwood logo, the date, shape number 946, an incised W for white (Iris)
glaze and the impressed monogram of the artist. Height 10 1/4 inches. A tiny amount of crazing is
confined to the slip decorated flower heads only.

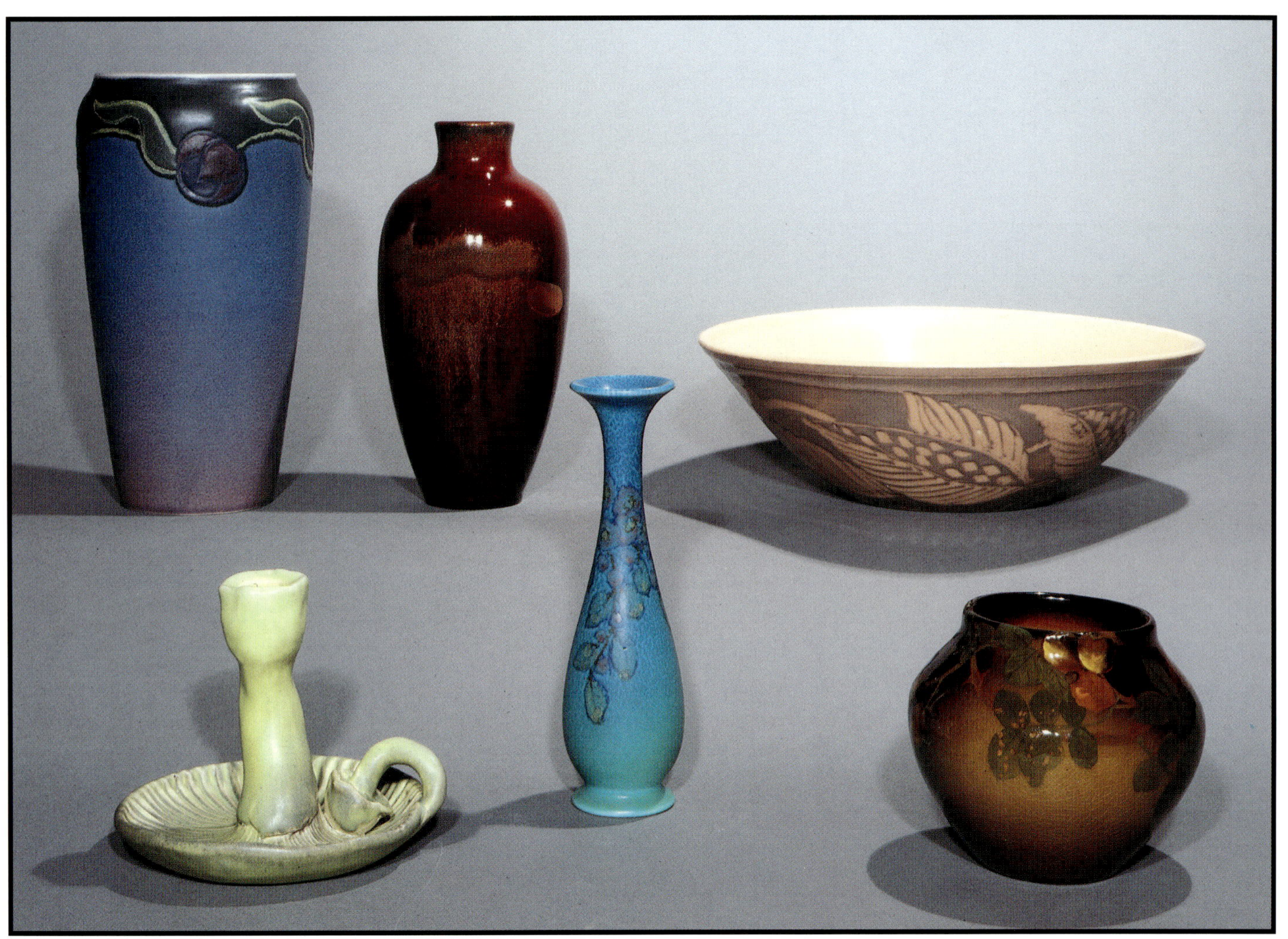

828   Handsome mat glaze vase incised and painted by C.S. Todd in 1920. Around the top of the vase, Todd has $800-1000
created a band of stylized roses which are outlined by incising and then brightly colored. Marks include the
Rookwood logo, the date, shape number 1369 D, V for Vellum glaze body and the incised initials of the
artist. Height 9 1/4 inches.

829   Experimental mat glaze candle holder in the form of a mushroom made in 1902 by Anna Valentien. Marks $400-500
include the Rookwood logo, the date, shape number 331 Z, experimental mark X 915 X and the incised
initials of the artist. Height 4 3/8 inches. Valentien made several versions of the mushroom candle holder,
some of which are probably unique pieces. This particular shape became production shape 1068.

830   Kenton Hills Porcelains Coromandel style glaze vase made, circa 1940. One side of the vase is loaded with $400-600
rich, copper-like crystals. Marks include the Kenton Hills logo and shape number 109. Height 8 1/4 inches.
There are a few small burst glaze bubbles near the base.

831   Bud vase in mat glaze with floral decoration done in 1927 by Katherine Jones. Marks include the Rook- $300-400
wood logo, the date, shape number 2545 F and the artist's initials, painted on in blue slip. Height 7 1/4
inches. Pictured: Rookwood Its Golden Era of Art Pottery 1880-1929 by Kircher and Agranoff, color plate
14, middle row, number 1.

832   Kenton Hills Unica bowl with leaf and berry decoration done in heavy slip on the outside of the piece by $400-600
Alza Stratton. Marks include the Kenton Hills logo, shape number 115 and the incised notation "Alza
Stratton Unica". Height is 3 5/8 inches and diameter is 11 1/4 inches.

833   Standard glaze vase with rose hip decoration painted by Carrie Steinle in 1904. Marks include the Rook- $200-300
wood logo, the date, shape number 906 E, a wheel ground x and the incised monogram of the artist.
Height 4 inches. The vase is x'ed because some of the green leaves have underglaze skips which really
look more like bug holes than glaze flaws.

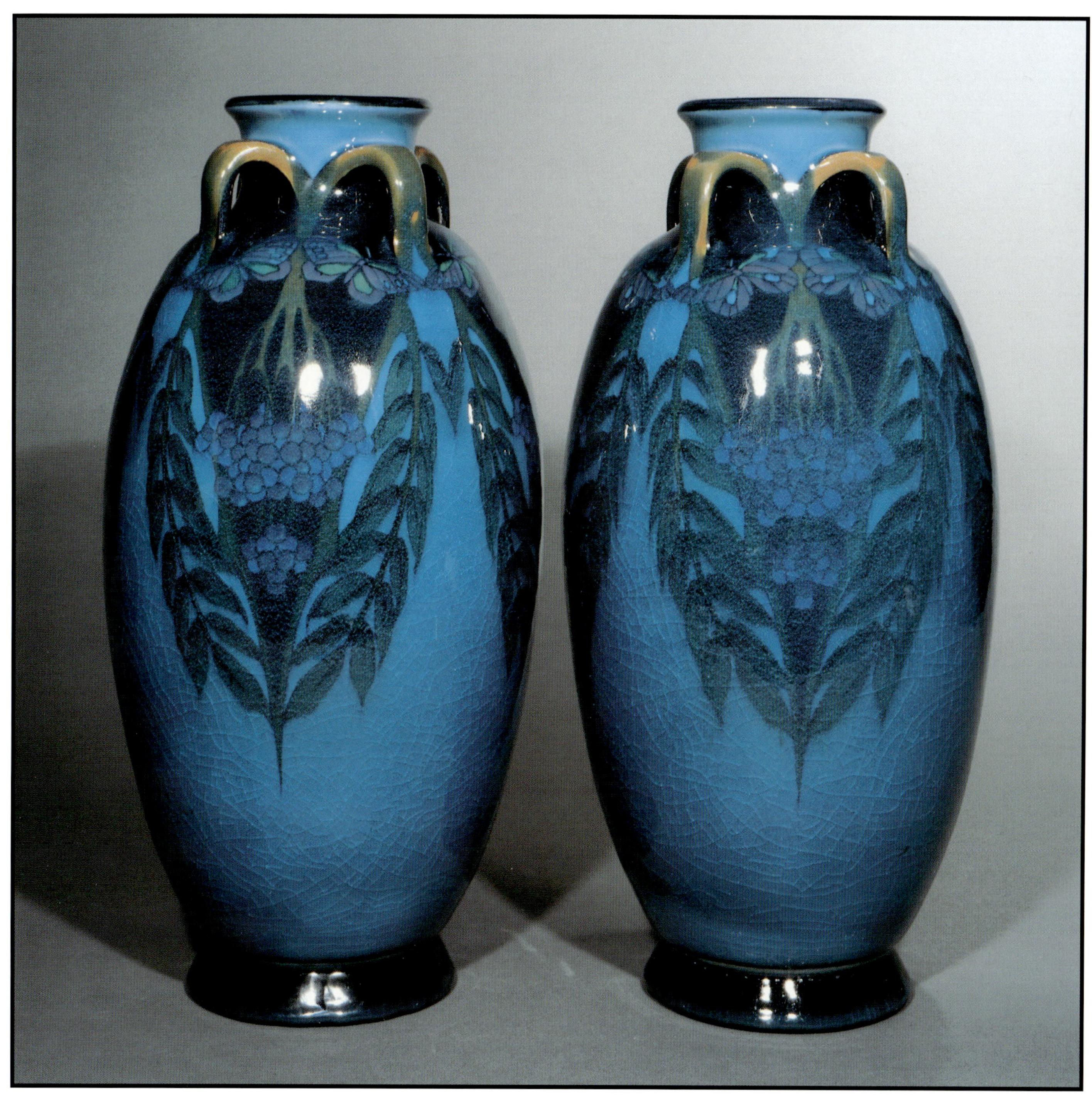

834   Rare, large and impressive pair of Turquoise Blue glaze vases decorated by Sara Sax in 1917. Each hand $7000-9000
thrown vase has four loop handles attaching the collar to the shoulder. The complex design features
repeating leaf and berry patterns with colorful butterflies, wing tip to wing tip, just below the handles.
Marks include the Rookwood logo, the date, shape number 2371, a sideways p for porcelain body and
the incised monogram of the artist. One of the vases has part of a Rookwood showroom paper label.
The other has the complete label with the price for the pair listed at $150 in 1917. Height of each is 17
inches. These vases have been in the same family since the early 1920's when they were purchased.

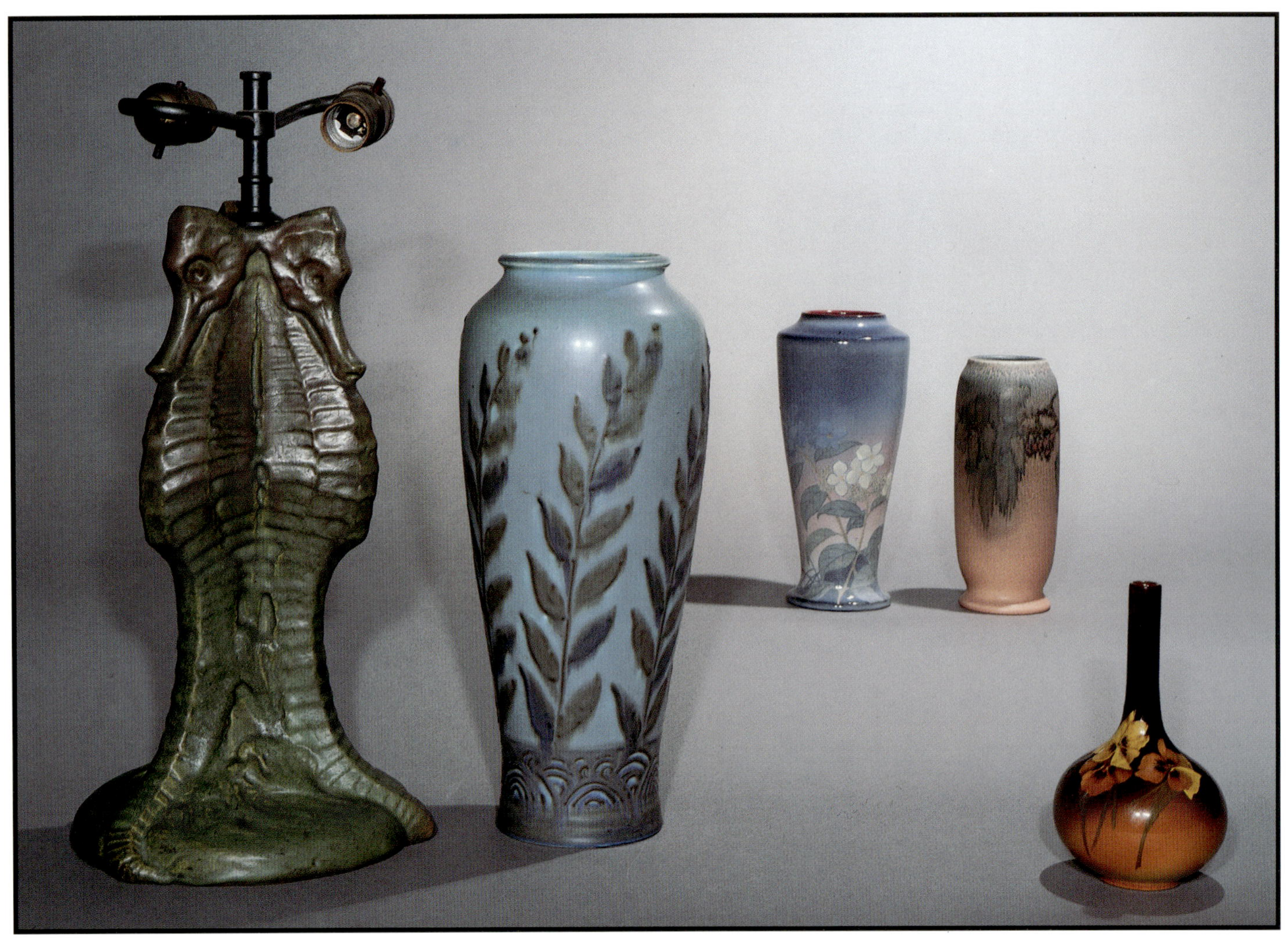

835   Rare triple seahorse lamp base done in brown over green mat glazes at Rookwood, circa 1905. Marks include the Rookwood logo and obscured date and shape numbers. Molded in the outside surface of the base is a large letter "F" which may be the mark of designer, Rose Fechheimer. Height of the ceramic portion is 15 1/4 inches. This is a rare and early production piece for Rookwood which has its original fittings. Only a handful of these have survived and this one is in excellent original condition. $1000-1500

836   Tall mat glaze vase with Art Deco floral designs painted in 1928 by Elizabeth Barrett. Barrett used slip trailing to outline the leaves and stems and the band around the bottom of the vase has repeating fan shaped designs done with slip trailing. Marks include the Rookwood logo, the date, shape number 2551 and the incised monogram of the artist. Height 14 1/8 inches. $700-900

837   High glaze vase with colorful floral decoration done by Kataro Shirayamadani in 1925. The vase is lined in a rich maroon glaze which seems to have been a color reserved for only Shirayamadani. Marks include the Rookwood logo, the date, shape number 1356 D and the incised cypher of the artist. Height 8 7/8 inches. A small glaze chip on the foot has been professionally repaired. $2500-3500

838   Mat glaze vase painted in 1926 by Margaret McDonald with red berries and green leaves on a pink ground. Marks include the Rookwood logo, the date, shape number 2070 and the monogram of the artist, painted on in black slip. Height 7 5/8 inches. $400-500

839   Standard glaze vase with a long, slender neck painted in 1899 by Elizabeth Lincoln. Decoration consists of red and yellow pansies with green stems. Marks include the Rookwood logo, the date, shape number 743 C and the incised initials of the artist. Height 6 7/8 inches. $400-500

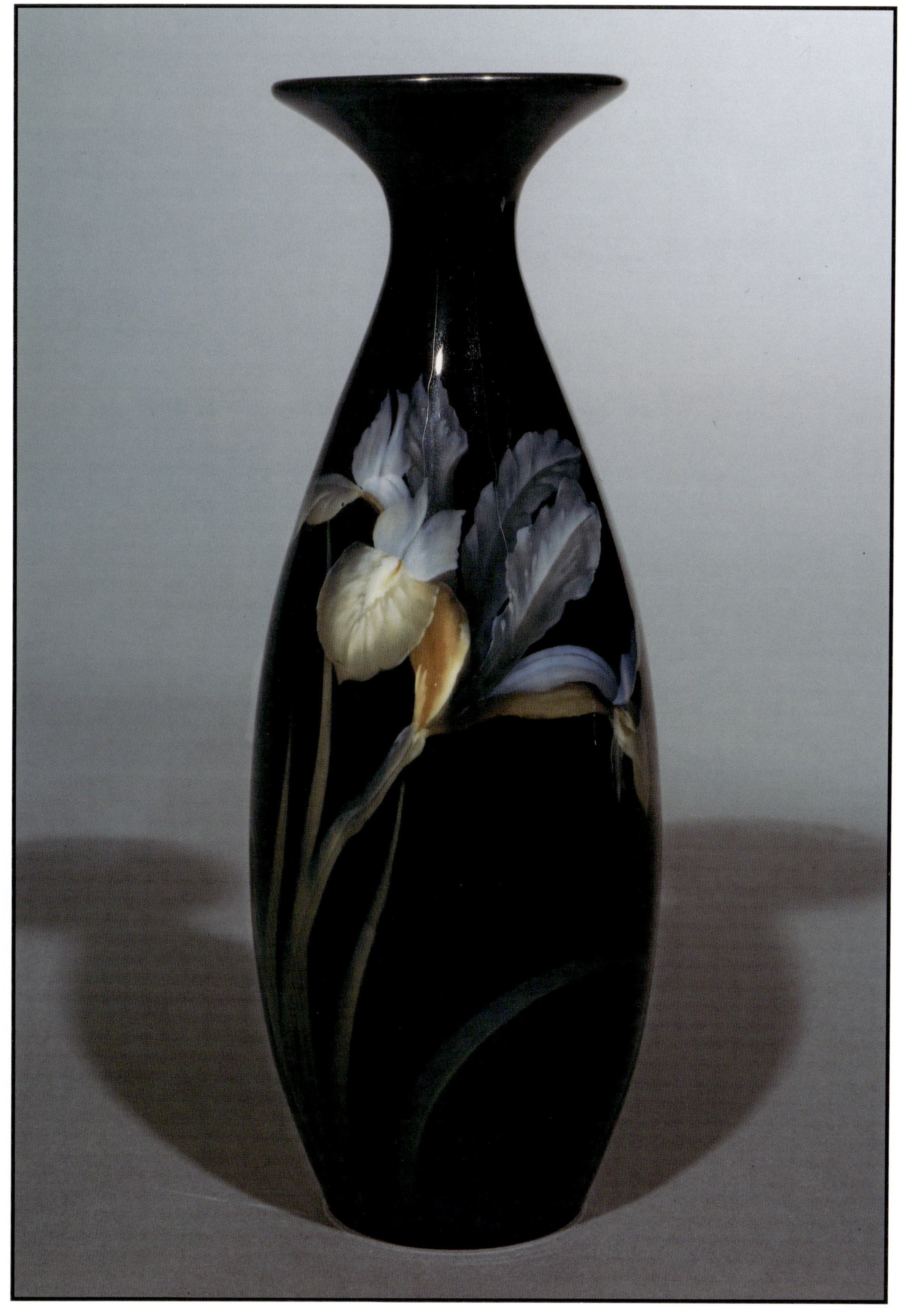

840   Stunning Black Iris glaze vase with delicate Japanese irises, painted by Carl Schmidt in 1907. Marks $10000-15000
      include the Rookwood logo, the date, shape number 482, an incised W for white (Iris) glaze and the
      impressed monogram of the artist. Height 9 3/4 inches. There are a few glaze scratches but the piece is
      uncrazed and extremely snappy.

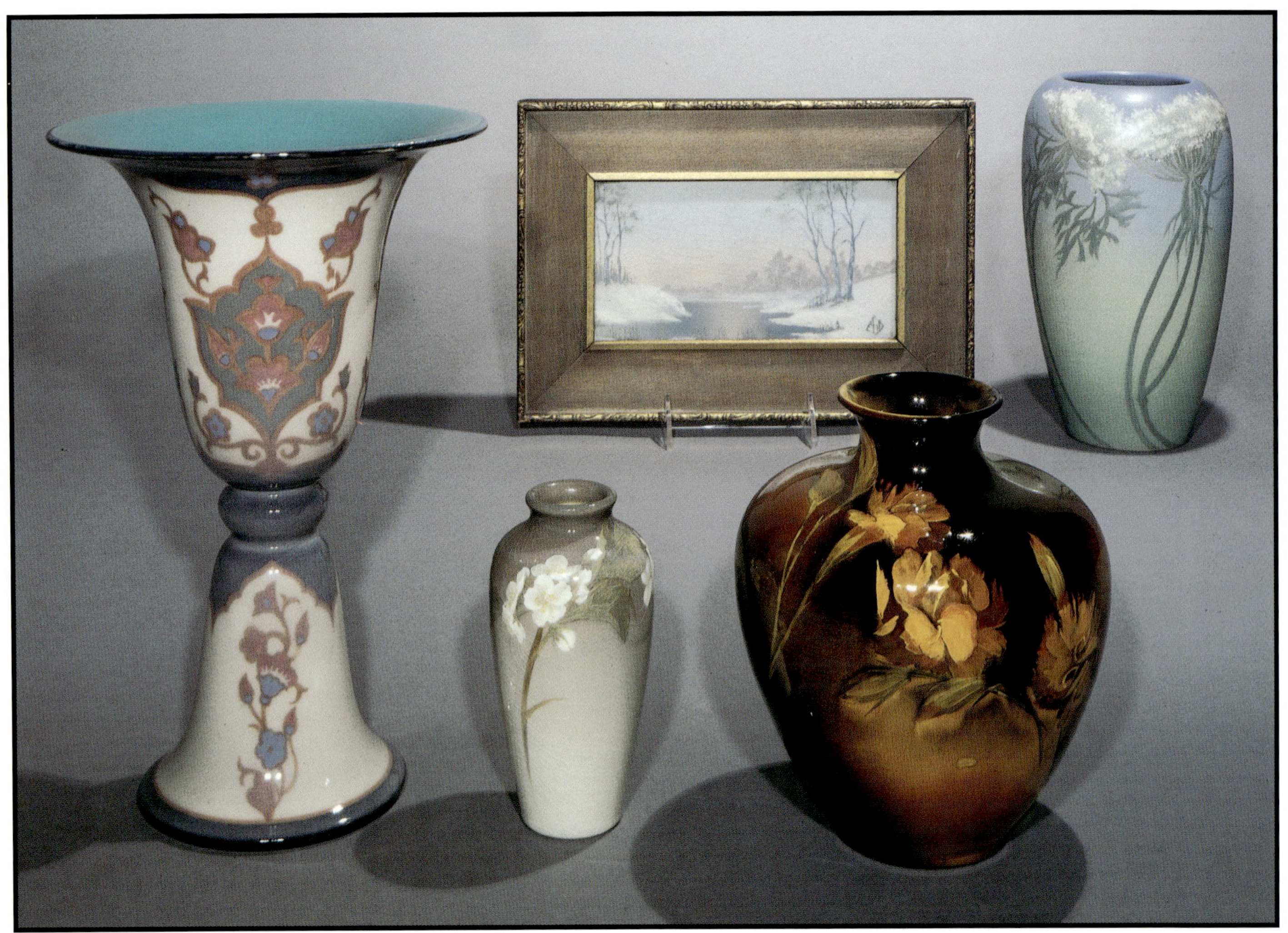

841   Tall urn-shaped vase with stylized floral decoration in many colors, the work of Arthur Conant in 1917. Marks include the Rookwood logo, the date, Special shape number S 1983, a sideways P for porcelain body, a paper label indicating this to be R 101 from the Born Collection and the incised monogram of the artist. Height 12 3/4 inches. The exterior of the vase is uncrazed. $2000-2500

842   Iris glaze vase with wild rose decoration painted by Ed Diers in 1904. Impressed marks include the Rookwood logo, the date, shape number 614 F and the artist's monogram. Incised on the base is a "W" for white (Iris) glaze. Height 6 1/8 inches. $700-900

843   Vellum glaze winter landscape plaque decorated by Mary Grace Denzler in 1914. Denzler's monogram is painted on the lower right hand corner of the piece. Marks on the back include the Rookwood logo, the date and an incised V for Vellum glaze. Size is 4 3/8 by 8 1/8 inches. Original frame. $1250-1750

844   Standard glaze vase with red carnation decoration by Artus Van Briggle, done in 1893. Marks include the Rookwood logo, the date, shape number 664 D, W for white clay and the incised monogram of the artist. Height 8 1/8 inches. There is a bit of dark crazing in the lighter background areas and a small glaze flaw just below the flowers. $400-600

845   Nicely detailed Vellum glaze vase with Queen Anne's lace decoration by Ed Diers, done in 1906. Marks include the Rookwood logo, the date, shape number 1126 C, V for Vellum glaze body, an incised V for Vellum glaze and the incised monogram of the artist. Height 9 inches. $1200-1500

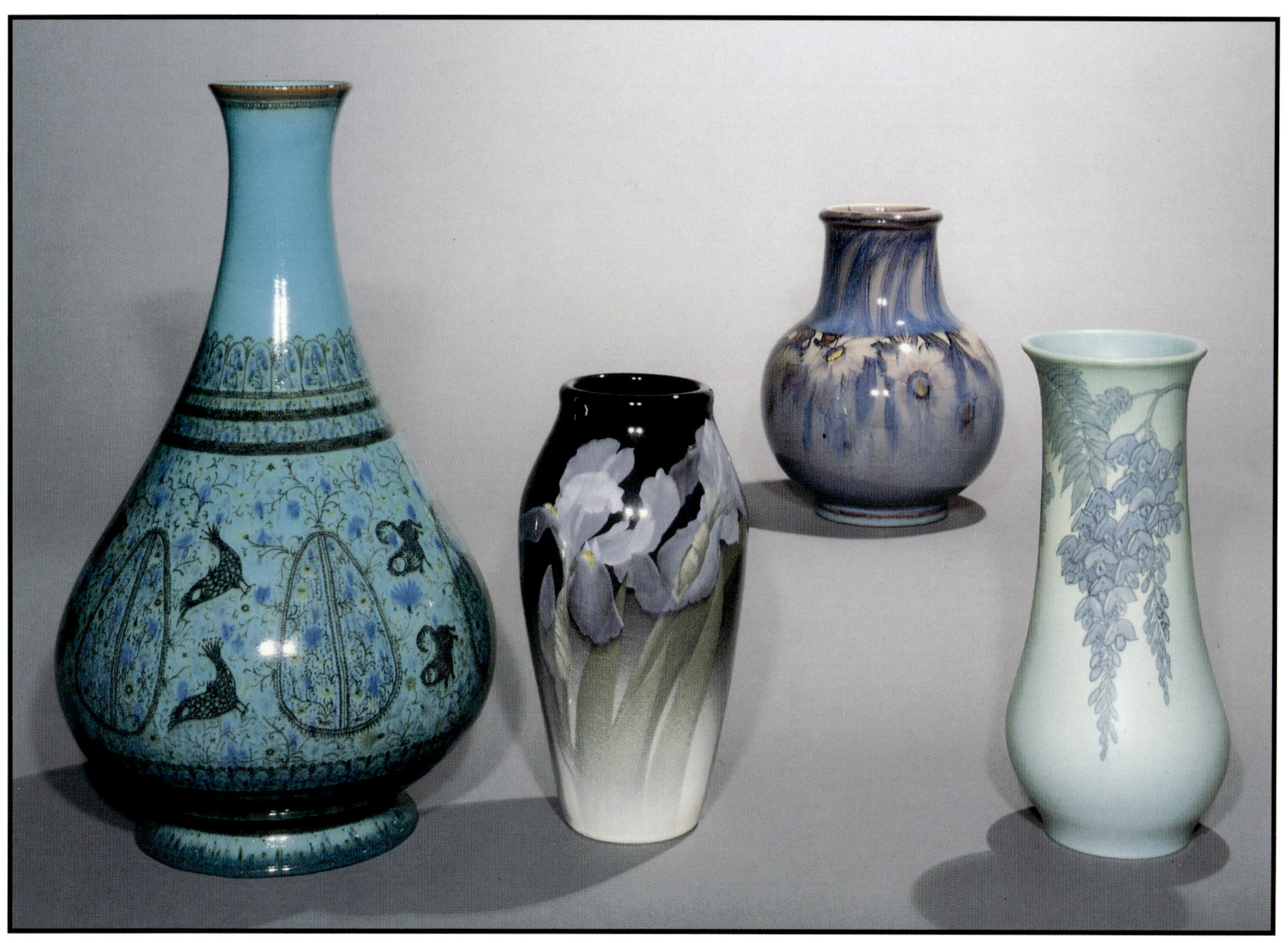

846   Large, blue tinted high glaze vase with intricate Islamic motifs consisting of bands of flowers, birds and lambs, painted in 1920 by William Hentschel. The base is impressed with the Rookwood logo, the date, shape number 2367 and incised with the artist's monogram. Height 15 1/2 inches. Very little crazing. We sold the mate to this piece in Rookwood V as Lot 935. $2000-2500

847   Showy Iris glaze vase with two large blue bearded irises in full bloom, painted in 1904 by Carl Schmidt. The black background color at the top of the vase contrasts nicely with the sharpness of the flowers. Marks include the Rookwood logo, the date, shape number 925 C, an incised W for white (Iris) glaze and the impressed monogram of the artist. Height 9 1/4 inches. $5000-7000

848   Fine Black Opal vase with daisy-like decoration done in 1927 by Sara Sax. Sax has combined a naturalistic use of flowers with a very stylized arrangement of the flower stems which are arrayed around the collar in a repeating pattern. Marks include the Rookwood logo, the date, shape number 2914 and the artist's monogram, painted on in black slip. Height 8 3/8 inches. Uncrazed and very clean. $4000-6000

849   Crisp and sharp Vellum glaze vase with profusions of wisteria painted in 1923 by Ed Diers. Three long wisteria flowers hand from vines and leaves which start under the rim. Marks include the Rookwood logo, the date, shape number 833, a sideways P for porcelain body, V for Vellum glaze and the incised monogram of the artist. Height 10 1/8 inches. Uncrazed. $2500-3500

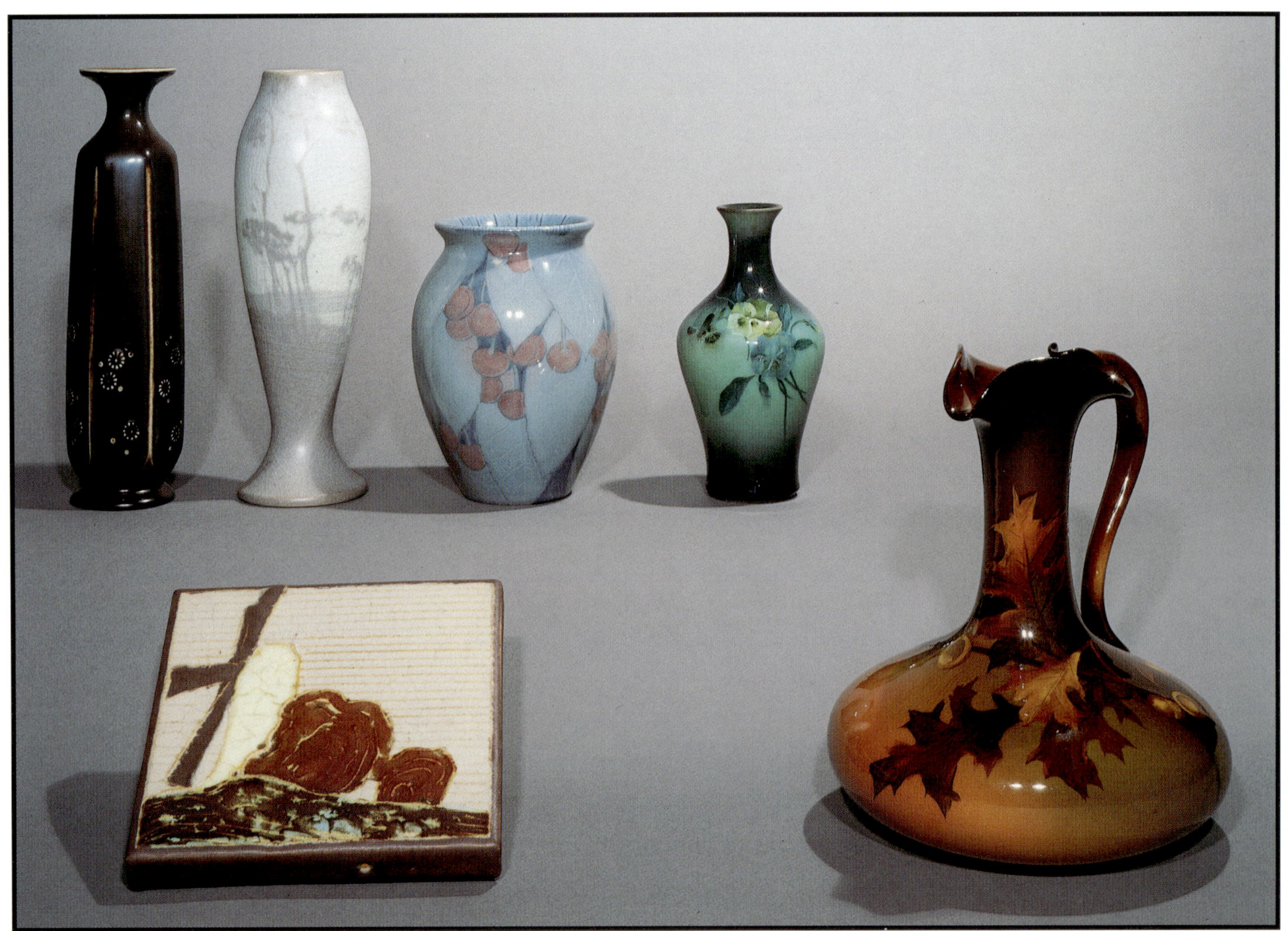

850   Unusual Glaze Effect vase made at Rookwood in 1924. The interior of the vase is done in an orange glaze $200-300
       which appears to also cover the exterior. A glaze akin to Black Opal has been applied over the orange
       exterior creating an unusual effect. Marks include the Rookwood logo, the date and shape number 2584.
       Height 9 5/8 inches. Minor glaze scratches. Uncrazed.

851   Early mat glaze trivet with unusual colors made at Rookwood, circa 1905. Most Rookwood trivets began in $400-500
       the Architectural Faience Department as tiles. Rookwood took many of the designs, put feet on the
       corners and used harder clay and glazes to produce both useful and attractive trivets. This tile with a
       windmill scene is a transitional piece. It bears the stamped "Rookwood Faience" logo and shape number
       1201 Y.1 but has already sprouted four feet on the corners and a fifth in the middle. Size is 6 1/8 by 6 1/8
       inches.

852   Vellum glaze scenic vase painted by Lorinda Epply in 1912. Impressed marks include the Rookwood logo, $700-900
       the date, shape number 949 D and V for Vellum glaze body. Incised marks include V for Vellum glaze and
       the artist's monogram. There is a wheel ground x on the base because of minor peppering at the rim and a
       1 inch by 1/8 inch area of glaze loss on the foot. Height 9 1/2 inches.

853   Good high glaze vase with cherries and overlapping leaves painted in 1919 by Kataro Shirayamadani. Marks $2000-2500
       include the Rookwood logo, the date, shape number 363 and the incised cypher of the artist. Height 6 1/8
       inches. Uncrazed and very stylish.

854   Pretty Sea Green glaze vase with blue and yellow pansy decoration, done in 1896 by Lenore Asbury. Marks $1000-1250
       include the Rookwood logo, the date, shape number 748 D, an incised G for Sea Green glaze and the
       incised initials of the artist. Height 6 3/8 inches. A horizontal crack in the neck of the vase has been
       professionally repaired.

855   Standard glaze ewer with oak leaf and acorn decoration painted in 1899 by Carrie Steinle. Marks include $500-800
       the Rookwood logo, the date, shape number 433 B and the incised monogram of the artist. Height 8 1/8
       inches. Nice size and condition.

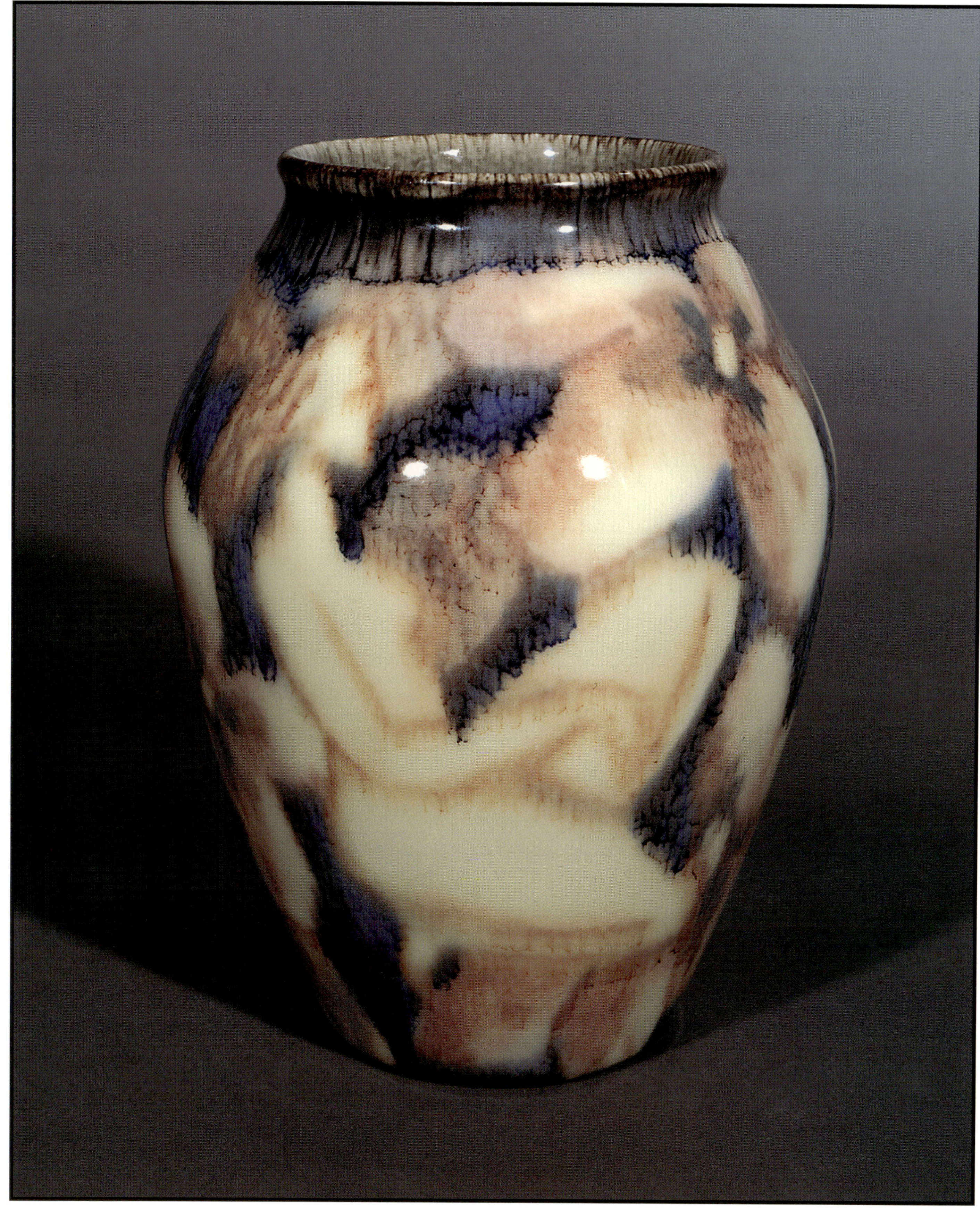

856   Colorful and extremely clean high glaze vase painted by Jens Jensen in 1931. The Art Deco piece $6000-8000
features three beautiful nudes in various poses, interspersed with large floral blossoms. The interior
and exterior rim are coated with a striated gray glaze. Marks include the Rookwood logo, the date,
shape number 915 C and the painted-on monogram of the artist. Height 7 7/8 inches. Jensen nudes
are highly prized and ones from the late 20's and early 30's are the rarest and best.

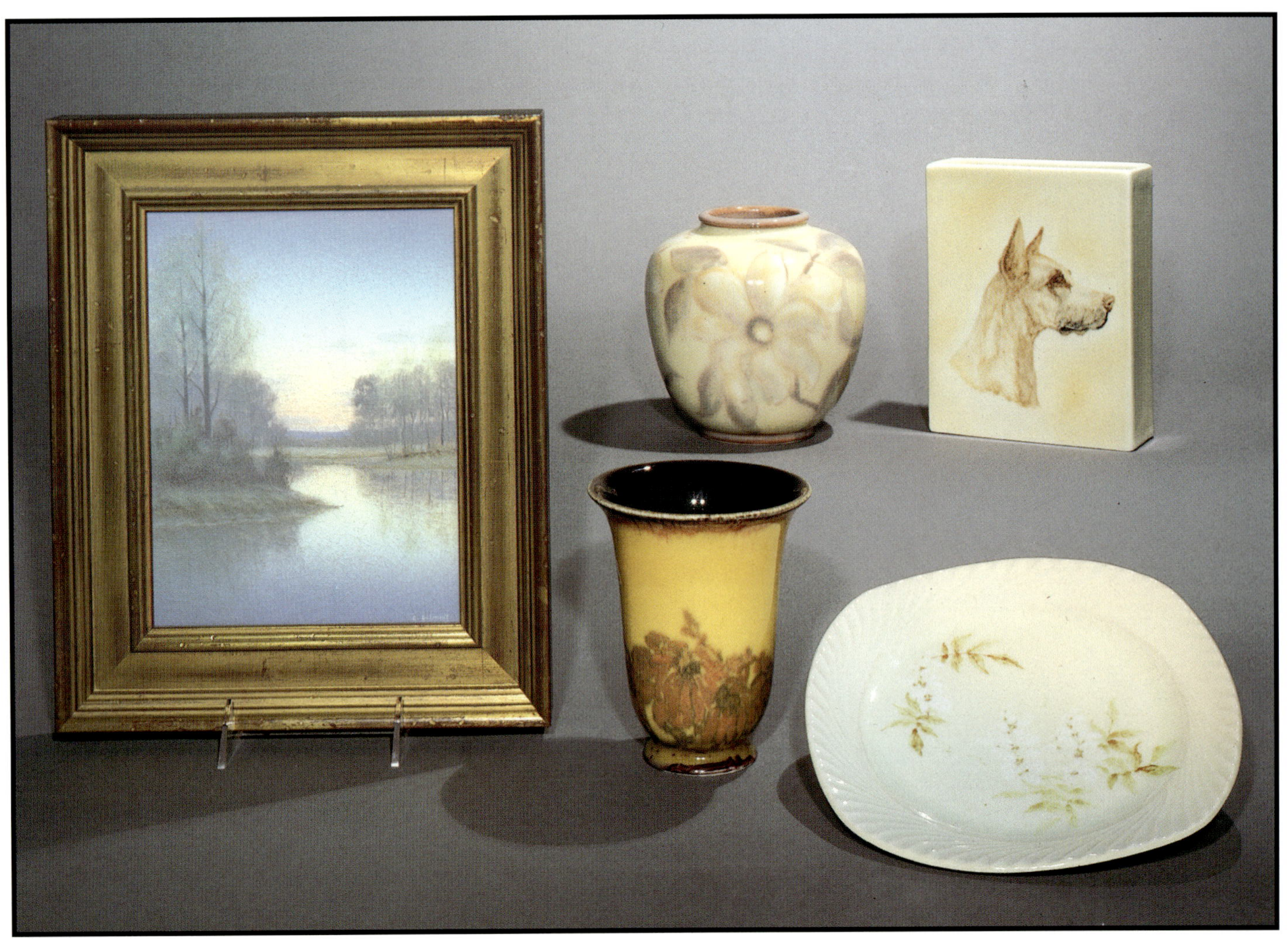

857 Pleasant Vellum glaze woodland scenic plaque painted by Carl Schmidt in 1917. Pictured are trees around a $3000-3500
lake with a pink blush of twilight in the sky. Schmidt's name appears in the lower right hand corner of the
plaque. Marks on the back include the impressed logo and date. Size is 9 1/2 by 7 1/4 inches. Minor burst
bubbles in the glaze.

858 High glaze vase with red chrysanthemums on a bright yellow ground painted in 1924 by Lorinda Epply. The $600-800
interior of the vase is glazed with a neat iridescence found on pieces from this period. Marks include the
Rookwood logo, the date, shape number 2237 and the artist's monogram painted on in black slip. Height 5
5/8 inches.

859 Pretty high glaze vase with magnolia blossoms on a yellow ground, done by Jens Jensen in 1948. Marks $1250-1500
include the Rookwood logo, the date, shape number S 2180 and the artist's monogram painted on in
brown slip. Height 6 1/4 inches. Very little crazing.

860 Cameo glaze plate with wisteria decoration, painted in 1887 by Sallie Toohey. Marks include the Rookwood $200-300
logo, the date, shape number 317 B, W for white clay, a small paper label indicating this to be lot 18 in the
Born Collection and the monogram of the artist, painted on in black slip. Diameter is 9 1/4 inches.

861 High glaze planter vase with the portrait of a Great Dane painted by an unknown artist, possibly a Junior $200-250
Decorator, in 1946. Marks include the Rookwood logo, the date, shape number 6292 C, the number 448
painted on in black slip and the artist's monogram, also painted on in black slip. Height 7 1/2 inches. There
is a crack on the back side of the piece.

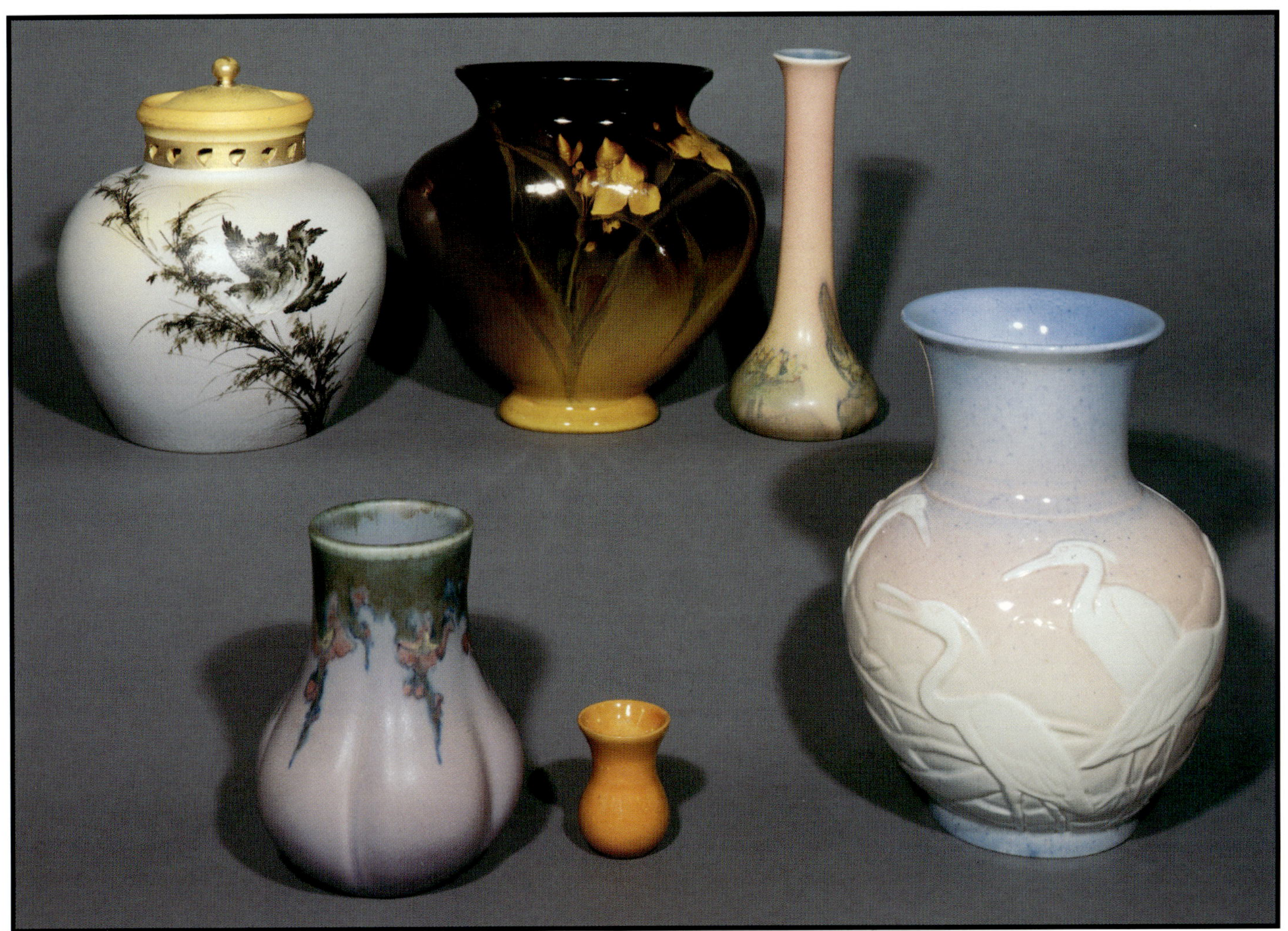

862	Handsome scent jar with reversible lid painted by Albert Valentien in 1886. Done in Rookwood's Dull Finish or smear glaze, the jar features a small flying sparrow and Oriental grasses with highlights on the lid in fired-on gold. Marks include "Rookwood" in block letters, the date, shape number 277, Y for yellow clay and the incised initials of the artist. Height 7 inches.	$1000-1500
863	Ribbed mat glaze vase with trailing fruit blossoms on a purple ground painted in 1929 by Elizabeth Lincoln. Marks include the Rookwood logo, the date, shape number 6101 and the initials of the artist, painted on in black slip. Height 4 3/4 inches.	$400-500
864	Standard glaze flat sided vase with yellow trillium decoration done by Ed Diers in 1899. Marks include the Rookwood logo, the date, shape number 797 and the incised monogram of the artist. Height 6 5/8 inches.	$300-500
865	Small test piece covered with Standard glaze over a speckled clay body, made at Rookwood in 1890. Marks include the Rookwood logo, the date, shape number 114 and remnants of red paint, most likely from a Cincinnati Art Museum acquisition number. Height 1 7/8 inches.	$50-100
866	Mat glaze bud vase with floral decoration done in 1931 by Sallie Coyne. Impressed marks include the Rookwood logo, the date, shape number 2309 and a fan shaped esoteric mark. The artist's monogram is painted on the bottom in blue slip. Height 7 inches.	$400-500
867	Rookwood popcorn vase designed by Shirayamadani and painted by an unknown artisan in 1943. The embossed scene of egrets standing on limbs has been hand colored in shades of blue and rose on the white body. We can only hope that the dark spots all over the inside and outside of the vase are there to represent ash from the explosion of a nearby volcano but we are more inclined to think something blew up in the kiln. Marks include the Rookwood logo, the date, shape number 6516 and a wheel ground line which likely indicates this to be a factory second.	$800-1000

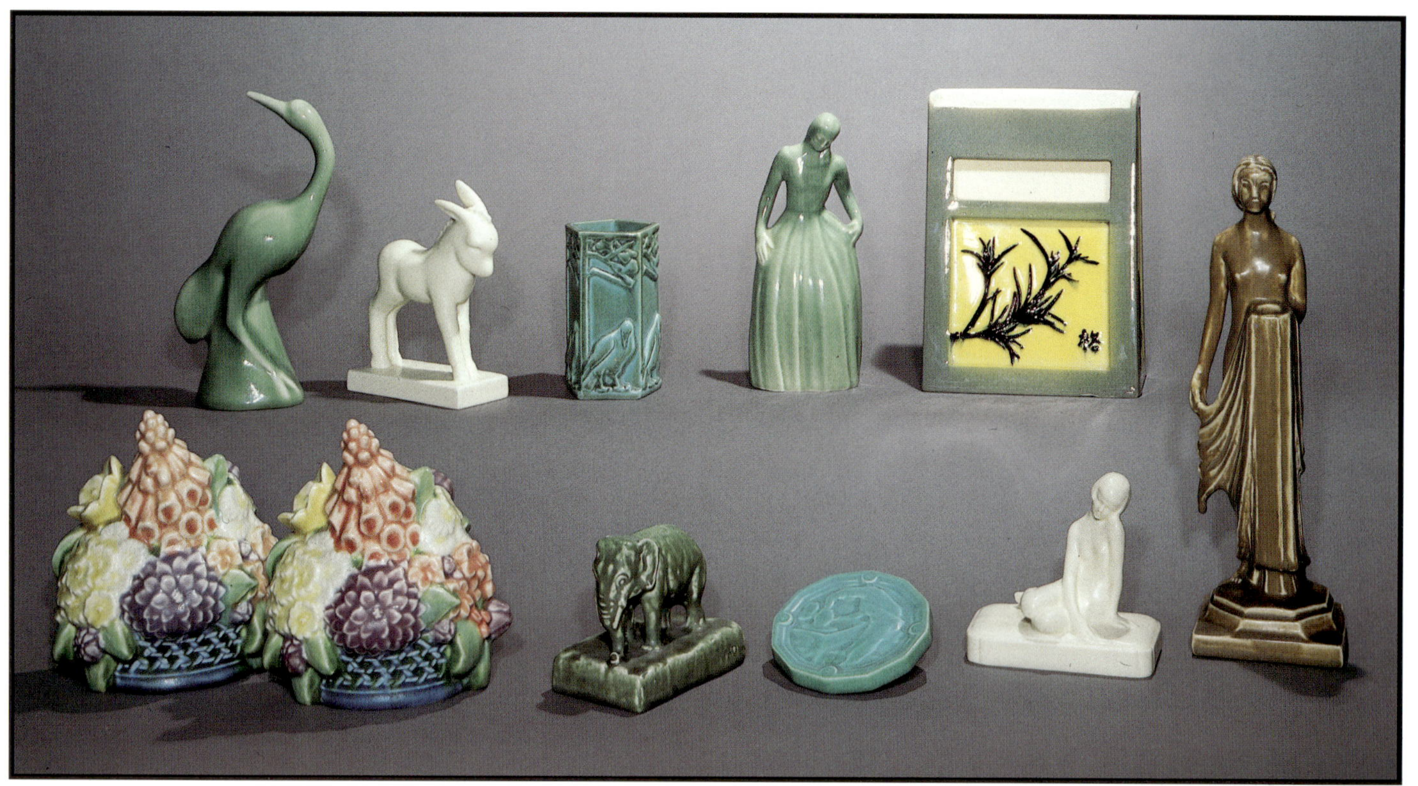

868 Pair of polychromed flower basket bookends made at Rookwood in 1929. Impressed marks include the Rookwood logo, the date and shape number 2837. Height 6 inches. Good mold and color.

$400-600

869 Green high glaze crane figurine made at Rookwood in 1948. Marks include the Rookwood logo, the date and shape number 6972. Incised on the bottom is the number 5. Height 8 1/2 inches.

$200-250

870 White mat glaze donkey paperweight made at Rookwood in 1942. Marks include the Rookwood logo, the date and shape number 6241. Height 6 inches.

$300-400

871 Green mat glaze elephant paperweight made at Rookwood in 1926. Marks include the Rookwood logo, the date and shape number 2797. Height 3 3/8 inches.

$300-400

872 Rook pencil holder in a crystalline green mat glaze made at Rookwood in 1934. Impressed marks include the Rookwood logo, the date and shape number 1795. Height 4 5/8 inches.

$200-250

873 Green high glaze Colonial woman figurine made at Rookwood circa 1955. Marks include the Rookwood logo and shape number 6907. Height 7 3/4 inches.

$300-400

874 Rookwood "Potter at the Wheel" paperweight made in 1940. Marks include the Rookwood logo, the date and the notation "Potter At The Wheel Rookwood Cincinnati Ohio". The Rookwood logo is embossed on the four circular high points on the front. Diameter is 3 3/4 inches.

$200-300

875 High glaze wallgreen or letter holder done in green, yellow and black with embossed leaves and Oriental characters, made at Rookwood in 1949. Impressed marks include the Rookwood logo, the date and shape number 7019. Height 8 1/8 inches. Uncrazed.

$300-400

876 Rookwood production paperweight in the form of a young nude woman, designed by Louise Abel and glazed in white mat in 1939. Marks include the Rookwood logo, the date, shape number 2868 and the cast in monogram of Abel. Height 4 inches.

$250-350

877 Tall and stylish Art Deco nude figural piece made in the form of a bud vase at Rookwood in 1920 in brown mat glaze. Marks include the Rookwood logo, the date and shape number 2345. Height 11 1/4 inches.

$600-800

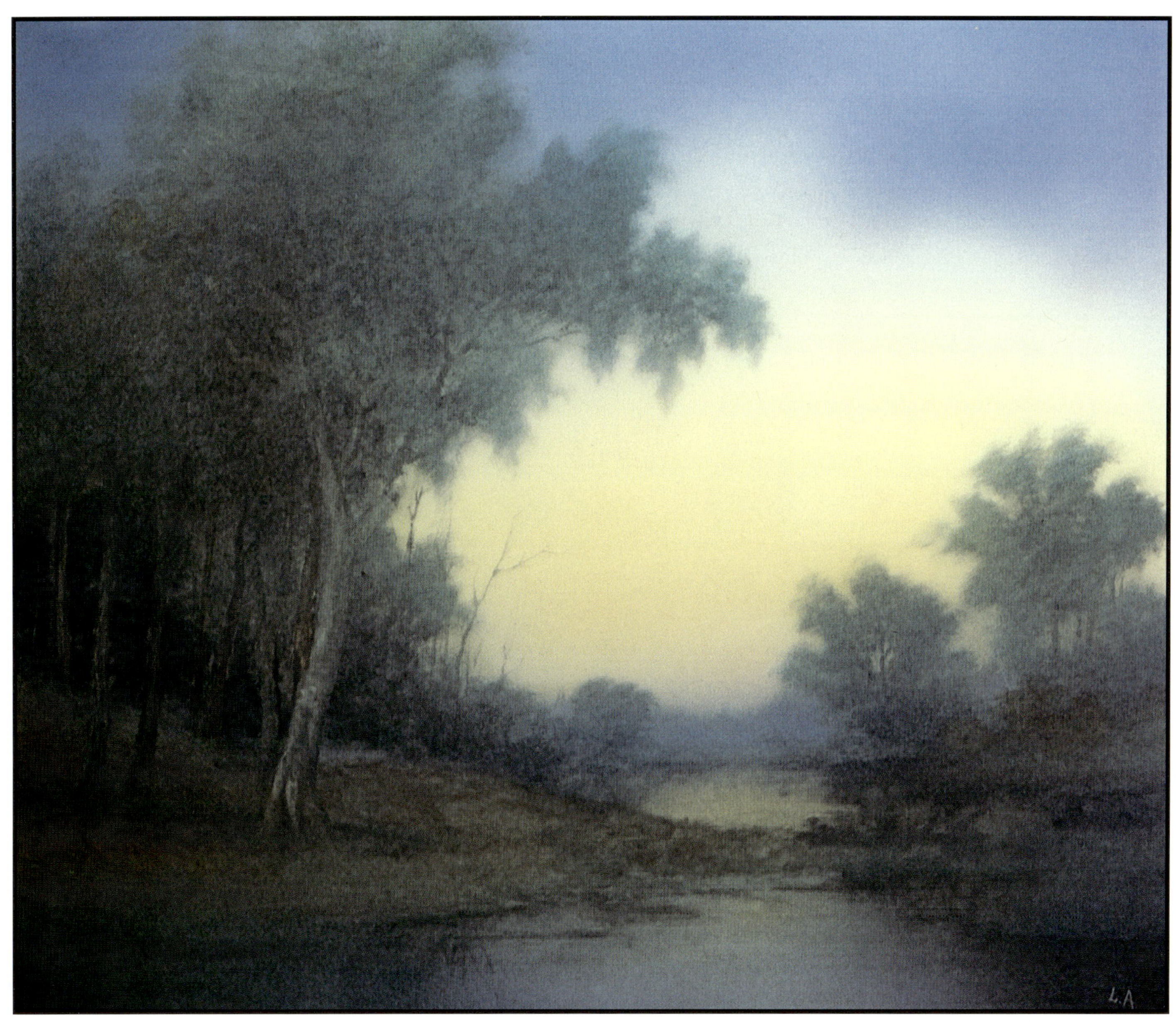

878   Large and beautiful Vellum glaze scenic plaque painted by Lenore Asbury in 1926. Pictured is a quiet $25000-30000
woodland setting with tall trees and a lake which is bisected by a small spit of land. The artist's initials
are painted on in the lower right hand corner in white slip. Impressed on the back are the Rookwood
logo and the date. Affixed to the original frame is a typewritten label with the title "Solitude L. Asbury".
Size is 14 1/4 by 16 3/8 inches. Uncrazed and very crisp. Plaques of this size were only entrusted to
senior decorators at Rookwood, people who could be counted on to do the job. Diers, Schmidt,
Rothenbusch and Hurley are known to have worked on the big plaques. This is the first time we have
seen an Asbury effort and I think she deserves the confidence shown.

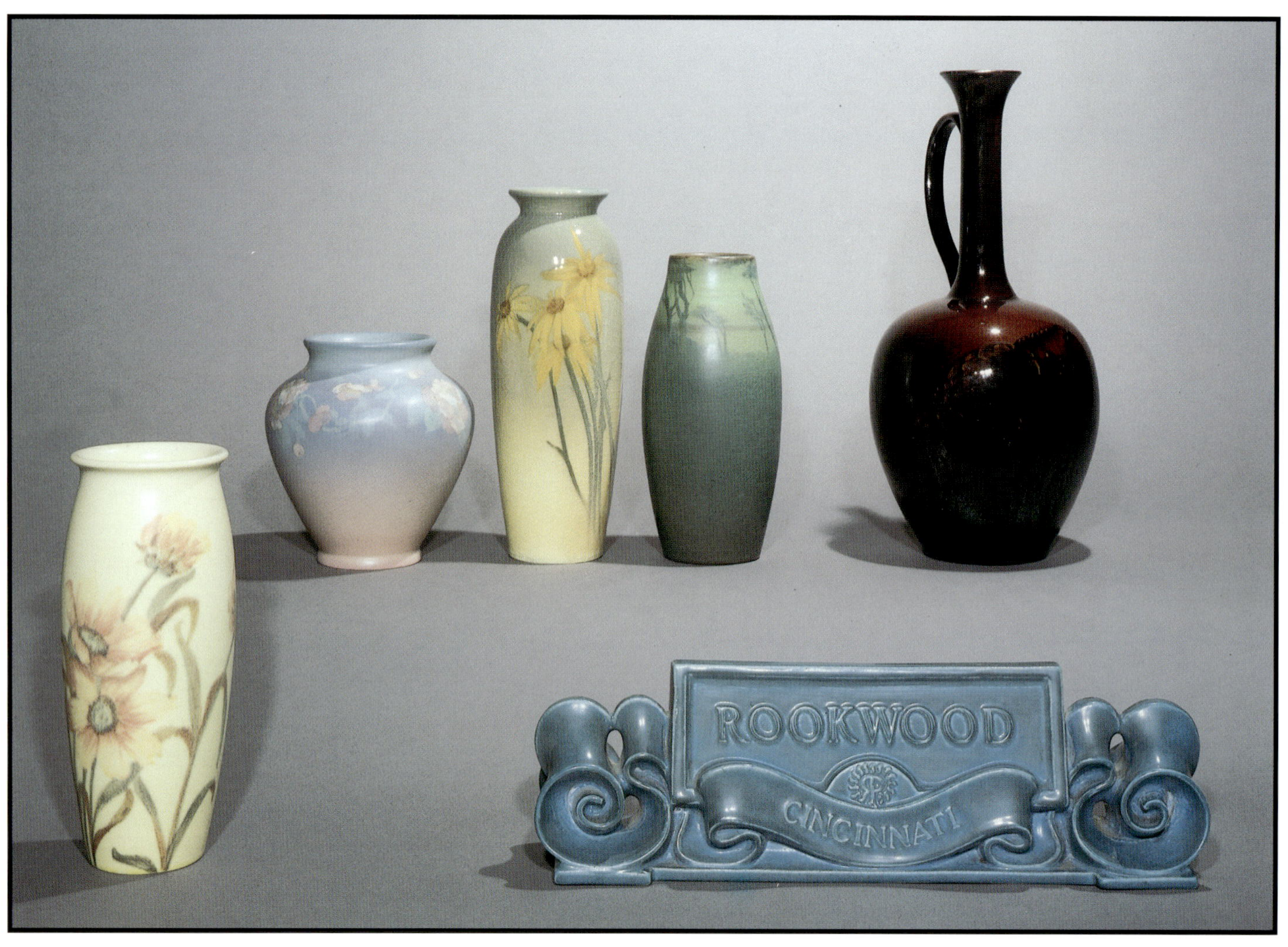

879   Pretty Vellum glaze vase with red, orange, green and brown daisies on a pale yellow ground, done in 1940 by Margaret McDonald. Marks include the Rookwood logo, the date, shape number 808 and the artist's monogram, painted on in brown slip. Height 7 3/4 inches. Uncrazed and very crisply painted. $700-900

880   Vellum glaze vase with red vining flowers encircling the shoulder, painted by Fred Rothenbusch in 1925. Marks include the Rookwood logo, the date, shape number 2831, an incised V for Vellum glaze and the incised monogram of the artist. Height 5 5/8 inches. Uncrazed and very clean. $700-900

881   Iris glaze vase with orange daisy decoration done in 1902 by Rose Fechheimer. Marks include the Rookwood logo, the date, shape number 829, an incised W for white (Iris) glaze and the incised monogram of the artist. Height 9 3/8 inches. $1500-2000

882   Blue mat glaze Rookwood double-sided advertising sign from 1924. Marks include the Rookwood logo, the date and shape number 2788. Height is 3 3/4 inches and length is 12 1/2 inches. This is an early casting of the sign which was introduced sometime between 1922 and 1924. $700-900

883   Rare Green Vellum scenic vase painted by Lenore Asbury in 1912. The decoration is in the upper third of the vase and consists of trees in the foreground and a lake behind. Marks include the Rookwood logo, the date, shape number 939 D, V for Vellum glaze body, an incised GV for Green Vellum glaze, the incised initials of the artist and an original Rookwood showroom paper label with the retail price $8.00. Height 7 3/4 inches. There is a pin-head size glaze skip at the base. $1000-1500

884   Standard glaze ewer with long, thin neck and flared rim decorated by Matt Daly in 1886. Under a glaze filled with lots of Goldstone lurks a turtle, walking past a flowering bush. Marks include "Rookwood" in block letters, the partially obscured date, shape number 26 or 262 and the incised initials of the artist. Height 12 1/4 inches. $1000-1250

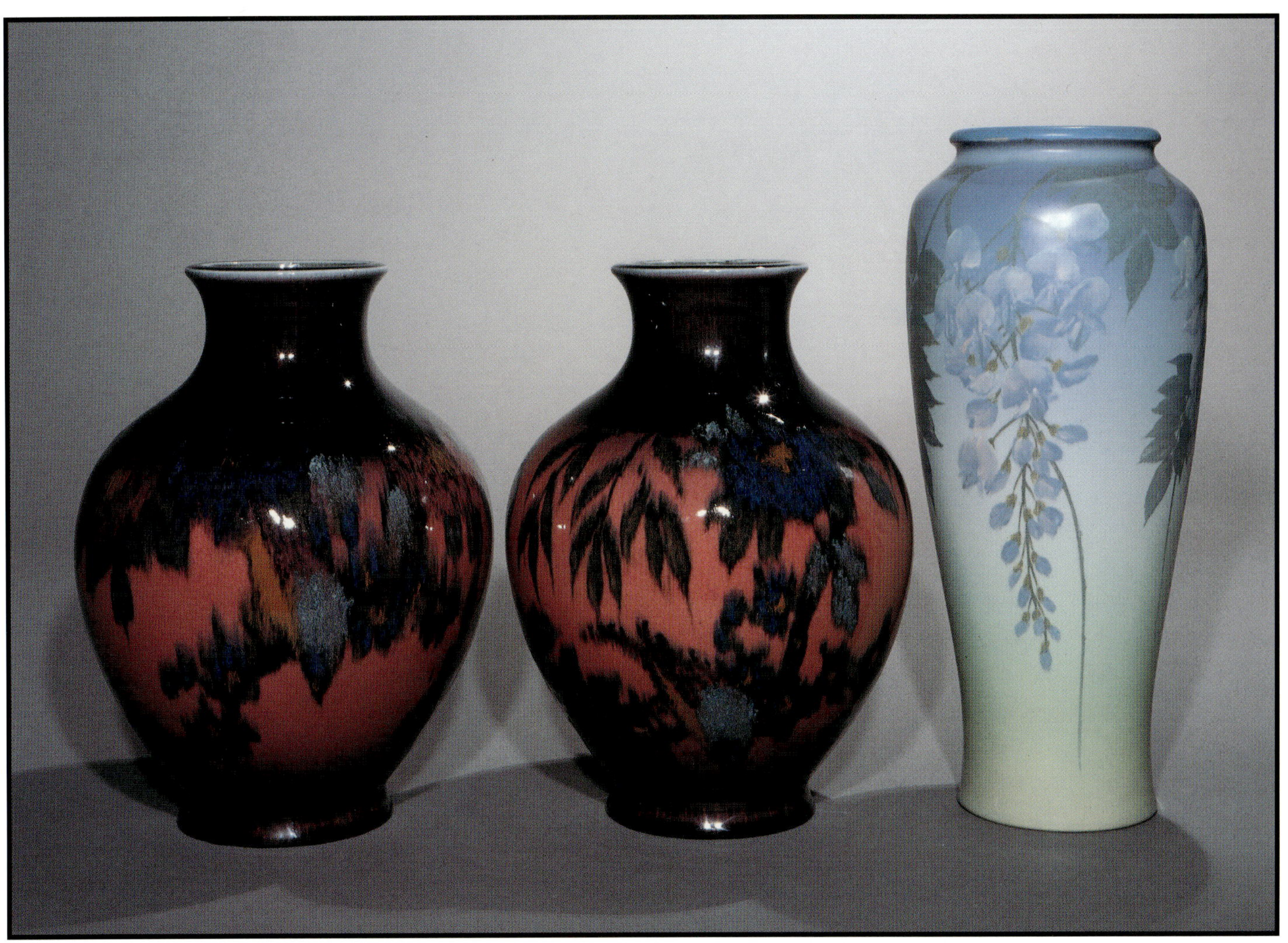

885 Large high glaze vase with lush foliage and exotic birds painted by E.T. Hurley in 1926. Pictured are two $4000-5000
     tropical birds perched amid multi- colored flowers and leaves, all set against a vibrant pink background.
     Marks include the Rookwood logo, the date, shape number 2918-B, remnants of a Rookwood showroom
     paper label and the artist's initials, painted on in black slip. Height 11 3/8 inches. The purchaser of this lot
     will be allowed to buy lot 886 for the same amount.

886 Large high glaze vase with lush foliage and exotic birds painted by E.T. Hurley in 1926. Pictured are two $4000-5000
     tropical birds perched amid multi- colored flowers and leaves, all set against a vibrant pink background.
     Marks include the Rookwood logo, the date, shape number 2918-B, remnants of a Rookwood showroom
     paper label and the artist's initials, painted on in black slip. Height 11 3/8 inches. There is a small grinding
     chip off the base. The purchaser of lot 885 will be allowed to buy this lot for the same amount.

887 Large and impressive Vellum glaze vase with lifelike wisteria decoration, done in 1928 by Ed Diers. Large $4000-5000
     clusters of wisteria cascade down all sides of the vase, all beautifully and exactingly detailed. Marks include
     the Rookwood logo, the date, shape number 2551, an incised V for Vellum glaze, a wheel ground x and the
     incised monogram of the artist. A small area of glaze on the underside of the rim (approximately 1/8 by 1
     inch long) came off in the firing, causing the vase to be x'ed. We felt it unnecessary to cover up this minor
     lapse on an otherwise stunning example of Vellum glaze floral decoration.

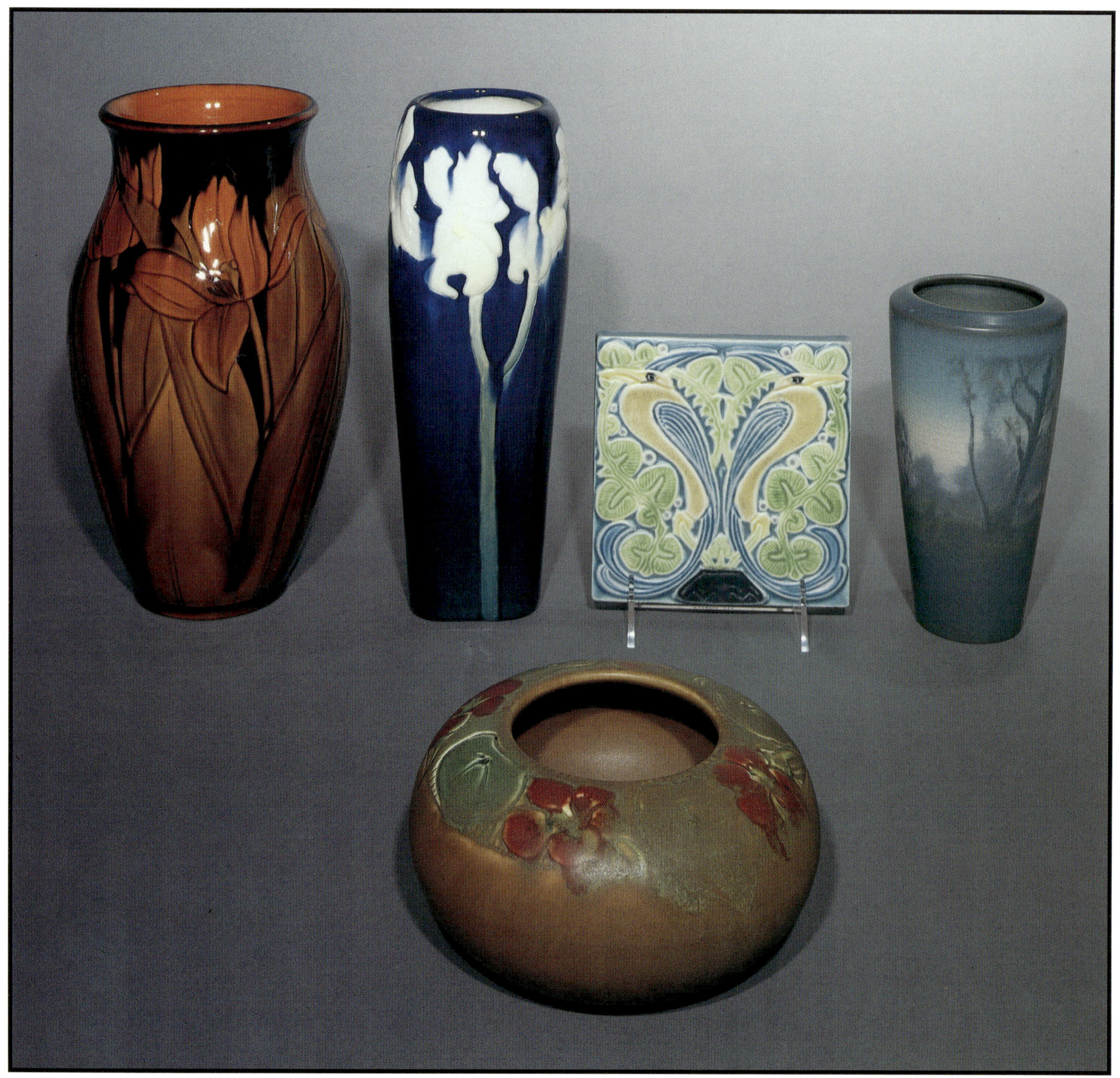

888   Handsome yellow tinted high glaze production vase hand colored by Lenore Asbury in 1929. The design of $1500-2000
embossed tulips is by Shirayamadani. Asbury has painted the flowers to her satisfaction and then called for
use of "Yellow Glaze", the reprise of Standard glaze, which seems to have appealed to Asbury. Marks include
the Rookwood logo, the date, shape number 6011, incised Y.G. for yellow glaze and the incised initials of the
artist. Height 10 7/8 inches.

889   Rare and impressive Black Iris glaze vase with lightly carved and painted irises, the work of John Dee $2000-3000
Wareham in 1898. Articles about Rookwood in this period referred to this style of decoration as Relief Dark
or Black Iris. The white flowers have pale yellow centers and bright green stems which contrast nicely with
the rare cobalt blue ground. The flowers and stems are painted on in heavy slip with modest modeling done
by Wareham to add dimension. Marks include the Rookwood logo, the date, shape number 821 C, an
experimental mark, "X 352 X" and the incised initials of the artist. Height 11 inches. Two cracks (each about
two inches long) descend from the rim and meet, forming a pie shaped wedge. The damage has been
professionally repaired.

890   Arts & Crafts style mat glaze vase with incised and painted nasturtiums, done in 1905 by Rose Fechheimer. $400-600
Marks include the Rookwood logo, the date, shape number 214 B and the incised monogram of the artist.
Height 3 1/4 inches.

891   Unusual Rookwood multicolored trivet with two exotic birds done in mat glaze in 1920. Marks include the $400-600
Rookwood logo, the date and shape number 1988. Size is 5 1/2 by 5 1/2 inches. Excellent mold and color but
with a small amount of peppering in the glaze.

892   Vellum glaze scenic vase painted by Fred Rothenbusch in 1918. Shown is a wooded setting with a lake in $800-1000
mid ground. Marked with the Rookwood logo, the date, shape number 2101 and the incised monogram of
the artist. Height 7 1/4 inches. A tight line descends from the rim.

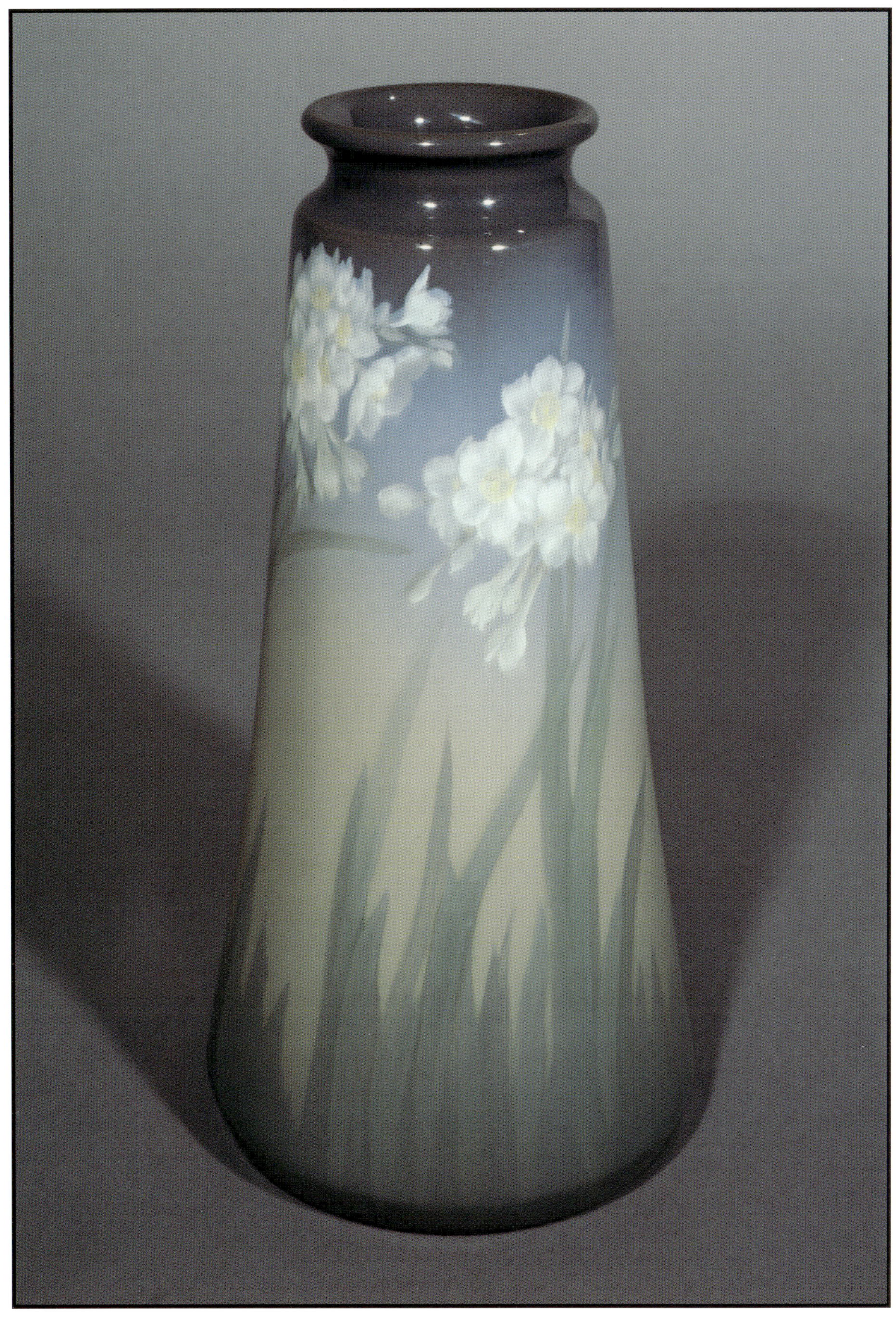

893   Handsome Iris glaze vase painted in 1911 by Ed Diers. Decoration consists of several sprays of white jonquils with many green leaves which encircle the base. Marks include the Rookwood logo, the date, shape number 1655 D, an impressed number "1" above the logo, an incised W for white (Iris) glaze and the incised monogram of the artist. Height 10 inches. An extremely minor amount of crazing is isolated in the white flower heads. A beautiful vase with delicate shading and strong image. $10000-12500

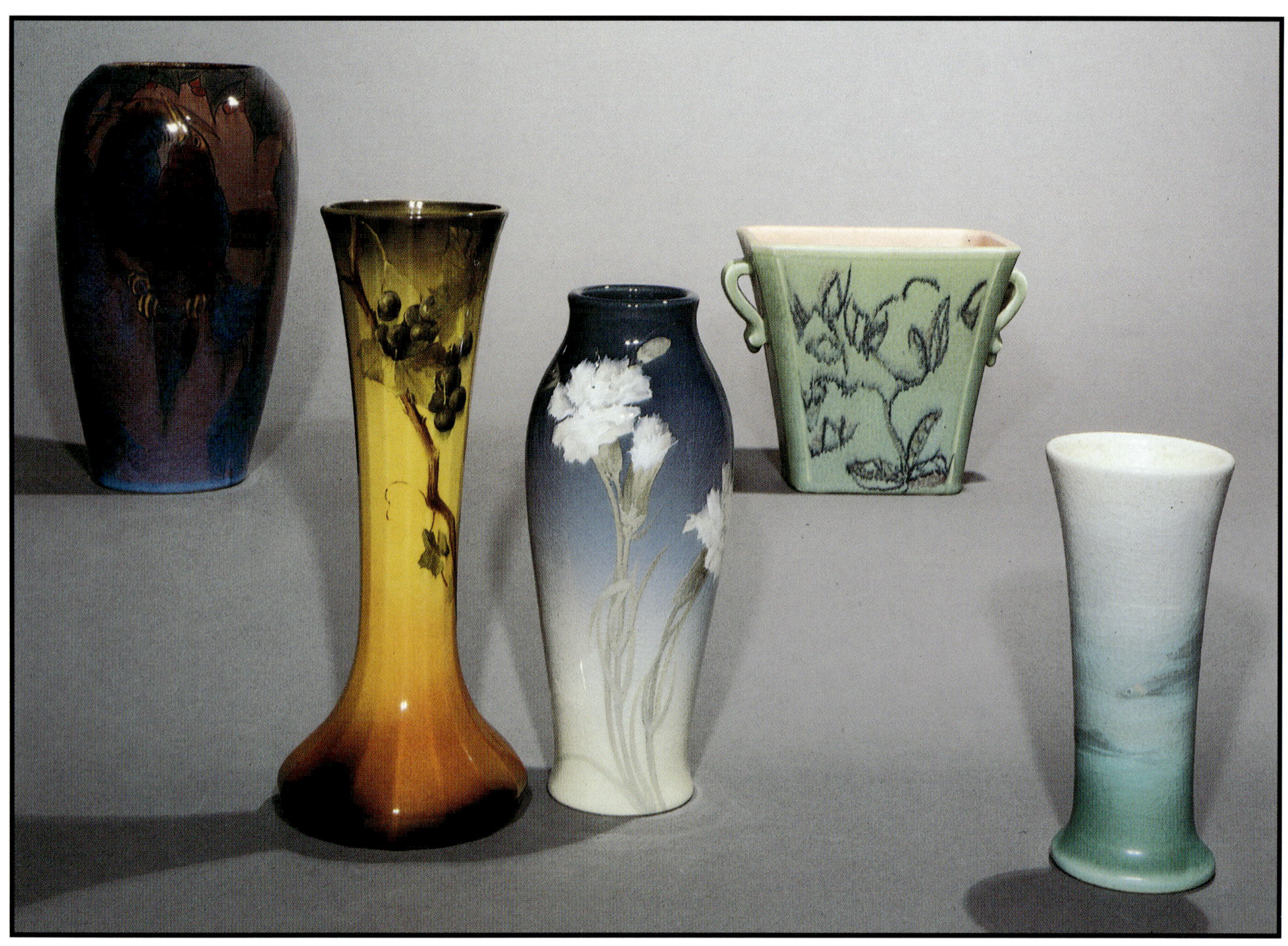

894   Interesting Black Opal glaze vase with three repeating sets of birds perched in exotic foliage, the work of $800-1200
Sara Sax in 1925. Done in strong reds and greens, the birds are crisply painted and outlined in black. Marks
include the Rookwood logo, the date, shape number 1126 C and the incised monogram of the artist.
Height 9 3/8 inches. A long curving crack descends from the rim.

895   Beautiful ribbed standard glaze vase with very life-like grape decoration done in 1894 by Harriette Strafer. $800-1200
Impressed marks include the Rookwood logo, the date, shape number 693 and a W for white clay. Incised
marks include the artist's monogram and L for light Standard glaze. Height 10 5/8 inches.

896   Iris glaze vase with white carnations on a medium blue ground, done in 1902 by Ed Diers. Marks include $1500-2000
the Rookwood logo, the date, shape number 937, an incised W for white (Iris) glaze and the incised
monogram of the artist. Height 9 inches.

897   Mat glaze planter vase with two handles painted with simple flowers by Katherine Jones in 1929. Marks $300-400
include the Rookwood logo, the date, shape number 6041 and the artist's initials, painted on in black slip.
Height 5 3/4 inches. Minor grinding chips off the base.

898   Vellum glaze vase painted by Edith Noonan in 1909. Several long fish swim through wavy water. Marks $500-700
include the Rookwood logo, the date, shape number 1357 E, an impressed V for Vellum glaze body, an
incised V for Vellum glaze and the incised initials of the artist. Height 7 inches. There is a fair amount of
peppering in the upper portion of the vase, both inside and out.

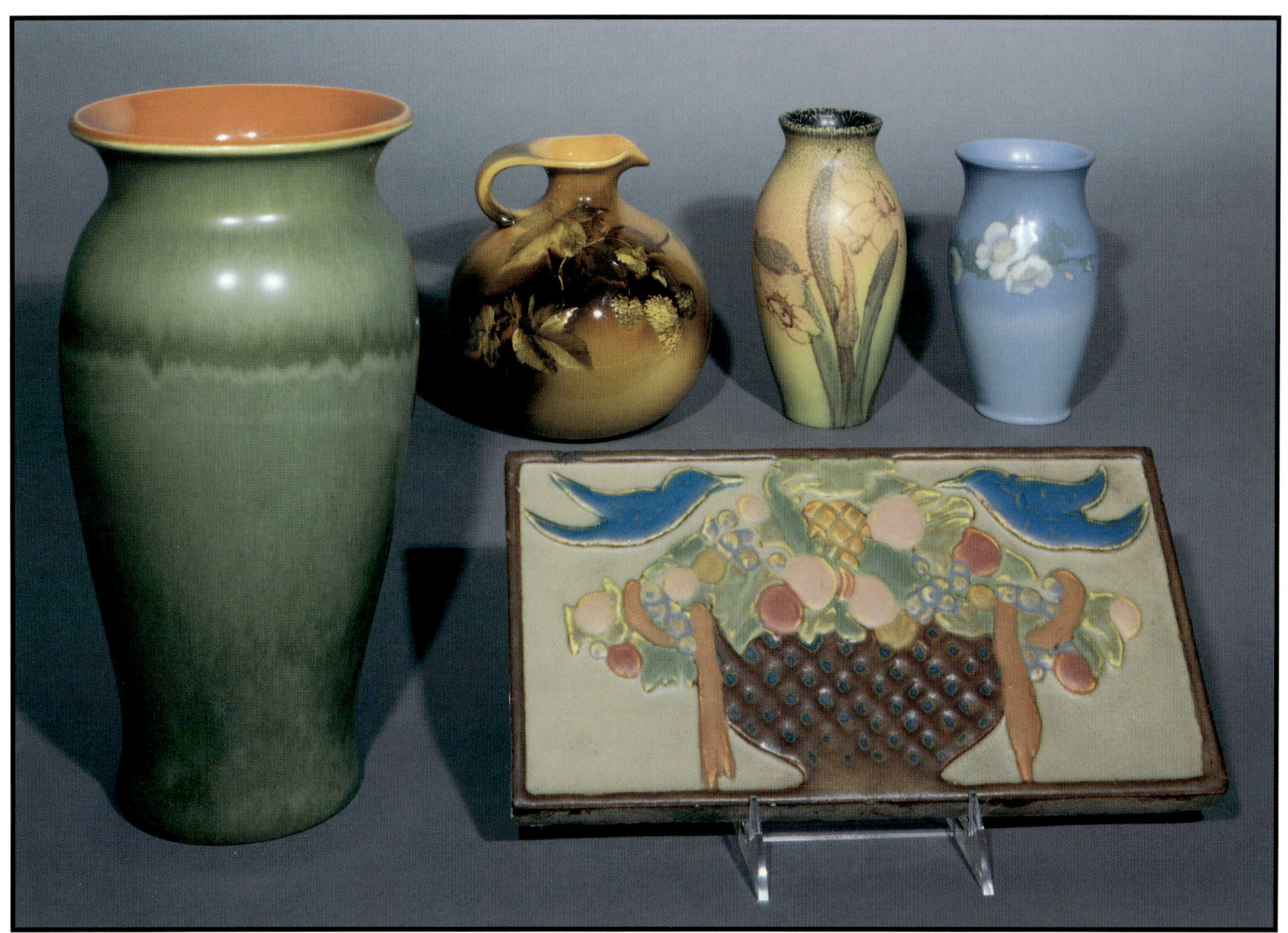

899 Large Rookwood production vase with a rich green crystalline mat glaze on the outside and a bright orange high glaze on the interior. The exterior glaze is loaded with crystals which cascade down the sides and can be felt as well as seen. Marks include the Rookwood logo, the date and shape number 2785. Height 11 1/2 inches. Minor grinding chips off the base.
$300-400

900 Nice Standard glaze pitcher with precise decoration of hops done in 1893 by Constance Baker. Marks include the Rookwood logo, the date, shape number 699, W for white clay and the incised initials of the artist. Height 6 inches. There is a very tight line on the back edge of the rim.
$400-500

901 Rookwood Architectural Faience tile in multicolored mat glaze showing a basket of fruit with two blue humming birds. Impressed marks on the back include the Rookwood logo and the numbers "G 527", "3084 Y" and "416". Size is 6 by 12 inches. Uncrazed and very clean with the exception of some edge chips which would mostly be hidden by a frame.
$600-800

902 Pretty and crisp mat glaze vase with jonquil decoration done in 1931 by Margaret McDonald. Marks include the Rookwood logo, the date, shape number 356 E and the monogram of the artist, painted on in reddish-brown slip. Height 6 1/2 inches.
$600-800

903 Crisp and clean Vellum glaze vase with wild rose decoration painted in 1926 by Ed Diers. Impressed marks include the Rookwood logo, the date and shape number 513. Incised on the bottom are the artist's monogram and V for Vellum glaze. Height 5 3/4 inches. Uncrazed.
$800-1000

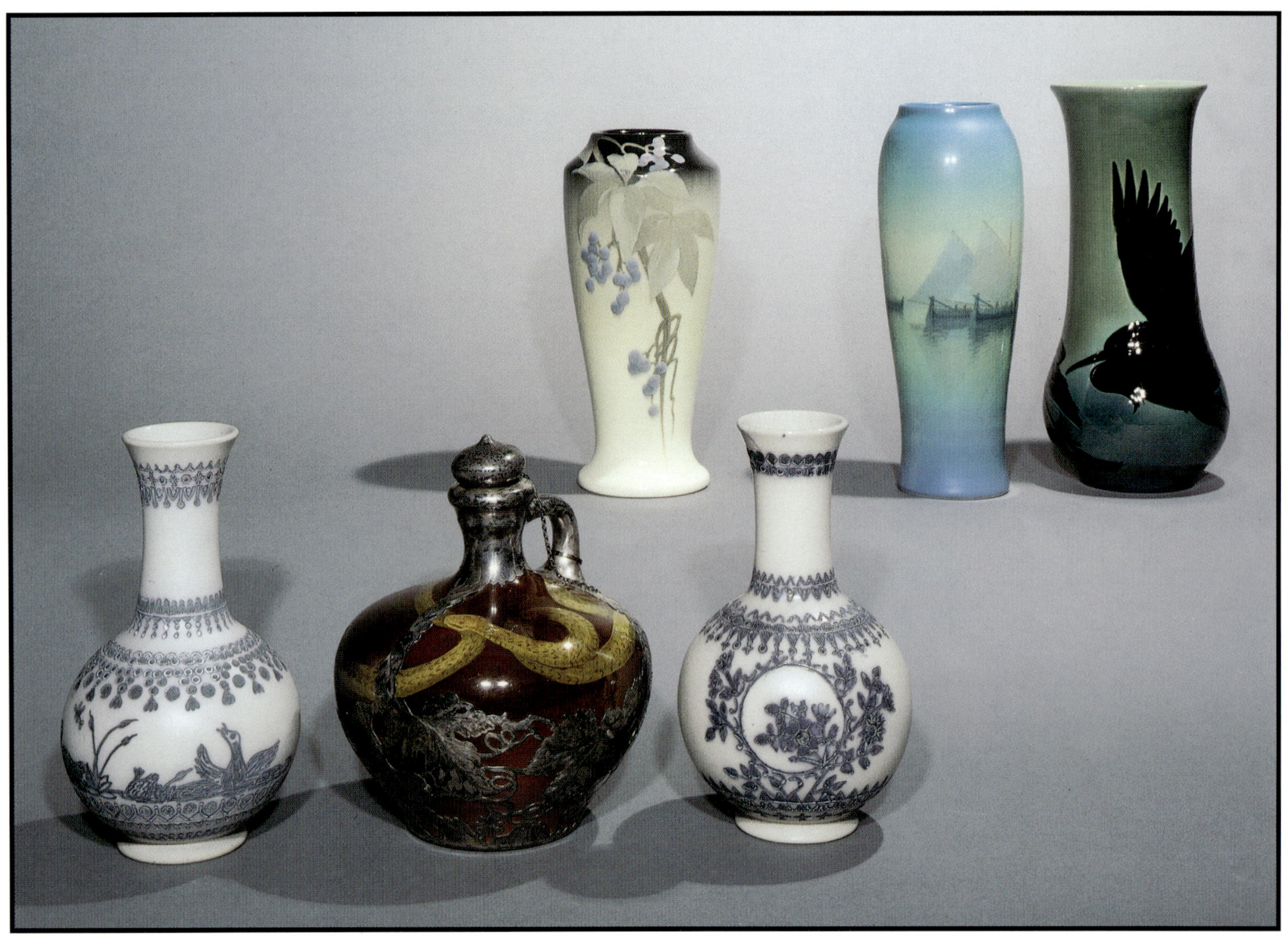

904	Rare Dull Finish glaze vase decorated in 1882 by Fannie Auckland. Only 14 in 1882, Auckland must hold the record for being the youngest decorator ever to work at Rookwood and one of the hardest to find. Her work consists of repeating designs of encircling bands done with filed nail heads pressed into the wet clay. In this example, some simple incising is done to show several ducks in a reed filled area, one of which is looking up at a dragonfly. A blue wash is applied, leaving the incised and stamped areas deeply colored against the gray clay body. The vase is incised "FA Rookwood 1882" on the bottom. Height 7 1/2 inches. Very minor surface irregularities which seem to be in the making. The purchaser of this lot will be allowed to purchase lot 907 for the same amount. These vases are obviously meant to be a pair and have been together since they were made.	$1500-2000
905	Rare Standard glaze stoppered whiskey jug decorated in 1892 by Ed Abel and overlayed with silver by Gorham. On a rather clear and bright surface, Abel has painted the creepy likeness of two green snakes with jaws open, tongues out and fangs at the ready. The Gorham overlay which encompasses the handle and spout is done in the form of grapes, grape leaves and vines. Marks include the Rookwood logo, the date, shape number 675, W for white clay, an incised L for light Standard glaze and the incised initials of the artist. The silver is stamped "Gorham Mfg.Co." and engraved with the number "R 1589". Height 7 1/4 inches. A link in the chain holding the stopper to the handle has broken.	$3000-4000
906	Pretty Iris glaze vase with well defined Virginia creeper decoration in good color, painted in 1908 by Sara Sax. Impressed marks include the Rookwood logo and date, shape number 1356 D and the artist's monogram. Incised is a W for white (Iris) glaze. Height 8 3/4 inches.	$1750-2250
907	The mate to lot 904 done in 1882 by Fannie Auckland. This vase is decorated with different nail head patterns and has as its main focus, a floral display. Marked in exactly the same manner as lot 904. Height 7 1/2 inches. Very minor surface irregularities which seem to be in the making. The purchaser of lot 904 will be allowed to purchase this lot for the same amount.	$1500-2000
908	Good Vellum glaze Venetian harbor scenic vase painted in 1921 by Carl Schmidt. Pictured are five sailing craft with the city of Venice in the background. Marks include the Rookwood logo, the date, shape number 2040 D, an impressed V for Vellum glaze and the impressed monogram of the artist. Height 9 1/2 inches.	$2500-3500
909	Rare and unusual incised and painted Sea Green vase with two flying cranes done in heavy slip in 1899 by John Dee Wareham. Wareham has incised the outlines for the birds and then painted them in, mostly in black slip against the green to blue background colors. Marks include the Rookwood logo, the date, shape number 833, a wheel ground x, an incised G for Sea Green glaze and the incised initials of Mr. Wareham. Height 10 inches. There are two glaze flaws which account for the X. One is an underglaze skip on the feathers of the bird not pictured and the other is a burst glaze bubble just above the skip. Uncrazed.	$4000-6000

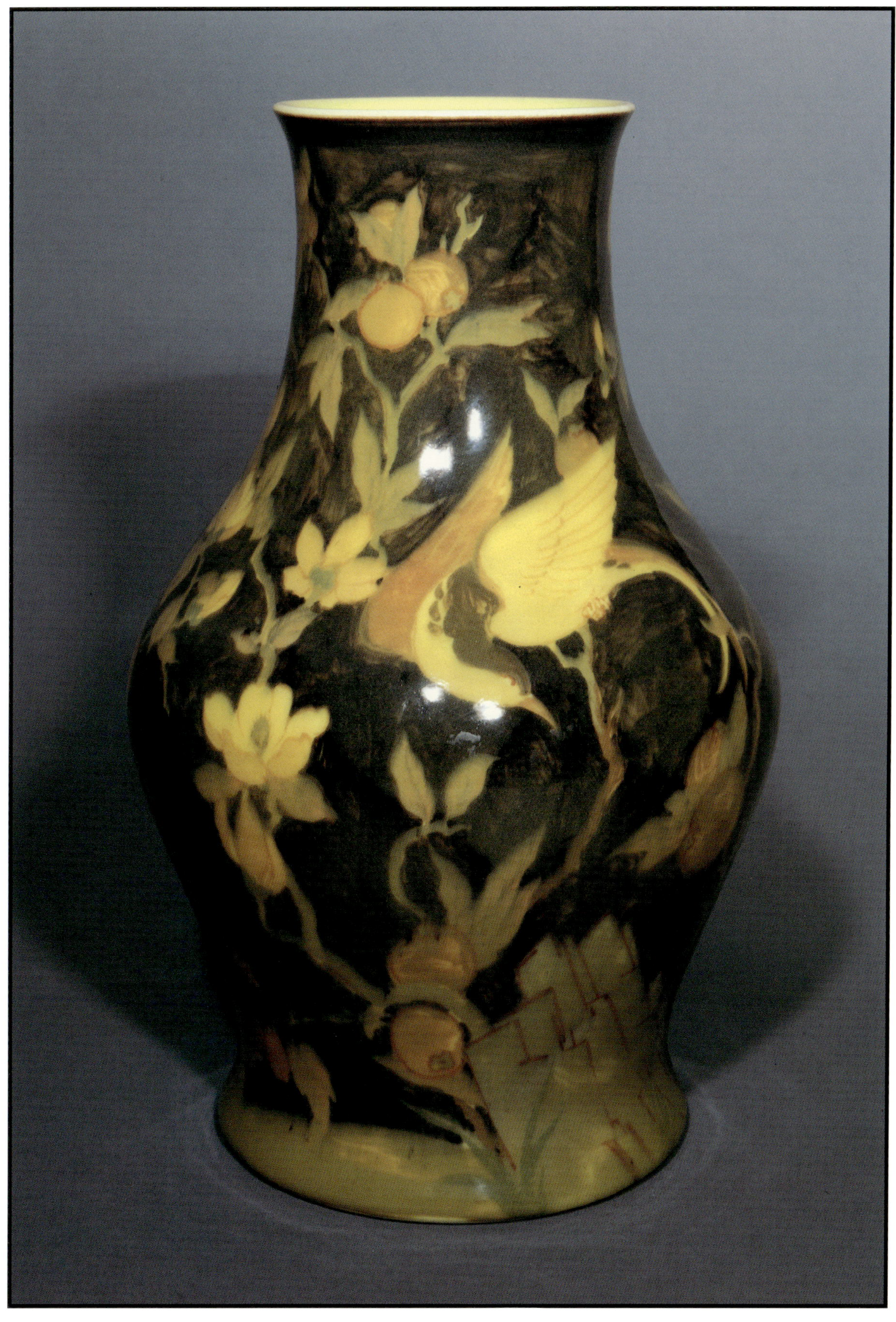

910   Tall yellow tinted high glaze vase done in Arthur Conant's unique style in 1921 depicting fruit, flowers and $5000-7500
         birds. Marks include the Rookwood logo, the date, shape number 2272 and the incised monogram of the
         artist. Height 12 1/2 inches. A neat drill hole in the bottom has been professionally repaired. On a black
         background are found dozens of yellow quince flowers and fruit with two birds perched in the branches.
         Angular rocks jut up from the ground. Uncrazed and done in very striking colors

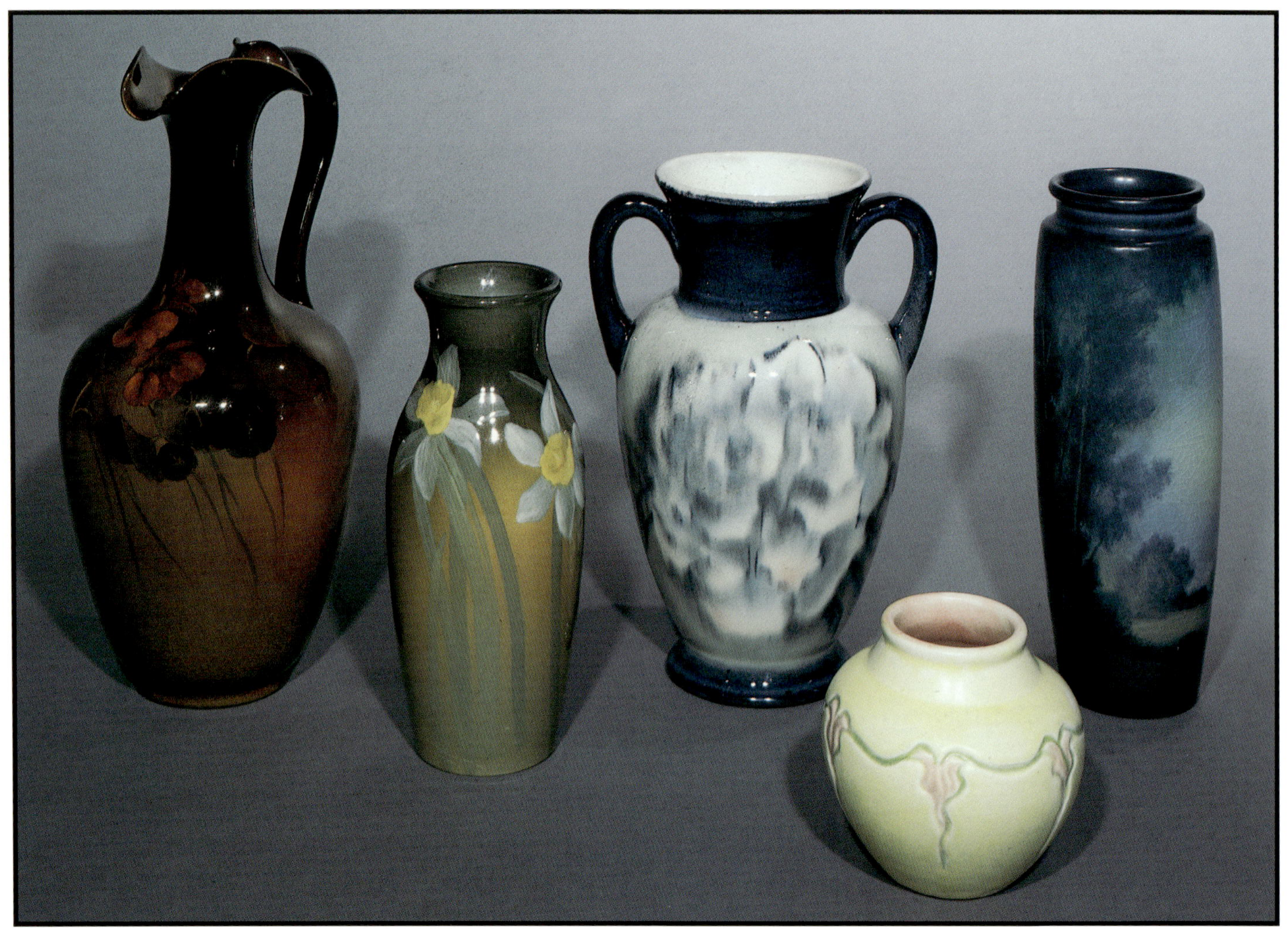

911	Good Standard glaze ewer with red nasturtium decoration painted in 1896 by Anna Valentien. Marks include the Rookwood logo, the date, shape number 504 C and the incised initials of the artist. Height 11 5/8 inches. Minor glaze scratches.	$800-1200
912	Iris glaze vase with yellow and white jonquils on a dark ground, painted in 1903 by Clara Lindeman. Marks include the Rookwood logo, the date, shape number 117 C, an incised W for white (Iris) glaze and the incised initials of the artist. Height 8 inches. Minimal crazing	$1250-1750
913	High glaze two-handled vase with floral decoration done by Kay Ley in 1946. Marks include the Rookwood logo, the date, shape number 2783, the number 4365 painted on in black slip and the artist's monogram, also painted on in black slip. Height 9 1/4 inches. Uncrazed.	$400-500
914	Early incised and painted mat glaze vase done in 1903 by Rose Fechheimer. Decoration consists of incised flowers in pink and green on a yellow ground. Marks include the Rookwood logo, the date, shape number 53 EZ and the artist's monogram, painted on in black slip. Height 3 3/4 inches. Minor glaze peppering.	$600-800
915	Vellum glaze scenic vase done by Ed Diers in 1917. The scene has a moody quality, almost like a pending summer storm, most likely because of the dark blues used by the artist. Marks include the Rookwood logo, the date, shape number 589 E and the incised monogram of the artist. Height 9 1/4 inches.	$1000-1500

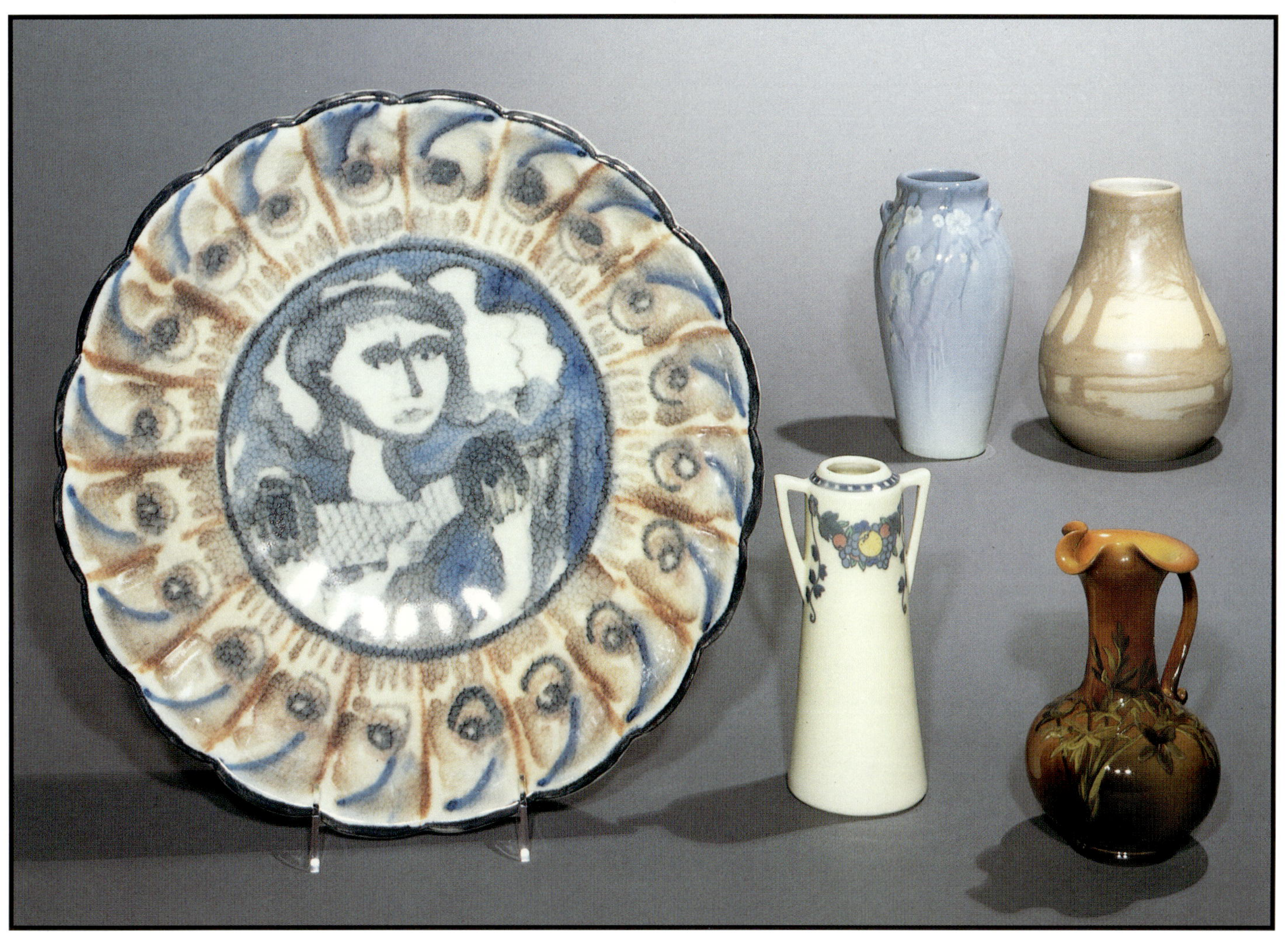

916   Stylish high glaze bowl with fluted edges painted by Jens Jensen in 1946. Jensen has decorated the fluted $1250-1750
panels of the bowl with a repeating geometric pattern. In the bowl's center, we find the portrait of a young
woman wearing a dress with puff sleeves, done as a typical Jensen allegory. Marks include the Rookwood
logo, the date, shape number 2813 C, the number "8752" painted on in black slip and the artist's monogram,
also painted on in black slip. Diameter is 13 1/4 inches.

917   Pretty Decorated Porcelain vase with two handles painted in 1916 by Arthur Conant. Conant has used at least $1000-1500
six different colors to apply the fruit, vines and alternating squares on the vase. Marks include the Rookwood
logo, the date, shape number 2018, a sideways p for porcelain body, the incised monogram of the artist and
an incised C just below the monogram. Height 6 1/8 inches. Uncrazed and very crisp.

918   Rare carved Iris glaze vase with trailing apple blossom decoration done by Clara Lindeman in 1907. Behind $3000-4000
the painted blossoms can be seen the limbs of the apple tree in relief. These limbs become three dimensional as they near the top, turning into ear-like handles at the shoulder. Overall, the vase has strong ties to
Japanese aesthetic and is a super effort by Lindeman. Marks include the Rookwood logo, the date, shape
number 925 E, an incised W for white (Iris) glaze and the incised initials of the artist. Height 6 1/2 inches.

919   Pretty Standard glaze ewer with blue flowers on an orange ground painted in 1893 by Bruce Horsfall. Im- $350-450
pressed marks include the Rookwood logo, the date, shape number 40 and W for white clay. Incised is the
monogram of the artist. Height 5 5/8 inches.

920   Early Arts & Crafts style Vellum glaze scenic vase painted by E.T. Hurley in 1906. Done in Hurley's tonalistic $2500-3000
style with trees which reflect in a small band of water in the foreground and several birds flying between
them. Impressed marks include the Rookwood logo, the date, shape number 969 C and V for Vellum glaze
body. Incised on the bottom are Hurley's initials and a V for Vellum glaze. Height 6 1/8 inches.

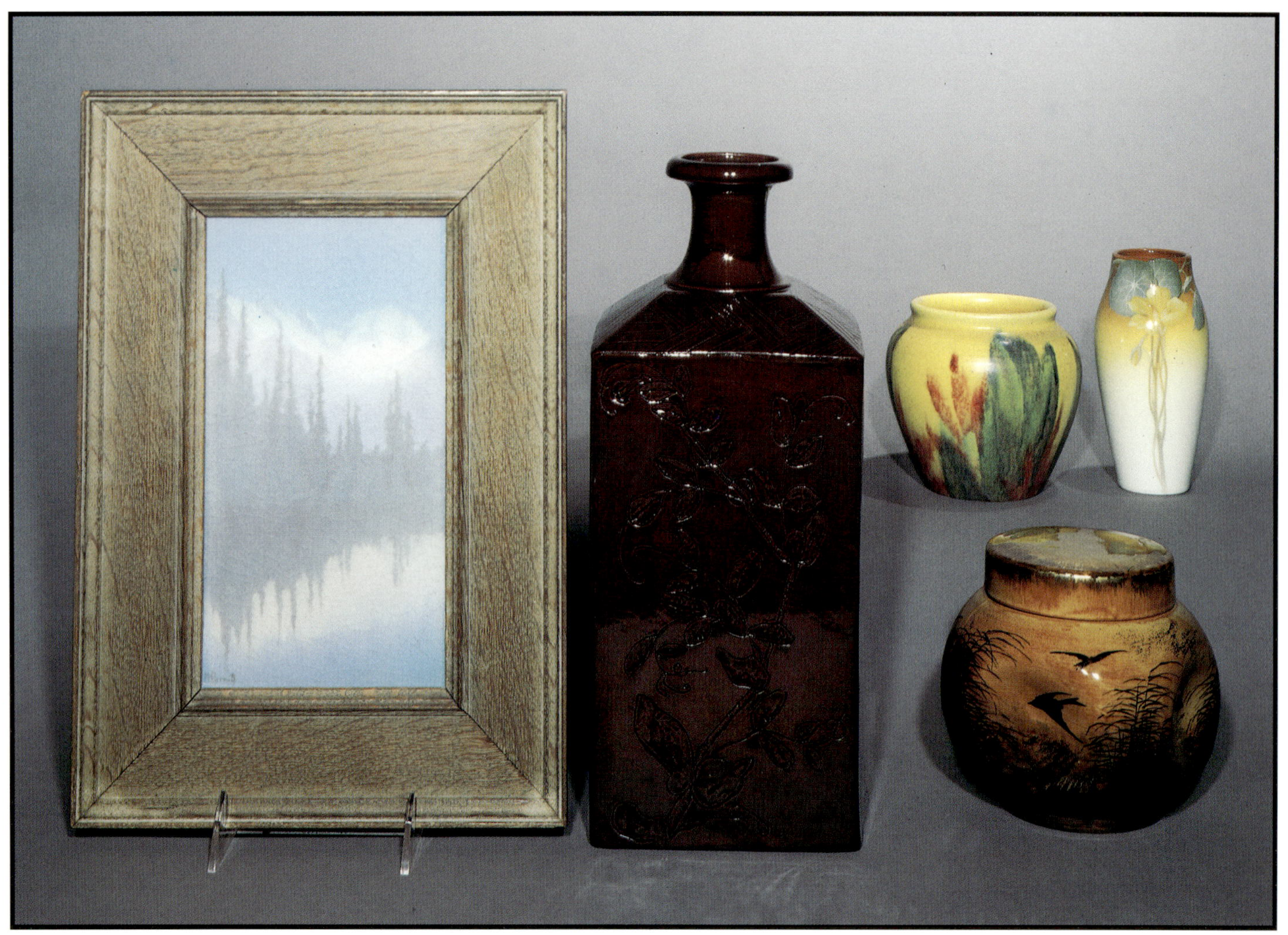

921   Vellum glaze scenic plaque showing tall fir trees with snow capped mountains behind, the work of Elizabeth McDermott. The artist's name appears in the lower left hand corner of the plaque. Marks on the back include the Rookwood logo, the date and V for Vellum glaze body. On the back of the frame is an original Rookwood paper logo and a typewritten Rookwood label with the title "Mirror Lake E.F. McDermott". Size is approximately 9 1/4 by 5 1/4 inches. $2500-3000

922   Square bottle shaped vase with leaf and vine carving on the four sides and geometric patterns incised in the shoulder, the work of Harriet Wenderoth in 1882. The vase is glazed with a yellow tinted high glaze, a precursor of Standard glaze. This style of Rookwood is known to collectors as being from Rookwood's Chocolate period. Marks include "Rookwood" in block letters, the date, shape number 192, R for red clay and the incised initials of the artist. Height 12 3/4 inches. Ex. The Glover Collection. $1000-1250

923   Mat glaze vase with flowers in red and green on a yellow ground painted by Louise Abel in 1927. Marks include the Rookwood logo, the date, shape number 931 and the monogram of the artist, painted on in brown slip. Height 4 3/4 inches. Minor grinding chips on the base. $300-400

924   Limoges style tea jar with lid decorated in 1882 by Albert Valentien. Several swallows glide through the tall grasses which are highlighted with fired-on gold. Impressed marks include Rookwood in block letters, the date, shape number 97, G for ginger clay and an anchor mark. Incised on the bottom are the artist's initials. Height 5 inches. The inner lid is missing but is of no visial consequence. $700-900

925   Delicate Iris glaze vase with yellow nasturtiums and green leaves on a yellow to cream ground, painted in 1901 by Carl Schmidt. Marks include the Rookwood logo, the date, shape number 30 F, an incised W for white (Iris) glaze and the incised monogram of the artist. Height 6 inches. A two inch crack descends from the rim. $1000-1250

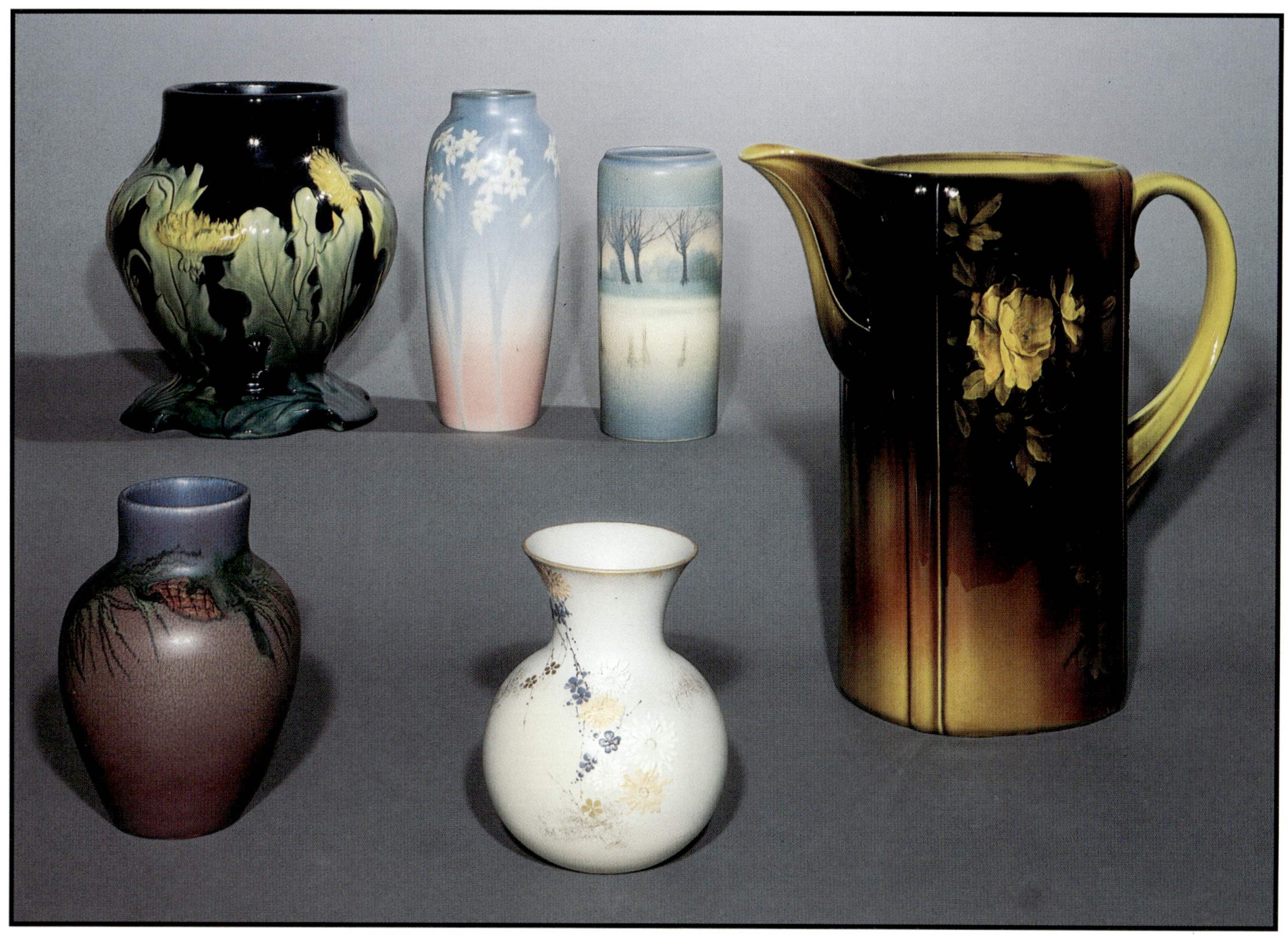

926   Mat glaze vase with nicely detailed pine cones and pine boughs painted in 1922 by Elizabeth Lincoln. Marks include the Rookwood logo, the date, shape number 927 F and the initials of the artist, painted on in black slip. Height 6 1/8 inches. $600-800

927   Wonderful and exceedingly rare carved Sea Green lamp base with yellow dandelions in high relief done in 1903 by Rose Fechheimer. Originally, this was an oil lamp, most likely with a ceramic font. Marks include the Rookwood logo, the date, trial shape number T 1272, an incised G for Sea Green glaze and the incised monogram of the artist. Height 9 1/8 inches. A large chip off one of the small feet has been professionally repaired as has damage to the rim. Pictured: Rookwood Its Golden Era of Art Pottery 1880-1929 by Kircher and Agranoff, color plate 8, middle row number 2. $3000-4000

928   Vellum glaze vase with lots of long stemmed jonquils in white and yellow, painted in 1929 by E.T. Hurley. Impressed marks include the Rookwood logo, the date and shape number 907 E. Hurley has incised his initials on the bottom. Height 9 1/8 inches. Uncrazed and very clean. There are jonquils all around the vase in different poses. $1750-2250

929   Pretty Dull Finish vase with stylized flowers in blue, white and salmon done by Artus Van Briggle in 1888. The decoration is chased with fired-on gold highlights. Marks include the Rookwood logo and date, shape number 402, W for white clay, an incised S for smear glaze (Dull Finish) and the incised initials of the artist. Height 5 1/2 inches. $500-700

930   Vellum glaze woodland scenic vase painted in 1911 by Kataro Shirayamadani. Against a peach colored sky are placed the black silhouettes of several trees which are faintly reflected in a body of water in the foreground. Marks include the Rookwood logo, the date, shape number 952 E, an impressed V for Vellum glaze body and the incised cypher of the artist. Height 7 5/8 inches. $2500-3000

931   Tall Standard glaze pitcher with exceptional yellow wild rose decoration done in 1890 by Harriet Wilcox. Marks include the Rookwood logo, the date, shape number 540, S for sage green clay, incised L.Y. for light yellow (Standard) glaze and the incised initials of the artist. Height 12 1/4 inches. Excellent artwork and condition. $1500-2000

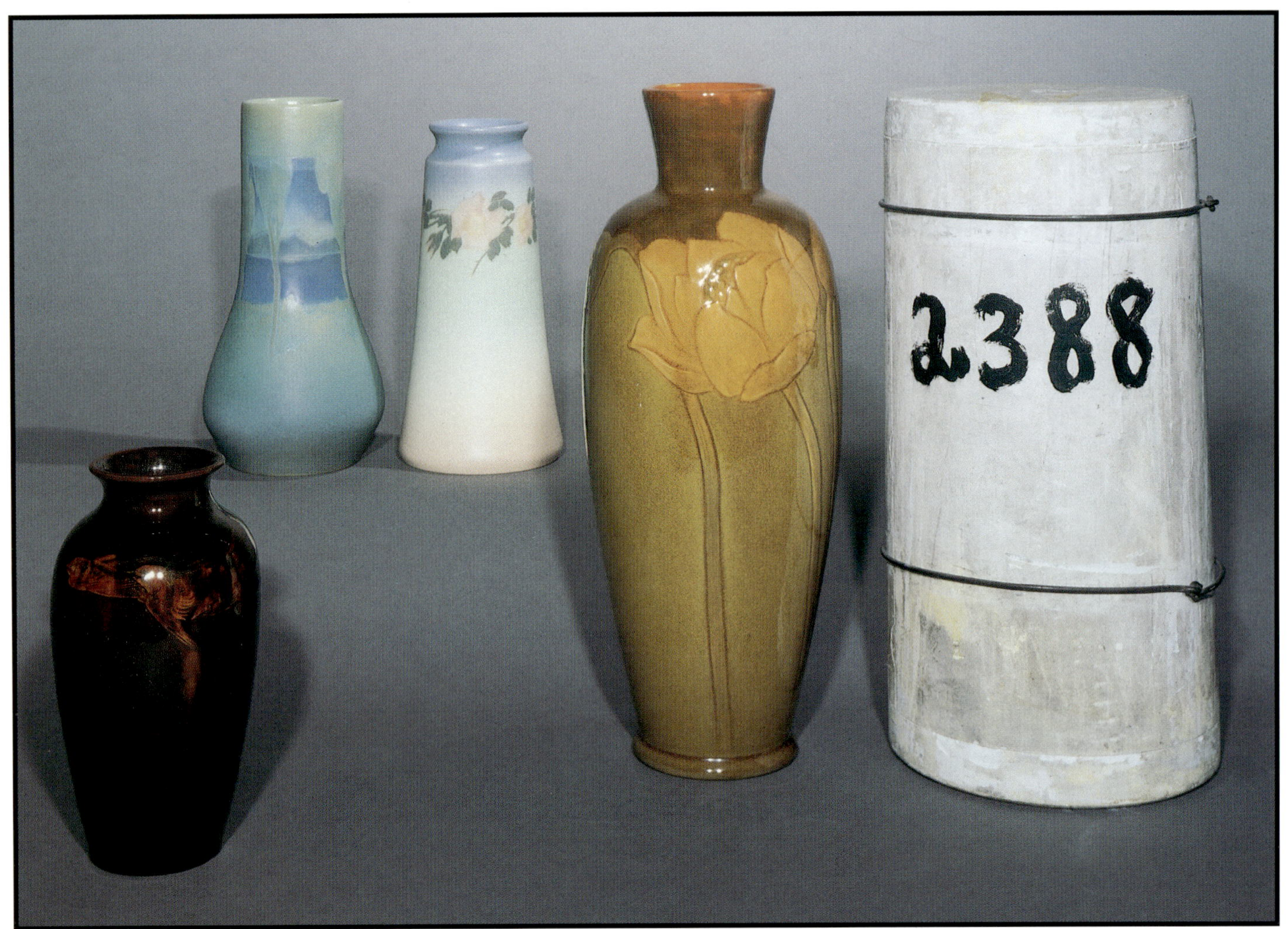

932   Good Standard glaze vase painted by Matt Daly in 1893 and loaded with Goldstone effect. Under the Mahogany glaze are five small birds in flight, each perfectly detailed by the artist. Marks include the Rookwood logo, the date, shape number 564 C, R for red clay and the incised initials of the artist. Height 6 3/4 inches. A small crack at the rim has been professionally repaired. $1000-1500

933   Very stylish, incised and painted Vellum glaze landscape vase, painted in 1908 by Kataro Shirayamadani. The scene, tall poplars and a lake in the background, was outlined by incising which helps to keep the flatly applied colors in place. Marks include the Rookwood logo, the date, shape number 1278 E, an impressed V for Vellum glaze body, a wheel ground x and the incised cypher of the artist. Damage to the rim has been repaired. Often, when a Vellum from this period is x'ed, the problem is missing glaze from the rim or foot. $1500-2000

934   Pretty Vellum glaze vase with a band of wild roses, done in 1917 by Ed Diers. Marks include the Rookwood logo, the date, shape number 1655 E, an impressed V for Vellum glaze body and the impressed monogram of the artist. Height 8 1/4 inches. $500-700

935   Standard glaze vase with poppy decoration, painted and incised by Matt Daly in 1898. Daly has opted for a two-dimensional, stylized treatment of the flowers rather then the more naturalistic style common to Rookwood. Marks include the Rookwood logo, the date, shape number 856 C and the incised initials of the artist. Height 13 1/8 inches. $2000-2500

936   Original Rookwood plaster mold for shape 2388, designed by Albert Munson, circa 1918. This original mold is made in five separate parts for ease of disassembly and is kept together by wire bands. The top and bottom plates are incised with the shape number and that same number is painted on the side in black. Inside the mold is a plaster casting of the vase itself. Height of the mold is 13 inches. $500-700

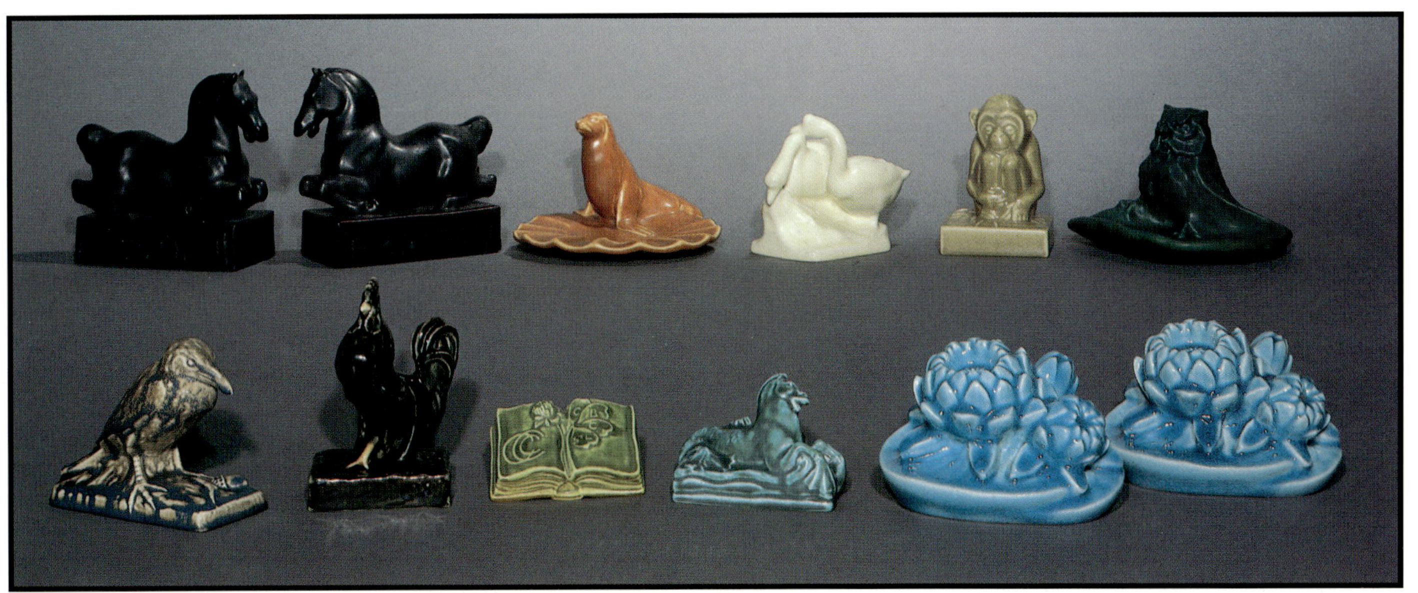

937 Great pair of kneeling horse bookends done in a fine black mat glaze at Rookwood in 1922. Marks include the Rookwood logo, the date and shape number 2588. Height 5 1/2 inches. $600-800

938 1930 Rookwood bird and acorn paperweight in a mottled blue over brown mat glaze. Marks include the Rookwood logo, the date and shape number 2810. Height 4 inches. $300-400

939 Unusual high glaze rooster paperweight in black, green and orange made at Rookwood in 1929. Marks include the Rookwood logo, the date, shape number 6030 and the cast-in monogram of designer William P. McDonald on the plinth. Height 5 inches. $400-500

940 Green mat glaze paperweight made at Rookwood in 1924. The front is embossed with clover and the initials "CCC" and "C B C St L". Marks on the back include the Rookwood logo and the notation "Reunion Commercial Clubs of Boston - Chicago - Cincinnati - St. Louis White Sulphur Springs W.Va. May 30 - June 1, 1924". Size is 2 1/4 by 3 5/8 inches. $250-350

941 Seal ashtray done in a rich burnt orange mat glaze at Rookwood in 1930. Impressed marks include the Rookwood logo, the date, shape number 2668 and a fan shaped esoteric mark. Height 4 inches. $300-400

942 Rare Rookwood Hippocampus paperweight in green mat glaze done in 1927. Marks include the Rookwood logo, the date and shape number 2796. Height 2 5/8 inches. $400-500

943 Double goose paperweight in white mat glaze made at Rookwood in 1927. Marks include the Rookwood logo, the date and shape number 1855. Height 4 1/8 inches. $300-400

944 Blue high glaze cactus flower bookends made at Rookwood in 1945. Marks include the Rookwood logo, the date, shape number 2836 and the incised number "65". Height 3 5/8 inches. $250-350

945 Tan mat glaze monkey paperweight made at Rookwood in 1935. Marks include the Rookwood logo, the date and shape number 6426. Height 4 1/2 inches. $350-450

946 Early Owl tray done in a rich, mottled green mat glaze at Rookwood in 1905. Marks include the Rookwood logo, the date and shape number 1084. Height 4 inches. Superb glaze, mold and color. Rookwood "offically" announced the production of multiples like this in 1905. $500-600

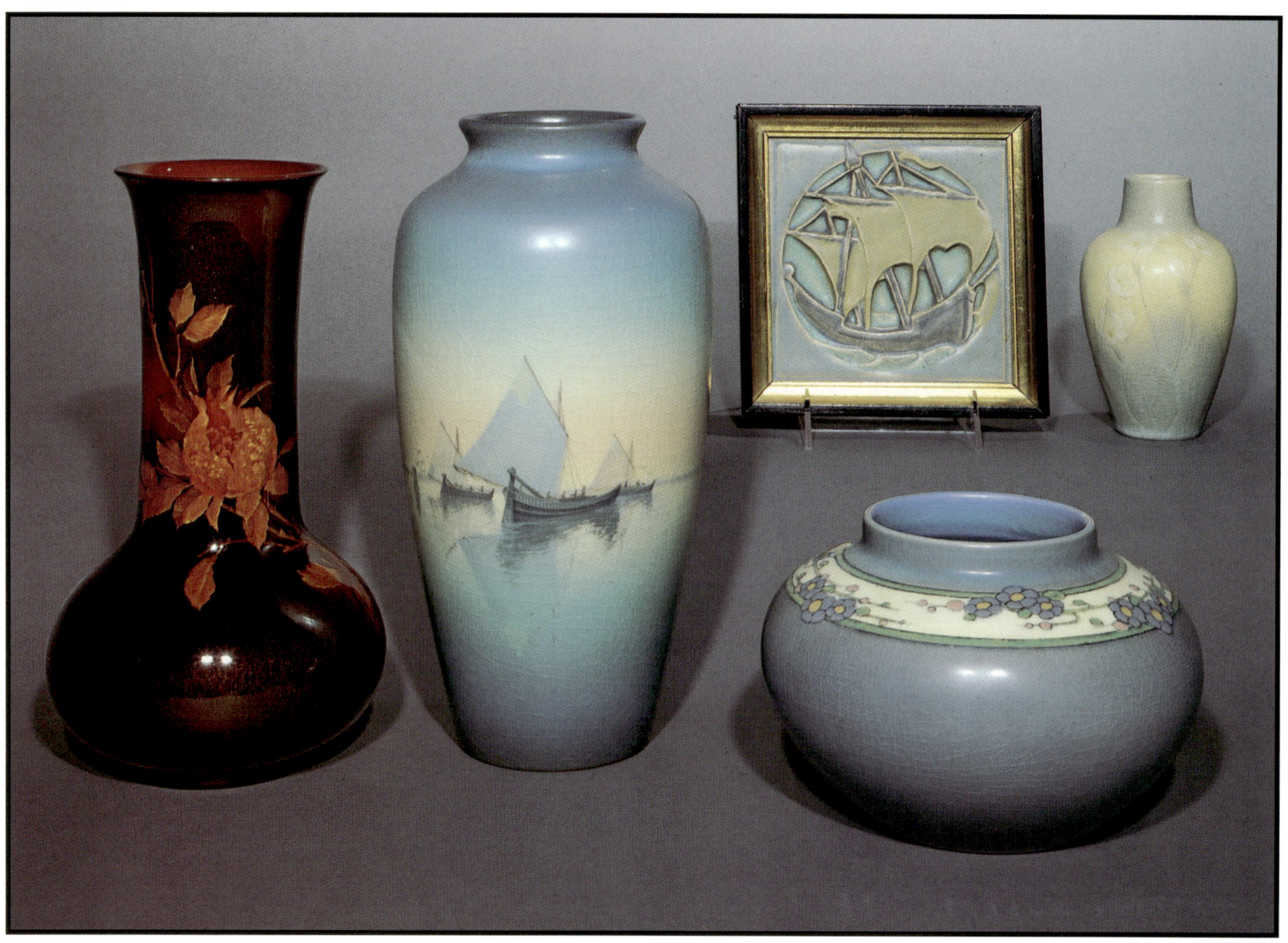

947   Good Standard glaze vase with what may be Buckeye decoration under patches of Tiger Eye effect, $800-1000
       painted by Albert Valentien in 1889. Marks include the Rookwood logo, the date, incised shape number
       486 C, R for red clay, an incised D for Dark Standard glaze and the incised initials of the artist. Height 10
       inches. Excellent artwork and fascinating glaze. Very minor glaze scratches.

948   Venetian harbor scene vase painted in 1921 by Carl Schmidt. There is no A or B side to this piece, as $2000-3000
       ships abound in every direction. Marks include the Rookwood logo, the date, shape number 614 D, an
       impressed V for Vellum glaze body and the impressed monogram of the artist. Height 10 3/4 inches.
       There are three 1/2 inch long cracks in the rim, none of which are loose but all of which can easily be
       seen and felt.

949   Multicolored mat glaze trivet with deeply embossed sailing vessel, made at Rookwood in 1917. Marks $400-500
       include the Rookwood logo, the date and shape number 1378. Size is 5 5/8 inches square.

950   Vellum glaze squat vase with a band of stylized flowers painted around the shoulder, done in 1917 by $800-1000
       Lenore Asbury. Marks include the Rookwood logo, the date, shape number 1929, an impressed V for
       Vellum glaze and the incised initials of the artist. Height is 4 5/8 inches and diameter is 7 1/4 inches.

951   Early carved and painted Vellum glaze floral vase done in 1904 by Kataro Shirayamadani. Marks include $700-900
       the Rookwood logo, the date, shape number 905 F, a wheel ground x and the incised cypher of the artist.
       Height 5 5/8 inches. Minor glaze flaws.

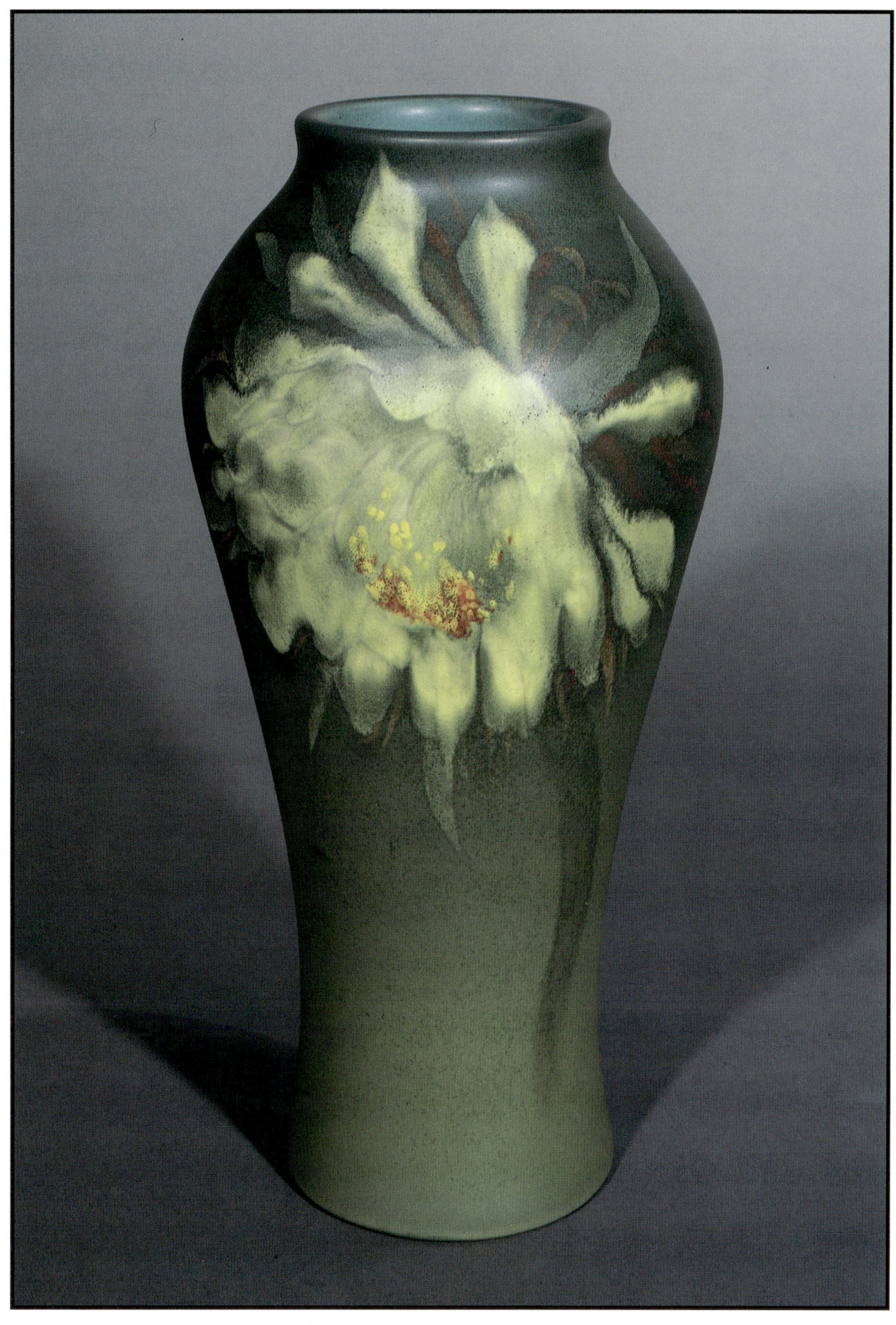

952   Large and beautiful Painted Mat vase done in 1900 by Albert Valentien. Valentien has depicted a large $12500-17500
white orchid with yellow and red stamen and bright red tendrils which trail from the back of the flower.
Also trailing from behind the flower are long green leaves which undulate around the vase in a sensuous
Art Nouveau fashion. Marks include the Rookwood logo, the date, shape number 909 B and the full
name of the artist, painted on in black slip. Height 11 3/8 inches. A neat drill hole has been professionally
repaired. The middle part of the artist's signature has been reconstructed in the repair process.

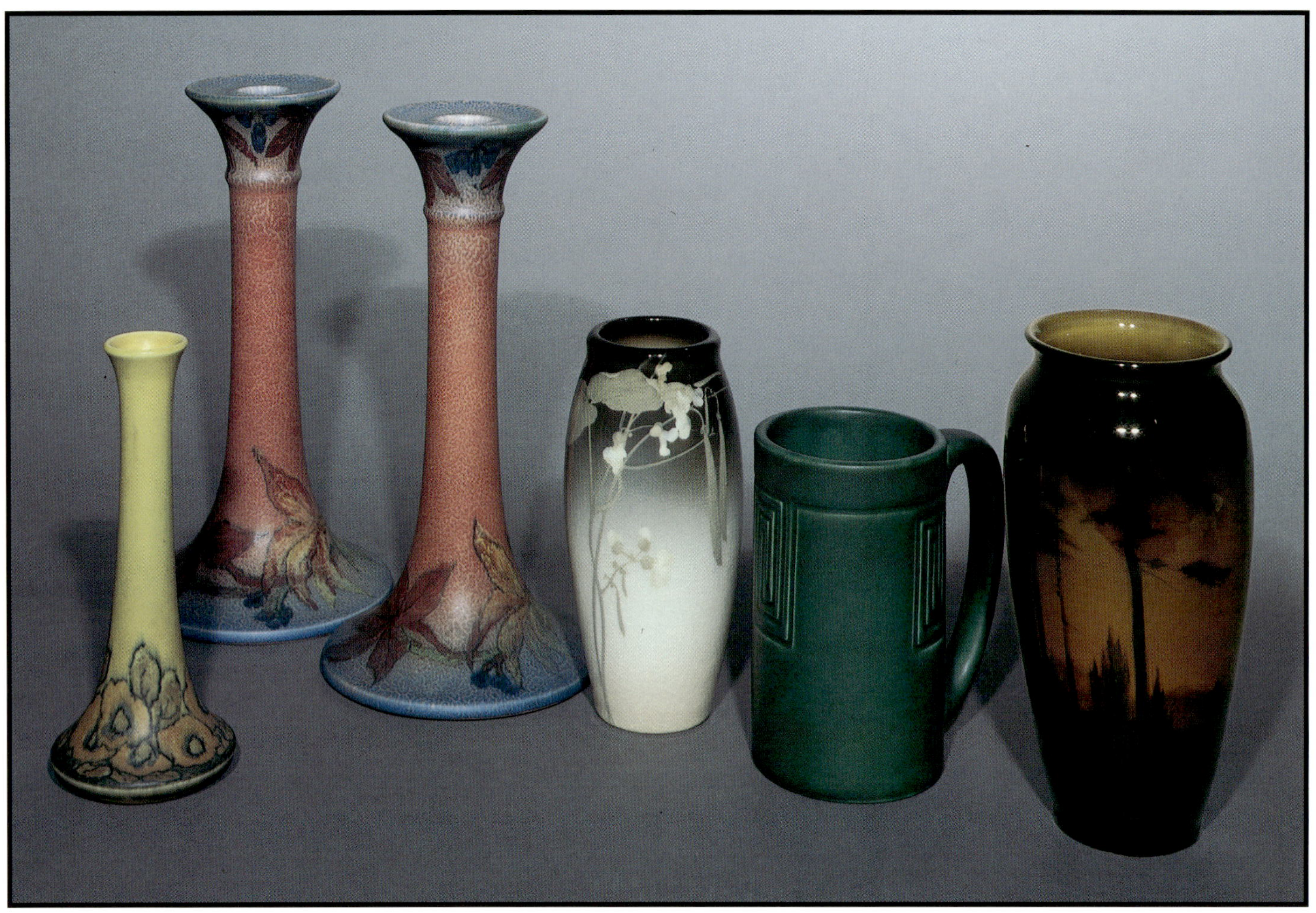

953   Mat glaze bud vase with orange flowers on a yellow ground, painted by Katherine Jones in 1925. The flowers and leaves are outlined in black slip. Marks include the Rookwood logo, the date, shape number 2307 and the artist's initials, painted on in black slip. Height 7 1/8 inches. $600-800

954   Unusual pair of mat glaze candlesticks with Virginia creeper decoration in bright colors done in 1925 by Elizabeth Lincoln. Marks on each include the Rookwood logo, the date, shape number 2598 and the incised initials of the artist. Height 10 1/4 inches. $600-800

955   Iris glaze vase decorated by Irene Bishop in 1907. Pictured are sweet pea flowers, leaves vines and pea pods. Marks include the Rookwood logo, the date, shape number 917 D, an incised W for white (Iris) glaze and the incised monogram of the artist. Height 6 3/4 inches. $1000-1250

956   Arts & Crafts style green mat glaze mug with embossed Greek Key designs, done at Rookwood in 1903. Marks include the Rookwood logo, the date and shape number 376 Z. Height 5 1/2 inches. $300-400

957   Rare yellow tinted high glaze scenic vase painted by Lenore Asbury in 1930. Marks include the Rookwood logo, the date, shape number 2544, a fan shaped esoteric mark, the incised initials of the artist and incised Y.G. for yellow glaze. Height 7 7/8 inches. Glaze scratches. Rookwood reprised yellow tinted glazes in the 1920's and Asbury, who started there in the 1890's and who worked with Standard glaze when it was first popular, seems to have been a strong advocate. This vase, which uses a nocturnal landscape theme rather than the traditional floral motif, is a bit unusual. $1750-2250

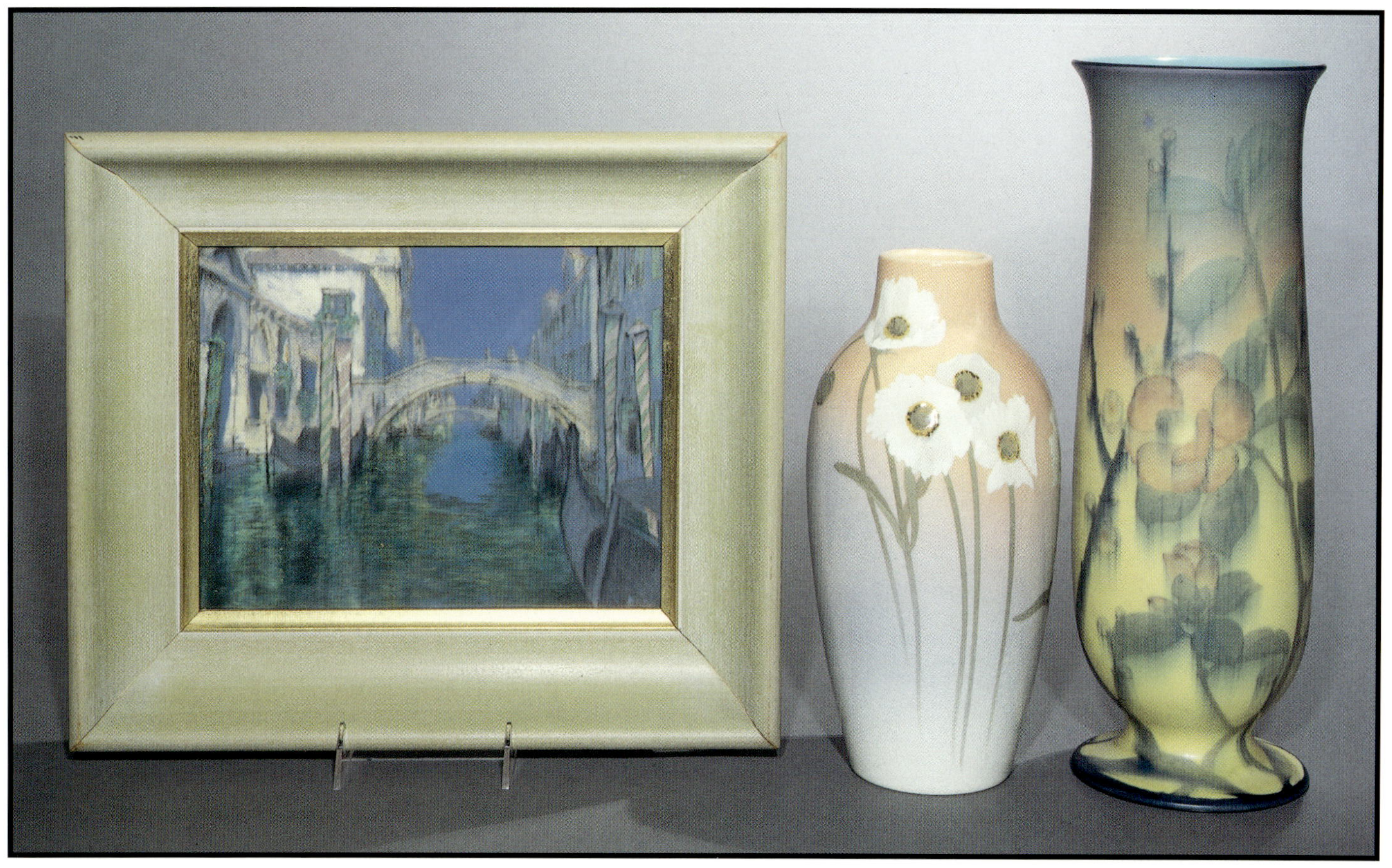

958   Rare Vellum glaze plaque showing a building lined canal in Venice, done in vibrant colors by E.T. Hurley in 1916. Hurley's initials are incised in the lower right hand corner of the piece. Marks on the back include the Rookwood logo, the date and V for Vellum glaze body. Size is approximately 9 by 11 inches. The frame is older but probably not original to the plaque. There are some burst glaze bubbles in the dark green color used on the poles and a flower box. $4000-6000

959   Good Iris glaze vase with white daisies on a coral to very pale blue ground painted in 1903 by Sara Sax. There are large groups of flowers on both sides of this vase. Sax seems to have liked painting daisies during her "Iris Glaze" years. We have seen a few other examples, all of which are nicely detailed and Art Nouveau-like in the way the flowers are arranged. This piece is no exception and is of above average size. Impressed marks include the Rookwood logo, the date, shape number 940 C, an incised W for white (Iris) glaze and the incised monogram of the artist. Height 11 1/8 inches. $8000-10000

960   Tall and showy Vellum glaze footed vase with bright red cherry blossoms on a mauve to green to yellow ground, painted by Kataro Shirayamadani in 1923. Marks include the Rookwood logo, the date, shape number 784 A and the incised cypher of the artist. Height 15 1/2 inches. Uncrazed. The underglaze colors have all run slightly but the overall effect is very, very nice. $4000-6000

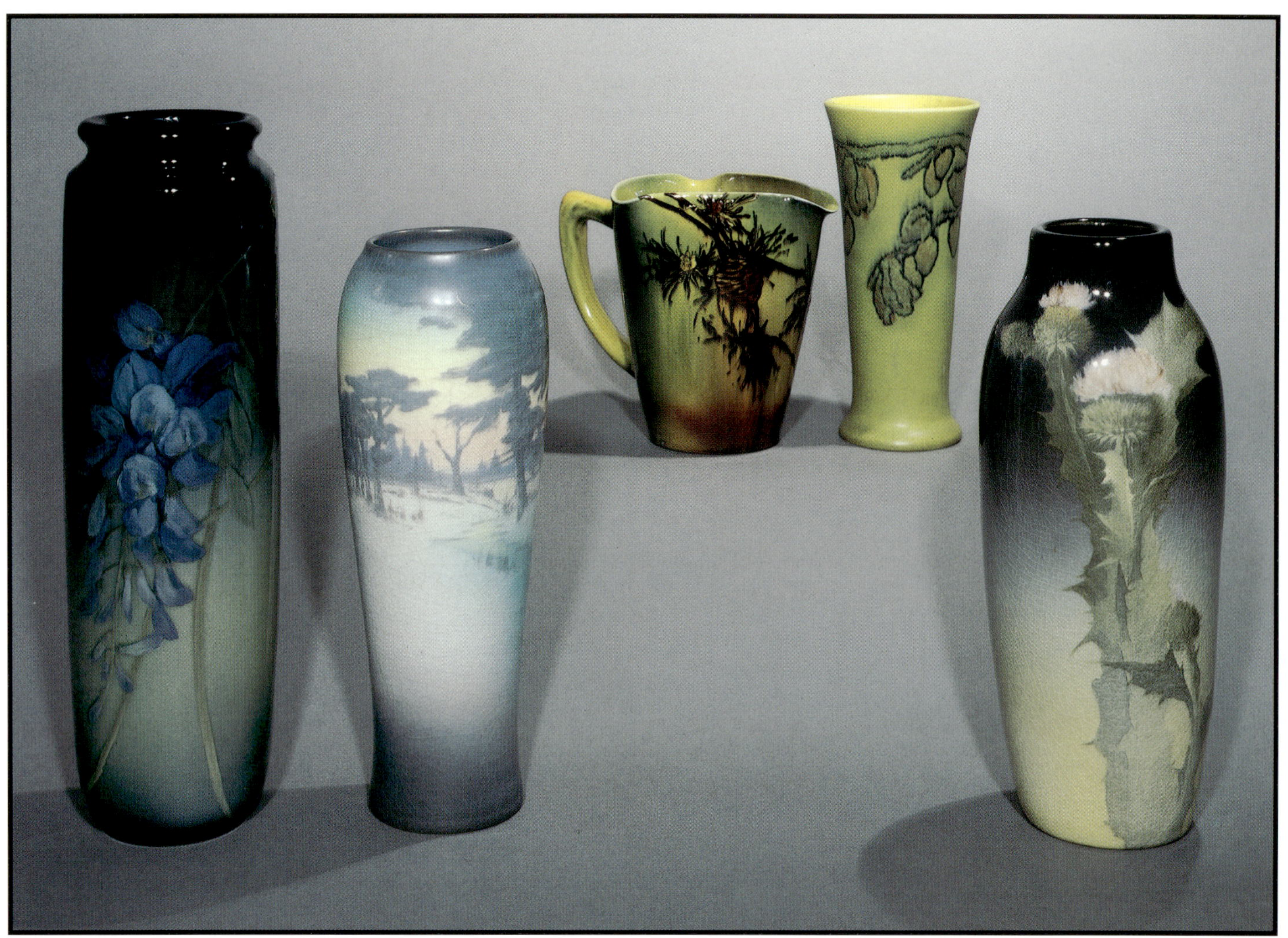

961   Good Sea Green glaze vase with vibrant, blue wisteria blossoms on a deep green ground, painted in 1900 $4000-5000
by Sallie Toohey. Marks include the Rookwood logo, the date, shape number 589 D, an incised G for Sea
Green glaze and the incised monogram of the artist. Height 11 1/2 inches. There is a very minor spot of
glaze burn on the back side of the vase. Strong color, good size and an uncommon glaze line.

962   Pretty Arts & Crafts Vellum glaze scenic vase showing pine trees in a snowy setting, the work of Sallie $1250-1750
Coyne in 1917. Impressed marks include the Rookwood logo and date, shape number 2040 D and V for
Vellum glaze body. Incised on the base is the artist's monogram. Height 9 3/8 inches

963   Light Standard glaze tri-cornered pitcher with pine cones and boughs painted by Ed Abel in 1891. Marks $600-800
include the Rookwood logo, the date, shape number 259 C, W for white clay, an incised L for light Standard glaze and the incised initials of the artist. Height 5 1/2 inches. There is a small burst bubble near the
bottom of the piece. Nice colors and decoration.

964   Mat glaze floral vase painted by Charles Klinger in 1925. Marks include the Rookwood logo, the date, $400-500
shape number 1357 E and the monogram of the artist, painted on in black slip. Height 7 1/4 inches.

965   Iris glaze vase with realistic thistle decoration done in 1903 by Fred Rothenbusch. Marks include the $2000-3000
Rookwood logo, the date, shape number 932 CC, an incised W for white (Iris) glaze and the incised
monogram of the artist. Height 9 5/8 inches.

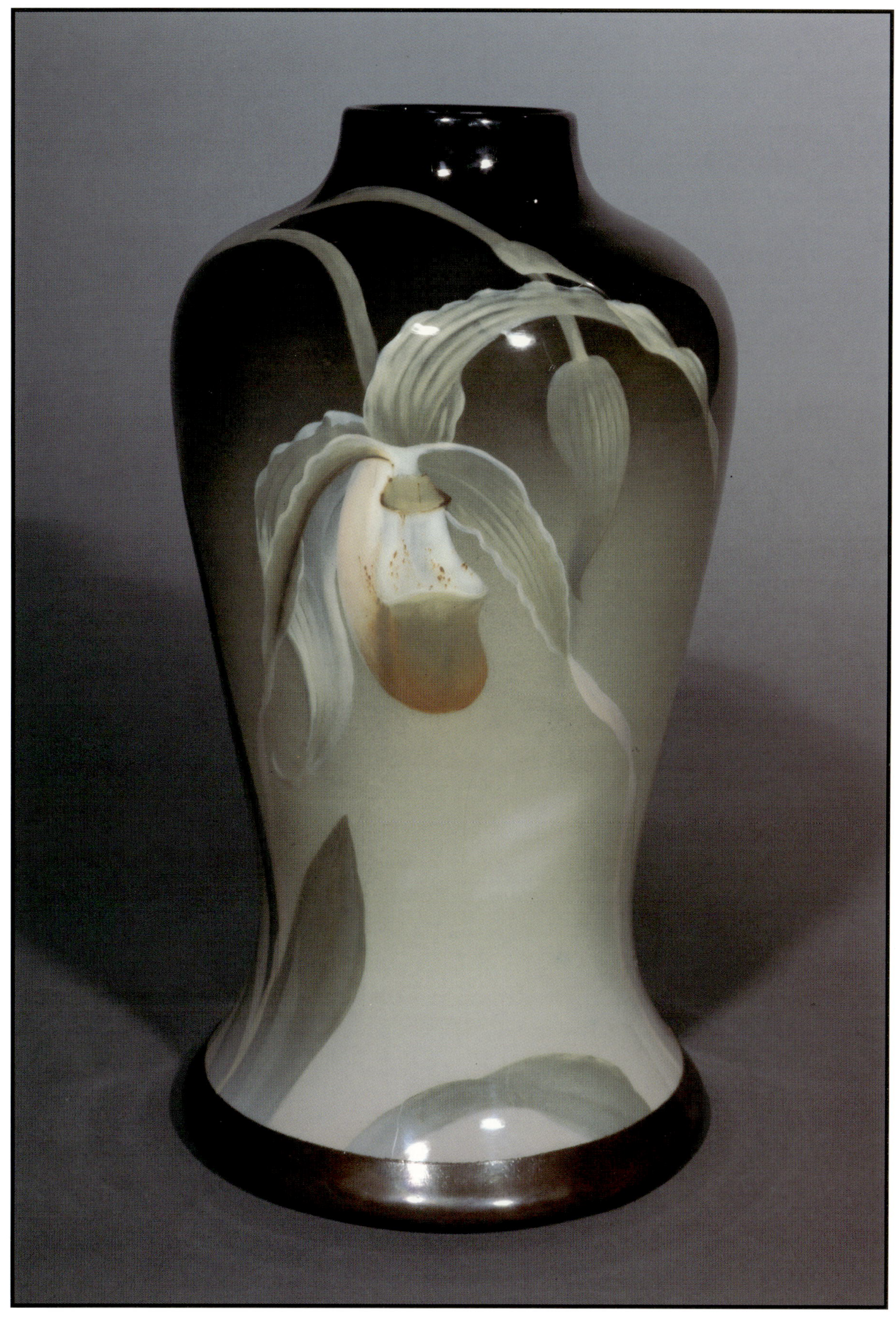

966 Stunning Iris glaze lamp vase with orchid decoration, done in 1906 by Carl Schmidt. A typically excellent work by Schmidt with unusual subject matter, an elaborate orchid in exotic colors. Marks include the Rookwood logo, the date, shape number 1038, an incised W for white (Iris) glaze and the impressed monogram of the artist. Cast holes in the base and low on the back side accommodate an electric cord and fittings should the piece ever be used as a lamp. The electroplated copper band at the base is an exact replacement for a badly decomposed original, applied at Rookwood to hide flaws in the glaze. The otherwise pristine surface of the vase was marred by dozens of fine bubbles in the glaze at the base, which had to be smoothed by grinding. Rather than mark the piece a second or scrap it, Rookwood chose to make the best of its misfortune by use of the copper band. Height 11 5/8 inches. Uncrazed.

$6000-8000

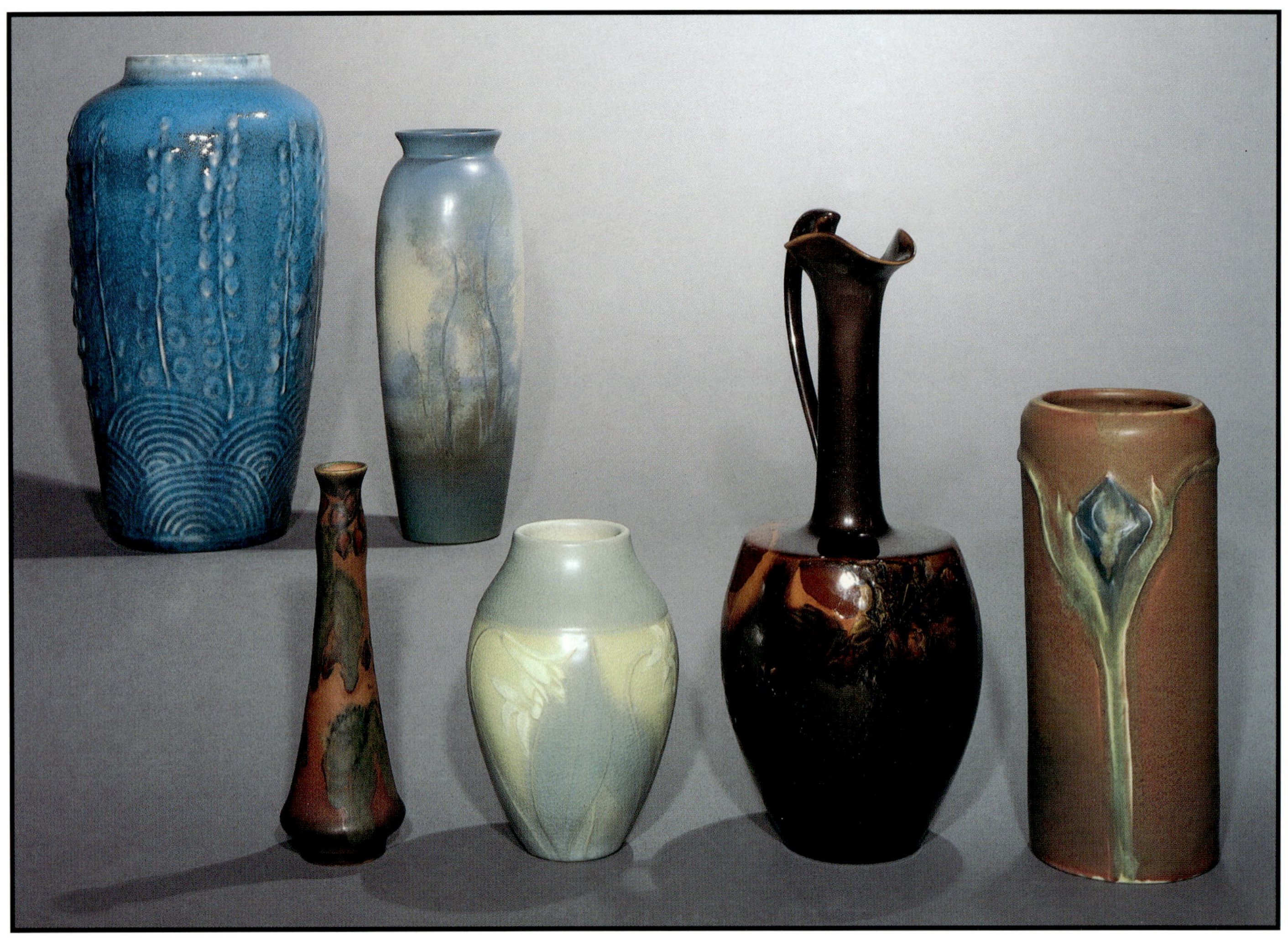

967	1944 Rookwood production vase with embossed Art Deco floral designs done in a strong blue crackle glaze with red highlights. Marks include the Rookwood logo, the date and shape number 6777. Height 11 3/4 inches.	$300-400
968	Mat glaze bud vase with floral decoration done in 1922 by Louise Abel. Impressed marks include the Rookwood logo, the date and shape number 2546 F. Painted on the bottom in black slip is the artist's monogram. Height 7 1/8 inches.	$500-700
969	Vellum glaze autumnal scenic vase painted by Ed Diers in 1921. Impressed marks include the Rookwood logo, the date, shape number 829 and V for Vellum glaze. The artist's monogram is incised on the base. Height 9 3/4 inches	$2000-2500
970	Early Vellum glaze floral vase carved and painted by Kataro Shirayamadani in 1904. Marks include the Rookwood logo, the date, shape number 604 E, V for Vellum glaze body and the incised cypher of the artist. Height 5 7/8 inches. A small base chip has been professionally repaired. 1904 is the first year for regular Vellum usage and carved pieces are uncommon at best.	$600-800
971	1889 Standard glaze ewer with floral decoration by Anna Valentien that has matured in the fire with some rather unexpected effects. Marks include the Rookwood logo, the date, shape number 441, R for red clay, an incised D for dark Standard glaze and the incised initials of the artist. Height 11 1/2 inches. Listed: 2,292 Pieces of Early Rookwood Pottery in the Cincinnati Art Museum in 1916 compiled by Stanley Burt as item 38 on page 87. Burt describes the ewer as follows: Ewer 441 - Maho(gany) - This piece had a slip dec(oration) which peeled off in spots from first fire - goldst(one) with dull gl(aze) - A.M.V." Things may not have worked quite as expected but the piece itself was nice enough for Rookwood to keep for over 40 years.	$600-800
972	Hand thrown Arts & Crafts style mat glaze vase with deeply carved jack-in-the-pulpit flowers done in 1905 by Sallie Toohey. Marks include the Rookwood logo, the date, shape number 952 and the impressed monogram of the artist. There is a blue, brown and green flower on each side of the vase. Height 8 3/8 inches.	$1000-15000

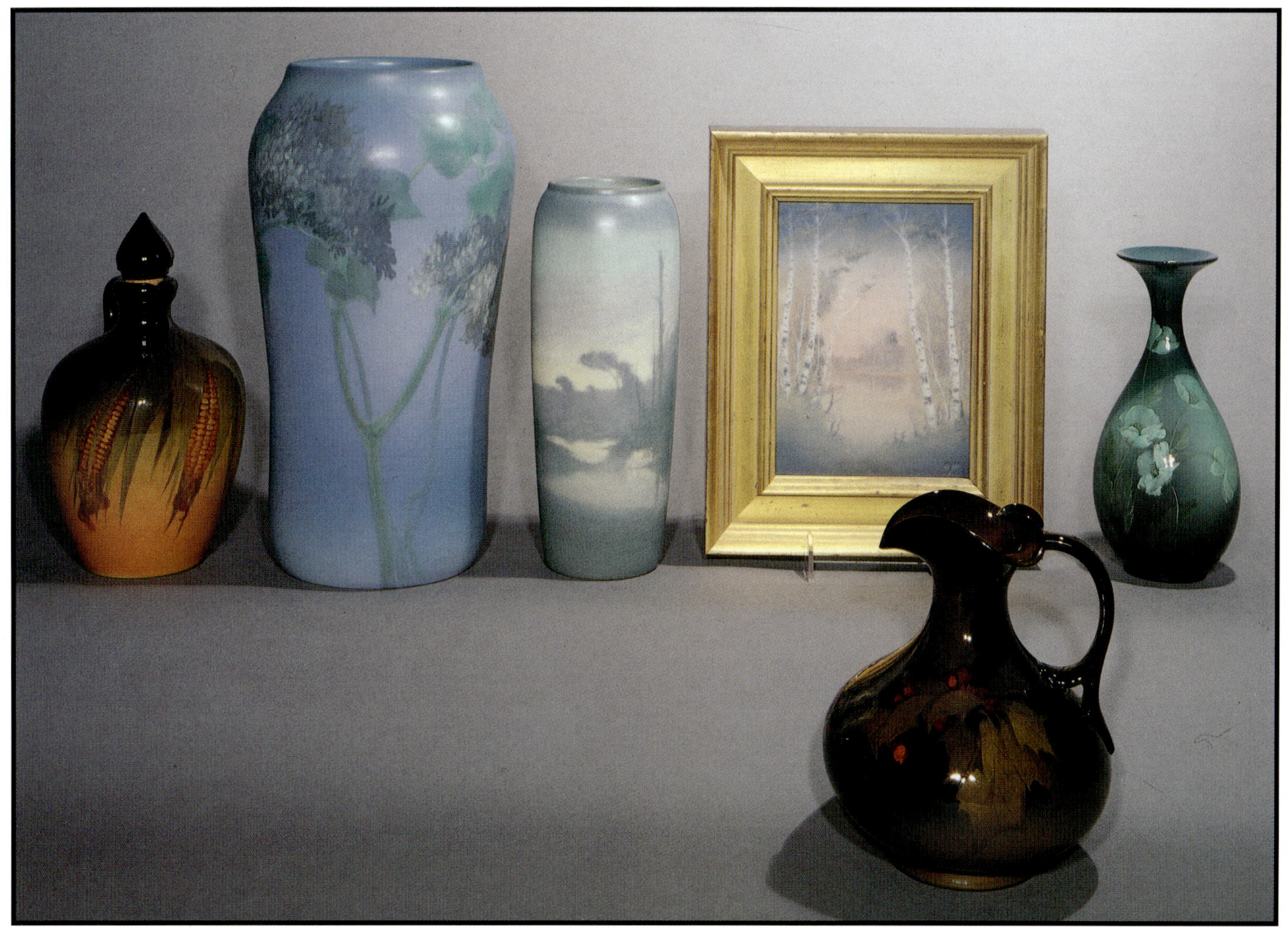

973	Standard glaze whiskey jug with corn decoration painted by Anna Valentien in 1898. Marks include the Rookwood logo, the date, shape number 512 B and the incised initials of the artist. Height 9 1/2 inches. There is a pin-head size nick off the very point of the stopper.	$700-900
974	Large Vellum glaze vase with purple and white lilacs on a medium blue ground, painted by Ed Diers in 1908. Marks include the Rookwood logo, the date, shape number 935 A, V for Vellum glaze body, an incised V for Vellum glaze and the incised monogram of the artist. Height 13 5/8 inches. A very tight line descends from the rim. Good artwork and nice contrast.	$1250-1750
975	Good tonalistic Vellum glaze landscape scenic vase painted in 1911 by Fred Rothenbusch. Rothenbusch has created a dusky scene with trees and stumps reflecting in water, done in shades of purple, gray, green and gray. Marks include the Rookwood logo, the date, shape number 951 C, V for Vellum glaze body, an incised V for Vellum glaze and the incised monogram of the artist. Height 10 1/2 inches.	$1000-1500
976	Crisp Vellum glaze birch tree scenic plaque painted in 1941 by E.T. Hurley. Hurley's initials are incised in the lower right hand corner of the plaque. Marks on the back include the Rookwood logo, the date and the notation "6 x 8". Size is actually 7 3/4 by 5 3/4 inches. Uncrazed and very colorful. Recently framed.	$3000-3500
977	Standard glaze ewer with holly decoration painted in 1903 by Lenore Asbury. Marks include the Rookwood logo, the date, shape number 718 and the incised initials of the artist. height 7 5/8 inches. There is a glaze burn on the lower tip of the handle.	$400-600
978	Pretty Sea Green vase with beautifully detailed poppies on a medium ground, painted in 1896 by Constance Baker. Marks include the Rookwood logo, the date, shape number 799, an incised G for Sea Green glaze and the incised initials of the artist. Height 8 5/8 inches. Glaze scratches. Damage to the rim has been professionally repaired. Excellent contrast.	$1250-1750

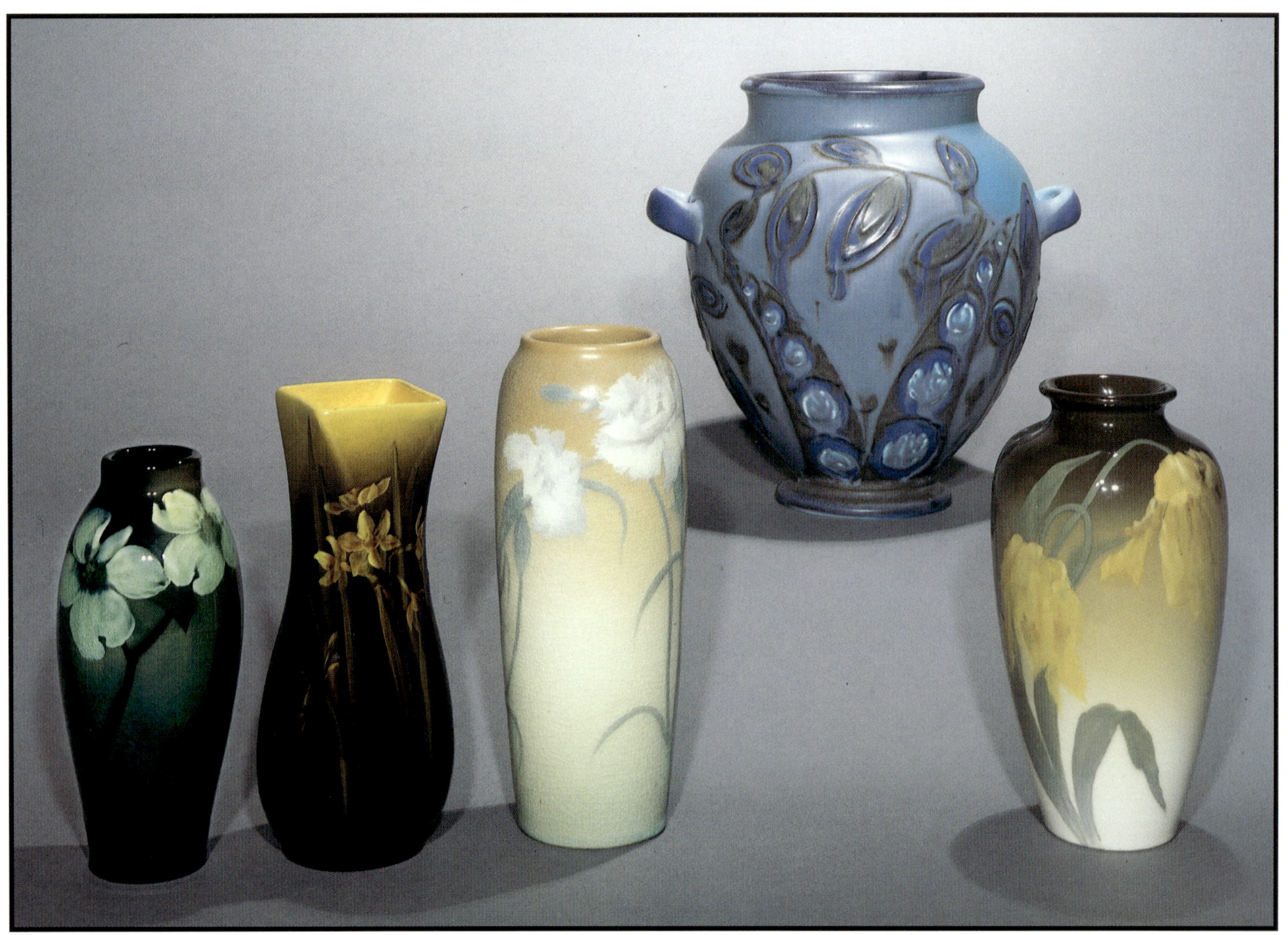

979   Nice Sea Green vase with dogwood flowers and limbs painted in 1900 by Sallie Toohey. There are two flowers on the front of the vase and one on the back. Marks include the Rookwood logo and date, shape number 901 D, an incised G for Sea Green glaze and the incised monogram of the artist. Height 7 inches. $1250-1750

980   Standard glaze vase in an unusual shape with jonquil decoration done in 1897 by Katharine Hickman. The body of the vase starts out round at the bottom and ends up square at the rim. Marks include the Rookwood logo, the date, shape number 817, an impressed triange-shaped esoteric mark and the incised monogram of the artist. Height 8 inches. There is a pin-head sized glaze nick off the rim. $300-400

981   Vellum glaze vase by Ed Diers painted in 1907 with white carnations on a cafe'-au-lait ground. Marks include the Rookwood logo, the date, shape number 951 D, V for Vellum glaze body, an incised V for Vellum glaze and the incised monogram of the artist. Height 9 7/8 inches. $700-900

982   Attractive mat glaze Art Deco vase with two handles, painted by Elizabeth Barrett in 1928. Flowers are outlined by slip trailing and painted in shades of blue, brown and white on a light blue ground. Marks include the Rookwood logo, the date, shape number 2949 and the incised monogram of the artist. Height 9 7/8 inches. A spiral crack in the body has been professionally repaired. $400-500

983   Nice Iris glaze vase with yellow parrot tulips painted by Irene Bishop in 1904. Marks include the Rookwood logo, the date, shape number 614 E, an incised W for white (Iris) glaze and the incised monogram of the artist. Height 8 inches. There is a small spot of dark brown on the back side of the vase. Uncrazed and very nice. $1500-2000

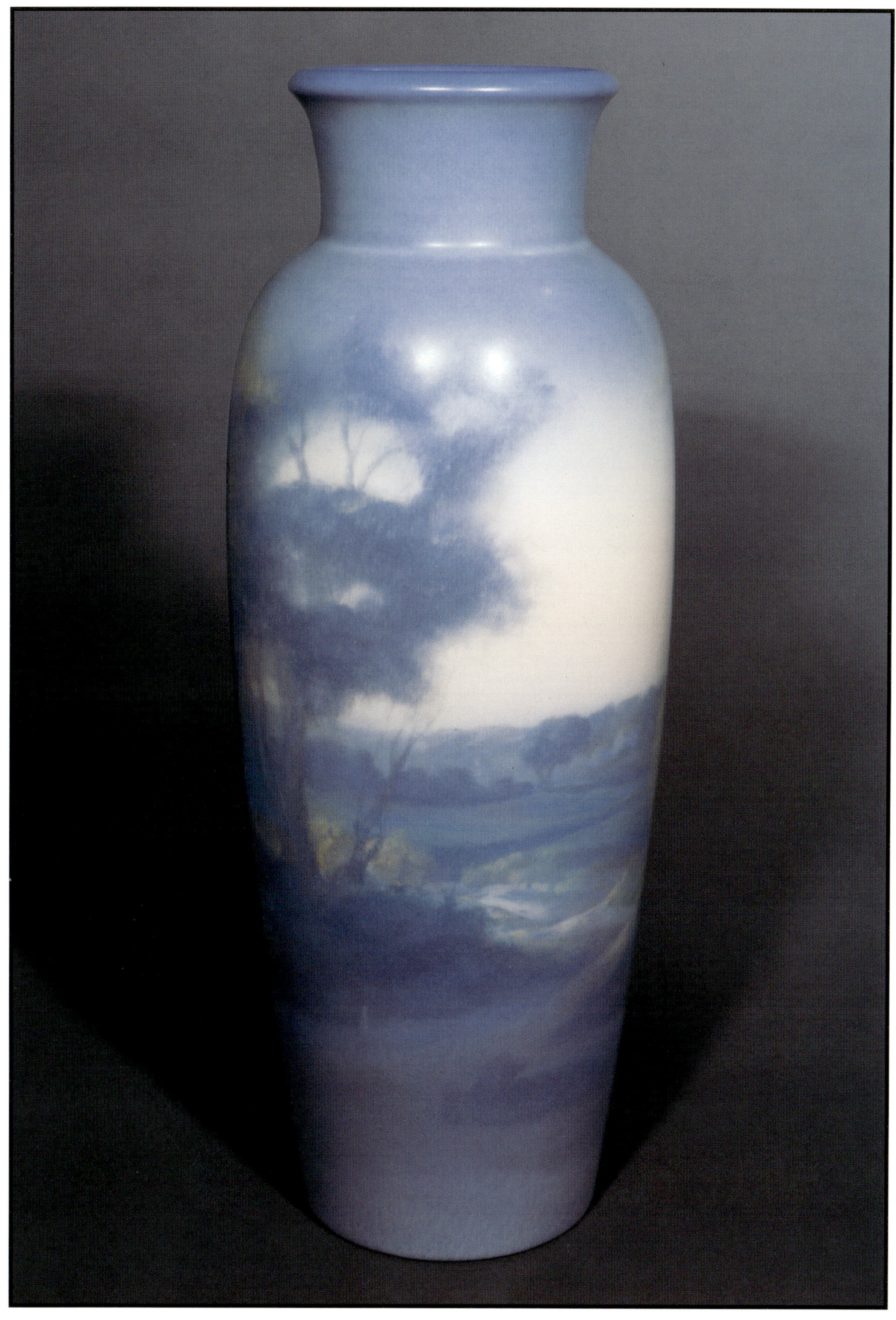

984   Tall, crisp and clean Vellum glaze scenic vase painted in 1929 by Fred Rothenbusch. A typically well executed Rothenbusch scenic complete with two small buildings in the distance and a small stream flowing toward the viewer. Marks include the Rookwood logo, the date, shape number 2785, an incised V for Vellum glaze, the impressed monogram of the artist and part of a Rookwood paper showroom label. Height 13 1/4 inches. Uncrazed. $6000-8000

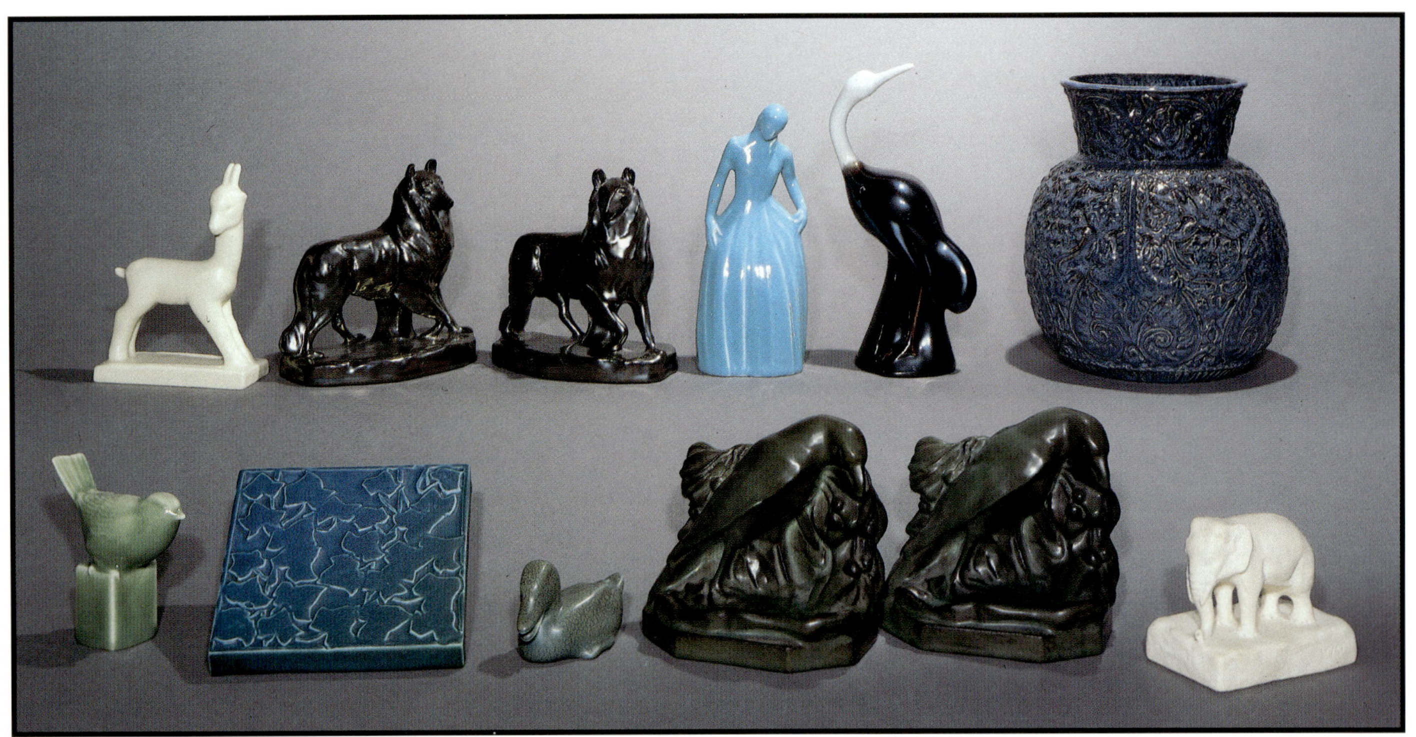

985   Green high glaze canary paperweight made at Rookwood in 1945. Marks include the Rookwood logo, the date and shape number 6383. Height 3 7/8 inches. $150-200

986   Art Deco white mat glaze goat designed by Louise Abel and made at Rookwood in 1944. Marks include the Rookwood logo, the date, shape number 6170 and Abel's cast-in logo. Height 6 1/8 inches. $300-400

987   Blue mat trivet with embossed English ivy decoration made at Rookwood in 1916. Marks include the Rookwood logo, the date and shape number 3083. Size is 5 3/4 inches square. $200-300

988   Rare pair of collie bookends made at Rookwood in 1930 and covered in Nubian Black glaze infused with many small crystals. Marks include the Rookwood logo, the date and shape number 2778. Height 6 inches. One ear on one bookend has been professionally repaired. $400-500

989   Duck paperweight done in a mottled green and blue mat glaze at Rookwood in 1931. Marks include the Rookwood logo, the date, shape number 6064 and a fan shaped esoteric mark. Height 2 1/8 inches. $200-300

990   Pair of rook bookends in a a wonderful green mat glaze that looks remarkably like weathered bronze. Made at Rookwood in 1925, the bookends bear the company logo, the date, shape number 2275 and designer William P. McDonald's monogram, molded into the flat backside. $300-500

991   Rookwood production female figurine done in 1953 and covered in a rich blue porcelain glaze. Marks include the Rookwood logo, the date and shape number 6907. Height 7 3/4 inches. Uncrazed. $200-250

992   Graceful Rookwood stork figurine in Clair de Lune over Nubian Black glazes made in 1954. Marks include the Rookwood logo, the date and shape number 6972. Height 8 7/8 inches. This is a pleasant and unusual use of these glaze colors. $200-300

993   Late Rookwood piece with embossed floral design covered with a rich, mottled blue-gray glaze in Starkville in 1963. Impressed marks include the Rookwood logo, the date, shape number 2556 and a C in a circle indicating copyright. Height 8 3/8 inches. $300-400

994   Unglazed Rookwood elephant paperweight made in 1925. Marks include the Rookwood logo, the date, shape number 2797 and the molded monogram of designer, William McDonald. Height 3 1/4 inches. Fired but never glazed, this piece gives insight into the detail of Rookwood commercial pieces before any glaze is applied. $150-200

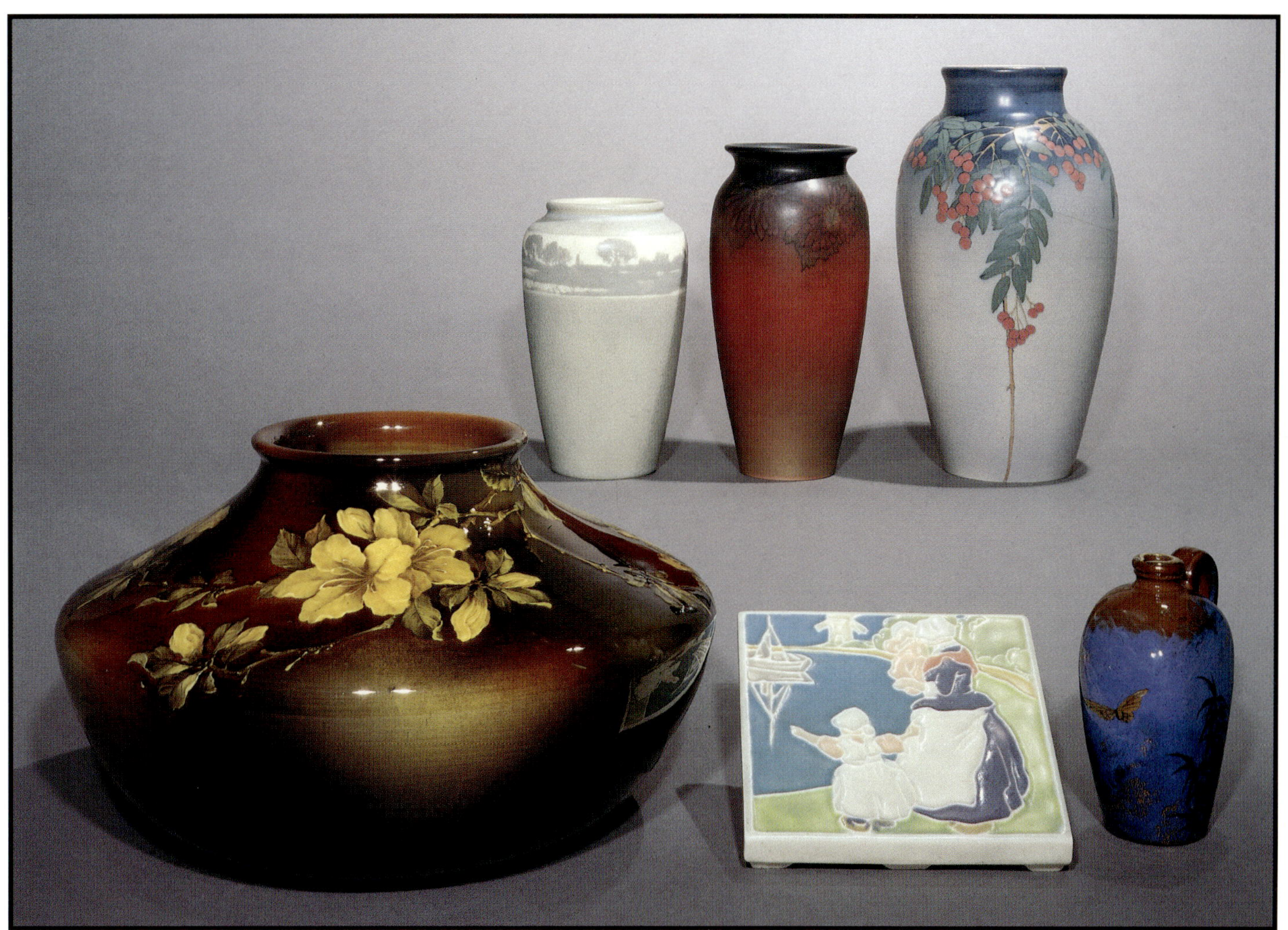

995   Large Standard glaze vase with snappy yellow rhododendron flowers, leaves and stems painted in 1888 by Matt Daly. Impressed marks include the Rookwood logo, the date, Special shape number 764 S and W for white clay. Daly has incised his initials and an L for light Standard glaze on the bottom. Height 6 7/8 inches and diameter 12 inches. There is a firing separation just below the shoulder on the back side of the piece. $1500-2000

996   Unusual banded Vellum glaze vase painted in 1910 by Sara Sax. Pictured in silhouette is a small village beside a lake. Marks include the Rookwood logo, the date, shape number 938 D, an impressed V for Vellum glaze body, an incised V for Vellum glaze and the impressed monogram of the artist. Height 6 5/8 inches. Glaze peppering and some discoloration in the glaze. $700-900

997   Mat glaze vase with red chrysanthemums on a red ground painted in 1925 by Elizabeth Lincoln. Marks include the Rookwood logo, the date, shape number 2544 and the incised initials of the artist. Height 8 1/8 inches. There is a small burst glaze bubble in mid body. $400-500

998   Unusually crisp and clean mat glaze trivet with Dutch scene made at Rookwood in 1927. Impressed with the Rookwood logo, the date and shape number 3204. Size is 5 3/4 by 5 3/4 inches. Uncrazed with excellent color and mold. $400-500

999   Pretty but troubled Vellum glaze floral vase decorated by Lenore Asbury in 1921. Colorful leaves and berries descend from the shoulder in profusion. Marks include the Rookwood logo, the date, shape number 243, a wheel ground x, a second wheel ground double x, a V for vellum glaze and the incised initials of the artist. Height 10 1/4 inches. A spiral firing crack winds down the vase from the rim to mid body. $400-500

1000   Limoges style perfume jug with oriental grasses and a single bright orange butterfly decorated by an unknown artist in 1883. Impressed marks include Rookwood in block letters, the date, shape number 60, a kiln mark and R for red clay. Height 4 3/4 inches. Good color and lots of fired-on gold trim. $300-400

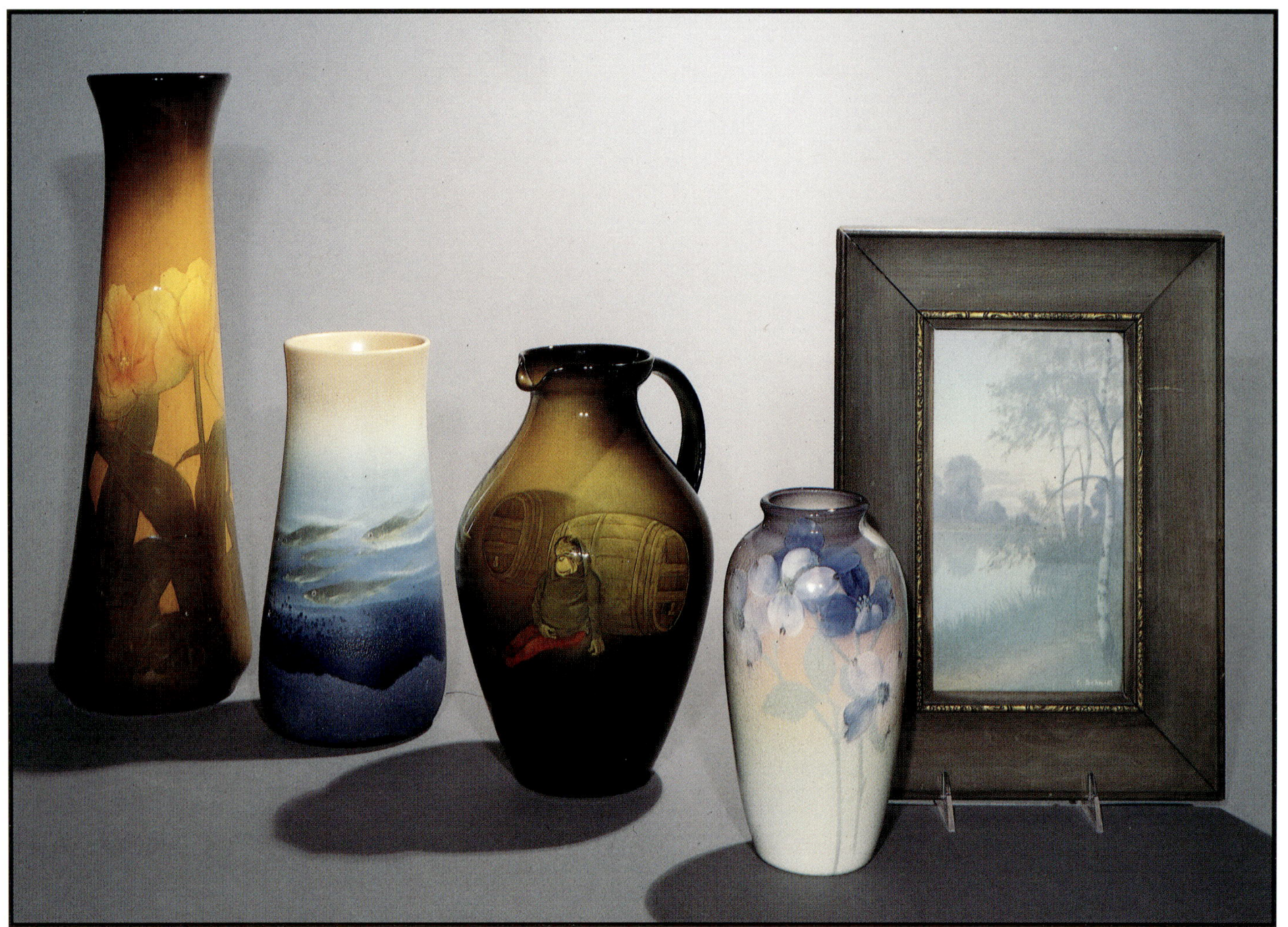

1001   Tall and impressive Standard glaze vase with yellow tulips in all stages of development, painted in 1899 $2000-2500
by Kataro Shirayamadani. Marks include the Rookwood logo, the date, shape number 804 A and the
incised cypher of the artist. Height 18 inches. A large piece of the rim was broken but has now been
professionally repaired as has a small nick on the base. Minor glaze scratches.

1002   Vellum glaze vase with undersea decoration done by E.T. Hurley in 1914. Pictured is a small school of $1500-2000
fish swimming through turbulent waters. Marks include the Rookwood logo, the date, shape number
1023 C, an incised V for Vellum glaze and the incised initials of the artist. Height 10 1/2 inches. At some
point in its life, the vase has lost a band of glaze and underglaze at its bottom. Since the band is
irregular, the overall effect is not unpleasant. There is also some staining to the glaze in the upper third
of the vase.

1003   Amusing Standard glaze pitcher showing a drunken monkey leaning against two oak barrels while $1250-1750
dreaming about cigars, cards, whiskey and beer. Deftly painted by Kataro Shirayamadani in 1894, the
piece is marked with the Rookwood logo, the date, shape number 423 and the incised cypher of the
artist. Height 10 3/4 inches. The handle was broken but has been beautifully restored.

1004   Pretty Iris glaze vase with pink and blue dogwood on a pastel ground, done in 1901 by Constance Baker. $1500-2000
Marks include the Rookwood logo, the date, shape number 922 C and the incised initials of the artist.
Height 8 3/8 inches.

1005   Vellum glaze landscape plaque showing birch trees beside a peaceful lake, painted in 1915 by $3000-3500
Carl Schmidt. The artist's name is painted on the front of the plaque in white slip. Marks on the back
include the Rookwood logo, the date and an impressed V for Vellum glaze body. Affixed to the original
frame is a paper label with the notation "A Quiet Lake C. Schmidt". Size is 9 1/4 by 5 1/8 inches

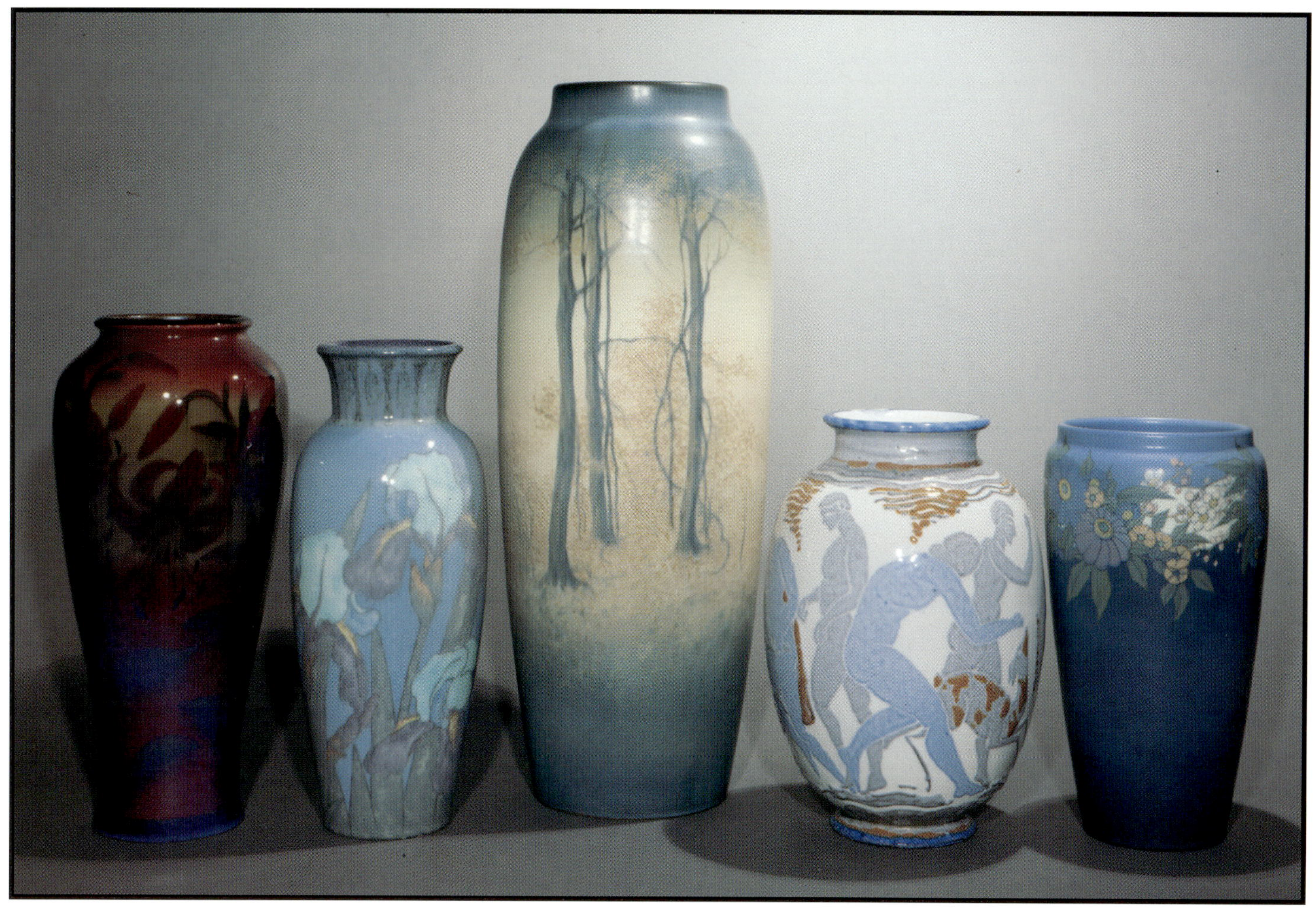

1006   Tall Black Opal vase decorated by Harriet Wilcox in 1928 with maroon lilies. The interior of the vase is $7000-9000
lined with a mottled brown to black glossy glaze. Marks include the Rookwood logo, the date, shape
number 2551, the initials of the artist painted on in black slip and part of an original Rookwood showroom
label. Height 14 inches. The vase has been drilled for use as a lamp but is in uncrazed and very clean
condition.

1007   Good high glaze vase painted by Sara Sax in 1928. Pictured are slightly stylized bearded irises and stems $8000-10000
which wrap around the surface of the vase. The collar of the vase is encircled with repeating geometric
designs while the interior is lined with a mottled blue and pink glaze unique to Sax's work. Marks include
the Rookwood logo, the date, shape number 2785 and the artist's monogram, painted on in black slip.
Height 13 1/4 inches. Uncrazed and very clean.

1008   Monumental fall landscape vase in Vellum glaze painted by E.T. Hurley in 1915. Pictured are hardwood $2500-3500
trees with rust colored leaves silhouetted on a peach ground. Marks include the Rookwood logo, the
date, shape number 907 A, an impressed V for Vellum glaze, an incised number "36-6", a wheel
ground x and the incised initials of the artist. Height 20 3/4 inches. A tight, horizontal firing crack about six
inches below the rim developed in the making and undoubtedly is the reason for the X. The crack runs
about half way around the vase but is very stable.

1009   Rare Art Deco style vase decorated by both Elizabeth Barrett and John Dee Wareham in 1935. $2500-3500
Pictured are seven classical Greek figures, both men and women, and two deer. The vase is done in Wax
Mat glazes of gray, light blue and rust on the white. porcelain body. Marks include the Rookwood logo,
the date, Special shape number S 2139 and the monogram of Barrett and Wareham's initials, painted on
in blue slip. Height 11 3/8 inches. The gray glaze has a tendency to bubble in places but the effect is quite
pleasant. While the vase has a neat drill hole through the base it is clean and uncrazed.

1010   Vellum glaze vase with floral decoration done in 1930 by Lenore Asbury. In a wide band starting at the $2000-3000
shoulder of the vase Asbury has applied both naturalistic and stylized flowers in many varieties and
colors. Marks include the Rookwood logo, the date, shape number 1369 C, an incised V for Vellum glaze,
an impressed fan shaped esoteric mark and the incised initials of the artist. Height 11 1/4 inches. There is
an inconsequential spider crack in the bottom of the vase which is not visible inside and does not come
near the sides. Uncrazed.

NOTES

NOTES

NOTES

NOTES

THE BOOKSTORE

Cincinnati Art Galleries is the largest publisher of classic books about Rookwood Pottery in the World. We also have available many important books about American Art Pottery and American arts and Crafts which are listed below. Orders can be placed by phone or mail with Visa or Master Card and by mail with a check. If you need assistance in selecting a particular book, please feel free to call us for more information.

☑ Please send me the following books:

☐ RW1   The Glover Collection of Rookwood Pottery - Cincinnati Art Galleries......................@ $45.00 each + $4.00 s/h
☐ RW2   Rookwood II - Auction 1992 - Cincinnati Art Galleries...@ $35.00 each + $4.00 s/h
☐ RW3   Rookwood III - Auction 1993 - Cincinnati Art Galleries.......................................@ $40.03 each + $4.00 s/h
☐ RW4   Rookwood IV & Keramics - Auction 1994 - Cincinnati Art Galleries....**SOLD OUT**......@ $35.00 each + $4.00 s/h
☐ RW5   Rookwood V & Keramics 1995 - Cincinnati Art Galleries.....................................@ $45.00 each + $4.00 s/h
☐ RW6   Rookwood VI & Keramics 1996 - Cincinnati Art Galleries...................................@ $45.00 each + $4.00 s/h
☐ RWset   **Special** - 5 Auction catalogues (I, II, III, V & VI) regularly $245...................@ $150.00 each + 6.00 s/h
☐ Ker93   Keramics 1993 - Auction 1993 - Cincinnati Art Galleries.....................................@ $30.00 each + $4.00 s/h
☐ PB1   The Book of Rookwood Pottery - Peck (softbound)...@ $25.95 each + $4.00 s/h
☐ PB1H   The Book of Rookwood Pottery - Peck (hardbound)..@ $45.00 each + $3.00 s/h
☐ PB2   Rookwood Pottery Potpourri - Cummins..@ $26.00 each + $3.00 s/h
☐ PB3   Rookwood Pottery - The Glorious Gamble - Cincinnati Art Museum - Ellis................@ $40.00 each + $3.00 s/h
☐ PB4   Rookwood Pottery - The Glaze Lines - Ellis..@ $69.95 each + $4.00 s/h
☐ PB5   Rookwood - Its Golden Era of Art Pottery 1880 to 1929 - Kircher & Argranoff............@ $60.00 each + $3.00 s/h
☐ PB6   The Mad Potter of Biloxi - (George Ohr) - Clark, Ellison & Hecht...........................@ $85.00 each + $4.00 s/h
☐ PB7   After the Fire - George Ohr an American Genius - Hecht....................................@ $37.50 each + $3.00 s/h
☐ PB8   American Art Pottery - Cooper-Hewitt Museum...@ $20.00 each + $3.00 s/h
☐ PB9   American Art Pottery - Kovel...@ $60.00 each + $3.00 s/h
☐ PB10   American Ceramics - The Collection of the Everson Museum of Art.........................@ $40.00 each + $3.00 s/h
☐ PB11   Art Pottery of America - Henzke...@ $45.00 each + $3.00 s/h
☐ PB13   U. S. Marks on Pottery, Porcelain & Clay - Lehner..@ $24.95 each + $3.00 s/h
☐ PB14   From Our Native Clay - Eidelberg..@ $24.95 each + $3.00 s/h
☐ PB15   The Newark Museum Collection of American Art Pottery....................................@ $19.95 each + $3.00 s/h
☐ PB16   The Book of Buffalo Pottery - Altman..@ $27.50 each + $3.00 s/h
☐ PB17   The Collector's Encyclopedia of California Pottery - Chipman...............................@ $24.95 each + $3.00 s/h
☐ PB18   Cowan Pottery - Saloff..@ $24.95 each + $3.00 s/h
☐ PB19   The Ceramics of William H. Grueby - Montgomery - (soft bound)..........................@ $40.00 each + $3.00 s/h
☐ PB19H   The Ceramics of William H. Grueby - Montgomery - (hard bound)..........................@ $55.00 each + $3.00 s/h
☐ PB20   Newcomb Pottery: An Enterprise for Southern Women - Poesch..........................@ $24.95 each + $3.00 s/h
☐ PB21   Frederick Hurten Rhead- An English Potter in America - Dale...............................@ $29.95 each + $3.00 s/h
☐ PB22   Early Roseville Pottery - Huxford..@ $7.95 each + $3.00 s/h
☐ PB23   The Collector's Encyclopedia of Roseville Pottery I - Huxford...............................@ $19.95 each + $3.00 s/h
☐ PB24   The Collector's Encyclopedia of Roseville Pottery II - Huxford..............................@ $19.95 each + $3.00 s/h
☐ PB25   Collector's Compendium of Roseville Pottery - Monsen.....................................@ $34.95 each + $3.00 s/h
☐ PB26   The Fulper Book - Hibel, Hibel, Defalco & Rago..@ $35.00 each + $3.00 s/h
☐ PB28   The Collector's Encyclopedia of Van Briggle Pottery - Sasicki & Fania.......................@ $24.95 each + $3.00 s/h

Bookstore continued on next page

Cincinnati Art Galleries

635 Main Street
Cincinnati, OH 45202
phone • 513-381-2128
email • cincar19@mail.idt.net

THE BOOKSTORE continued

- ☐ PB29   All About Weller - McDonald..@ $28.95 each + $3.00 s/h
- ☐ PB30   Collector's Encyclopedia of Weller Pottery - Huxford.......................................@ $29.95 each + $3.00 s/h
- ☐ PB31   Owens Pottery Unearthed - Kristy & Rick McKibben & Jeanette & Marvin Stoft.........@ $39.95 each + $3.00 s/h
- ☐ PB32   A Collector's Guide to Owens Pottery - Frank Hahn..@ $34.95 each + $3.00 s/h
- ☐ CB1   The Arts & Crafts Movement in California, Living the Good Life - Trapp.....................@ $55.00 each + $4.00 s/h
- ☐ CB2   Arts & Crafts Movement in Western New York 1900 to 1920 - RIT- Austin.................@ $16.00 each + $3.00 s/h
- ☐ CB3   The Collected works of Gustav Stickley (reprints of several catalogues).....................@ $20.00 each + $3.00 s/h
- ☐ CB4   The Early Works of Gustav Stickley (selections from early catalogues)........................@ $20.00 each + $3.00 s/h
- ☐ CB5   Gustav Stickley After 1909 (reprint of 1909 catalogue)..@ $18.50 each + $3.00 s/h
- ☐ CB6   The Mission Furniture of L. & J. G. Stickley (reprints of several catalogues).................@ $20.00 each + $3.00 s/h
- ☐ CB7   *Stickley Brothers of Grand Rapids (selections of several catalogues)*...........................@ $16.50 each + $3.00 s/h
- ☐ CB8   Quaint Furniture Arts & Crafts (reprint of ca. 1908 catalogue)...............................@ $7.95 each + $3.00 s/h
- ☐ CB9   What Is Wrought In Craftsman Workshops (reprint of 1904 catalogue).......................@ $15.00 each + $3.00 s/h
- ☐ CB10   Limberts Arts & Crafts Furniture (selections from several catalogues).......................@ $20.00 each + $3.00 s/h
- ☐ CB11   Roycroft Furniture (reprint of 1906 catalogue)..@ $7.95 each + $3.00 s/h
- ☐ CB12   A Catalog of the Roycrofters (features metalwork and lighting)...............................@ $11.95 each + $3.00 s/h
- ☐ CB13   Shop of the Crafters at Cincinnati (reprint of 1906 catalogue)...............................@ $8.95 each + $3.00 s/h
- ☐ CB14   Lifetime Furniture (reprint of ca. 1910 catalogue)...@ $10.95 each + $3.00 s/h
- ☐ CB15   Furniture of the American Arts and Crafts Movement - David M. Cathers..................@ $27.50 each + $3.00 s/h
- ☐ CB16   The Pegged Joint - Restoring Arts & Crafts Furniture - B. Johnson.........................@ $14.00 each + $3.00 s/h
- ☐ AB1   American Artists at Auction - 1/83 - 1/93 - Franklin & James......................................@ $150.00 each + $4.00 s/h
- ☐ ETH   The Etchings of E. T. Hurley - (exhibition catalog)...@ $15.00 each + $3.00 s/h

Subtotal.. $______________

Shipping and Handling.. $______________

Ohio Shipments add 6% Sales Tax.. $______________

Total..$______________

Name____

Address____

City_______________________________State____________Zip____________

Daytime Phone #_______________________________

Check, Visa or MasterCard only please

☐ Visa   ☐ MasterCard

____   __________________
                    number   expiration date

Cincinnati Art Galleries

635 Main Street
Cincinnati, OH 45202
phone • 513-381-2128
email • cincar19@mail.idt.net

ABSENTEE BID ORDER FORM

I wish to place the following bids with Cincinnati Art Galleries to be executed during its Rookwood VII and Keramics 1997 Auction, June 7th and 8th, 1997.

I understand that Cincinnati Art Galleries will execute my absentee bids as a convenience and will not be held responsible for any errors or failure to execute bids. I also understand that my absentee bids are subject to all parts of the "Conditions of Sale" which appear in this catalog, and that I am responsible for the purchase price and 10% buyer's premium and the 6.0% Ohio State Sales Tax for all items purchased. NOTE: Purchasers of items shipped out-of-state are subject (where applicable) to report and pay use tax to the state into which the items are being shipped.

I understand that I am responsible for packing and shipping costs of my purchases. Cincinnati Art Galleries will ship my purchases in the best way possible as soon as full payment has been received, and I understand that four to six weeks should be allowed for delivery.

Lot #   **Description**   **Bid Price**

Cincinnati Art Galleries will always attempt to purchase designated lots for the lowest possible amount in competition with other bidders, but we cannot be held responsible for errors or failure to bid. All terms of "Condition of Sale" apply to absentee bidders as well as those present.

Name ____ **Bidder** ____________________________

Address ____

____

Phone Number ____

Ohio Resale Number ____

Signature ____ **Date** ________________________

Cincinnati Art Galleries

635 Main Street
Cincinnati, OH 45202

phone • (513) 381-2128   fax • (513) 381-7527   email • cincar19@mail.idt.net